AQA A-Level Psychology 2015 (7182)

Published and distributed by: OSC Ltd.

First published in Aug 2015

Edition Number: 2018/v2

© OSC Ltd.

Printed under licence by CloudLearn Ltd.

Disclaimer

The authors of this text believe the contents of this course to be accurate and correct. While all possible care has been taken in producing this work, no guarantee can be given.

Contents

Introduction

Welcome to the start of your study of A Level Psychology.

The reasons students have for starting any new academic endeavour are many and various, and are dependent on their own particular circumstances and hopes for the future. In that regard, you are most likely no different. However, there are also common themes that unite students in their desire to return to academic work. Often, students cite the need to gain a qualification necessary for career progression, the desire to improve skills that are felt to be a bit 'rusty', or the wish for a new and different challenge.

These are all excellent reasons for returning to study, but beyond all of them there often also lies the desire to study a subject for its own sake, and for the interest that it can spark.

Although you may be feeling a little daunted by the prospect of working towards a new qualification, rest assured that you have made an excellent choice in UKDLP. This course has been designed with the needs of the specification in mind, and as such is tailored to the requirements of this particular examination. You will find that all the study tasks, all the Tutor Marked Assignments (TMAs) and all the study advice given is structured around the expectations of the AQA examination format. Provided you are committed to completing the course and to using the opportunities given here to think and develop, you will find yourself very well prepared for examination indeed.

Furthermore, UKDLP Ltd aims to provide all the flexibility you would expect of distance learning with all the support you would find in a more traditional 'face-to-face' classroom context. It is often not possible for students to find local teaching in the subjects they require, nor do all have the necessary fixed time to dedicate; indeed, you would not be here already if that were not the case.

Since your needs are more complex, we understand that you particularly require guidance, support and advice in order that you can approach examination with confidence. In order to set things going, we will give an introduction to what to expect on this course.

1.1 Social Influence

Paper 1: Compulsory Content

Key Areas:

- **Types of Conformity**
  - Internalisation
  - Identification and compliance
- **Explanations for Conformity**
  - Informational social influence
  - Normative social influence
  - Variables affecting conformity, including group size
  - *Asch*, unanimity and task difficulty
- **Conformity to social roles**
  - Social roles as investigated by *Zimbardo*
- **Explanations of Obedience**
  - Agentic state and legitimacy of authority
  - *Milgram* - situational variables affecting obedience including proximity, location, uniform
  - Dispositional explanation for obedience – the Authoritarian Personality
- **Explanations of resistance to social influence**
  - Including social support and locus control
- **Minority influence**
  - Including reference to consistency, commitment and flexibility
- **The Role of social influence processes in social change**

Introduction

In the social world, whether we are aware of it or not, as social beings, our thoughts, feelings, actions, beliefs and perceptions are invariably influenced by social groups and social interaction; these are known as social influences. This is of significant interest to the discipline of Psychology. Social influences can take many forms and can be seen in types of **conformity**, **obedience**, **resistance** and so on. These will be addressed in detail in the sections that follow.

Conformity

Conformity is a type of social influence where an individual or individuals yield to group pressure, either real or imagined. Conformity can result in a change in a person's behaviour, beliefs or both.

Conformity is a necessary part of everyday life. In society we conform to unwritten rules which we all know and follow.   To illustrate the power of everyday conformity, consider the following scenarios:

What would happen if...

- You pushed into the middle of a queue *by yourself* and stayed in the queue for at least 2 minutes?
- You sang loudly on a bus?
- You positioned yourself 6 inches from an acquaintance's nose during a conversation?
- You laughed during a funeral?

Consider...

- How would other people behave?
- How would that make you feel?

In each of the above cases, we would be breaking the rules or norms of society. When we do that, we get menacing looks or comments from other people which make us feel embarrassed and humiliated. This keeps us in line and ensures that we conform.

Group Norms

Group norms are the informal rules that groups adopt to regulate group members' behaviour. Sanctions exist to punish those who do not comply. We can identify norms when they are violated:

- Wait for your turn

- Remain quiet on the bus
- Maintain interpersonal distance
- Assume a somber demeanour during a funeral

Why do norms exist?

Think about the following statements. Do you agree with them? If not, what are your reasons?

- All norms are useful

- Norms ensure the survival of the group

- Some norms persist despite the fact that they are dysfunctional

Research Studies

One of the first studies into conformity was carried out by Sherif (1936). The study is summarised below:

Measured	Individual and group judgments in an ambiguous situation.
Technique	Due to autokinetic effect, in a dark room without any external frame of reference, a stationary point of light appears to move. Participants were first asked to estimate how far the light moved alone, and then again as a member of a group.
Findings (individuals)	Individuals established a personal norm that guided their judgments about how far the light was moving. Each individual had their own estimate of distance based on his personal experience.
Question	Would each individual's judgments become more similar when making estimates as a group?
Findings (groups)	The group formed a new estimate of how far the light was moving that was *unique to the group* and different from the judgment of each individual. Over time the group *agreed* on

	how far the light moved, despite the fact that the light *never actually moved* at all.

Rohrer *et al* (1954) used Sherif's method and found that group answers formed in the experiment persisted even up to a year after the experiment had taken place and even though the group no longer existed. This shows the strength and persistence of group norms. Sherif's study can therefore be said to demonstrate a type of conformity known as internalisation. This means that all members of the group believed and accepted that the group answer was correct; they internalised the answer so that it became part of their individual belief systems.

Types of Conformity

Internalisation

As shown by Sherif, this occurs when there is a true change of private beliefs to match those of the group. Therefore, the beliefs and norms of a group are internalised by an individual, and subsequently become part of the individual's own belief system, e.g. an individual may become a vegan after having lived with a group of people who believe in vegan related principles which that individual may take on board and agree with, thus conforming to the group.

Identification

Here a person accepts the norms of a group both privately and publicly because he or she values membership of that group. An individual will conform due to a social role they have within a given social setting. Often the social role is exhibited in different aspects of social behaviour, but does not necessarily have an impact upon the individual's internal personal view or opinion. A good example is a young teenager taking on the dress code and beliefs of the 'Goth' culture because all his friends do. Once he leaves College and goes to work, this is likely to change again. Norms and values taken on in this way are not as robust as those acquired through internalisation. They can shift as we get older and find ourselves members of different groups.

Compliance

An individual may agree publicly with a group but may privately disagree. For example, during a class debate an individual may agree with the majority but deep down hold a contrary point of view.

Activity 1

Look at the everyday scenarios given in the table below. For each one, decide whether it would result in internalisation, compliance or identification. The answers are given at the bottom of the table.

Situation	Type of Conformity
1. You are in a lift which gets stuck between the tenth and eleventh floors. People look at one another but no one moves. Eventually the group decides to press the alarm button and shout.	
2. The teacher asks a question that Sally is sure she knows the answer to. The teacher asks each person in the group for their answer, and Sally is sure the whole class is wrong. When it comes to her turn, however, she gives the class answer.	
3. The teacher is asking each person in the class to read out the marks they have received for a test. Patrick's marks are much higher than anyone else's. However, when it comes to his turn, he takes ten marks off his score.	
4. You are in a restaurant with your boyfriend/girlfriend for the first time and you are not sure what to do. Are you supposed to order food at the bar or wait at your table for a menu? You watch the older couple in front of you to see what they do.	
5. David has just started a new junior school. It is summer and all the other boys are wearing shorts, something he would have never done as his old school for fear of ridicule. The next day, David wears his shorts.	

6. You are taking part in a psychology experiment in which you and some other students are being asked to judge which line of a series matches a comparison line. Your fellow students call out their answers, and you are to answer last but one. To your surprise, the other students all seem to be choosing an obviously wrong answer. When it comes to your turn, you call out the same answer as everyone else.	
7. You are walking down the road and suddenly the person in front of you starts to run. Then you see two others have joined in and are also running. You think perhaps something must have happened and that they are running away from danger. You begin to run in the same direction.	

1. Internalisation

2. Compliance

3. Identification

4. Internalisation

5. Identification

6. Compliance

7. Internalisation

Identification and the Zimbardo experiment

We have seen that identification occurs when a person takes on the values and behaviour of a group he admires. He may be a member of the group or simply feel an affiliation with the group and its members. The norms of a group can be seen in the roles that members within that group play. We expect certain roles to have specific characteristics that apply to the *role* rather than the person playing that role. For example, we would expect a nurse to show more kindness and compassion than a prison officer and for a teacher to dress more conservatively than a dancer in a nightclub.

One of the most controversial studies ever carried out in social psychology was Philip Zimbardo's (1971) prison experiment.

The experiment was commissioned to look at the psychological effects of prison life, and Zimbardo was particularly interested to find out if the brutality often found in American jails at that time was a consequence of certain personality traits of prison guards or of the role to which they were assigned.

Zimbardo set up a mock prison in his university's basement and observed the participants through hidden cameras. The experiment had to be stopped after only six days (out of the proposed 2 weeks). Some argue that it should have been stopped much earlier.

Zimbardo (1971)

Participants:	24 volunteer male students
State of mental and physical health of participants:	Only the most stable were selected (those with no violent or anti-social tendencies)
Allocation to roles:	Random allocation to either a 'prisoner' or a 'guard' role
Clothing:	Guards given uniforms and night sticks. Prisoners dressed in smocks and referred to by number
Instructions to guards:	Keep prisoners under control without using physical violence
Behaviour of guards:	Escalating punishments, including humiliation, sleep deprivation and even force feeding
Duration of experiment:	6 days (out of proposed 2 weeks)
Findings:	Situations enforce conformity. Those assigned the role of guard abused their power and behaved violently, despite being selected for their stability and knowing that it was an experiment

After the experiment, Zimbardo interviewed the participants:

'Most of the participants said they had felt involved and committed. The research had felt "real" to them. One guard said, "I was surprised at myself. I made them call each other names and clean the toilets out with their bare hands. I practically considered the prisoners cattle and I kept thinking I had to watch out for them in case they tried something." Another guard said, "Acting authoritatively can be fun. Power can be a great pleasure." And another: "... during the inspection I went to Cell Two to mess up a bed which a prisoner had just made and he grabbed me, screaming that he had just made it and that he was not going to let me mess it up. He grabbed me by the throat and although he was laughing I was pretty scared. I lashed out with my stick and hit him on the chin although not very hard, and when I freed myself I became angry."'

Commentary/Evaluation

Why did such behaviour occur?

Zimbardo and Ruch (1977) believe that the behaviour can be explained by the strong 'prisoner' and 'guard' stereotypes that we learn from the media both in real-life situations and in fiction. Secondly, the environmental situation (i.e. the mock prison) acted to fuel the behaviour by providing cues for the role-play exercise.

Ethical Issues

One of the fiercest critics of Zimbardo is Savin (1973). He claims that the benefits resulting from the experiment do not outweigh the terrible distress caused to the participants.

However, Zimbardo defends his position by saying that all the participants were told exactly what would happen, and they all signed consent forms. They were given a thorough debrief, and Zimbardo was certain that the distress felt in the experiment did not go beyond the mock prison to affect the participant's real lives.

Historical and Social Context

Zimbardo's original experiment was replicated by Haslam and Reicher in 2002 and shown on British television as a programme called 'The Experiment'. In this replication:

- Guards were uncomfortable about exercising power. Consequently, they never developed any group identity.
- Prisoners were unhappy about the inequalities they faced. They supported each other, shared a social identity and challenged the guards' authority.
- Eventually, a commune of ex-guards and ex-prisoners was established but broke down because some members of the group wished to return to a more tyrannical regime. At this point the study was ended.

This may be because social roles and the way in which we view authority and human rights have all changed since the 1970s. Reicher and Haslam (2006) believe the study proved that a shared social identity need not always lead to negative outcomes. Zimbardo (2006) points out, however, that the participants in the modern study were tougher and more streetwise than the participants in the original study had been. In addition, all participants had microphones and were aware that their actions were constantly being filmed, unlike in the original study where participants were filmed in secret. This could have affected their behaviour. You can read more and view original film footage of Zimbardo's prison experiment at: http://www.prisonexp.org.

Variables Affecting Conformity

There are various factors that can affect the extent to which and if individuals will, conform. Solomon Asch (1951) conducted a series of experiments where he asked participants to complete what appeared to be a relatively simple perceptual task. Asch believed that there was a difference between what he called 'true' conformity and compliance. Compliance is shown when a person 'goes along' with a group because he wishes to be accepted by the group or does not wish to appear foolish. It involves a public 'out loud' conformity even though the individual does not believe what he is saying (his public behaviour and private beliefs are not the same). He claimed that the power of social influence would be better demonstrated if he could get participants to conform by complying with an obviously incorrect answer during a simple task, simply because the rest of the group did the same.

Asch told 50 male students that they were taking part in a test of visual perception. They were put into groups of between 7 and 9 and seated around a table. They were then shown two cards (see the figure below) with lines drawn on them. The first card had a single standard line and participants were asked to match the length of this standard line to one of three comparison lines (A, B or C) shown on a second card. The task was easy and obvious.

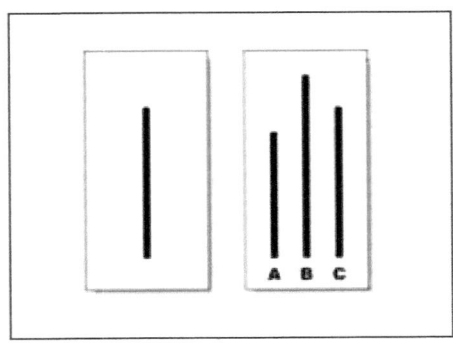

However, not all the participants were genuine, 'naive' participants. Some were non-participants who had been briefed by the experimenter to answer in a particular way. In psychology experiments, these non-participants are called 'confederates'.

There were 18 trials for each group. In 12 out of the 18 trials, Asch used confederates to give obviously wrong answers. The naive participant was seated second to last around the table so that they would hear the incorrect answer repeatedly before giving their own.

The naive participants gave the same incorrect answer as the group in about one third of trials. However, there were large variations between individuals. The most conformist (5%) conformed on every single trial, whereas 25% remained independent despite considerable group pressure to conform. During the experiment, some participants began to appear self-conscious and to show increasing signs of stress.

After the experiment, when asked why they had conformed, some participants said they doubted their own perception, while others admitted that they didn't want to stand out from the group.

The findings from these studies are shown below:

- *A non-unanimous majority* - One other person gave the correct answer on the critical trials and conformity dropped to 5%. This shows the effects of having social support
- *Size of the majority* – When the majority consisted of just two people, conformity dropped to 12.8%. 32% conformity occurred with a majority of three and, thereafter increasing the group size made no difference

- *Losing a partner* – The naive participant had a 'partner' who originally gave the correct answer but then conformed to the majority in the middle of the procedure. This gave conformity levels of 28.5%
- *Gaining a partner* – One of the confederates switched to giving the correct answers half way through. This resulted in conformity levels of 8.7%
- *Nature of the task* – Conformity increased as the task was made more and more difficult (by making the length of the lines more similar)
- *Mode of response* – Conformity rates dropped to low levels when naïve participants were allowed to write their answers down rather than shouting them out loud

So, the following has been identified as factors that can affect conformity:

- *Size of group* – the larger the group, the more likely the individual is to conform though the extent to which this may occur is not definitive
- *Unanimity/Social Support* – a unanimous response is likely to lead to individual conformity
- *Difficulty of task* – when individuals are uncertain, they are more inclined to look to others for conformity
- *Privacy* – individuals are less likely to conform if they are able to make choices/decisions in private
- *Status of the group* – the higher the group status the more likely an individual is to conform

Other factors affecting conformity:

- *Culture* – collective culture results in greater degrees of conformity
- *Age* – younger individuals are likely to conform more than older ones due to factors such as life experience and confidence
- *Features of the situation an individual is presented with* – people are more likely to conform if they are presented with a situation that is ambiguous to them

Methodological Issues

This type of laboratory experiment isolates a particular aspect of behaviour for study. It is well-controlled and easy to replicate. However, the groups and tasks are artificial and lack ecological validity.

Ethical Issues

Deception was used, and the true nature of the experiment was not revealed to the participants. Fully informed consent was therefore not possible. There was some stress caused to participants in Asch's study.

Variations on Asch

Asch wanted to look at factors affecting conformity. He asked questions such as 'Does the nature of the group or the type of task influence conformity rates?' and 'How can we manipulate the experiment to increase/decrease conformity?'

Imagined Pressure

Crutchfield (1955) replicated Asch's work but sat participants in booths so that they could see each other. They could see what they thought were other people's responses on a control panel in front of them. Despite the participants having no face-to-face contact, Crutchfield still recorded conformity rates of 30% on Asch's line task. He also found that conformity increased as the task was made more difficult. This shows that imagined pressure from a group is enough to get people to conform.

Historical Context

Asch's experiments were conducted in the early 1950s in the USA during the McCarthy era. Can the results be generalised to other times and other places? The relatively high levels of conformity in Asch's research were seen by some as a reflection of American society in the 1950s. Indeed, some psychologists have called the Asch phenomenon a 'child of its time'. There is some evidence to suggest that Asch's results may, in part, reflect the society of his day. Nicholson *et al* (1985) replicated Asch's experiment (repeated it under the same conditions) and found lower levels of conformity. This may be due to changes in American society, but it could also be due to other factors such as individual differences in the participants used. Despite these differences, most social psychologists agree with Elliot Aronson that 'decades of research indicate that conformity for normative reasons can occur simply because we do not want to risk social disapproval even from complete strangers we will never see again' (Aronson, 1999).

Cultural Context

Asch's experiments have been replicated in 13 countries outside the USA. In the original experiments, there was 37% conformity. However, in the experiments conducted on students in other societies, the conformity rates varied considerably, from 14% in Belgium to 51% in Zimbabwe (Smith and Bond, 1998). Many reasons have been given for these variations, including minor changes in experimental design. However, the main reason put forward to explain these variations is cultural differences. Social psychologists make the distinction between *individualist* and *collectivist* cultures. In individualist cultures, high value is placed on individual freedom, self-help, self-reliance and individual responsibility. By comparison, collectivist cultures place more emphasis on collective responsibility, group co-operation, collective effort and dependence on social groups. As a result, group pressure to conform is greater in collectivist cultures. Results from these experiments show that the conformity rate is higher in collectivist cultures. Therefore, culture is an important variable affecting human behaviour.

Gender Differences

Asch and Crutchfield used male participants. This revealed nothing about conformity in women. For many years it was assumed that women were more conforming than men. However, research into gender differences in conformity has not found this to be true. Eagly and Carli (1981) found that male researchers were more likely to find higher levels of conformity in women than female researchers. This may be due to male researchers using tasks which were more familiar to male participants. Support for this view comes from a conformity experiment conducted by Sistrunk and McDavid (1971) in which male and female participants were asked to identify various objects while being subjected to group pressure to give the wrong answer, and so to conform. Some participants were given traditionally male items (e.g. a wrench), others were given traditionally female items (e.g. different types of needlework), while others were given 'neutral' items (e.g. identifying rock stars). Conformity for women was highest on male items, conformity for men was highest on female items and, for 'neutral' items, conformity levels were similar for both sexes. This study indicates that there are no significant differences in conformity behaviour between women and men.

Why Do People Conform?

Dependency

Deutsch and Gerard (1955) explain conformity in terms of a 'dual-process dependency model'. This model suggests that people conform because they depend on others for two distinct reasons: for social approval and for information. They went on to describe two types of social influence which can lead to conformity for the two different reasons given above:

- **Normative influence** (the need to be accepted and to belong) - This leads to compliance and is shown in Asch's experiment. An individual will make a decision according to the influence of the majority because of its normative influence. The individual in this case will act according to the behaviour of the majority because they do not want to be left out – they do not want to go against the norm. Also, as can be seen by Asch's study, individuals may go with the majority opinion for fear of feeling uncomfortable and being in the minority. From a psychological perspective, this occurs because of a basic need to be accepted and the need to belong

- **Informational influence** (the need to get it right and to gain information) - This leads to internalisation and is shown in Sherif's experiment. In this case an individual may find themselves in a position where they are not sure what the right or correct answer or response should be, so they will look to the majority opinion, believe that to be correct and make a decision according to the majority. The individual therefore, internalises the majority opinion believing that the information received is right. An example would be not knowing which way to vote in a general election and voting according to majority opinion

Evaluation of Deutsch and Gerard

Deutsch and Gerard's explanation has been criticised for implying that normative and social influence are separate and independent. Insko *et al* (1983) have shown that often the two types of influence can interact and work together to increase conformity. For example, in the case of 'Sally' (from the earlier task on types of conformity) you will recall that she went along with what she believed was an incorrect answer given by the class. This could be due to normative influence in that she does not want to be rejected by the group and appear to be different. It could also be due to informational influence; she may begin to doubt whether her answer is correct when so many people have chosen a different one (what do they know that she doesn't?). These two types of influence will act together to make Sally even more likely to conform. The two types can also be seen working together in variations of Asch where the task is made more difficult. This increases informational influence and, therefore conformity increases.

Their explanation has been further criticised for failing to recognise the importance of belonging to a group. Many studies have shown that conformity to group norms can persist for many years even if the group has since disbanded.

Social Identity Theory

Social Identity Theory was developed by Tajfel and Turner in 1979. It claims that apart from the level of 'self' or personal identity, an individual has multiple social identities. Social identity is the individual's self-concept derived from perceived membership of social groups (Hogg and Vaughan, 2002). In other words, it is the "us" associated with any *internalised group membership*.

Social Identity Theory suggests that group membership creates in-group self-categorisation. This self-categorisation can be seen in the minimal group studies of Tajfel and Turner (1986) in which the mere act of individuals *categorising themselves* as group members was sufficient to lead them to display in-group favouritism.

Once an individual sees himself as belonging to a group, he will seek to achieve positive self-esteem by beginning to perceive strong similarities between himself and other members of his group and to see large differences between his own group and other similar groups (seen often in rival football supporters). This tendency to maximise perceived differences is known as the *meta-contrast principle*. In other words, people's sense of who they are is defined in terms of 'we' rather than 'I'.

Social groups provide us with norms or rules which regulate the behaviour of the group's members. Not only will members conform to such norms whilst with the group but they will also refer to them and abide by them even when other group members are not present.

Evaluation

Social Identity Theory has had a considerable impact on social psychology. It is tested in a wide range of fields and settings, including prejudice, stereotyping, negotiation and language use. The theory also has implications for the way people deal with social and organizational change.

This approach can be used to explain the findings of Rohrer's follow-up to a Sherif-type study where participants conformed to group norms up to one year after the study had ended.

It also has support from Asch-type studies in which participants are allowed to write down their responses, rather than calling them out (removing normative influence). In such cases, conformity is dependent on the nature of the group. If the confederates are perceived as belonging to the naïve participant's 'in-group', conformity is higher than if they are perceived as belonging to the 'out-group' (Hogg and Turner, 1987).

Introduction

Obedience can be defined as a form of social influence that causes an individual to comply with a direct order given by another individual who is usually regarded as an authority figure.

Authority is hierarchically based, so from a young age we are all taught to obey authority figures: our parents when we are very young, and then our teachers, police, and other figures of authority. Such obedience is necessary for society to be able to function. Imagine, for example, if people decided not to obey a red traffic light because they didn't feel like it or to throw a chair at the teacher when she asked for the class to be quiet. Clearly, such wanton acts of disobedience would soon lead to a breakdown in society.

But what about when someone is asked to carry out an order which violates his own sense of justice or moral code, e.g. killing or causing harm to another person? Such things do happen in times of war. We are all aware of the slaughter of six million Jews, Poles and political prisoners during World War II and, more recently, with the torture and humiliation of Iraqi prisoners by American soldiers (some of whom were women) at Abu Ghraib prison.

For decades, social psychologists have been trying to answer the question: 'What makes ordinary people commit such atrocities?' If we look at the trials of those who have engaged in the most depraved treatment of their fellow human beings, a common theme emerges: they were ordinary people simply following orders.

Research into Obedience

One of the most notable studies into obedience was conducted by Stanley Milgram (1963). He became interested in what he called the 'situational determinants' of obedience. He wanted to find out what factors could make a person obey an authority figure to the point of harming (perhaps even killing) another human being. His starting point was to look at the justifications offered by those accused of acts of genocide during World War II (the Nuremburg War Criminal Trials). The defence of the accused was based on 'obedience' in that the accused were following orders given.

Milgram (1963) conducted what has become the most infamous social psychology experiment ever. Milgram selected a range of male participants, from different occupations and backgrounds, who had responded to an advert for paid research into 'punishment and learning'.

Each participant arrived at the laboratory in Yale University, where they were introduced to another participant, Mr. Wallace, who was in fact a confederate. The 'experimenter', a 31 year-old man in a white lab-coat, then explained that they would each be allocated to the role of 'teacher' or 'learner' by drawing lots. The participants believed this allocation was random, but in fact it was rigged so that the participant would always be the teacher.

The experimenter then told the teacher that they had to teach the learner a series of word pairs. The learner's recall would then be tested. If the learner got any of the word pairs wrong, they would be given an electric shock starting at 15V and increasing by one increment each time. The participant was given a small shock to show that the equipment was real. The anxious teacher was told that 'the shocks may be painful but they are not dangerous'. The teacher then watched the learner having the electrodes strapped to their wrists and was then led into a separate room where he could hear but not see the learner.

The learner gave a predetermined set of answers to the word pair exercise, with 3 wrong answers for every 1 correct. As the shocks increased in voltage, the (pre-recorded) screams of the learner became more intense and dramatic. At 180V the learner complained of a weak heart and at 300V he banged on the door and demanded to be let out. At 315V he refused to answer.

When the teacher demonstrated reluctance or refused to continue the shocks, he was given a series of prompts/orders. There were 4 prompts and if one was not obeyed then the experimenter would state the next prompt and so on. They were:

- First prompt – *'Please continue'*
- Second Prompt – *'The experiment requires you to continue'*
- Third Prompt – *'It is absolutely essential that you continue, teacher'*
- Fourth Prompt – *'You have no other choice but to continue'*

Although many of the participants expressed extreme agitation (including sweating, shaking and nervous laughing fits), and many argued with the experimenter, they usually continued to obey. In fact, Milgram found that all 40 participants went to 300V and 65% administered the maximum shock of 450V.

This was a surprising result for Milgram. He and the psychiatrists that he consulted had predicted that only 2.6% of people would administer a strong shock of even 240V.

However, it should also be noted that, despite the considerable pressure to obey, 35% of the participants showed disobedience and would not administer the maximum shock.

Milgram's Variations/Situational Variables

In order to explore the relevance of the various situational factors/variables that led to obedience, Milgram performed replications (636 participants; 18 variations) of his basic protocol in which he changed elements in the surroundings and the proximity of the 'teacher' and 'learner'. The results of some of these variations are shown below:

Variation	Obedience Rate (% continuing to 450V)
Original experiment Learner pounds the wall at 300V. After 300V, he stops pounding the wall and gives no further answers.	65%
Institutional context/Change of Location	47.5%

Experiment moved to down-town office rather than prestigious university.	
Proximity Teacher and learner in the same room	40%
Touch proximity Teacher made to force learner's hand down onto shock plate when he refuses to continue.	30%
Remote authority/ Authority figure is distant Experimenter leaves the room and gives orders by telephone.	20.5%
Two peers rebel Teacher paired with two 'actor' teachers. One 'actor' teacher refuses to go past 150V, the other leaves at 210V.	10%
Peer administers shocks Naïve participant reads the word pairs while 'actor' teacher presses the buttons.	92.5%

These variations show that obedience levels in the laboratory can be manipulated by changing situational variables.

The conclusion of these studies were that ordinary people, when given orders from an authority figure, even if the order was contrary to their own sense of morality or they were aware that their action could result in harm to or death of another, would still obey the orders given.

Evaluation

Methodological Issues

Orne and Holland (1968) have criticised Milgram's experiment for lacking both of the following:

- Internal validity: Participants succumbed to the demand characteristics of the situation. They could not possibly have thought the shocks were real; they realised what was going on and played along with it to please the experimenter.
- External validity: Milgram's lab and elaborate deception was unlike anything seen in real life. Participants would never behave like that in a real-life setting.

However, further research has revealed some disturbing answers to these criticisms.

Internal Validity (The Believability of the Situation)

Sheridan and King (1972) replicated Milgram's experiment but replaced the 'learner' with a real-life cute puppy. The puppy yelped in pain and struggled when participants shocked him and yet, much like in the Milgram experiment, most participants carried on shocking to the end of the scale even though many of them were in extreme distress and some of them even wept. It would seem that the need to obey is stronger than our feelings for the victim.

External Validity (Obedience in a Real-life setting)

Hofling *et al* (1966) got a bogus doctor to telephone nurses on a ward and ask them to give a patient three times the maximum stated dose of a drug (Astroten). The request broke hospital rules since the doctor was not identified, the drug was not signed for and nurses should not accept such requests by telephone. Nevertheless, 21 out of 22 nurses obeyed the request (a higher obedience rate than in the Milgram experiment).

This is worrying, since it shows that such blind obedience can indeed occur in a real-life setting. However, Hofling *et al*"s study has itself been criticised for lacking ecological validity since, in real life, nurses would not be asked to break rules in this way. Also, they would have had no knowledge of the drug Astroten (a fictional drug) to help them decide whether or not to obey. Rank and Jacobsen (1977) replicated Hofling *et al*"'s study using a known drug, Valium. In this study, only two out of 18 nurses obeyed.

Ethical Issues

Milgram's work raised much controversy in the psychological community. Some called his work 'vile' whilst others said it was the most morally significant research ever done. One of Milgram's fiercest critics was Diana Baumrind. She published a paper in 1964 in which she levelled a number of ethical 'charges' against his work. Milgram was quick to publish a 'defence' to these charges in which he justified his work. Baumrind's 'charges' and Milgram's 'defence' are shown below:

Ethical Issue	Charge	Defence
Deception	Milgram told his participants that his study was about the effects of punishment on learning when, in fact, it was to see how far someone would go in obeying an authority figure's instructions to harm another individual. Nothing in the experiment was real: the 'learner' was an actor, the shock generator was fake and the screams were scripted. Milgram referred to this as his 'technical illusion'.	The experiment would not have worked without this deception. The finding that an ordinary human being could be made to harm another human given the right situational determinants is of huge benefit to mankind and has far-reaching social implications for how we might be educated to resist such pressures.

Lack of informed consent	Participants could not give informed consent as they were not aware of the true nature of the experiment.	Milgram got around this by obtaining *presumptive consent*. This means that he asked similar people to those who eventually took part in the experiment how 'far' they would go. Most said they would break off and no-one said they would carry on shocking to the end.
Psychological harm to participants	Milgram's experiment caused extreme distress to some of the participants involved. This was displayed as participants laughing uncontrollably, shaking, or digging their fingernails into the flesh of their palms.	Milgram said he could not have known that such high levels of stress would be caused. He gave participants a full debrief and reunited them with the learner so they could see he was unharmed. He offered psychological counselling and followed his participants for many months after the study to ensure there was no lasting harm. In a questionnaire, over 80% of his participants said they were glad to have taken part in the research.
Right to withdraw	Milgram's participants were told that they could leave at any time but the 'prods' read	Milgram argued that all participants were free to leave and that one-third of the

	out to them during the procedure (such as 'the experiment requires that you continue') made it difficult for participants to exercise that right.	participants *did leave* before the end of the experiment.

Moral Conversion

Further criticism comes from John Darley (1992) who believes that evil is latent in all of us. Innocent people can be turned into torturers by taking part in the kind of activities that Milgram asked of his participants. As people get used to committing such acts, they are asked to carry out more and more depraved ones until they are able to torture others without empathy or remorse. Darley believes that, by taking part in his experiments, Milgram's participants could have undergone a process that morally altered them and started them on the 'road to evil'.

The Obedience Alibi

David Mandel (1998) argues that claiming the atrocities committed during war are simply due to someone following orders is misleading and oversimplified. It ignores other factors which may motivate the perpetrators of atrocities, including personal gain. Analysis of the behaviours of those who killed and tortured Jews during World War II reveals some findings which do not concur with Milgram, namely:

- Perpetrators would often torture and kill in the absence of supervision by their superiors
- They were not inhibited by seeing the pain and suffering of their victims
- They were often willing to continue killing even when offered the chance to quit

Support for Milgram

Supporters of Milgram argue that his work has the potential to inculcate a healthy scepticism in all of us (so that we don't blindly obey authority). It is therefore of the highest moral significance.

Darley's claims that Milgram's participants may have entered a slippery slope towards evil can be countered by the lengthy debriefing procedure that Milgram used. He arranged for a psychiatrist to interview a sample of participants to assess for psychological damage. None was detected.

Mandel's criticism that Milgram's findings were oversimplified and that people could misuse them as an excuse for atrocities was recognised by Milgram himself. He was careful to point out that his study could not provide an adequate explanation of the Nazis' behaviour towards the Jews during the holocaust. He himself said we must be 'cautious in generalising' (Blass, 2004).

Finally, the outcry following Milgram's work has led to the formulation of written codes of conduct and strict ethical guidelines which must be adhered to when carrying out psychological research. This has helped to improve the quality and standard of subsequent psychological research.

Why do people obey?

In Milgram's original experiment not everyone obeyed the experimenter; 35% of people broke off before reaching 450V. Does this mean that some people are naturally more obedient than others? Or are some people not susceptible to the situational determinants of obedience? A number of explanations have been put forward to explain why people obey. These can be divided into situational factors and personality factors. We will now look at these in detail.

Legitimate Authority

One idea is that people tend to obey authority figures whose role is defined by society because they are seen as 'legitimate' and, therefore people believe they know what they are doing. Being in a legitimate position of authority gives them a right to tell others what to do.

In Milgram's experiment, the prestige of Yale university in which the experiment was carried out and the authority of the researcher dressed in his technician's coat would have imbued trust in the participants, making them more likely to obey. When the experiment was transferred to a less prestigious down-town office, obedience fell.

The problem is we are so conditioned to obey and trust authority that we often accept a person's credentials based on very little information. A good example of this is shown in the studies by Bickman (1974) and Sedikides and Jackson (1990) on the power of uniforms. In both studies a researcher was able to get passers-by to perform tasks such as picking up litter or refrain from leaning on a zoo exhibit, simply by being dressed in the appropriate uniform.

Gradual Commitment

An important feature of Milgram's procedure was the gradual nature in which participants were drawn into giving higher and higher levels of shock. This is called the *foot-in-the-door effect*. Once people have complied with a small request (e.g. giving a 15V shock) it is difficult for them to refuse a subsequent similar request. This comes from a desire to appear consistent.

Contractual Obligation

In addition, there is a feeling of contractual obligation that keeps participants in the study. Having agreed to take part and accepted the role, people feel bound to continue or face having to re-evaluate their view of themselves as someone who quits or gives up.

The Agentic State

Milgram explained that the participant's responses suggested we operate on one of two levels in a social situation. Either we are:

- *Autonomous* – behaving independently and aware of the consequences of our actions (e.g. we are giving another human being painful shocks of increasing intensity) and being responsible for their own actions
- *Agentic* – acting as the agents of others and, therefore not responsible for our actions (e.g. we are helping a researcher with an experiment over which he has full control and responsibility), allowing oneself to be directed by others, passing on the responsibility to another by claiming to 'follow orders'

We undergo an *agentic shift* in certain circumstances because we have been trained from an early age to 'do as we are told' by figures of authority. When we obey, we become 'agents' of authority. The set up that Milgram used was designed to look scientific and technical. The participants would have trusted that the experimenters knew better than them and therefore shifted into an agentic state in which they acted without question.

In addition, because of the way in which we are raised to respect authority, leaving the experiment and refusing to obey further has high costs. When we choose to disobey, we risk appearing rude or arrogant, something which we are taught is socially unacceptable. This can be seen in the Milgram experiment where even when participants said they didn't want to go on, and were obviously experiencing high levels of distress, their protests were always couched in the politest language, e.g. 'With all due respect to your experiment, would you please take a look at the guy in that room, sir?'

Buffers

Milgram uses the term 'buffer' to describe any aspect of a situation that protects people from having to confront the consequences of their actions. This is shown in Milgram's remote victim (original experiment) variation where obedience reached 65% compared with the touch proximity condition in which it fell to 30%. Similarly, in war, it is easier for a person to launch a missile by pressing a button in a control room if they can't see the devastation it causes.

Dispositional Explanation for Obedience: The Authoritarian Personality (Adorno, 1950)

Adorno was among a group of European psychologists who fled Nazi persecution during World War II. He believed that an authoritarian personality was developed in early childhood as a result of being raised by parents who were rigid, punitive and strict and as such was the result of an individual's personality type. He believed that while people with this personality were often hostile to authority, they were extremely obedient to people in positions of power. However, they would often project their feelings of hostility towards their parents onto another (safer) target (often a group of a different race or religion).

As a result of his research, Adorno constructed a number of scales designed to measure various personality characteristics. His most famous is the F Scale, for potential for fascism, which measures the authoritarian personality.

Adorno suggests that some deep-rooted personality traits predisposed some individuals to be highly prejudicial. He used case studies (e.g. Nazis), psychometric testing (the F Scale) and clinical interviews to support his theory.[1]

From his findings, those with Authoritarian Personalities exhibited:

- Hostility to those they consider to be of inferior status
- Obedience to those they consider to be of a higher status
- Inflexible and rigid beliefs and opinions
- Conservative and traditional values

These individuals were more likely to develop an 'us and them' mindset. This, according to Adorno could be traced back to a strict childhood upbringing by authoritarian parents and not being able to express frustration or hostility to the

---

[1] Have a look at the original F scale at http://www.anesi.com/fscale.htm

parents. This later exhibited itself through aggression toward those considered weaker.

Obedience and Obedience Atrocities

As we have seen, extreme obedience to authority is sometimes used as an explanation for genocide or the massacre of civilians during war. However, Smith and Mackie (2000) and Cardwell (2001) believe that obedience alone cannot explain these atrocities and that other important factors must be considered in explaining such acts. Three main factors have been identified:

- The context of inter-group hostility – Social Identity Theory argues that people see themselves as members of groups and tend to maximise differences between their own group and others. Many obedience atrocities have taken place within a context of strong inter-group hostility

- The importance of self-justification – People who carry out atrocities often convince themselves that their victims deserved their fate. This is also known as blaming the victim. The perpetrators are therefore able to continue to view themselves as decent and moral people, despite what they have done. Some of Milgram's participants argued that the learners 'deserved' to be shocked for failing to learn (Milgram, 1974)

- The role of motivational factors – Cardwell (2001) has argued that Milgram's research ignores the role of motivational factors in extreme obedience. He argues that personal gain was an important motivational factor in Nazi Germany, where jewellery, gold teeth and even hair were looted from the deceased

Activity 2

- Explain the term 'situational determinants'
- Outline two reasons why people obey

Answer to activity 2

1. 'Situational determinants' are cues which arise from the situation a person is in, giving them hints as to how they should behave.

2. *Legitimate authority:*

People tend to obey authority figures whose role is defined by society because they see them as 'legitimate' and believe they must know what they are doing.

Gradual commitment (foot-in-the-door-effect):

Participants are drawn into giving higher and higher levels of shock due to a desire to remain consistent. Once they have complied with a small request (e.g. giving a 15V shock) it is difficult for them to refuse a subsequent similar request.

Explanations of Resistance to Social Influence

Independent Behaviour

In the studies of both conformity and obedience, there were always those participants who refused to go along with the group, or refused to continue obeying the malicious authority figure. This raises the question: 'What was it about these people that allowed them to demonstrate independent behaviour and stand up for what they believed in?' or, as Milgram would put it, 'Why didn't they slip from an autonomous into an agentic state?' We shall now explore the factors that may contribute to independent behaviour.

Individual Factors

In Asch's study, many participants did not conform to the group in all the trials, and some (24%) managed to stick to their own judgement in all trials. There appear to be two important individual factors which determine ability to resist pressures to conform: the need to be an individual and the need to remain in control. These are discussed in more detail below.

The Need to be an Individual

In some, the desire to be 'their own person' and be seen as an individual outweighs the need to conform. It seems that, in Western cultures particularly, some people feel uncomfortable if they appear to be 'like everyone else'. Snyder and Fromkin (1980) 'deindividuated' a group of students by telling them that their beliefs and attitudes were identical to those of 10 000 others. They 'individuated' a second group by telling them their attitudes and beliefs were different. In a later Asch-type experiment, the deindividuated students were less likely to conform. The researchers believe that they were trying to re-assert their individual identities.

The Need to Remain in Control

Most people need to feel that they have freedom of choice and can control their own environment. This need, however, is stronger in some people than others, depending on their personality and past experiences. Burger (1992) has found that people with a high need for control are more likely to resist conformity pressures than those who have a lower need. This has been investigated by Daubman (1993) who tested participants in two groups: those who scored highly on a 'need for control' scale and those who scored nearer the bottom. The participants worked in pairs to solve puzzles. At the end of the task all participants were all told they were average at solving puzzles and that their partner had done better. They were then given hints and tips for how to do better next time. The findings showed that those with a high score on the need for control scale often became irritated and angered by the feedback, while those with a low score welcomed it and were grateful to receive it. This supports the idea that attempts to influence are seen as threats to the personal freedom of those who need a high level of personal control.

Situational Factors

Gaining Social Support

In variations to the original Asch experiment, he manipulated situational variables to look at the factors affecting conformity. You will recall that when the naïve participant gained a partner (one of the confederates switched to giving the correct answers half way through), conformity dropped to 8.7%. This appears to be the best way to resist conformity; the social support provided by an ally acts as a *buffer* against the pressures to conform.

Prior Commitment

Once we have made a commitment to a decision, it is very difficult to change our minds. Reversing a previous decision may make us look foolish or indecisive and these are not desirable traits. In a variation of Asch's study, he asked naïve participants to give their judgements before the other confederates, who then gave a unanimous wrong answer. Asch then gave the naïve participants the opportunity to change their minds. Not a single one did. This demonstrates the power of prior commitment.

Resisting Pressures to Obey

In Milgram's work, we looked at the power of social influence in making people obey. However, it is important to remember that 35% of participants disobeyed the instructions given to them and refused to continue giving shocks. Again, there must be individual and situational factors at work that allow a person to refuse to obey.

Individual Factors

Personality Characteristics

Following Milgram's experiment, Elms and Milgram (1966) set out to discover the background and personality of the 35% of participants who had refused to obey. They found that disobedient participants scored highly on a social responsibility scale and had a high internal locus of control.

Locus of Control

"A locus of control orientation is a belief about whether the outcomes of our actions are contingent on what we do (internal control orientation) or on events outside our personal control (external control orientation)." (Zimbardo, 1985)

Locus of Control is considered to be an important aspect of personality. The concept was developed originally Julian Rotter (1966).

Locus of Control refers to a person's perception about the underlying causes of events in his/her life. If you believe that your successes and failures are controlled by *yourself* and that things happen because you make them happen, then you have an ***internal locus*** of control.

Alternatively, if you believe that they are controlled by ***external forces*** (such as God, fate or the planets) over which you have little control, you are said to have an external locus of control.

The locus of control is a continuum, so people can have a mixture of internal/external loci or be at either end.

This idea is shown in the following diagram:

External Locus of Control Individual believes that his/her behaviour is guided by fate, luck, or other external circumstances	**Internal Locus of Control** Individual believes that his/her behaviour is guided by his/her personal decisions and efforts Associated with self-determination and personal agency

Research Studies

- Avtgis (1998) - Meta analysis - Found those with an external locus of control were more likely to conform. Correlation between external locus of control (ELC) and conformity 0.37 i.e. higher conformity in externals
- Holland (1967) - Found no such relationship between an ELC and obedience
- Blass (1991) - Re-analysed Holland's data and found those with an internal locus of control were more resistant to pressures to obey, and this was especially true if they felt they were being coerced or manipulated by the experimenter

Comments

Many studies find tentative links between 'internals' and the ability to resist both conformity and obedience pressures. However, many studies show no such relationship.

Moral Reasoning

Kohlberg (1969), cited in Elms (1972), was a colleague of Milgram who studied moral development. He found that those participants using a more advanced level of moral reasoning were more able to resist the experimenter's verbal 'prods' and consequently showed higher levels of disobedience. However, other research has found that a higher level of moral reasoning does not always lead to disobedience. Some people may hold certain principles but the power of the situation may overwhelm them.

What makes an Effective Dissenter?

David Levy (1990) set up a filmed reconstruction of the Milgram experiment. His aim was to find out what characteristics an effective dissenter should have. His film showed the participant either politely refusing to carry on, or being rude to the experimenter (calling him a jerk) and angrily storming out. People who watched the film preferred the polite dissenter. This implies that it is acceptable to disobey as long as the social conventions of courtesy and respect are followed.

Situational Factors

Activity 3

Answer the questions below to find situational that factors might help a person resist pressures to obey.

1. Milgram (1974) said: 'When an individual wishes to stand in opposition to authority, he does best to find support for his position from others in his group. The mutual support provided by men for each other is the strongest bulwark we have against the excesses of authority.'

Which variation of Milgram's obedience study demonstrates this and why?

2. In Milgram's study, one female participant disobeyed the experimenter and refused to continue giving shocks. When asked why, she said that she had had enough pain in her life (she was a holocaust survivor) and did not want to inflict pain on someone else. Milgram explained her behaviour in terms of her having being awakened from her 'agentic state'. What did he mean by this?

3. Questioning the motives, legitimacy and expertise of authority figures has been proposed as a way to prevent automatic obedience. Remember that when Milgram's experiment was transferred to a down-town office block, the levels of obedience dropped. What explanations have been given for this?

4. A study conducted by Gamson *et al* (1982) demonstrated the effectiveness of education in helping participants to question the expertise of an authority figure. It involved people making a video and signing statements that could be used against a person in court. As the study progressed, participants became more suspicious about the real purpose of the experiment. Participants who worked in groups refused to obey the requests of the experimenter and one person actually quoted Milgram's findings as a reason for disobedience. He became aware that he was becoming the victim of the foot-in-the-door effect (gradual commitment). What did he mean by this?

The Role of Social Influence Processes in Social Change

A great deal has been learned about obedience and the processes involved in social influence from experiments such as Zimbardo's prison study and Milgram's experiments. Such processes are used every day when products are advertised through the media and when companies attempt to get us to buy their products using the foot-in-the-door technique during cold calling. They are also used as propaganda by the government to get us to change our behaviour, e.g. cutting down on smoking and drinking, practising safe sex, etc.

We shall now consider how the processes we have learned can be used in society to produce social change.

Social Change and Minority Influence

Minority groups use a variety of methods to get themselves heard. We are all familiar with demonstrations, campaigns and protest marches used by minority groups to address issues of discrimination and inequality, but how do minorities influence the majority view?

Research has shown that minorities can be influential as long as they adopt the appropriate style of behaviour.

Moscovici (1985) claims that to influence a majority, minorities must:

- Be consistent in their views and never waiver from them
- Avoid dogmatism (they must be willing to listen to others' views)
- Use moderate language, e.g. 'alternatives to animal testing' rather than 'death to the animal torturers'

Hogg and Vaughn (1998) state that minorities must be seen to:

- Be acting out of principle rather than self-interest
- Have made sacrifices for their cause
- Be similar to the majority in terms of class, age and gender
- Advocate views which are in line with the current zeitgeist (spirit of the times) e.g. views in line with saving the environment are popular at the moment. Therefore minorities holding views consistent with this idea will have more power

How does this behavioural style help?

The following explanations have been offered as to why these behaviours make minorities effective:

Consistency

This is the single most important factor in minority influence. It makes the minority appear confident and assured and can lead to the majority taking the minority view more seriously. A consistent minority disrupts established norms creating uncertainty and doubt.

The Snowball Effect (Van Avermaet, 1996)

Once a few members of the majority begin to move to the minority position, others quickly follow. Clark (1998/1999) demonstrated this by simulating the jury situation from the film *12 Angry Men*. He found that the participants were influenced by the number of defectors to the minority position. Interestingly, however, this was only true up to the 'ceiling of influence', and 7 jurors changing their mind had no more influence than 4.

Group Membership (Hogg and Vaughn, 1998)

We are most likely to be influenced by a minority we perceive as belonging to our 'in group'. As with social identity theory, we are most likely to conform with members of our own group.

Social Cryptomnesia (Mugny and Perez, 1991)

This suggests that minority groups exert their influence through a process known as social cryptomnesia. The ideas of a minority may be too radical when they are first aired, but as time goes by the rest of society 'catches up with them' and they are eventually accepted. However, the idea and the source of the idea become dissociated so that no-one is really sure where the idea came from in the first place. A good example is the idea that the earth is round. This idea was preposterous at the time but is now so well-accepted that today there is no-one who still believes the earth is flat. However, although many different astronomers and mathematicians have been credited, no-one is really sure who made the initial discovery. This is useful because it means that the idea can be taken into mainstream thinking without having to adopt the negative identity of the source (at the time people who thought the earth was round were labelled either as mad or heretical). It also explains why minority views often take a long time to assimilate into mainstream society.

Moscovici *et al* (1969)

We have seen that consistency is the most important factor in minority influence. Moscovici *et al* (1969) carried out an experiment to see if a consistent minority could influence a majority to give an incorrect answer in a perception task.

Moscovici selected groups of 6 containing 4 naive participants and 2 confederates. The groups were then shown 36 slides of different shade of blue and were asked to name the colour.

In one condition, the confederates consistently said that all 36 slides were green. Just over 8% of the participants agreed that the slides were green.

In the second condition, the confederates stated that 24 (of the 36) slides were green. Only 1.26% of the participants agreed that these slides were green.

This study therefore suggests that consistent minorities are more effective at influencing the majority.

However, the study has been criticised for lacking ecological validity since the participants are aware they are being studied and the task is unlike any required in real-life.

Comments

According to Moscovici (1980), minorities use informational social influence to persuade those in the majority to change their views. Minorities want to bring about conversion. They hope that by focusing on the issue, the majority will come to examine the arguments posed by the minority. In turn, this may start the process of conversion whereby, at least in private, attitudes genuinely begin to shift.

A consistent minority may plant the seed of doubt in the mind of someone holding a majority viewpoint. Over time, that doubt may lead to a change of view especially if other members of the majority are seen converting to the minority view.

Evaluation

Most of the research on minority influence is based on laboratory experiments which do not adequately represent the conditions under which real minorities operate. Most minorities have a lower social status than the majority, and we have seen many historical examples of how majorities are able to crush minorities who express a different view (Sampson, 1991).

In the real world, it is unlikely that minorities succeed simply because they are consistent, flexible or willing to compromise. More often their success results from massive protests such as the civil rights demonstrations by African Americans in the 1950s and the uprisings in Eastern Europe which overthrew communist rule in 1989. Sampson believes that we should not ignore laboratory findings on minority influence but reminds us that we need to see the broader social contexts in which minorities operate.

Resisting Unwanted Influences

Milgram and Zimbardo's studies showed us that ordinary people put under pressure to obey an authority figure or placed in powerful positions without structural constraints, could commit evil acts. To reduce the likelihood of such behaviour, there is a need for all of us to be aware of the circumstances that can lead to blind obedience or a failure to empathise with the suffering of others.

In his book 'The Lucifer Effect', Zimbardo (2007) recommends that we all try to adopt a ten-step programme to resist unwanted influence.

- *Admit mistakes* – Don't justify past actions; apologise and move on
- *Be mindful* - Evaluate the words and actions of people who are trying to influence us. Ask 'Will there be a positive outcome if this course of action is seen through to the end?' Educate children to be critical thinkers
- *Be responsible* – Take responsibility for your own actions and decisions
- *Assert your individuality* – Be clear about your own identity. Politely state your own name and credentials and get others to do the same. Make eye

contact and offer information about yourself that reinforces your own unique identity. This helps to avoid the anonymity that breeds tyranny

- *Respect just authority but rebel against unjust authority* – Try to distinguish between those who have authority based on expertise and those who do not. Often self-proclaimed authority figures are false-prophets who should be disobeyed and openly exposed to critical evaluation
- *Balance need for group acceptance with value of own identity* – Know when to follow group norms and when to reject them
- *Be frame-vigilant* – Be mindful of how issues are described (framed) e.g. being asked to 'go the extra mile to defend our country' does not sound as sinister as being asked to 'torture suspects for information'
- *Develop a balanced time perspective* – Don't become trapped in the 'heat of the moment'. If others are behaving badly, think about past commitments/values and future consequences
- *Don't sacrifice freedoms for the illusion of security* – For example, 'I will keep you safe if you...'. Sacrifices are real and immediate and security is often a distant illusion
- *Oppose unjust systems* – Get others to join your cause and don't be afraid to 'whistle-blow' if necessary

These steps can help us to be more aware of possible malignant or harmful influences in society. As Milgram put it:

"It may be that we are puppets - puppets controlled by the strings of society. But at least we are puppets with perception, with awareness. And perhaps our awareness is the first step to our liberation." Stanley Milgram (1974)

Activity 4

1. Define the term 'independent behaviour'

2. Name two situational factors which can help to resist conformity

3. Define the term 'locus of control'

4. Name two ways in which we can resist unwanted social influences

1.2 Memory

Key Areas:

In this unit we will be looking at the following areas:

- **The multi-store model of memory**: sensory register, short-term memory and long-term memory. Features of each store: coding, capacity and duration

- **Types of long-term memory**: episodic, semantic, procedural

- **The working memory model**: central executive, phonological loop, visuo-spatial sketchpad and episodic buffer. Features of the model: coding and capacity

- **Explanations for forgetting**: proactive and retroactive interference and retrieval failure due to absence of cues

- **Factors affecting the accuracy of eyewitness testimony**: misleading information, including leading questions and post-event discussion; anxiety

- **Improving the accuracy of eyewitness testimony**, including the use of the cognitive interview

The aim of this topic is to look at how memory works in terms of its ability to take in information, encode it, store it and retrieve it.

We will be looking at the following:

- What memory is and types of memory

- The multi-store model of memory

- The working memory model

- Explanations for forgetting

- Eyewitness testimonies (EWT)

Introduction

Memory is something familiar to us all. For example, we may hear people saying things such as: 'My memory isn't very good today' or 'I'm no good at remembering names'. If we take a moment to consider what memory is, we soon realise that without it we would have no concept of ourselves, what experiences we have had during our lives and how that links up to our current identity.

It is difficult to imagine how we would get through even one day without memory. Suppose we lost all of our memory during the night. The next morning, with no knowledge of what toast and orange juice are, our breakfast might just as well have arrived from Mars! We would have no idea where the bathroom was or even what it was for. We wouldn't have a clue where we were supposed to be going that day or how to get there.

Activity 5

Think back to yesterday afternoon, this morning or to another recent time in your life which you can still recall easily. Choose a 4-5 hour time period and consider what you did over that whole time. Make a note of everything you can remember. Now reflect on all the occasions where you had to make use of your memory. What different types of information do you need to be able to recall in order to function normally in day-to-day life?

How Does Our Memory Work?

Scientists have been able to discover more about normal memory from those people who have suffered head trauma. Tellingly, even those who have had the most horrific head injuries rarely lose all the knowledge they have gained in a lifetime. Instead, they might suffer impairment to different parts of memory: the short or long term memory. This gives rise to the idea that our memory is made up of different components or has different functions.

Indeed, it is better to understand our memory as if it were **not** a single entity. It performs so many varied tasks and deals with so many different types of information that psychologists believe it is, in fact, a collection of different information processing systems. A number of models or theories have been put forward to describe these systems.

The Process of Memory

Memories are formed in a way that involves a number of processes. Firstly we have to have an experience and then the following happens:

- Encoding – the process whereby we transform information received into a meaningful form that allows us to store it

- Storage – holding or storing the information. Note, however, that some psychological changes occur in order for the information received to be stored

- Retrieval – bringing the memory out of storage and restoring the information so that it can be used where needed

The Multi-Store Model

Atkinson and Shiffrin (1968)

This is one of the best known early models of memory. It assumes that memory consists of three separate 'stores': **sensory memory** (SM),[2] **short-term memory** (STM) and **long-term memory** (LTM). Research into these stores has concentrated on the type of **encoding** (the form in which information is represented e.g. acoustic or visual), the **capacity** (how much it can hold) and **duration** (how long it lasts) of each one. This model assumes that information must flow through the stores in a fixed linear sequence, being re-coded as it passes through each one.

For example, a friend tells you her phone number. Your pen and paper are in the car so you must try and remember it until you can write it down. This information

---

[2] Also referred to as Sensory Register

has come to you via your sensory memory – you heard your friend say her phone number. Because you wish to remember it you give it attention, which serves to pull it into your STM. However, you must keep it looping round in your STM by repeating it over and over again to yourself until you can get to the car.

This is known as **maintenance rehearsal**. If you can get to the car with no further distractions, you will be fine because you can write the number down. But suppose you meet another friend and start talking to him. Now the number is lost; it has been displaced because you had to use your STM to hold the new conversation, and you cannot hold both the phone number and the conversation in your STM at the same time.

According to Atkinson and Shiffrin, rehearsal or repetition of material is the key to getting information from the STM into the LTM. We shall now look at the components of the Multi-Store Model in more detail.

Sensory Memory (SM)

This involves input from the environment. There is a large amount of information available to our senses at any given time. When we wish to remember something (such as a phone number), we select the relevant information for processing in the memory system. Sensory memory consists of a set of **modality specific stores** which store information coming from the environment for fractions of a second.

All this means is that the information we wish to remember is stored in the form in which it was received, that is either in the **iconic store** (for visual information, such as if we have seen a poster or picture we want to recall), the **echoic store** (for auditory information, as in a friend telling us their phone number) or the **haptic store** (for tactile information – as in remembering our pin number by remembering the sequence of buttons we have to press on an ATM).

Sperling (1960) tested iconic memory by presenting participants with grids of letters for very short periods of time (50 milliseconds). He found people could retain four items for up to one second.

Later studies of sensory memory have confirmed Sperling's findings and have concluded that sensory memory can:

- Retain items for about two seconds

- Only record information passively (i.e. we can't control it)

- Only retain information in a relatively unprocessed form

In conclusion, the sensory memory is made up of separate stores for visual information, auditory information and tactile information, and only a fraction of the items registered here are ever passed on to the STM; the rest are lost.

Short-term Memory (STM)

When psychologists study memory, they are interested in answering three questions: how much can it hold, for how long and in what form the information is stored.

In other words, the factors of capacity, duration and encoding. The capacity of the STM has been known for a long time. Jacobs (1887) devised a technique to measure the capacity of STM. The technique has been widely used ever since, and has become known as the **digit-span technique**.

Activity 6

Try a digit-span task for yourself. Get a friend to read each of the number series to you. The digits must be read in the same monotone, and there must be an equal space of about half a second between each digit.

Once the series has been read, you should repeat it immediately in the correct order. Your friend begins and says '5' so you repeat 'five', then your friend says '6,2' and again, you repeat, 'six, two', and so on.   The capacity of your short-term memory is equal to the last series which you can remember in the correct order without jumbling any of the digits.

5

6 2

7 5 3

4 3 8 7

2 4 7 3 6

8 5 4 1 6 9

7 8 1 5 9 2 3

6 8 2 4 6 2 7 4

1 8 7 4 1 5 6 3 8

7 5 4 1 6 5 2 3 4 6

1 2 4 9 6 1 9 4 8 3 7

Capacity

Using this serial recall technique, Jacobs found that the average STM capacity is around seven items. Later, Miller (1956) termed this the 'magic number seven'. He also showed that capacity could be increased by **chunking** items together. That is, digits could be **chunked** into memorable dates, so a number string of: 1 0 6 6 1 9 8 4 1 9 9 7 becomes: 1066 (battle of Hastings) 1984 (a book by George Orwell) and 1997 (death of Princess Diana). This has converted a meaningless number string into three meaningful 'chunks' which take up only three slots of precious STM capacity, in contrast to the twelve needed for each digit in the number string if recalled separately. However, the notion of a 'chunk' as the basic unit of STM has been questioned by Simon (1974) who found that STM capacity was smaller for larger chunks of information (eight word phrases) than for smaller ones (single words). Therefore, it would seem that size of chunk matters; we can't hold as many large 'chunks' as we can smaller ones. Forgetting occurs in STM due to displacement. In other words, once STM capacity is reached, any new information 'displaces' or pushes out information already stored there, which suggests that our STM typically has a maximum capacity.

Duration

The duration of STM appears to be around 6-12 seconds according to Peterson and Peterson (1959). They believed that the STM consists of a **memory trace** which decays if it is not rehearsed. Their experiment consisted of participants seeing trigrams (groups of three unrelated consonants, for example 'RBQ') and then attempting to repeat them after intervals of 3, 6, 9, 12 or 18 seconds, during which time rehearsal was prevented. The longer the time between learning and recall, the more trigrams were lost, suggesting that the memory trace did indeed decay with time. However, this experiment has been criticised because it is not possible to rule out the influence of limited capacity. The design has also been criticised since the same participants were used for each trial, and it is possible that trigrams learned on earlier trials interfered with the processing of new ones on subsequent trials.

Note: Whenever you read about psychological experiments, it is always vital to examine the experiment design for possible methodological flaws or bias (as above). This is an important part of learning about How Science Works, and will inform our later study of research methods. Researchers interested in memory have investigated whether the following factors affect the capacity of the STM:

- The influence of our LTM (whether or not we want to transfer information from the STM into our LTM)

- Reading aloud (can this help expand the capacity of our STM?)

- Pronunciation time (does this have an impact on our auditory store in our sensory memory?)

- Individual differences (can we generalise about memory or is this a quality that varies greatly from individual to individual, in the way that physical characteristics do?)

And for duration, the following factors have been researched:

- Rehearsal (does rehearsing – repeating – information to ourselves prolong the length of time we can remember it for?)

- Intention to recall (if we want to recall something because it has significance or importance for us – such a friend's phone number, a birthday or a special event – does that increase the length of time we can remember it?)

- Amount of information to be recalled (can we remember many items for a short time or one item for a long time – or are these factors not related in this way?)

Moreover, encoding (the way in which information is stored) in the STM has also been investigated. Conrad (1964) found that, on STM tasks, participants made acoustic errors, i.e. they substituted letters which **sound** alike rather than ones which **look** alike, even when the letters were presented visually. This experiment shows that the **STM encodes acoustically**: that is, regardless of the original format of the information we want to remember, it is encoded into acoustic data when transferred into the STM.

Activity 7

Write a sentence describing what you understand by the following terms:

- Memory duration

- Capacity

- Encoding

- Encoding – The way in which information is represented in memory, e.g. acoustic, visual, semantic

- Capacity – The amount of information that each memory component can hold at any one time

- Duration – The length of time that information can be held in memory

Long-term Memory (LTM)

It is not possible to quantify the exact capacity of the LTM as there seems to be no upper limit to what we can store. The LTM is highly organised and consists of a number of different memory systems, each of which is responsible for storing different kinds of information. Because of its seemingly limitless capacity, forgetting in LTM does not often occur due to displacement (as it does in the STM). However, it can occur when similar types of information are stored, causing confusion. This is known as **interference**.

Tulving (1972) proposed that there were the following types of long term memory:

- *Episodic* - a part of the long-term memory responsible for storing information about events (i.e. episodes) that we have experienced in our lives. It involves conscious thought such as a memory of an 18th birthday

- *Procedural* - a part of the long-term memory that is responsible for knowing how to do things so it is not conscious but rather automatic. For example, procedural memory would involve knowledge of how to drive a car

- *Semantic* - a part of the long-term memory responsible for storing information about the world that involves conscious thought. This would include things like knowing about the meaning of words

Establishing the duration of LTM is also problematic since it can last a whole lifetime. Bahrick *et al* (1975) found that participants tested on recall of photographs of their classmates, performed well even at around 34 years after graduation, although they did better on recognition tasks where they had to match a photo to a name, rather than recall tasks in which they simply had to list their classmates without the aid of picture cues. However, there was a decline in performance of this test after about 47 years. Unlike most studies of memory, this used meaningful stimulus material (memories from participants' own lives) rather than unrelated lists of letters or words; this could indicate that information which is emotionally/personally significant to us is easier for us to remember. However, it was difficult to establish whether the decline in memory after 47 years reflected the limits of LTM duration or a more general decline in memory processing with age.

Note: Remember, being able to examine the limitations of experiment design and critique this where necessary is an important part of your A-level study.

Researchers have investigated whether the following factors have an impact on the duration of the LTM:

- The depth of learning (does how well we think we have learnt something make a difference to the length of time we can remember it for?)

- The pattern of learning (does the learning method impact on the LTM duration?)

- The nature of the material to be remembered (do we remember some kinds of information in our LTM more easily than others, and if so, why is this?)

Encoding in LTM is believed to be mainly **semantic** (that is, according to meaning). Baddeley (1966) found participants performing LTM tasks made more errors when recalling lists of **semantically similar** words (such as big and huge) than when recalling lists of **semantically dissimilar** ones.

However, it is also known that the LTM can use acoustic and visual encoding as well as semantic.

Activity 8

Look at Figure 1 (below) and use the following to label the diagram:

Arrows: Environmental stimuli; Attention; Retrieval; Elaborative rehearsal; Information retrieval; Maintenance rehearsal

Boxes: Sensory Memory; Short Term Memory; Long Term Memory

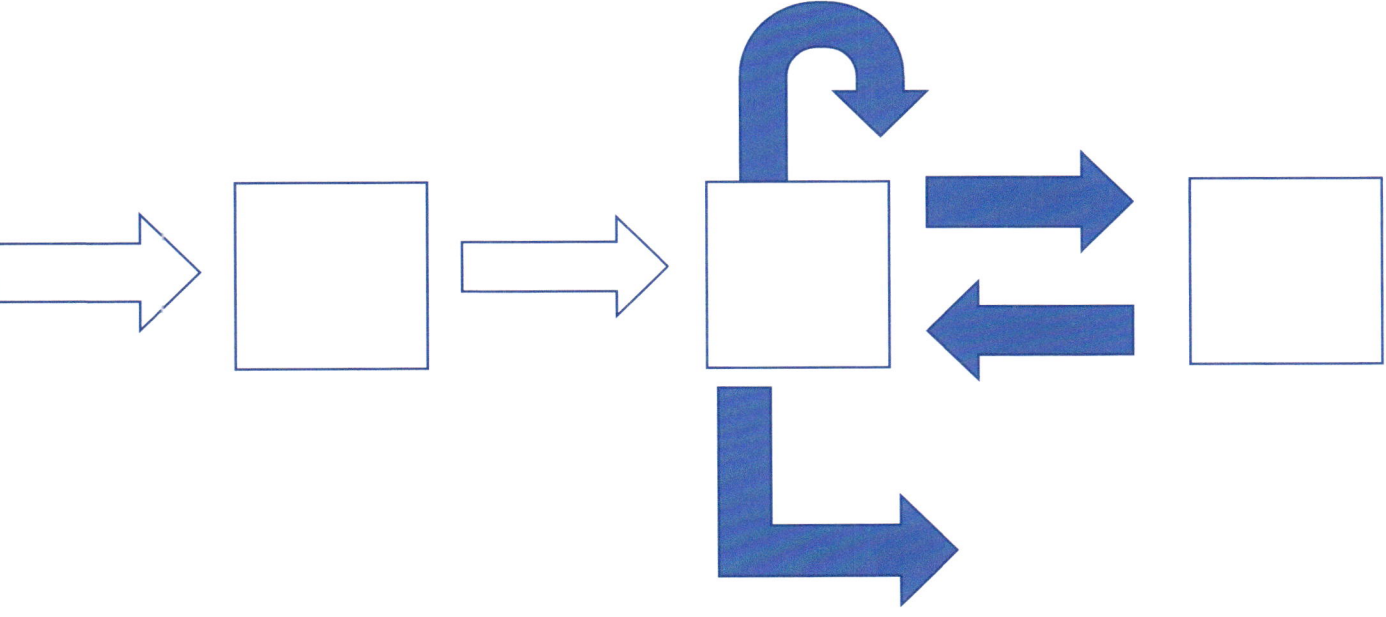

This is an outline diagram for the Multi-Store Model.

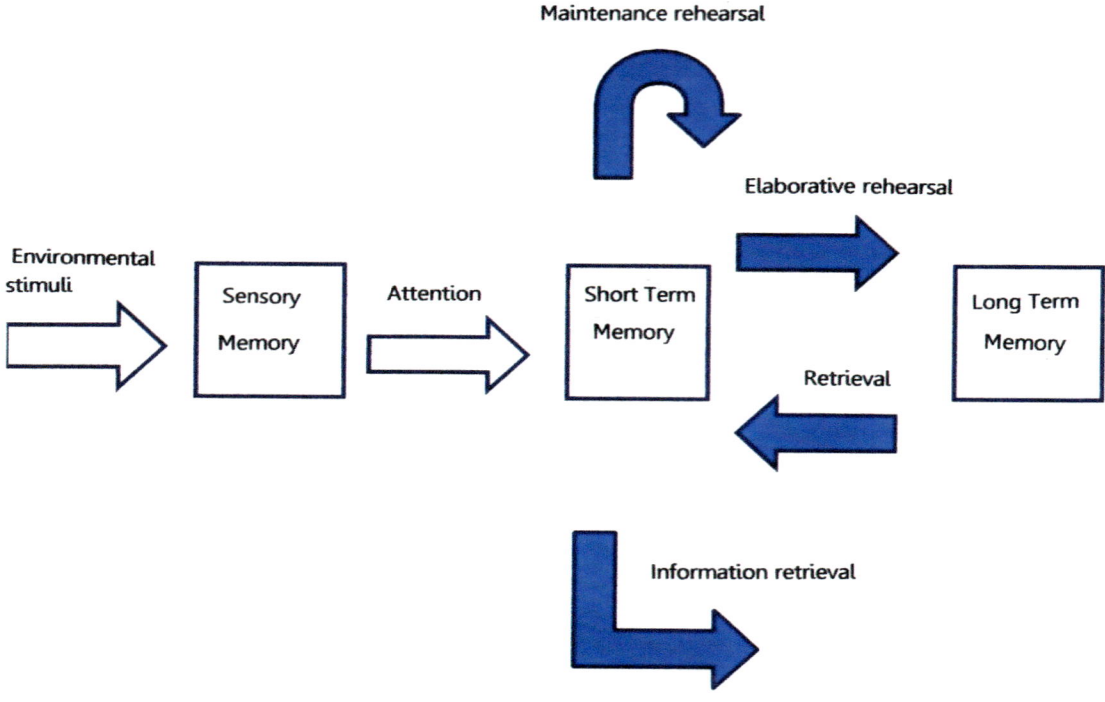

Evidence for a Distinction between STM and LTM

That the STM and LTM are two distinct stores has been shown using tasks where participants are given words and then allowed to recall them in any order (this is known as **free recall**). When the frequency of recall of each word is plotted against its position in the list, a characteristic **serial position curve** is produced. This describes the fact that words at the beginning and end of the list are retained well but those in the middle of the list are often lost. This is because participants start to rehearse the words at the beginning of the list until the capacity of their STM is exceeded. These words have therefore been processed in the LTM (this is the **primacy effect**). However, words at the end of the list are remembered because they are still active in STM (this is the **recency effect**).

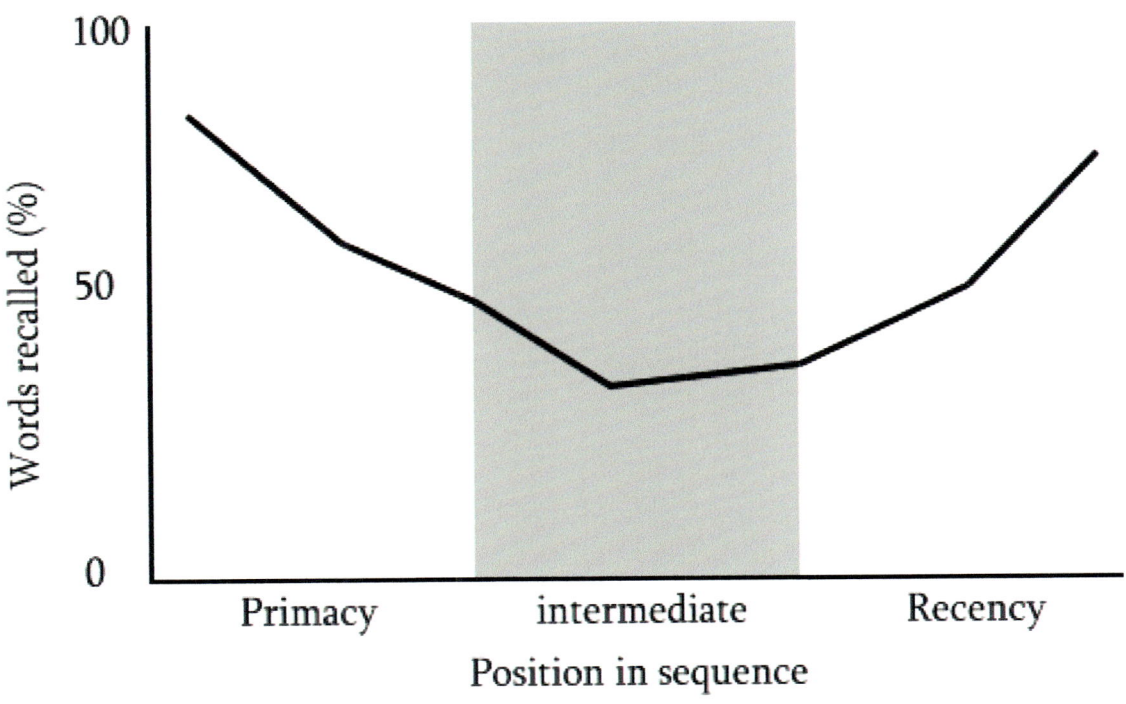

Glanzer and Cunitz (1966) gave participants a distractor task after presenting them with a word list which they then had to recall. The task was designed to prevent rehearsal of the last few items on the list. They found that the recency part of the curve was lost whilst the primacy part remained unaffected: immediate recall of the words gave a standard serial position curve, whereas recall after a 30 second delay and the distraction tasks successfully disrupted the recency effect. The fact that researchers were able to manipulate the ability of one memory store whilst leaving the other intact provides support for there being two separate stores or a functional dissociation in memory.

Further support comes from neurophysiological case studies on people who have suffered brain damage. A patient known as HM (Milner, 1966) underwent surgery to remove his hippocampus on both sides in an attempt to cure his epilepsy. This left him with severe **anterograde amnesia** (which meant that he could not store new memories). His STM was left intact and he could retain verbal information for about 15 seconds. However, he could not transfer information into his LTM or, if he could, he could not retrieve it. Blakemore (1988) describes his memory for new events, faces, phone numbers and places as settling in his mind for just a few seconds before trickling away again.

Brain scanning studies also support this distinction. Squire *et al* (1992) used PET scans to show that the pre-frontal cortex of the brain is active during STM tasks while the hippocampus is active during LTM tasks.

Activity 9

What are the two key features of the Multi-Store Model of memory? Make sure you can explain these before continuing.

Now complete the table below with these key terms: unlimited; up to a lifetime; 7 +/- 2 items; mainly acoustic; seconds; mainly semantic

	Short-term memory (STM)	Long-term memory (LTM)
Capacity		
Duration		
Encoding		

The Multi-Store Model has a series of stages, SM, STM and LTM, and information flows through these in a fixed, linear sequence. Information is transferred from STM to LTM via rehearsal.

	Short-term memory (STM)	Long-term memory (LTM)
Capacity	7 +/- 2 items	unlimited
Duration	seconds	up to a lifetime
Encoding	mainly acoustic	mainly semantic

Evaluating the Multi-Store Model

In order to evaluate the Multi-Store Model of memory, it is necessary to compare studies which both support and challenge the model. Evidence from laboratory studies on primacy/recency and from case studies of brain damaged patients provides good support for a functional dissociation or a distinction between STM and LTM. There is also support from neurophysiological studies which show that different areas of the brain are active when participants are performing STM and LTM tasks.

However, there are a number of criticisms of the model. One of the main criticisms is that the model is oversimplified and does not take into account the full complexity of memory. Evidence that the model is oversimplified comes from the study of a patient known as KF (Shallice and Warrington, 1970). KF suffered brain damage in a motorcycle accident which severely impaired his STM but left his LTM intact. The Multi-Store Model would predict that this could not happen since all information in LTM must pass through STM. The fact that he could make new long-term memories (providing the information was presented visually) refutes this idea and thus one of the core assumptions of the Multi-Store Model. Further evidence refuting the notion that information only flows one way through the system is provided by Ruchkin *et al* (1999) who found that participants' brain activity when recalling words or pseudo-words (nonsense words) was different. Evidently, when processing words, they were activating information stored in LTM. This suggests that LTM must be activated before certain stages of STM processing can occur. Another criticism is that the role of rehearsal has been overstated. Theorists today believe that memory is an active process and that simple repetition of information to be remembered is the least effective strategy of all. Craik and Tulving (1975) found that better retention in LTM was achieved when participants processed information semantically (by meaning). This means that people had better LTM retention when they gave meanings to otherwise meaningless data – as with the meaningless number string becoming meaningful dates in an earlier task.

Additionally, Brown and Kulik (1977) have shown that memories for events which were highly emotionally charged, extremely traumatic or personally significant in some way are imprinted in LTM with little effort at all to remember them having taken place. Such memories have become known as flash-bulb memories, since the emotion surrounding the event seems to evoke a special mechanism causing the memory to be imprinted on LTM without rehearsal.

An easy demonstration of this is to think about your memory of 9/11. You can probably recall in vivid detail what you were doing at the time you heard the news, how you felt and who you were with, because it was a highly charged and highly significant, emotional event.

If you also think about personal/emotionally significant times or moments in your own life (these can be either good or bad), such as a wedding, a funeral, a special birthday, important childhood event or other personal event, then it is highly likely that you can recall what happened, what was said and so on, even if the event happened a long time ago. This shows that for your LTM, storing 'emotional' memories such as these is relatively easy and straightforward in a way in which storing passwords, PIN numbers, phone numbers and so on is not.

Activity 10

Give one strength and one weakness of the Multi-Store Model of memory.

Answer to activity 10

The Multi-Store Model made an important contribution to memory research and has provided the foundation for future work on memory.

The main weakness of the Multi-Store Model is that it is oversimplified. For example, it takes no account of LTM activation in the storage of information and it cannot explain evidence such as that provided by the case study of KF.

The following example illustrates this simplification in the form of a case study: Some students read through their revision notes lots of times before an examination, but still find it difficult to remember the information. However, the same students can remember the information in a celebrity magazine, even though they read it only once. **Why do you think this is the case?**

Evaluating Memory Research

Much of the work on the Multi-Store Model is laboratory based. This allows good control of variables and ensures that research can be replicated, thus increasing **reliability**. However, many of the tasks used were not things participants would normally be asked to do in real life (e.g. learning trigrams or nonsense words). Therefore, this questions the ability of such experiments to represent memory for everyday situations. In other words, they lack **ecological validity**. Further work has concentrated on looking at memory as an active and interactive process as well as looking at the possibility of separate stores for different types of information within STM and LTM.

How Science Works

Before continuing our study of memory, let us check now those two key terms: **reliable** and **valid**. It is important that you understand what these terms mean, since it is part of your understanding of How Science Works.

Reliability: Psychologists must ask themselves the following whenever they design their research: if another psychologist repeated any piece of research, following the same methodology, would he or she obtain the same results? It is expected that if research is **reliable,** then the answer to this question would be: yes.

In other words, **reliable** research and the data that results from it is that which conforms to the scientific method and the principle of repeatability. In general, quantitative data is more **reliable** than qualitative, if we follow this definition of reliability.

Validity: The next question psychologists ask themselves when evaluating research is this: how far does this data give us a true or **valid** picture of the subject of research? In order to answer this question, psychologists must do some analysis of the methodology used to obtain the data. For example: how well does the method used match the research subject in question? Is it appropriate for the topic? Was the research carried out ethically and correctly? This is how a psychologist evaluates whether or not data is **valid**.

When we next meet an example of psychological research, don't forget to ask yourself whether the design is both **reliable** and **valid**.

The Working Memory Model

In 1974 Baddeley and Hitch developed a model of short term memory, which they called working memory. This model was an alternative to the short-term store as referred to in Atkinson and Shiffrin's 'multi-store' **memory model** (1968). Baddeley and Hitch argued that the STM as seen in relation to the Multi-Store Model was far too simple an explanation, and as such needed to be developed further. Baddeley and Hitch were interested in the function (what is it for?) rather than structure (what is it like?) of the STM. They argued that the working memory is short term memory, and instead of all information going into one single store, there are different systems for different types of information. They proposed that a more useful view of the STM was as a working memory with sub-components designed to perform a series of different functions. This idea emphasises the fact that the STM is an active store used to hold information both from sensory memory and from long-term memory whilst it is being manipulated for present use. It is also involved in reasoning, understanding and learning. The Working Memory is the process that takes place when we continually focus on material for longer than STM alone will allow. Alan Baddeley and his colleagues have carried out a number of investigations which show that working memory consists of several components. These are:

- **Central executive** – This is involved in all tasks requiring attention. It allocates resources to the other stores and acts as the controller for working memory

- **Visuo-spatial sketchpad** (also known as the inner eye) – This holds visual information such as size, shape and colour. It consists of two sub-components; an active rehearsal mechanism called the **inner scribe** which is linked to a passive visual store called the **visual cache**. The visuo-spatial sketchpad is assumed to be responsible for manipulating visual images

- **Phonological loop** (inner voice) – This holds verbal information in speech-based form. Again, it has two sub-components; an active **articulatory loop** which maintains auditory information by sub-vocal repetition, and a passive storage system known as the **phonological store**

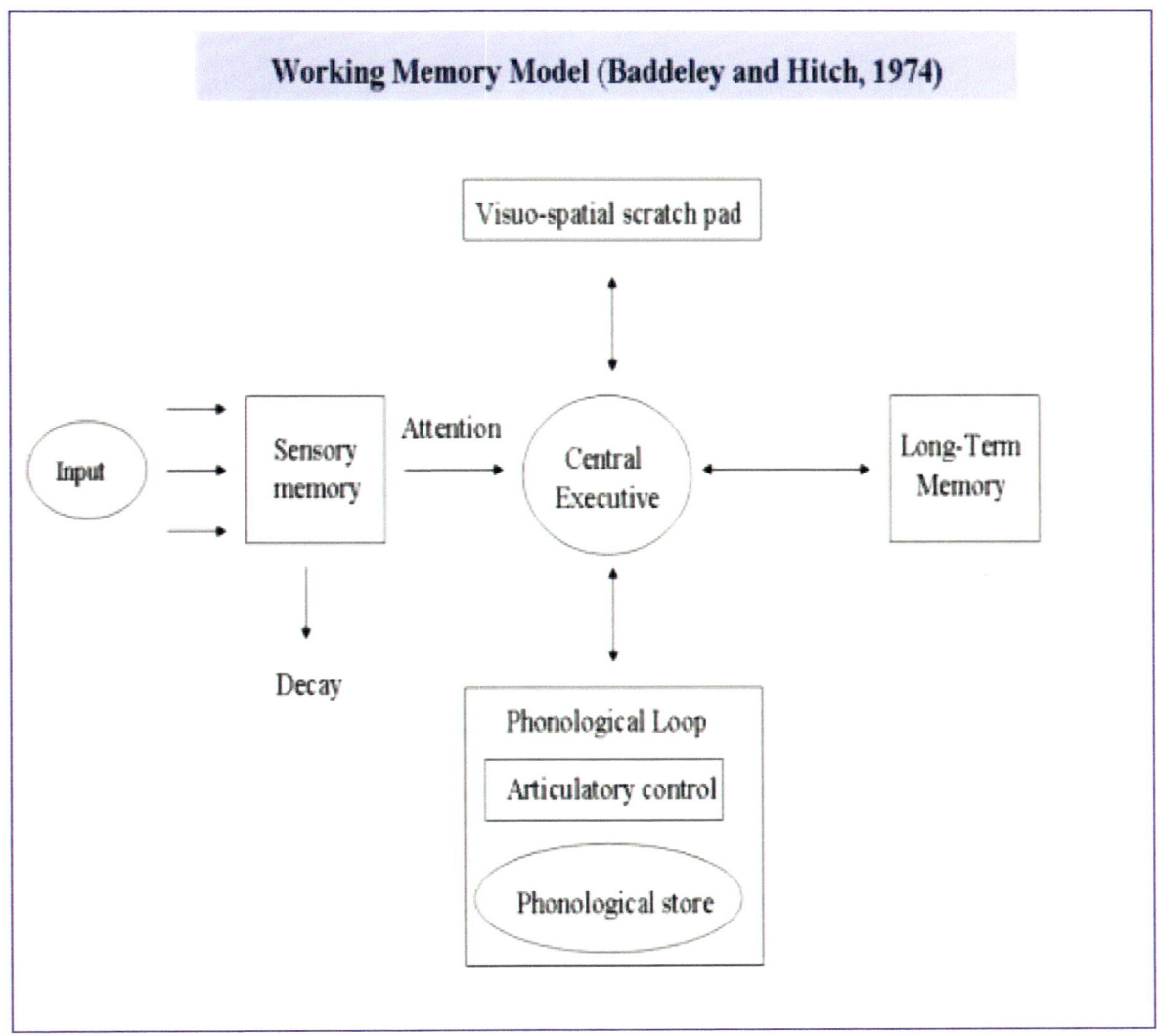

Working Memory Model (Baddeley and Hitch, 1974)

To illustrate how the components work, imagine you have been asked to count the number of windows in your house, from memory. Think about the front of the house where you live right now.

The image of your house is retrieved from your LTM and held in the **visual cache** where it can be manipulated and rotated, whilst you use the **articulatory loop** to count the windows **sub-vocally** (in other words, you do this silently rather than out loud, unless perhaps you are alone).

You need to be able to define and describe the components of the Working Memory Model. Make sure that you understand them before you continue.

Much of the research into working memory has been carried out using an experimental method known as the **dual task technique**, which has been designed to show that two tasks can be carried out simultaneously with little or no effect on performance of either task, providing they use different components of STM. On the other hand, performance of two tasks that do use the same components of STM will be adversely affected in the dual task, which can show researchers which parts of memory are used for completing which kind of tasks. What follows is an example of two dual process tasks to show this in practice.

Activity 12

1. Stand up and walk around. While you are walking, recite the alphabet out loud. Then sit down and recite the alphabet out loud a second time. Is there a difference in your ability to complete the task while walking compared to sitting?
2. Now imagine that you are writing a letter to a friend of yours. Take a piece of paper and start writing this letter. While you are doing this, recite the alphabet out loud. Then stop writing the letter, and recite the alphabet out loud again. Is there a difference in your ability to complete the task while writing compared to not writing?

Experiment Interpretation

If you have completed the dual process tasks, you should have found it much easier to recite the alphabet while walking compared to when writing a letter, or you will have found that your ability to write the letter was significantly slowed down by the task of reciting the alphabet. Think now about why this is. Psychologists researching memory have concluded from experimentation of this kind that the same memory stores are being accessed in alphabet recitation and letter writing (verbal/language processing skills), whereas the kind of memory required for walking is found in a very different store, meaning that in this dual process task no interference can take place.

Further evidence has suggested that the capacity of the phonological loop is determined by time rather than number of items. Baddeley *et al* (1975) found that the capacity of the phonological loop is the number of words that can be articulated in 1.5 seconds.

There is further substantial evidence to support the idea that we can't perform two tasks which require the same processing system. Baddeley *et al* (1973) found that participants could not correctly identify top or bottom angles of imagined capital letters at the same time as performing a light-tracking task, since both tasks used the visuo-spatial sketchpad. However, they had no problem with the tracking task at the same time as performing a verbal task. This shows that there are separate components in working memory and that each component has a limited capacity.

Studies using PET scans which measure blood flow through and, therefore, determine the activity of different parts of the brain at a given time also lend support to the idea of separate sub-systems in working memory. Some researchers believe that the visual cache stores form (shape) and colour information and the inner scribe processes spatial and movement information. Klauer and Zhao (2004) found more activity on the left side of the brain when performing visual working memory tasks and more on the right side when performing spatial tasks. This supports the idea of separate subsystems within the visuo-spatial sketchpad since they appear to have different functions and are located in different areas of the brain.

Using a similar technique, Bunge *et al* (2000) found greater activity in the pre-frontal cortex when performing two working memory tasks than when performing only one. This supports the idea that the central executive (the pre-frontal cortex) works harder to allocate memory resources appropriately in dual-task conditions, thus also supporting the hypothesis that there are different components of working memory.

Evaluation of the Working Memory Model

The Working Memory Model has a number of advantages over the concept of STM described by the Multi-Store Model. It explains our ability to carry out tasks such as mental arithmetic by holding information both from sensory memory (e.g. the factors in the sum) and long term memory (the knowledge of how to solve it) whilst being able to manipulate it. It also offers a new interpretation of the study of the patient KF. He had damage to just the verbal part of his short term memory, which is why he could still retain information that was presented visually.

There is also a large amount of empirical evidence supporting the model. The dual process tasks of Baddeley and Hitch (1974) demonstrate the existence of various sub-systems in working memory, and there are numerous studies which demonstrate the functions of the phonological loop and visuospatial sketchpad. For example, Baddeley and Hitch (1974) found that participants could perform almost as well on a dual task (e.g. reciting a list of digits and a reasoning task) as they could when completing the tasks separately, even though reciting the digits should use up the limited capacity of their STM.

The Working Memory Model has had useful applications to real-life. Working memory capacity has been shown to be linked to reading comprehension and note-taking (Engle *et al*, 1999) and phonological loop deficit has been identified as an underlying factor in children with dyslexia, thus potentially linking research in cognitive psychology with issues in developmental or educational psychology.

However, a weakness of the model is that the central executive has been more difficult to investigate and, although tasks have been devised which demonstrate the function of the central executive (see Baddeley, 1996), its exact role remains unclear.

In which case, the Working Memory Model is not able to offer a complete understanding of how memory works and it does little to explain the role of long-term memory activation in processing information. With this in mind the original model was updated by Baddeley (2000) with the concept of the **Episodic Buffer.** The Episodic Buffer acts as a 'backup' store which communicates with both long-term memory and the components of the working memory. Baddeley described this model as a system that stores information that is fed by the visual, spatial, verbal (sub-systems) and perception, that links to the central executive and plays an essential role in conscious awareness. The buffer part of this concept refers how information is temporarily held in a multi-dimensional way. Episodic refers to how information is bound together in chucks or episodes which in turn links to the central executive and is responsible for our conscious awareness.

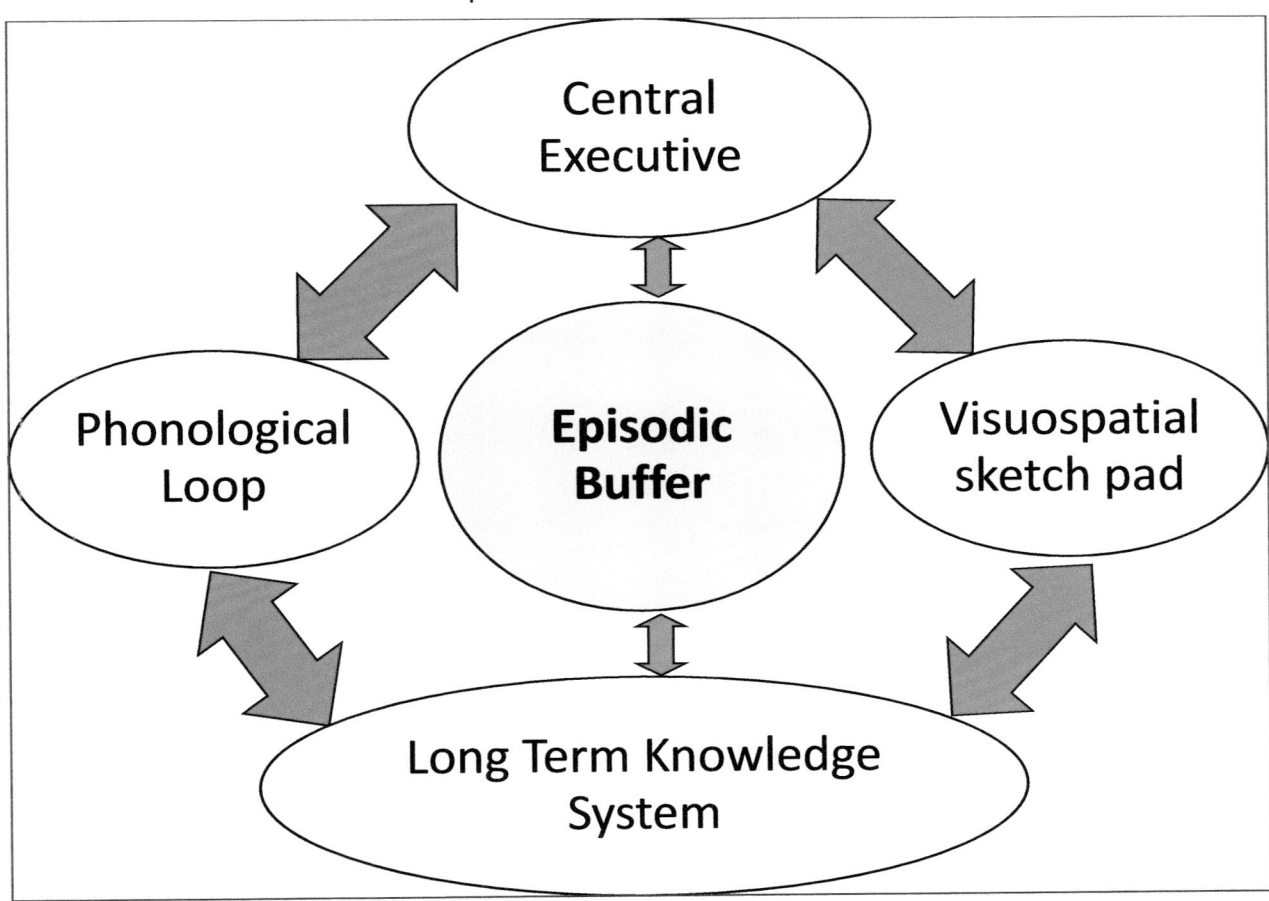

Figure: The updated model now includes the Episodic Buffer

Finally, much of the work on this model has used laboratory studies which are well controlled and produce reliable results. However, these experiments can lack ecological validity since the tests participants are asked to perform are rather artificial and do not represent memory in everyday life. This reminds us that appropriate experiment design is key, and trying to replicate real-life memory in experimental conditions (where possible) increases the validity of the resulting data.

Activity 13

Outline one weakness and one strength of the Working Memory Model.

One strength of the Working Memory Model is that it explains our ability to carry out tasks using information both from sensory memory and long term memory. It also offers a new interpretation of the study of the patient KF.

One weakness of the model is that it cannot yet explain the role of long-term memory activation in processing information.

Explanations for forgetting

Why do we 'forget'? Why is it for example, that you could rush up the stairs to get something and then by the time you get to the top of the stairs you've forgotten why you ran up there in the first place? Or, after being introduced to someone and actually having a conversation with them, by the following day you have forgotten their name but you can remember the colour and style of the shoes they were wearing? As we have seen from some of the previous points made in this unit, there are many explanations or attempted explanations regarding how memory works, but how does psychology explain forgetting. There two main explanations given as to why we 'forget'.

- First, we forget because the information that was stored in our memories is no longer available – which sounds a bit like leaving the office, going out to lunch and not being available until you get back. But this explanation is not too dissimilar to that idea – the information is not available when you need it but it may be accessible at a later date

- Secondly, the memory or information that has been forgotten has been permanently forgotten and, as such, any physical traces of the memory cease to be. In such instances the information is not available at all

How we forget

In terms of how we forget, it is argued that this is very much dependent upon whether what has been forgotten was stored in the long term or short term memory. In the 1930s to 1950s psychologists of the time would argue that what caused forgetting was something called **interference.** This was based on the notion that memory can be interfered with in some way by what we have learnt previously or by what we learn in the future. The suggestion therefore being that the memory can become combined with some other information or confused by distorted memories. According to interference theory, memories can interfere with each other and cause forgetting.

Interference theory suggests that there are two ways interference can occur:

1. **Proactive interference (pro=forward) -** the inability to be able to learn something new because something that had been learnt previously (an old memory) interferes with the learning of something new (a new memory). (See figure 1 below)

Figure 1: Proactive interference

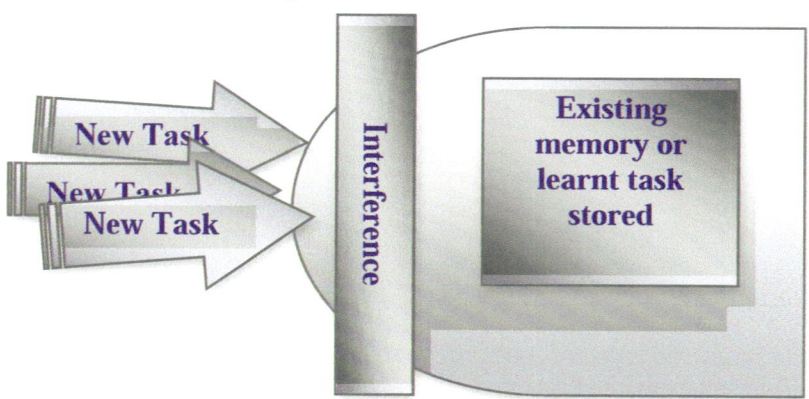

2. **Retroactive interference** (retro=backward) - forgetting something learnt previously because of learning a new task. The later learning interferes with earlier learning. (See figure 2 below)

Figure 2: Retroactive interference

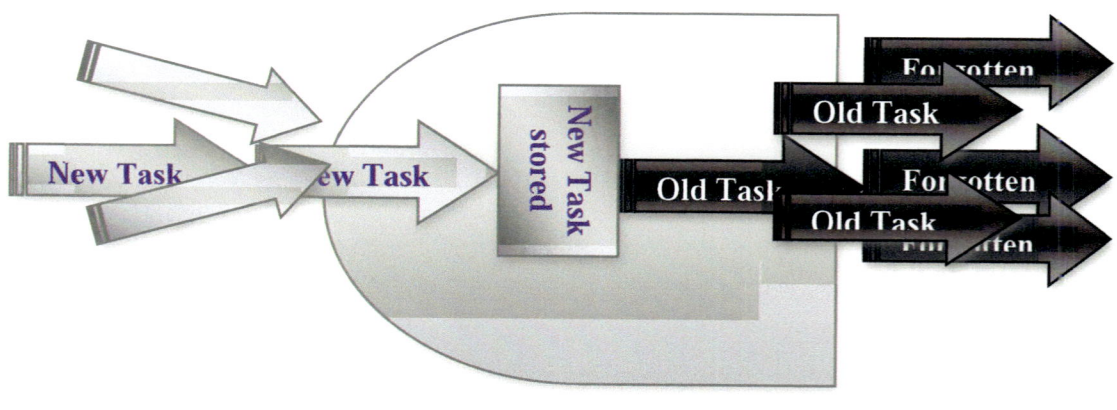

Study:

Author/Date	Underwood and Postman (1960)
Aims	To investigate and test how retroactive interference affects learning.
Procedure	Participants were split into two groups. Half of the group (Group A) had to learn and remember a list of paired words, e.g. cat/tree, jelly/moss, book/tractor. They were then asked to learn a second list of paired words e.g. cat/glass, jelly/time. Here the paired words were different to the first list. The other half of the group (Group B), the control group, had to learn the first list of words only and not given the second list. All of the participants were then asked to recall the words on the first list.
Findings	The recall of Group B was more accurate than that of Group A.
Conclusion	What is being suggested by the findings of this experiment is that having to learn a second list interfered with the ability to recall the first list and is therefore an example of retroactive interference.
Evaluation	This was a laboratory study and therefore artificial. Baddeley (1990) states that the tasks given to participants were too close to each other and, in real life; these kinds of events are more spaced out. More recent research (Anderson, 2000) has tried to address the issues raised above by investigating actual 'real-life' occurrences and the outcome of these studies support for interference theory. Whilst it is generally accepted is that interference does play a part in forgetting, the extent of this part is not definitive.

Proactive and retroactive interference is thought to be more likely to occur where the memories are similar. Baddeley (1999) found that people sometimes forgot things and found it difficult to remember certain information if elements of what was being remembered were similar. For example, trying to remember the name of a place you visited that is very similar to the name of somewhere else.

Retrieval Failure

Retrieval failure is when information in the long-term memory cannot be accessed or retrieved, and the reason for this is because the '**retrieval cues**' are not present at the time.

When we store a new memory, that memory will be stored with details and information associated with it, and these are **retrieval cues**. These cues can be, for example, seeing something or smelling something that is associated with the memory; this can trigger off a cue/s (**external/context**). Experiencing an emotion, feeling or mood can also act as a cue (**internal/state**).

Laboratory based experiments suggest that in terms of long term memory, memories are more likely to be retrievable if appropriate retrieval cues are present. These cues act as a trigger or clue that enables an individual to gain access to the memory. Tulving (1974) argues that information from a memory is more likely to be retrievable if the actual cue was present at the time at which the information was encoded. So, if a man proposed to a woman when their favourite song was playing in the background, both are more likely to remember details of that event when they hear the song (which can now be regarded as the retrieval cue) again.

Eyewitness Testimony

One practical application of memory research has been in the field of eyewitness testimony (EWT). EWT refers to an account given by an individual of an event or occurrence they have witnessed. Inaccurate EWT can have serious consequences, leading to wrongful convictions and even the death penalty in the US. For example, Rattner (1988) reviewed 205 cases of wrongful arrest and found that this was due to mistaken EWT in 52% of cases. Understandably, there has been much research carried out into why EWT can be unreliable and the various factors that can affect it.

The problem is that memory is not a static record of an event. Unlike photographic or CCTV evidence, memory is an active process, and there is evidence that our previous experiences, the stereotypes we hold and the emotion we felt at the time of an event, can change the way in which that memory is laid down. If that were not bad enough, post-event information can change our memories of an event. It is therefore very difficult to know which is the original memory and which is the one that has been altered by the passage of time and the overlay of your later life experiences (such as information about the same events which you receive from other sources, or your changed emotions about the event in question).

For example, suppose you have a memory of your fifth birthday party, and one day (as an adult) you are discussing this with your mother. You talk about a gift you received from Uncle Frank and how much you liked it at the time. However, your mother says 'no, that was from Uncle Steven; Uncle Frank didn't come to your fifth party.'

Now your memory for the event has been challenged with the post-event information given to you by your mother. You will now return your memory of your fifth birthday party to your LTM in an altered form i.e. with Uncle Steven giving you the gift instead.

Consider why it is that your mother's version of events is considered more accurate by you than your own version. The fact that you are inclined to believe your mother's version of events rather than your own is an indication that the authority of other sources of information can have a huge impact on how we record events and our subsequent interpretation of them; in this case, because you were a child at the time of your fifth birthday party, once you are also an adult you consider your adult mother's memory of the same event more authoritative.

This alteration of memory *after the event* has far reaching implications for the accuracy of EWT. If witnesses were given wrong or misleading information during questioning, perhaps by a source they considered more authoritative (for whatever reason), it could have the potential to change their recollection of an event. One of the most prolific researchers into EWT is an American psychologist, Elizabeth Loftus, she wanted to examine the influence of (mis)leading information in relation to this. Her findings indicated that memory of an event that had been witnessed can be extremely flexible. Loftus suggested that if a person was exposed to new information during the interval between witnessing an event and recalling it, the new information may affect what they were able to recall and the accuracy of it. In other words the original memory can be modified, altered or supplemented.

In a study by Loftus and Palmer (1974), *Reconstruction of Automobile Destruction,* they devised an experiment to find out if **leading questions** could bias how a witness answers. They showed participants a film of a car accident and then asked them how fast the cars were travelling when they hit each other. All participants were asked the same question except that the verb 'hit' was replaced with 'smashed', collided, 'bumped' or 'contacted'. Their findings showed that the word used in questioning affected the estimations of speed given by the participants. The results are given below:

Verb used in questioning	Average speed estimates (mph)
Contacted	31
Hit	34
Bumped	38
Collided	39
Smashed	41

When asked one week later if they had seen any broken glass in the original film, participants who had been given the word 'smashed' were more likely to answer 'yes', even though there had been no glass in the film at all!

The results showed that subtle changes in the wording of questions changed the participant's perceptions. In some cases the participant may change their eyewitness testimony because of the way questions were asked after a crime was committed, which influenced the r response. For Loftus and Palmer there were two possible explanations for this:

1. **Response-bias factors**: The information provided may have simply influenced the answer a person gave (a 'response-bias') which in itself was not actually false but the words used influenced or generated a bias in terms of the

person's response. For example, when a witness is trying to recall the amount of force exerted by one person in relation to another in a physical altercation, their account can be influenced or biased by the words used to describe the occurrence – such as the difference between someone being 'slapped' and being 'struck'.

2. **The memory representation is altered**: The critical verb changes an individual's perception of the accident. Critical verbs could result in someone having a perception of an incident that is more serious than the actual incident itself and this is then stored in the individual's memory of the incident. e.g. 'the victim suffered a broken nose' when compared to 'the victim suffered a facial fracture'.

This shows that even subtle changes to the wording of a question can affect EWT.

Study note: A good way to summarise psychological studies is to make a note framework, such as the one given below. This note framework shows another study into misleading post-event information and the impact this can have on EWT. In future, when making your own notes on psychological studies or doing your own research, consider using this framework for summarising the key information you find.

Studies on Misleading Post-Event Information

Author/Date	Loftus (1975) 'Barn Study'
Aims	To see if false information given post-event can change the original memory.
Procedure	Participants were asked about the speed of a white sports car after watching a film showing this car travelling along a road. Half the participants were asked about the car passing a stop sign whereas the other half were asked about it passing a barn.

Findings	17% in the 'barn' group reported seeing a barn in the film compared to only 3% in the 'stop sign' group. There had been no barn in the original film.
Conclusions	The 'barn' group had added the misleading post-event information to their original memory, whereas the non-barn group had not.
Evaluation	This was a laboratory study and therefore artificial; it lacked ecological validity. There were high demand characteristics (this means that there was a high demand that participants act the way they think they should within the context of this study). Deception was used: the researchers were not able to give away the precise nature of study beforehand, but participants were debriefed afterwards.

The Effects of Misleading Information

Misleading information can cause inaccurate recall of events because it leads to a phenomenon known as 'source misattribution'. In other words, participants who are given post-event information that is not consistent with their original memory (e.g. being asked about a barn instead of a stop sign) get confused as to where they encountered each item. In the study above, some of the participants misattributed the source of the barn and thought they had seen it in the original film, whereas in fact the source of the barn was the misinformation of the researchers who were deliberately feeding the participants false information. Loftus concludes that this is because the original memory is overwritten or altered and is replaced by the new, false memory, which the participants now believe to be the correct record of events.

However, not all people are equally prone to source misattribution errors. Tomes and Katz (1997) have found that people with poorer general recall for an event are more susceptible to misleading information, as are people who score highly on tests of imagery vividness and empathy with other people. This research therefore links the psychology of memory to social and behavioural psychology, reminding us of the connections that are frequently made between different subdivisions of the subject.

Also, Loftus found that people are not easily misled by blatantly wrong information. She showed participants sets of slides in which a red purse was stolen from a handbag. Later, she gave participants an account of the theft which contained deliberate errors. One of the errors referred to the purse as being brown in colour. Most of the participants were not misled by the error relating to the colour of the purse. This shows that people are not always affected by misleading information, especially when the information refers to central rather than peripheral details of an event.

Evaluation of Research on Misleading Information

Loftus has made an important contribution to our understanding of the inaccuracy of eyewitness testimony. It seems clear from her research that memory for events can be altered in the light of misleading information. However, her studies have been criticised for artificiality. It is also possible that participants in experiments are less accurate than real-life witnesses because they know inaccuracies will not lead to serious consequences, and because the artificiality of the situation has meant that the memory is not powerfully imprinted on their LTM.

Foster *et al* (1994) tested this first possibility in a study where participants were shown a video of a bank robbery and subsequently asked to identify the robber in an identity parade. One group of participants were led to believe that the robbery was a real event and that their responses would influence the trial, while the second group were told that it was a simulation. Identification of the robber was more accurate for the first group, suggesting that consequences and context are an important factor for witnesses.

It has also been suggested that the method of testing witnesses' recall could be a factor in explaining some of Loftus' findings. For example, she often used forced-choice tests where participants had to pick one slide from a choice of two. Koriat and Goldsmith (1996) have shown that witness accuracy can be dramatically increased if tests do not rely on forced-choice format and if witnesses are allowed to leave out a question if they feel unsure (that is, they are not forced to make a choice). It is also the case that witnesses can produce far more accurate memories if they are given the appropriate cues.

Loftus has been further criticised for her explanation of the effects of post-event information. She believes that the original memory is re-written by the incorporation of misleading information: the original memory is deleted and replaced by the new, false memory. Other researchers have disputed this and believe that the original memory is still available, even though it has been obscured by the new information.

Bekerian and Bowers (1983) replicated a study by Loftus *et al* (1978) where a car is shown stopping at either a 'stop' or a 'give way' sign. Participants are then asked questions which are consistent or inconsistent with what they have seen. In the recognition phase of the study, the participants were presented with the pairs of slides in chronological order (i.e. the order they were first shown). This was not like the original study where Loftus showed them in any order. In the original study, recall was poor but in the replication, recall for those given misleading information was as accurate as a control group who were given non-leading information.

Bekerian and Bowers concluded that the original memory had not been lost for the experimental group. This was because using slides in the correct order provided enough cues to reactivate the original memory regardless of having been given misleading information after the event. However, other researchers have failed to replicate this result, so it remains unclear whether the memory trace is in fact destroyed or whether it is only obscured and can later be retrieved.

Further work on EWT has shown that it is not just the retrieval stage of memory that is vulnerable. Let us now look at the stages of memory after the event itself and the things that can affect the accuracy of the record at each stage.

Encoding	Storage	Retrieval
• Poor viewing conditions • Effect of schemas • Anxiety and the weapons effect	• Misleading information • Misattribution errors	• Leading questions
Another key factor: The age of the witness		

We will now consider the encoding and storage stages in more detail and how different factors can impact on the accuracy of the memory.

Encoding: Effect of Schemas

Frederick Bartlett (1932) showed that, instead of storing an exact replica of events, we store what he termed a 'reconstructive memory' based on our interpretation of events. This interpretation is created using knowledge that we have already stored in our memory, which is stored in discreet entities called schemas. Schemas help us to make sense of the world. If we had to analyse every new event or object from scratch, it would take ages to process the information and would be a waste of resources. Schemas enable us to process new information according to what we have already stored about previous similar situations and help us to fill in any 'gaps' in the information available to us.

For example, let's suppose your friend tells you that the film he saw last night was good but he missed the start because the service at the 'Taj Mahal' was slow. You somehow know that 'service' and 'Taj Mahal' refer to an Indian restaurant (rather than the actual Taj Mahal, or any other kind of establishment such as a bar or cafe) without really giving it a second thought. This is because you have a restaurant schema stored in your memory to which you can refer, and you are able to 'fill in the gaps' or infer information based on the cues you receive from others and your surroundings and with the aid of your schemas. In particular, schemas we have stored about other groups of people, often containing negative information, are called stereotypes. Brewer and Treyens (1981) investigated the effects of schemas on visual memory. They asked individual participants to wait in a room for 35 seconds. The room was designed to look like an office and contained 61 objects, some of which were consistent with an office schema (desk, typewriter etc.) and some of which were not (including a skull, a brick and a pair of pliers). In a later unexpected recall test, they found that participants were most likely to recall the typical office items and less likely to recall items inconsistent with an office schema, such as the pliers. They also found that errors in recall typically involved substituting schema-consistent items, i.e. falsely recalling things like pens and a telephone, which fit in with an office schema but were not actually present in the office. Eight participants recalled the bizarre item, the skull, which shows that we do use schemas when encoding information but will also pay attention to highly bizarre or atypical details.

List (1986) applied schemas to EWT. She asked people to rate various events in terms of their probability in a shoplifting scenario (thus eliciting their shoplifting schema; that is, what people expect would happen in a shoplifting scenario). She then devised a video showing eight different acts of shoplifting, each of which incorporated some of the events previously rated as high-probability and some rated as low-probability.

She then showed the video to a new set of participants and tested their recall one week later. She found they were more likely to recall high-probability events than low-probability events and that any substitution errors made tended to involve high-probability events. This study further demonstrates the impact schemas can have on EWT.

Based on research such as this, Cohen (1993) has suggested five ways that schemas can lead to reconstructive memory:

1. We tend to ignore elements of an event that don't fit in with our currently activated schema
2. We can store the central features of an event without having to store the exact details
3. We can make sense of what we have seen by 'filling in' (inferring) missing information
4. We distort memories of events to fit in with prior expectations (e.g. we may remember a robber wearing a balaclava when, in fact, he wore a cap, because our schema of a robber is powerful enough to create interference with our memory of the event)
5. We may use our schemas to provide us with a best guess if we can't recall the exact information

The Impact of Stress and Anxiety on EWT and Memory Recall

Evidence about the effects of anxiety and stress on the accuracy of EWT is contradictory. Laboratory studies suggest that anxiety can impair recall whereas real-life studies often show that the anxiety of an event can enhance recall. This may be because events are so traumatic that they are 'seared' into LTM, making memories highly accurate and long-lasting (though of course, from a behavioural psychological perspective, potentially hugely damaging to an individual and potentially requiring therapeutic intervention in order to neutralise them as far as possible).

In a study by Clifford and Scott (1978) they had a group of people watch a film of a violent attack. They found that people remembered fewer of the 40 items of information about the event than a control group who saw a less violent and stressful version. Witnessing a real violent crime, it can be assumed, is likely to be more stressful and as such it could be suggested that the level of memory accuracy may be diminished somewhat due to the anxiety/stress of witnessing a real situation.

However, a study by Yuille and Cutshall (1986) suggests that we should reconsider the extent to which stress influences eyewitness memories. In their study, they found that witnesses, who had seen a real life shooting outside a shop in Canada, were able to recall and give high levels of accuracy regarding the incident. And even when witnesses were re-interviewed some 5 months later they still had a good level of recall, despite the level of stress and anxiety they had experienced at the time.

In one laboratory study, Loftus (1979) had some participants sitting outside a laboratory. The participants were led to believe that they were listening to genuine conversations inside the laboratory, followed by them witnessing a man leaving the laboratory. In one condition, participants heard a calm discussion and saw a man with greasy hands and a pen leave. In another condition, there was a heated exchange accompanied by the sound of smashing glass and furniture being turned over. The man leaving the lab was holding a bloody knife.

Later, the group who had heard the calm exchange were much better at identifying the man from a series of photographs than the group who had heard the heated exchange. Loftus believed that the anxiety caused by seeing the weapon in the second condition had affected participants' ability to identify the man. She called this the 'weapons effect' since the presence of the weapon had drawn the focus away from the face of the perpetrator onto the weapon. (An implication of this for EWT is that witnesses may be better at identifying weapons than faces – also possibly useful for the police.)

Later research by Loftus and Burns (1982) provided support for this finding. Participants saw either a film of a violent crime in which a boy was shot in the face, or a non-violent version. Those who had seen the violent version were less accurate in recalling the details of the crime, again implying that the weapons effect interferes with witnesses' ability to recall the faces of people they have seen. However, Christianson and Hubinette (1993) questioned 110 witnesses who had witnessed genuine bank robberies. Some of the witnesses had been bank employees who had been directly threatened during the robberies. The rest were onlookers. They found that:

- Victims gave more accurate recall of the event and remembered more details than people who had been onlookers
- This superior recall was evident even after a 15-month interval

Their study shows that even though an individual/s may experience high levels of stress or anxiety during an incident, such as witnessing a crime, this does not necessarily mean they will not be able to recall details of the incident with a good level of accuracy. Also, misleading questions, as addressed by Loftus and Palmer, does not necessarily have the effect suggested, as the witness may still be able to recall details, despite any attempts to redirect or mislead them. This would suggest that people (especially victims) are good at remembering highly stressful and traumatic events if they occur in real-life rather than in the artificial surroundings of a laboratory, even where they are led to believe that the events they are witnessing are real (as in the calm conversation, heated argument and bloody knife scenario).

The Age of the Witness

It is generally believed that children do not make as reliable witnesses as adults. This schema was most likely at work in your decision to overwrite your own memory of your fifth birthday party with that of your mother's in our earlier example. Yet there are some crimes where only child witnesses were present (e.g. in some abuse cases). It makes sense then, for psychologists to study the accuracy of children's testimony at each stage of the process, i.e. encoding, storage and retrieval, and also to make a careful consideration of the impact of this on children's EWT.

Encoding: Ceci and Bruck (1993) believe that children may be inaccurate at providing EWT because they lack the appropriate schemas to help them interpret a situation. However, this could make them more accurate than an adult, since without an appropriate schema, they are not susceptible to inferring information which is consistent with a particular schema but was not actually there during the event. We already know that adults are susceptible to this.

Storage: The longer the time between the encoding of a memory and its later retrieval, the more likely retrieval is to be inaccurate. This is the case for both adults and children, although it would seem that children's memories are more affected by a retrieval delay than are adults' memories (Thomson 1988). The type of information stored is also a factor. For example, as storage interval increases, descriptions of people become less accurate than details of actions.

Retrieval: Children leave out more details than adults, but relevant cues can help to jog their memory. However, children are more susceptible to leading questions than adults, so they are more likely to recall information implied by the question. Leichtman and Ceci (1995) found that if 3 and 6 year-old children were given misleading information in questions, they incorporated it into their memory. Similarly, Poole and Lindsay (2001) found that children aged 3 to 8 incorporated elements of a story read to them by their parents into their memories of a science demonstration watched earlier. When asked about the source of the information (source monitoring), older children were able to remove the post-event items. This suggests that younger children are more susceptible than older children to the effects of misleading post-event information.

Elderly Witnesses

Elderly witnesses may also experience errors of recall. In a study by Yarnley (1984), participants were shown a staged event. When questioned afterwards, the study found that 80% of elderly participants failed to mention that the attacker held a knife, compared to only 20% of younger adults.

Cohen and Faulkner (1989) conducted a similar study where participants were shown a film of a kidnapping. A narrative account of the events shown was then read to participants, with half being given an accurate account of the film and half given a misleading one. The elderly participants' recall was found to be much more susceptible to the effects of the misleading information than that of the middle-aged participants.

Improving the accuracy of EWT

The Cognitive Interview

The reliability of eyewitness recall has been of great concern, not surprisingly when we consider that in many instances the making or breaking of a case or the 'catching' of a perpetrator of a crime, is very much dependent upon an individual's ability to recall the details of an incident or perpetrator. Fisher and Geiselmen *et al* (1985) suggest that one of the methods that could be used in order to retrieve the information needed, particularly in terms of getting accurate witness testimony during police questioning, is to use the **cognitive interview technique**. This method uses four techniques in order to retrieve the memory needed. They are:

- *Cognitive reinstatement* – to recreate the context: The interviewer may try to get the individual to mentally create the environment as well as placing the time within some sort of personal context at the time of the incident, such as asking the individual: what they were doing at the time or prior to the incident; what the day or weather was like, whether it was raining or sunny; how they were feeling at the time. This taps into the specific environmental cues that were present and may help 'jog' the memory
- *Change Perspective*: The interviewer may ask the individual to recall the incident from a different perspective, such as asking the witness what they think other people may have seen. This may enable the individual to recall something from a different recall route
- *Reverse Order*: The interviewer may ask the individual to recount the incident in an order different to how it occurred – a difference narrative order. As with 'change

perspective', this may enable the individual to recall something from a different recall route

- *Report everything*: The interviewer would ask the individual to recollect every little detail, even the ones that may seem trivial. Irrelevant details may help to trigger more significant ones. Doing this can elicit other memories linked to seemingly insignificant details

Activity 14

Do you think the Cognitive Interview technique would be effective? Consider the technique now. Can you think of any potential problems? In particular, consider the research you have already studied which shows the circumstances under which witnesses are more likely to give inaccurate testimony.

When you have done this, continue reading below.

Does the cognitive interview approach work?

Yes, because...

1. Retrieval cues enhance and improve memory recall
2. This approach gives individuals time to recall and retrieve information with a higher degree of accuracy
3. Milne and Bull (2002) found that used singularly, the four techniques improved recall
4. Godden and Baddeley (1975), found that memory can be significantly improved when encoding and recall takes place in an environment not too dissimilar, if not the same as where the incident occurred

But...

1. According to Geiselman (1999) this is not the best approach to use in all cases. Geiselman found that in reviewing cases where the witnesses were under the age of 6, the recall was not as accurate. This suggests that a different approach would have to be used according to whom the information was being retrieved from
2. There is also an ethical issue to be considered: using this approach to recall in detail, violent, sexual or gruesome events could be too traumatic for the witness concerned

In general, there are studies which show that the Cognitive Interview (CI) elicits more information than other types of questioning both in laboratory and real-life situations. However, it also seems to elicit more **inaccurate** information. It has also been found that the techniques of context reinstatement and reporting every detail found within the CI seem to be the most effective combination of elements in terms of eliciting accurate recall (Milne and Bull, 2002). However, it has proved to be effective with children over the age of 8 but not so useful with children under 6, perhaps because young children fail to understand the instructions (Geiselman, 1999).

In order to minimise the amount of inaccurate information given by interviewees in a CI, Fisher (1987) recommends using an Enhanced Cognitive Interview technique in which police actively listen to the witness, minimise distractions, use open-ended questions, encourage the use of imagery and avoid making judgemental comments. Overall, researchers have found that the Cognitive Interview has been useful in increasing the accuracy of EWT.

Strategies for Memory Improvement

Research into memory has provided us with various techniques that we can use to improve our retention of information. The following techniques will also be useful to you when you come to revise for the exam! This section will describe how the techniques work and relate them back to the memory research that underpins them. The techniques are based on:

- Organisation of information
- Encoding and retrieval strategies
- Active processing

Organisation of Information

The way we organise information that we wish to remember is central to remembering it effectively. One of the best known organisational strategies is using **mnemonics**. This uses verbal rhymes or visual images to organise information such as processes or events which need to be remembered in order. For example, the easiest way to remember the planets of the solar system is to make up a rhyme which uses the first letter of each name of the planet. This is much easier than simply trying to remember the names themselves by repetition or 'rote'. The more silly or bizarre you make the rhyme, the more likely you are to remember it. A typical rhyme could be:

Many **V**ets **E**at **M**onkey **J**am **S**aid **U**ncle **N**ick **P**recisely

Take the first letter from each of the rhyme words and you have:

Mercury, Venus, Earth, Mars, Jupiter, Saturn, Uranus, Neptune, Pluto.

Because LTM loves the unusual and bizarre (after all, there is no such thing as monkey jam and, if there were, would many vets want to eat it?) the rhyme will be stored with little effort. You have also 'chunked' the nine planets into a single item (the single phrase, which is one unit of semantic sense) rather than into nine discrete entries (the nine separate names of the planets), which will thus take up only one slot of precious STM when you recall it.

Some mnemonic techniques are based on visual imagery. These involve linking a visual image to the information you wish to remember. One of the most fun visual techniques is called the method of **loci** (plural of locus, meaning place). This allows us to remember things like shopping lists by visualising a familiar place already stored in LTM and 'hanging' the new information from it.

Activity 15

Imagine that you are going to the shops and you have a list of items to purchase, as follows:

- Eggs
- Bread
- Milk
- Biscuits
- Jam
- Sausages
- Bananas
- Chocolate

Once you have done that, consider how easy or difficult it is to remember the list by rote. It was not a lengthy list, but using rote memory means that you need to make eight separate entries in your STM in order to recall the information, but this is not the best allocation of your memory resources.

Now let us try the loci technique and compare how easy it was to remember the shopping list. First, think of a familiar routine which you do in the same order every day and which is therefore already easily available to you in STM. Consider now what that would be. A common one is getting ready for work in the morning, though you could also use a familiar route you walk every day (such as from your home to your school or office).

Now, use your imagination to make each of the items on the shopping list **interact** with the different stages of your routine. Here is an example of how this would work in practice, using my own familiar morning routine:

- My alarm goes off; I yawn and stretch out my hand, but eurgh! The clock is slippery; it is covered in egg! I am out of bed quicker than ever before but when I put my feet on the floor, something strange is underfoot: sausages!

- This is the strangest day of my life; I go to the bathroom, but the bath is full of biscuits!

Now carry on imagining each stage of your usual morning routine (or familiar walking route) whilst interacting with each of the items on the shopping list (notice that the ordering of the shopping list items is not important in this case – feel free to choose which ever food item fits the best with each stage in your own routine or journey).

When you have reached the end of the list, cover this sheet of paper and try to recall the items. Memory using this technique is typically robust; you will find that you can recall them tomorrow, next week and also next month, provided that you have made the interactions sufficiently bizarre and therefore memorable.

For this reason, using loci (and mnemonics) are highly recommended for recall of key information for your A-level examinations, such as names and dates of important studies. Try it and see if it works for you.

Psychological Research into Memory in Real World Applications

You may have already heard or read about individuals who can perform great feats of memory such as accurately recalling the order of a pack of playing cards they have seen for only one second for each card, or being able to recite the decimal places of pi (a mathematical quantity) to hundreds (or even thousands) of decimal places.

You may also think that such individuals are born with the gift of extraordinary memory, and that these kinds of feats are unavailable to everyday people. Psychological research has shown that if you think this, you are wrong. In fact, such individuals do not have a memory that is qualitatively different to yours in any way, shape or form. Instead, they have simply trained their memory to such an extent that they are able to recall a great quantity of information, but being able to do this is something that any individual could also do with the same memory training. You will also now be unsurprised to learn that this memory training is the advanced application of techniques such as loci and mnemonics.

In fact, recalling the order of a pack of playing cards is commonly undertaken by memory 'athletes' by using loci. A very familiar routine or route (such as those of the type described, or else a walk around a very familiar place, such as your own home) is used to hang each playing card (each of which are conceptualised as if people, using a further memorisation strategy) to a stage of the familiar route or part of the familiar place. It is particularly important to make the interactions as bizarre as possible so they are highly memorable.

An example of this follows, using the example of a walk around your own home:

I walk into my bedroom and see a man wearing a jumper with **10 diamonds** on it lying on the bed. He is lying flat on his back and the jumper is black with each diamond shape shining a brilliant white on it: I can see the pattern clearly and that there are two columns of five diamonds. He smiles at me and tells me to look in the wardrobe.

I then open the wardrobe and instead of seeing clothes I see a woman wearing a crown and two giant spades are hanging from her ears and she is wearing a necklace also made of spades. She is the **Queen of Spades**. She shouts at me to get out of her space and to look under the bed.

Tentatively, I look under the bed. There is another young man lying there, but he is asleep. He is also wearing black and a name badge which tells me he is called **Jack**. The room falls entirely silent apart from the sound of his beating heart which pounds louder and louder until it is the only thing I can hear; he is the **Jack of Hearts**.

In this way, a memory athlete trains him or herself to remember the order of a deck of randomly shuffled playing cards by pre-conceptualising each card as a person (as in the three examples above) and then linking each 'person' (card) to a place or stage in the familiar route (the loci) in a memorable way. The difficulty is to be able to do this very quickly and yet in a highly memorable fashion (as in the three bizarre examples given), and it is this that takes the practice and mental preparation and training that memory athletes need to undergo.

Indeed, many studies have shown that this type of highly visual imagery enhances recall. For example, Paivio (1965) found that participants were better at recalling concrete nouns than abstract ones. He linked this to the **dual coding hypothesis** where concrete nouns are encoded twice, first using a verbal code and then again, using a visual image. De Bene and Moè (2003) found the use of visual imagery to especially help memory when information is presented verbally, since conjuring up a visual image can be done whilst holding the word in the articulatory loop and, therefore, making use of two separate working memory systems. Studies like these seem to show that visual imagery enhances recall, but they have been criticised for lacking realism since it is not very often that we have to learn lists of unrelated words (except perhaps when memory athletes are deliberately training themselves for competitions!).

However, having some kind of organisational strategy for remembering the more typical complex information we are more likely to be faced with in real-life (such as psychological concepts and theories for A-level examination), still seems to improve our recall.

Bransford and Johnson (1972) devised an experiment to test this theory. They asked two groups of participants to read a long paragraph and then to try and remember the main details. For one group the passage was given the title 'Doing the Laundry', while the other group were not given a title. The study found that the group who were given the title performed significantly better on the recall test. This suggests that understanding the material significantly improves a person's ability to remember it. It also suggests that knowing the context of the information, i.e. 'Doing the Laundry', helped the participants to remember the passage because they were able to make use of their existing knowledge of doing laundry (their **schema**) to recall the information.

Encoding and Retrieval Strategies

Many memory strategies are based on the **encoding specificity principle** (Tulving and Thompson, 1973), which states that when we acquire memories, we encode them with links to the context we were in at the time. Thus, the context becomes a retrieval cue which can help recall information stored in LTM. To illustrate this idea, Tulving and Osler (1968) gave participants lists of words, each of which was paired with cue word, e.g. 'city–dirty'. Participants were then asked to recall the original list either by free recall or cued recall (they were presented with the cue words and had to remember the word associated with it). The findings showed that cued recall produced consistently better performance than free recall.

The Role of Context

Another interesting study shows that even the context in which learning took place can act as a retrieval cue. A study which looked specifically at context-dependent retrieval was carried out by Godden and Baddeley (1975).

They asked divers to learn a list of 40 unrelated words either on land or 15 feet under water. Later, half the divers recalled the words in their original context whilst the other half recalled in a different context (i.e. those who had learned the list on land recalled under water and vice versa). The findings were that those who recalled in the same context as the one in which learning had taken place remembered more words. This supports the encoding specificity principle. Information about the context must have been encoded along with the words. These cues were not available to those who recalled in a different environment, therefore, their recall was poorer. Perhaps this research into memory tells us something important about cognitive functioning: our memories are not abstractions of our experiences but are instead a more holistic picture of what has happened to us and what we have done. Similarly, Smith (1979) gave participants a list of 80 words to learn whilst sitting in a distinctive basement. The following day he tested some of the participants in the same basement, some in an upstairs room and a third group who were tested in the upstairs room but were asked to 'imagine' they were in the original basement room. The findings were that those in the original context recalled the most words, followed by those who imagined they were in the original context. The worst recall was produced by those in a different context. The findings from studies such as these have implications for students doing exams, since they seem to suggest that students will do better if they recall the information in the same context in which they learned it (something that hardly ever happens), or if they attempt to 'cue' key information to aid recall. However, most studies report that environmental differences need to be substantial before any significant difference in recall is noticed. Nevertheless, it has also been shown that students simply imagining the original room in which the information was learned can help with retrieval during the exam. For this reason, experimentation with cueing and environmental context to aid recall is also strongly recommended for A-level examination revision.

The Role of an Individual's State

There is also evidence that physiological state or mood can affect recall. Surprisingly, Goodwin *et al* (1969) found that heavy drinkers who learn things in a drunken state are more likely to recall them when in a similar state. Eich (1980) has also found this effect with marijuana.

In general, there is less conclusive evidence that mood affects recall. However, in a meta-study, a review of research studies into mood, Ucros (1989), found a moderately strong relationship between mood at the learning stage and at the retrieval stage. She also found that mood was more likely to affect memories of real-life rather than artificially constructed material, and that adults were more affected by mood dependence than children.

Active Processing

We are more likely to remember material that we have actively processed by interacting with material on what Craik and Tulving (1975) called a 'deep' level. They identified three levels on which we can take in information: structural (what does it look like?), phonological (what does it sound like?) and semantic (what does it mean?). Craik and Tulving argued that taking in information on a structural level involves a very shallow level of processing, resulting in a memory trace that is not very robust. Deep processing (resulting in good retention) comes from understanding material semantically.

To demonstrate this, Craik and Tulving (1975) gave participants a list of words to which they had to answer questions requiring shallow, medium or deep processing. They then gave the participants a surprise recall task. Words which had been associated with deep processing on a semantic level were the best remembered. This shows that meaningful interaction with material gives better retention and that the learning is incidental (participants did not know they were going to be tested so made no special effort to remember the material). In fact, they performed as well as a control group who made a particular effort to remember the words on the list.

A possible conclusion to draw is that this kind of interaction works because it activates material stored in LTM and therefore makes numerous associations which can later act as retrieval cues. For that reason, taking the time to reflect on the material presented here and to think about it yourself is highly recommended as a way to activate deep engagement and thus a more profound memory of the material.

However, Tyler *et al* (1979) questioned the notion of levels of processing. They believed that the semantic tasks required more effort and it was the effort required in processing the information which improved recall. To test this idea, they gave participants two sets of anagrams to solve: 'difficult' and 'easy'. Participants were later given an unexpected recall test. They found that significantly more of the difficult anagram words were recalled and concluded that since all words were processed at the same level (semantically, therefore at a deep level) the better recall in the difficult anagram group must have been due to the effort put into processing them and not the depth of processing.

Nevertheless, most studies show that the more you interact with the material and the more elaborate and organised you make it, the more likely you are to remember it in the long term.

Activity 16

A student teacher finds it very difficult to remember pupils' names. She decides to look in a psychology book to find some useful strategies for improving her memory.

Thinking about memory techniques, outline one strategy the student teacher could use, and explain why this might improve her memory for pupils' names.

Answer to activity 16

Mnemonics could help the teacher to remember the names. She could use the first letters of the names and where the children sit to make up a funny rhyme or phrase. The more bizarre the rhyme is, the easier it will be to remember it. When she has to recall the names, the rhyme will only take up one chunk of short-term memory. It is therefore more efficient than trying to remember all the names separately.

1.3 Attachment

Key Areas:

- **Caregiver-infant interactions in humans**: reciprocity and interactional synchrony. Stages of attachment identified by Schaffer. Multiple attachments and the role of the father
- **Animal studies of attachment**: Lorenz and Harlow
- **Explanations of attachment**: learning theory and Bowlby's monotropic theory. The concepts of a critical period and an internal working model
- **Ainsworth's 'Strange Situation'. Types of attachment**: secure, insecure-avoidant and insecure resistant. Cultural variations in attachment, including van Ijzendoorn
- **Bowlby's theory of maternal deprivation. Romanian orphan studies**: effects of institutionalisation
- **The influence of early attachment on childhood and adult relationships**, including the role of an internal working model

Introduction

An attachment is a strong emotional bond that develops over time between an infant and its caregiver or caregivers. It is reciprocal since each partner is attached to the other, and behaviour is reciprocated. For example, this means that when an infant smiles at its caregiver, the caregiver smiles back. Likewise, if a caregiver smiles at an infant, then the infant will smile back – and this occurs from a very young age indeed Research by Meltzoff and Moore (1997) and Feldman (2007) have shown that infants as young as a few days old seek to reciprocate the facial or physical gestures of their caregivers. This pattern of reciprocity should continue to strengthen over the first few months of the infant's life (provided that the infant is receiving good quality, consistent care), such that interactional synchrony then develops. This is where both the infant's and the caregiver's behaviour are harmonised to a high degree, such that each is in tune with the other, and responds accordingly.

Feldman (2007) describes the process of interactional synchrony in her research as follows:

"Interaction synchrony in the context of parent–infant relatedness, the focus of this review, addresses the matching of behavior, affective states, and biological rhythms between parent and child that together form a single relational unit. Synchrony describes the intricate 'dance' that occurs during short, intense, playful interactions; builds on familiarity with the partner's behavioral repertoire and interaction rhythms; and depicts the underlying temporal structure of highly aroused moments of interpersonal exchange that are clearly separated from the stream of daily life (Beebe, 1982; Fogel, 1993; Stern, 1977; Tronick, 1989; Trevarthen, 1979). Synchrony, therefore, provides one window to the nature of early relationships that is different from the angle captured by more global constructs such as sensitivity or responsiveness and highlights a distinct component in the attachment theory's focus on predictable caregiving as a critical feature of early infant care (Bowlby, 1969). Just as the laws of thermodynamics demonstrate that heat increases the speed of physiological processes, the high level of positive arousal that infants co-construct with their parents during the short daily episodes of face-to-face play, a level reached only during such shared moments, accelerates the maturation of the infant's relational skills and provides essential environmental inputs for the development of self-regulation and social fittedness (Feldman, 2003). The intensity of these moments, in turn, requires the external regulatory framework afforded by the organisational parameters of synchrony."

In other words, interactional synchrony is an important feature of secure attachment, and infants who lack interactional synchrony with their caregivers are more likely to be insecurely attached.

Maccoby (1980) identified four behaviours which demonstrate attachment in young children. These are:

- Seeking proximity (closeness) especially in times of stress
- Distress on separation
- Pleasure when reunited
- General orientation towards the caregiver

Explanations of Attachment

We are going to look at two different approaches to understanding why babies develop attachments. These are **Learning Theory** and **Evolutionary Theory**.

Learning Theory

To understand learning theory, we must first look at two types of learning: **operant** and **classical conditioning**. The concept of **operant conditioning** stems from the work of Burrhus F. Skinner. Often referred to as the father of behaviourism, BF Skinner worked on learned behaviour in animals. He designed a piece of apparatus which consisted of a special cage called a Skinner box. The cage had a lever on one wall which, when accidentally pressed by the animal (usually a rat) during its exploration of the cage, released a pellet of food. The animal soon learned to voluntarily press the lever in order to gain a food reward. This is an example of positive reinforcement: action plus reward (reinforcer) causes the action to be repeated. We experience positive reinforcement in real life. For example, we work and get paid, or we try hard at sport and get a trophy. Skinner also worked on negative reinforcement. He electrified one half of the grid in the bottom of the animal's cage and sounded a buzzer just before he administered a shock to the animal's feet. The rat soon learned to move to the non-electrified side of the box on hearing the buzzer sound. Thus negative reinforcement is avoidance learning: warning followed by action equals avoidance.

A real life example of negative reinforcement is smoking. The reduction in nicotine causes cravings which are satisfied by having another cigarette. The cigarette switches off the unpleasant feelings of the craving and so smoking behaviour is likely to be repeated.

Learning Theory

This theory can be applied to attachment. A new-born child cries, for example, because it is hungry. This is negatively reinforcing for parents because the sound of the baby crying makes them feel uncomfortable. Therefore, the parent will feed and cuddle the baby. The baby stops crying, thus reducing the feelings of discomfort in the parent. From the baby's point of view, the crying produces a reward or positive reinforcement, which makes crying likely to be chosen again the next time the baby experiences discomfort.

Classical conditioning is based on an involuntary association between two stimuli. Russian physiologist Ivan Pavlov noticed that the dogs in his lab salivated in response to the keepers' footsteps as they approached with their food. Since dogs don't normally salivate to the sound of footsteps, it was clear that they had associated the sound with the anticipation of the food that was to come. You may have noticed the same thing in your pet dog who comes running when you open his food cupboard.

There are some terms you need to know to understand classical conditioning. These are:

- Unconditioned stimulus (US)
- Unconditioned response (UR)
- Conditioned stimulus (CS)
- Conditioned response (CR)

Using these terms to explain Pavlov's observations would give:

Food (US) → Salivation (UR) (This is the normal reflex)

Food (US) + Sound of footsteps (CS) → Salivation

Eventually:

Sound of footsteps (CS) → Salivation (CR)

We can explain attachment behaviour in terms of classical conditioning. The stimulus of the milk (US) produces pleasure (UR). The person who feeds the baby becomes associated (CS) with the milk since they always seem to be present when the milk is given.

Therefore, eventually, the baby feels secondary pleasure in the company of the person who normally feeds it (CR) even on the occasions when food is not offered. According to learning theory, this is the basis of the attachment bond. This idea has become known as the 'cupboard love hypothesis', since it sees food as the main reason for attachment.

Stages of Attachment

Schaffer and Emerson (1964) conducted a longitudinal study in which they studied 60 babies at monthly intervals for the first 18 months of their life. From their observations they were able to identify four phases of attachment:

1. *The pre-attachment phase* – here the infant does not form any particular attachment to any particular person; rather they will respond to any care giving
2. *Indiscriminate attachment phase* – from about 6 weeks to 7 months the infant will show a preference for one care giver over another – they have learnt to distinguish between a primary care giver and a secondary one
3. *The discriminate attachment phase* – from about 7 to 11 months the infant will have a strong preference for one particular person and look to that person for comfort and security. The infant may also show signs of fear or anxiety when separated from the main caregiver or if they find themselves with someone they do not know. It is at this stage an infant may experience what is known as separation anxiety
4. *Multiple attachment phase* – evident after about 9 months, where the infant begins to become more independent and form attachments with others such as grandparents,

fathers, older siblings, even other care givers, such as nursery staff, if the infant is placed in such an environment

It's worth noting that whilst Schaffer's attachment theory does give us some idea of how this process can occur during the early stages of life, there are other factors to consider that can have an impact upon the extent to which attachment of this nature can occur. For example, we would need to consider the fact that some children do not necessarily have a primary care giver, as a child could be raised in an orphanage, so the opportunity for attachment is diminished somewhat. Also, we cannot assume that the quality of care giving is any good. Responses of the care giver to the needs of the infant could be slow, inconsistent and even negligent.

Reciprocity

The word reciprocal means two-way, or something that is mutual. Infant and caregiver are both active contributors in the interaction and are responding to each other. This is referred to as reciprocity.

Interactional synchrony

The word synchrony means a simultaneous action or occurrence. Interactional synchrony relates to the timing and pattern of the interaction. The interaction is rhythmic and can include infant and caregiver mirroring each other's behaviour and emotion. The infant and caregiver's behaviours and affect are synchronised because they are moving in the same, or a similar, pattern.

Condon and Sander (1974) have investigated interactions between infants and caregivers in particular in relation to responses to adult speech. In their paper they report "As early as the first day of life, the human neonate moves in precise and sustained segments of movement that are synchronous with the articulated structure of adult speech".

According to research by Meltzoff and Moore (1983) infants as young as 3 days imitate the facial expression of adults. This implies that this ability to mirror is an innate behaviour.

Evaluation of Learning Theory as an Explanation of Attachment

Learning theory predicts that the strongest attachment will be with the person who offers the greatest pleasure to the infant; most likely this will be the person who feeds it. However, Shaffer and Emerson (1964) found that this was not always true. They found that fewer than half the infants they observed had a primary (preferred, strongest) attachment to the person who fed them and took care of their physical needs. In addition, these theories can't explain why many children become attached to abusive or neglectful parents (Schaffer 1971).

The importance of fathers

Often discussion of this nature focuses on the mother as the primary care giver and therefore the one where attachment theory is likely to be applied, but what about the importance of fathers in this context? As we have seen, it is possible for an infant to have more than one attachment after seven months. However, just as infants can form what is seen to be a significant attachment to the mother figure, the father figure can also become an attachment figure. According to Bowlby (1988), fathers can be very significant when it comes to attachment and development. Theories of human evolution suggest that the key role of the father was to protect and provide for the family unit whilst the role of the mother was that of nurturer and care giver. However, as societies have clearly developed and the process of socialisation has changed in terms of some aspects of gender roles, it has become increasingly evident over time that fathers are capable of providing the care giving role and therefore attaching to their children. Nothing can detract from the fact that generally, mothers are biologically and hormonally programmed to bond, but it is accepted in many quarters that fathers are able to replicate behaviours of 'mothering'. According to Greenberg and Morris (1974), fathers who are actively involved in the pregnancy, delivery and holds the infant after birth, are more likely to be actively and positively involved during the attachment phases. It is worth noting that on a psychological level, we need to be aware of the impact absent fathers can have on a child's psychological and social development, potentially causing long term, irreparable damage.

Animal studies of attachment

Lorenz's Imprinting Theory

Lorenz (1935) started from the premise that social bonds in animals are formed by imprinting and in order to demonstrate how this worked he took a large clutch of goose eggs and kept them until they were about to hatch out. Half of the eggs were placed with a goose mother, and Lorenz kept the other half beside himself for several hours.

When the geese hatched Lorenz imitated the actions and noises of a mother goose such as making quacking sounds, resulting in the baby geese regarding him as their mother, following him. The other group followed the mother goose.

Lorenz found that geese followed the first moving object they saw after hatching and it was this process he referred to as *imprinting*. On the basis of this, he suggested that the process of attachment is innate and, as such, imprinting occurs without any feeding taking place. Lorenz theorised, based on his observations, that if attachment did not occur within the first 32 hours then attachment would not develop.

Perhaps one of the most convincing pieces of evidence that food is not the main reason for attachment comes from Harlow and Zimmerman's (1959) work with rhesus monkeys. It was clear that these infant monkeys relied upon their mothers for food, protection, socialisation and comfort, but what Harlow and Zimmerman wanted to know was what the basis of this attachment was.

Infant monkeys were taken from mother shortly after birth and raised in a cage with two 'surrogate' mothers. The 'surrogate' mothers were not living mammals but rather made of wire, with one having a feeding bottle attached and the other covered with terry towelling cloth.

Behavioural theory of attachment suggests that infants form attachments with a carer that provides food, so the purpose of this test was to see if food theories were correct; that the monkeys would attach to the wire mother since it provided food. Contrary evolutionary theory suggests that infants have a biological need for touch and physical contact for comfort.

The findings of this experiment was, all monkeys preferred the soft towel covered surrogate mother and would spend many hours clinging to it, only briefly leaving it to feed from the wire mother. In addition, the baby monkeys were very distressed if the soft mother was removed from the cage; the infants would explore new toys but only if soft mother was in the room and they ran to the soft mother and hid their face when a clockwork teddy bear was introduced to the cage.

This work suggests that rather than food being the centre of attachment behaviour, the need to keep proximity to a 'tactile-comfort' mother-figure seems to be the main factor in attachment behaviour. This study supports the evolutionary explanations (discussed further in the next section) of attachment. Harlow and Zimmerman's findings suggest that clinging was a natural response and that the need for physical interaction was critical during the first months of life. However, we must remember that although this work has many parallels with observations on humans, it does use primates and therefore, can't be directly generalised to humans.

Also, the monkeys were placed in a highly unrealistic situation in which they were deprived of all social contact; a situation which is particularly damaging. This could have affected the results.

Ethics of Harlow's experiment

This study raised questions about 'unethical' issues, such as, causing actual emotional harm and distress not only to the infant monkeys but their actual mothers.

Evolutionary Explanations

Bowlby's Theory: The work of Harlow influenced the work of Bowlby, a famous child psychologist who began working on attachment in the 1940s. After looking closely at the behaviour of children who were evacuated during World War II, he put forward a theory of attachment in 1959.

His theory was based on the work of ethologist Konrad Lorenz (1935) who found that Greylag geese and other birds, which are mobile after hatching, have evolved a special survival mechanism called **imprinting**. This mechanism makes the bird instinctively follow the first thing it sees (even if that happened to be Lorenz himself!). He also found that this must occur within a critical period of 32 hours after hatching or it would not occur at all.

It is clear that imprinting has survival value in animals which are mobile soon after birth as it keeps them close to their parents and safe from predators. But how does this relate to humans? Bowlby believed that human infants have a similar survival mechanism: an innate drive to become attached, which makes them want to keep proximity to a preferred attachment figure. He believed that, although a child might have many attachments, he or she had the tendency to seek out one special attachment to his preferred or primary attachment figure (usually this is still the mother, though there is no reason why a primary caregiver could not also be the father). This idea is called **monotropy**: that the primary caregiver can only bond with one infant at a time, and that having one primary caregiver is how a child attaches.

In order to establish an attachment, Bowlby further believed that the baby was born with innate mechanisms called social releasers (such as crying and smiling) specifically designed to make their parents want to care for them. Like Lorenz, Bowlby believed that attachment must happen within an optimal window of development known as the **sensitive period**. He believed that, in humans, this period was during the first three years of life.

He also believed that the attachment a child formed with his or her primary caregiver gave the child an internal working model or blueprint on which all his or her future relationships would be based (the **continuity hypothesis**) and that disruption to or lack of an attachment bond during the sensitive period could have serious consequences for the mental health of the child in later life. This period is not surprisingly referred to as the **critical period** – a time when a child's exposure to certain stimuli or experiences encourages and results in proper development. Bowlby said, because of this critical period a child should stay with his/her primary caregiver for at least 2 ½ years.

Observations

Evolutionary adaptive behaviours in children which support Bowlby's ideas:

- Having an intense stranger fear protects infants from predators; this is usually strongest from 9 to 18 months when child is mobile and able to move away from caregiver
- Seeking proximity and having separation anxiety when the primary caregiver is removed; this reinforces the adaptive behaviour that the child cannot be left behind by the caregiver

Evidence for and against the main tenets of Bowlby's theory:

Idea	Evidence
Social releasers	**Support** Schaffer and Emerson (1964) Babies become sociable at around 6 weeks. By 7 months show separation anxiety and fear of strangers.
Monotropy	**Refute** Schaffer and Emerson (1964) By 18 months 87% of babies had multiple attachments. Strongest bond not always with the mother.
Continuity hypothesis (internal working model)	**Support** Hazan and Shaver (1987) Through studying respondents to a newspaper 'Love Quiz' and a group of undergraduates, Harzan and Shaver found a strong

	relationship between childhood attachment type and adult attachment type.
	Black and Schutte (2006)
	A study of 205 young adults found that those who recalled positive relationships with their mothers were more likely to seek comfort from their partners. Those who recalled positive relationships with their fathers were more likely to rely on their partners.
	Refute
	Zimmerman *et al* (2000)
	Assessment of children's attachment type at 12-18 months and again at 16 years suggested that childhood attachment was not a good predictor of adolescent attachment. Major life events such as death and divorce have an important impact on later attachment and continuity may only exist in the absence of such events.
	Main and Goldwyn (1984)
	Many people who experience difficult childhoods and insecure attachments go on to develop positive and secure relationships in later life. Positive school experiences and strong adult attachments may be helpful in developing trust and security.

Other Attachments

Bowlby's ideas were formulated in the 1950s when society was very different. Most mothers at this time stayed at home to raise children while the father went out to work. It is therefore understandable why he believed the mother was the most important attachment figure in a child's life, and focussed on the role of the mother as being the primary caregiver.

However, modern research has shown that it is desirable for a child to have multiple attachments, each attachment figure providing another type of care or relationship for the child. For example, Lamb (1983) found that fathers are more likely to be chosen as playmates, and Schaffer (1996) showed that as well as vertical attachments with parents and other authority figures, a child's horizontal attachments (i.e. with siblings or cousins of a similar age) are very important for their understanding of the world. Bowlby's emphasis on the mother led to these important attachments being ignored. However, Bowlby and his co-workers have had a huge impact on the way in which we raise children and the provisions we make to care for them when we have to be apart, e.g. for parents to work or when a parent or child has to go into hospital.

Types of Attachment

The role of an internal working model

As discussed previously we have seen that according to attachment theory, a fundamental basic feature of development, is the quality of early attachment which can determine how an individual interacts and attaches with others in later life (in adulthood for example). So, according to Bowlby (1969) attachment at an early age, especially emotional bonds between an infant and the main caregiver can impact upon how an individual functions on a social, psychological and biological level and these manifest themselves through the construction of what is referred to as **internal working models** (IWMs). IWMs are internal representation of the 'self' and 'other' based on a child's interactions with their main caregiver/s.

For Bowlby, if a child has the experience of their primary care giver (e.g. a parent) being emotionally available and open, supporting and responsive to their needs, they are more likely to construct a self-model that mirrors these qualities. On the flip side, if the opposite is experienced by an individual, in that as a child the primary caregiver was emotionally unavailable, rejected the infant and was detached, this would have the effect of a self-model being constructed that focuses on the individual seeing themselves as unworthy, unlovable and so on.

After the influence of Bowlby's work, developmental psychologists started to ask what factors made an attachment secure and what happened if a child developed an insecure attachment to its caregivers.

The Strange Situation

One of the most influential studies on individual differences in attachment type was conducted by Mary Ainsworth (1970). According to Ainsworth's, "Strange

Situation" study, different attachment experiences may result in difference expressions of attachment. She set up the 'Strange Situation' laboratory observation in which she observed babies between one year and 18 months of age interacting with their mother and a stranger. She also observed the babies to see how they behaved when left alone for a short period of time and how they greeted their mother when she returned.

Ainsworth measured four main behaviours in the infants:

- General orientation to the mother (did the children use her as a secure base?)
- Stranger anxiety
- Separation anxiety
- Behaviour towards mother on reunion

Ainsworth's experiment

In Ainsworth's 'Strange Situation', infants aged from 12 to 18 months, together with their mothers, were placed in a purpose-built playroom and were observed through a video camera. The room had two chairs and a play area with a selection of toys.

The following procedure was then followed:

1) Mother and infant go into the room. Infant is placed near the toys and is free to play with them. Mother sits in one of the chairs

2) Three minutes later a stranger enters, sits down in the other chair and speaks to the mother

3) The stranger approaches the infant and tries to engage with them

4) The mother leaves the room, leaving the infant alone with the stranger. The stranger comforts the infant if they are upset

5) After about three minutes, the mother returns and the stranger leaves

6) Three minutes later the mother again leaves the room. The infant is briefly alone in the room

7) The stranger returns and offers to comfort the infant

8) The mother returns and the stranger leaves

9) It is important to note that the experiment was stopped if the infant became too distressed

Using this method, Ainsworth was able to identify three attachment types in the infants she studied:

Type B Secure (70% of sample): These children were generally oriented towards the mother, used her as a secure base to explore the room and brought toys to show her. They became distressed when mother left, showed joy and were easily comforted when she returned. They were wary of the stranger. These children could therefore be described as being securely attached children to their primary caregiver.

Type A Insecure Avoidant (15% of sample): These children ignored mother and played happily with the toys alone. Showed some distress at her departure but did not want comfort from her when she returned. They also rejected the stranger when she tried to comfort them.

Type C Insecure Ambivalent/Resistant (15% of sample): These children cling to mother. They showed extreme distress when mother left but when she returned, although they appeared to want her close (putting out their arms to be picked up etc.), they seemed to be angry and rejected her attempts to comfort them.

So, according to attachment theory, IWMs are significant because they form part of the individual's sense of self-worth and subsequently how they operate in terms of their expectations of others. Overall, what is being suggested here is that how a child interacts with their primary caregiver has a significant impact on how an individual sees themselves, others and the world in general.

Overall the IVMs provide the foundation for understanding how the attachment process operates in and affects adult relationships.

Criticisms

Ainsworth's study was well controlled and therefore easily replicated, making it a reliable method for studying attachment behaviour. Using her methods, Main and Cassidy (1988) were able to identify a fourth type: **Type D** or 'disorganised'. Children of this type tended to come from abusive homes. They had little idea how to cope when their carer left the room and often became extremely distressed. They tended to comfort themselves by freezing or rocking backwards and forwards.

However, some have argued that the method lacks validity because the Strange Situation is so unlike anything the baby would have to go through in real life, although others claim it is not unlike the situation a child faces when being left at nursery or with a babysitter. Another criticism is that it would be unreasonable to make generalisations about all infants based on this research.

That is, Ainsworth used middle-class American babies, which makes the findings culturally biased, i.e. they only tell us about middle-class American children and, therefore, lack population validity.

Other studies challenge the validity of the Strange Situation, claiming that infants behave differently depending on who they are with when they are tested. For example, a child might be classed as securely attached to its mother but insecurely attached to its father. If this is the case, then the Strange Situation is only measuring particular relationships and not some central characteristic of the child. This implies, therefore, that attachment is more a relationship quality, rather than a fundamental personality trait, which a child either has or does not have.

Ainsworth's work also raises ethical questions, since the situation was stressful for the babies. However, the observers were asked to stop the study if the babies became unduly distressed. Nevertheless, the Strange Situation raises an interesting question for research ethics. Under what circumstances should research be stopped, and how can ethical judgements be made regarding the limits of research?

Further Research

Ainsworth went on to look for reasons for different types of attachment behaviour. She wondered whether a child's attachment behaviour is determined by the carer, the child or by something else.

After many observations using the Strange Situation, she formulated the **Sensitivity Hypothesis**. This states that sensitive mothers have securely attached infants.

Ainsworth found that she could often match the mother's behaviour to the type of attachment shown by the infant. Securely attached infants tended to have mothers who understood their needs and were consistently good at meeting them. Insecurely attached infants tended to have mothers who ignored them (avoidant types) or who were, at times, neglectful and at other times overly fussy (ambivalent types).

This view is supported by De Wolff and van Ijzendoorn (1997) who found a correlation of 0.24 between sensitivity of the mother (though this assumes it is the mother who is also the primary caregiver) and secure attachment. This suggests there is a relationship, albeit a very weak one.

There is an alternative explanation. Some infants may form attachments more readily than others because they are naturally more friendly or easier to care for. This explanation is known as the **Temperament Hypothesis** (Kagan, 1982).

There is some evidence to support this view. Belsky and Rovine (1987) found that infants who showed signs of behavioural instability, such as tremors or shaking, were less likely to become attached to their mothers than infants who did not. Similarly, Fox (1991) found that there was a strong correlation between the attachment types of the child to both parents (i.e. if a child was securely attached to his or her mother, he or she would very likely have the same attachment with the father). This further suggests that attachment types are caused by some inherent characteristic of the infant, and therefore contradicts the theory that attachment is more a quality of relationship that a child has with different significant adults.

Conclusion

Evidence is presented here to support both the sensitivity and temperament hypotheses. It is likely, therefore, that attachment type is determined by an interaction between the temperament of the baby and the sensitivity, or even prior care-giving experience, of the mother (again, assuming it is the mother who is the primary caregiver of the child). A difficult infant that tends to cry a lot and is difficult to soothe, for example, paired with an anxious or neglectful caregiver, may well be more likely to have an insecure attachment than if he or she were paired with a sensitive primary caregiver who is consistently attentive.

Activity 17

Why might the Strange Situation be unsuitable for comparing attachment in different cultures? Think about this now and then continue reading.

Cultural Variations in Attachment

Most of the research into attachments was carried out in America. This means that most of the theories are based solely on one culture, and it has been assumed that types of attachment and how they arise are similar all over the world. In the last few decades, however, psychologists have come to realise that this is a very narrow view of human behaviour. To try to redress the balance and to investigate whether their theories of attachment are universal (that is, apply to everyone regardless of culture/nationality) they have conducted a number of studies in other European and non-European countries using Ainsworth's standard Strange Situation protocol.

Van Ijzendoorn and Kroonenberg (1988) conducted a meta-analysis in which they analysed the results of 32 Strange Situation studies conducted in 8 different countries. The study found that there are large differences between different cultures.

The study found that secure attachment (Type B) was the most common type overall. However, the percentage of infants with secure attachment varied considerably, from 50% in China to around 75% in Great Britain and Sweden.

Avoidant attachments (Type A) were most common in West Germany (35.5%) and in the Nederlands (26.3%). Avoidant attachments were rare in Japan (5.2%) and Israel (6.8%).

Ambivalent attachments (Type C) were most common in Israel (28.8%), Japan (27.1%) and China (25%). Ambivalent attachments were very rare in Great Britain (2.8%) and Sweden (3.9%).

Explaining the Differences

The researchers found that the differences between cultures were often related to the differing child-rearing styles and the economy of the country studied. For example, Germany is classed as an individualist culture. Parents bring their children up to be independent and stand on their own two feet. German mothers would view what we would call 'securely attached' as weak, clingy behaviour (Grossmann and Grossmann, 1991). On the other hand, Japanese culture is a collectivist one, therefore parents tend to have grandparents or other family members they can call on to share child-care during the first few years of an infant's life. Consequently, the Japanese infants have extreme fear of strangers and don't cope well with being left alone in the Strange Situation (Takahashi, 1990). We would classify their behaviour as Type C or ambivalent.

This research therefore strongly suggests that the Ainsworth standard of attachment is, in fact, culturally determined, and based on American cultural norms of child-rearing, rather than being universally applicable. What is secure in one culture is undesirable or 'clingy' behaviour in another; what is insecure in one culture is socially acceptable and the product of family norms in another.

However, Van Ijzendoorn and Kroonenberg also found that the differences within cultures were greater than the differences between them. In other words, it would be wrong to assume that a particular culture raises children in exactly the same way, and that individual differences between families in child-rearing styles are also important.

<u>Criticisms</u>

On the positive side, this study used a large sample that makes the findings generalisable. However, twenty-seven of them were carried out in individualist cultures and only five in collectivist ones, so the sample may not be representative in this respect.

<u>Bowlby's theory of Maternal Deprivation</u>

Disruption of Attachment

This section looks at the effects on children of disruption to their attachment bonds, such as when parents divorce or when parents separate temporarily from their children each day, for example, so that parents can work. It also looks at the rare phenomenon of privation (which is where a child has never had the opportunity to form an attachment) and the effects of institutionalisation on children in orphanages or children's homes.

In 1953, John Bowlby proposed his maternal deprivation hypothesis. This hypothesis stated that a child should form a 'warm, intimate and continuous relationship with his or her mother or permanent mother-substitute'. He believed that disruption to that relationship could put the child at risk of future mental health problems and make it difficult for him or her to form proper adult relationships.

This hypothesis was the precursor to Bowlby's later attachment theory, and has three main elements which state that the relationship must be:

- **Continuous** (with few or no separations for the first five years)

- Made before the **critical period** of two and a half years (he later accepted that this was more flexible and called it a sensitive period)
- Should be with **one main carer** (either the natural mother or mother-substitute)

Bowlby based his ideas on research carried out in the late 1940s which looked at the effects on children of separation from their caregiver during the first five years of life. Bowlby termed this **maternal deprivation**. One of the most famous pieces of research is given below.

Bowlby's 44 Juvenile Thieves

Bowlby (1944) looked at the cases of 44 juveniles who had been referred to his child guidance clinic for stealing. Of the 44 cases, 40% had been separated from their mothers for six months or more before they were five years old. Bowlby diagnosed these juveniles as suffering from a condition he termed 'affectionless psychopathy'. The symptoms they shared included showing no remorse for their crimes and no concern for their victims or themselves. This led Bowlby to conclude that maternal deprivation was a factor contributing to delinquency in children. Another study which demonstrated the effects of separation on children was carried out by Rene Spitz and Katherine Wolf (1946). They looked at 123 babies during their first year of life who were being looked after by their unmarried mothers in an American prison. After about nine months, babies were taken away from their mothers to be cared for in the prison nursery. While the mothers were away, the babies were observed to cry more, lose their appetites and fail to gain weight. When reunited with their mothers, the babies' conditions returned to what they had been before the separation.

Critics have argued that these studies are extreme examples of separation possibly coupled with poor parenting and, therefore, don't tell us much about children in ordinary families who experience perhaps one or two weeks of separation at most (perhaps to go into hospital or a residential nursery while their mother has a second child, for example) from loving and supportive parents.

However, one of the most notable studies looking into such short periods of separation tells a very different story. The study was carried out by husband and wife team James and Joyce Robertson (1948). In the 1940s, children in hospital or other forms of child care had their physical needs met, but it was deemed unnecessary to do anything about their emotional needs. In order to convince the medical profession that children suffered emotionally, the Robertsons went into hospitals and nurseries armed with a cine camera and began to observe the children. One of these children was John, a 17 month old infant who was placed in a residential nursery during the birth of his mother's second child. The film demonstrated how John's condition deteriorated as the separation continued; what they observed has become known as the **protest-despair-detachment or PDD model.**

For the first few days John **protested** as best he could and tried to obtain attention. When this failed he showed distress. He tried to make attachments with the nurses but the system of working meant that a different person would look after him at different times of the day, making it very difficult to bond with a particular individual. After a few days, John's condition passed from distress to **despair**. He cried constantly and refused food. He had difficulty sleeping. His condition changed again when he gave up trying to attract attention and became less and less interested in either the nurses or his father when he came to visit. When his mother finally came to collect him, he ignored her and wouldn't allow her to comfort him **- detachment.**

The PDD model clearly outlines the short-term effects of separation. However, James and Joyce Robertson noted that such effects could persist over months or even years following the separation. When John returned home he carried what Joyce Robertson referred to as a nub of anxiety; he was worried about his mother going out and wanted to know when she would return and he wouldn't sleep without a light on.

Separation anxiety of the type John experienced is a longer-term effect of earlier separation and may persist long after the separation is over. It is marked by:

- Extreme clinginess
- Detachment
- Being more demanding

Other long-term effects include lower levels of academic achievement and self-esteem, a higher incidence of conduct disorder and other problems of psychological adjustment, earlier social maturity, a higher frequency of depression and more distant relationships in adulthood with parents and other relatives (Richards, 1995).

Evaluation

Rutter (1981) believes that Bowlby's view that the effects of separation are due solely to the disruption of a continuous bond with the caregiver is oversimplified, and that it is necessary to look at other factors, such as the strength of attachment before the child is separated, the child's home circumstances and the reason for the separation. Rutter also believes that Bowlby failed to distinguish between what he referred to as maternal deprivation and privation. **Privation** is where a child has made no bond at all with his or her caregiver (such as may happen through neglect). This has much more serious consequences for the child's later emotional, social and cognitive development.

Certainly, not all children are affected in the same way by separation. More recent research has shown that there are a range of factors which affect a child's ability to cope with separation. The following table shows some of these factors and their effects.

Factor	Effect
Age of child at time of separation	Schaffer and Callender (1959) In a study of children in hospital, the researchers found that children under 7 months suffered minimal upset and the most severe reaction occurred between 12 to 18 months. This may be related to the development of language skills and the ability to understand that caregiver will return.
Type of attachment	Barrett (1997) Individuals with secure attachment are best able to tolerate short separations. This may be because they believe that the caregiver will return.
Sex of child	Gross and McIlveen (1997) Boys seem to respond more strongly to separation than girls. However, there are also significant differences within, as well as between, sexes.
Multiple attachments and quality of care	Children older than 10 months may have multiple attachments and so can be left with another attachment figure with minimal effect.
Experience of previous separations	If a child is used to brief separations, then they are likely to respond less strongly to separation than a child who is not used to separation.

The Effects of Privation

As mentioned, privation is a term used to describe a child who has failed to form a bond with an adult caregiver. At its extreme, it can happen when young children lose both parents and are brought up in under-staffed, un-stimulating institutions. However, it more commonly occurs when the child is neglected by parents who do not have the ability to care for them, and so no attachment forms.

Studies into privation have centred on case studies of children brought up in isolation and institutional studies in which children have spent much of their early life in orphanages and are later adopted.

Case Studies

Susan Curtiss (1977) is professor of linguistics at UCLA. She studied the case of Genie, a young girl who suffered extreme privation. Genie was thought to have learning difficulties at birth, and as a result was locked away in an upstairs room by her parents. She spent every day alone and had little opportunity to make an attachment. She had no toys to play with and nothing to look at. By day she was tied to a potty chair and by night she was tied into a sleeping bag. Genie was found at the age of thirteen. Sadly, she was malnourished and had suffered delays in her physical development; she could not chew solid food and was not potty trained. She found it difficult to relate to others and had a very low IQ.

A similar case was reported by Koluchova in 1972 of Czechoslovakian twin boys who had suffered privation. However, the difference between them and Genie was that they were not isolated until they were about eighteen months old, they had each other to form a bond with and they were removed from their state of privation earlier (at the age of seven).

Both the boys and Genie had attachment experiences that were far from normal and both should have suffered severe consequences in later life. However, there were marked differences in the recovery rates of the children in the two cases. Genie did learn some language, although her grammar was always below normal. She could make attachment bonds and her IQ improved but never reached normal levels. However, the researchers into her case found it difficult to establish whether her lack of development was due to the privation or her learning difficulties, which were possibly present at birth.

However, the twin boys went on to make successful attachment bonds, improved in their intellectual development (measured by IQ score) and went on to lead reasonably normal lives.

Evaluation of Privation Case Study Research

Ethics

- Often intrusive – By necessity, researchers have to follow children for many years to gather evidence on the long-term effects of privation

- Concerns over informed consent – Children are both too damaged and too young to give their consent to being studied

- Researchers must be careful not to exploit the children for their own ends

Methodological Issues

- If case studies are used effectively and robustly, then researchers can gain very valuable information which is rich and detailed

- It can be hard to unpick cause and effect, since privation often also goes alongside physical neglect or abuse. For example, is it the lack of an attachment or the un-stimulating physical environment that is the cause of the child's later problems?

- A case study is by nature retrospective, since it can only begin once privation has been established and the child removed from the neglectful environment. Therefore researchers often have to make a best guess as to child's past. However, this may not be accurate and many variables may be unknown

Institutional Studies – The Tizard and Hodges Study

One of the most important studies into privation was carried out by Tizard and Hodges (1984 and 1989). This study was important because it examined the long-term effects of emotional privation. The advantage of this study over the case study method was that it was possible to use a relatively large sample of 65 English working-class children, and the researchers also had detailed records obtained from the children's home of the children's early lives, so they did not have to rely on retrospective data.

The home provided the children with a good standard of physical care and mental stimulation. The only thing it did not provide was emotional care. Therefore, the researchers had the chance to study the effects of emotional privation without the influence of other factors, such as physical abuse.

Although the physical needs of the children were met, staff at the children's home were discouraged from forming attachments with the children, because of the high staff-turnover rates. Indeed, on average, the children had had 24 different carers by the age of two, and by the age of four, they had had around 50.

At the age of two, the children showed unusual patterns of attachment. They would run up to any adult who entered the room and demand their attention. They would then cry when the adult left, even though they had formed no relationship with them. They also had no fear of strangers. This pattern is known as 'disinhibited attachment' and is characteristic of children in institutions.

When the children were four, 25 of them were returned to their biological parents, 33 were adopted and 7 remained in the home, sometimes being fostered for varying periods of time. This unusual situation created what is known as a 'natural experiment'.

Tizard and Hodges visited the children when they were aged 8, and interviewed them again at age 16. They found that almost all of the adopted children and most of those who had been returned to their original parents had formed close attachments at age 8. At age 16, more of the adopted children were close to their parents than the returned children. All the groups had difficulty with peer relationships and siblings, with the adoptees having slightly better relationships with their siblings than the returned children.

Conclusion

Surprisingly perhaps, early care in an institution does not have the drastically damaging effects predicted by Bowlby. The high quality care and stimulation in the English nursery ensured that cognitive development was normal, even though there had been no chance to make an attachment. Attachments to the adoptive parents were made after the age of two and a half, Bowlby's proposed critical period for attachment formation. However, there are some lasting effects of privation which continued until at least 16 and probably longer, but these effects are not inevitable and seem to depend on individual differences. In conclusion, such effects can be seen as differences in the children, and as such are not necessarily due to privation. (Remember, we would expect the same outcomes for all children who experienced privation, regardless of individual differences, if we are to establish privation as a cause of damaging effects later in life.)

Evaluation of the Tizard and Hodges Study

Methodological Issues

- There was a good range of research methods used, including interviews, questionnaires and self-reporting

- There is an inevitable attrition rate or participant 'drop out' in longitudinal studies, which may mean that the final sample is not representative of the original group. This makes it less valid when it comes to drawing conclusions about the effects of privation on a child
- This was a natural rather than a laboratory experiment.Since the researchers had no control over which children were adopted, there could be a bias in the group that were adopted. It is possible that the more sociable children may have been easier to place in adoptive families and that this is why they did so well later, rather than due to any other factor

Ethical Issues

- This is a very sensitive issue since it deals with both privation and children; researchers must not put pressure on the families and the children studied
- Researchers need to be impartial and non-judgemental, despite the fact that they are dealing with a difficult, sensitive and emotive issue

Romanian Orphan Studies

Tizard and Hodges found **disinhibited attachment** in their studies of institutionalised children. Disinhibited attachment is where children don't discriminate between people they choose as attachment figures. The child doesn't seem to prefer his or her parents over other people, even strangers. The child seeks comfort and attention from virtually anyone, without distinction. They will treat strangers with overfriendliness and may be attention seeking. This type of attachment has been also reported in ongoing studies by Rutter *et al* (2007) which follow the progress of Romanian orphans adopted by English families.

Rutter (1998) studied Romanian orphans who had been placed in orphanages, aged 1-2 weeks old, with minimal adult contact. This was a Longitudinal study and natural experiment, using a group of around 111 Romanian orphans and assessed at ages 4, 6 and 11, then re-assesed 21 years later. (**Note**: study still ongoing)

58 babies were adopted before 6 months old and 59 between the ages of 6-24 months old. 48 babies were adopted late between 2-4 years old. These were the 3 conditions Rutter used in his study.

Those who were adopted by British families before 6 months old showed 'normal' emotional development compared with UK children adopted at the same age. Many adopted after 6 months old showed disinhibited attachments (e.g. attention seeking behaviour towards all adults, lack of fear of strangers, inappropriate physical contact, lack of checking back to the parent in stressful situations) and had problems with peers.

Rutter et al. (1998) found that **the sooner the children were adopted, the faster their developmental progress.**

This study suggests long-term consequences may be less severe than was once thought if children have the opportunity to form attachments. When children don't form attachments, the consequences are likely to be severe.

In Rutter's subsequent research in 2007, he assessed children reared in profoundly depriving institutions in Romania and subsequently adopted into UK families. **Institutionally deprived adoptees** were compared at 11 years with children who had not experienced institutional deprivation and who had been adopted within the UK before the age of 6 months. Parental reports, a modified Strange Situation and investigator ratings of the children's behaviour were all assessed. Results revealed that disinhibited attachment was strongly associated with institutional rearing but there was not a significant increase in relation to duration of institutional deprivation beyond the age of 6 months. In contrast only mild disinhibited attachment was more frequent in non-institutionalised adopted children. The most recent observation at age 11 has shown that over half the children still showed disinhibited attachment and that many of these children were receiving special help from education or mental health services.

It must be remembered, however, that orphanages in Romania were very poorly equipped and children often had only their basic physical needs met, and sometimes not even these. Most of the time, they were often left in cots with no toys or other stimulation. It is therefore difficult to assess whether these effects are due to privation or the poor environmental conditions in which the children spent their early lives.

The Bucharest Early Intervention Project

Zeanah et al. (2005) assessed the attachment in 95 children aged between 12-31 months who had spent an average of 90% of their life in an institution and compared them to a control group who spend their life in a "normal family". The attachment type was measured using the Strange Situation.

Findings: 74% of the control group was found to be securely attached but only 19% of the institutionalised group. 65% of this group were classified as disorganised attachment (a type of insecure attachment were the children display an inconsistent pattern of behaviour; sometimes they show strong attachment other times they avoid the caregiver).

Summary

The factors which can help children to recover from the early effects of privation are:

- High quality of care during privation
- Removal from privation at a younger age
- High quality of care after privation
- Positive later life experiences

Activity 18

1) Define the term 'attachment'

2) List four characteristics seen in an 'attached child'

3) Define the term 'privation'

4) Decide whether these statements are true or false:

    a) Privation always has serious consequences for a child's social and emotional development

    b) The effects of privation cannot be overcome

    c) It is difficult to study the effects of privation

Answers to activity 18

1. An attachment is a strong emotional bond that develops over time between an infant and its caregiver or caregivers. It is reciprocal since each partner is attached to the other

2. - Seeking proximity (closeness) especially in times of stress

    - Distress on separation

    - Pleasure when reunited

    - General orientation towards the caregiver

3. Privation is the lack of attachment in a child who has never had the opportunity to form one

4. (a) False: many factors, such as early environment, age of child and quality of care given after privation will affect how well the child recovers

    (b) False: to some extent, they can be. Many of the Romanian children adopted into English families are doing very well (Rutter, 2007)

    (c) True: it is very difficult to study privation in the absence of confounding factors such as individual differences in the children, early experience and quality of any institution they may have been raised in

Attachment in Everyday Life

In this section we will look at the effects of different types of day care on the social development of children. We will consider the effects of day care on their relationship to their peers and on aggressive behaviours.

Day Care

There are several different types of day care. These are usually classified as either nursery-based care or family-based care.

Nursery-based Care

Nursery-based care is available to all children aged three and above. Nurseries are often attached to primary schools and use the primary school's facilities. They are regularly inspected by Ofsted and have trained staff and planned activities.

Family-Based Care

Registered Childminders

Registered childminders are also registered and inspected by Ofsted. They provide day care in their own homes, and the child will be taken to the childminder's house each day. Usually, the childminder will mind several children or have children of their own, so the day care provides opportunities for the child to socialise with others.

Au-pair/Nanny

An au-pair or nanny is employed by a family to help care for their child. The child will be cared for in their own home. The child will be cared for alongside their siblings (if they have any) or alone. It is unlikely that there will be any other children present.

Informal Arrangements

Some children are cared for informally by friends, relatives or neighbours, often on an unpaid basis. There has been very little research conducted into the effects of this type of day care.

Activity 19

What was your own experience of day care, if any?

There are numerous studies which examine the question of whether day care is harmful to young children. Many of them show mixed results.

- Andersson (1989, 1992) looked at nursery care in Sweden and found that children who attended day care were more sociable and better able to get along with peers than those who did not attend day care. Similarly, Schindler, Moely and Frank (1998) found that children who spend time in day care play more pro-socially. These studies suggest that day care is good for children's social development

- However, other studies have found that children spending time in day care were less co-operative and that this got worse the longer they spent in day care each day (DiLalla, 1988). One suggestion for these contradictory results is that most studies examine the quantity rather than the quality of day care. For this reason Campbell, Lamb and Hwang (2000) carried out a longitudinal study which studied the effects on children of both the quality and quantity of day care

Campbell, Lamb and Hwang (2000)

Campbell *et al* carried out a longitudinal study of a group of children in Gothenburg, Sweden who attended day dare continuously between the ages of 18 months and 3 ½ years. Of this group, 30 attended nursery-based care and 9 attended family-based care. A further 9 switched from nursery-based to family-based care during the study. This group were compared against a group who had applied for day care places but had been turned down.

Before the children started day care, at age 18 months, they were observed at home playing with familiar peers. The researchers also measured the quality of the children's home environment using Caldwell's HOME inventory.

The children were then observed playing with other children in the day care setting for 30 minutes. This observation was conducted at age 18 months (before they had started day care) and at ages 2 ½ and 3 ½. At age 6 ½ the children's social competence was assessed by their care provider. It was assessed again by their class teacher at age 8 ½ and at age 15 by self-report questionnaires.

Findings

The researchers found that:

- Children who spent long sessions in day care (e.g. 8am-6pm) were less pro-social than those who spent shorter sessions
- Children who experienced high quality care were more socially competent
- Social competence seemed to be stable (i.e. social competence at 3 ½ correlated with that at 15)

Conclusion

Short sessions of good quality day care have positive effects on children's social development.

Methodological Issues

- 'Prospective' approach used to observe long-term effects
- Baseline taken so later comparisons valid
- Range of assessment measures used increases validity
- Conducted in Sweden where lots of funding available for child care, therefore, difficult to generalise

Ethical Issues

- Sensitivity required
- Informed parental consent essential

Negative Effects of Day Care – Aggressive Behaviours

Belsky (2006) carried out a similar longitudinal study in America. He has observed that children in day care have enhanced cognitive abilities but tend to be more aggressive than those who have not experienced day care. Perhaps this is because children have to fight over toys and adult attention. He also believes that such children have problems with aggression towards peers as they grow older and are less obedient to authority figures.

However, Clarke-Stewart (1990, 1992) argues that this is simply a sign that children in day care learn how to look after themselves from an earlier age and this is an advantage rather than a problem. Furthermore, Borge *et al* (2004) found that aggression was higher in home reared-children than those attending day care. Again this implies that quality of care is important.

Comparing Different Types of Day Care

Melhuish (1990) conducted quasi-experimental research in London in which different types of day care were compared. The research is described as 'quasi-experimental' because the independent variable (the day care setting) was not set by the investigator. (We will learn more about experimental techniques in the next topic.). Melhuish compared three groups of children who started day care before the age of 9 months. The study included different day care settings, including informal arrangements. These settings were private nursery care, childminder care and care by relatives. Care by relatives had the highest adult to child ratio and the least contact with other children. Nursery care had the lowest adult to child ratio (where many children were cared for by fewer adults) and the greatest contact with other children. At age 18 months, children who had been cared for by relatives showed the highest levels of language development. At the same age, children who had been cared for in the nursery showed the lowest levels of language development. At age 3 years, the nursery group were still less skilled in language than the group cared for by relatives, but they showed higher levels of pro-social behaviours, such as sharing and co-operation.

Evaluation

- Different types of day care may show different types of gain for children
- Time spent in day care and length of day can have an effect
- Day care settings vary in quality
- Individual differences (e.g. type of attachment and home circumstances) will affect the experience of day care
- Individual differences in the parents will affect the type of care chosen (e.g. women who chose family care tended to have stronger identities as mothers)

Activity 20

1. Name two different types of day care and comment on differences in:

   ➢ The likely amount of adult attention

   ➢ The ability to socialise with other children outside the family

2. Suggest four factors that have been shown to affect a child's experience of day care

1. Care by relative: more one to one adult attention, little or no opportunity to meet children outside family.

Care in nursery: less one to one adult attention, more opportunity to socialise with children outside the home.

2. Four factors that affect a child's experience of day care are:

- Security of existing attachments
- Type of care chosen
- Length of time spent in day care
- Quality of care

Implications of Research into Attachment and Day Care for Child Care Practices

Research into attachment has been influencing child care practices since the 1950s. The first major change was in the medical profession. After being shown overwhelming evidence by researchers such as James and Joyce Robertson, who filmed the distress experienced by children in hospital, they gradually changed their practices so that today, parents are able to stay in hospital with their children, often sleeping on a camp bed alongside them. Parents also provide most of the physical care such as washing and dressing.

In terms of day care, Bowlby's theory has led to establishments adopting a 'key worker' approach so that the child has the same carer (mother-substitute) wherever possible. This allows the child to develop a secure emotional bond with someone who cares for them outside the home.

Quality of care is also important and establishments are required by law to provide:

- Appropriate adult to child ratios depending on the age of the child
- Small group sizes
- Well-trained staff and incentives to ensure low staff turnover

- A well-structured day with plenty of activities and time to engage in free play
- A happy and loving environment where home routines are followed as closely as possible

The impact of childhood attachment on adult relationships

Whilst Bowlby's work primarily focused on understanding attachment in infancy – the infant/caregiver relationship - he did believe that the experience in terms of early attachment would impact upon human experience throughout an individual's lifetime.

Hazan and Shaver (1987) embarked upon exploring some of Bowlby's ideas and noted the significance of the view that there was a possible connection between the attachment process and adulthood experiences. Hazan and Shaver suggest that when it comes to adult romantic relationships, the emotional bond and connection that occur between adults is similar to the attachment behavioural system that is seen between infants and their primary caregivers. Both types of relationship demonstrated that the individuals involved in the relationships (whether infant or consenting adults) would, feel safe and secure when the other person was present, and they would rely on and look to the other person in times of significant emotional challenges such as distress or fear. Also the other person would be a 'secure base' from which the world could be explored. And finally, communication between these individuals would have an element that is unique to the relationship, sometimes referred to as 'baby talk'. On the basis of Hazan and Shavers analysis, the infant/caregiver relationship eventually moves from parent (for the infant) to peers and romantic partners, turning to such individuals as opposed to a parent, in times of distress, illness, when there is need for comfort, security and so on.

What we do have to bear in mind, when looking at studies conducted by thinkers such as Hazan and Shavers, is that their research is based on the recollection of adults of their childhood. Therefore, being dependent on an individual's memory of their attachment during infancy, in itself can be problematic in terms of accuracy. However, attachment theorists who look at the connection between infancy attachment and adult attachments and connections, suggest that this is probable and not deterministic. In other words there is not a definitive correlation but a possible one.

1.4 Psychopathology

Psychopathology is the scientific study of mental disorders, and there are a variety of ways in which psychological abnormalities and problems associated with defining them can be addressed.

- Definitions of abnormality, including deviation from social norms, failure to function adequately, statistical infrequency and deviation from ideal mental health

- The behavioural, emotional and cognitive characteristics of phobias, depression and obsessive compulsive disorder (OCD)

- The behavioural approach to explaining and treating phobias: the two-process model, including classical and operant conditioning; systematic desensitisation, including relaxation and use of hierarchy; flooding

- The cognitive approach to explaining and treating depression: Beck's negative triad and Ellis's ABC model; cognitive behaviour therapy (CBT), including challenging irrational thoughts

- The biological approach to explaining and treating OCD: genetic and neural explanations; drug therapy

Psychological Abnormality

For many years psychiatry lagged behind mainstream medicine in finding the underlying causes of and appropriate treatments for abnormal behaviour. During the early twentieth century, treatment for abnormal behaviour was nothing short of barbaric with patients being held indefinitely in 'lunatic asylums' where they would often be restrained for long periods. When not restrained, they would be whirled around in various wooden contraptions or dunked in water in an effort to stun the brain into behaving itself.

During this time, efforts were being made to define exactly what abnormal behaviour was and to work towards providing a classification system which could group sets of symptoms together into recognisable mental disorders.

We will now look at some attempts to define abnormal behaviour and the limitations associated with such attempts.

Definitions of Abnormality

Deviation from Social Norms

- Behaviour is abnormal if it goes against *approved of and expected* ways of behaving, e.g. singing loudly in a supermarket queue or washing hands 100 times a day
- Abnormality is therefore a relative concept. What is normal in one situation could be abnormal in another

Limitations

- Behaviour may simply be eccentric
- Definition may be used for political or social control, e.g. dissidents in the former USSR labelled 'insane' and locked away for having counter-political views
- Definition may vary over time. What is classed as a mental illness today, may well be normal tomorrow, e.g. homosexuality was classed as a mental illness in the USA until 1973
- Social norms are culturally relative. For example, in some tribal societies it is normal to hear the voices of dead relatives; we would class this as schizophrenia

Failure to Function Adequately

- A more practical definition
- Abnormality viewed as disability/dysfunction

- A characteristic or behaviour is defined as abnormal if it interferes with the ability to pursue some desired goal, or if the person is unable to engage in their normal range of behaviour
- Rosenhan and Seligman (1989) list some characteristics of abnormal behaviour related to the failure to function definition, including observer discomfort, unpredictability, irrationality and maladaptiveness

Limitations

- The context is important, e.g. prisoners on hunger strike are not failing to function
- Failure to function may be for other reasons, e.g. discrimination, oppression, economic conditions
- Some disorders may not impair failure to function e.g. obsessive-compulsive disorder can be well hidden by some sufferers
- Again, behaviour is culturally relative

Deviation from Ideal Mental Health

- This definition approaches the issue from the opposite side, by first attempting to define mental health. Therefore, psychological abnormality deviates from this ideal state
- Jahoda (1958) suggests self-acceptance, potential for growth and development (self-actualisation), resistance to stress, autonomy, accurate perception of reality, environmental competence and having positive interpersonal relationships
- Atkinson *et al* (1983) include self-knowledge/self-awareness

Limitations

- Jahoda's characteristics[3] (especially autonomy and self-actualisation) reflect a Western view of personal growth and achievement not recognised in collectivist cultures
- These characteristics represent an ideal state. Many people are not able to self-actualise but this does not mean they are abnormal
- It is unclear by how much a person has to deviate before being classed as mentally ill

Statistical infrequency

- This definition uses population data or statistics to make a definition of abnormality. A person's behavioural traits or behaviours are considered abnormal if it is statistically infrequent. For example, in the case of IQ we could say that you are of average IQ if your IQ falls around the mean. Intelligence follows a **normal** distribution.
- Using statistics can be a particularly robust and helpful way to make diagnoses, since they provide clear cut off points. Statistics will also give us a picture of what is actually rare (or not) in terms of mental health.

Limitations

We may still need a statistical benchmark or cut-off to define abnormality. For example, if your behaviour is shared by 1% of the population, is it abnormal? What about .1%? or .01%? The problem with using statistical limits is that they can appear arbitrary. If we have defined abnormality as being shared by 1% of the population or less, what if we then find a behavioural trait which 1.02% of the population share? Can this legitimately be classed as normal?

This definition also does not help us to decide between rarity and undesirability. Some behaviours or traits may be rare (very high intelligence), but also highly desirable. Is high intelligence really also a psychopathology?

---

[3] Refers to 6 characteristics for positive mental health – 1)Positive attitude toward self; 2)self-actualisation; 3)resistant to stress; 4)Personal autonomy; 5)accurate perception of reality; 6)understanding of others

This definition also does not help us where a psychopathology is actually quite common. For example, the incidence of depression, particularly among some groups, is quite high. Likewise, suicide (an abnormal behaviour) is one of the leading causes of death for men aged 20-34 in England and Wales. Suicide is actually quite statistically frequent in which case, but does this also mean that it is also psychologically normal to commit suicide?

Activity 21

For each example below, consider the extent to which the behaviour fits each of the attempts at defining abnormality. Then decide whether or not you think the behaviour is abnormal and give reasons.

	Deviation from social norms	Failure to function	Deviation from ideal mental health	Abnormal? Why/why not?
A religious woman, who is praying, hears the voice of God speaking to her.				
A businessman who has recently been made redundant experiences a loss of motivation and fails to get out of bed most days.				

A family go shopping naked in the supermarket of a nudist holiday resort.				
A teenager stands in the middle of a busy street trying to control the approaching vehicles with his special mental powers.				

The Context of Culture and Sub-culture

As you will have discovered, it is difficult to decide whether someone is abnormal unless you see the behaviour in its situational or cultural context. This is because abnormality means different things in different situations. The person in the first example, above, may have been deemed abnormal if you hadn't known she were religious. The businessman obviously has depression but that is a 'normal' reaction to what he has just experienced and will pass. The only one of the four actually suffering from a mental disorder is the teenager trying to control traffic; he has schizophrenia.

The following factors may also influence this problem of definition and diagnosis:

- **Race** In the UK, African-Caribbean immigrants are 7 times more likely to be diagnosed as schizophrenic than whites (Cochrane, 1977). These differences cannot be explained in terms of biological/genetic factors as similar rates are not found in their countries of origin. It is likely, therefore, that these differences are due to bias in diagnosis and stress. Stress may arise from poorer living conditions, prejudice and/or the stress of learning to live in a foreign and possibly hostile culture

- **Gender** Women are more likely to suffer from depression, specific phobias and eating disorders. Howell (1981) explains that women's experience in British culture predisposes them to depression, and therefore clinicians are diagnosing a situation rather than a person. Similarly, Cochrane (1995) believes that depression in women can be linked to problems in childhood (e.g. sexual or physical abuse) and female gender-role socialisation, which increases vulnerability. Men are more likely to suffer from alcohol abuse and anti-social disorder. Bennett (1995) blames this finding on the socialisation of men in industrialised societies. The masculine role they are expected to fulfil alienates men from seeking help for psychological problems

- **Social Class** Cochrane and Stopes-Roe (1980) found that lower social class was linked to higher incidence of psychiatric problems. Several explanations have been offered

  - Clinicians may be less willing to label middle-class individuals with mental disorders. Johnstone (1989) found this was the case when comparing middle- and lower-class patients with the same symptoms
  - The living conditions for lower-class individuals may be more stressful and this leads to more mental illness
  - The Social Drift Hypothesis proposes that people who are mentally ill drift downwards due to their inability to function. The higher incidence of schizophrenia in poor areas could reflect the fact that people with the disorder move to poorer areas. In other words, their disorder causes them to be poor (inability to hold down a job, etc.) rather than poverty causing the disorder (Cochrane, 1983)

Approaches to Psychopathology

Approaches to understanding psychopathology can be divided into two broad areas:

- Biological (or medical)
- Psychological (psychodynamic, behavioural, cognitive)

Having so many different perspectives may seem unwieldy, but human beings are very complex organisms and human behaviour is often an interaction between genes (biological approach), environment (behavioural approach) and thought processes (cognitive approach). Often one or more perspectives will be used to explain certain disorders and this is reflected in the treatments prescribed. For example, depression will often be treated with medication and cognitive-behavioural therapy; better outcomes in terms of recovery are usually achieved with a combined approach.

Biological Approach

This approach sees mental disorders as being caused by some underlying abnormal physiology. It has dominated the field of mental health for the past 200 years. In medieval times, people with a mental illness were thought to be possessed by the devil. Gradually, in the early nineteenth century, people began to realise that mental symptoms could follow a physical disease such as syphilis and so underlying biological causes were examined. However, there was still little knowledge of how to treat these poor souls and the hospitals, such as the infamous Bethlehem Hospital in London (Bedlam), originally built to house them, became little more than tourist attractions. Since then, with advances in diagnostics and medical imaging, as well as the advent of psychoactive drugs in the 1950s, people have tended to feel more and more comfortable with this approach, especially as it was the first to view those with a mental illness as 'sick' rather than 'bad' or 'evil'.

Physical Causes of Mental Disorders

- Brain damage – The structure of brain may be altered in some way, e.g. due to infection or injury. General paresis (a type of dementia common in the nineteenth century) was found to be caused by the syphilis bacterium attacking the nervous system
- Biochemistry – Neurotransmitters are chemicals that transfer nerve impulses from one neurone to another. There are hundreds of these in the brain but the two most commonly studied are associated with

schizophrenia (excess of the neurotransmitter dopamine) and depression (lack of the neurotransmitter serotonin). Hormones are also implicated in mental disorders, e.g. the hormone cortisol is often elevated in stressed individuals

- Genes – Some mental disorders have a strong genetic basis, which means that the tendency (or predisposition) to suffer a mental disorder can be passed on in the genes. It also means that if one family member has the disorder, others are at greater risk of developing it and the closer the genetic relationship, the higher the risk. This has been demonstrated for schizophrenia where Shields (1978) found the concordance rate (the probability that a pair of individuals will both have a certain characteristic, given that one of the pair has the characteristic) to be 48% for identical twins (share 100% of their genes) compared with only 9% for ordinary siblings (share 50% of their genes)

Evaluation of the Biological Approach

The biological approach may be able to pinpoint the brain damage or neurotransmitter associated with a particular disorder but it cannot always determine the cause. For example, someone may inherit a faulty gene which causes them to make too little serotonin, in which case their depression is genetic. However, studies have shown that environmental triggers such as losing a job or breakdown of a relationship can also reduce serotonin levels.

This has even been shown experimentally using monkeys. When isolated from their group, monkeys tended to show a marked reduction in blood levels of serotonin (Watson *et al,* 1998). For this reason, a diathesis-stress model is often used to explain mental illness. This involves a genetic predisposition (diathesis) and an environmental trigger (stress), which interact to produce the disorder.

Psychodynamic Approach

Sigmund Freud (1856-1939) was one of the most influential figures of the early twentieth century. During this time, medicine could offer little explanation for mental disorders and Freud set about looking for underlying unconscious causes. He believed that we are all born with raw animal instincts such as the drive for sex, food and aggression, which have to be tamed to allow us to live in society. During childhood, we go through a series of stages during which we must deal with conflict between our instincts and pressures to conform to the rules of society. Eventually, we learn to subjugate these instincts and become moral citizens. However, at times, unresolved conflict which has been pushed down into the unconscious can resurface and cause neurotic symptoms. Freud developed what he called a 'talking cure' (psychoanalysis) during which these unresolved conflicts could be uncovered and dealt with, allowing the person to 'move on'.

Evaluation of the Psychodynamic Approach

- The model tries to find the underlying causes for abnormal behaviour, rather than just treating the symptoms
- It focuses on the individual. Rather than merely seeing a patient as a list of symptoms, it tries to understand the patient's own, unique experiences
- It still has a vast influence today and is widely recognized as one of the most influential theories of the twentieth century
- It created greater sympathy for people with psychological disorders
- It is impossible to test scientifically and is not based on scientific evidence
- It is deterministic in that it sees behaviour as being determined by instincts over which the patient has no control
- It deals with the past rather than the here and now
- It is culture-specific in that it may only apply to sexually-repressed Victorian women
- Psychoanalysis is not appropriate for disorders such as schizophrenia

Phobias

Phobias are an irrational fear which generate a feeling of dread, fear and foreboding of a thing and/or situation, resulting in an individual's going to some lengths to avoid the 'thing' or situation. So, a phobia can be acquired by pairing of a neutral object with a feared one. The neutral object then becomes associated with the fear and a phobia is born. The phobia can be as a result of biological, psychological or social factors.

Types of Phobia		
Specific	**Social (Social Anxiety Disorder**	**Agoraphobia**
An intense, irrational fear of a thing and/or object e.g. mice, spiders, blood, enclosed spaces.	Fear of social situations; of being embarrassed; meeting new people	Fear of being in open, public or enclosed spaces

Characteristics of Phobias

Behavioural	Emotional	Cognitive
The response will be avoidance of the phobic object, thing or situation that generates a severe anxiety response.	Severe fear and anxiety can become or cause distress if presented with the phobic thing, object or situation	Fearful thoughts about the phobic thing, object or situation.

The Behavioural approach to explaining phobias

The aim under this approach is to identify the behaviours that are causing problems and replace them with more appropriate ones.

Phobias can be a learned response or can be acquired by modelling the behaviour of another or others. Watson and Rayner (1920) conducted what is known as the 'Little Albert' experiment. In this experiment a 9 month old child was presented with a white rat, a monkey, a rabbit and various other items, none of which he had any particular response to or exhibited any fear toward, showing the expected level of curiosity for a child of his age. However, every time he touched the white rat a metal bar that was suspended behind him was struck with a large steel hammer generating a loud and sudden sound which startled the child causing him to burst into tears. This was done consistently over a period of time. The result being, that after a while it was no longer necessary for the metal bar to be struck to cause the child to be afraid, at simply seeing the white rat and anything that was white and fluffy would generate an irrational fear response (phobia) in the child. The outcome of this experiment suggested that phobias can be attributed to classical conditioning.

What we do need to bear in mind, is that some phobias are not attributable to classical conditioning, and in fact Ost (1987) suggests that some people with extreme phobias e.g. fear of snakes, germs, closed spaces etc., have no recollection or any experience of the thing that generates a fear response associated with the phobia.

Mowrer (1947) suggested a two-factor theory of avoidance and phobias, also known as the **two-process model**, which is _classical conditioning plus operant conditioning_. Operant conditioning is negative reinforcement through avoidance, making it more likely that that phobia will be experienced again resulting in the same fear response. Therefore, avoidance of the 'thing' that triggers the phobic response may reduce the fear at the time but reinforce that fear as a result of the avoidance.

The Behavioural approach to treating phobias

The two main behavioural therapies in use today are systematic desensitisation (SD) and aversion therapy. Both these techniques work on the principle of classical conditioning.

Systematic Desensitisation

You will also recall that Pavlov demonstrated this association by getting dogs to salivate to the sound of a bell rung at the same time that they were given food. If the bell is rung continuously however, in the absence of food, the association weakens and eventually disappears. This is known as *extinction*. Extinction never happens in the case of a phobia, since the person avoids the feared object. The aim of therapy is to present the feared object at the same time as getting the person to relax. After enough presentations, the association between the fear and the neutral object will be lost and the phobia will be cured. Flooding is a quick way to achieve this. The person is put into an inescapable situation with the feared object. The person reaches a heightened state of anxiety but, eventually, the fear subsides (probably due to exhaustion on the part of the patient). Wolpe (1960) forced an adolescent girl with a fear of cars into the back of a car and drove her around for four hours; her fear reached hysterical heights but then receded. By the end of the journey, her fear had completely disappeared. Understandably, this method raises ethical issues, so Systematic Desensitisation (a much kinder method) is used instead. In SD therapy, the client is asked to list the scenarios that frighten them most, with the least frightening first. For example, a client with a fear of dogs might list seeing a picture of a dog as least frightening and being trapped in a room with one as most frightening. The client then learns a relaxation technique. Next, the client imagines the first level of fear (seeing a picture of a dog) while practising the relaxation technique. As the client becomes comfortable at that level, they are then able to move onto the next level, until they are able to visualise all of the situations without fear. Sometimes, real animals are used as part of SD therapy (for example, real dogs or real spiders) but it is uncertain whether this is more effective than visualisation.

Aversion Therapy

This is perhaps the most controversial of all the therapies since it involves using the principles of classical conditioning to instil a fear of some object or behaviour (often an addiction) that the therapist wishes to remove.

Typically, the person will have an addiction e.g. to alcohol. The therapist will get them to take an emetic drug (induces severe nausea and vomiting) at the same time as drinking alcohol. Eventually an association is acquired between the alcohol and the unpleasant feeling of being sick. Thus the person learns to avoid alcohol in the future.

The problem with this therapy is that the person's desire to drink alcohol is so strong that extinction will often take place. The footballer George Best, who underwent aversion therapy for alcoholism, said that he could bear the sickness he felt when he took a drink after therapy because he knew that, after a few drinks, it would subside.

Evaluation of Behavioural Therapies

- Only targets the behaviour, and does not cure underlying causes
- SD has extremely effective success rates of 60-90% for spider and blood infection phobias (Barlow *et al,* 2002)
- Significant ethical issues, especially with aversion therapy

Behaviour Modification

These techniques use the principles of operant conditioning to train desired behaviour.

Token Economy (TE)

This is based on the principle of secondary reinforcement whereby tokens (secondary reinforcers) are given for socially acceptable behaviour. The tokens can then be exchanged for certain primary reinforcers such as sweets and cigarettes. The founders of this technique, Ayllon and Azrin (1968) tried the technique with a group of chronic schizophrenics. At the start of the trial, some of the patients screamed for long periods, some were mute and most could no longer eat with a knife and fork. Some buried their faces in their food. They were systematically rewarded for ward work and self-care with tokens that could later be exchanged for special privileges. In all cases, behaviour improved.

Since then hundreds of studies have been carried out comparing TE with other forms of therapy, including drugs. In one study, Paul and Lentz (1977) used a social learning/token economy in which patients were rewarded for good behaviour as well as having the opportunity to see appropriate behaviour modelled by staff and other patients. They found that the number of patients using neuroleptics (anti-schizophrenia drugs) fell to 11% after TE compared with a group under routine hospital care, 100% of whom remained on drugs.

Evaluation of Behaviour Modification

- Token economies are a useful way of improving antisocial behaviour
- Early studies on TE also helped to highlight the fact that poor patient handling by staff actually contributed to antisocial behaviour
- Often behaviour returns once out in the community where no such programme operates
- Reductionist approach – Treats behaviours but not underlying cause

Depression

Depression is a disorder that negatively affects an individual's mood and how they feel. It is often equated with feelings of sadness at the extreme end of the spectrum where an individual may feel worthless and lack the ability or desire to engage in day-to-day or pleasurable activities. It can occur as a result of biological, psychological and social factors.

Behavioural	Emotional	Cognitive
Individuals may exhibit changes in behaviour, from eating habits (eating more or less or not eating at all) to changes in physical activity, from extreme hyperactivity to extreme lethargy.	The extent and enormity of the negative emotion being experienced is what distinguishes depression from just feeling 'upset' or 'a little down or sad'. Feelings of helplessness, hopelessness, frustration, irritation, powerlessness, infiltrate all facets of an individual's life and their ability to function fully on a daily basis.	An individual's past negative schema, developed during childhood can result in negative and pessimistic views of themselves or situations and circumstances that may result in a negative interpretation of facts that places the individual at the centre of blame (see Beck below). This could generate feelings of suicide.

The Cognitive approach to explaining depression

Cognitive-behavioural therapies (CBT) emphasise the need to alter the thinking and reasoning processes of the client, but also make use of some of the techniques of traditional behaviour therapies. They assume that mental disorders are caused in part by the way the client views themselves and the world. The therapist tries to help people to control symptoms, such as anxiety and depression, by teaching them more adaptive ways of thinking about their experiences. Although past events are not disregarded, cognitive therapists focus on the patient's current state of functioning. There are several approaches to cognitive-behavioural therapy.

The two of the most notable explanations of depression from a cognitive perspective with its examination of peoples thought processes, judgements, perceptions, come from Albert Ellis and Aaron Beck.

Albert Ellis

Ellis suggests that those who suffer from depression experience what he calls '**basic irrational assumptions**', which means an individual may irrationally regard themselves as being a failure or have a negative view of themselves which is not grounded in anything factual. The result of this may be the individual seeking the approval of others so as not to feel rejected but still viewing themselves negatively. Ellis's **ABC Model** is fundamental to our understanding the cognitive therapy when dealing with depression. The model works as follows:

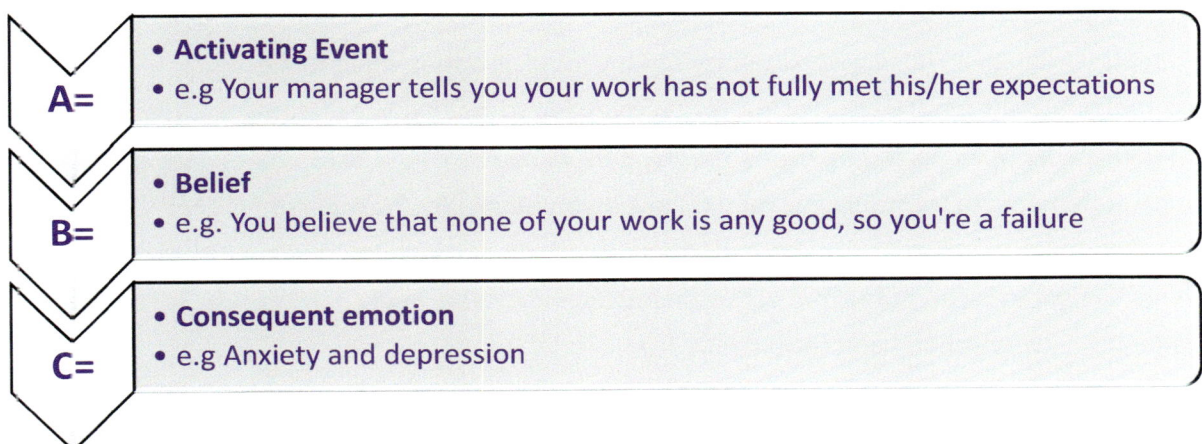

A=
- **Activating Event**
- e.g Your manager tells you your work has not fully met his/her expectations

B=
- **Belief**
- e.g. You believe that none of your work is any good, so you're a failure

C=
- **Consequent emotion**
- e.g Anxiety and depression

A+B=C

A triggers **B**, resulting in **C**

It is the irrational belief or thought (not the event itself) that causes the consequences.

Ellis's treatment of depression – Rational Emotive Behaviour Therapy (REBT)

REBT is a form of cognitive therapy that encourages and teaches an individual who harbours irrational beliefs to actively identify and dispute them and to assimilate rational beliefs and thoughts that are positive – to actively act against the irrational thought/belief.

Developed by Albert Ellis (1962), this is now a widely used therapeutic approach. The task of REBT is to restructure the client's faulty belief systems and to substitute 'positive self-talk' for irrational self-statements. The therapist actively disputes false beliefs through rational confrontation, and teaches the client to identify and dispute such beliefs themselves (see dialogue below).

Behaviourally-oriented techniques are also employed, often in the form of 'homework assignments', for example, to reward themselves with an external reinforcer, e.g. a food treat, after working for 15 minutes at disputing their beliefs.

Dialogue of REBT (taken from Ellis, 1984)

Therapist: The same crap! It's always the same crap. Now, if you would look at the crap - instead of 'Oh, how stupid I am! He hates me! I think I'll kill myself!' - then you'd get better right away.

Patient: You've been listening! (laughs)

Therapist: Listening to what?

Patient: (laughs) Those wild statements in my mind, like that, that I make.

Therapist: That's right! Because I know that you have to make those statements - because I have a good theory. And according to my theory, people couldn't get upset unless they made those nutty statements to themselves... Even if I loved you madly, the next person is likely to hate you. So I like brown eyes and he likes blue eyes, or something. So then you're dead! Because you really think: 'I've got to be accepted! I've got to act intelligently!' Well, why?

Patient: (very soberly and reflectively) True.

Therapist: You see?

Patient: Yes.

Therapist: Now, if you will learn that lesson, then you've had a very valuable session. Because you don't have to upset yourself. As I said before: if I thought you were the worst [expletive deleted] who ever existed, well that's my opinion. But does that make you a turd?

Patient: (reflective silence)

Therapist: Does it?

Patient: No.

Therapist: What makes you a turd?

Patient: Thinking that you are.

Therapist: That's right! Your belief that you are. That's the only thing that could ever do it. And you never have to believe that, see? You control your thinking. I control my thinking - my belief

---

about you. But you don't have to be affected by that. You always control what you think.

Source: Gross and Mcilveen (1998)

Overall, the focus of this approach is to get an individual to realise that when presented with difficult or challenging events in their life that they have a choice in terms of how they respond to it and how they feel - they are in control of their response, not the response in control of them.

Beck's treatment of depression

Developed initially for the treatment of depression (Beck *et al, 1979*), this therapy has since been extended to the treatment of anxiety disorders and phobias (Beck, *1985*).

Beck identified 3 negative thoughts present in depression, and it is these negative thoughts that underlie depression as a mental disorder. These negative thoughts were:

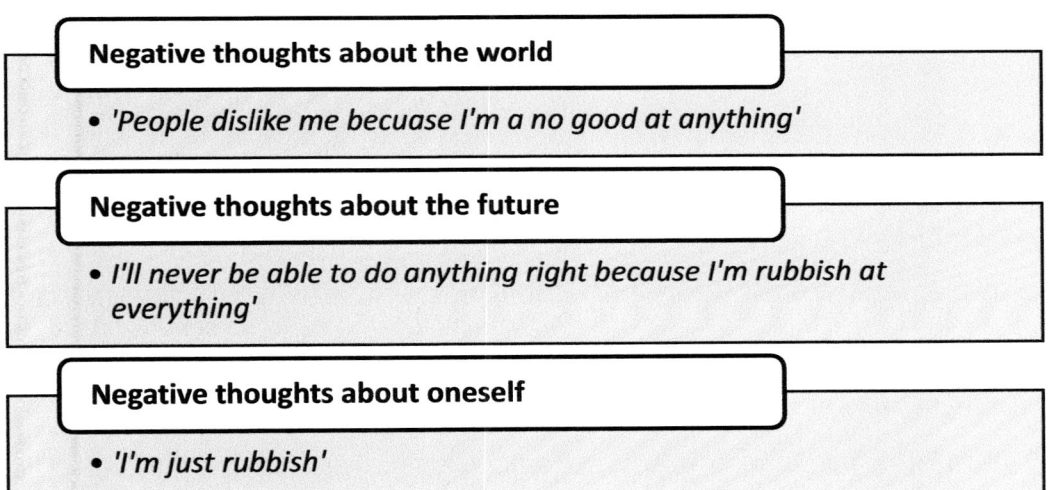

Negative thoughts about the world

• *'People dislike me becuase I'm a no good at anything'*

Negative thoughts about the future

• *I'll never be able to do anything right because I'm rubbish at everything'*

Negative thoughts about oneself

• *'I'm just rubbish'*

In contrast to the challenging and confrontational approach of REBT, Beck's approach to therapy is to more gently point out errors of logic and contradictory evidence, encouraging patients to 'reality test' for themselves, i.e. to gather information about themselves through unbiased observation and experimentation. Irrational beliefs are converted into hypotheses which can be tested and falsified though experience, and the client is encouraged to decide for themselves whether or not their thinking is accurate. Again, behavioural techniques are employed, in that activities for such hypothesis testing are designed, and pleasurable activities are scheduled to provide reinforcement.

Dialogue of Cognitive-Restructuring Therapy (taken from Beck et al, 1979)

Therapist: Why do you think you won't be able to get into the university of your choice?

Patient: Because my grades were not very good.

Therapist: Well, what was your grade average?

Patient: As and Bs.

Therapist: How many of each?

Patient: I got two As and Two Bs.

Therapist: Have you found out what the average grades are for admission to the university?

Patient: Somebody told me that a B average would suffice.

Therapist: Isn't your average better than that?

Patient: I guess so.

Source: Gross and Mcilveen (1998)

What makes these negative thoughts particularly significant is that they may still be in the mind of the individual even if there is evidence that suggests that the contrary is true. This for Beck is an illogical thinking process that is self-denigrating, self-defeating, causing anxiety and depression. So the individual is helped to identify and recognise illogical thoughts and is 'encouraged' to question those thoughts and even challenge them by trying to apply new interpretations and ways of thinking.

Evaluation of CT

Strengths	Weaknesses
Good success rates for depression and anxiety. May be more successful than drug treatments in some cases.	Less effective for conditions such as schizophrenia, although may help sufferers to cope with their condition.
More cost-effective and less time consuming than psychoanalysis.	In focusing on the cognitive, it ignores genetic or biological factors. There is no real understanding of where the negative thoughts come from in the first place.

Obsessive Compulsive Disorder (OCD)

OCD is a type of behaviour that is associated with cognitive bias. If we are to accept that cognitive bias occurs during decision-making when an individual processing information has an error of thinking that causes them to make judgements based on biases and irrational thoughts, then we can apply these elements to the condition of OCD.

OCD is a condition that affects 12 in every 1000 people and is an anxiety disorder that causes an individual to have repetitive feelings, ideas, thoughts, sensations, obsessions or behaviours that makes them feel compelled to act in a certain way that may take the form of performing repetitive or ritualistic behaviour. Performing repetitive or ritualistic behaviour may provide some short-term relief for the individual affected, as not to do so can cause great anxiety. Understandably this condition (examples of which can be exhibited by hand washing, not touching certain things, placing things in a certain order, checking and rechecking things), can cause disruption to everyday functions such as going to work or school, and can be anything from mild to severe. There are many causes for this type of cognitive bias behaviour which can stem from social pressures, stress, emotional difficulties and individual motivation.

Characteristics of OCD

Behavioural	Emotional	Cognitive
Mower argues that, as with phobias, the fears associated with OCD are learned, in that something that was once considered a neutral and non-distinct thing or object becomes associated with a negative event which causes an individual to feel compelled to complete a certain action in order to prevent the negative outcome. This action becomes ritualistic and repetitive, alleviating, temporarily, the anxiety experienced.	Due to obsessional thinking an individual may experience, this can result in feelings of anxiety, distress, powerlessness, frustration etc.	Intrusive, negative thoughts may be exaggerated and given greater significance than the thought actually warrants – the individual sees the thought as actually representing a threat. He/she may come to fear their own thoughts and try to diffuse or abate them by engaging in ritualistic or routine activities that they associate with neutralising the negative thought e.g. an individual may think, *"I may cause harm to someone because I've had thoughts about poisoning people. I must be a danger to others."* In order to combat this fear, the individual may conduct ritualistic behaviour, such as washing things in the kitchen in a certain way in an

		attempt to avoid contamination and possibly food poisoning, repeatedly checking that medication is locked away and so on.

The Biological approach to explaining OCD

Genetic – Family and twin studies suggest that family members who suffer with OCD may have a predisposition to the condition. However, causes could be attributable to social rather than biological influences. Children whose parents suffer from OCD, if experienced by the child itself, are often different in terms of the symptoms exhibited. The gene Sapap3, associated with the ability to plan and process, when lacking, has been suggested by Feng *et al* (2007) to be implicated in OCD.

Biochemistry studies have found that lower levels or deficiency of serotonin (neurotransmitter) were found in people who suffered from OCD. Pigott *et al* suggested that drugs that increased the levels of serotonin reduced OCD symptoms.[4]

Neuroanatomy/Brain Structure – The Orbital-frontal Cortex (OFC) of the brain is associated with decision-making, judgement and the moderation of behaviour. The signals sent by the OFC are normally filtered by the Caudate Nucleus. However, in sufferers of OCD, the Caudate Nucleus is damaged or malfunctioning resulting in signals being overloaded, causing heightened levels of anxiety and compulsion. Another significant part of the brains structure is the Basal Ganglia, which is associated with pattern recognition, emotion and memory. Where there

---

[4] Note: research in relation to this is varied.

are abnormalities in the Prefrontal Cortex, this can result in a predisposition to OCD. One way to address this is to disconnect the Prefrontal Cortex from the Basal Ganglia.

General ways of treating OCD

The type of treatment applied to an individual affected by OCD will be dependent on the type of disorder being treated and the extent to which it affects the individual concerned. Examples are:

- Cognitive Behavioural Therapy
- Medication Treatment
- Exposure and Response Prevention (ERP)
- A combination of all of the above.

The Biological approach to treating OCD

Drug Treatments – increasing levels of serotonin reducing levels of dopamine; anti-anxiety and anti-depression medication – interacts with the chemicals in the brain to generate balance. Drug treatment is often the first line of treatment offered for many mental disorders. This is because drugs are effective at alleviating symptoms relatively quickly, and it is a treatment with which people feel familiar and comfortable.

The three main types of drugs are listed below:

- Anti-anxiety (minor tranquilisers), e.g. benzodiazepines such as Librium and Valium. These increase the action of an inhibitory neurotransmitter, GABA, which quietens the nervous system and brings about muscle relaxation. Used to treat anxiety
- Anti-depressants e.g. selective serotonin reuptake inhibitors (SSRIs). These block the re-uptake of serotonin at the synapse (junction between two neurones) making more available. Increasing serotonin levels improves mood. Used to treat depression

- Anti-psychotics (major tranquilisers), e.g. phenothiazines such as Chlorpromazine. These block dopamine (D2) receptors, reducing levels of dopamine. Used to treat schizophrenia. Clozapine is now often used, as it has fewer side effects than chlorpromazine and works on a wider range of neurotransmitters

Evaluation of Drug Treatments

Many of the drugs used to treat psychological disorders have serious and unpleasant side effects. The long-term use of Clorpromazine to treat schizophrenia leads to a movement disorder similar to Parkinson's disease, while Clozapine lowers the white blood cell count and thus reduces the effectiveness of the immune system.

Treatment for schizophrenia is on-going and there is no cure. Therefore patients must continue to take medication, or they will suffer a relapse. However, the very serious side effects often deter patients from continuing treatment, especially once they begin to feel well.

Some anti-depressants also have dangerous side effects. Patients taking monoamine-oxidase inhibitors (MAOIs) must be extremely cautious as to what they eat as many foods can cause severe reactions. The long-term use of tricyclic anti-depressants has been associated with heart problems. The more recently developed and most commonly prescribed class of anti-depressant, the SSRIs, have fewer side effects and are generally considered safer than the earlier anti-depressants. However, even these have sometimes been linked to suicide, and should be prescribed discerningly.

There are also ethical issues involved in drug treatment, as people who are very ill may not be able to give informed consent.

Psycho-surgery – surgical intervention - aims to disconnect the thinking/planning part of the brain (frontal lobes) from the older, emotional parts (the amygdala). The first systematic attempts at human psychosurgery occurred from 1935, when neurosurgeon Egas Moniz performed the first prefrontal lobotomy - a procedure severing the connection between the prefrontal cortex and the rest of the brain.

Moniz deemed the procedure a success, especially in the treatment of depression, even though about 6% of patients did not survive the operation, and there were often marked and adverse changes in the patients' personality and social functioning. Nevertheless, Moniz received a Nobel Prize in 1949.

American physician Walter Freeman (Freeman, 1942) was impressed with Moniz's technique but, having no surgical background, he invented the "ice pick lobotomy" whereby he tapped an ice pick up through the patient's eye socket with a rubber mallet and wiggled it around to destroy the pre-frontal tissue. He used the technique to treat aggression, schizophrenia and depression. Leaving no visible scars, the ice pick lobotomy was heralded as a great advance in surgery, and was done under local anaesthesia or after having been rendered unconscious using electroshock. His youngest patient was a 12 year-old boy, Howard Dully, treated for hyperactivity and aggression after his step-mother claimed she could not handle him. From 1936 through the 1950s, he advocated lobotomies throughout the United States. Ultimately, between 40,000 and 50,000 patients were lobotomised.

Nowadays, psychosurgery is used as a last resort, usually to treat severe depression and where other treatments have failed. The procedure is carried out using modern surgical techniques and radiographic imaging which can precisely pinpoint the nerves to be targeted (often cauterised or destroyed with small radioactive pellets), leaving the rest of the frontal lobe intact.

Evaluation of Psychosurgery

- Psychosurgery is now very rare, so it is hard to judge its effectiveness. It has been beneficial in alleviating the symptoms of severe anxiety or obsessive-compulsive disorders (Beck and Cowley, 1990)
- However, there are major ethical issues as damage is irreversible and changes to personality are unpredictable. Patients may be too ill to understand the implications of the treatment and therefore can't give informed consent

Electro-Convulsive Therapy (ECT) - In 1933, Polish psychiatrist Manfred Sakel (Sakel, 1956) was treating a schizophrenic patient who was also diabetic. The patient was accidentally given an overdose of insulin, and once he had recovered from the resulting hyperglycaemic seizure, Sakel noticed that his schizophrenic symptoms seemed to have improved. This led to the development of inducing seizures or convulsions to treat schizophrenia and, later, depression. Gradually, passing an electric current across the brain became the preferred method to induce such seizures and ECT was born (Cerletti, 1940).

In the early days, ECT was a dangerous procedure. The resulting convulsion was so powerful that it caused the patient to flail around, often breaking bones and causing lacerations to the tongue. Afterwards, patients often experienced periods of disorientation and memory loss.

Nowadays, the use of muscle-relaxants during the procedure has made the seizure almost imperceptible save for perhaps a twitching of the patient's toes. In addition, the shock (of 70-130 V) is now usually applied unilaterally (to one side of the brain) for around half a second, which minimises memory loss. However, how ECT actually works is still a mystery. Many believe the assault on the brain causes the release of various neurotransmitters which can improve symptoms (especially in depression) but, beyond that, little is known about why or how it works.

Today, in the UK, ECT is only used for the most severe forms of depression where other treatments have failed. Nevertheless, over 11,000 patients in England and Wales were given ECT in 1999 (Johnstone, 2003) usually in a course of 6-12 treatments administered 2 or 3 times a week. Two thirds of these were women. An estimated 1 million people worldwide receive ECT every year.

Evaluation of ECT

- Often quicker than drugs or psychological therapies. The effects are immediate

- Effective, short-term treatment for depression. However, in one study 60-70% of patients improved but a large proportion became depressed again the following year (Sackheim, 1988)

- Requires consent or second opinion before it can be administered, and the Mental Health Act (2007) now states that a patient can refuse ECT unless its use is necessary to save life or prevent serious deterioration in the person's condition

- Criticised on ethical grounds. Fears it may have been used (especially in the early days) to punish or control patients in mental hospitals (as highlighted in the novel, *One Flew Over the Cuckoo's Nest* by Ken Kesey)

- No scientific basis (Heather, 1976)

- Brain damage occurs in animals given ECT (Breggin, 1979)

Treating Abnormality

As discussed previously, there are various therapeutic approaches available to treat psychological abnormalities and during the past one hundred years, more and more treatments for abnormality have been discovered. Although underpinned by the medical model, these have broadly followed the various trends in psychology, from psychodynamic psychology through behaviourism and cognitive psychology.

Today, it is recognised that some disorders respond better to certain types of therapy. It is also recognised that a combined therapeutic approach is often more effective than using one approach alone. For example, much better outcomes are achieved for depression if drugs, such as SSRIs, and cognitive-behavioural therapy are used together. The drugs improve mood, which enable the person to begin to tackle the negative thinking which often underlies the disorder.

Therapies Based on the Psychodynamic Approach

Psychodynamic therapies were initially developed by Freud. In the belief that abnormality is a result of unconscious conflicts, the goal of psychoanalysis is to drain this 'psychic abscess' by bringing repressed conflicts into awareness where they can be confronted and dealt with. Therefore, the aim is not to 'cure', but rather to enable the person to gain insight into the reasons for their behavior, so that their ego can better cope with the inner conflicts causing their disturbance.

A number of methods are used, but all involve delving into the client's past in the belief that problems originate in childhood events. Present difficulties were not seen as relevant by Freud since he believed that these could be dealt with by sympathy and advice from family and friends.

Techniques used in classical psychoanalysis include the following:

- Free association – Client talks freely about whatever thoughts and feelings come to mind, regardless of how painful, personal or seemingly irrelevant they might be. This removes the normal 'censorship' of the ego and enables the contents of the preconscious to be explored. During this process, the analyst usually sits quietly behind the client. Sometimes the analyst 'interprets' the client's comments in order to follow a train of thought and delve deeper into the client's psyche

- Analysis of dreams - Freud viewed dreams as 'the royal road to the unconscious'. During sleep, Ego defences are lowered allowing repressed material to come through in a disguised form. The symbols (manifest content) contained within dreams are analysed to reveal unconscious desires (latent content), which are often sexual or aggressive in nature. The *dream work* is the process of converting latent into manifest content through processes such as displacement and symbolisation

- Analysis of transference - Often the relationship between the analyst and client becomes emotionally charged. The client may get upset and say something like 'I was never good enough for you.' This obviously represents repressed feelings towards a parent or 'significant other' which have been transferred onto the analyst. It is the analyst's job to probe further the source of the childhood problems and bring them into the present so they can be discussed

- Analysis of resistance - during free association, resistance may occur, in the form of unwillingness to talk about certain thoughts or feelings. The client may become distractible, joke about something as if it were not important, arrive late for the session or miss the session altogether. Events like this are important because they indicate possible areas of repression and must be overcome for the analysis to succeed

Evaluation of Psychoanalysis

- Tends to be very time consuming (up to three years) and expensive. Therefore it is not available to everyone
- Not suitable for psychotic disorders such as schizophrenia where the person may not be in touch with reality. Fonagy (2000) found it consistently helped to improve symptoms in patients with mild neurotic disorders but results were not so clear-cut for more serious disorders
- Eysenck (1952) called psychoanalysis a waste of time and money, claiming that patients on a waiting list for the treatment showed as much improvement as those receiving it. However, Corsini and Wedding (1995) have shown that the success rate varies from 30 to 60 percent depending on how success is measured
- Disparity in power between the analyst and client is open to abuse. Survey data from 575 psychotherapists in America reveal that 87% (95% of men, 76% of women) therapists have been sexually attracted to their clients (Pope *et al*, 1986)

Projective Tests

Psychologists use projective tests to try to examine the personality characteristics and emotional functioning of their patients. Designed by Herman Rorschach (pronounced raw-shock) in 1921, the inkblot test is the second most widely used test by members of the Society for Personality Assessment. It has been employed in diagnosing underlying thought disorder and differentiating psychotic from non-psychotic thinking. Patients are asked to look at various inkblots and say what the shape means to them. By repeating this with a series of different ink blots, various themes (such as preoccupation with aggression) and anxieties emerge.

- Supporters of Rorschach believe that the subject's response to an ambiguous and meaningless stimulus can provide insight into their thought processes
- However, it is not clear *how* this occurs
- Validity of the test has been questioned
- Rigorous procedures surrounding the administration of the test seen as unwieldy and many psychologists cut corners, making the test unreliable

Summary

You have looked in some detail at the treatments and therapies which stem from the four models of abnormal behaviour. Here is a brief resume of the strengths and weaknesses of each approach.

Biological Approach

Some symptoms are caused by brain abnormalities but some are caused by problems with living. Some are combinations of both. Where the symptoms are wholly organic (i.e. caused by physical abnormalities), drug therapy will be appropriate.

However, the methods by which some drugs work is not fully understood so the question arises: 'Is it unethical to give a patient a drug when we are not sure of possible long-term side effects?' We are not sure how ECT works and, where psychosurgery is involved, we do not fully understand the changes that may occur in personality when we chop bits of people's brains out! Worse still, many patients do not really understand what the surgery involves.

Psychodynamic Approach

This approach is based on the assumption that emotional and personality disorders are caused by childhood experiences. If we reject this theory, then techniques designed to relive childhood cannot produce a 'cure' for adult problems. Sometimes it is argued that by looking backwards for the origins of problems, we may miss the real causes of problems in the here and now. For example, if being trapped in a tower block with two small children is what's making me miserable, there seems little point in analysing my early relationship with my mother. However, the use of psychoanalytical techniques still has benefits if used correctly.

Behavioural Approach

Behaviourist techniques have produced considerable success in dealing with phobias and addictions. However, behaviour shaping in the treatment room (a highly controlled environment) does not always persist when the patient returns to his/her normal social context. The idea of changing 'abnormal' behaviour for that which is more socially acceptable raises serious ethical concerns. Imagine using aversion therapy to 'cure' a gay man by showing him pictures of his naked lover and giving him a strong electric shock! Yet this would have been an acceptable cure in 1960s America. Behavioural therapies have been criticised for being based on an oversimplified picture of human behaviour where people react to stimuli and learned associations. They do not seem to reason, think or make sense of their experiences. Another criticism is that behavioural therapies are not able to change the behaviour of some psychotic people whose problems lie in thinking and interpreting things differently from others.

Cognitive Approaches

Cognitive restructuring theories tend to direct the client's perceptions and cognitions to focus on positive, rather than negative thoughts. Gaining a better understanding of ourselves is good but understanding our thoughts isn't the same as changing our actions. The emphasis in therapy must be on changing undesired behaviour into desired behaviour. Thought influences behaviour and behaviour influences thought. Since these two are inseparable, cognitive therapy should emphasise behaviour as well as thought processes. Most modern therapies are described as cognitive-behavioural therapies, and there is mounting evidence that they are successful in treating depressive/anxiety disorders and those where low self-image and poor self-control lead to difficulties in coping with life.

Effectiveness of Therapies

We have already seen that some therapies are more effective for certain disorders, and that some disorders benefit from a combined treatment approach. The best way to compare the effectiveness of therapies is to carry out studies in which patients diagnosed with the same disorder are put into different treatment groups and monitored over a period of time.

Using this method, Elkin *et al* (1989) found that drugs, CBT and psychotherapy are all more effective than a placebo (dummy pill) in treating depression. Similarly, Davidson *et al* (2004) found CBT and drugs are equally effective in treating depression and that combining them does not improve their effectiveness, although Otto *et al* (2000) found that the benefits of CBT last longer than those of drugs. In all studies there are some patients who do not respond to therapy.

Activity 22

1. Give one strength and one weakness of psychoanalysis

2. Outline one behavioural therapy based on classical conditioning and one based on operant conditioning

3. Give one strength and one weakness of using behavioural techniques in the treatment of mental illness

1) Give one strength and one weakness of psychoanalysis.

Psychoanalysis tends to be very time consuming (up to three years) and expensive. Therefore it is not available to everyone. It is not suitable for psychotic disorders, such as schizophrenia, where the person may not be in touch with reality.

2) Outline one behavioural therapy based on classical conditioning and one based on operant conditioning.

Aversion therapy is based on classical conditioning and aims to pair unwanted behaviour with some unpleasant stimulus in order to bring about extinction.

Token economy is based on operant conditioning. It aims to teach desired behaviour by rewarding such actions as self care with tokens (secondary reinforcers) which can be swapped for privileges and/or commodities such as sweets (primary reinforcers).

3) Give one strength and one weakness of using behavioural techniques in the treatment of mental illness.

Strength: Behavioural techniques are more cost-effective than many other treatments. They have good success rates in the treatment of depression and anxiety.

Weakness: Behavioural techniques require the awareness and commitment of the client. They are less effective in the treatment of conditions such as schizophrenia, where the client has less awareness of the external world.

Tutor Marked Assignment 1

(Mock Exam)

Now go to CloudPort to download your mock exam. Answers should be word processed and uploaded via CloudPort

Please note: If you are pursuing the AS Level qualification only then you will only sit Papers 1 and 2, which correspond to TMAs 1 and 2. If however you are pursuing full A Level qualification you will sit the second set of exam papers which correspond to TMAs 3, 4 and 5. As level no longer counts towards the A level qualification.

2 Psychology in Context

For this portion of the course you will be looking at the following areas:

1.2.1 – **Approaches in Psychology**

1.2.2 - Biopsychology

4.2.3 – Research Methods

> ➢ 4.2.3.1 Scientific processes

> ➢ 4.2.3.2 Data handling and analysis

> ➢ 4.2.3.3 Inferential testing

After going through these units you will be expected to:

- Demonstrate knowledge and understanding of psychological concepts, theories, research studies, research methods and ethical issues

- Apply psychological knowledge and understanding of social influence, memory and attachment in range of contexts

- Analyse, interpret and evaluate psychological concepts, theories, research studies and research methods in relation to social influence, memory and attachment

- Evaluate therapies and treatments, looking at their appropriateness and effectiveness

During the course of your studies you will develop knowledge and understanding of research methods in the general sense as well as engaging in practical and mathematical skills that will engage you in looking at:

- Research design

- Conducting Research

- Analysing and interpreting data

2.1 Approaches in Psychology

Paper 2: Compulsory Content

When we refer to approaches in Psychology, we are looking at the various ways in which Psychology tries to explain behaviour. There is no one approach that can provide all of the answers; as such, this section looks at some of the main approaches that are associated with Psychology. The ones discussed in this section are:

- Learning Approaches
- Cognitive Approaches
- Biological Approaches
- Psychodynamic Approaches
- Humanistic Psychology
- Comparison Approaches
- Origins of psychology: Wundt, introspection and the emergence of psychology as a science

Origins of Psychology

The study of the mind dates back many centuries. In fact there is evidence that can trace psychology back to the ancient Greeks. For example, in the pre-Socratic writings; in the empirical tradition of the proto-scientist and philosopher Aristotle, or else in Plato's work on human nature and the constitution of the 'soul' (in Greek: *psyche*, hence 'psychology') or animating part of the person: what we may now term 'mind'. However, historians of psychology typically date the foundation of *modern* psychology to around the 1870s onwards, with the advent of the more systematic application of the experimental/laboratory method and data analysis to the study of human behaviour and mind, by pioneers such as Wilhelm Wundt: an area formally considered suitable for philosophical speculation (or introspection) rather than experimentation. In 1874, Wilhelm Wundt (considered to be one of the 'founding fathers' of psychology) published *Principles of Physiological Psychology, and in his works he identified and discussed the connections between human thought and behaviour and the science of physiology. So began the emergence of psychology as a science.*

Activity 23

Research the psychological career of Wilhelm Wundt, by reading the following article. Make sure that you can describe the key features of his research.

http://www.simplypsychology.org/wundt.html

Historical beginnings of Psychology

Psychology as a late nineteenth century science thus represented a new application of existing methodological practices (that is, experimental and laboratory based) alongside the rigour of data analysis. For example, an early psychologist, Norman Triplett (1898) commonly credited with carrying out the first sports or social psychology experiment, where he analysed the pacing effect (running/cycling a race with a pacer improves performance compared to running without a pacer) presented the data he had gathered on the winning times in sports races, with "the feeling that they have **almost** the force of a scientific experiment." From the time of the Enlightenment and what is now recognised as the birth of the modern physical sciences (e.g., physics or chemistry), these methods had previously only been applied to studying the physical, rather than the mental or social worlds.

However, the development of psychology as a science, rather than a mode of philosophical enquiry, was initially marked by some theoretical disagreement as to how best to interpret human behaviour. The influential theory of evolution in Darwin's *Origin of Species* (1859), suggested that human behaviour should be understood in reductive terms: if the ultimate origins of humanity were in the animal kingdom, then animal behaviour (and the process of evolution) should be the key to explaining human behaviour. This can be seen as the foundation of both early twentieth century behaviourism and later, the discipline of Evolutionary Psychology. The advantage to psychology of grounding itself in evolutionary thinking in the late nineteenth century and early twentieth, was that psychology's future direction as an offshoot of the biological sciences (rather than a domain of philosophy) was made clear. However, the disadvantage of this would be confusion over psychology's precise future relationship to the scientific method of laboratory experimentation, since an evolutionary approach implied that understanding human behaviour was merely a subset of extrapolations drawn from studying animal behaviours in the field, or animal behaviour in the laboratory. But where would this leave data collection from human participants in experimental paradigms, which is a familiar experimental method in contemporary psychology?

Moreover, the subjectivity of the human condition was quickly subsumed in the evolutionary or behaviourist approach which saw all behaviours as the outcome of learning based on a stimulus and a response. This state of affairs provided the context for an alternative approach to understanding the human mind: that pioneered by Sigmund Freud, in the form of psychoanalysis.

Freud was first educated in the medical sciences, and actually advocated for a 'scientific psychology' (1895), by which he meant an understanding of the unconscious which was also firmly grounded in neurophysiology. However, he was also convinced that the way to understand the primarily subjective nature of human experience, feeling and behaviour (and especially psychopathology) was through case studies of patients undergoing psychoanalysis, using techniques such as symbolic dream interpretation (Freud, 1899). This ultimately led Freud away from the objective experimental and laboratory method. However, psychoanalysis, though hugely influential as both a therapy and as a cultural movement (such as the then shocking revelation that unconscious drives underlie a substantial portion of human conscious behaviour), is not usually considered scientific in traditional terms.

Contemporary Approach

The eventual formalisation of psychology as a unified scientific discipline by the early twentieth century as distinct from, on the one hand, biology, and on the other, philosophy or psychoanalysis, can now perhaps serve to mask the fundamentally interdisciplinary nature of contemporary psychology. This is most evident in the practice of the modern discipline, where the health sciences, other social sciences, biology and philosophy (among others) have all been brought to bear on the subject to produce the multiple fields that constitute the current range of academic psychology, unified by a scientific methodological approach. Furthermore, psychology as a scientific endeavour is still predicated on important questions within the philosophy of mind, which links back to its philosophical origins: what is mind and what is its relationship both to the brain, and to the body?

These latter are the famous 'Hard Problem' of human consciousness (why does it *feel* like something to be a person; that is, why do we have consciousness in the first place?) and the mind-body problem, respectively (how can a material body and the seemingly non-material mind interact?). In which case, the concept of 'mind' is also a unifying force to psychology: though how mind is conceptualised and operationalised has varied both across fields of psychology and through time.

The Basic Assumptions of psychological approaches

Learning Approaches - The Behaviourist Approach

This approach emphasises the role of *learning* in causing 'maladaptive' behaviour which can then lead to mental disorders. Behaviourists deal with three main types of learning:

- Classical conditioning
- Operant conditioning

- Social learning

Classical Conditioning

Classical conditioning is learning by *association*. It is based on involuntary behaviour, i.e. behaviour elicited by a stimulus without conscious control. If another stimulus is present at the same time, it too will eventually elicit the original response.

In Pavlov's experiment on dogs, for example, pairing the sound of a bell with food caused the dog to associate the two stimuli. Eventually, the dog would salivate to the bell alone; it had acquired a conditioned response.

Classical conditioning has been used to explain the acquisition of phobias, e.g. a fear of flowers could be explained thus:

Bee sting (US) → fear and pain (UR)

Bee sting + rose (CS) → fear and pain

Rose → fear and pain (CR)

- Unconditioned stimulus (**US**)
- Unconditioned response (**UR**)
- Conditioned stimulus (**CS**)
- Conditioned response (**CR**)

This fear can generalise to all flowers, or in the case of other phobias, all spiders, all heights, etc. However, not all people with a phobia can remember having a traumatic experience associated with the feared object. Seligman (1971) explains this in terms of biological preparedness i.e. we inherit an inbuilt fear of things that were dangerous to our ancestors, making us more likely (prepared) to fear certain animals or objects. Evidence that people can be more easily conditioned to fear spiders than flowers supports this idea (Ohman *et al,* 2000).

Operant Conditioning

Operant conditioning is a theory developed by B.F. Skinner (1974) who demonstrated that animals could be made to learn quite complex behaviour by rewarding required actions. When a learner performs a behaviour, there are three possible consequences:

- Positive reinforcement which is pleasurable e.g. a rat receiving food after pushing a lever
- Negative reinforcement (avoidance learning) e.g. cleaning your bedroom to avoid being nagged by your parents
- Punishment e.g. receiving a fine for speeding

Maladaptive behaviour could be learned through operant conditioning, e.g. if behaviours such as depression are reinforced through increased attention, they may be repeated. Also Mowrer (1947) believes that although phobias may be acquired by classical conditioning, they may be maintained by operant conditioning as the person avoids the feared object (negative reinforcement).

Social Learning Theory

Bandura (1969) showed that humans could not only learn directly through operant conditioning but indirectly by observational learning and modelling. Individuals can therefore learn abnormal behaviours through observing others and then modelling (copying) their behaviour, especially if they see behaviour rewarded (vicarious reinforcement). This may explain how eating disorders develop.

Coward (1984) points out that earlier in history food was often scarce. During these times, big bodies were a sign of wealth and status. Nowadays, food is in plentiful supply to most Westerners, so different standards in beauty have developed. The ideal shape portrayed in the media is not that of a mature woman but of a pre-pubescent girl. Yet young women will do anything to match this ideal since they see thin models rewarded with power and status.

Social learning theory can also be seen as an intermediate point between behaviourism and the cognitive approach to learning (to be covered). Bandura held a different perspective to Skinner – he saw the human mind as like a computer, or an information processor of some kind. Therefore, because we are actively involved in learning, cognitive processes must be involved. These cognitive factors **mediate** in the learning process, between the stimulus and the behaviour, and also help determine whether learning is successful.

Learning is therefore not automatic, based purely on observation and imitation. Bandura described four major mediating factors could be:

- **Attention**. Do we even notice the stimulus behaviour? For a person to imitate or learn a behaviour, they first need to find it interesting enough to pay attention to. You may see several behaviours every single day, but not ever imitate or learn any of these since they never become salient

- **Retention**. Do you remember the stimulus? If you notice a behaviour, you may not also remember and recall it. This may prevent effective imitation

- **Reproduction**. Can you yourself carry out the behaviour performed in the stimulus? Perhaps we are constrained in our own abilities to imitate other behaviour. There could be many reasons for this, such as our own level of physical ability

- **Motivation** Do you want to carry out the behaviour yourself? Perhaps there is not enough of a reward for imitating and carrying out the behaviour. Perhaps there is a punishment for do so. In which case, you will not be motivated to learn the behaviour

Vicarious Conditioning

Bandura noted that reinforcers need not be direct. Children can learn simply by observing what happens to others. By watching what happens to a model, observers develop an *expectation* about the likely outcome of performing the behaviour themselves. If the models in the study described above had been punished for acting aggressively, the children would have developed an expectation that punishment would follow aggressive behaviour, which would have caused them to be less likely to imitate this behaviour when placed in a room with a Bobo doll.

If, on the other hand, the models had been reinforced for acting aggressively, the children would have developed an expectation that reinforcement would follow aggressive behaviour, which would have caused them to be more likely to imitate this behaviour when placed in a room with a Bobo doll.

Bandura concluded from his experiments with the Bobo doll that Children may acquire aggressive behaviour but will not perform it unless they are reinforced or vicariously reinforced for it. Therefore, *the child's social context regulates aggressive behaviour.* (Albert Bandura (1975)

Evaluation of Social Learning Theory

Methodological Issues

- The Bobo doll affords aggression. In other words, its very nature invites you to knock it over and watch it bounce back

- Pre-school children are naturally more aggressive than older children

- Most of the children belonged to colleagues of Bandura – a limited sample

- The children already knew that you were supposed to hit the Bobo doll

Strengths

- Social learning theory can explain inconsistencies in aggressive behaviour, such as how a person may be aggressive in one situation (e.g. at home) but meek and mild in another (e.g. work). This is because they have been rewarded for different types of behaviour in the two different situations

- It also explains how children might be influenced by watching actions on television. (The theory is often used to criticise parents for allowing their children to watch unsuitable programming or the media more generally.)

Social learning theory can also be seen as an intermediate point between behaviourism and the cognitive approach to learning (to be covered). Bandura held a different perspective to Skinner – he saw the human mind as like a computer, or an information processor of some kind. Therefore, because we are actively involved in learning, cognitive processes must be involved. These cognitive factors **mediate** in the learning process, between the stimulus and the behaviour, and also help determine whether learning is successful.

Activity 24

Check your understanding of social learning theory by applying it to the following scenario:

Michael has an older brother whom he admires. Michael's brother is involved with some aggressive boys at school. On one occasion, he saw his brother trying to take a younger child's pocket money away from him. His brother and his 'gang' were then able to buy cigarettes with the money. The next day, Michael tried to take money from a smaller child but the child hit him hard on the nose and caused it to bleed. The child's father also came to his house and complained to his parents, causing Michael to be 'grounded' for a week.

Explain Michael's behaviour using the following terms:

- Observational learning
- Modelling
- Vicarious learning

Questions

1) Which of the two brothers is more likely to continue being aggressive and violent towards younger children?

2) What other social influences are at work in the case of Michael's brother?

Answers to activity 24

Michael has seen his brother taking money from a child (observational learning) and tries to copy this behaviour (modelling). He sees his brother rewarded with money from this behaviour (vicarious learning).

1) Michael receives punishment after trying to steal money. First, he is hit on the nose and then grounded. Thus, operant conditioning suggests that Michael will be deterred from trying to steal money again. Michael's brother, however, has received a reward for his behaviour (positive reinforcement) so is more likely to continue being aggressive and violent towards younger children

2) Michael's brother is influenced by the aggressive children in his 'gang'. He is under pressure to conform to this group's behaviour

Evaluation of the Behavioural Approach

- The behavioural model overcomes labelling someone as ill or abnormal, because it focuses on behaviour being adaptive or maladaptive
- The model provides convincing explanations for the cause of some mental disorders e.g. phobias
- It has provided effective treatments for some disorders
- Some critics claim that behavioural therapies are de-humanising and unethical. For example, aversion therapy has sometimes been imposed on people without consent and can be very distressing
- The behavioural approach has also been criticised as being too simplistic and reductionist, as its ideas of behaviour are quite narrow, e.g. 'all behaviour is learned through the process of conditioning'
- It is deterministic, since it sees human behaviour in terms of stimulus and response with no room for conscious choice

Evaluation of the Behavioural approach

- Treatments can be effective. Especially when treating phobia

- There is a lot of experimental evidence supporting the behavioural model

- However a lot of it has been conducted on animals or is unethical

- Treats the symptoms and not the cause, underlying fear is often transferred to another object after treatment of the original phobia

Cognitive Approach

As you know from studying the history of psychology, there was always an interest in studying the processes of the mind from the nineteenth century onwards. However, a dramatic shift took place in psychology in the 1950s – this is sometimes known as 'the cognitive revolution', which went on to initiate cognitive psychology as a distinct field of psychology. Essentially, what happened was that American psychologists in particular rejected behaviourism (which you know about from studying, for example, Skinner) and instead started thinking of the mind as more like a computer.

Cognitive psychology is now an important field within psychology: people study cognitive processes such as memory, perception, thinking and language. The key theoretical underpinning of the cognitive approach is that the mind is computational. This means that in the cognitive approach, the brain is likened to a computer, which processes input (such as sensory information from perceptions) and then makes calculations or determinations as to how the organism (you!) should behave (the output).

The computations made by the brain directly determine our behaviour. However, it is impossible to see the brain thinking thoughts: we can only make inferences about the thoughts of others based on how their behaviour, or what they tell us about their thoughts. Moreover, some people think that it is too simplistic to liken the human brain to a computer: what about other factors, such as culture or our memories of what has happened before? Surely they also inform our behaviour, as well as immediate processing of sensory inputs? Some people therefore think that the computational cognitive approach is too mechanical and reductionist: reductionism is the idea that complex phenomena (such as cognition or behaviour) can be reduced to simpler parts (such as inputs, processes and outputs on a computer model).

The Role of Mediational processes

Mediational process are those thoughts, decision making processes and judgements which occur internally as a response to an external stimulus, and help influence our actions/response to the stimulus. Cognitive psychologists attempt the scientific study of internal mental processes through controlled experiments, and believe that they can be determined by comparing the different 'output' (behaviour) of subjects whilst controlling the 'input' (external environment/stimulus). Behavioural psychology makes direct links with environment and observed behaviour, with no attempt to study the influence of mediational processes, which cannot be observed.

Neuroscience

Cognitive neuroscience is a more recent field of psychological research, which studies links between brain function and cognitive processes. The development of technology such as Electroencephalogram (EEG), Functional Magnetic resonance Imaging, (FMRI) and event-related potentials (ERP's) has enabled new scientific study and provided a new evidence base for existing theory, e.g localisation of function. The next lesson on Biopsychology will cover this in more detail.

Use of the Cognitive Approach to in Mental Health

The cognitive approach (sometimes known as cognitive-behavioural) is one of the most widely used approaches to understanding and treating mental disorder.

The cognitive model assumes that emotional problems can be attributed directly to distortions in our thinking processes (cognitions). These take the form of negative thoughts, irrational beliefs and logical errors (or fallacies), such as polarised (black and white) thinking and overgeneralization. Such thinking is thought to be automatic and unconscious. Examples of these could be thoughts such as, "I must be perfect in all I do" or "I must get three grade As in my A levels or I am worthless".

This way of thinking is known as a cognitive bias.

This approach to understanding abnormality was founded by Albert Ellis (1962) and Aaron Beck (1963) who criticised the behavioural model for not taking mental processes into account. The rationale behind the cognitive model is that the thinking (cognition) processes that occur between a stimulus and a response are responsible for the *feeling* component of the response.

Ellis believed that maladaptive behaviour results when people operate on misguided and inaccurate assumptions, or irrational beliefs. These beliefs cannot possibly be validated, and so the person experiences misery and depression.

Some common irrational beliefs are listed below:

1) I must perform well and win the approval of others, or else I am an inadequate or worthless person

2) You must treat me fairly and considerately and not frustrate me, or it's awful and you are a rotten person

3) My life conditions must give me the things I want easily and with little frustration and must keep me from harm, or else life is not worth living and I can't be happy at all

Ellis went on to develop the irrational-emotive model in which an activating event is interpreted in an irrational way, leaving a person feeling worthless and depressed.

According to Ellis, it is not the event which causes depression but the person's *irrational interpretation* of the event. Ellis called this the ABC model in which *private beliefs* (B) about the *activating event* (A) determine the emotional *consequences* (C). Beck (1976) also believed that errors in thinking underpin mental disorders. He found that depressed people tend to draw illogical conclusions when they evaluate themselves. Such negative thoughts lead to negative feelings which in turn can result in depression. Beck identified three forms of negative thinking surrounding the self, the world and the future (the cognitive triad) that he thought were typical of those suffering from depression.

Example

Poor Exam Grades

Negative Views about Oneself: "Because I've got a poor grade, I'm useless and worthless."

Negative Views about The World: "Because I've got poor exam grades, everyone hates me."

Negative Views about the Future: "Because of my poor exam grades, I'll never ever be good at anything."

Beck also looked at the attributional style of depressed people.

Attributions can be:

- Global/specific
- Internal/external
- Stable/unstable

Beck found that depressed people tended to attribute negative events, such as failing a driving test, to internal, global and stable factors (I'm no good, at anything, and never will be). Positive events, such as gaining an award, are interpreted as external, specific and unstable (it was a fluke, right place and time, just this once).

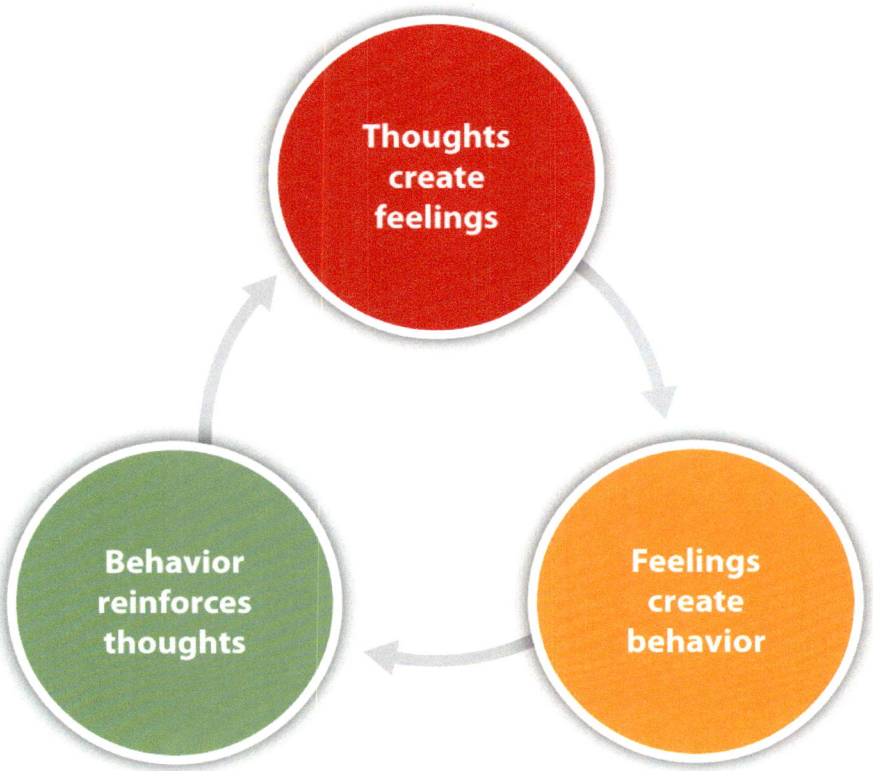

Activity 25

Read the case study of Tina and identify the features of the cognitive triad:

Tina, a 43 year-old depressed woman, had left the orchestra she had previously loved. She had been a good cellist but claimed that when she arrived home from work these days she was too tired to do anything else and that work 'took it out of her'. All she wanted to do was sleep in the evening and she hadn't picked up her cello for months. She believed that playing had become too much of an effort, and anyway she had never really been good enough to join the orchestra; she had been fooling herself and the rest of the orchestra had carried her and covered her mistakes. She was sure they would be glad to see the back of her.

Views about Self: Too tired to practise, not good enough cellist for orchestra.

Views about World: Rest of orchestra covering her mistakes. Orchestra would be glad she had left.

Views about Future: Never play in orchestra again.

Her views also demonstrate the attributional style of depressed people that Beck identified as internal, global and stable.

Evidence

There is clear evidence that depressed people describe their world in the way that Beck suggested. The key question, however, is whether negative thinking *causes* depression or whether depression *causes* negative thinking. The Temple-Wisconsin study of cognitive vulnerability to depression (discussed in Barlow and Durand, 1999) provides some answers. This longitudinal study followed a group of students whose thinking styles were assessed every few months. The researchers found that students prone to negative thinking were more likely to become depressed. 17% of students who scored high on tests of negative thinking went on to experience severe depression compared with only 1% of those with low scores. This suggests that a negative cognitive style precedes depression.

The Role of Schema

As described in the earlier section of the course on memory, Schemas can be described as 'ready made' stores of knowledge that we have stored in our memory in discreet entities. Schemas help us to make sense of the world. If we had to analyse every new event or object from scratch, it would take ages to process the information and would be a waste of resources. Schemas enable us to process new information according to what we have already stored about previous similar situations and help us to fill in any 'gaps' in the information available to us.

Cognitive abilities develop through the processes of assimilation and accommodation. **Assimilation** is the process of fitting new information into an existing schema. **Accommodation** occurs when the new information will not fit into the existing schema. The schema will be altered to fit the new information.

Evaluation of the Cognitive Approach

- Clinically useful and effective (especially for anxiety and depression)
- Clear supporting evidence
- Correlation between symptoms and maladaptive cognition
- Narrow focus (does not take account of biology or genes)
- Overemphasis on the present
- Limited effectiveness
- Measuring cognitions is difficult
- Negative thinking may be a more accurate view of reality

The emergence of cognitive neuroscience

This is a fairly new scientific discipline, which emerged out of the conversation between cognitive psychology and neuroscience which took place from the 1990s onwards. That is, people interested in studying the processes of memory, language or perception shared their research with those people who had been studying the neurology and physiological processes of the brain. Together, they were interested in determining which regions of the brain were activated when, for example, people performed cognitive tasks such as face recognition, recalling information from STM or recognising a stimulus. As such, cognitive neuroscience draws on neuroanatomy and neurophysiology as well as on research into memory, language or perception. Cognitive neuroscience can make use of techniques such as functional brain imaging, (fMRI), position emission tomography (PET) and electroencephalography (EEG) and magnetoencephalography (MEG) as well as the existing and continuing research into computational neuroscience. You will be learning more about some of these techniques for studying the brain in the Biopsychology topic.

Activity 26

Draw a table summarising the main assumptions and two criticisms (one positive, one negative) of each of the following models of abnormality:

- **Biological**

- **Psychodynamic**

- **Behavioural**

- **Cognitive**

Answer to activity 26

Model	Assumptions	Positive criticisms	Negative criticisms
Biological (medical)	- Internal causes - Genes - Neurotransmitters Hormones - Nervous system damage	- Abnormal behaviour viewed as sickness rather than insanity	- Treats symptoms rather than cause
Psychodynamic	- Internal causes - Unresolved conflict - Overwhelms ego, spills over into neurotic symptoms - Fixation at one of the psychosexual stages	- Tries to find the underlying causes for abnormal behavior, rather than just treating the symptoms	- Deterministic in that it sees behaviour being determined by instincts over which the patient has no control
Behavioural	- External causes - Maladaptive behaviour learned via classical and operant conditioning and social learning	- Provides convincing explanations for the cause of some mental disorders e.g. phobias	- Is reductionist in that it takes no account of biological or cognitive factors
Cognitive	- Internal causes - Sees negative, irrational thinking as the cause of conditions such as anxiety and depression	- Correlation between symptoms and maladaptive cognition	- Treatments have limited effectiveness

Biological Approach

This approach addresses the relationship between psychology and biology. Looking at the functions of the brain and the nervous system and how these biological factors influence behaviour. For example, it is generally accepted that genetics has a part to play in terms of certain psychological traits and individual characteristics. As such, there is a body of evidence to suggest that genetics and biology generally can determine and affect how we behave. It is in this context you will see the variations in approaches in terms of various areas of discussion such as the nature/nurture debate in psychology.

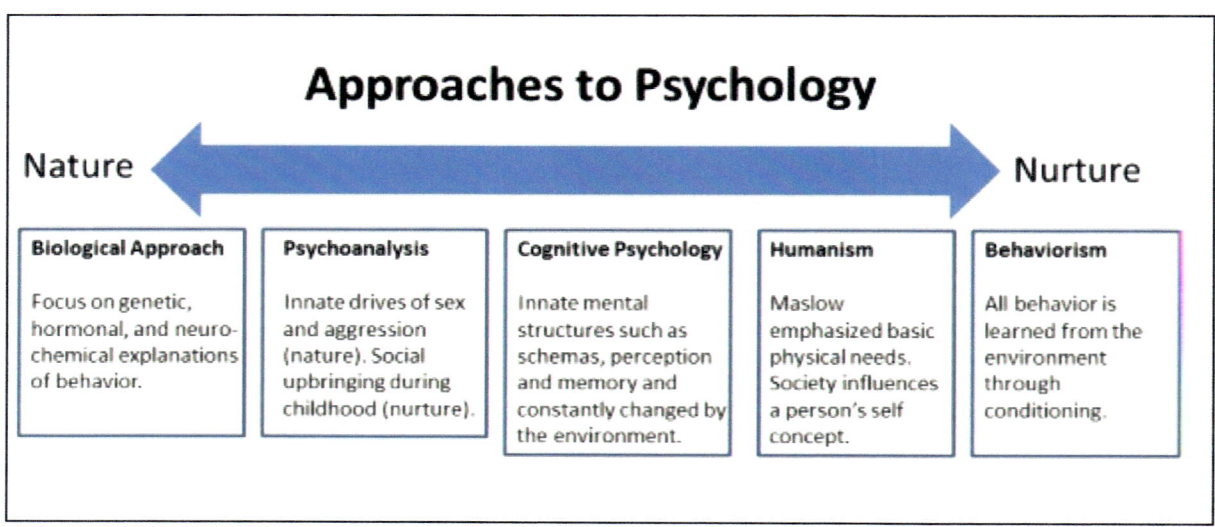

A branch of psychology referred to as **Biopsychology** is an approach that looks at the brain and its anatomical and physiological functions, such as how neurotransmitters, which are functions of the brain that transmits chemical messages throughout the body, enable it to respond in certain ways in difference situations. The brain also can have an impact upon and influence feelings and emotions, thoughts and subsequently behaviour.

One area where Biopsychology has contributed to our understanding of behaviour has been in relation to stress and anxiety by looking at its effects on the body. This section will look at studies of the pituitary-adrenal system and the sympathomedullary pathway in outline, as well as looking at stress in everyday life, looking at the effects of stress on the immune system.

One significant point to make at this stage is that stress and anxiety generate the same chemical reactions in the body even though the definition of stress and anxiety differ, with stress being the response or reaction an individual has usually in a threatening situation (see below for an explanation of the flight and fight response) and anxiety is associated with fear of possible, as opposed to an actual, danger or threat. Therefore an individual may be on heightened alert with no real reason to be in such a state. For example, conditions such as Obsessive Compulsive Disorder (OCD) is an anxiety disorder that can be associated with the same/similar chemical and physiological reactions in the body as stress.

The genetic basis of behaviour and personality

It may surprise you to learn that intelligence (as measured by IQ) is highly **heritable**. That is, intelligence is at least 50% determined by your genes, rather than by your environment or upbringing (this includes factors such as the schooling you received, and whether or not your parents were supportive of your education). The research of the psychologist Ian Deary, and the Scottish Mental Surveys of 1932 and 1947, have revealed a huge amount about the stability (and instability) of traits such as intelligence over time. And if a trait is stable over time, this suggests that it is influenced more by genetic factors than by environmental ones, which can and do change over the life course.

Activity 27A

Research the Scottish Mental Surveys here:

http://www.psychologicalscience.org/index.php/publications/observer/2016/february-16/intelligence-over-time.html

Twin studies and family studies are often used in this field, to try to separate out environmental or social/cultural factors from genetic ones. A very good way to do this is through comparing the personality, intelligence or incidence of psychopathology in monozygotic (MZ – these are identical) twins reared **apart**. (MZA).

Monozygotic twins share a **genotype**: this means that they share the same set of genes in their DNA. However, biological psychologists are interested in whether they also share the same **phenotype**: this is the physical expression of traits, characteristics or features. It is particularly interesting to compare MZA twins since they share the same genetic inheritance.

However, MZA twins did not share the same **environmental** or social features of their upbringing, since each twin would have been adopted by a different family.

What is interesting from studies of MZA twins is that they often perform very comparably on tests of intelligence, but also on tests of personality or behaviour. Indeed, in some famous studies, MZA twins who are reunited in adulthood even have the same physical appearance (in terms of dress or style, that is), the same jobs, have chosen similar partners, and have similar families, have the same hobbies or behavioural traits and even share very similar life experiences, based on having made the same kind of choices or decisions about their lives. See the Minnesota Twin Family Study for more on the similarities between twins, including research into MZA twins by Bouchard (1979).

Psychodynamic Approach

Sigmund Freud (1856-1939) was one of the most influential figures of the early twentieth century. During this time, medicine could offer little explanation for mental disorders, and Freud set about looking for underlying unconscious causes. As we have already seen, he believed that we are all born with raw animal instincts (such as the drive for sex, food, and aggression) which have to be tamed to allow us to live in society. During childhood, we go through a series of stages during which we must deal with conflict between our instincts and pressures to conform to the rules of society. Eventually, we learn to subjugate these instincts and become moral citizens. However, at times unresolved conflict which has been pushed down into the unconscious can resurface and cause neurotic symptoms. Freud developed what he called a 'talking cure' (psychoanalysis) during which these unresolved conflicts could be uncovered and dealt with, allowing the person to 'move on'. We will now examine the main principles of Freud's theory.

The Structure of Personality

Freud believed that there are three main interacting parts to our basic personality:

ID	unconscious	pleasure principle	contains raw animal instinct
EGO	conscious	reality principle	delays gratification of instincts until more appropriate time
SUPEREGO	conscious	internalises morals and values of society	makes us feel guilty when we have done wrong and proud when we have upheld our values

Each of the parts can experience conflict, e.g. conflict between innate desires and the need to live in a structured society. If the conflict becomes great enough, it could threaten to overwhelm the ego. Therefore, according to Freud, there are four main ways that the unconscious mind could turn this conflict into an acceptable form.

These are:

- Parapraxes, or slips of the tongue, where some unconscious worry is 'let out' by the person unconsciously substituting a word for the word they meant to say. For example, someone with money problems might say at breakfast 'please pass the money' instead of 'please pass the honey'

- Dreams - The person can dream about the unconscious wish in symbolic form (manifest content) rather than dream about the real worry (latent content) and thereby avoid damaging the sensitive ego. Freud believed that many dreams were of a sexual nature, e.g. a man worried about being impotent might dream of a broken candlestick or a woman afraid of being raped might dream about her purse being stolen. Here the candlestick and purse represent male and female genitals

- Neurotic symptoms – These arise when too many traumatic memories or wishes have been repressed and threaten to overwhelm the ego. Freud did not make the distinction between neuroses and psychoses, so any abnormal disorder would be classed as a neurotic symptom
- Defence mechanisms - Freud believed that defence mechanisms are used by the ego in the face of conflict. The defences help us to deal with anxiety, prevent us from being overwhelmed by temporary threats or traumas and can provide 'breathing space' in which to come to terms with conflict or find alternative ways of coping. As a short-term measure, they are necessary and normal but, as long-term solutions to life's problems, they are usually regarded as unhealthy and undesirable

Below are Freud's defence mechanisms. You may recognise some of them since we all use them.

Name of Defence Mechanism	Description
Repression	Forcing a dangerous/threatening memory/idea/feeling/wish out of consciousness and making it unconscious.
Displacement	Choosing a substitute object for the expression of your feelings because you cannot express them openly towards their real target. You transfer your feelings onto something quite innocent that will not retaliate.
Denial	Refusing to acknowledge certain aspects of reality or refusing to perceive something because it is painful, distressing or threatening.
Rationalisation	Finding an acceptable excuse for something which is really quite unacceptable, or in other words creating a 'cover story' which preserves your self-image.

Reaction Formation	Consciously feeling/thinking the very opposite of what you truly (unconsciously) think.
Sublimation	A form of displacement in which a substitute activity is found to express an unacceptable impulse. The activity is usually socially acceptable.
Identification	The incorporation of an external object (usually another person) into your own personality so that you come to think and act as they would.
Projection	Displacing your own unwanted feelings and characteristics onto someone else.
Regression	Engaging in behaviour characteristic of an earlier stage of behaviour. Reverting to childlike behaviour.
Isolation	Separating thoughts and emotions that usually go together so that no conflict is experienced.

Activity 27B

Choose the correct defence mechanism for the following behaviours:

1. A traumatic memory of which the person has no recollection.	
2. You are angry with your partner so you kick the cat.	
3. A friend who admires you starts to wear the same clothes as you.	
4. Your father says you can't go out with your friends. You lie on the floor and kick your arms and legs.	
5. You are trying to get a colleague you hate sacked, but you come to believe they are doing the same to you.	
6. You enjoy football. It is an outlet for your aggression.	
7. I stole your sweets to stop you getting tooth decay.	
8. What a lovely shirt you're wearing (yuk!!).	
9. You know your friend has an A level exam tomorrow but he says: "Oh, it's only a little test, the marks don't really count".	
10. You get a letter to say you are going to be taken to court. You laugh.	

1. Repression

2. Displacement

3. Identification

4. Regression

5. Projection

6. Sublimation

7. Rationalisation

8. Reaction formation

9. Denial

10. Isolation

Psychosexual Development

Freud believed that we pass through a series of developmental stages during childhood. During each stage, the instinctual energy of the id centres on a particular part of the body (or erogenous zone). The attempts by parents and others to channel this energy towards the needs of society causes conflict. This conflict can either be resolved (person develops and moves on) or becomes fixated (leading to specific adult behaviours).

Stage	Age	Description	Fixation
Oral	0-18 months	Pleasure gained from sucking and biting	Oral adult e.g. a smoker may be over-dependent on oral gratification
Anal	18 months to 3 years	Activities revolve around faeces. Infant gains pleasure and control from retaining or expelling faeces	A fixation on anal retention may lead to obsession with hygiene and neatness, even perhaps obsessive-compulsive disorder. Alternatively, a fixation on expelling faeces may lead to reckless, careless or disorganised behaviours.

Phallic	From end of anal stage to ages 4 or 5	Interest in own genitalia	Oedipus complex: Intense affection for mother causes rivalry with father and fear of castration. Eventually, boy begins to identify with father. Elektra complex: Absence of penis in girls causes penis envy.
Latency	From end of phallic period to puberty	Psychosexual development enters a latency period and re-emerges at puberty	Lack of sexual fulfilment in adulthood if become fixated in latency period.

Case Study

Little Hans

The one and only child studied by Freud was Little Hans (1909) who developed a phobia of horses. Hans was 5 years old and developed his fear after seeing a horse that was pulling a carriage fall over and kick his feet in the air. Little Hans was terrified and thought that the horse was dead. According to Freud, Little Hans was experiencing unresolved oedipal conflict (wanting to possess his mother, and seeing his father as a rival) which he had displaced onto horses. The fear of horses, therefore, represented his fear of castration at the hands of his father. The blinkers on the horse reminded Little Hans of his father's glasses, and the black around the horse's mouth reminded him of his father's beard and moustache!

Evaluation of the Psychodynamic Approach

- The model tries to find the underlying causes for abnormal behavior, rather than just treating the symptoms
- It focuses on the individual. Rather than merely seeing a patient as a list of symptoms, it tries to understand the patient's own, unique experiences
- It still has a vast influence today and is widely recognized as one of the most

influential theories of the twentieth century

- It created greater sympathy for people with psychological disorders
- It is impossible to test scientifically and is not based on scientific evidence
- It is deterministic in that it sees behaviour as being determined by instincts over which the patient has no control
- It deals with the past rather than the here and now
- It is culture-specific in that it may only apply to sexually-repressed Victorian women
- Psychoanalysis is not appropriate for disorders such as schizophrenia

Humanistic Psychology

Humanistic psychology starts with the premise that people have free will to make choices in their lives - personal agency, and stresses the value of the individual. Rogers (1959) and Maslow (1943) argue that people strive to grow and gain fulfilment, referred to as self-actualisation. They argue that in terms of understanding the individual, scientific psychology's methodology of using laboratories to investigate human behaviour does not give real insight into subjective perception, whether this is doing research into human or animal behaviour. Humanists therefore favour qualitative methods because as far as they are concerned, to really understand human behaviour requires a researcher to talk to the subject of a study in order to gain an understanding their feelings, reasons etc. From a humanist perspective, the use of comparative psychology, which focuses on the study of animals, is not really a sound approach when trying to offer explanations for human behaviour as it cannot take into account thoughts, reasoning and so on. Maslow (1943) wanted to understand what motivates people, and he developed what is referred to as a hierarchal theory of human motivation. People are motivated to fulfil certain needs, and when those needs are fulfilled, they then aim to fulfil the next one, and so the process continues. According to Maslow there are 5 hierarchical needs:

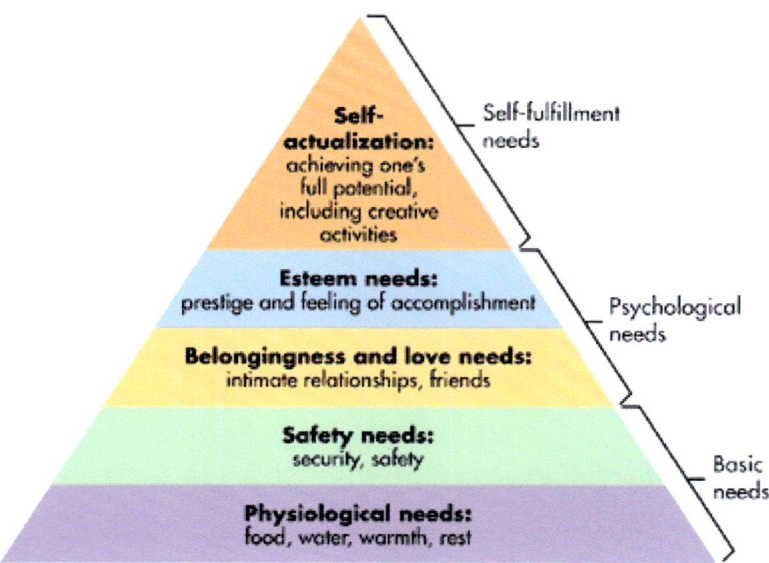

- Physiological - The need for food, drink, sleep, shelter, sex
- Safety - The need for security, law, order, protection from the elements, being free from fear
- Love/Belonging - The need for intimacy, love, affection, friendship
- Esteem - The need for independence, prestige, self-respect, achievement, respect from others
- Self-Actualisation - The need to realise person potential, personal growth, self-
- fulfilment

Lower level basic needs have to be met in order for an individual to reach self-actualisation. According to Maslow all individuals are capable of progression to self-actualisation; however, their ability to do so may be inhibited by a failure to meet all of the basic needs. Life experiences and unexpected occurrences can result in an individual fluctuating between needs. For example, a person who gets a promotion and acquires status and respect would have reached the esteem level, but if they then lose their job and become unemployed, this could result in them moving to one of the levels below the esteem one.

Maslow suggests that one in a hundred people become self-actualised as society rewards motivation, primarily based on esteem, love and other social needs.

Comparison of approaches

Draw a table summarising the main assumptions and two criticisms (one positive, one negative) of each of the following models of abnormality:

- Biological
- Psychodynamic
- Behavioural
- Cognitive

Answer to activity 27C

Model	Assumptions	Positive criticisms	Negative criticisms
Biological (medical)	- Internal causes - Genes -Neurotransmitters Hormones - Nervous system damage	- Abnormal behaviour viewed as sickness rather than insanity	- Treats symptoms rather than cause
Psychodynamic	- Internal causes - Unresolved conflict - Overwhelms ego, spills over into neurotic symptoms - Fixation at one of the psychosexual stages	- Tries to find the underlying causes for abnormal behaviour, rather than just treating the symptoms	- Deterministic in that it sees behaviour being determined by instincts over which the patient has no control
Behavioural	- External causes - Maladaptive behaviour learned via classical and operant conditioning and social learning	- Provides convincing explanations for the cause of some mental disorders e.g. phobias	- Is reductionist in that it takes no account of biological or cognitive factors
Cognitive	- Internal causes - Sees negative, irrational thinking as the cause of conditions such as anxiety and depression	- Correlation between symptoms and maladaptive cognition	- Treatments have limited effectiveness

2.2 Biopsychology

This approach addresses the relationship between psychology and biology, looking at the functions of the brain and the nervous system and how these biological factors influence behaviour. For example, it is generally accepted that genetics has a part to play in terms of certain psychological traits and individual characteristics. As such, there is a body of evidence to suggest that genetics and biology generally can determine and affect how we behave. It is in this context you will see the variations in approaches in terms of various areas of discussion such as the nature/nurture debate in psychology.

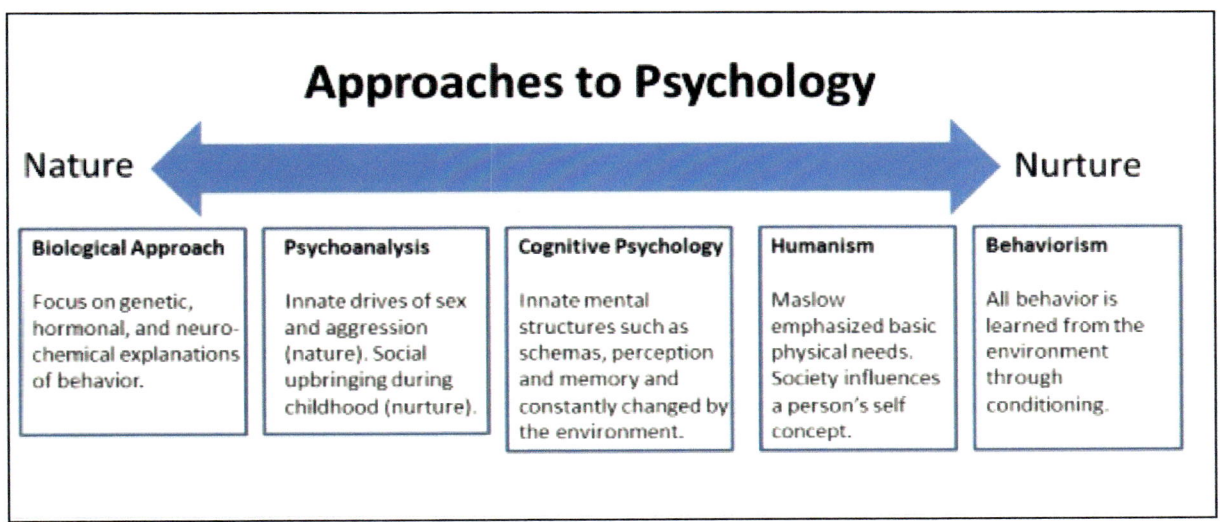

The branch of psychology referred to as **Biopsychology** is an approach which requires detailed knowledge of the brain and its anatomical and physiological functions. **Neurotransmitters**, for example, are chemicals within the brain that transmit messages throughout the body, enabling it to respond in certain ways in different situations. The brain can also have a significant impact upon feelings and emotions, thoughts and subsequently behaviour. This unit will examine the structure and function of the human brain, ways of studying the brain, and the effects of biological rhythms on human behaviour.

The nervous system is the system within the body which receives, transmits and responds to stimuli, and contains all of the neural tissue in the body. This includes nerve cells (neurons), the supporting cells (neuroglia) and organs of the nervous system (the brain and spinal cord); all of which can be divided into two separate systems.

The central nervous system (CNS) consists of the brain and spinal cord, whilst the peripheral nervous system (PNS) consists of all of the remainder of nervous tissue within the body. The nervous system is one of the most complex systems in the human body, but it is relatively small and accounts for only approximately three percent of bodyweight.

The peripheral nervous system can further be divided into two distinct parts: the somatic and the autonomic systems.

The somatic nervous system controls all voluntary body movements, processing sensory information and sending signals to the skeleton and muscles. It is responsible for sensory information processing from each of the five senses; receiving nerve impulses from the tongue, skin, ears, eyes and nose. It may help to remember that the word 'soma' means 'body': this system picks up information from the body and makes it act.

In movement, the somatic nervous system carries impulses from the brain to the muscle to be moved, while in its sensory capacity it carries impulses from the sensory organs to the brain. There are therefore two 'limbs' of the somatic nervous system: the afferent and the efferent. The afferent (or sensory) neurons carry impulses to the CNS, while the efferent, or motor neurons, carry impulses from the central nervous system to the muscles.

The autonomic nervous system controls involuntary (automatic) body processes.

Neurons

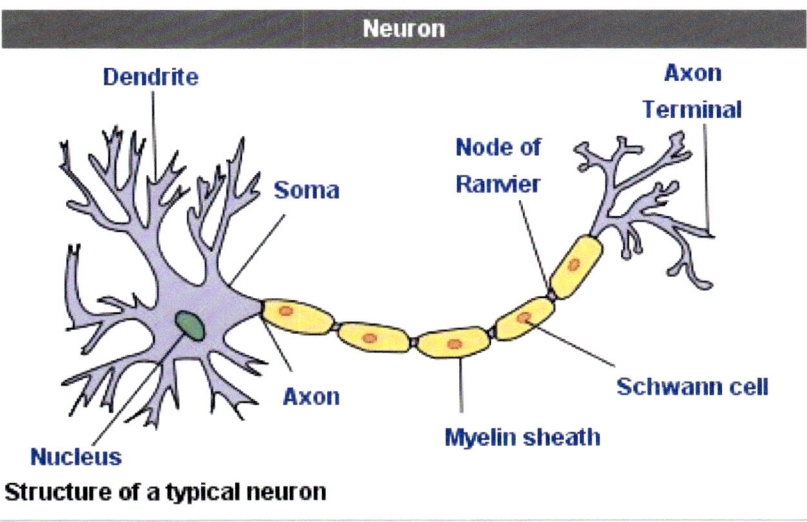

Structure of a typical neuron

Neurons are specialised to be able to transmit nerve impulses and are divided into three different categories; sensory, motor and association neurons.

Sensory neurons transmit information received from the sensory receptors throughout the body to the brain and CNS. As they carry information towards the CNS, they are classed as afferent neurons.

The receptors of sensory neurons are subdivided further into three groups:

- Exteroceptors – these provide information regarding the external environment, through touch, temperature, etc.
- Interoceptors – these provide information regarding the internal environment, such as the digestive and cardiovascular systems
- Proprioceptors – these provide information regarding the position and movement of skeletal muscles and joints

Motor neurons transmit information from the CNS to parts of the body which have to respond to sensory stimulus. The responsive body parts are called effectors and are either muscles or glands; where muscles are stimulated to contract and glands stimulated to produce a secretion. As they carry information away from the CNS they are classed as efferent neurons.

Association (connecting) neurons carry nerve impulses from one neuron to another, and as such do not contact sensory receptors or effectors. These account for approximately 90% of the neurons within the body and the majority of them are located within the brain and spinal cord.

They are responsible for both the distribution of sensory information (from sensory neurons) and the coordination of motor activity (to motor neurons).

The above neurons, although different in function, all contain the same basic component parts. These parts are dendrites, cell body, nucleus, axon and axon terminal. Dendrites are branched processes which extend out from the cell body at one end of a neuron, which are sensitive and receive nerve impulses.

The cell body (soma) is a relatively large section of the neuron which is filled with cytoplasm and organelles (components within a cell that have different functions, such as processing nutrients). The cell body also contains a nucleus.

The central section of a neuron is called an axon, which is a long cytoplasmic process which carries nerve impulses away from the dendrites and towards the opposite end of the structure. It contains cytoplasm (called axoplasm within an axon), neurotubules, mitochondria and various enzymes, and is surrounded by a myelin sheath which is composed of lipids (fats) and proteins, and insulates the axon whilst increasing the speed of conduction.

At the opposite end of the neuron to the dendrites, the axon branches into multiple sections called axon terminals which end with synaptic end-bulbs. The end-bulbs contain synaptic vesicles which in turn contain a neurotransmitter that is responsible for transmitting the nerve impulse towards the next adjacent neuron, via a synapse.

Serotonin is a neurotransmitter produced by the pineal gland, deep in the centre of the brain. It plays an important role in the control of appetite, sleep, memory and learning, temperature regulation, mood, behaviour, cardiovascular function, muscle contraction, endocrine regulation and depression. It also influences aggressive and violent behaviour.

The organisation of these component parts varies between the different types of neuron, and is largely dictated by the positioning of the cell body:

- Sensory neuron – the cell body is positioned to one side of the axon and is separate from the dendrites
- Motor neuron – the cell body is positioned in the centre of the dendrites
- Association neuron – the cell body is separate from the dendrites, and is positioned in line with the dendrites and axon

Synapses

Neurons link together to form a network which is capable of transmitting nerve impulses throughout the body, and the links between them are called synapses.

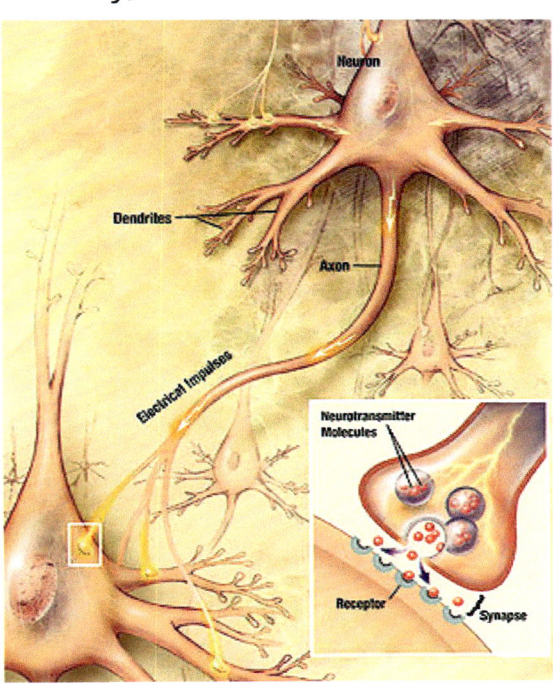

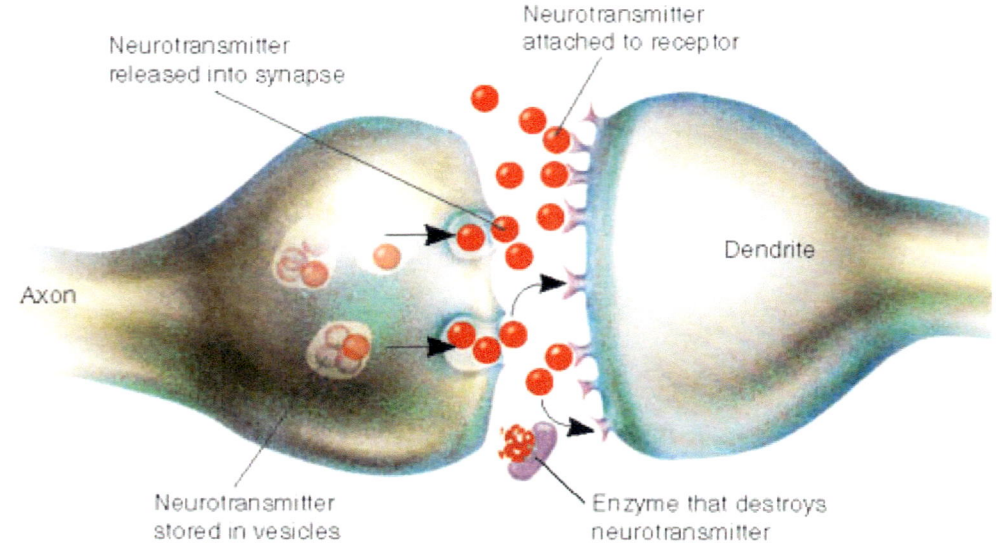

Neurotransmitter released into synapse

Neurotransmitter attached to receptor

Dendrite

Axon

Neurotransmitter stored in vesicles

Enzyme that destroys neurotransmitter

The neuron that carries the impulse to the synapse is called the presynaptic neuron and the neuron which receives the message and conducts the impulse away from the synapse is called the postsynaptic neuron. The nerve impulse can be transported over the synapse in one of two ways – electrical and chemical:

- Electrical – in an electrical synapse there is contact between the two (pre and post synaptic) neurons. The contact is made at a gap junction with contains approximately 100 tubular protein structures called connexons, and allows the impulse to conduct directly from one neuron to another

- Chemical – in a chemical synapse there is no contact between the neurons. They are separated by a space called a synaptic cleft which is approximately 0.02µm in width, and is filled with extracellular fluid. Nerve impulses are unable to cross the synaptic cleft and so must be converted to a chemical signal by interaction with a chemical called a neurotransmitter. The neurotransmitter is released by the presynaptic neuron, diffuses across the synaptic cleft and then is able to act upon the postsynaptic neuron to create a nerve impulse

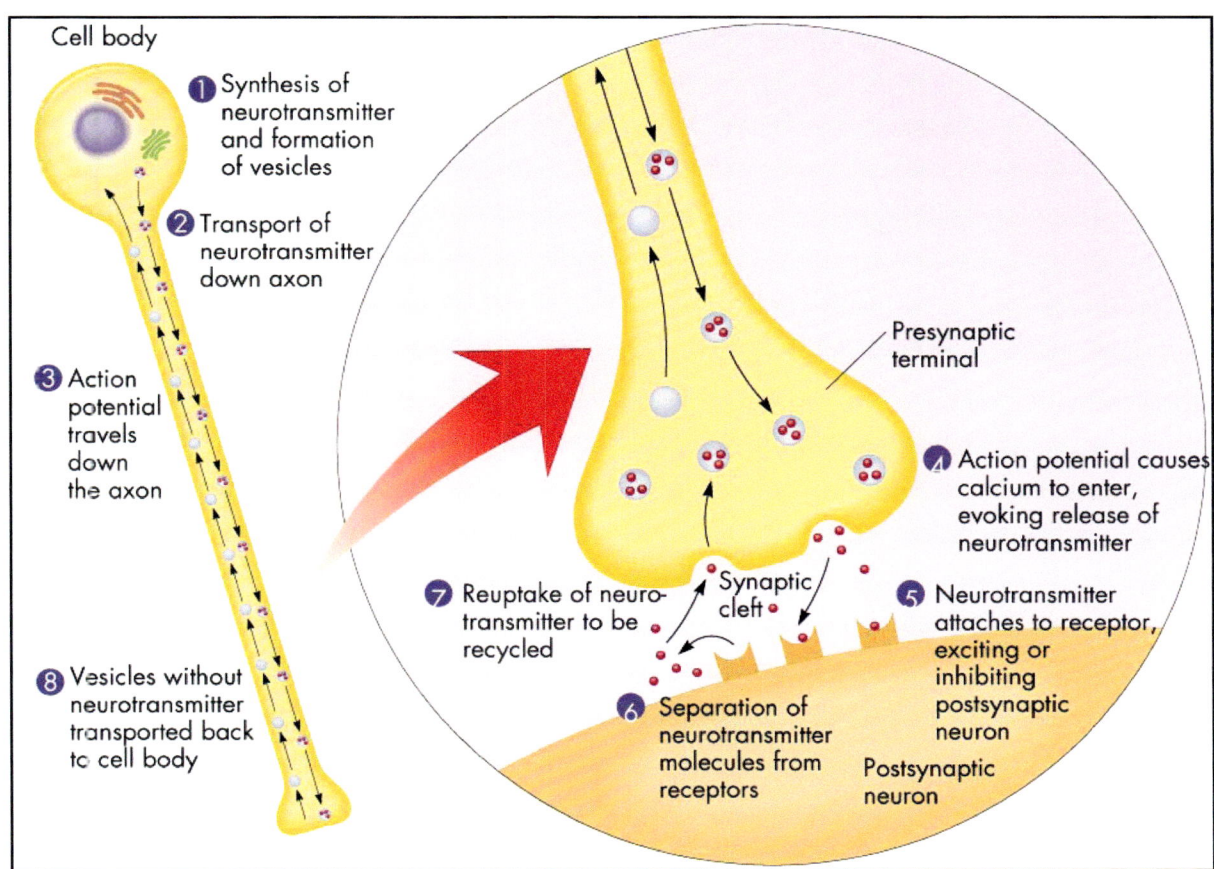

As chemical synapses require the electrical impulse to be converted into a chemical signal and then back into an electrical signal, they are relatively slow at transmitting a signal in comparison to electrical synapses, and they can only transfer information in one direction.

However, chemical synapses are much more selectable in which impulses are transmitted than electrical synapses, as with the electrical synapse the impulse is always carried across to the following neuron, but with a chemical synapse the arriving impulse may or may not release sufficient neurotransmitter to continue the impulse. This allows chemical synapses to be adjusted for different purposes in different parts of the body, such as those which require a greater amount of sensitivity.

Motor neurons communicate with muscles at chemical synapses called a neuromuscular junction. The region of muscle adjacent to the neuron is called the motor end plate which contains specialised (acetylcholine) receptors, and the motor neuron releases a neurotransmitter called acetylcholine. Upon detection of acetylcholine, the receptors within the muscle tissue trigger muscular contraction.

Central Nervous System

The central nervous system contains only two main components; the brain and the spinal cord. Although there are few component parts, the complexity, especially of the brain, is large.

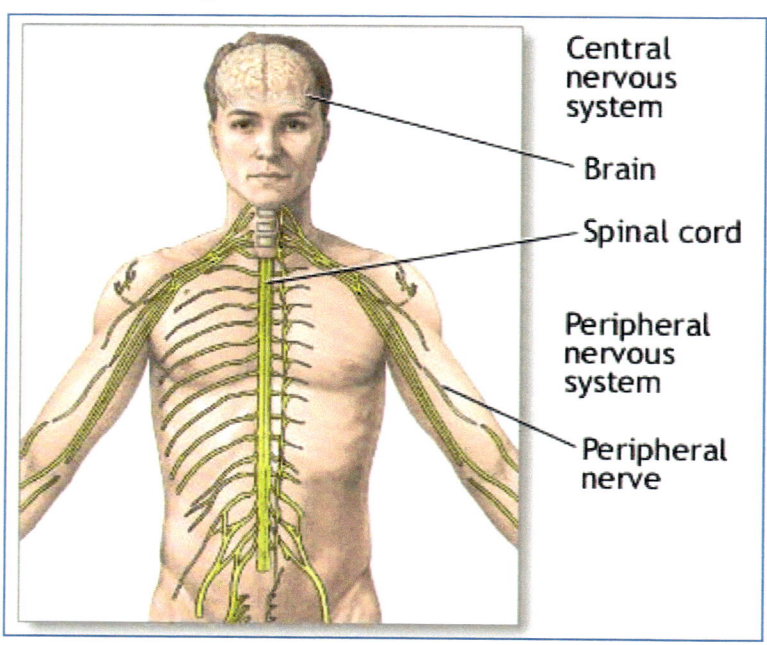

The spinal cord is a long mass of nerve tissue that extends from the inferior section of the brain (medulla oblongata) and down through the vertebral column to the superior border of the second lumbar vertebra. The spinal cord is composed of both grey and white matter (white matter forms an approximately cylindrical shape with grey matter forming a 'butterfly' shape inside it) and is surrounded by three meninges which are membranes that provide stability and absorption from shocks.

The three meninges are dura mater (outermost), arachnoid (central layer) and pia mater (innermost).

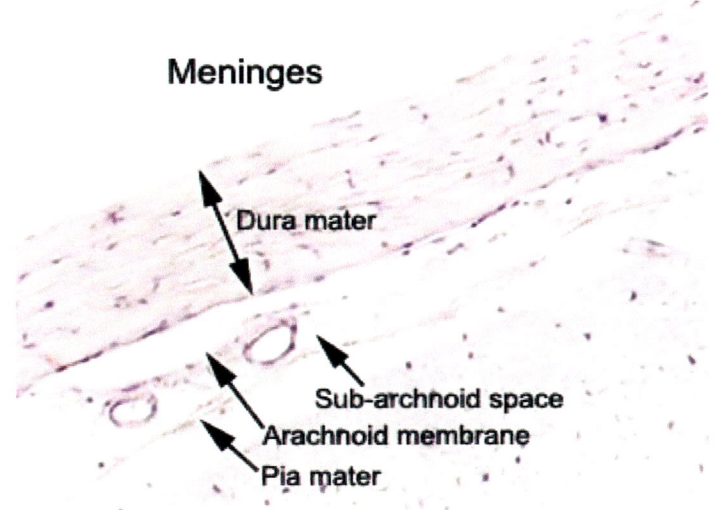

Meninges

Dura mater

Sub-archnoid space
Arachnoid membrane
Pia mater

In the centre of the spinal cord is a canal which runs the length of the spinal cord and is continuous with the fourth ventricle of the brain. The grey matter of the spinal cord is responsible for analysing each piece of sensory information, which then may be stored and a decision made as to an appropriate response.

It is used in the process of integration and facilitates memory and learning. Grey matter consists of either neuron cell bodies, dendrites and axon terminals, or bundles of unmyelinated axons and neuroglia.

White matter is composed of bundles of myelinated axons and is responsible for conducting nerve impulses. The white matter of the spinal cord contains bundles of nerve fibres (from a common origin or destination) called nerve tracts, which carry similar information to or from the brain. There are two different types of nerve tract within white mater:

- Sensory tracts – these consist of nerve fibres which carry information from sensory receptors towards the brain, and are called ascending tracts
- Motor tracts – these consist of nerve fibres which carry information from the brain to effectors (muscles or glands) and are called descending tracts

The Brain

The brain is the most highly developed section of the nervous system and as it requires a large proportion of the body's resting oxygen (approximately 20%), it is also highly vascular. It contains a vast network of arteries and veins, which supply blood and nutrients (such as glucose, oxygen and water) for the brain to function effectively.

The passage of substances from the blood stream to the brain takes place through a semi-permeable barrier of specialised capillaries, which are unlike other capillaries throughout the body in the way that they are more selective as to what will pass through.

Also within the barrier are astrocytes (neurological cells that support neurons in the brain and spinal cord, and attach neurons to blood vessels) and a continuous basement membrane.

The barrier allows free passage of vital nutrients, such as glucose, oxygen and water, whilst slowing the passage of creatine, urea and various ions. It also prevents the passage of proteins and most antibiotics, which helps to protect the brain from harmful substances and pathogens, however lipid-soluble substances such as alcohol, caffeine, nicotine, heroin and anaesthetics can pass rapidly into the brain cells.

The brain is protected by the cranium and is also surrounded by three meninges in the same way as the spinal cord; by dura mater, arachnoid and pia mater. The brain can be divided into four different sections:

- Cerebrum
- Cerebellum
- Diencephalon
- Brain stem

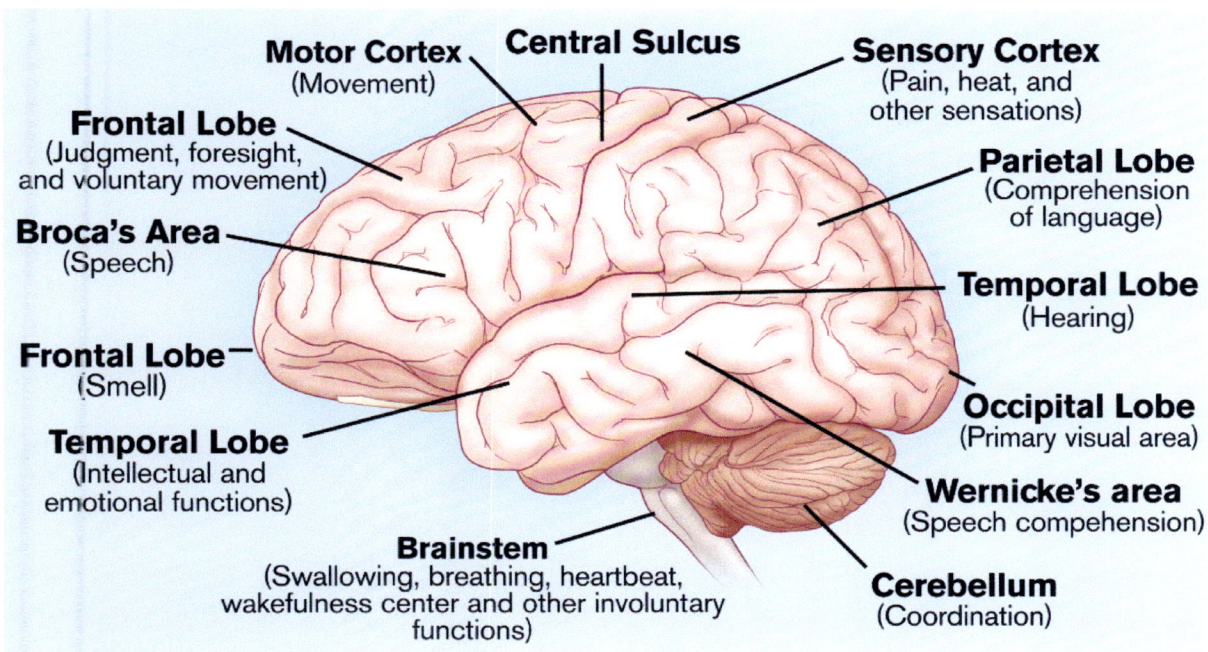

It also contains four cavities (ventricles) which are filled with cerebrospinal fluid. There are two lateral ventricles, one in each of the cerebral hemispheres, a ventricle within the diencephalon and a ventricle located between the brain stem and cerebellum.

The cerebrospinal fluid performs a number of functions, including protecting the brain by acting as a shock absorber, and assisting in nourishing the brain by providing the medium through which nutrients and waste products are exchanged between the blood and nervous tissue. It also provides an optimal chemical environment for neurons to transmit their nerve impulses.

The cerebrum is the largest section of the brain, occupying the majority of the superior region within the cranium. It is divided into two cerebral hemispheres (left and right) which are joined by a band of nerve fibres. The surface of each hemisphere is made of grey matter, called the cerebral cortex, and underneath this is white matter.

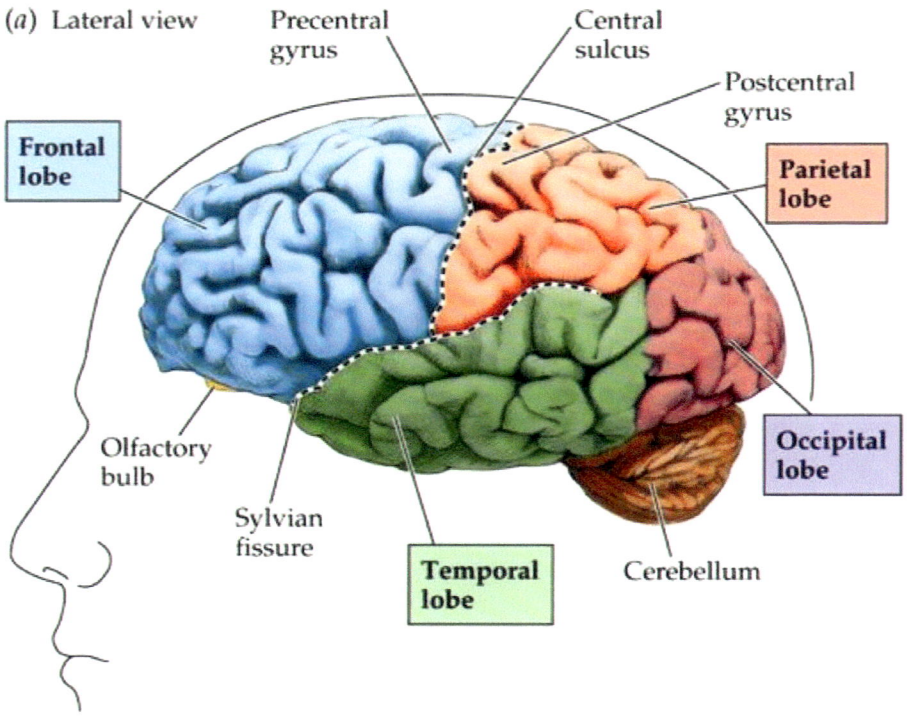

(a) Lateral view

Precentral gyrus

Central sulcus

Postcentral gyrus

Frontal lobe

Parietal lobe

Olfactory bulb

Sylvian fissure

Temporal lobe

Cerebellum

Occipital lobe

The cerebrum is split into four lobes, each of which are used for a variety of different functions:

- Frontal lobe – this is the anterior section of the cerebrum and is used in the planning and execution of activities. It sends messages through efferent nerves to the muscles and also controls facial and neck muscles, voluntary eye movement and speech
- Parietal lobe – the parietal lobe is located towards the posterior of the cerebrum and is the site for sensory reception and perception. It receives information about taste, touch, pressure, joint and muscle position, temperature and pain. It is also used for processing memory and thought
- Occipital lobe – the occipital lobe is located on the inferior/posterior section of the cerebrum, and is used in the processing of visual information from the eyes

- Temporal lobe – these are located on the lateral sides of the cerebrum and process information from the ears and nose (aural and olfactory information)

Second in size to the cerebrum is the cerebellum, which is the posterior section of the brain, inferior to the cerebrum, and is partially hidden by the cerebral hemispheres.

Its major function is monitoring the position of the limbs and tension within their associated muscles. It controls fine movements, posture, balance and locomotion by making adjustments to the messages sent out by the cerebrum towards the voluntary muscles.

The diencephalon is located in the central section of the brain and consists of the thalamus and hypothalamus. The thalamus is composed mostly from grey matter and is used to relay sensory and motor impulses to and from the appropriate centres of the cerebral hemispheres. It is also used in some sensations of pain, pressure and temperature. The hypothalamus is situated inferior to the thalamus and its primary role is in the regulation of homeostasis, which it is able to do as it links the nervous and endocrine systems.

The hypothalamus receives information from sound, taste and smell receptors, and also monitors various aspects of the internal environment, such as blood pressure and temperature. It also functions in anger, aggression, hunger and thirst.

The fourth section of the brain is the brain stem, which is located on the inferior section of the brain and superior to the spinal cord. It consists of three different sections; the midbrain, pons and medulla oblongata.

The midbrain is the most superior section and extends from the pons to the inferior portion of the diencephalon. It relays motor impulses from the cerebral cortex to the pons, medulla oblongata and the spinal cord, as well as impulses from the spinal cord to the thalamus. It is used in the co-ordination of eye movement in response to visual stimuli and the head and trunk in response to auditory stimuli.

The pons is situated in the centre of the brain stem, in between the midbrain and medulla oblongata. It consists of a thick band of nerve fibres and forms a link/bridge between the brain and spinal cord, and also links the two hemispheres of the cerebrum.

The medulla oblongata forms the most inferior section of the brain stem, and is a continuation of the spinal cord. It contains all of the nerve tracts which connect the spinal cord to various parts of the brain, and also the majority of nerve tracts cross over to the opposite side as they pass through this region.

Therefore some sensory impulses from one side of the body are received in the opposite side off the cerebral cortex (i.e. impulses from the left side of the body would be received by the right hemisphere).

The medulla oblongata is used in such actions as swallowing, vomiting and sneezing, and also regulates some vital processes such as heartbeat, blood vessel diameter and the basic rhythm of breathing. Also connected to the brain stem is a section of the brain called the limbic system, which consists of a ring of structures that encircle the brain stem.

They are on the inner border of the cerebrum and the floor of the diencephalon. The function of this system is in relation to the emotional aspects of behaviour and memory, such as those found in pleasure, pain, anger and fear.

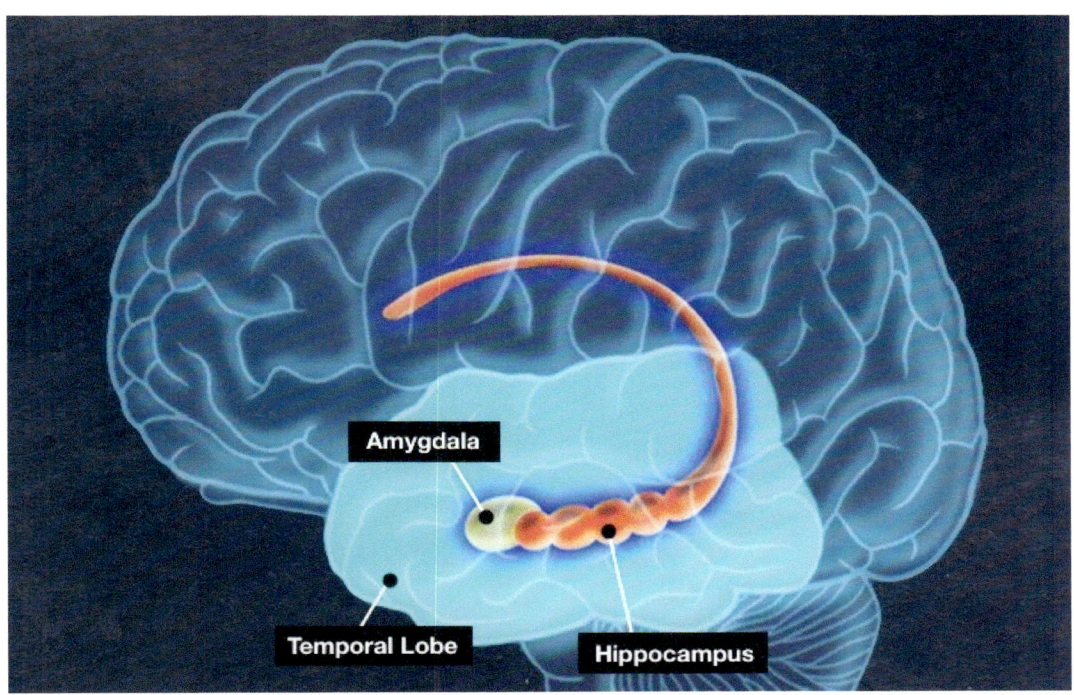

Localisation of Function in the Brain

We touched on this idea in the previous section but will expand on it further now. The concept of localisation of function is the theory that certain areas of the brain correspond to certain functions; that is to say that specific areas of the brain control different functions of the body.

The theory of localisation refers to the idea that factors like behaviour, emotions and thoughts originate in the brain in different and specific locations. Therefore, damage to relevant areas of the brain can cause drastic loss of that corresponding function. With this in mind, we can say that many functions of the brain are strictly localised.

Centres of the brain: language

Language provides us with a complex, creative and powerful system of communication and is the vehicle for thought; one of the key factors which makes us human.

The first region of the brain to be linked with language was Broca's area, names after Paul Broca who, in 1861, performed an autopsy on a patient who had been unable to produce meaningful speech for over 20 years. The examination showed there was a large area of damaged tissue to the posterior part of the left frontal lobe, an area which is adjacent to the motor cortex that controls the muscles of the face, mouth and vocal cords.

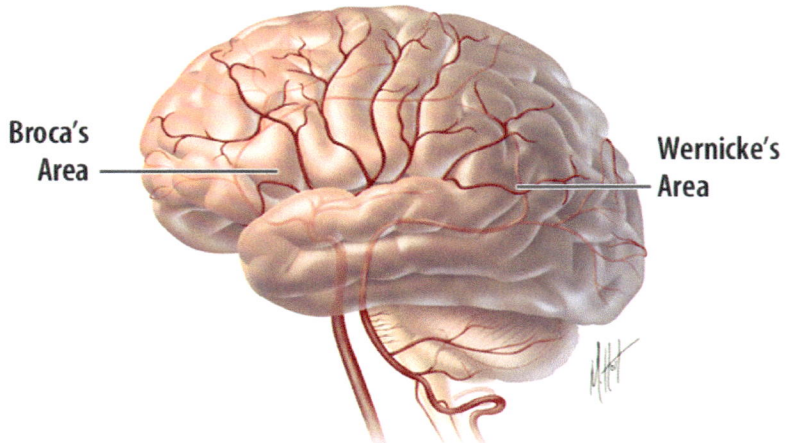

People who suffer from Broca's aphasia generally exhibit language which is slow, laboured and lacking in grammatical structure or inflection, although verbal comprehension is normally intact.

A little later, in 1874, Carl Wernicke described a second type of aphasia in which patients appeared to utter grammatically correct speech, although content was largely devoid of meaning, and had severe comprehension defects. This deficit is now called Wernicke's aphasia and is associated with damage to a region of the temporal lobe that is adjacent to the primary auditory cortex.

A neural pathway called the arcuate fasciculus passes from the Wernicke's area to the Broca's area, and damage to this route, which produces a third type of aphasia – called conduction aphasia – is characterised by an inability to repeat abstract words.

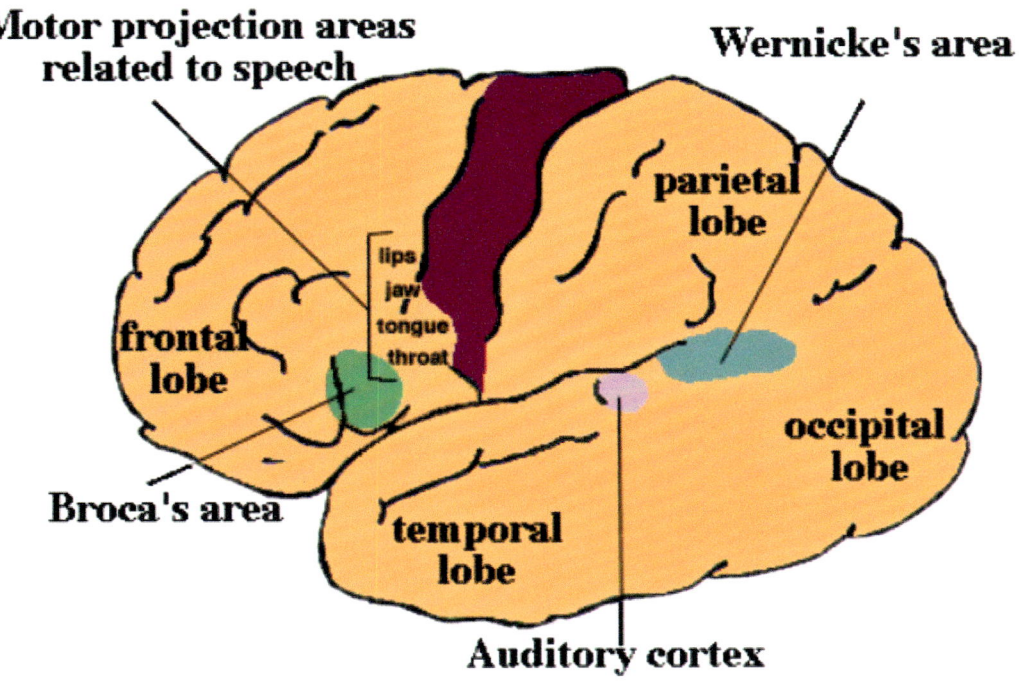

The theory that is most commonly used to explain how the brain processes language is the Wernicke-Geschwind model; this proposes that both the primary auditory cortex (for speech) and visual cortex (for reading) project to Wernicke's area where word recognition and comprehension takes place.

This translation of mental thoughts into verbal codes is also believed to take place in Wernicke's area, and this information can be passed to Broca's area, which produces the motor output necessary for speech.

The Wernicke-Geschwind Model of Language

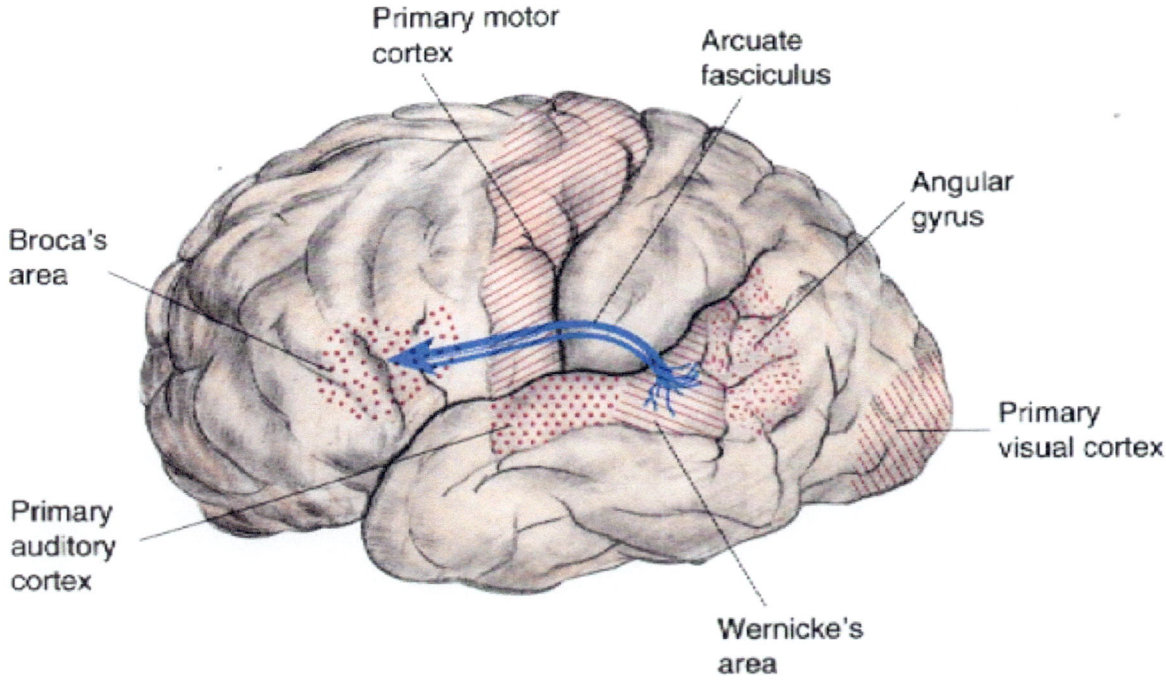

Hemispheric lateralisation of function

It is generally accepted that the left hemisphere of the cerebral cortex is predominantly involved in language, and the right hemisphere more concerned with visuospatial skills and emotion. Evidence supporting this theory was provided by Roger Serry and his associates in the 1960's. They examined patients who had received a commissurotomy, or severing of the corpus callosum. This is an operation that stops the two hemispheres of the brain from directly communicating with each other. It was found that if a written word was presented to the left hemisphere, split-brain subjects typically had no problem reading it, although they often reported seeing nothing when the word was presented to the right. In contrast the right hemisphere was found to be much better than the left at copying drawings or completing jigsaws.

In addition, pictures presented to the right hemisphere were more likely to elicit an emotional response (for example, blushing or arousal) than when presented to the left. However, language) or other cognitive functions) are not always lateralised to one side of the brain. For example, around 90% of people are right-handed, which is controlled by the left hemisphere of the brain. Studies using the Wada test, where one of the hemispheres is temporarily anaesthetised by an injection of sodium amytal into the carotid artery, have shown that around 95% of right-handed people have language strongly localised to the left hemisphere; but, in left-handed subjects this figure drops to about 70%. Moreover, about 15% of left-handers have language lateralised to the right hemisphere, and the remaining 15% show mixed dominance.

It has been suggested that if high levels of testosterone occur during the last trimester of foetal development, this may slow maturation of the left hemisphere, with the right more likely to take over some of its function.

Brain Plasticity

Brain plasticity, also known as neuroplasticity, is a term that refers to the brain's ability to change and adapt as a result of experience. When people say that the brain possesses plasticity, they are not suggesting that the brain is similar to plastic. Neuro represents neurons, the nerve cells that are the building blocks of the brain and nervous system, and plasticity refers to the brain's malleability.

Up until the 1960s, researchers believed that changes in the brain could only take place during infancy and childhood. By early adulthood, it was believed that the brain's physical structure was mostly permanent.

Modern research has demonstrated that the brain continues to create new neural pathways and alter existing ones in order to adapt to new experiences, learn new information and create new memories.[5]

The human brain is composed of approximately 86 billion neurons. Early researchers believed that neurogenesis, or the creation of new neurons, stopped

_____

[5] http://www.aqa.org.uk/resources/psychology/as-and-a-level/psychology/teach/lesson-plan-plasticity

shortly after birth. Today, it is understood that the brain possesses the remarkable capacity to reorganize pathways, create new connections and, in some cases, even create new neurons.

There are a few defining characteristics of neuroplasticity:

1) It can vary by age; while plasticity occurs throughout the lifetime, certain types of changes are more predominant during specific life ages. The brain tends to change a great deal during the early years of life, for example, as the immature brain grows and organizes itself. Generally, young brain's tend to be more sensitive and responsive to experiences than much older brains

2) It involves a variety of processes; plasticity is ongoing throughout life and involves brain cells other than neurons, including glial and vascular cells

3) It can happen for two different reasons; as a result of learning, experience and memory formation, or as a result of damage to the brain. While people used to believe that the brain became fixed after a certain age, newer research has revealed that the brain never stops changing in response to learning. In instances of damage to the brain, such as during a stroke, the areas of the brain associated with certain functions may be damaged. Eventually, healthy parts of the brain may take over those functions and the abilities can be restored

4) Environment plays an essential role in the process, but genetics can also have an influence. The interaction between the environment and genetics also plays a role in shaping the brain's plasticity

5) Brain plasticity is not always good. Brain changes are often seen as improvements, but this is not always the case. In some instances, the brain might be influenced by psychoactive substances or pathological conditions that can lead to detrimental effects on the brain and behaviour

Types of Brain Plasticity

- Functional Plasticity: Refers to the brain's ability to move functions from a damaged area of the brain to other undamaged areas
- Structural Plasticity: Refers to the brain's ability to actually change its physical structure as a result of learning

The first few years of a child's life are a time of rapid brain growth. At birth, every neuron in the cerebral cortex has an estimated 2,500 synapses; by age of three, this number has grown to a whopping 15,000 synapses per neuron.

The average adult, however, has about half that number of synapses. Why? Because as we gain new experiences, some connections are strengthened while others are eliminated. This process is known as synaptic pruning. Neurons that are used frequently develop stronger connections and those that are rarely or never used eventually die. By developing new connections and pruning away weak ones, the brain is able to adapt to the changing environment.[6]

Functional recovery of the brain after trauma

Recovery from a Traumatic Brain Injury (TBI) varies based on the individual and the brain injury. Attempts at predicting the degree of TBI recovery remain crude. Recovery can be seen months, and even years, after the initial injury. Devastating and fatal injuries can be easier to ascertain than other injuries.

These are the indicators the medical team uses for prognosis:

- Duration of Coma - The shorter the coma, the better the prognosis
- Post-traumatic amnesia - The shorter the amnesia, the better the prognosis
- Age - Patients over 60 or under age 2 have the worst prognosis, even if they suffer the same injury as someone not in those age groups

---

[6] http://psychology.about.com/od/biopsychology/f/brain-plasticity.htm

Recovery of brain function is thought to occur by several mechanisms. Some common theories are:

- Diaschisis - Depressed areas of the brain that are not injured but linked to injured areas begin functioning again
- The function is taken over by a part of the brain that does not usually perform that task
- Redundancy in the function performed so another area of the brain takes over
- Behavioural substitution - The individual learns new strategies to compensate for deficits

Ways of Studying the Brain

In this section we will look at four key method of studying the brain:

- Functional magnetic resonance imaging (fMRI)
- Electroencephalogram (EEG)
- Event-related potentials (ERP's)
- Post-mortem examinations

Functional magnetic resonance imaging (fMRI)

Functional magnetic resonance imaging is a technique for measuring brain activity. It works by detecting the changes in blood oxygenation and blood flow that occur in response to neural activity – it utilises the fact that when a brain area is more active it consumes more oxygen and to meet this increased demand blood flow increases to the active area. fMRI can be used to produce activation maps showing which parts of the brain are involved in a particular mental process. The development of FMRI in the 1990s, generally credited to Seiji Ogawa and Ken Kwong, is the latest in long line of innovations, including positron emission tomography (PET) and near infrared spectroscopy (NIRS), which use blood flow and oxygen metabolism to infer brain activity. As a brain imaging technique FMRI has several significant advantages:

1) It is non-invasive and doesn't involve radiation, making it safe for the subject
2) It has excellent spatial and good temporal resolution
3) It is easy for the experimenter to use

The attractions of fMRI have made it a popular tool for imaging normal brain function – especially for psychologists. Over the last decade it has provided new insight to the investigation of how memories are formed, language, pain, learning and emotion to name but a few areas of research. fMRI is also being applied in clinical and commercial settings.[7]

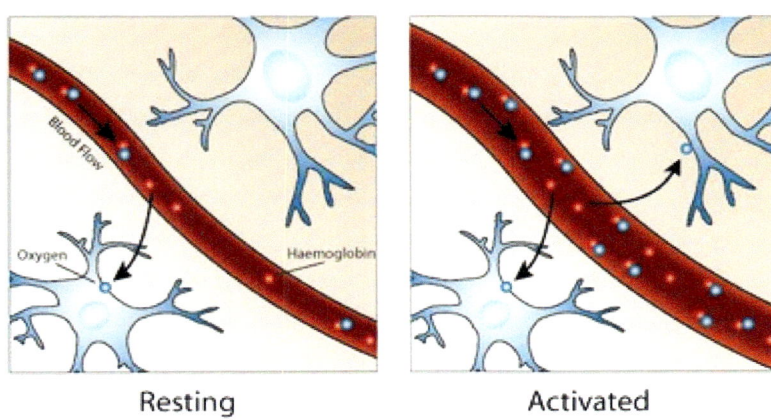

Resting   Activated

Eectroencephalogram (ECG)

An electroencephalogram (EEG) is a non-invasive technique for measuring brain activity. It involves placing small sensors on the head that record changes in potential difference (measured in micro-volts). This electrical activity originates in the brain and therefore provides a unique insight how the brain reacts to external stimuli. It is a completely safe and painless procedure.

EEG is a particularly useful tool in the discipline of cognitive science, as it can reveal changes in brain state associated with differing levels of arousal or under different experimental conditions. It operates with excellent temporal precision

[7] http://psychcentral.com/lib/what-is-functional-magnetic-resonance-imaging-fmri/

(recording data at a rate of up to 2000 data points per second), and therefore reveals much about the chronology of mental processes. Much psychological research is based on measuring the speed and accuracy of participants' responses, i.e. recording how long it takes to press a button in response to a particular stimulus. EEG can expand upon this method of indexing cognitive processing by showing us what happens in the brain before, during and after a response button is pressed.[8]

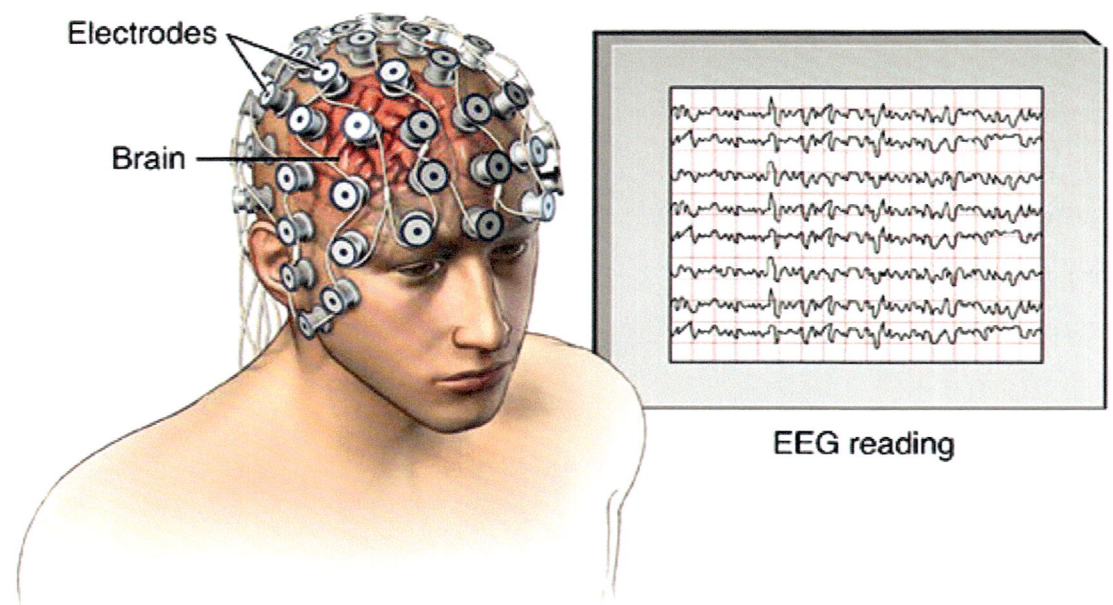

Event-related potentials (ERP's)

The event-related potential (ERP) technique in cognitive neuroscience allows scientists to observe human brain activity that reflects specific cognitive processes.

_____

[8] https://www.sheffield.ac.uk/psychology/research/groups/eeg

ERPs are very small voltages generated in the brain structures in response to specific events or stimuli. They are EEG changes that are time locked to sensory, motor or cognitive events that provide safe and non-invasive approach to study psychophysiological correlates of mental processes. Event-related potentials can be elicited by a wide variety of sensory, cognitive or motor events. They are thought to reflect the summed activity of postsynaptic potentials produced when a large number of similarly oriented cortical pyramidal neurons (in the order of thousands or millions) fire in synchrony while processing information.

ERPs in humans can be divided into 2 categories. The early waves, or components peaking roughly within the first 100 milliseconds after stimulus, are termed 'sensory' or 'exogenous' as they depend largely on the physical parameters of the stimulus. In contrast, ERPs generated in later parts reflect the manner in which the subject evaluates the stimulus and are termed 'cognitive' or 'endogenous' ERPs as they examine information processing. The waveforms are described according to latency and amplitude.[9]

Post-mortem examinations

We touched on post mortem examinations earlier so we will here only look briefly at some of the advantages and disadvantages of this technique:

- Useful for looking at the brain closely and in detail
- Post-mortem studies provide understanding of rare disorders
- Useful for studying the brains of people with specific psychological problems. e.g. schizophrenia, speech problems
- Participant needs to die before the brain can be examined

---

[9] http://www.ncbi.nlm.nih.gov/pmc/articles/PMC3016705/

The peripheral nervous system (PNS) contains all of the components of the nervous system apart from the brain and spinal cord (which make up the central nervous system). Included within PNS is a network of nerves which connects to all organs and peripheral regions of the body, and originate from the cranial and spinal nerves. It also includes ganglia (a group of nerves) situated outside of the brain and spinal cord.

The PNS conveys sensory impulses from various stimuli towards the central nervous system, and then transmits the appropriate motor response towards the required muscles and glands. The majority of these responses are automatic and used in response to environmental changes to maintain homeostasis.

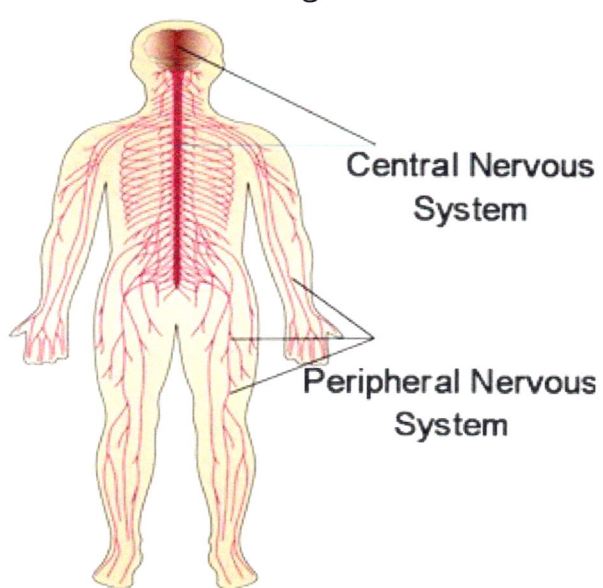

Cranial nerves originate from the brain and in general they supply the sense organs and muscles of the head. In total there are twelve pairs of cranial nerves which consist of either sensory fibres (sensory nerves) or sensory and motor fibres (mixed nerves). The numbering of the nerves begins with the cranial nerve that originates at the anterior of the brain:

   i.   Olfactory – This is a sensory nerve that is associated with smell

   ii.   Optic – This is a sensory nerve that is associated with vision

iii. Oculomotor – This is a mixed nerve where the motor action controls the movement of the eyelid and eyeball, adjusts the lens for near vision and constricts the pupil. The sensory function is for proprioception ('muscle sense,' which is the subconscious awareness of the positions of bones, joints and muscles in relation to the rest of the body)

iv. Trochlear – A mixed nerve where the motor function is related to movement of the eyeball and sensory function is for proprioception

v. Trigeminal – A mixed nerve which is used in the action of chewing and the sensory function of conveying the sensation of touch, pain and temperature

vi. Abducens – A mixed nerve where the motor function is related to movement of the eyeball and sensory function is for proprioception

vii. Facial – A mixed nerve where the motor function provides facial expression and secretion of saliva/tears. The sensory function relates to taste and proprioception

viii. Vestibulocochlear – A sensory nerve that conveys impulses associated with hearing and equilibrium

ix. Glossopharyngeal – A mixed nerve which is used in the motor function of secretion of saliva and the sensory functions of taste, regulation of blood pressure and proprioception

x. Vagus – A mixed nerve which is used in the motor functions of smooth muscle contraction/relaxation and secretion of digestive fluids. It is also used in the sensory functions of transmitting sensations from organs and in proprioception

xi. Accessory – This is a mixed nerve which is used in swallowing and movement of the head, and the sensory function of proprioception

xii. Hypoglossal – A mixed nerve which is used in the movement of the tongue and the sensory function of proprioception

The spinal nerves originate from the spinal cord, and they consist of a total of thirty-one pairs of nerves which are numbered/named according to the area of the spinal cord from which they emerge, starting at the most superior point. There are eight cervical spinal nerves, twelve thoracic, five lumbar, five sacral and one coccygeal nerves. Each spinal nerve has two points of attachment on the spinal cord; a posterior root and an anterior root. The posterior root contains sensory fibres and the anterior root contains motor fibres, and as the two roots converge before emerging from the vertebral column to form a nerve trunk, all spinal nerves are mixed nerves.

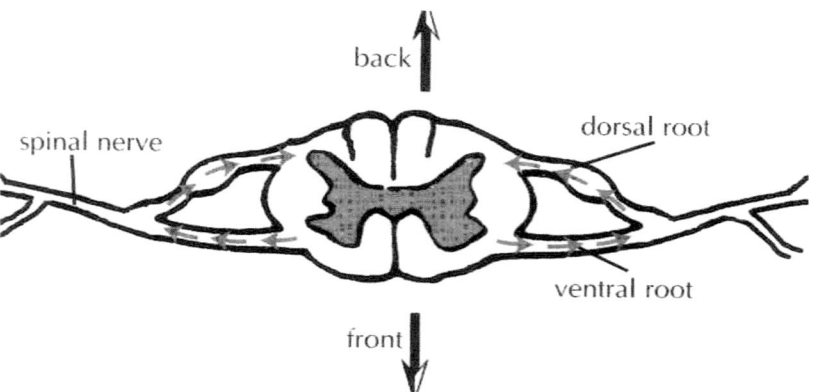

After emerging from the vertebrae, the nerve trunks branch into smaller units called rami.

The dorsal ramus funs to the deep muscles and skin of the posterior surface of the trunk, whilst the ventral ramus serves the muscles and structures of the upper and lower extremities, along with the lateral and anterior surface of the trunk.

All nerves (except the thoracic nerves) join together to form networks on both sides of the body, which are called plexuses. Nerves then emerge from the plexuses for the relevant parts of the body. The main plexuses are the cervical, brachial, lumbar, sacral and coccygeal plexuses.

- Cervical plexus – Originates at the ventral rami of C1-C4 and some C5. It supplies the skin and muscles of the neck, head and upper part of the shoulder

- Brachial plexus – Originates at the ventral rami of C5-C8 and T1. It extends down and laterally on either side of the inferior four cervical and first thoracic vertebrae, and provides the nerve supply to the shoulder and upper limbs
- Lumbar plexus – Originates at the ventral rami of L1-L4 and supplies the anterolateral abdominal wall, external genitals and some of the lower extremities
- Sacral plexus – Originates at the ventral rami of L4-L5 and S1-S4 and supplies the buttocks, perineum and lower extremities
- Coccygeal plexus – Originates at the ventral rami of S4-S5 and the coccygeal ventral ramus. It supplies the skin over the coccyx

Function of the Nervous System

The nervous system has three main functions; senses changes (internally and external to the body), analyses the changes and responds to the changes.

Neurons located in receptors throughout the body detect changes in the environment and transmit the information towards the brain for processing, and then motor commands are sent from the brain to effectors in specific parts of the body, and may be muscles or glands.

The central nervous system (CNS) as a whole performs a wide variety of functions which range from planning and execution of activities to regulating heartbeat and other vital actions.

A brief summary of functions is as follows:
- Frontal lobe of cerebrum – planning and execution of activities, and control of facial and neck muscles
- Parietal lobe of cerebrum – sensory reception and perception
- Occipital lobe of cerebrum – receives visual information
- Temporal lobe of cerebrum – sensory perception; receives auditory and olfactory information
- Thalamus – relays sensory and motor impulses

- Hypothalamus – regulates homeostasis
- Cerebellum – monitors limb position (proprioception)
- Midbrain – relays motor and sensory impulses, and co-ordinates movements of the eyeballs
- Pons – links the cerebral hemispheres
- Medulla oblongata – regulates heartbeat, blood vessel diameter and breathing rhythm. Also co-ordinates swallowing, coughing and sneezing, and helps to maintain posture and equilibrium

The peripheral nervous system has the functions of transmitting sensory information towards the CNS and motor impulses from the CNS to effectors (muscles and glands) throughout the body. This action is called a reflex arc and has five components:

- Receptor – the receptor in the neuron responds to a stimulus by triggering a nerve impulse. The stimulus is either a change in the internal or external environment
- Sensory neuron – the nerve impulse is conducted through neurons and synapses to the axon terminals of the sensory neuron, located in the grey matter of the spinal cord or brain stem
- Integrating centre – within the grey matter of the CNS, the sensory information is analysed and the appropriate response is determined
- Motor neuron – an impulse is generated by the CNS following analysis of the information, which is conducted along the motor neuron to a specific part of the body which is required to respond to the stimulus
- Effector – the generated impulse results either in the contraction of a muscle or the secretion of a substance by a gland, as is called the reflex action

Motor commands through efferent nerves can pass into two different divisions of the PNS, which are the somatic nervous system and the autonomic nervous system. The somatic nervous system relays motor impulses to skeletal muscles, whereas the autonomic nervous system relays motor impulses to smooth muscle, cardiac muscle and to glands. Within the autonomic nervous system, there are two pathways in which impulses can travel, which are sympathetic and parasympathetic.

The sympathetic nervous system is responsible for the 'fight or flight' reactions that prepare the body for action, which it does by stimulating an increase in heart and respiratory rates, blood pressure and conversion of glycogen in the liver.

Digestion rate is also reduced so that blood can be diverted from the digestive system to other areas of the body which require the extra supply. The endings of the nerves which originate from the spinal nerves in the thoracic and lumbar regions release noradrenaline which assist in the fight or flight reaction.

The medulla of the adrenals is supplied with sympathetic fibres which trigger the release of adrenaline into the blood, which also enhances this reaction.

The parasympathetic nervous system operates in parallel with the sympathetic nervous system and acts as an antagonist, which causes the body to 'rest and relax' by restoring the body's systems to normal operating conditions once the original stress has been removed.

The motor nerves of the parasympathetic nervous system originate from cranial nerves and some spinal nerves in the sacral region. They release acetylcholine which decreases heart and respiratory rate, and blood pressure.

Each organ in the body receives input from both the sympathetic and parasympathetic nervous systems, and the response created depends on the relative stimulation received from each one.

Life Cycle Developments

During the embryonic stage of development, there is an abundance of electrical synapses which provides a simple means of synchronising activity of the interconnected neurons and ensures that all impulses are processed. However, as the nervous system develops in the foetus, electrical synapses are replaced in favour of more selective chemical synapses.

Following birth, the spinal cord enlarges and elongates in proportion with the growth of the vertebral column, up until the age of approximately four years. During this period, the ventral and dorsal roots are very short as they enter the intervertebral foramina (an opening in the bone) immediately adjacent to their spinal region. Following the age of four years, the vertebral column continues to grow but the spinal cord does not.

Due to this, the distance between the dorsal roots and spinal nerves becomes greater which results in elongation of the dorsal and ventral roots, and correspondence between spinal and vertebral segments is lost. For example, the sacral segment of the spinal cord in a child under four years of age would correspond to the sacrum, but in an adult the sacral segment of the spinal cord is at the level of vertebrae L1-L2.

Various reflexes and motor pathways develop early in childhood, such as a reflex called the Babinski Reflex. When an infant's foot is stroked on the sole, the motor response produces a fanning apart of the toes (a positive response), but a healthy adult would produce a different response where the toes would curl in a plantar action (a negative response). However, in adults suffering a CNS injury, a positive Babinski reflex would be observed.

As the body ages a reduction in the number of cortical neurons within the brain takes place. For example, a new-born female has approximately 19.3 billion cortical neurons and a male has 22.8 billion.

The average rate of decline from birth is approximately 85 000 per day (31 million per year) and continues to decline throughout the life cycle. The brain also reduces in size and weight, primarily due to a decrease in the volume of the cerebral cortex.

Over time, deposits will accumulate in the walls of blood vessels within the body, which leads to an overall decrease in blood flow. The reduction in blood flow itself does not adversely affect the brain, but it increases the chances of strokes occurring.

Functional changes also occur as the body ages, such as reduced efficiency of neural processing and accessing memory, especially of the recent past. Sensory systems become less acute and require greater stimuli to produce nervous impulses, for example lights need to be brighter and sounds need to be louder before they are perceived.

The precision of motor control decreases with age, as does the time it takes to perform a motor action, which is due to the reduced efficiency of the motor pathways from the central nervous system.

A further age-related issue which increases as the body ages is that requirements for certain vitamins/minerals increases due to changes within the physiology of the body. For example, as the body ages, there is a reduction in the utilisation of vitamin B6 which increases the requirement for this vitamin, and a reduced rate of secretion of stomach acid has an adverse effect on the absorption of vitamin B12, folic acid, iron, calcium and zinc, which mean that supplements may have to be used.

The Endocrine System

The endocrine system is an information signal system like the nervous system, yet its effects and mechanism are classifiably different. The endocrine system's effects are slow to initiate, and prolonged in their response, lasting from a few hours up to weeks. The nervous system sends information very quickly, and responses are generally short lived. In vertebrates, the hypothalamus is the neural control centre for all endocrine systems.

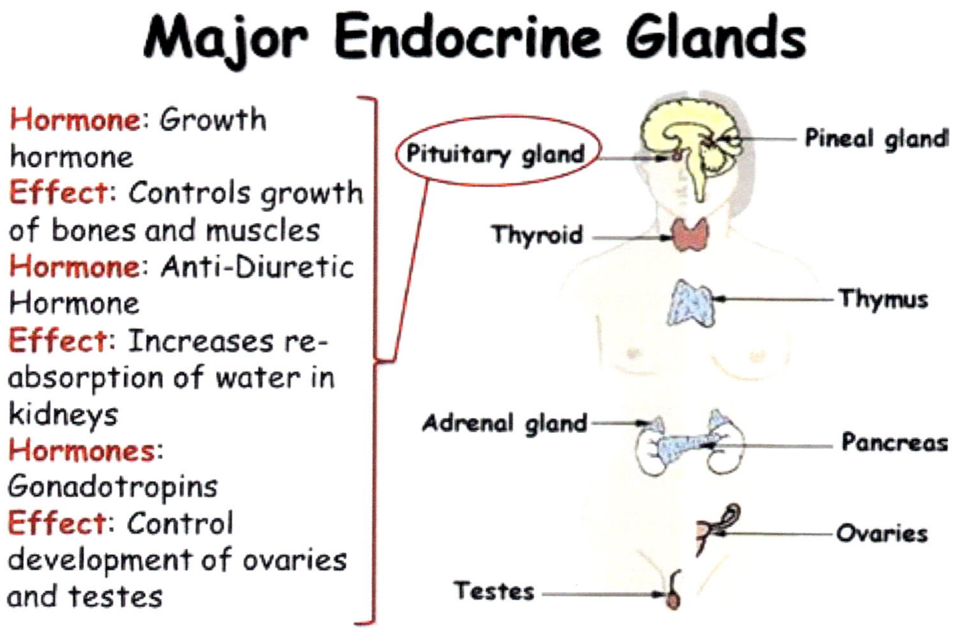

Major Endocrine Glands

Hormone: Growth hormone
Effect: Controls growth of bones and muscles
Hormone: Anti-Diuretic Hormone
Effect: Increases re-absorption of water in kidneys
Hormones: Gonadotropins
Effect: Control development of ovaries and testes

Pituitary gland

Pineal gland

Thyroid

Thymus

Adrenal gland

Pancreas

Ovaries

Testes

The endocrine system is a network of ductless glands that secrete hormones directly into the bloodstream, when certain signals are triggered. The trigger signals can come from chemical changes in the blood, different levels of other hormones or signals from the nervous system, to which it is connected to by the hypothalamus.

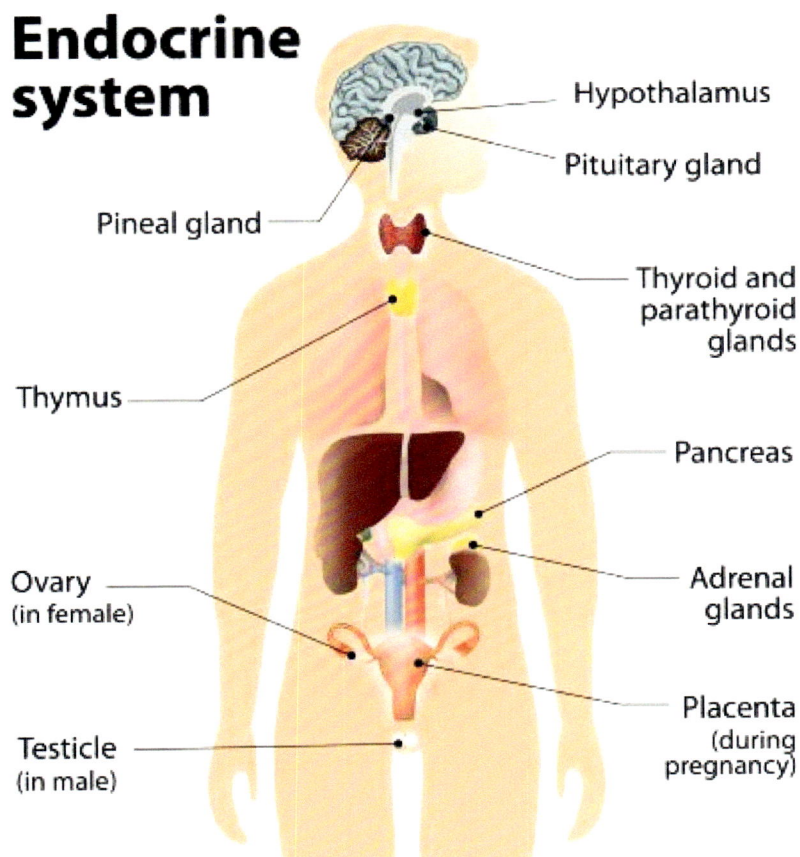

Endocrine system

- Hypothalamus
- Pituitary gland
- Pineal gland
- Thyroid and parathyroid glands
- Thymus
- Pancreas
- Ovary (in female)
- Adrenal glands
- Testicle (in male)
- Placenta (during pregnancy)

The foundations of the endocrine system are the network of endocrine **glands** and the **hormones** they produce, store and secrete. The glands are controlled directly by stimulation from the nervous system as well as by chemical receptors in the blood and hormones produced by other glands. The diagram shows the main glands of the endocrine system: Pituitary, thyroid, adrenal, reproductive (testes- male; ovaries – female), pineal and pancreas.

As the endocrine glands are ductless, they are all highly vascular (contain a large amount of blood vessels) because they secrete their hormones directly through the thin capillary walls into the bloodstream.

There are ten major endocrine glands in the body, which are; hypothalamus, pituitary gland, thyroid gland, parathyroid glands, adrenals, pancreas, ovaries, testes, pineal gland and thymus.

Endocrine glands release more than 20 major hormones directly into the bloodstream where they can be transported to cells in other parts of the body. As the body's chemical messengers, **hormones** transfer information and instructions from one set of cells to another. Many different hormones move through the bloodstream, but each type of hormone is designed to affect only certain cells. The endocrine glands must release the correct amount of hormones to keep the body working efficiently. If they release too much or too little, a hormone imbalance will result, which leads to ill health. Endocrine diseases, e.g. diabetes and hyperthyroid disease, are quite common.

The endocrine system helps control the following processes and systems

- Growth and development

- Homeostasis (the internal balance of body systems)

- Metabolism (body energy levels)

- Reproduction

- Response to stimuli (stress and/or injury)

Hypothalamus

The central part of the endocrine system is the hypothalamus, which is regarded as the 'master' of this system. It is situated in the diencephalon which is a section of the brain, posterior to the mid-brain. As well as being an endocrine gland, it also receives information about many processes within the body and provides a link between the nervous and endocrine systems.

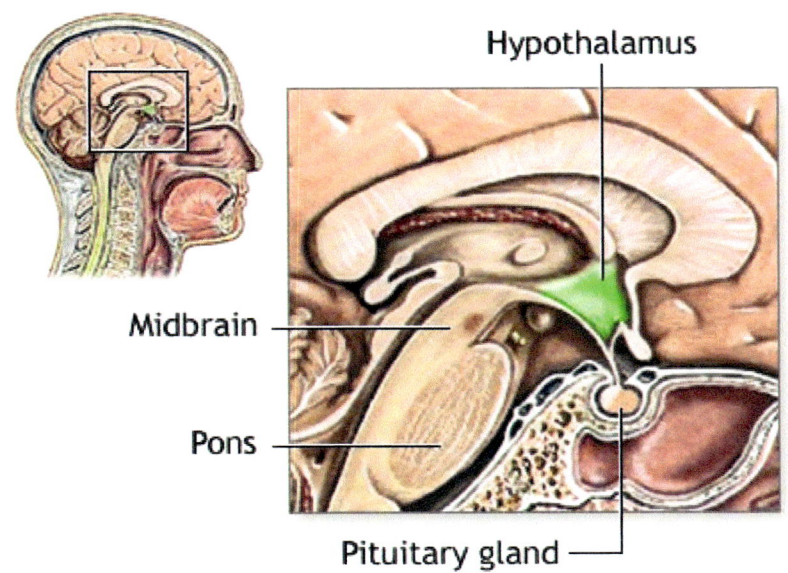

This link allows it to be a predominant part of homeostasis within the body, because should one of the processes which it is measuring start to alter, and then it is able to signal an appropriate hormonal response. This can then be measured through a negative feedback system, where once the change in homeostasis has been successfully resolved, an inhibiting hormone is secreted which would temporarily stop further release of the active hormone that affected the change. As the hypothalamus links the nervous and endocrine systems, it has the ability to perform many functions, such as controlling the autonomic nervous system, govern many of the body's drives (such as hunger and thirst), influences emotions and receives sensory information from internal (within the body) and external (e.g. temperature and sunlight) environments.

The hypothalamus secretes several hormones, which include:

- Oxytocin – stimulates contraction of uterine muscles during the birth process, and milk ejection after birth
- Anti-diuretic hormone (ADH) – also known as vasopressin, this hormone regulates water retention within the body. It decreases urine production and causes contraction of the arteries when low levels of water are detected

The hormones which are produced by the hypothalamus are transported, in the blood, to the pituitary gland for storage and release

Pituitary Gland

The pituitary gland is located inferior to the hypothalamus and consists of two lobes; the anterior and posterior lobes. The posterior lobe does not produce hormones, but it stores and releases oxytocin and vasopressin, which are produced by the hypothalamus and transported to the posterior lobe of the pituitary gland.

The anterior lobe produces six major hormones, and releases them when instructed by the hypothalamus. This is because the hypothalamus constantly monitors the bloodstream for appropriate levels of hormones (in this instance, those which are produced by the anterior lobe) and when one of the levels declines, the hypothalamus secretes a releasing hormone which is transported to the anterior lobe of the pituitary gland, and stimulates release of the appropriate hormone.

As noted above, the detection of increased/decreased levels of hormones is controlled by a negative feedback system, where, once the correct levels of a particular hormone have been restored, the hypothalamus stops the anterior lobe releasing further hormones by secreting a selective inhibiting hormone.

The six major hormones secreted by the anterior lobe are:

- Growth hormone (somatotrophin) – controls body growth
- Prolactin – stimulates production of milk from the mammary glands
- Adrenocorticotrophic hormone (ACTH) – stimulates secretions from the adrenal glands
- Thyroid stimulating hormone (TSH) – stimulates secretions from the thyroid gland
- Gonadotrophic hormones – includes follicle stimulating hormone (FSH) and luteinising hormone (LH), which stimulate activities relating to the ovaries and testes

- Melanocyte stimulating hormone – stimulates production of melanin, which is a pigment within skin and hair

Along with the hypothalamus, the pituitary gland and its hormones have a direct effect on most of the other endocrine glands within the body. For example, the thyroid gland will only secrete its hormones when it receives TSH (thyroid stimulating hormone) from the anterior lobe of the pituitary gland.

Thyroid and Parathyroid Glands

The thyroid and parathyroid glands are both located in the neck, inferior to the larynx. The thyroid gland curves across the anterior surface of the trachea (windpipe), with one lobe to either side.

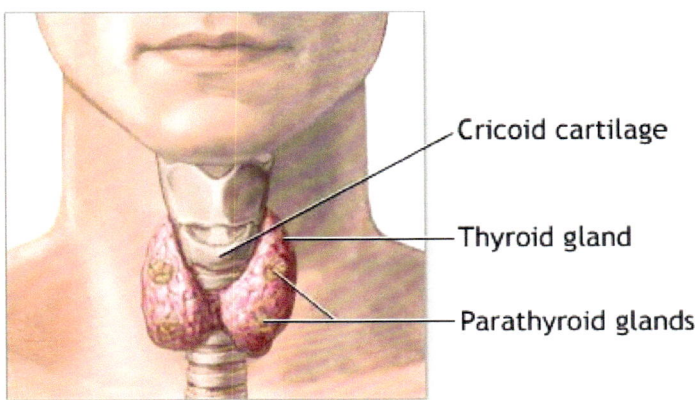

There are four parathyroid glands which are relatively small in comparison to the thyroid and oval in shape, which are embedded in the posterior surface of the thyroid gland (two on each lobe).

The average weight of the thyroid gland in an adult is approximately 35 grams, whereas the average weight of the four parathyroid glands combined together is approximately 1.5 grams.

Within the thyroid gland are a large number of follicles, which are spheres that are lined with a simple cuboidal epithelium. The follicles are surrounded by a network of capillaries which enable nutrients and hormones to diffuse to and from the bloodstream.

The thyroid gland is responsible for regulating growth and development within the body, and its hormones also control metabolic rate and activity of the nervous system.

Upon receiving TSH from the anterior lobe of the pituitary gland, the thyroid removes iodine from the blood, where it can produce thyroid hormones such as Thyroxine, by reacting iodine molecules with the amino acid tyrosine. Tyrosine is present in all thyroid hormones. Another hormone which the thyroid secretes is calcitonin, which lowers levels of calcium and phosphates within the blood by accelerating their absorption into bone tissue and therefore inhibits bone breakdown.

The parathyroid glands produce a hormone called 'parathyroid hormone' (PTH) which acts to decrease the blood phosphate levels whilst increasing the blood calcium levels. PTH also increases the number and activity of bone-destroying cells (osteoclasts), inhibits osteoblasts by reducing the rate of calcium deposits in bone, and increases the re-absorption of calcium in the kidneys.

Adrenal Glands

There are two adrenal glands within the body which are located on the superior border of each kidney, and as such they are also referred to as suprarenal glands. The adrenal glands are roughly pyramid-shaped which allows them to in between the space between the kidney, diaphragm and abdominal cavity. Each gland is divided into two sections; the outer layer is called the adrenal cortex, and the inner section is the adrenal medulla.

The adrenal medulla contains two types of secretory cells, each of which produces one particular hormone, but both are released when the body is under stress to help it cope with and prepare for an emergency.

These hormones are:

- Adrenaline (epinephrine) – causes an increase in metabolic, heart and respiratory rates as well as increased blood pressure and constriction of blood vessels. Adrenaline is the major secretion from the adrenal glands, representing approximately 80 % of the output

- Noradrenaline (norepinephrine) – has the same effects as adrenaline and is also a neurotransmitter, secreted from the nerve endings of the sympathetic nervous system

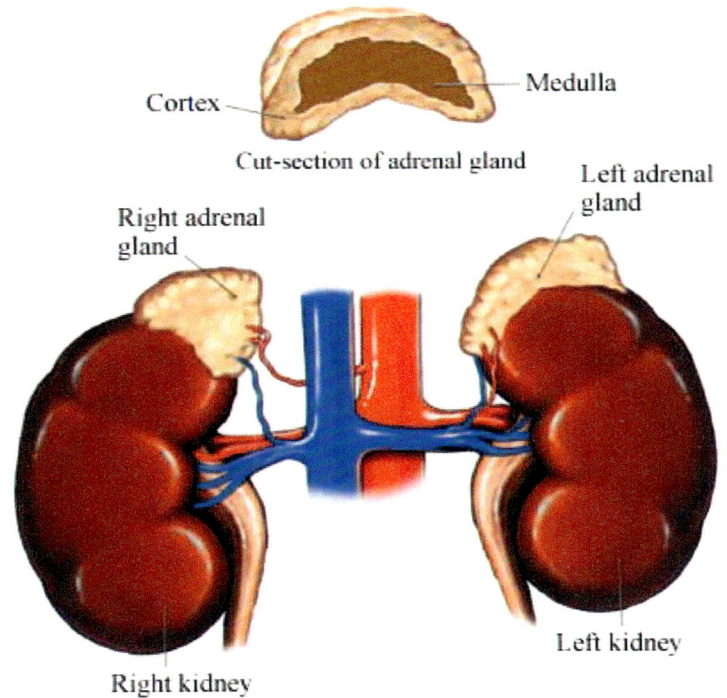

The adrenal cortex forms the outer section of the adrenal glands, and is rich in vitamin C and lipids (fats), especially cholesterol. Several hormones are produced by the adrenal cortex, all of which are steroid based and collectively called corticosteroids or adrenocortical steroids (a steroid being a chemical structure based around four co-joined carbon rings, three of which have 6-carbon atoms and one has 5-carbon atoms).

The major hormones produced in the adrenal cortex are:

- Cortisol and corticosterone – stimulate the conversion of fats and proteins to glucose
- Aldosterone – controls sodium and potassium concentrations

- Androgens and Oestrogens – male and female sex hormones

Pancreas

The pancreas is situated in the abdominopelvic cavity between the stomach and small intestine (duodenum), and is approximately 12-15cm long. It is primarily a digestive organ as around 99% of pancreatic tissue is involved in producing digestive enzymes which are transported via a duct to the digestive system, which classifies the pancreas as an exocrine gland (use of a duct).

The endocrine section of the pancreas therefore accounts for around 1% of its tissue, which are scattered in clusters throughout the pancreas amongst the exocrine cells.

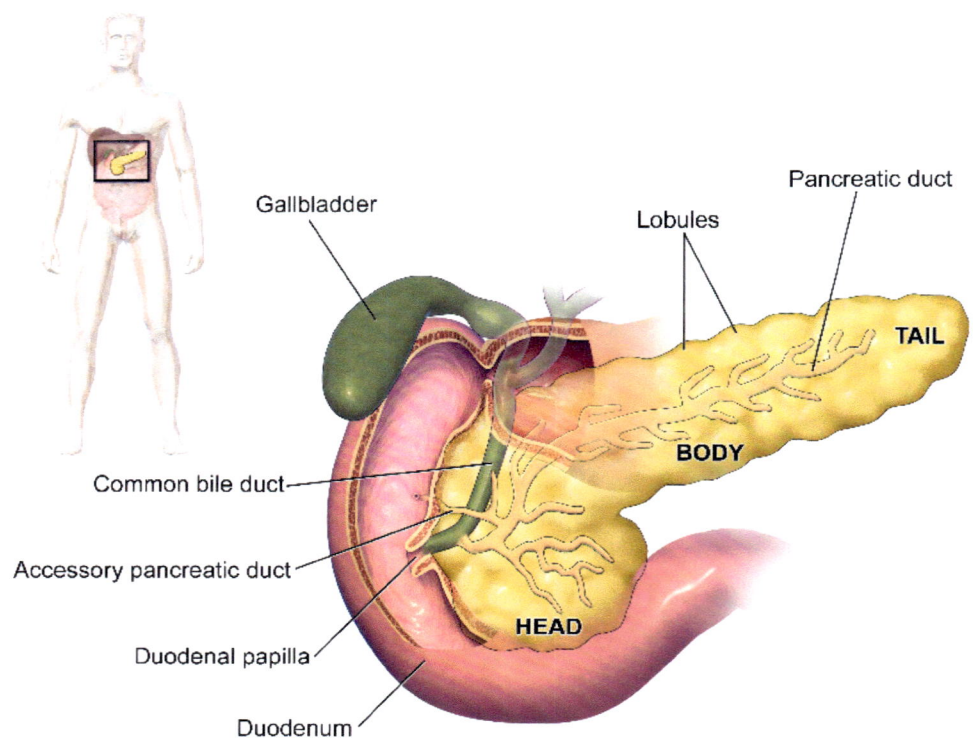

These clusters are called pancreatic islets or islets of Langerhans, and contain four different types of cells:

- Alpha cells – produce the hormone glucagon, which raises blood glucose levels by causing the release of glucose in the blood and accelerates the breakdown of glycogen into glucose within the liver
- Beta cells – produce the hormone insulin, which decreases the blood glucose levels by accelerating the transport of glucose from the blood into cells, converting glucose into glycogen and decreasing the amount of glycogen that is converted into glucose
- Delta cells – produce a hormone that suppresses the release of glucagon and insulin by the alpha and beta cells, and slows the rates of food absorption along the digestive tract
- F cells – produce the hormone pancreatic polypeptide (PP), which inhibits gallbladder contractions and regulates the production of some pancreatic enzymes

Ovaries/Testes

The ovaries and testes are the principle structures of the reproductive system in females and males, respectively, and can both be referred to as gonads. The two ovaries are located in the upper pelvic cavity, one on each side of the uterus, and are suspended in place by ligaments.

The ovaries contain 'eggs' or follicles which are immature ova encased in a sac, which are transported through the fallopian tubes to the uterus during menstruation. The endocrine cells within the ovaries secrete four hormones, which are controlled by secretions of follicle-stimulating hormone (FSH) and luteinising hormone (LH) from the anterior lobe of the pituitary gland.

- Oestrogen – this is the sex hormone concerned with development and maintenance of the reproductive system, as well as secondary sex characteristics (such as fat distribution, voice pitch and width of the pelvis). Oestrogen takes part in the menstrual cycle and helps to control fluid balance

- Progesterone – this is the second female sex hormone and is produced after ovulation. It helps to prepare the uterus for the implantation of fertilised ovum, develops the placenta and prepares the mammary glands for milk secretion. Progesterone also takes part in the menstrual cycle
- Inhibin – towards the end of the menstrual cycle, this hormone inhibits the secretion of FSH from the pituitary gland
- Relaxin – during childbirth, this hormone dilates the cervix and helps the pelvic girdle to widen

The testes are located outside of the body at the inferior section of the abdomen, in two pouches of skin called scrotal sacs. They are suspended by spermatic cords and act to produce sperm in a process called spermatogenesis.

The endocrine cells of the testes are controlled by secretions of FSH and LH from the pituitary gland, and produce two hormones:

- Testosterone – this is the primary male sex hormone. It controls development, growth and maintenance of the reproductive system as well as the development of secondary sex characteristics (such as facial/chest hair, thickening of the skin and enlargement of the larynx, which deepens the voice)
- Inhibin – this hormone is used to control sperm production

Pineal and Thymus glands

The pineal gland is located in the brain, on the roof of the third cerebral ventricle. It consists of neuroglia (nerve cells) and secretory cells called pinealocytes, which produce and secrete melatonin. Melatonin is a hormone which is thought to induce sleep, maintain body rhythms and inhibit sexual activity. The production of melatonin is at its greatest during the night/darkness.

Pineal Gland

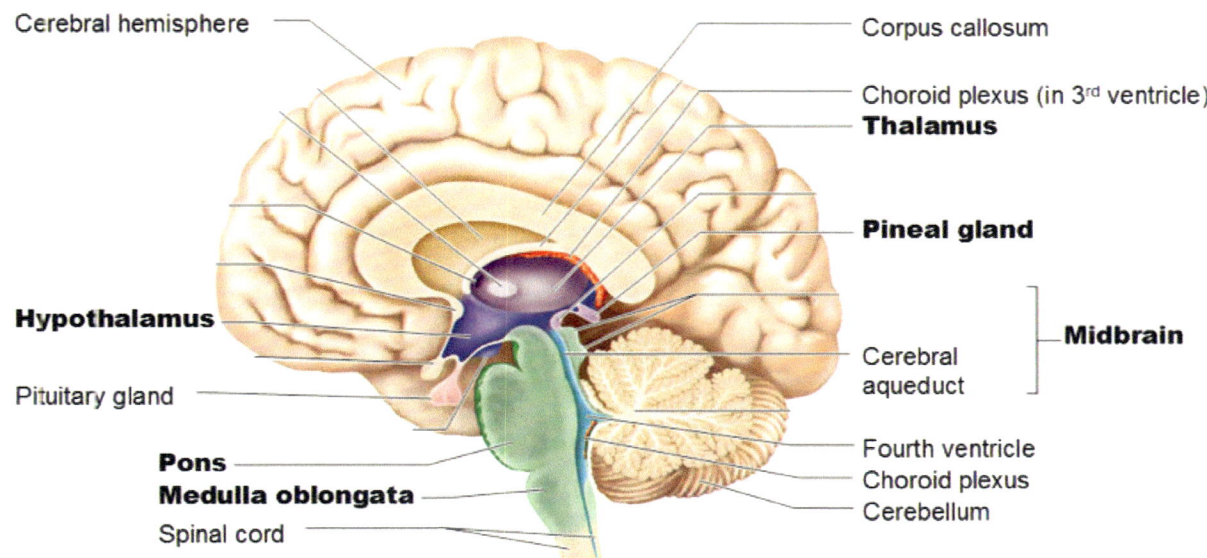

The thymus gland consists of two lobes which are located in the upper chest posterior to the sternum (breast bone) and anterior to the lungs.

The thymus secretes several hormones which are collectively called thymus stimulating hormones (TSH) or thymosins. These hormones are produced in the thymus and also act upon the thymus itself as it produces and matures T-cell lymphocytes (white blood cells).

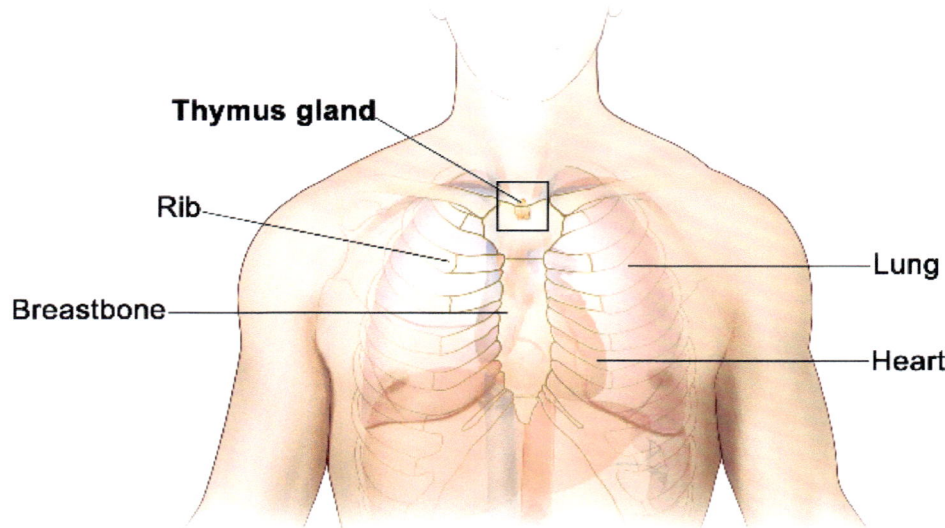

An excellent answer, top quality. The key elements are identified and a good explanation is given of each. Pass.

Function of the Endocrine System

The endocrine system consists of cells, tissues and glands within the body which secrete hormones directly into the blood, by diffusing through capillary walls, and which regulate many of the body's processes and homeostasis. As the hormones are secreted directly into the blood, they have the ability to travel quickly throughout the body to the target cells/organs.

The secreted hormones 'saturate' the extracellular fluid and therefore exposes cells throughout the body to these hormones, however for hormones to have any effect, there must be a specific receptor which is capable of utilising the hormone. If the specific receptor is not present, then the hormone will not have any effect on that particular cell/tissue, e.g. anti-diuretic hormone (ADH) secreted from the pituitary gland will affect the kidneys as it has specific receptors, but ADH will not have any effect on the thyroid gland or the reproductive system.

Endocrine hormones circulate freely throughout the body, but only have a limited period of functionality, which in general can be less than one hour (apart from thyroid and steroid hormones which circulate much longer due to them becoming attached to special transport proteins).

Hormones become inactivated in three ways:

- Diffusion out of the bloodstream and binding to its target receptor cells
- Absorption by the cells of the liver or kidney, which break them down
- Enzymes breaking them down in plasma or extracellular fluids

Both endocrine and exocrine glands produce secretions, but whereas endocrine glands are ductless and secrete their hormones directly into the blood, exocrine glands transport their secretions via a duct onto epithelial surfaces, such as within body cavities

The hormones produced within the endocrine system control many systems and functions within the body, for example:

- They regulate the composition and volume of extracellular fluid (the fluid which surrounds cells)
- They help to regulate metabolism and energy balance
- Regulate contraction of smooth and cardiac muscles
- Regulate secretions by glands
- Help to maintain homeostasis
- Help to regulate growth and development
- Contribute to the processes of the reproductive system

An important function which the endocrine system takes part in is dealing with stresses (e.g. physical or emotional) and especially the 'flight or fight' reaction. There is a response system within the body called the general adaptation syndrome (GAS) which relates to all stresses which face the body, and not specifically related to the endocrine system.

There are three phases to GAS, which are the alarm phase, resistance phase and exhaustion phase. When a new stress is imposed upon the body, the alarm phase begins, and for example within the endocrine system the brain sends signals to the adrenal gland (adrenal medulla) to secrete epinephrine and norepinephrine. This produces increased mental alertness, mobilisation of energy reserves, increased blood flow to the muscles and increased blood pressure/heart rate. This provides the body a better environment to deal with short-term stresses, but these conditions cannot be maintained for long.

The resistance phase relates to long-term stresses which can include starvation, anxiety or illness, and therefore adrenal gland secretions would not be sufficient or appropriate.

In cases such as these, the hypothalamus could stimulate secretions of anti-diuretic hormone (ADH) which would help preserve water levels within the body and blood, and the islets of Langerhans within the pancreas could produce hormones which help conserve levels of glucose within the body. The resistance phase also cannot be maintained indefinitely and the body is required to achieve homeostasis before this phase can end. For example, when starving, there is only a limited period of time the body can survive without food, and when there are adequate supplies of food and the body's reserves have been revived, the GAS can stop and homeostasis return.

The third stage is called the exhaustion stage, and is only reached when the resistance phase cannot continue further. Within this stage, the body will begin to malfunction and unless homeostasis is returned, then systems within the body will begin to fail which leads ultimately to death.

With the example of starving, once the body's reserves have been exhausted, there will not be sufficient nutrients to provide energy or produce further hormones/secretions, which would lead to death.

The endocrine system shows few development changes throughout the human life cycle, with the exception of reproductive hormones and puberty. Blood and tissue concentrations of many other hormones, such as various thyroid hormones and anti-diuretic hormone, remain relatively unchanged within the body throughout the life-cycle.

Prior to puberty, levels of luteinising hormone (LH), follicle stimulating hormone (FSH) and testosterone (in males) are relatively low. During puberty, levels of these hormones increase which stimulates the ovaries to secrete oestrogens (in females) and the production of sperm (in males).

These hormones also produce secondary sex characteristics, which produce greater physical differences between men and women, than there are between boys and girls. For example, within females, the secondary sex characteristics include development of breasts, promotion of fat distribution to the breasts, abdomen and hips, and affects the distribution of hair.

In males, the secondary sex characteristics include growth of facial and chest hair, enlargement of the larynx and increased sebaceous gland (an oil producing gland in the skin) secretions.

As the body ages, there is a decline in the concentration of the reproductive hormones in both males and females. At approximately 55 years of age, the level of testosterone in males declines which leads to less muscle strength and a decrease in sexual desire and viable sperm. In females, between the ages of 40 and 50, menopause occurs and the ovaries become less responsive to FSH and LH, which leads to a reduction in oestrogen and progesterone.

Within females, pregnancy affects the hormonal balance within the body, which includes an increased secretion of oestrogen and progesterone from the ovaries, and the placenta produces a substance which mimics LH, and as such provides the same effects. Towards the end of gestation, the level of progesterone declines, which allows uterine contractions to begin occurring (progesterone inhibits uterine contractions). Also, oxytocin is secreted from the pituitary gland which stimulates the uterine contractions, and relaxin helps to dilate the cervix and relax appropriate ligaments and joints, ready for labour.

During childhood, as the skeletal structure grows and develops, the thyroid gland produces a hormone called calcitonin (CT) which aids the regulation of calcium (Ca^{2+}) concentrations in body fluids. As calcitonin is secreted, osteoclasts (bone cells involved in re-absorption of bone cells) are inhibited, which slows the rate of calcium release from bone. This hormone helps to stimulate bone growth and mineral deposits in the skeleton. It is also prevalent throughout the life-cycle as this hormone helps to reduce the loss of bone mass as well as controlling calcium levels during pregnancy between the mother and foetus.

ADRENALINE and the FIGHT OR FLIGHT RESPONSE

The human body has an in-built mechanism to enable us to cope with dangerous, life threatening situations. This mechanism is known as the 'fight or flight' response, or 'stress response'. It is an instantaneous reaction to perceived physical threat which mobilises the body to either flee, or become aggressive. In times when danger was ever-present, this was an important survival reaction. However, in modern life, many perceived threats cannot be managed this way. Nevertheless, our endocrine system continues to pump out the hormones it deems necessary when our brains perceive a threat. This can lead to continued stress response, sometimes over long periods of time, resulting in ill health. You can learn more about Psychological research into stress management in unit 4 of this course.

Fight-or-Flight Response

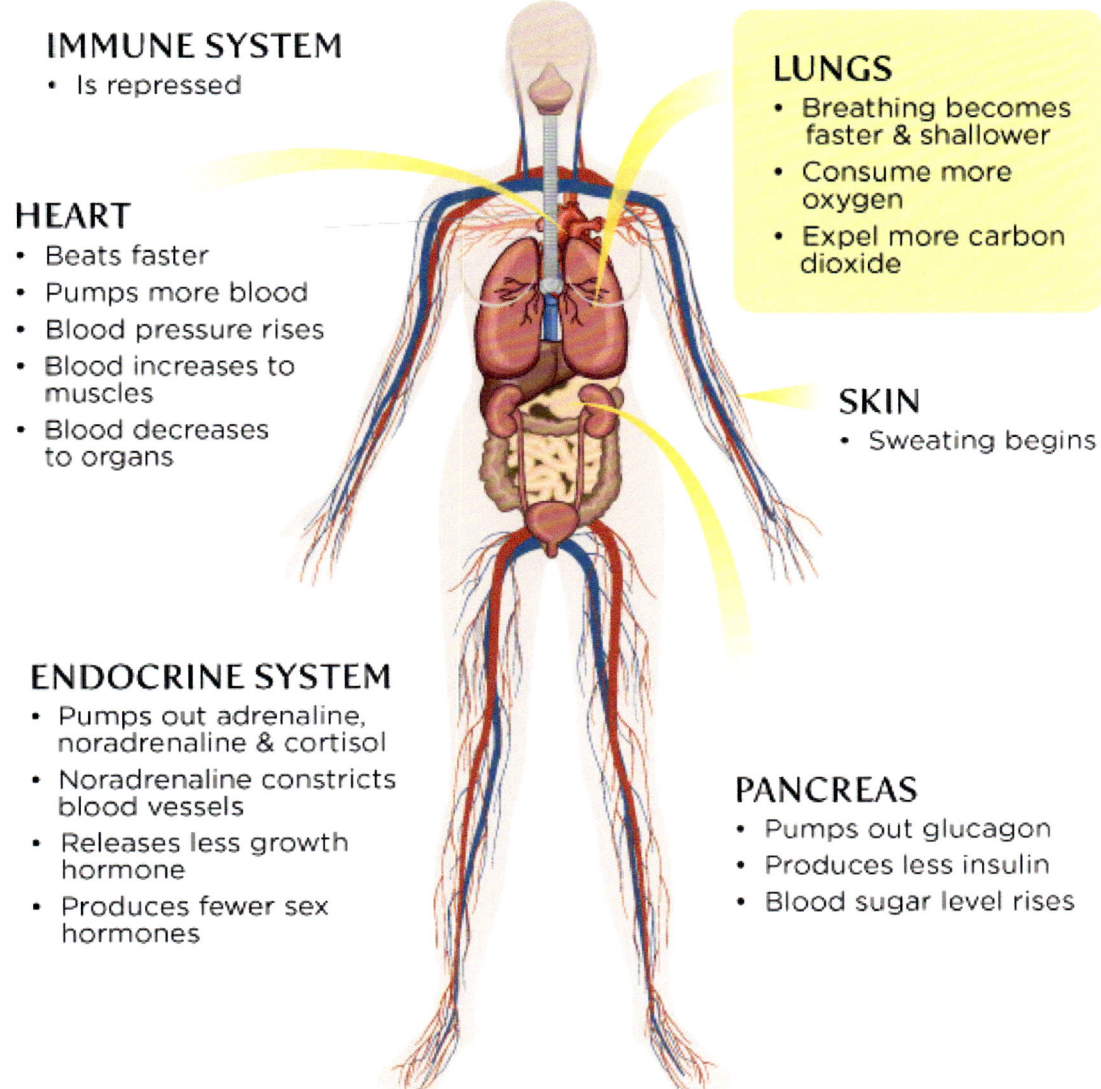

IMMUNE SYSTEM
- Is repressed

HEART
- Beats faster
- Pumps more blood
- Blood pressure rises
- Blood increases to muscles
- Blood decreases to organs

LUNGS
- Breathing becomes faster & shallower
- Consume more oxygen
- Expel more carbon dioxide

SKIN
- Sweating begins

ENDOCRINE SYSTEM
- Pumps out adrenaline, noradrenaline & cortisol
- Noradrenaline constricts blood vessels
- Releases less growth hormone
- Produces fewer sex hormones

PANCREAS
- Pumps out glucagon
- Produces less insulin
- Blood sugar level rises

Neurotransmitters

Serotonin is a neurotransmitter produced by the pineal gland, deep in the centre of the brain. It plays an important role in the control of appetite, sleep, memory and learning, temperature regulation, mood, behaviour, cardiovascular function, muscle contraction, endocrine regulation and depression. It also influences aggressive and violent behaviour.

Circadian Rhythms

The word circadian comes from the Latin words *circa* and *dies* meaning 'around a day'. These rhythms affect the daily physiology and behaviour of both humans and non-human animals. Body temperature, blood pressure and production of cortisol (a hormone produced by the adrenal gland, which mobilises your body to cope with the demands and stresses of everyday life) all reach a peak in the late afternoon and reach their lowest values early in the morning. These patterns persist even if the pattern of activity is reversed. The human body has more than 100 circadian rhythms. Each rhythm follows its own unique 24 hour cycle, but individual rhythms also interact to affect your body's function throughout the day. The circadian rhythm most studied is the sleep-wake cycle.

Keeping Time

The obvious external control mechanism for a 24 hour circadian rhythm is light. We are active during the daylight hours and inactive (asleep) at night. One of the most dramatic observations that light is an important **exogenous zeitgeber** (external time giver) can be seen when there is a solar eclipse; animals and birds are tricked into believing it is night, which is why an eerie silence always seems to accompany the event.

This observation was backed by a case study carried out in 1975 by Michel Siffre, a French geologist and speleologist (a specialist in the science of caves).

Siffre went to live in a cave in Texas for 6 months (179 days). The cave had no natural light, and Siffre could use a telephone to ask for the artificial light to be turned on or off and he could sleep and eat whenever he wanted. His physiological functions, such as heart rate and body temperature, were monitored, as well as his sleep-wake cycle. In the absence of natural light, Siffre's biological rhythms became free running (separated from the natural rhythms of daylight). His days became longer and lasted from 25 to 32 hours. However, his body temperature maintained the same (24 hour) rhythm and became out of sync with his wake-sleep cycle.

Evaluation

This is a one-participant study, so may not be generalisable to all humans. Also, Siffre's living conditions were unusual in other ways than simply lacking time signals, and other factors such as loneliness could have affected his behaviour. In addition, Siffre was allowed to turn on an electric light during his waking hours and this may have delayed his rhythm artificially. Indeed, modern studies with humans completely isolated from artificial light suggest that, although our rhythm has a tendency to run on a little, it is closer to 24 hours than early studies suggest (Czeisler cited in Cromie, 1999). However, supporting evidence comes from Groblewski *et al* (1980) who found that rats exhibit a 25 hour cycle when kept under dim illumination. A strength of the study is that it was conducted over a period of six months, allowing Siffre's rhythms to settle down into a natural pattern.

These experiments show that circadian rhythms are set using light and, therefore, light acts as an exogenous zeitgeber to reset our clocks to a 24 hour rhythm. In the absence of light, these rhythms tend to lengthen; nevertheless, a definite rhythm is still maintained. This must mean that there is an internal control mechanism which maintains the circadian cycle. Biologists have named this mechanism the 'biological clock'.

Activity 28

Joshua is studying for his A-levels. He enjoys college and is a reliable student who completes his work on time. His teacher, however, is fed up with him yawning all through the lesson first thing Monday morning.

1) Using your knowledge of how light affects the sleep-wake cycle, can you suggest why Joshua is so sleepy on Mondays?

2) What could he do to improve the situation?

Answer to activity 28

1) Joshua probably stays up later at the weekends and is exposed to more electric light than he is during the week. This delays the onset of melatonin production and shifts his sleep-wake cycle forwards. This will make it very difficult to get to sleep when he attempts to go to bed earlier on Sunday evening, leaving him fatigued and groggy on Monday morning

2) Joshua should use dim light in the evenings if he is staying up. He should also try not to go to bed much later than he does during the week

The Biological Clock

The search for the location of the biological clock in mammals began in earnest in the 1960s when Curt Richter found that damaging the hypothalamus in rats made them wake, run, sleep and eat at odd times. In other words, their circadian rhythms were destroyed. In 1972, Robert Moore probed this area further using radioactive amino acids. He traced their path along the nerves leading from the eye to the hypothalamus and found they terminated in two tiny, paired nuclei located in the ventromedial hypothalamus just above the optic chiasm (part of the optic nerve where nerve pathways from the retina of each eye cross over to reach the opposite hemisphere of the brain). These paired structures were named the suprachiasmatic nuclei (from *supra* meaning 'above', and *chiasmatic* referring to the optic chiasm) or SCN.

The Biological Clock and Its External Control

The retinae at the back of the eyes contain photoreceptor (light-sensing) cells called rods and cones which enable us to see. In addition, there are retinal ganglion cells also which respond to light and which serve a different purpose other than vision. When these nerve cells are stimulated by light, they relay their signals along the optic nerve to the SCN; the greater the intensity of the light, the stronger the signal. This allows the SCN to initiate adjustments to organs and cells involved in maintaining circadian rhythms. For example, in response to light flooding the bedroom in the morning, the SCN will instruct the pineal gland to switch off melatonin (a chemical which initiates sleep) production so that we can wake to begin a new day. As light levels fall during the evening, it will send signals to begin the production of melatonin once more.

Genetic Mutant Hamsters

Martin Ralph (1988) was a neuroscientist working on circadian rhythms in the golden hamster. This animal has a fairly dependable circadian period of around 24 hours, even if kept in the dark for weeks on end. When a mutant male hamster appeared, therefore, with a circadian period of around 22 hours, it was easy to spot. Further testing and cross breeding experiments by Ralph and his colleagues uncovered a faulty gene (named *tau*) in the 'short period' hamsters. Furthermore, hamsters with one copy of the faulty gene had circadian periods of around 22 hours, while the circadian periods of the hamsters with two copies of the gene were around 20 hours. This mutant strain of hamster provided the researchers with the opportunity to study the effects of transplanting mutant hamster SCNs into normal hamsters. If the normal hamster's circadian rhythm changed as a result of the transplant, there would be considerable evidence that the SCN was indeed the biological clock. Ralph's study is outlined below:

Aims: To establish whether the SCN is the biological clock. Procedure: Normal hamsters had their circadian periods destroyed by removal of the SCN on both sides. They were then transplanted with donor SCNs from the mutant hamster strain.

Findings: After a period of about a week, the recipient hamsters began to show circadian rhythms once again. The key finding is that the newly established rhythm matched the donor hamster and not the normal rhythm with which they were born. If the recipient received an SCN from a mutant hamster with one copy of the faulty gene, its new rhythm was around 22 hours; an SCN with two copies of the gene reset the hamster's rhythm to around 20 hours.

Conclusion: This shows that the SCN is indeed the biological clock.

Evaluation: Although this experiment was carried out on animals, and it is difficult to generalise directly to humans, there is evidence that patients with tumours of the hypothalamus also experience disruption to their circadian rhythms, while elderly people tend to feel sleepy in the early afternoon and to wake early in the morning due to loss of SCN cells with age. Further evidence comes from the observation that animal SCN cells maintain a circadian rhythm in their rate of firing of action potentials, utilisation of oxygen and protein synthesis even when removed from the brain and cultured in a Petri dish.

Infradian Rhythms

Infradian rhythms are defined as an endogenous pattern that has a cycle duration of longer than a day. The female menstrual cycle is an example of an infradian rhythm. It is a cyclical biological event that occurs in a fairly regular pattern on a monthly basis. The average cycle length is 28 days.

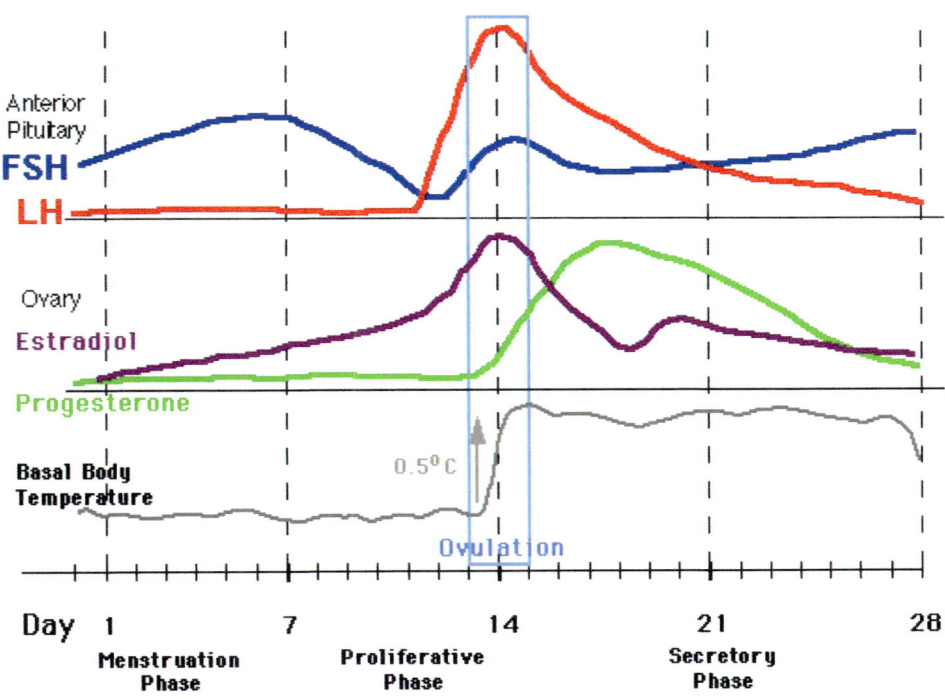

Source: www.mrothery.co.uk/images/Mcycle.gif

Role of Endogenous Pacemakers

Endogenous control of this complex cycle is regulated by a tiny, pea-sized gland, the pituitary gland, which rests in a small bony cavity just under the hypothalamus. The pituitary serves as the **endogenous pacemaker** by regulating the interplay between four important hormones: oestrogen, progesterone, follicle stimulating hormone (FSH) and luteinising hormone (LH). The graph above illustrates a typical menstrual cycle

Day one of a new cycle is the first day of menstruation, and you will see from the graph that most of the hormones during this phase are either level or falling. During this phase, a new follicle is ripening in the ovary. The new follicle secretes oestrogen (estrodiol). As the follicle grows bigger during the proliforative phase, it secretes larger amounts of oestrogen which signals the pituitary to switch off production of FSH so that no new follicles will grow. It also acts on the uterus to make the lining thicker. The rise in oestrogen triggers the release of LH from the pituitary; this LH surge pops the follicle and the ovum (egg) is released in an event called ovulation. The slight rise in FSH at this time is thought to be important for initiating the growth of a new follicle in the subsequent cycle.

After ovulation, the remains of the popped follicle in the ovary become a corpus luteum (yellow body); this body produces large amounts of progesterone. Under the influence of progesterone, the endometrium (uterine lining) changes to prepare for potential implantation of an embryo to establish a pregnancy. If implantation does not occur within approximately two weeks, the corpus luteum will die, causing sharp drops in levels of both progesterone and oestrogen. The drop in these hormone levels causes the uterus to shed its lining in a process termed menstruation. The drop in oestrogen means that FSH production in the pituitary gland is no longer inhibited and so the cycle will begin again.

In the menstrual cycle, changes occur in the female reproductive system as well as other systems (which lead to breast tenderness or mood changes, for example). A woman's first menstruation is termed menarche, and occurs typically somewhere around age 12. The end of the reproductive phase of a woman is called the menopause, which occurs somewhere between the ages of 45 and 55. Medical problems such as anaemia and infertility can be due to disorders of the menstrual cycle.

This model describes the way that the female body would function in a world with fewer external factors to confound natural biorhythms. Nowadays, however, the strictly biological control of our menstrual cycles has been distorted by the effects of exogenous hormones, such as hormone replacement therapy (HRT) and the contraceptive pill, plastics and pesticides, hormones in meat and dairy and the influence of electric lighting on the pineal gland. For instance, oral contraceptives suppress ovarian function by keeping estrodiol artificially high and inhibiting FSH. Also, Miyauchi, F. *et al* (1992) found working the night shift (i.e. nocturnal exposure to artificial light) suppresses ovarian function by altering the circadian rhythm of prolactin and melatonin, leading to irregular periods in women working at night. These are just two examples of the derangement of natural cycles by external influences which are likely to have profound effects on fertility, longevity, and general health.

Role of Exogenous Zeitgebers

There are many historical and cultural references which link ovulation with the full moon. Indeed, it may be no coincidence that the average menstrual cycle is 28 days and the lunar cycle just over 29 days. But could the moon affect the menstrual cycle and if so, how?

The answer could be light. You will recall from your knowledge of the circadian rhythm that light acts as an exogenogenous zeitgeber which resets the biological clock to keep our rhythms in line with a 24 hour day. During hours of darkness, the pineal gland produces melatonin which not only initiates sleep but also inhibits the production of LH required to pop the follicle and bring about ovulation. Therefore, it makes sense that, during a full moon, when there is more light, melatonin levels are lower, the inhibitory effect on LH is released and that, therefore, women are more likely to ovulate during a full moon. This is an interesting notion and explains why ancient people linked the moon with fertility, but is unlikely to have much of an effect in modern times due to our constant exposure to artificial lighting.

However, that light does affect the menstrual cycle is shown in a study carried out in Finland by Kivela *et al* (1988) who measured LH levels in women and found them to be higher in summer months where there are 22 hours of daylight than in winter months where there are only 5 hours of daylight. In a similar study, Wojtowicz and Jakiel (2002) also reported an increase in the number of irregular anovulatory (failure to ovulate) cycles in winter compared to summer.

The role of pheromones as exogenous zeitgebers in the human menstrual cycle has also been studied. Pheromones are natural chemicals which can trigger a behavioural response in other members of the same species. In insects, pheromones attract mates, alert others of danger and signal the location of food. Could human pheromones reset the menstrual cycle? Stern and McClintock (1998) carried out an experiment to find out:

- **Aims:** To see if pheromones taken from donor females could reset the menstrual cycles of recipient females

- **Method:** The researchers collected samples of sweat from a donor female and swabbed them onto the upper lip of other females

- **Findings:** These women's menstrual cycles started to synchronise with that of the donor female

Ultradian Rhythms

Ultradian rhythms are defined as an endogenous pattern that has a cycle duration of shorter than a day. They can be seen in many physiological and behavioural processes, e.g. smoking cigarettes, renal excretion and heart rate. The most widely studied ultradian rhythm is that which occurs during sleep.

<u>A Typical Night's Sleep</u>

Most people don't think very much about what happens during sleep. For most of us, we shut our eyes and open them again approximately eight hours later. However, during sleep, a number of shorter cycles occur during which we experience different types of sleep. These sleep stages can be measured in sleeping volunteers using three different pieces of equipment:

- Electroencephalogram (EEG) – This measures brainwaves
- Electroocculogram (EOG) – This measures eye movements
- Electromyogram (EMG) – This measures muscle tone

Here are the stages involved in a typical night's sleep.

<u>Relaxation</u>

EEG – Normal beta waves (alert brain) replaced by slower, higher amplitude alpha waves. Muscles relaxed. Person feels drowsy.

Stage 1 – Falling Asleep

EEG – Theta waves (irregular, slower)

EMG – Muscles still active

EOG – Eyes closed. Gentle rolling eye movements

Heart rate slows and temperature falls. The eyes are closed during Stage 1 sleep, but if aroused from it, a person may feel as if he or she has not slept. Stage 1 may last for five to 10 minutes. The person may experience fleeting dream-like (hypnagogic) images.

Stage 2 – Light Sleep

EEG – Theta waves with brief bursts of activity (sleep spindles)

EMG - Spontaneous periods of muscle tone mixed with periods of muscle relaxation. Muscle tone of this kind can be seen in other stages of sleep as a reaction to auditory stimuli (e.g. saying the person's name). After about 20 minutes in Stage 2, heart rate slows, and body temperature decreases. At this point, the body prepares to enter deep sleep.

Stages 3 and 4 – Deep Sleep (or Slow-Wave Sleep)

EEG – Delta (slow) waves. Some sleep spindles in stage 3

EMG – Muscles relaxed

EOG – Virtually no eye movement

During Stages 3 and 4, we are extremely unresponsive to the environment and very difficult to wake. Stage 3 is brief. Stage 4 lasts about 40 minutes.

Non-REM Sleep

The period of non-REM sleep (NREM) is comprised of Stages 1-4 and lasts from 90 to 120 minutes, with each stage lasting anywhere from 5 to 15 minutes. Surprisingly, however, Stages 2 and 3 repeat backwards before REM sleep is attained. So, a normal sleep cycle has this pattern: Waking, Stage 1, 2, 3, 4, 3, 2, REM. Usually, REM sleep occurs 90 minutes after sleep onset.

REM

REM sleep is distinguishable from NREM sleep by changes in physiological states, including its characteristic rapid eye movements. Heart rate and respiration speed up and become erratic, while the face, fingers, and legs may twitch.

EEG - Intense dreaming occurs during REM sleep as a result of heightened brain activity

EMG – Muscles paralysed (to prevent us acting out our dreams)

EOG – Rapid eye movements

Because the brain is so active (virtually indistinguishable from an active waking state), yet the muscles are paralysed, REM is often referred to as paradoxical sleep. The first period of REM typically lasts 10 minutes, with each recurring REM stage lengthening, and the final one lasting an hour.

Sleep Cycle

A person completes five cycles of sleep in a typical night. The nature of these cycles is summarised below:

Cycle one: 1 2 3 4 3 2 REM

Cycle two: 2 3 4 3 2 REM

Cycle three: 2   REM

Cycle four: 2   REM

Cycle five: 2   REM

Features:

- Each cycle lasts about 90 minutes
- Stage 3 and 4 sleep only occur in the first two cycles
- Time spent in REM increases as sleep progresses
- The last three cycles consist of alternating cycles of Stage 2 and REM sleep

Research Studies: EEG

Loomis, Harvey and Hobart (1937) used the EEG to record the electrical activity in the brain of a sleeping person for the first time. They found that far from being asleep itself, the brain was highly active during sleep and that certain types of electrical activity seemed to be related to changes in the type of sleep a person was having. They found that the waves got 'bigger' as sleep got 'deeper'.

Eugene Aserinsky (1952) connected his sleeping 8-year-old son to an EEG machine to see if repairs he had carried out to it had been successful. Electrodes were also placed near the child's eyes to try and record the rolling eye movements that were believed to occur during sleep. After a while, the EOG started to record wildly oscillating waves. Aserinsky thought that the machine must still be broken but, after several minutes, the EOG fell silent. These periods of what became known as rapid eye movement or REM continued throughout the night, and when Aserinsky woke his son during these periods he reported that he had been dreaming.

The EEG during these REM periods showed that the brain was highly active as well even though the child was sound asleep. Aserinsky and Kleitman (1953) repeated these observations using adult volunteers and found strikingly similar patterns in all participants observed.

Dement and Kleitman (1957) showed that when people were woken during REM sleep and asked if they were dreaming, more often than not they reported that they were. When they were woken at other times (during what became known as non-REM sleep or NREM), they occasionally reported dream-like experiences but their descriptions lacked the vivid images and themes which characterised periods of REM.

Individual Differences in Ultradian Rhythms

The typical person has around five cycles of sleep a night, each of which lasts on average for around 90 minutes. The exact pattern varies from person to person, and the time between REM and NREM varies between and within people, so as well as distinct individuals differing in terms of their sleep cycles, the pattern changes within the same person from night to night.

Despite individual variations however, there are some consistencies. It seems that, in all humans, Stage 3 and 4 sleep only occurs in the first two cycles and that episodes of REM increase in length over the course of the night.

Some other differences are:

- New-born infants sleep around 16 hours a day~50% of this is REM
- One year-old infants sleep for around 12 hours a day~^{1}/3 of this is REM
- Adults spend ¼ of an eight-hour period in REM
- At 60, Stage 4 sleep has virtually disappeared

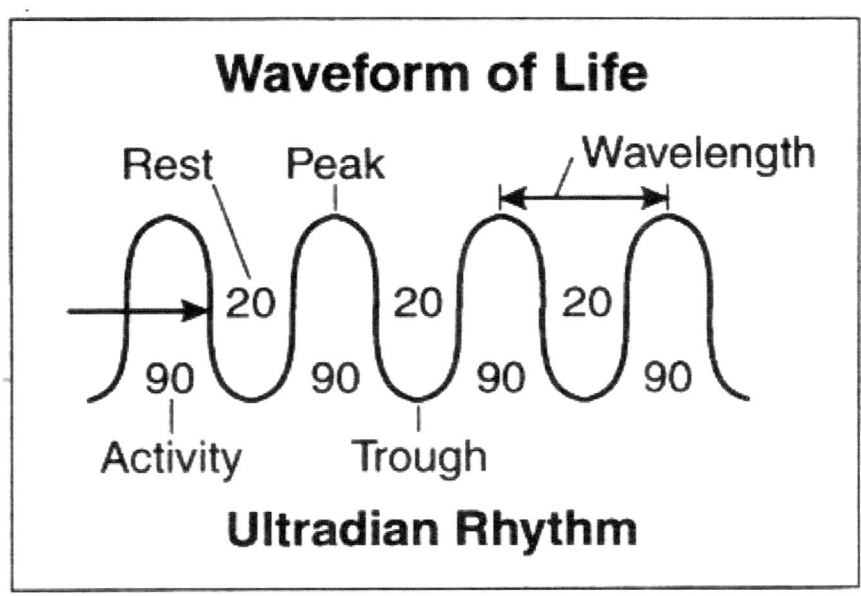

- Objective evidence - The EEG, EOG, and EMG provide objective measures of the physiology of sleep, and have greatly advanced our understanding
- Artificiality of the sleep laboratory - A significant weakness is that such physiological measures are gathered in a sleep laboratory, where the artificial conditions and the fact that research participants are wired up to machines, may affect sleep patterns
- Weaknesses of the self-report method – The self-report method yields subjective data, compared to the objective measurements of the EEG, EOG, and EMG
- Individual differences - Most people have five sleep cycles, which last approximately 90 minutes each. However, there is great variation in sleep patterns, as evidenced by individual differences in the total amount of sleep
- Universality - There are some universal characteristics of sleep

Role of Endogenous Pacemakers

The alternating pattern of NREM and REM sleep that characterises the ultradian rhythm is due to the alternating activity of two small nuclei, the raphe nuclei and locus coeruleus, situated in the brain stem.

A simplified version of endogenous control follows:

- As night falls, melatonin is released from the pineal gland.
- Melatonin acts on the raphe nuclei causing them to release serotonin.
- This brings on slow wave (NREM) sleep and inhibits activity in the locus coeruleous (LC).
- As serotonin is used up, inhibition of the LC ceases allowing it to release acetylcholine (Ach) and noradrenaline both of which are involved in REM sleep.
- Meanwhile, serotonin levels are replenished until they are high enough to, once again, inhibit LC activity. This brings about another NREM cycle.

Evidence

Jouvet (1967) cut out various bits of cats' brains, especially the hypothalamus, to find out which areas were responsible for the various parts of the ultradian rhythm. He found that:

- Lesions to the *raphe nuclei* - Absence of slow-wave sleep
- Removal of the *raphe nuclei* – No sleep
- Lesions to the *locus coeruleus* – No REM sleep
- Lesions to the *pons*, which makes a neurotransmitter called acetylcholine - Reduced REM sleep
- Severing the connection between the *pons and spinal cord* - Cats ran around during dreaming as if they were chasing invisible mice!

Human Studies

- REM sleep is increased in people who take drugs which increase levels of *acetylcholine (Ach)*
- Stoyva and Metcalf (1968) studied people who had been exposed to insecticides which increased *Ach* activity. Those who had been exposed reported increased REM activity

- People who take selective serotonin reuptake inhibitors (SSRIs) for treatment of depression have less REM sleep since the increased serotonin interferes with release of Ach from the LC (Jasper and Tessier, 1969)

Role of Exogenous Zeitgebers

There isn't much of a role for exogenous zeitgebers in the ultradian cycle, apart from the role of light (discussed as part of the section on circadian rhythm) which helps to set the sleep-wake cycle and governs melotonin secretion (melotonin is needed to fall asleep).

Consequences of Disrupting Biological Rhythms

Research into disruption of biological rhythms has centred largely on the circadian rhythm. Disturbances in circadian rhythms occur when we make rapid **phase shifts**. A phase shift is the displacement of a biological rhythm along its time axis, which causes a dissociation between exogenous and endogenous components. An easy way to think of this is when we have to get up at 3.00am to catch a plane. The sensible thing to do is to go to bed at 7.00pm. The problem is that we are not tired at 7.00pm, and our bodies are telling us we should still be active. Melatonin, the hormone we need to initiate sleep, is not active at this time and so it is impossible to get our usual eight hours sleep. This is an example of trying to perform a rapid **phase advance**, where we attempt to set our body clock earlier; the exogenous and endogenous components of our normal rhythm have become desynchronised and we are left feeling irritable and exhausted. Two of the commonest causes of these rapid phase shifts are:

- Shift work
- Long, eastward flights which can give rise to **jet lag**

Shift Work

It is thought that as many as 20% of people living in developed countries work during the night and at varying times from week to week. Unfortunately, this type of work often causes health problems since the exogenous zeitgebers stay the same but workers are forced to adjust their natural circadian rhythm in order to meet the demands of the new work schedule. For the first few days, until their natural rhythms adjust, they are working when their heart and breathing rate, metabolic rate, temperature and cortisol secretion are all at their lowest, since their bodies think it is the middle of the night. Some shift workers report gastrointestinal problems (such as indigestion and nausea), irritability, insomnia and even depression. There are also the social problems associated with shift work leading to the disruption of domestic and family life. These factors, coupled with the medical symptoms, mean shift workers often perform poorly, especially in the first few days of a new shift pattern.

Hawkins and Armstrong-Esther (1978) studied 11 nurses during the first seven nights of a new night shift. They found that performance was significantly impaired on the first night but improved gradually over successive nights. Furthermore, the nurses' body temperature had not fully adjusted to night working after seven nights. They also found individual differences in response to the change in shift pattern; some nurses seemed to adjust very quickly to working nights whilst others never really adjusted at all.

Charles Czeisler (1982) was able to use data from studies such as these, and from his own research on circadian rhythms at Harvard University, to improve workers' health and productivity at a large corporation in Utah. The company worked a three-weekly schedule which rotated between day, night and evening shift.

This pattern not only required workers to make two phase advances (night to evening and evening to day) but the weekly rotation allowed no time for circadian rhythms to adjust. Czeisler recommended rotating the shifts in such a way that they always produced a phase delay (taking advantage of the body's tendency to run on a longer cycle) shifting the biological clock forwards in time rather than backwards. He also favoured spending three weeks in each shift, since most people take more than a week to adjust. The results after Czeisler's intervention were dramatic; workers liked the new schedules, were healthier and made better use of their leisure time. Productivity rose by an astounding 22%. It would appear that many shift patterns that were common in industry did little to take into account the devastating effects on workers of constant and rapid phase shifts, but nowadays, thanks to the work of circadian rhythm specialists such as Charles Czeisler, companies are more adept at using shift patterns which work *with* the circadian rhythm rather than against it.

Activity 29

You are working as an occupational psychologist, and Sam, a shift worker, comes to see you complaining of tiredness and lack of ability to concentrate at work. When he does have leisure time, he feels too tired to do anything much and usually spends it watching television. Here are Sam's shifts:

Week one: 10pm to 6 am

Week two: 6 am to 2 pm

Week three: 2 pm to 10 pm

1) Name two things which are wrong with Sam's current shift pattern

2) Explain how you would change his shift pattern to help overcome his problems

Answer to activity 29

1) Sam's shift pattern is wrong for two reasons. First of all, there is a phase advance between the first two shifts, which will give him typical shift-work symptoms. Secondly, the week in each shift is not long enough to allow his body to adjust to working at the new time.

2) The shifts should be rotated to always produce a phase delay. In other words, Sam should start work later with each new shift.

i.e. 6am to 2 pm

   2pm to 10pm

   10pm to 6 am

He should also stay in each shift for three weeks to allow time for his circadian rhythm to adjust.

Jet Lag

Jet lag is the result of making a rapid phase shift by flying across time zones. It is much worse when flying west to east than east to west. This is because an eastward flight shortens the day (phase advance) whereas a western flight lengthens the day (phase delay). You will recall that it is much easier for the body to cope with a phase delay, due to the natural tendency towards a longer cycle. The symptoms of jet lag include sleep disturbances, irritability, lethargy, drowsiness in the middle of the day and gastrointestinal problems such as indigestion and nausea. Further symptoms can include poor performance on cognitive and physical tasks for a few days, especially after eastward flights; not so useful if you have an important business meeting to attend or you are an athlete travelling to a competition.

A study by Wright *et al* (1983) looked at the effects of travel across time zones (jet lag) on exercise capacity and performance in a group of eighty-one healthy male soldiers, aged 18-34. The soldiers were studied for 5 days before and 5 days after an eastward deployment across six time zones to determine the effects of jet lag on exercise capacity and performance. Measurements of strength in the upper body, leg and trunk muscles were unchanged but performance on running and lifting and carrying exercises were worse for five days after the trip. Performance on a 6.5 m rope climb did not change. These findings suggest there could be more than one biological clock, with each organ in the body having its own rhythm as well as being controlled by the master clock.

Evidence to support this idea comes from work by Hava Siegelmann (2006) in which she and her colleagues analysed the data from years of jet lag experiments on rats. Siegelmann found that rats could endure a four-hour time jump before their internal clocks jumbled and jet lag set in. She also found that although the master clock in the brain could be reset fairly quickly, the individual clocks in the lungs or the liver, for example, can take several days to adjust, explaining why jet lag seems to affect some abilities more than others.

Practical Applications

Research into circadian rhythms has given us a number of possible ways of lessening the effects of jet lag, although these are not always successful, and different techniques work for different people.

Travellers could travel in small steps of no more than four hours and allow time for the entrainment (synchronisation of exogenous and endogenous cues) of their biological clocks before moving on.

They could also pre-adapt their biological clock to the time zone of the destination to which they are travelling by going to sleep a few hours earlier for travelling eastwards and a few hours later for westward flights. However, these solutions are time consuming, awkward and sometimes just out of the question. Therefore, people have begun to look for new means of ridding themselves of jet lag.

One of the simplest ways is for travellers to force themselves to adjust to the new time zone. After an eastward flight, they should set their watch to the new time zone, try and stay up as late as possible and think in terms of what the time actually is, not what it is back home.

A good workout early in the morning after an eastward flight could help with adaptation to the new time zone. Mrosovsky and Salmon (1987) found that hamsters forced to run on a wheel for a period of three hours on the day of an eight hour phase advance in their light-dark cycle, had adapted to the new conditions in one day, whereas those not given exercise adapted gradually over a ten day period.

Exposure to bright light at carefully calculated times of day (depending on how many time zones the traveller is crossing and in what direction) is also useful, as this can help to delay the production of melatonin and therefore help the person to remain awake for longer.

In addition, much research has been done into the use of **chronobiotics**: compounds that are capable of quickly shifting biological clocks and, therefore, useful in alleviating jet lag. Melatonin is used in the USA as a cure for jet lag, although the evidence for melatonin as a chronobiotic is often inconclusive; many individuals find it helps but a similar number find it has little effect. Some studies have shown that travellers given melatonin 3 days before and 4 days after an eastward flight reported little jet lag. Other studies have shown little or no effect. It is possible that in some cases melatonin is reducing jet lag, but this may be because it is acting as a hypnotic and so increasing the amount of sleep during the flight, thereby removing the feelings of fatigue and other symptoms associated with jet lag.

The main problem with melatonin as a cure for jet lag, and any other rhythm disorders, is that long-term toxicological tests have not been carried out on it, so its safety is unknown. At the moment, what seems to be the best way to alleviate jet lag is to try and fit in with the new time zone. Failing that, it seems jet lag will remain an occupational hazard of the long distance flyer.

Activity 30

1) Suggest five things the UK Olympic athletes could have done to help alleviate jet lag when they travelled to the Beijing Olympics in 2008. Beijing's time zone is GMT+8 hours.

1.

2.

3.

4.

5.

2) Explain the possible detrimental effects of jet lag on the athletes' performance.

1) 1. Getting up earlier a few days before the flight. 2. Setting their watches to Beijing time before leaving the airport. 3. Having a good workout on the morning after the flight. 4. Exposing themselves to as much light as possible before and after the flight. 5. Arriving three weeks before competition to allow a new circadian rhythm to become established

2) They could have sleep disturbances and feel fatigued and disorientated. They could also experience gastrointestinal problems for a few days until their circadian rhythms are entrained to the new time. It could also affect their athletic performance and add valuable seconds to their competitive times (Wright, 1983)

Issues Debates and Approaches

Ethics

Much of the work carried out into circadian rhythms uses the **biological approach**, a comparative approach where different species of animal can be studied and compared. This is useful since we can do things to animals that it would be unethical to do to humans. We would not know as much today about the SCN and the circadian rhythm if it were not for early experiments with rats and mice in which SCN tissue was destroyed or transplanted in order to learn more about the biological clock and animals were kept in the dark to discover the role of light as an exogenous zeitgeber.

The biological approach is also useful because it looks at how genes, neurotransmitters and hormones affect behaviour. It can also map specific parts of the brain to certain functions. The discovery that the SCN was the biological clock, for example, has led to treatments for jet lag, seasonal affective disorder (winter depression) and many sleep disorders.

It is also **deterministic** in that it sees the effects of shift work and jet lag as being *caused* by physiological factors alone, when it is well known that some people cope with shift work and jet lag more easily than others. The influence of a person's cognitions, personality and past experiences will all affect their ability to cope. These factors are not taken into account by the biological approach.

In terms of **ethics** regarding the use of non-human animals in research, many of the early studies into the SCN and circadian rhythms involved ablation studies where the SCN was destroyed or studies in which animals were surgically blinded. Clearly, such research would not meet the strict guidelines in place today and would be considered

unethical.

Today, all animal research must be approved by the Home Office and must adhere to the Animals (Scientific Procedures) Act 1986. This law states that animal research must be fully justified, in that the benefits to humans outweigh the suffering of the animals. The Act gives strict rules on how animals should be kept and the level of suffering they should be made to endure, asks that the smallest number of animals possible is used and, finally, only allows animals to be used if alternatives such as tissue culture and computer models are not suitable. Researchers contravening this act can be struck off professional registers and can even receive custodial sentences. For this reason, many of the early animal experiments into circadian rhythms can no longer be replicated and therefore today's researchers have to rely on re-analysing data collected in the past, rather than conducting similar experiments themselves.

Activity 31

It is wise to get as much essay practice as you can before the exam. Each question should take you 30 minutes to complete; you will not only be tested on your knowledge but also on your ability to organise your material to answer the question set.

Consider the following question:

Discuss the role of endogenous pacemakers and exogenous zeitgebers in the circadian rhythm. (25 marks)

The 25 marks available are awarded in the following areas.

AO1 = 9 marks for description of the role of endogenous pacemakers and exogenous zeitgebers.

AO2 = 12 marks for commentary on the significance of the studies you have selected and evaluation of their usefulness in explaining the roles of endogenous and exogenous factors.

AO3 = 4 marks for evaluation or interpretation of research, e.g. interpretation of results and methodological criticisms. Further, to achieve AO2/AO3 marks above basic, you must refer to issues, debates and approaches relevant to this area.

Expectations

The examiner will expect to see a **clear** and **accurate** description of the role of endogenous pacemakers and exogenous zeitgebers in circadian rhythms. To achieve the best marks your description must be accurate and detailed. Remember to include **psychological terms**, describe studies **concisely** and write as clearly as possible.

Evaluation and Analysis

Here, the examiner is looking for your ability to **analyse** (break down into its component parts) the endogenous and exogenous components of the rhythm which you have described. It is time to think about the usefulness of the research by comparing it with the findings of other studies, which may support or refute the work, and take into account any methodological criticisms which may affect the validity or reliability of the study. You may bring in research into 'consequences of disrupting circadian rhythms' but you must make this material **relevant** to the question. In other words, only use it to comment on endogenous and exogenous factors.

Think carefully about approaches, issues and debates to achieve top marks. How useful is the biological approach in this case? Could other factors affect endogenous and exogenous control which can't be explained using this reductionist and deterministic approach? Why could some of the early experiments on non-human animals not be carried out today and how does this affect future research into circadian rhythms? It would be prudent to explain that you are going to focus on the sleep-wake cycle, since much of the research into circadian rhythms has focused on this area.

Organising Material

Make yourself a note table before you attempt your essay. This allows you to organise your material and structure your answer carefully. You can also add information which you remember as you are working. The first column is done for you.

	Endogenous pacemaker	Exogenous zeitgeber
Description/explanation	SCN Location Function Relationship with circadian rhythm and sleep-wake cycle	
Supporting evidence	Richter 1960s Moore 1972 Ralph 1988	
Commentary	Significance of the studies. What do they tell us about the SCN? Support from humans with hypothalamic tumours	
Criticisms	Animal studies: animals not as complex as humans. May be other factors Studies well-controlled Support each other	

Approaches	Biological approach looks at physiology but does not take into account cognitive or emotional factors and the role of past experience	
Issues	Ethics: could not repeat the experiments today to test their reliability and validity; must use alternative methods	
Debates	Many experiments reductionist deterministic	

Essay Skills

When writing the essay, be sure to bear in mind that, in an exam situation, you only have 30 minutes. It is a good idea to practise writing an essay within these time constraints at home. You will probably take a couple of minutes to plan the material you are going to use. That means, in this case, you should aim to spend fourteen minutes each on exogenous pacemakers and exogenous zeitgebers. You should aim to write about three to four sides in this time and to cover each of the three skill areas. Sixteen marks are awarded for AO2/AO3 material, so don't spend too long writing a lengthy description for which only nine marks are available. It is better to describe one study chosen from your note table and then use the other studies as commentary or evaluation.

When you have finished, construct a similar table for the following question:

Describe and evaluate research into the consequences of disrupting circadian rhythms. (25 marks)

The Nature of Sleep

As we have seen in the previous section, sleep is an ultradian rhythm of around eight hours which consists of five stages, each lasting approximately 90 minutes.

Activity 32

Use your ultradian rhythm notes to name the stages of sleep given below:

a) Lasting approximately 30 minutes, this stage is also known as slow wave sleep (SWS) because of the long, slow delta waves of the EEG. The EOG and EMG show very little activity. This is deep sleep from which it is difficult to be woken.   Stage?

b) Lasting approximately 15 minutes, the body relaxes and the individual feels drowsy. The EEG activity is characterised by theta waves. The EOG indicates slow rolling eye movements and the EMG shows reductions in muscle tension. Heart rate and temperature also fall. A hypnagogic state may occur during the transition from wakefulness to sleep in which fleeting dream-like images may be experienced, e.g. the feeling of falling. As this is the lightest stage of sleep, we are easily awakened and may feel as if we have been jolted awake. Stage?

c) Lasting approximately 10 minutes in the first cycle and building up to an hour by the fourth and fifth cycles, this stage is characterised by brain activity which is reminiscent of an alert, waking state during which, if woken, a person reports that they were dreaming. This type of sleep has been called paradoxical sleep because EEG readings show that the brain is very active, while the EMG readings show that the body is paralysed. Stage?

d) Lasting approximately 15 minutes, the EEG activity is characterised by long, slow delta waves (1–5 Hz) with some sleep spindles. The EOG and EMG are the same as Stage 2. Stage?

e) Lasting approximately 20 minutes, the EEG activity is characterised by larger and slower theta waves (4–8 Hz) and high frequency sleep spindles, which are our responses to external stimuli (e.g. noise). The EOG shows little eye movement and the EMG shows the muscles are relaxed. It is still easy to be awakened. Stage?

Answer to activity 32

a) Stage 4

b) Stage 1

c) REM

d) Stage 3

e) Stage 2

Research Studies

Once again, you can review the research studies given in the section on the ultradian rhythm to describe and explain the nature of sleep. These are:

- Loomis, Harvey and Hobart (1937)

- Eugene Aserinsky (1952)

- Aserinsky and Kleitman (1953)

- Dement and Kleitman (1957)

You can also comment on individual differences in sleep, e.g. new-borns spend over 50% of their sleep time in REM, and Stage 4 has virtually disappeared by the time we are over 60.

The physiology of sleep may be useful (endogenous control), and the studies by Jouvet which helped to uncover the parts of the brain involved.

Functions of Sleep

The idea that sleep must serve some function comes from studies on sleep deprivation. It is well known that, in torture, sleep deprivation serves as a tool to dehumanise and disorient individuals who will eventually provide confessions or information just to be allowed to sleep.

Human Studies

In 1959, New York DJ Peter Tripp attempted to set a Guinness world record for sleeplessness to raise money for the March of Dimes charity. For much of the stunt, he sat in a glass booth in Times Square broadcasting 24 hours a day. After a few days, he began to experience sleep deprivation psychosis. He had hallucinations in which he believed that he was an impostor pretending to be the real Peter Tripp! He also saw spiders crawling in his shoes. Remarkably, the hallucinations occurred on a 90 minute cycle corresponding with the time he would have been in REM sleep. As time went on, Tripp also experienced a drop in body temperature. For the last 66 hours, the observing scientists and doctors gave him drugs to help him stay awake.

After reaching the 200 hours, Tripp slept for 24 hours and reported feeling fine. However, his wife claimed that his personality had changed; he was moody, irritable and no longer able to hold down a job. His marriage ended in divorce soon after. To add insult to injury, his record attempt was broken six years later by high school student Randy Gardner, who lasted 11 days and, although he suffered similar effects (e.g. hallucinations) during the sleep deprivation, he recovered with no ill effects.

Evaluation of Human Studies

Such studies make interesting reading but they are not easy to control. For example, although researchers kept Peter Tripp and Randy Gardener awake, they could have taken small cat-naps without the researchers knowing.

Summary

A study which nicely summarises the effects of sleep deprivation is a meta-analysis carried out by Huber-Wiedman (1976). The findings are summarised below:

Nights without sleep	Symptoms
1	Discomfort
2	Urge to sleep, especially between 3 and 5 am when body temperature is lowest
3	Cognitive tasks requiring concentration are seriously impaired, especially if they are repetitive or boring
4	Periods of micro sleep occur and the volunteer becomes irritable and confused. The 'hat phenomenon' occurs. This is a tightening around the head which feels like wearing a hat that is too small
5	May become delusional
6	Person becomes depersonalised with a loss of self identity (sleep deprivation psychosis), hand tremors, droopy eye-lids, difficulty focusing the eyes and increased sensitivity to pain

Animal Studies

Rechtschaffen *et al* (1983) studied sleep deprivation in rats.

Aims:

To discover if sleep deprivation is harmful.

Procedure:

Each rat was placed on a rotating disc which protruded from a small bucket of water. An EEG machine monitored the rat's brain activity. When the rat showed brain activity that would indicate sleep, the disc would rotate, making the animal work to stay on the disc and avoid falling off into the water. Consequently, the animal was denied sleep. As a control, another rat was present on the disc. However, when this rat's brainwave activity showed sleep, the disc did not rotate, allowing it to sleep normally.

Findings:

After 33 days, all of the sleep-deprived rats had died. Post-mortems performed on the dead rats were inconclusive but researchers did notice that the sleep deprived animals seemed unable to regulate their own body temperatures, and this got worse as time went on.

Comments

Animal studies are useful but they tell us little about the effects of sleep deprivation in humans. Even when humans attempt to go without sleep, the hallucinations they experience demonstrate that the need for REM sleep is so strong that the brain will still attempt to snatch it, even if the person is awake. Furthermore, it is difficult to separate the effects of sleep deprivation from the effects of stress caused by the methods used to keep the animals awake.

However, a case study came to light in 1992 which answered this question. High school music teacher Michael Corke suffered from a condition known as **Fatal Familial Insomnia**. Damage to the part of his thalamus, which controls sleep, sensory and motor functions, caused him to go without sleeping at all for six months, despite doctors prescribing high doses of barbiturates and sedatives.

During the six months, his condition deteriorated. He lost the ability to maintain his body temperature, lost his centre of gravity and could not perform even the most basic cognitive tasks. Eventually, he slipped into a coma and died.

Studies such as this prove, irrefutably, that sleep is necessary for normal functioning.

Theories of Sleep

There are two main theories of sleep.

Evolutionary Theories:

- Sleep helps to protect us from harm at night
- Sleep helps us to conserve energy

Restoration Theory:

- Sleep helps us to repair damage done to our bodies during the day
- Sleep restores the brain's levels of neurotransmitters

Evolutionary Theories

Evolutionary explanations of sleep are based on the assumption that animals have evolved particular sleep patterns because it is **adaptive**; in other words, it increases their chances of survival in the specific ecological niche they occupy. The niche an animal occupies refers to its method of food gathering (e.g. herbivore or carnivore, predator or prey), the place it lives (e.g. in a burrow or in trees), its metabolism (whether it must eat often or little) and whether it is active during the day or night.

Protection from Harm (Meddis, 1975)

Meddis believes that sleep evolved to keep animals safe from predators at times when foraging for food was not productive i.e. at night time (for humans). However, he also recognises the importance of the predator/prey status of the animal. For example, lions are not predated upon and therefore can afford to sleep for long periods, whereas the prey species such as sheep and cattle must stay awake to remain vigilant. Of course, the theory could also predict that sheep and cattle would remain asleep for much of the day to stay out of harm's way. However, since they are herbivores, they must constantly graze to get enough food.

Evaluation of Meddis' theory

This theory can explain why some prey animals sleep a lot and others sleep very little. It is, therefore, non-falsifiable. Another problem with the theory is that sleeping is a risky activity that puts us in a very vulnerable position. Therefore, if protection from harm was the only reason for sleep, it would surely be better to adopt a strategy which allowed us to stay out of harm's way but remain vigilant. During a lot of sleep time we are 'paralysed and senseless' (Blakemore, 1988), and the inevitable vulnerability this causes seems at odds with evolutionary survival. Sleep can also be dangerous in other respects, as these two dolphin examples illustrate:

- The Indus dolphin is at constant risk from being hit by logs and other big river debris being swept down the River Indus. Clearly, loss of consciousness is life threatening since it means loss of vigilance. However, despite this, it still grabs quick naps of a few seconds at a time (Pilleri, 1979)
- The Bottlenose dolphin sleeps with one hemisphere of its brain at a time so it can remain partly conscious and return to the surface to breathe (Mukhametov, 1984).

Clearly sleep in these animals is not characterised by the muscle paralysis that occurs in humans. The fact that the animals illustrated above go to extraordinary lengths to sleep, indicates that it must serve some function other than simply to keep us out of harm's way.

Conservation of Energy (Webb, 1982)

A variation on Meddis is the Hibernation Theory, which also sees sleep as an adaptive behaviour, but this time designed to conserve energy. It compares sleep to hibernation. During hibernation, body temperature falls and the animal becomes inactive as a way of conserving energy when food is scarce. The more at risk we are from predators, the longer we will sleep. Other factors will also affect the time spent sleeping such as the time we need to spend each day searching for food. Again, in the case of early human species, night time would have been an unproductive period when we would have been unable to forage. Sleep would have been one way of conserving our resources by lowering our metabolic rate. According to Webb, sleep in humans is a hangover from our more vulnerable evolutionary past.

Evaluation of Webb's Theory

Meddis criticises the theory on the grounds that it is simplistic. According to Meddis (as seen above), the amount of time spent sleeping is a compromise between protecting from danger and dietary requirements.

In fact, sleep provides little in the way of conservation of energy. Just being inactive at night would save almost as much energy but without the added danger of loss of vigilance. It is estimated that the calories we save by sleeping, rather than simply resting, is equal to the calories in a slice of bread! This theory would also suggest that animals which do not use much energy during the day would need to sleep less, yet the giant sloth, a large inactive animal, sleeps for about 20 hours a day.

Research Evidence

A study by Lesku *et al* (2006) illustrates the complex relationship between an animal's body mass, brain mass, basal metabolic rate (BMR), sleep-exposure index (safety of sleep site) and trophic position (herbivore/carnivore). It also nicely demonstrates why both Meddis' and Webb's theories are inadequate at explaining why animals sleep.

Lesku's study found that:

- Brain mass was positively correlated with REM sleep, but has no relationship with NREM

- The more dangerous the sleeping site, the less REM sleep (a negative correlation between the sleep exposure index and REM)
- Herbivores generally had less total sleep and less REM sleep than carnivores
- Basal metabolic rate (BMR) is negatively correlated with NREM and total sleep time. Note that this contradicts studies by Zepelin and Rechstaffen (1974), possibly due to different ways of calculating BMR. Savage and West (2007) suggest that it is the brain's BMR that is significant

There are, however, certain methodological problems with correlational study. Strong correlations can indicate a relationship between variables, but they cannot establish cause and effect. The study has high ecological validity, as many of the animals were originally studied in their natural environment. Meta-analysis of this type raises no ethical issues.

Summary:

Lesku *et al* show that a range of factors determine the sleep patterns of different species and that these factors need to be considered separately for different species.

Problems with Evolutionary Theories

Evolutionary theories fail to explain:
- The physical and psychological effects of sleep deprivation
- The fact that some animals and humans die without sleep (Rechtschaffen, Michael Corke)
- The complex nature of sleep, which has five stages including different types of sleep (i.e. NREM and REM)
- Lifespan changes in sleep

Restoration Theory (Oswald, 1980)

Oswald (1980) suggests that sleep restores both mind and body. NREM sleep helps to restore the body and repair damage whereas REM sleep helps to replenish neurotransmitters in the brain.

According to Oswald, NREM sleep is a time for replenishing the body. He points out that most NREM sleep, especially Stages 3 and 4, occur at the start of the night when the body is most tired. During Stages 3 and 4, we secrete greater levels of growth hormone into the blood, which would help in the repair process. We do know that many restorative functions appear to occur during sleep, for example digestion, removal of waste from muscles etc. and protein synthesis for repair and growth. However, these processes also occur whilst we are awake.

Support for this idea is provided by Shapiro (1981) who studied ultra-marathon runners after completing a 57 mile run. It was found that they slept for 90 minutes longer than usual for the next two nights. REM sleep decreased, whilst Stage 4 of quiet or NREM sleep increased dramatically from 25% of the night's sleep to 45%. That REM sleep is necessary for brain repair, and restoration is supported by the observation that REM sleep makes up 50% of the total sleep time in new-borns (who are making vast numbers of new neural connections) but falls to 25% of the total sleep time as the child grows.

Further support for this view comes from laboratory studies of REM deprivation. Dement (1960) deprived volunteers of either REM or NREM sleep and observed the consequences. He found that the effects of REM deprivation were most dramatic with participants becoming more aggressive and having very poor concentration. He also reported REM rebound effects in which participants would try and catch up on lost REM sleep by going straight into REM when allowed to go back to sleep.

By the seventh night, Dement reported that participants were averaging 26 attempts per night to enter REM. After the procedure, when they were allowed an uninterrupted night's sleep, they spent much longer in REM. This is known as REM rebound.

Furthermore, Stern and Morgane (1974) point out that anti-depressant drugs, such as SSRIs, remove REM sleep in those who take them, sometimes for many months. However, once people stop taking the drugs they do not have REM rebound. This is because the drugs increase levels of serotonin and dopamine that are normally replenished by REM sleep. Since they have increased levels anyway, they don't need REM sleep and do not experience REM rebound.

Evaluation of Restoration Theory

Activity 33

Oswald's Restoration Theory neatly answers the question 'Why is there more than one type of sleep?' since it gives different functions for NREM and REM sleep. Read the following research study summaries and decide which findings support or refute Oswald's restoration theory.

a) Empson (1989) found that fibrositis sufferers experience an acute lack of Stage 4 sleep. Fibrositis is a chronic back condition where the patient experiences severe inflammation and pain of the back muscles and their sheaths. He also found that people who are deprived of Stage 4 sleep, experience symptoms which are similar to those found in fibrositis sufferers.

b) Kales et al (1974) found that insomniacs suffer from far more psychological problems than healthy people

c) Empson and Clarke (1970) found that participants who heard unusual phrases before bedtime, remembered more than those who heard the same phrases but were then deprived of REM sleep. Participants deprived of the same amount of NREM sleep remembered more than REM-deprived participants

d) REM sleep requires the expenditure of energy. During REM sleep, blood flow to the brain increases and the temperature of the brain is elevated. Such activity would actually prevent high levels of protein synthesis needed for neurogenesis

e) Ryback and Lewis (1971) asked healthy individuals to spend six weeks resting in bed. They found no changes to their normal sleep patterns during this period

f) Prolonged increases in REM sleep have been found in patients who have undergone intensive electro-convulsive therapy. These increases are consistent with the estimated time for the half-life of proteins in the brain

In a six-week period, about half the brain's total protein is replaced and this is the approximate length of the increased REM period

g) Cell repair goes on 24 hours-a-day but reaches a peak at nigh

Answers to activity 33

a) Supports

b) Supports

c) Supports

d) Refutes

e) Refutes

f) Supports

g) Refutes

Horne's Theory

Horne has adapted Oswald's Restoration Theory. He believes there is little evidence for the restoration of the body during sleep and that:

- REM and deep NREM are essential for normal brain function. Horne calls this **core sleep**
- Light NREM sleep serves no function. Horne calls this **optional sleep**
- The restoration of the body doesn't take place during sleep but during relaxed periods of wakefulness during the day

Evidence

Horne and Pettitt (1985)

Aims: To see if incentives help participants overcome the effects of sleep deprivation

Procedure:

G1 72 hour sleep deprivation

G2 72 hour sleep deprivation + incentives

G3 no sleep deprivation or incentives

All groups tested on auditory tone discrimination task

Findings: G2 performance was as good as control after one night of sleep deprivation. After two nights, still performed significantly better than G1.

Conclusion: Sleep deprivation initially affects our motivation to perform a cognitive task but when motivation is provided, effects of sleep deprivation are minimised.

Methodological Issues: Small group sizes, therefore difficult to generalise; no checking to see if participants were having microsleeps; no control group with incentive but no sleep deprivation

Comments

There is a lack of convincing evidence that NREM restores the body. Horne's theory neatly explains the findings of Ryback and Lewis (1971) who found no change in the sleep patterns of individuals resting in bed for six weeks. If NREM sleep is so important for restoration of the body, one would expect to see less NREM sleep in these participants, since they were not taking exercise.

Horne therefore provides a more convincing explanation for the function of sleep.

Issues Debates and Approaches

Much of the work carried out into functions of sleep uses the **biological approach**, a comparative approach where different species of animal can be studied and compared. As we have seen, this is useful since we can do things to animals that it would be unethical to do to humans. We would not know as much about the effects of total sleep deprivation if it were not for early experiments with rats using the technique described by Rechtschaffen *et al* (1983). However, some claim that the techniques used in such experiments are so stressful for the animals that it is impossible to rule out effects caused by the techniques themselves. By today's standards, such approaches are seen as unethical, so it is not possible to replicate them.

The **evolutionary approach** uses less invasive techniques since it observes animals in their natural habitats or in captivity (i.e. in zoos). However, merely being present in an animal's natural habitat can disturb its natural behaviour, and behaviour in captivity may not be the same as behaviour in the wild.

The evolutionary approach is often seen as **reductionist** although it has recently broadened out to include a variety of ecological and physiological variables which could influence sleep patterns. It is therefore no longer reductionist in its outlook. Psychology aims to be scientific, generating hypotheses which can be tested and falsified. Early evolutionary theories of sleep such as those by Meddis and Webb could explain both why animals slept a lot or very little. Such theories are **non-falsifiable** since they are very difficult to test precisely. The restoration theory of sleep lends itself to specific hypotheses which can be tested. Studies based on these hypotheses can be well-controlled and generate findings which lead to conclusions. Such conclusions help to refine and further sleep research.

Disorders of Sleep

Sleep disorders can be divided into two distinct categories:
- Dyssomnias, e.g. insomnia and narcolepsy
- Parasomnias, e.g. sleep walking and nightmares

Insomnia

Insomnia involves problems in falling asleep, staying asleep and with poor quality of sleep, so that people suffer from daytime tiredness.

To provide a diagnosis of insomnia, practitioners ask patients questions about how many times they wake at night and how long it takes to fall asleep. Practitioners will also ask the patient how long they have had symptoms and how often it occurs.

Morin *et al* (1999) have provided the following definition of clinical insomnia. For insomnia to be diagnosed, one or more of the following must be present:
- Sleep onset latency (time taken to fall asleep) of more than 30 minutes
- Sleep efficiency (time in bed actually spent asleep) of less than 85%
- Increased number of night-time awakenings
- Symptoms occurring three or more times a week

Additionally:

- Transient insomnia lass less than a week. It is often due to a particular cause, such as jet lag or exam stress
- Short-term insomnia lasts for between one and four weeks
- Chronic or clinical insomnia lasts for more than one month and has a significant effect on daytime work and social functioning as a result of tiredness and irritability

Practitioners also make a distinction between:

- Primary insomnia
- Secondary insomnia

Primary Insomnia

Primary insomnia is sleeplessness that has no underlying medical, psychiatric, or environmental cause (such as drug abuse or medications).

It is characterised by the following:

- A 1 month or longer history of at least one of the following: a) difficulty initiating or maintaining sleep or b) non-restorative sleep
- Sleep disturbance (or associated daytime fatigue) causing significant reduction in day-to-day functioning

Idiopathic Insomnia

- Often begins in early childhood
- People with idiopathic insomnia often have difficulties with attention, concentration or hyperactivity
- Emotionally, people with childhood-onset insomnia are often repressors, denying and minimising emotional problems
- Individuals often show atypical reactions, such as hypersensitivity or insensitivity, to medications
- Insomnia tends to persist over the entire life span and can be aggravated by stress or tension

Lifelong sleeplessness is attributed to an abnormality in the neurological control of the sleep-wake cycle involving areas of the brain responsible for wakefulness and sleep. Possibly, the sleep system possesses a lesion (change due to disease) that predisposes the person towards arousal. There is also some evidence that idiopathic insomnia has a genetic basis (ICSD, 2005).

Secondary Insomnia

Secondary insomnia differs from primary insomnia in that a specific condition can be identified as the *cause* of the sleep problem.

Some examples of secondary insomnia are:

- **Sleep apnoea** - A sleep disorder caused by difficulty breathing during sleep. Persistent, loud snoring and frequent long pauses in breathing during sleep, followed by choking or gasping for breath are the main signs of sleep apnoea. It is often associated with dry mouth and headaches in the morning. Two types exist:
  - **Obstructive type** caused by narrowing of the airways due to enlargement of tissue at the back of the throat. Occurs most often in those who are overweight and in those who smoke or drink alcohol
  - **Central type** often associated with malfunctions in the brains control of breathing and heat function
- **Sleep-wake schedule** or **circadian rhythm disorders** are sleep disorders caused by having sleep-wake schedules that do not match up with your natural sleep schedule. People who work the night shift may suffer from this problem
- **Insomnia due to medical conditions** - Many common medical problems and the drugs that treat them can cause insomnia, including allergies, arthritis, heart disease, hypertension, asthma, Parkinson's disease, attention deficit hyperactivity disorder or hyperthyroidism. Physical discomfort (e.g. chronic pain) may also cause problems sleeping

- **Insomnia due to an emotional problem** - Insomnia can be a symptom of a number of emotional difficulties, e.g. depression or anxiety
- **FFI (Fatal Familial Insomnia)** - See the case of Michael Corke described earlier in this chapter

Explanations for Insomnia

Research Evidence

It is well known that people suffering from depression and anxiety are more likely to suffer from insomnia. The following study looks at family conflict, anxiety and insomnia.

Gregory *et al* (2006)

Aims: To see if insomnia is related to family conflict and therefore, anxiety and depression.

Procedure: Longitudinal study, children, New Zealand. Assessed on family conflict using questionnaires to measure levels of tension, hostility and distress.

Findings: Family conflict at age 15 significantly correlated with frequency of insomnia at age 18.

Conclusion: Demonstrates possible link between family conflict and later sleep problems. Possibly due to increases in levels of anxiety and tendency to worry about family difficulties.

Methodological issues: Large sample but gender biased (mostly females). Correlational, therefore difficult to establish cause and effect. Possible links with some other factor causing both family conflict *and* insomnia.

Other Explanations for Insomnia

There are many additional causes of insomnia. Unfortunately, for some patients the stress of knowing that they need to get to sleep at night can cause them to become very tense. This distress therefore contributes to their wakefulness. These patients may benefit from CBT to help them identify and challenge their faulty cognitions.

Other patients may find that their bedtime routine has become associated with insomnia. In other words, they have learned or become conditioned to associate going to bed with sleeplessness. These patients can be helped by Stimulus Control Therapy, which can help them to break this conditioning. In this therapy, patients are encouraged to only go to bed when they feel sleepy and to avoid undertaking other tasks such as reading or answering emails in the bedroom.

Psychologists have also looked at genetic and personality factors to explain insomnia. Clinical anxiety is a personality factor that may contribute to insomnia and neuroticism is highly correlated with insomnia (Heath *et al*, 1998). Anxious people are in a constant state of physiological arousal, and they may benefit from learning relaxation techniques (such as muscle relaxation) and from CBT that aims to reduce their general anxiety.

Genetic factors may also regulate sleep, and recent research has looked into the role of 'clock genes' in regulating the sleep-wake cycle. Indeed, some people are 'larks' (who feel most awake early in the morning) and some are 'owls' (who feel more awake in the evening). This is known as **chronotype** and it is genetically determined. It is therefore important to work with your natural lark or owl tendencies, rather than against them.

Activity 34

Melissa is 17 and suffers from insomnia. She is worried about the lack of quality of sleep she is experiencing as she is studying for her A-levels and often feels so sleepy in class that she finds it very hard to concentrate.

Melissa usually catches up on her favourite soaps when she comes in from school so she leaves her homework until a couple of hours before bed. She often feels quite sleepy during this time so she will have four or five cups of coffee to help her concentrate. Melissa feels tired when she goes to bed but she never manages to get the eight hours she believes she needs to cope with the following day. The more she worries about not getting enough sleep, the more she lays awake. It takes her a long time to get to sleep and she wakes feeling exhausted in the morning.

Use your notes to diagnose Melissa's insomnia and come up with a treatment plan to help improve her situation.

Melissa needs to adopt better sleep hygiene habits. She should do her work as soon as she gets in from school to prevent over-arousal later in the evening. She should avoid stimulants such as caffeine for the last couple of hours before bed and must try to think differently about the amount of sleep she needs. For example, she may not actually need eight hours sleep, and worrying about this will only cause her to experience anxiety which will in turn keep her awake. If she still has difficulties after trying these methods, it may be worth discussing things with her G.P. who may prescribe drugs to help her sleep or a course of cognitive-behavioural therapy.

Other Sleep Disorders

Narcolepsy

Narcolepsy is a condition where normal elements of sleep, specifically elements of REM (Rapid Eye Movement) or dream sleep, suddenly occur during a person's wakeful state.

Main Symptoms:

- Excessive daytime sleepiness and falling asleep suddenly
- Sleep paralysis, a frightening symptom considered to be an abnormal episode of REM sleep atonia (loss of muscle tone) where the patient suddenly finds himself unable to move for a few minutes, most often upon falling asleep or waking up
- Hypnagogic hallucinations in which patients experience dream-like auditory or visual hallucinations while dozing or falling asleep
- Cataplexy, a pathological equivalent of REM sleep atonia unique to narcolepsy, is a striking, sudden episode of muscle weakness triggered by emotions. Typically, the patient's knees buckle and may give way upon laughing, elation, surprise or anger. In other typical cataplectic attacks the head may drop or the jaw may become slack. In severe cases, the patient

might fall down and become completely paralyzed for a few seconds to several minutes. Reflexes are abolished during the attack

These attacks can last for seconds or many minutes and can occur many times a day.

Schoolchildren with narcolepsy may become the focus of ridicule and bullying in school, and it becomes difficult for them to engage in usual school activities and study. Later in life, it can affect someone's education, relationships and career prospects. Consequently, someone with narcolepsy often also has low self-esteem, depression and relationship problems.

Explanations for Narcolepsy

Narcolepsy in humans and dogs seems to be the result of lack of a brain chemical called hypocretin (orexin). This was confirmed in humans by Thannickal, Moore and Niehuis (2000). Indeed, when orexin is injected into the areas of the brain involved with sleep, REM increases. In dogs, a defective gene is responsible for the lack of orexin. In humans, however, narcolepsy is not entirely inherited, and monozygotic (identical) twins have only a 30% higher concordance rate than dizygotic twins (who develop from two eggs). This suggests that environmental factors are also important is understanding narcolepsy. Currently, narcolepsy is treated with stimulant drugs such as methylphenidate.

Sleepwalking

Sleepwalking (somnambulism) is a parasomnia that causes people to get up and walk during their sleep. Sleepwalking can occur at any age but is most common in children, with the first episodes usually between the ages of four and eight years. Sleepwalking disorder is seen in only 1–5% of children and occurs more frequently in boys. Adults who sleepwalk typically have a history of sleepwalking that stems back to childhood.

Episodes of sleepwalking typically occur when a person is in the deep stages of NREM sleep. The sleepwalker is unable to respond during the event and does not remember sleepwalking. In some cases, sleepwalking is associated with incoherent talking.

Symptoms

Episodes of sleepwalking can range from quiet walking about the room to agitated running or attempts to 'escape'. Typically, the eyes are open with a glassy, staring appearance as the person quietly roams the house. On questioning, responses are slow, absent or incoherent. If the person is returned to bed without awakening, the person usually does not remember the event.

Explanations

One theory, popular until the 1960s, was that sleepwalkers were acting out dreams caused by deeply suppressed anxieties or psychic trauma. But research conducted in sleep laboratories has shown that it occurs in the slow-wave, 'deep sleep' period and not in the rapid eye movement (REM) phase of sleep, which is when we dream.

Genetics

Sleepwalking occurs more frequently in identical twins, and is 10 times more likely to occur if a first-degree relative has a history of sleepwalking. Therefore, it is thought the condition can be inherited.

Environmental Factors

Certain factors which cause a person to be temporarily aroused during sleep may cause a person to sleepwalk. Some examples are:

- Sleep deprivation
- Unfixed or chaotic sleep schedules
- Stress
- Alcohol intoxication
- Drugs such as sedatives/hypnotics (drugs that promote relaxation or sleep), neuroleptics (drugs used to treat psychosis), stimulants (drugs that increase activity) and antihistamines (drugs used to treat symptoms of allergy)

Medical Conditions

Medical conditions that have been linked to sleepwalking include:

- Arrhythmias (abnormal heart rhythms)
- Fever
- Gastroesophageal reflux (food or liquid regurgitating from the stomach into the food pipe)
- Night-time asthma
- Night-time seizures (convulsions)
- Obstructive sleep apnoea
- Psychiatric disorders, for example, post-traumatic stress disorder, panic attack, or dissociative states.

So far there hasn't been much research looking at the causes of sleepwalking. One problem has been the difficulty getting people to sleepwalk while they're asleep in sleep laboratories being observed by researchers. When they do, EEGs don't show much except that the brain state is similar to slow-wave sleep.

A more recent theory is that sleepwalking is a state of incomplete arousal – a twilight zone between sleep and waking – caused when someone who should be asleep is prematurely aroused.

Pilon *et al* (2008) at the University of Montreal conducted an experiment in a sleep lab on a group of 10 known sleepwalkers and 10 non-sleepwalkers.

Aims: To look at the impact of sleep deprivation and forced arousals on sleepwalking.

Procedure: They observed both groups in a period of normal sleep, and during a period of deeper-than-normal sleep, after the participants had been kept awake for 25 hours. Both groups were subjected to intermittent loud noises while sleeping.

Findings: The noises had no effect on the non-sleepwalkers; they kept sleeping. But the noises caused three of the first group to sleepwalk during the normal sleep, and all 10 to sleepwalk during the deeper sleep that followed sleep deprivation.

Conclusion: This supports the idea that sleepwalking is caused, or at least triggered, by sleep deprivation, caused for example by a disruption to normal sleep patterns by the external environment.

Comments: This would explain why sleepwalking is more common in shift-workers and other people whose sleep is frequently disrupted, and in people who have medical conditions that interfere with sleep.

It also explains why treatments such as psychotherapy and sedatives don't work very well as treatments for sleepwalking. A more sensible approach, the researchers say, is to minimise sleep deprivation, maintain regular sleep cycles, and avoid potential disturbances during sleep.

Evaluation: Limited sample, lab conditions could have affected normal sleep patterns, making sleepwalking more likely. Nevertheless, the study provides a good explanation for the disorder.

2.3 Research Methods

Paper 2: Compulsory Content

Key Areas

- Experimental Methods
- Observational Techniques
- Self Report Techniques
- Correlations
- Content analysis
- Case Studies

Introduction

In this section, we will look at choosing research methods and designing experiments, scientific processes, techniques of data handling, data analysis and the strengths and limitations of them all. We will look at different types of research such as laboratory and field experiments, and we will learn about different types of experimental design. We will then consider observational and correlational methods and look at interviews, questionnaires and case studies.

Experimental Method

There are 3 main types of experimental methods. They are:

- Laboratory experiments

- Field Experiments

- Quasi (natural) experiments

The Experimental (Laboratory) Method

An experiment is the most rigorous of all techniques used in psychology. This is because the experimenter has full control over the independent variable (IV) which can be manipulated to produce a change in the dependent variable (DV) and has the best chance to control extraneous variables. A good way to achieve this within an experiment is to have a control group which remains untreated. The control group provides a baseline against which to measure the findings.

Laboratory experiments are conducted under controlled conditions where the environment and variables are controlled making it easier to measure the outcomes of the experiment and in some instances, to replicate it.

Field Experiments

The field experiment meets all the criteria for an experiment but is carried out in a natural setting. This means that the researcher cannot control the extraneous variable to the same extent as in a laboratory setting. The advantages of field experiments are that they often have higher levels of ecological validity and reduced demand characteristics. However, participants are often not allocated randomly, and there is less control over the extraneous variables.

Natural Experiments/Quasi-experiments

The researcher uses pre-existing conditions (such as age, sex etc.) and takes advantage of naturally occurring events that the researcher has no control over. An example is the adoption studies of Heston (1966) which compared incidents of schizophrenia in children of schizophrenic parents who were adopted before the age of one month, with children of parents without schizophrenia raised in their own home.

Such studies have the advantage of being able to study situations that it would not be ethical to set up but can be utilised as they happen which makes them as a research methodology quite common in psychology. The main disadvantage is that the experimenter has no control over allocation of participants to conditions. Therefore, internal validity is low.

Observational Techniques

These focus on naturally occurring behaviour. There are many different types of observational study. The two being focused on here are:

- Naturalistic observation - Naturalistic observation involves the researcher observing behaviour as it occurs in the natural environment. The observer has no control over the experiment and cannot manipulate the IV. However, it does have high ecological validity and overcomes the artificial environment of the laboratory

- Controlled observation - Controlled observation is observational study in which the researcher attempts to control certain variables in order to be able to observe behaviour under a certain set of circumstances. In the 'Strange Situation', Ainsworth (1970) performed a controlled observation to look at attachment behaviour in infants

Methods of Observation

Participant observation	Observer joins and becomes part of the group being observed. Therefore, the observer participates in the activity being observed.
Non-participant observation	Observer remains outside the group being observed. Unlike the above form of observation, here the observer is somewhat detached and does not participate in any way.

Disclosed observation/Covert obs.	Participants aware they are being observed. The researcher/observer does not inform the subjects of the observation e.g. Bandura's 1961 Bobo doll study.
Undisclosed observation/Overt obs.	Participants unaware they are being observed. Here the researcher conducting the observation makes this known to those being observed. So, the researcher is open about their intentions e.g. Williams (1986) and his study of the media and anti-social behaviour.
Structured observation/Controlled	Researcher determines precisely what types of behaviour are to be observed and constructs a standardised checklist.
Unstructured observation/Naturalistic	Data gathered in unplanned, ad hoc way.

Systems Used for Written Observations

Rating Scale

Behaviour rated on a pre-designed scale, e.g. coding of an aggressive act on a scale of 1 to 10 (mild to severe).

Coding System

Behaviour recorded using number or letter system e.g. V for verbal aggression, P for physical aggression.

Categorisation System (Tally Chart)

Pre-categorised behaviour recorded as frequency of occurrence.

See overleaf for an example:

Child	Hits or shoves another child	Shouts at another child	Withdraws
A	III		
B			IIII
C	I	II	

Advantages

High ecological validity and avoids demand characteristics.

Disadvantages

There may be observer effects, and replication may be difficult.

Self-Report Techniques

Interviews and Surveys

Interviews

Interviews can be **structured** where every respondent answers the same questions and is more formal in terms of the interaction between the interviewer and interviewee, or **unstructured** where there is more flexibility in what is asked and additional questions may be asked in order to establish meaning and/or clarity. Alternatively, the **semi-structured approach** has the advantages of both the structured and unstructured approaches. An example of a semi-structured approach is the **clinical interview**, used to assess a person with a mental disorder. The technique allows the respondent to provide detailed information about his/her family history and symptoms; at the same time, structured tests can be administered to provide information on the person's cognitive or social functioning. This approach allows the clinical interview to be used for diagnosis and treatment, although one of its disadvantages is that it can still be limited by the respondent's inability to express himself clearly. In addition, the interviewer must be sensitive or he may create demand characteristics, especially if the person's future depends on their responses in the interview.

Designing Interviews

Interviews must be planned carefully, taking procedural and ethical issues into account. Below is a checklist for planning interviews.

Before the Interview

- Clearly describe the research problem
- State the aim
- Link the problem to an appropriate theory

- Identify the categories of data to be collected

The Questions

- Generate an appropriate set of questions
- Plan the order in which questions will be presented
- Plan the interview to obtain the right balance between structured and unstructured items

The Interview

- Consider how you will present yourself
- Identify and approach potential respondents
- Plan a pre-interview meeting
- Plan a post-interview debriefing
- Decide how much information is to be collected during the interview
- Consider the ethical issues raised by the research and seek advice as necessary

Evaluation

- Detailed information can be obtained and the interviewer can clarify data collected at the time
- Unstructured interviews can raise new lines of psychological inquiry
- Unstructured interviews produce qualitative data, which can be difficult to analyse
- Interpersonal factors may create increased risk of investigator effects, e.g. participants may alter their responses to make themselves look better

Questionnaires

Questionnaires used in surveys may use **closed-ended** questions whereby the respondent is provided with alternative answer choices and must pick one, or **open-ended** questions which allow them to answer in any way they wish. Both of these have advantages and disadvantages. Closed questions are easier to analyse quantitatively, since the respondents' choices are arranged in categories, but the researcher may not get access to each respondent's true feelings towards a particular topic and could miss important information they have not pre-categorised. Alternatively, open questions allow the researcher to collect rich, detailed information but are much more difficult to analyse.

Designing Questionnaires

Care must be taken when designing questionnaires since you will not be there to clarify any questions which respondents may find ambiguous or difficult. Again, a checklist for designing questionnaires is presented below.

Type of Question

- Closed questions are easy to analyse since you can provide a box for respondents to tick e.g. 'yes' or 'no'. Alternatively you can offer a scale along which respondents can indicate the strength of their feelings towards a particular topic or a list of options from which to choose.

- Open questions do not constrain respondents but allow them to answer in any way they like. They are much harder to analyse but may give access to information you have not thought of and pre-categorised

Number of Questions

- Only include questions which are necessary for the purpose of the research
- Include demographic questions (on age, sex, marital status, etc.) at the end of the questionnaire
- Don't put highly sensitive questions at the beginning of the questionnaire

Language

- Use language which is clear and unambiguous
- Avoid jargon or technical language

Leading Questions

- Never word a question that leads a respondent in a particular way, e.g. it is better to ask 'What was the young boy wearing?' than 'Was the young boy wearing trousers or jeans?'
- Never include value-judgements in questions such as 'Do you think using the death penalty is playing God?'

Ask one question at a time

- Take care that you don't ask two questions rolled into one. You will not be sure which part of the question the participant has answered. For example, avoid asking: 'Do you think that mothers should work or should they stay at home to look after their children?' Instead, ask two separate questions

Avoid using emotive language

- Using emotive language can bias responses, e.g. don't use: 'Do you think defenceless animals should be used in psychological research?' Instead ask, 'What are your views towards using animals in psychological research?'

Avoid Making Inappropriate or Insensitive Assumptions

- Avoid questions which include assumptions that could cause embarrassment. For example, asking 'What is your occupation?' assumes that everyone is employed. It is better to ask 'Are you currently in paid employment?'

Evaluation

- Questionnaires can be used to question a large sample of people relatively quickly and can collect large amounts of data
- They reduce investigator effects, as the researcher does to need to be present.
- Answers may be affected by social desirability
- Low response rates
- Self-selecting sample

Activity 35

Design a questionnaire consisting of ten questions that could be used to investigate a person's experience of day care when they were a child.

When you have finished, review your questions against the checklist above.

Case Study

The case study provides a detailed account, usually of a single participant. It contains detailed personal history, background, test results (e.g. IQ score or personality profile), ratings and records of interviews. This method gives rich information about the person, but the data are often qualitative and therefore it is difficult to make inferences about cause and effect. Below is an extract from a famous case study of a patient with multiple personality disorder, Eve White:

As if seized by sudden pain, she put both hands to her head. After a tense moment of silence, both hands dropped. There was a quick, reckless smile, and, in a bright voice that sparkled, she said, "Hi there, doc!" The demure and constrained posture of Eve White had melted into buoyant repose.... This new and apparently carefree girl spoke casually of Eve White and her problems, always using 'she' or 'her' in every reference, always respecting the strict bounds of a separate identity. When asked her name, she immediately replied, "Oh I'm Eve Black."

Source: "The Three Faces of Eve" Thigpen and Cleckley (1954) p. 137

Advantages

Case studies such as this one can be used to study an unusual set of circumstances and lend themselves to a longitudinal approach where the person is followed up over time. They are also useful when investigating a new line of psychological research.

Problems

Data collection for case studies relies on the memory of the participant and close family. Also a close relationship develops between experimenter and client which may lead to bias. Cause and effect are difficult to establish, especially if there is no way to prove the details of the individual's past. The limited sample makes it difficult to generalise, and they can be extremely time consuming and expensive.

Correlations

A **correlation** is an *association* or *relationship* between two variables (co-variables). An example is the study by Rahe *et al* (1970) which found a correlation between LCU (life change unit) scores and illness scores. Rahe found a positive correlation. That is, the higher the number of LCUs, the greater the risk of developing illness. Alternatively, we can have negative correlations where more of one thing leads to less of another (e.g. the hotter it gets the less clothes we wear). Correlations are measured from +1 to –1. +1 is a perfect positive correlation and -1 is a perfect negative correlation. 0 means there is no correlation at all.

In practice, perfect correlations are rarely found but usually fall somewhere between these extreme values. A correlation of 0.7 would show a fairly strong positive relationship between two variables, while a correlation of –0.3 would show a fairly weak negative one. A scattergram can be used to determine visually if there is a relationship between two variables. The scores on one variable are plotted against the scores on the second variable. This is an example of a scattergram showing a positive correlation:

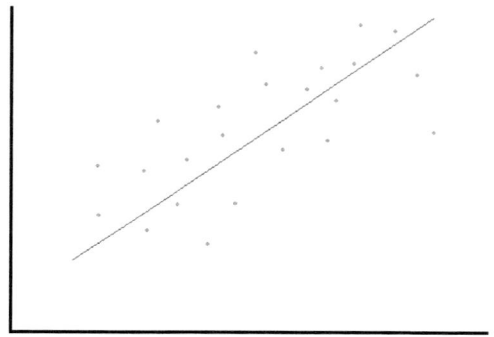

Correlation can be used to establish a relationship between two variables and can allow researchers to conduct a statistical analysis. However, it must be remembered that correlation is not the same as causation. Correlation only establishes a relationship between two variables; it does not establish cause and effect. For example, there could be a third variable that creates the relationship. Correlation also cannot be used to detect curvilinear relationships, only linear relationships. Curvilinear relationships occur where correlation is only positive up to a point.

The difference between correlations and experiments

An experiment allows the researcher to control and isolate the variables in order to observe possible effects on a dependent variable – so it looks at cause and effect. For example, giving someone over 150 grams of fat per day in their diet will increase levels of cholesterol.

Here the researcher can control some aspects of this experiment in order to see what impact this may have. Therefore, the researcher could increase or decrease the fat consumption by 10% to see if that would have any impact on the cholesterol levels of those taking part in the experiment – cause and effect - the aim of the experiment is to identify an independent variable, manipulate it and then to see how it affects a dependent variable.

Because of researcher control, it is also possible for the researcher to eliminate certain variables in the experiment.

A correlation identifies two variables and looks for a **relationship** between them. To use a fictional example - those living in hotter countries (variable 1) are more likely live beyond the age of 80 (variable 2). A correlation looks for relationships and associations between two naturally occurring variables and, unlike experiments, correlations can only predict relationships, unlike experiments which can predict cause and effect (causation).

Content Analysis

This is a research method where words, images or concepts used in the media are analysed and quantified. For example, the number of times a gender specific word is used in a newspaper article could give some indication of gender bias in that particular newspaper.

Case Studies

These provide an in-depth investigation of a single person, group, event or community. Data is gathered using various sources and methods.

Case studies are widely used in psychology. Freud for example used case studies one of his most famous being include his Little Hans study.

Strengths	Limitations
Provides an insight other research does not provide	Difficult to make generalisations about the population as a whole
Provides detailed information	Researcher bias could be an issue
Very good for illustrating theories	Difficult to replicate
	Time and cost

2.3.1 Scientific Processes

The Application of Scientific Method in Psychology

The key features of science are that it is **empirical** (objective and replicable), **systematic**, **controlled** and **testable**.

THE SCIENTIFIC METHOD

REPLICABILITY

When psychologists report what they have found through their research, they also describe in detail how they made their discoveries. Following a recognised and established research method enables other psychologists to repeat the research in order to see if they can replicate the findings. Scientific theories are tested over and over again to ensure replicability.

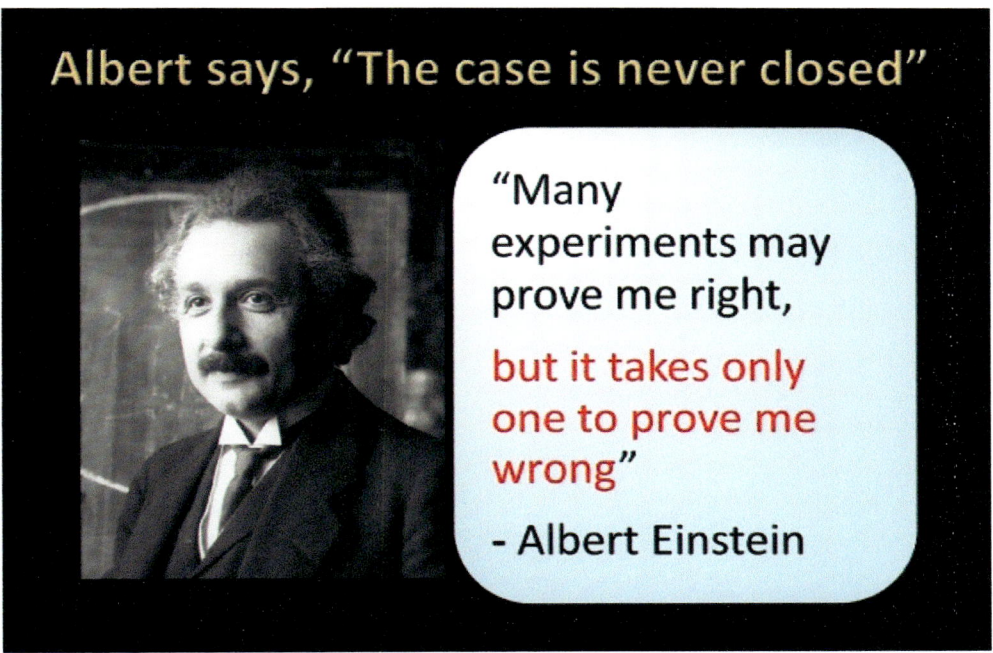

Traditionally, scientists gathered data using empirical methods and then used **induction** or **deduction** to develop theories.

- INDUCTION – THE DEVELOPMENT OF GENERAL TRUTHS OR THEORIES BASED ON THE DATA OBSERVED. THIS ONLY EXPLAINS EXISTING DATA AND MAKES NO PREDICTIONS ABOUT WHAT MIGHT BE FOUND.
- DEDUCTION – THEORIES ARE DEVELOPED WHICH RESULT IN PREDICTIONS (HYPOTHESES) THAT CAN BE TESTED.

Philosopher Karl Popper (1959) rejected this idea and claimed that a host of different experiments could be generated in order to support a theory. However, no amount of evidence can 'prove' that a theory is right and it only takes one piece of evidence to 'disprove' it.

Popper used the example of black swans. He explained that a scientist who only ever saw white swans would hypothesise that 'All swans are white' based on the observational data. However, it would be impossible to prove this hypothesis. If one black swan was found, it would invalidate the hypothesis.

Popper came up with a different model of how science progresses based on the **hypothetico-deductive** method. It is both a model of how science should be done and how science progresses.

The model has the following stages:

1. Identify a problem
2. Develop a hypothesis
3. Devise a study
4. Analyse and evaluate the results
5. Modify and repeat
6. Develop a theory

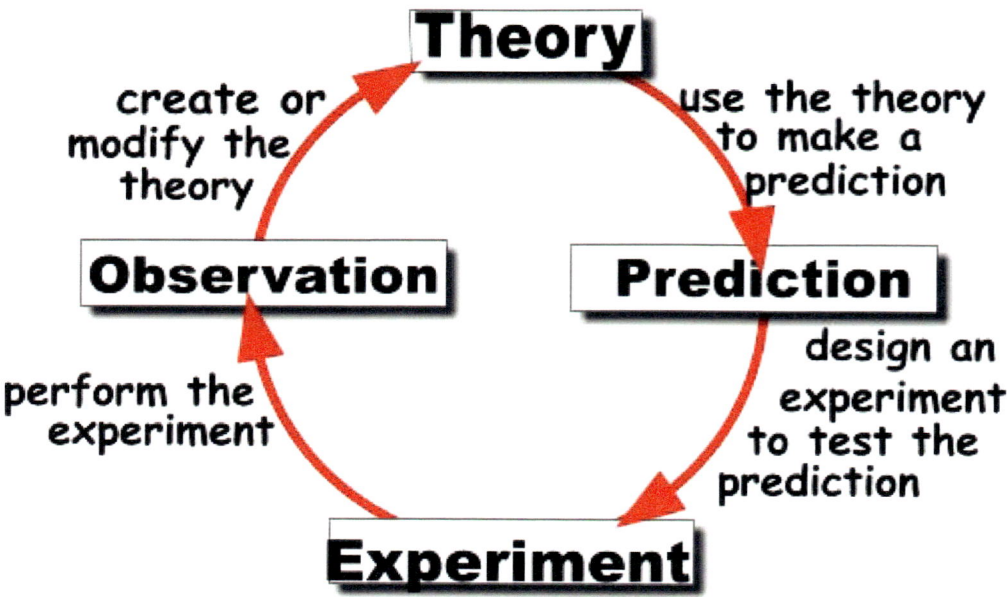

The crucial element in the hypothetico-deductive method is the issue of **falsifiability**. In other words, researchers should set out to *disprove* their theories. If a theory can't be disproved it is said to be **non-falsifiable**, which means it is probably not possible to test it and, therefore, it is a weak theory. The more researchers attempt and fail to disprove a theory, the stronger that theory becomes. If a theory is disproved, it must be replaced with a better one. This shows the gradual and systematic way that science progresses.

⬜ Launch CloudPort for interactive content

Paradigms

The philosopher Thomas Kuhn disagreed with the steady progress of science proposed by Popper. He believed that science progresses through long periods of what he calls 'normal science' until there is a revolution during which old ideas are overturned and a new paradigm emerges. In other words, there is resistance to change followed by sudden and major change.

We can see an example of this in the history of psychology. In psychology, the first paradigm was introspection, followed by psychodynamic psychology (1900s), until that paradigm gave way to behaviourism (1930s) and that gave way to cognitive psychology in the 1960s, and so on.

Neither Popper nor Kuhn's version is dominant. Dyer (2006) believes this is because Popper's view exists outside a social context whereas Kuhn's model takes social change into account.

Alternatives to the Scientific Approach

Towards the end of the 20th century, some psychologists questioned the use of the traditional scientific method in psychology. This is for several reasons:

- PSYCHOLOGISTS INTERACT WITH THE PEOPLE THEY STUDY. THEREFORE, PEOPLE CANNOT BE OBJECTIVELY STUDIED IN THE SAME WAY AS PHYSICAL PHENOMENA.

- BEHAVIOUR IN LABORATORIES IS UNUSUAL. IT IS SEPARATED FROM ITS SOCIAL CONTEXT AND IS NOT ALWAYS APPLICABLE TO REAL-LIFE SCENARIOS.
- THE NEED FOR CONTROL MEANS THAT A SINGLE VARIABLE SHOULD BE STUDIED IN ISOLATION. THIS IS NOT POSSIBLE IN PEOPLE, WHOSE BEHAVIOUR IS A PART OF THEIR WHOLE PERSONALITY.
- PEOPLE ARE TREATED AS PASSIVE PARTICIPANTS AND THEIR SUBJECTIVE EXPERIENCE IS OFTEN IGNORED.
- OBJECTIVITY IS A MYTH. ALL SCIENTISTS ARE INFLUENCED BY THEIR OWN EXPERIENCES AND IDEAS. THIS IS ESPECIALLY TRUE FOR PSYCHOLOGISTS, WHO ARE COLLECTING DATA IN A SOCIAL CONTEXT.

Postmodernists argue that knowledge is a social construct and is, therefore, subjective and shaped by the cultural context and language that is used to describe it **(social constructionism)**. The alternative approach that has emerged from this is 'new paradigm research'. This approach relies on methods which attempt to understand the social world of the participant by analysing discursive material such as in depth interviews and written material such as diaries and blogs. This research is qualitative rather than quantitative and uses language rather than numbers.

However, this does not mean that there is going to be a paradigm shift in which the scientific method is replaced. For example, we might look at a young girl's blog to understand her experience with an eating disorder but use a more traditional method involving blood tests or brain scans to discover a neurochemical cause. For this reason, it is likely that the two approaches will add to the multi-method discipline that psychology has become (Dyer, 2006)

The difference between aims and hypotheses

Aim = a statement of the general purpose of an investigation or experiment. .

A Hypothesis = a specific statement about the expected outcome of an investigation or experiment.

Generating Hypotheses

When psychologists carry out research, they are hoping to answer certain questions. In order to do this, they must write the question in a formalised, testable way called a hypothesis. The hypothesis is stated at the start of the experiment and predicts the outcome.

There are two types of hypotheses that you need to be aware of:

The **null hypothesis** states that there will be **no difference** between the conditions or **no relationship** between two variables. We set out to disprove or reject this hypothesis.

The **alternative (or experimental) hypothesis** states that there will be **a difference** between the conditions or **a relationship** between two variables.

Alternative hypotheses can be **one-tailed** or **directional** (where the direction in which the results will go is predicted), or **two-tailed or non-directional** (where a difference is predicted but without direction).

For example, in a memory experiment, participants are asked to recall a list of words after: a) learning mnemonic techniques or: b) learning no techniques. Since we know that such techniques improve memory, we could predict that the participants who learn the technique will recall *more words* than those who do not (one-tailed).

If we wished to hedge our bets, we could use a two-tailed hypothesis which would simply state that there will be *a difference in recall* between the two conditions.

Sampling

When we decide to do an experiment, we would like to get results that tell us something about the population we wish to study. A population includes all individuals of a particular group that is being studied. For example, we might wish to know how managers motivate their work force. We can't possibly interview all managers as the size of the population of managers in terms of the research would be difficult to co-ordinate in terms of time, money and resources. So we must select a sample from which we can draw conclusions that we can extrapolate to the population. The sample is a portion of the population, having as many of the same characteristics as possible as the population. The population from which we draw this sample is known as the target population.

Sampling Techniques:

Random Sampling

A random sample is, as its name suggests, when a sample of the population is selected at random.

Stratified Sampling

A population would be classified according to a set or sets of categories; then participants would be selected from each category in the same proportions as they are in the population. This should guarantee that there are samples that are representative of the population.

Quota Sampling

We may not want to sample a random selection of the general population. Instead, we might want a specific sample on which to test our hypothesis. A quota sample reflects the *exact proportions* of specific characteristics as they occur in the target population. For example, if we are looking at study habits of psychology students at a college, we may have 30 females and 10 males in their second year of studying psychology, and 40 females and 20 males in their first year. A quota sample would select a sample of males and females in the ratio of 3:1 from the second year and 2:1 from the first year.

Systematic Sampling

Here, participants are picked on the basis of some system. A sample of five year-olds, for example, could be selected by picking *every fifth name* on the register. This is not a random sample (as discussed earlier) since not everybody has an equal chance of being chosen. However, it is likely to be relatively unbiased and is often faster than random sampling. It is sometimes called a **quasi-random sample**.

Opportunity Sampling

Here we simply grab people who happen to be near us at the time (e.g. students sitting in the canteen). However, there is a high chance that the sample will be biased, leading to low population validity.

The Volunteer (or Self-selecting) Sample

This is a type of sampling to be particularly wary of. If we advertise for participants, the volunteers who turn up are a self-selecting sample and, therefore, a biased one. Research has found that a particular type of person volunteers for such research. Consequently, we cannot generalise to the target population, leading to low population validity.

Activity 36

1) Which of the following procedures do you think would produce a group of people who would form a random sample?

- Picking anybody off the street to answer a questionnaire (target population: the general public)
- Selecting every 10th name of the register (target population: school)
- Sticking a pin in a list of names (target population: the names on the list)

2) Why is an opportunity sample unlikely to be representative of the target population?

Answer to activity 36

1) None of these methods will generate a random sample: selecting people off the street is opportunity sampling, picking every 5th name off a register is systematic sampling and pin-sticking may seem random but the middle names are more likely to be chosen than those at the top or bottom.

2) An opportunity sample is more likely to sample certain groups of people, for example, people who are not working or otherwise have time to take part. Consequently, it is difficult to generalise to the target population and there is low population validity.

Implications of Sampling Techniques:

Sampling Bias

We need our sample to be typical of the population about which we wish to generalise. If we decided to interview managers in a local firm that was struggling to make a profit, we would not obtain a realistic view of the question we wanted to study. This is known as a biased sample.

Representative Samples

To avoid bias, we need samples that are representative of the population from which they are drawn. The target population for each sample depends on the hypothesis we wish to test. For example, we might need one sample of men and one of women, or we may want a group of children who watch more than twenty hours of TV a week and one watching less than five hours. How can we be sure that the participants we select will be representative of their category?

The answer is that we can never be sure. The truly representative sample is an abstract ideal which is impossible to achieve. The only practical thing we can do is to remove as much sampling bias as possible. We need to ensure that no members of the target population are more likely than others to get chosen. One way to achieve this is to take a truly random sample. This is defined as *a sample in which every member of the target population has an equal chance of being included.*

It is difficult to select a truly random sample. Most psychological research does not use random samples. A common method is to advertise in the local press; more common still is to acquire people by personal contact, and most common of all is to use students.

Conducting Pilot Studies

Once the hypothesis has been written and the variables have been operationalised, the researcher must choose a suitable research method that is capable of testing the hypothesis. Once the research method has been chosen, it will be tested in a pilot study.

A pilot study is a small-scale study carried out with a few participants to assess and eliminate any possible problems with the planned study, for example:

- Are the instructions clear? Do all participants understand them?
- How much time should participants be given to complete a task?

Pilot Studies

A pilot study provides a way of enabling the researcher to do a 'run-through' of the procedures that the researcher was planning to use as part of their investigation. Once the hypothesis has been written and the variables have been operationalised, the researcher must choose a suitable research method that is capable of testing the hypothesis. Once the research method has been chosen, it will be tested in a pilot study. It is effectively the study on a smaller scale whereby the researcher may try out a social experiment, for example, on a few people rather than on a larger scale basis. The benefit of this is that it can flag up any potential anomalies or problems with the study and method of research. It can also save time and resources e.g. money.

A pilot study as a small-scale study is carried out with a few participants in order to assess and eliminate any possible problems with the planned study. For example:

- Are the instructions clear? Do all participants understand them?
- How much time should participants be given to complete a task?

Experimental Designs

Repeated Measures Designs

(Sometimes called **related** or **within–groups** designs.)

Suppose we overheard a conversation in a coffee shop that more wars seem to take place in hot countries. From this chance conversation, we decide to test the theory that heat makes people aggressive. We could ask participants to perform a problem-solving task in cold conditions and again in hot conditions. We could then look for signs of aggression in the participants when the task became difficult and compare the results. In this design, each participant is tested in each of the two conditions.

Activity 37

Think carefully about the design of this experiment and write down some advantages and disadvantages of having the same people performing in both conditions.

After you have done this, carry on reading below.

Advantages of Repeated Measures Designs

The main advantage of a repeated measures design is that it eliminates the influence of individual differences since the same people are tested *in each condition.*

Problems with Repeated Measures Designs

Order Effects

These can be a problem if the same people perform a task under two different conditions. Performance may improve through practice (**practice effects**) or worsen due to fatigue or boredom (**fatigue effects**). Demand characteristics may also be a problem since the participant may guess the true purpose of the experiment by the time he participates in the second condition. One solution to this problem is **counterbalancing**. Therefore, half the participants would complete the experiment under condition A first, followed by condition B. The other half would complete the experiment under condition B first, followed by A. You can remember this as ABBA.

Independent groups design

(Sometimes called **unrelated** or **within-groups** designs.)

Sometimes an experiment cannot be counterbalanced to get rid of order effects. In this case an independent groups design (where different people participate in the two conditions) must be used. Such cases could be:

- When order effects cannot be dealt with or are asymmetrical
- When testing differences e.g. between males and females or introverts and extroverts
- Where a naïve participant must be used because the real purpose of the experiment can be guessed after the first condition
- Where a control group is needed e.g. testing a new drug against a placebo

Activity 38

Returning to the heat/aggression experiment, let's suppose that a group of psychology students are used for the 'hot' condition while a group of nursery nurses are used for the 'cold' condition. The 'cold' group turn out to be less aggressive. This is what our hypothesis predicted so our results are correct. But how can we be sure that nothing has confounded our experiment? Write down some factors that may have affected the results.

The nursery nurses may be less aggressive and generally better able to deal with frustration than the psychology students. After all, their job requires them to be patient and calm when dealing with the tantrums of small children.

Advantages of Independent Measures Designs

The main advantage of this type of design is that it eliminates order effects, since fresh participants take part in the two conditions. It also reduces the effects of demand characteristics since the participant only takes part in one condition.

Problems with Independent Measures Designs

The main drawback with this design type is that individual differences can never be totally eliminated. Another problem is that independent measures designs require twice as many people, which can be expensive and time consuming.

Matched Pairs Designs

Sometimes the way to avoid fatigue and practice effects is to find different people but match them for certain criteria, e.g. race, age, sex, intellectual ability and socio-economic status. This type of experiment is called a matched pairs design. It is a related design because the *pairs* of scores are treated just as if one person had obtained a set of scores by participating in each condition. The pairs of participants are assigned randomly to the different conditions.

Activity 39

Monozygotic (identical) twins are the perfect matched pair for this type of experimental design. Explain why you think this is.

Identical twins are already perfectly matched in age, sex, race, intelligence and socio-economic status. They have the same genes and upbringing, thus eliminating many of the possible extraneous variables.

Advantages and Problems of Matched Pairs Designs

This type of design utilises the advantages of both the repeated measures and independent measures designs while avoiding some of the problems. However, this type of design can be expensive since, if one person drops out of the study, the paired participant is also lost.

Observational Designs

Observation as a methodology for research is often used within the realms of Psychological research and analysis and can be a good starting point for any research. The purpose of this approach is for the researcher to observe a given situation/s without having an impact upon any aspect of what is being observed. Observation can enable the researcher to observe verbal as well as non-verbal behaviour. The observer may attempt to record everything that they are observing in detail, using recording devises to capture all events and actions. Researchers may also apply a sampling technique as it can be difficult to record everything, and as such there are two techniques that can be used:

Event Sampling – where the researcher records a particular event every time it occurs. For example in a classroom observation, ticking a box every time a student raised his/her hand to ask a question. This approach could potentially be problematic if there many occurrences of the event being observed, which can make it difficult to record everything at once.

Time Sampling – here the researcher will record what is happening at regular fixed time intervals in order to note what is happening at that particular moment in time. For example, a researcher may note the number of times there is evidence of confrontational interaction within a particular group during 10 minute intervals.

A potential problem with this approach is that something may be missed during the period of time when the observation is not occurring (in between intervals).

Questionnaire Construction

Questionnaires can be a very versatile way of gathering information on a given area of study, and as such are often used by researchers in various fields and disciplines. They can be an effective way of gaining an insight into and measuring attitudes, preferences and opinions of a large number of respondents. By using this approach, information can be gathered and collated relatively quickly. There are, however, some aspects of questionnaires that can be regarded as problematic, such as:

- Confusion – the language used in the questionnaire may be confusing to the respondent and as such their response may be unreliable

- The respondent may give responses that they feel the researcher wants rather than what they really think or believe

- The respondent may want to present themselves in a favourable or positive light, and thus may respond to questions in a way that is somewhat misleading

When questionnaires are designed or constructed, there are important distinctions to be considered in terms of the types of questions being asked. The researcher, therefore, may design or construct a questionnaire that uses open or closed questions or in some instances a combination of the two.

Closed questions are often structured in a way where the response/s fit into categories that have already been decided by the researcher in advance. So, the response to questions may require a simple 'yes' or 'no' or questions may be presented in a way where the respondent can only select one of two or three predetermined answers; or the questions provide a ranking in terms of how the respondent may feel about a particular issue e.g. agree/disagree/strongly agree/strongly disagree. This approach is often associated with quantitative research methods as the responses are easily quantifiable and statistics can therefore be generated from them.

Open questions offer a deeper insight into the respondent's answers to the questions given as it often allows the respondent to express themselves in their own words, not being restricted by prescribed, predetermined answers e.g. 'How do you feel about…?' This approach is often used to gain an insight into more complex issues that require a deeper understanding and therefore is associated with a qualitative approach/methodology.

Activity 40

Think about closed and open questions, and identify at least five strengths and five weaknesses that can be associated with each approach.

Open Questions	
Strengths	**Weaknesses**

Closed Questions	
Strengths	**Weaknesses**

When designing a questionnaire the researcher would aim to address and apply the following factors:

- Define the aims of the research so as to ensure that questions asked are pertinent to those aims
- Identify the sample population – depending on the nature of the research it may not be possible, viable or practical to try to question the whole population so a population sample would need to be identified
- Decide the length of the questionnaire
- Types of questions: open/closed; formal/informal; colloquial/conversational in tone or technical and jargonized etc.
- Presentation – professional with clear and concise instructions
- Possibly run a pilot study in order to test out the above – this is a good way to establish whether or not the questions the researcher is proposing to use are workable and understandable

Variables

A variable is something that may change or vary in some way and which can be categorised or measured. The control, manipulation and measurement of variables are central to psychological research. Psychologists must precisely define or **operationalise** variables if their research is to be scientifically credible. Before a hypothesis can be written, the variables in a piece of research need to be operationalised. This means that the way the variables will be used must be clearly defined. Variables are classified as independent variables (IV), dependent variables (DV) and extraneous variables (EV).

The **independent variable (IV)** is the variable that the researchers will manipulate as part of the experiment. The independent variable is expected to have a direct effect on the dependent variable. It can be thought of as the 'cause' of the change in the dependent variable.

The **dependent variable (DV)** is affected by the manipulation of the independent variable. The dependent variable is the variable measured in an experiment.

The experiment is the best method in which to control **extraneous variables (EV)**. These are variables over which the researcher has little control but which could affect the outcome of the experiment by affecting the DV.

Activity 41

Identify the IV and DV in the following statements:

- Attitudes can be influenced by propaganda messages

- Noise affects efficiency of work

- Time of day affects attention span

- Performance is improved with practice

- Smiles tend to produce smiles in return

- Aggression can be the result of frustration

- Birth order in the family influences the individual's personality and intellectual achievement

- People's behaviour in crowds is different from behaviour when alone

Answer to activity 41

IV propaganda messages; DV attitudes

IV noise; DV efficiency of work

IV time of day; DV attention span

IV practice; DV performance

IV smiles; DV smiles

IV frustration; DV aggression

IV birth order; DV personality and intellectual achievement

IV in crowd/alone; DV behaviour

Another example: we may wish to test the idea that women take fewer risks when driving than men. In order to test this idea, we need to define exactly how we are going to measure the behaviour and identify the independent variable (IV) and dependent variable (DV). One way we could do this is to observe behaviour of men and women at traffic lights and count how many 'jump' the light as it turns red.

Thus:

IV = men and women

DV = number jumping the red light

Way to operationalise = keep a tally chart into which a mark is written either in the male or female column if a driver passes over the white line and carries on driving or after the red light shows.

Alternative (experimental) hypothesis = 'men will be observed to jump red traffic lights more often than women'.

Activity 42A

Look at the hypotheses below, which are taken from some of the psychological studies we have met so far. For each one, decide if it is a null or alternative (experimental) hypothesis and whether it is directional or non-directional.

1. Loftus and Palmer, 1974

As the severity of the verb increases there will be no difference in the estimates of the speeds of the car.

2. Bowlby, 1944

There will be a difference in the frequency of affectionless psychopathy in the 44 thieves and 44 boys with emotional problems.

3. Harlow and Zimmerman, 1959

When monkeys are deliberately scared, they will seek comfort from the cloth mother.

4. Tizard, 1984

People raised in an institution will be less likely to form meaningful attachments in later life than those raised at home.

1. Loftus and Palmer, 1974

Null. Non-directional.

2. Bowlby, 1944

Alternative (experimental). Non-directional.

3. Harlow and Zimmerman, 1959

Alternative (experimental). Directional.

4. Tizard, 1984

Alternative (experimental). Directional.

Types of Extraneous (or Confounding) Variables

Extraneous variables may come from the participants themselves **(participant variables)** or from the conditions under which the participants are tested **(situation variables)**. For example, suppose we attempted to measure frustration levels in participants solving a difficult anagram and we picked participants from an English class going on in the next classroom. It is likely that many of these participants will be above average at solving anagrams and therefore will show less frustration. Such **participant variables** will therefore confound our results or give us an unrealistic idea of the effects of anagram solving on frustration.

Similarly, if we were to test groups of people at different times of the day, say one early in the morning and one late at night, we may have a **situation variable** since people are generally more alert at certain times of the day, and those tested at night may well be tired.

There are also other types of variable which arise from using people in experiments. These are **demand characteristics** and **investigator effects**.

Demand characteristics arise when the participant picks up on cues that lead the participant to behave in a certain way. **Investigator effects** arise when the investigator knows the desired outcome of the experiment. This can lead the investigator to affect a participant's behaviour in a certain way or even to record results in such a way that the desired effect is shown. These variables are both threats to the **internal validity** of the experiment.

Demand characteristics can be overcome by the use of the **single blind technique** where the participants do not know the hypothesis being tested or which group they are in. Investigator effects can be overcome by the use of **double blind technique** where neither the participants nor the researcher knows the hypothesis or the conditions of the experiment. In such experiments, the data is collected by a research assistant on behalf of the experimenter.

Control

In order to ensure the validity of experiments, one way is to have experimental controls that can be utilised in order to prevent other factors from affecting the outcome of an experiment, to prevent one variable from being affected by the dominance of another variable.

Any experiment needs to be carefully organised and have standardised procedures. Therefore, there are various ways in which controls can be applied to experiments as follows:

Random allocation aims to remove the possible effects of individual and choice bias by researchers dividing participants into comparison groups e.g. by using a computer-generated random sequence. So every member of the population has an equal chance of being selected. Therefore they have the same chance of receiving each of the possible interventions without bias.

Counterbalancing occurs when all possible orders of presenting the variables are included. So, if you have two groups of participants (group A and group B) and two types of independent variables (Type 1 and Type 2), you would present one possible order (group A gets Type 1, group B gets Type 2) first and then present the opposite order (group A gets Type 2, group B gets Type 1). This enables the researcher to measure the effects in all possible situations. However, one limitation is that not all studies can be designed this way – the larger the number of variables the more difficult it is to coordinate and manage.

Randomisation as a sampling method is when participants are randomly allocated, and there is an equal chance of a participant being allocated to one or the other of an experimental group.

Standardisation is an approach that applies a consistent set of procedures that is applied to all participants or variables in an experiment. This enables participants to be tested under the same conditions

Demand Characteristics and Investigator Effects

In any form of research, it is possible that variables other than those referred to previously can have an impact upon the quality and outcome of the research. Factors such as demand characteristics and investigator effects will be addressed briefly in this context.

Demand characteristics

This term was first introduced by Martin T Orne (1959). Demand characteristics refer to a situation whereby the subject being researched becomes somewhat concerned with the extent to which the experiment he/she is a part of meets the desired requirements of the researcher. Therefore, the greater the demands of the research the more effort the individual will put into meeting the needs of the demand. In other words the individuals become invested in the researcher in a way that has an impact upon their behaviour and thus throws into question the validity of the results.

If the researcher is aware that the individuals' responses are affected in this way, he/she may try to 'disguise' in some way the true nature of the research, but there can be no guarantee that the subject has been 'distracted' from the true purpose of the experiment or research.

Investigator effects is when the researcher behaves in a way (usually unconsciously) that brings about the result predicted. The researcher/investigator's methodology and procedures are designed in such a way that the investigator's bias brings about the result predicted.

Ethics

The main ethical issues involved in psychological research are **deception**, **informed consent** and the **protection of participants**. These issues are problematic because deception is sometimes necessary to experiments where knowing what is being investigated may alter the behaviour of the participant. However, deceiving participants as to the nature of the research impairs their ability to give their informed consent. It must be remembered that psychological research can directly or indirectly cause harm to participants. It is therefore vital that researchers conduct their research ethically in order to minimise the risk of injuring participants.

Developing Codes of Conduct

During the 1960s and 1970s, there were growing demands for explicit and detailed ethical guidelines for psychological research. Partly as a result of this debate, professional associations of psychologists in a number of countries published codes of conduct for research with human participants. In 1978, the British Psychological Society (BPS) published its 'Ethical Principles for Research on Human Subjects'. This was revised in 1990 and 1992 and republished in 1993 and 1998 with the title 'Ethical Principles for Conducting Research with Human Participants'.

Ethical considerations are now a major concern in research. The BPS (1998) states that, 'In all circumstances, investigators must consider the ethical implications and psychological consequences for the participants in their research'. The investigation should be considered from the viewpoint of all participants and threats to their psychological health, well-being, values or dignity should be eliminated.

These codes are considered to be so important that psychological associations now have committees which are responsible for ethical issues, and continuously monitor and update ethical guidelines. In addition, universities have ethics committees which examine research proposals to ensure they are in line with codes of conduct. If they are not, they will be rejected.

Some of the most important ethical guidelines are that participants must be debriefed after the experiment and allowed to withdraw their data if they no longer consent to participate. The participants also have the right to withdraw from the experiment at any time. Experiments should also be stopped if they begin to cause harm or distress.

You can read the full version of the BPS research guidelines on their website:

http://www.bps.org.uk/sites/default/files/documents/code_of_human_research_ethics.pdf

Peer Review

The most effective way of looking at the quality and validation of research or proposed research is by peer review, with the peers being professionals in the same field and/or discipline, such as fellow psychologists.

According to the Parliamentary Office of Science and Technology, peer review in the UK serves three main functions:

1. **Allocation of research funding**. Peer review is used in order to establish which research projects should be funded. It is also used to "assess the progress of funded projects"

2. **Publication of research in scientific journals**. The quality and importance of the research submitted will be assessed before publication

3. **Assess the research rating of university departments**. A lot of research is conducted by university departments, and as such peer review is used to judge the quality of research conducted by each department[10]

"Peer review is designed to improve the quality of research reporting and to prevent poor research from taking place."[11]

Implications of psychological research for the economy

For this aspect of your studies you can utilise topics covered elsewhere in the course in order to demonstrate the impact of psychological research on the economy. The economic implications will be briefly addressed in terms of the following areas:

- Attachment research

- Psychopathological research

- Memory research

Remember to review these areas in your course materials

Attachment research

There are many aspects of Psychological Research that can be connected to gaining a better understanding and subsequent introduction of social policy in terms of the impact psychological research can have on the economy. One such areas of research is based around Attachment. In 1951, Bowlby, prepared a report on behalf of the World Health Organization (WHO) looking at the impact of maternal deprivation on the lives of homeless or disturbed children and how significant the mother/child relationship was. Bowlby's findings and conclusions in relation to attachment were presented to governments, social and public agencies. He suggested the need for social policy change that would provide family support – financial, psychological and social. Bowlby's work brought about changes to social work; for

---

[10] www.parliament.uk/post/home.htm Parliamentary Office of Science and Technology, September 2002, Number 182 Peer Review

[11] www.parliament.uk/post/home.htm Parliamentary Office of Science and Technology, September 2002, Number 182 Peer Review

example mother/child separation was to be an absolute last resort unless there was evidence to suggest that separation would be the better option in terms of the well-being of the child i.e. if there was evident of abuse or neglect.

The work of Bowlby has had a significant impact in many areas of attachment - parent/child relations, adoptions, fostering, hospitalisation, parenting behaviours in general and so on. Even in terms of childcare and maternal employment, Bowlby's work has greatly influenced society's approach to this (at times controversial) area. Not surprisingly, maternal employment has a significant impact on the economy.

Evidence in the 1980s showed that substituted childcare (that being childcare provided by someone other than the mother, such as day care, nurseries, grandparents, child minders, fathers), had no significant negative impact on a child's psychological and social development, thereby enabling the mother to be able to be economically active through the work place.

Psychopathology research

In research conducted in 2011, the House of Commons found that:

- Potential loss of earnings from depression was £8.97bn per year
- Loss of earnings from suicides was £1.47bn per year
- Cost to the NHS to treat depression was £520m per year (some of the breakdown is as follows:
  - ➤ £237m for hospital care
  - ➤ £230m for anti-depressant drugs
  - ➤ £46m for doctors time
  - ➤ £9m for outpatients appointments
- NHS statistics found that in 2010-2011, 43.4m prescriptions for anti-depressants were distributed; 10.2m sleeping pills were prescribed

In the light of the above figures and the potential economic impact due to time lost from work, whilst more expensive than drug therapy (which is regarded by many as a short term solution), other forms of therapy such as CBT are being utilised and seen as more economically sound – in that in the long term, if treated appropriately and effectively, people would take less time off work and therefore be more economically productive.

Memory research

If you recall from the section on eyewitness testimonies, this is a very significant area of study in terms of finding ways to improve memory. The economic implications of this can be seen in relation to costs associated with legal processes such as time and resources spent in terms of police investigations, interview facilities, court cases, documentation and recording of statements and so on. Being confident about the reliability of EWT can save time meaning that police time and resources could be utilised in other areas of investigation.

Reliability across all methods of investigation

What is reliability? This is shown in stability or consistency of a test both over time, and also within the test itself. To show that a test is reliable, we first have to be sure that what we are measuring is not changing, with variations in the result being due to measurement error. However, reliability is not an all or nothing concept. We can talk about the degree of reliability.

Reliability is shown by the following:

- Consistency of instrument (e.g., a questionnaire or scientific apparatus used to take a measurement)
  - How much error is there in the measurements?
- Results must be repeatable
  - i.e. If same individual were to take test on multiple occasions, their score should be similar

All tests have a reliability coefficient (a statistical measure) that we can use in interpretation.

Ways of assessing reliability:

There are three different ways of assessing reliability:

- Test-Retest
- Internal Consistency
- Scorer Reliability and Agreement

If you are carrying out a psychometric test (a test which measures, for example, intelligence, or personality, the test manual will state which method(s) were used to determine reliability. Often, more than one method is used to determine whether a test is reliable.

Test-Retest

Test-retest is a measure of reliability, whereby the same test is given to the same participants at two different points in time. What are the limitations of this measure of reliability?

- Practice effects then become an issue, since we can expect participants to improve on their second test compared to their first test.
- Motivation to take the same test twice is also an issue, especially where you need to actively recruit participants. Having to do this may put some people off taking part in the experiment at all.
- Furthermore, there is a problem with the timing of delay between administrations:
  - Too short: participants more likely to remember previous responses
  - Too long: individual may change with regard to the dimension being measured
- Also, what if the dimension is expected to fluctuate over time (e.g., state anxiety – the measure of an individual's level of anxiety due to circumstances)? We would therefore not expect a huge amount of stability between certain constructs such as state anxiety from one time to the next, but this does not necessarily indicate that our test of anxiety (for example, a questionnaire) is unreliable.

Inter-rater (or observer) Reliability

This is a measure of the degree of consistency among scorers' judgements, and can be broken down further as follows:
- **Inter**-rater reliability: Relationship between scores on same test of 2 or more scorers
- **Intra**-rater reliability: Relationship between scores on same test by same scorer on 2 or more occasions

Improving reliability

- Reliability estimates are subject to error, and this error is a function of sample size. One way to improve the measurement of reliability is to increase the sample size
- 50 to 100 are typical sample sizes for test-retest or parallel form measures
- To obtain acceptable internal consistency reliability coefficients (e.g., of around 0.8 or above), we typically require sample sizes > 200

Statistical calculations of reliability

These are essentially a correlation, and is known as the 'reliability coefficient':
- Test-Retest: Correlate score at 'Time 1' with score at 'Time 2'
- Alternate forms: Correlate score on 'Form A' with score on 'Form B'
- Split-Half: Correlate score on 'Half 1' with 'Half 2'

Conclusions

Reliability refers to the 'consistency' of a test, both over time and within the test itself. Test-retest, internal consistency and scorer reliability are three main means to measure reliability. The reliability coefficient can be calculated statistically, which is essentially a measurement of correlation. Researchers would be looking for a reliability coefficient of at least 0.8, to be confident that the test or measurement they have administered is reliable.

What is validity?

Validity is the technical term given to whether a test measures what it claims to measure. If a test for anxiety *does* measure anxiety (rather than, e.g, stress, depression or another factor) then we can say it is valid. We can also look at the extent of the validity of a given test – how well does the test measure a construct? However, unlike reliability, there is no single, straightforward statistic which measures validity. Instead, assessing validity depends on accumulation of research evidence investigating the relationship between scores on the test and other independently observed behaviours.

There are also different forms of validity:

- Content validity: does a test include all representative aspects of particular facet? For example, if we are measuring levels of anxiety, does the anxiety questionnaire include items on anxiety across a range of different scenarios, or not?
- Ecological validity: can the test results be generalised to real-life or real world situations?
- Face validity: what does test appear to measure to respondents?
- Temporal validity: can we generalise the results of a study across time?
- Criterion related validity:
  - Predictive validity: Can score predict future performance?
  - Concurrent validity: Is score related to other test scores?
- Construct validity: Does the test match the theory?

Face validity

This form of validity looks at the way in which the test appear to the test subject (testee). That is, does the test seem fair? For example, some tests of intelligence include questions about general knowledge or culture. However, this domain is quite subjective: whose culture? What counts as general knowledge? This may mean the test lacks face validity for some participants, who are still intelligent but do not have access to these forms of knowledge. Face validity therefore influences how the test subject responds – if they feel the test is unfair, then they will lose motivation and will perhaps not complete the test. This has obvious implications for testing and for accuracy. Face validity is therefore important as a means of 'selling' the test to potential participants. Recruiting participants for an experiment can be an issue, so it is important that participants do not feel unduly frustrated by the test you ask them to complete.

Concurrent validity

Concurrent validity is an assessment of the validity of a test at this moment. That is, it relates to the extent to which the results of a given test or measurement correspond to those of a measurement already established for the same construct. IQ is a good example: there already exist standard measurements or tests for IQ. If you devise your own test for IQ, then one way to assess concurrent validity would be to give your participants both a standard IQ test and your own one (at roughly the same time – this is important), then to correlate the results of both. If your test of IQ has high concurrent validity, it should correlate strongly with the existing IQ test.

Ecological validity

This term refers to the extent to which we can make generalisations about a test or findings from a research study to the real world or real-life scenarios. In any experimental paradigm, there is always a trade-off between experimental control (e.g., minimising extraneous variables, having a clear task) and ecological validity (making a task, test or experimental procedure match what would actually happen in real life). That is, in order to create a clear experimental procedure, researchers often present a single outcome task to participants. For example, in cognitive psychology, researchers may ask participants to repeat a string of numbers from memory, having presented them with a stimulus number string a few seconds before. The number of digits correctly recalled is therefore a measure of STM. This task is clear and controlled: the researchers would minimise for other extraneous variables which might improve or hinder memory (such as the nature of the conditions under which the task was performed). However, does this task have ecological validity? This may be a valid concern. In the real world, you rarely have to use your STM to recall a list of digits in this way. Can we really extrapolate from participant performance in this task, therefore, to how we use our STM to solve real world problems?

Temporal validity

Temporal validity refers to how relevant the time period of a test or research study is to the findings. This means that this measure of validity is particularly pertinent to those areas of psychology which investigate how social attitudes change over time, since these kinds of studies usually have low temporal validity. We can't really expect a study on society to produce the same results now as it did 20 or 30 years ago (in many cases), so usually researchers need to revise the questions in accordance with changing times and norms.

Activity 42B

Read the following article on ways to assess and improve validity
http://www.simplypsychology.org/validity.html

Features of science: objectivity and the empirical method

Two examples of natural sciences are biology and chemistry. These are characterised by empirical, objective inquiry. These are important terms:

- Objectivity is the extent to which a test or experiment is free of bias and prejudice
- Empiricism is the name given to the method of using observable facts to test theories

Scientists aim to discover natural laws, which explain patterns in the natural world. They conduct research through experiments and statistical methods. In order for their laws to become accepted, scientific knowledge, they must test their hypotheses using **replication.** A scientific study should aim to have replicability: It should be possible to repeat the experiment (using the same protocol, different participants but the same research procedure) and receive statistically similar results.

The philosopher of science Karl Popper expanded on his positivist predecessors in 1959, arguing that sociology could only be a valid science if based on **falsification**. Falsification is the idea that researchers should aim to refute hypotheses. Scientists thus needed to use testable hypotheses.

The longer that these hypotheses are not falsified, the truer they are. Scientists should use deductive methods (as opposed to the positivist **inductive** methods), starting with a theory and testing it against evidence, rather than gathering evidence and then formulating a theory.

Theory construction and hypothesis testing

The sciences will start with a hypothesis and from there conduct experiments, observations and measurements in order to establish the hypothesis and ultimately to test the underlying theory.

One of the key features favoured by science is that of objectivity, therefore, personal opinions and points of views are not encouraged or valued, and as such the results generated from scientific experiments are seen as more credible than any other form of evidence. Note, however, some thinkers such as Lyotard (1984), a post-modernist, argue that it is not possible to be completely objective even in science. However, scientific positivists or realists think that science can be objective, and that it is possible for findings to be value-free.

The research process

The stages in the research process of academic Psychology are broadly as follows:

- Choose a subject for research – define the nature of the problem for investigation. This could be done by considering gaps in existing research. What variables have yet to be tested under which conditions?

- Find and then read the existing research on the topic

- Decide what you think is the relationship between the variables being tested, so you can formulate a hypothesis

- Decide on the research plan – what are the most suitable methods of data collection? For example, quantitative or qualitative? Why do these methods suit the research?

- Carry out the research according to this plan

- Record the results and analyse the findings

- Report the research, discuss the findings in terms of your preliminary thoughts – do they match up or not? This is usually through publication of your results in the form of a journal article

- Discuss your findings with the wider psychological research community, such as academic colleagues or at conferences

Paradigms and paradigm shifts

Another history and philosopher of science, Thomas Kuhn, made famous the concept of **'paradigm shifts'**. Kuhn argued that science transitions through 'paradigm shifts', moving from one stage to the next. These stages are: pre-science, normal science and revolutionary science. Born out of 'pre-science', or an experimental period of science with no central paradigm, 'normal science' is a period in which scientists use a shared set of techniques and theoretical values. Normal science, therefore, reflects the description of the natural and psychological sciences, based on empirical, objective modes of inquiry. When normal science reaches a 'crisis point', in which its underlying explanations are scrutinised, it will shift to 'revolutionary science'. So to summarise: normal science operates within a specific paradigm, which will eventually shift; the pursuit of objective truths through universally recognised techniques and theoretical values is combined to a specific paradigm, which is subject to change.

Reporting psychological investigations

The results of academic scientific investigations are published in Psychology journals, such as the *British Journal of Psychology*, or in journals which cover individual fields of psychology, such as the *British Journal of Social Psychology*. These journals are essentially collections of the results of different research, conducted by different psychologists. If you go on to study Psychology at a higher level, then you will be required to start reading Psychology journals which contain articles reporting the results of psychological experiments. Scientific journals are one of the key ways in which psychologists (and all scientists) communicate their results to one another. Scientific journals vary in terms of prestige and the kinds of articles they typically favour: some have a higher 'impact factor' compared to others. An impact factor is a measure of the number of times an average article in a journal has been cited (referred to in another study) in a year. Typically psychologists, in common with all scientists, desire to publish their work in journals which have a high impact factor. This is because it is in the interests of a psychologist to produce work which stands a good chance of being widely read and cited, by publishing it in a widely read and respected scientific journal.

Sections of a scientific report: abstract, introduction, method, results, discussion and referencing

In order for the publishers to include the results of a scientific study in a journal, it must conform to some fairly narrow requirements. In particular, these relate to the way the work is formatted and presented. Scientific results must be published in the following format of a scientific article:

Abstract

This is a short statement of around 200 words of less at the start of the article, and it summarises the article with the main aim of interesting the reader enough to read the full article. Most people decide whether or not an article is worth reading in full, based on the details given in the abstract. The abstract should include some theoretical background, some explanation of the methods, the key result and a brief discussion point. It should make the aims and the results of the experiment clear, while also enticing the reader enough to read the full article.

Introduction

In this section, the authors set out the theoretical or conceptual background for their study, and explain what the existing research shows about a given topic, and also why their experiment was necessary. This is usually because the researchers have spotted a gap in the literature: nobody has yet tested this particular group of people, under these conditions, using this particular experimental protocol. In which case, the researchers aim to contextualise their research within the wider body of existing research into the subject. This could be any topic in psychology, such as research into memory, psychopathology, attachment or any other field. The authors will need to cite existing relevant studies and their results, and also to include the full reference to each study cited in a references list at the end of the article.

Method

In this section, the authors explain in more detail how they carried out their research. This section is often divided into the following subsections: design, participants, materials/apparatus and procedure. In the design section, the authors will comment on whether a repeated measures or independent groups design was used (for example) and what the IV and DV are. In the participants section, the authors will go into more detail about the number of participants, how they were selected, the gender and age of the participants, any give other factors relevant to the particular experiment. This will depend on what is under study.

The authors will NOT name individual participants, but will instead refer to them only as 'participants' and describe the group in general (e.g., by giving the mean age or age range of the participants) rather than saying 'one participant, Mr Smith, was 46, whereas another participant, Ms Brown, was 34…' In the materials and apparatus section, the authors comment on the materials and apparatus used in the study. This could be the use of a questionnaire, the use of a computer test of memory, the use of a stimulus of some kind, or anything else which related to the way the experiment was carried out.

In many cases, the authors will cross reference the reader to a copy of the questionnaires used (for example), which will be given in an appendix at the end of the article. In the procedure section, the authors go into a lot more detail about how the experiment was actually run, including how they controlled for EVs and reduced demand characteristics, order effects or investigator effects (where relevant). There should be enough detail in this section for another scientist to replicate the experiment themselves. The aim is to be clear about the methods used, with the justification for why these methods were selected already contained in the introduction section.

Results

In this section, the authors state their results. This section is largely statistical, and the researchers will report descriptive statistics, such as the means and standard deviations of the DV under each condition (independent groups design) or for each participant in the repeated measures design. The authors will also apply statistical tests, and will report the results of their findings. They may refer to graphs, charts or other pictorial representations of the data, and will present key data in the form of tables so it can be easily read and different statistics easily compared. The authors will not, at this stage, try to explain their results. For example, if there is a significant difference between one condition compared to another, the authors will state the level of significance as a percentage, using null-hypothesis significance testing, but will not seek to explain why they found this difference at this stage.

Discussion and Conclusion

This should be one of the longer sections of the overall article. Here, the authors discuss their findings in the light of the existing literature. Broadly speaking, they will have either confirmed or failed to confirm their hypothesis. This section will link in clearly with the introduction, which first established the theoretical background and then explained the rationale for this particular study. In this section, the authors will comment on what surprised them about the results, what was expected, and why this was so. The authors will also comment on any limitations of their research design, will propose future research leading on from their results, and will also explain some of the consequences or impact of their results. This section will also refer heavily to the existing literature on the subject, since the results will need to be compared against other similar and relevant studies. These studies will also be cited and referenced in a references list.

Referencing

Each journal has its own convention about referencing style and how it expects references to appear in an article, before it can be published. In Psychology, it is common to use so-called 'APA' referencing. This is the referencing style formulated by the American Psychological Association, who have produced guidelines on how to set out the name of the author, the date, the title of the article, publisher and so on in a standard format throughout the article. A full list of the references to the articles which the authors have cited in their own article must appear at the end of the article, in an alphabetical list ordered by the surname of the lead author. This is so the reader can then follow up the sources cited in the article if they want to, by using the reference to find and then read any of the articles which have been cited by the authors.

Activity 42C

In 1963, Peter Medawar (a Nobel Prize winner in medicine) broadcast and then published 'Is the Scientific Paper a Fraud'? In this influential broadcast and later article, he criticised the convention of scientific journal publishing. You can read this short article here:

http://www.albany.edu/~scifraud/data/sci_fraud_2927.html

Do you agree with Medawar's criticisms?

2.3.2 Data Handling and Analysis

Key Areas:

- **Quantitative and Qualitative Data**

- **Primary and Secondary Data**

- **Descriptive Statistics**

- **Presentation and display of quantitative data**

- **Distributions**

- **Analysis and interpretation**

- **Levels of measurement**

In this topic, we will look at how data can be analysed and presented in psychology. We will look at ways of analysing quantitative data, including measures of central tendency and dispersion. We will then look at how to represent data graphically as bar charts, histograms and scattergrams. Finally, we will briefly consider qualitative data.

Levels of Measurement

This section will discuss the analysis of **quantitative data.** The first important consideration is to decide at what level the data are to be measured. The **level of data** measurement refers to the **precision** with which the data have been measured.

Nominal Data

The collection of **nominal data** involves dividing participants into **categories** and counting how many are in each category. This is the most basic level of measurement and is really no more than a tally or a head count. An example of nominal data would be to ask all the people in the room to assign themselves to one of two categories as either 'tall' or 'short'. We would then know how many people were in the 'tall' group and how many were in the 'short' group, but we would know little else. We would have a very crude measurement of height.

Ordinal Data

The next level of measurement we could perform would involve asking all the people in the two groups to form a line with the 'tallest' person at the start and the 'shortest' person at the end. In this way we would now know something about the **position** of the people in the room with regard to height. For example, we would know that the second person was taller than the third and the last person was the shortest in the room. This is known as **ordinal data** since we now know the position in the rank of all the participants.

Interval data

To get the most precise measurement of height, we could measure each person to find their *exact height* in metres. Now we have the most precise measurement of all and we have a lot more information about each person. For example, we could establish that person 2 in the line was exactly 5cm shorter than person 1, and that the tallest person was 50cm taller than the shortest person. We could also be confident that the **intervals** on the ruler were exactly the same distance apart and that 2cm would be exactly double the distance of 1cm.

Measures of Central Tendency

Measures of central tendency are used to reduce a set of numerical data down to a single value which represents the whole set.

The Mean

This value is often referred to as the *average* value. It is what we get if we add up all the scores in a sample and divide the answer by the number of scores. It should only be used on interval data, i.e. data which you have obtained by measuring something which has a scale such as temperature, time or height.

Activity 43

The following scores represent the time taken to solve an anagram:

135, 109, 95, 121, 140

Find the mean.

1. Add up all the values

2. Divide by total number of values

Answer to activity 43

135+109+95+121+140 = 600

600 / 5 = 120

Advantages

Very often the mean is not the same value as any of the values in the group. It acts like the fulcrum of a balance see-saw, sitting exactly at the centre of all the deviations from itself. This makes it the most sensitive measure of central tendency.

Disadvantages

This sensitivity can be a disadvantage in certain circumstances. Suppose we add a sixth person's score to our set of anagram-solving times. This person is not very good at anagram solving and had a bad night's sleep. This person stares at the anagram for exactly 600 seconds.

Activity 44

Add this person's score to the earlier scores and find the mean value.

Answer to activity 44

135+109+95+121+140+600 = 1200

1200 / 6 = 200

Now the mean value is not representative of the group in general. A single extreme score in one direction has distorted the mean.

Activity 45

The managing director in a company earns £300,000 per annum.

Her personal assistant earns £14,000.

The four secretaries earn £12,000 each.

- What is the mean wage for an employee in the company?

- Why is this not a representative figure?

300000 + 14000 + (4x12000) = 362000

362000 / 6 = 60333.33

The mean wage is £60,333.33

However, this is not a representative figure because the managing director earns vastly more than her employees. The mean has been affected by an extreme value in one direction.

The Median

The median is the **central** value of a set. If we have an odd number of values, it is easy to find. We simply put all the values in numerical order and find the central value.

The scores from the anagram-solving exercise were:

95, 109, 121, 135, 140   The median is 121.

If there is an even number of values, as with the sixth person's time added, we take the mean of the two central values.

95, 109, 121, 135, 140, 480   The median is (121+135)/2 = 128

Notice that this value is still reasonably representative of the group of values.

Advantages

- Can be used on interval or ordinal level data. (Ordinal data are measured on a scale which you have designed for the purposes of your experiment e.g. how aggressive a person feels on a scale of 1-10)
- Easier to calculate than the mean
- Unaffected by extreme values in one direction

Disadvantages

- Doesn't take into account the exact values of each item
- If values are few, it can be unrepresentative e.g. with values of 2, 3, 5, 98, 112 the median would be 5

The Mode

The **mode** is the most frequent, most common value. We use this if we have nominal data which are measured as frequencies (such as the number of men who do the washing up). For example, if we assign a category number 1, 2, 3, 4, 5, 6, 7, 8 to types of play observed in children, we cannot calculate a mean or a median. What we can do is to say which type of play was most frequently engaged in.

For this set of numbers:

1, 2, 3, 3, 3, 4, 4, 4, 5, 5, 5, 5, 5, 5, 6, 6, 7, 7, 7, 8

The mode is 5, as this value occurs most often.

For the set of numbers:

7, 7, 7, 8, 8, 9, 9, 9, 10, 10

There are two modes, 7 and 9, and the set is said to be **bimodal**.

Advantages

- Can be used on interval, ordinal or nominal (frequency) data
- Shows the most important value of a set
- Unaffected by extreme values in one direction

Disadvantages

- Doesn't take into account the exact value of each item
- Not useful for relatively small sets of data where several values occur equally frequently (e.g. 1, 1, 2, 3, 4, 4)

Measures of Dispersion

A measure of dispersion is another way of summarising data. This measure tells us how 'spread-out' the scores are.

The simplest way to express the spread of a set of scores is to use the **range**. This tells us over how many numbers a set of scores is spread, and is calculated simply by taking the smallest number away from the largest. The problem with this is that extreme values affect the result.

e.g.

10, 11, 11, 12, 12, 13, 13, 13, 14

10, 11, 11, 12, 12, 13, 13, 13, 20

One single figure changes the range from 4 to 10. To overcome this problem, the **interquartile range** can be calculated. This is calculated using the 25% of scores immediately below the median and the 25% of scores immediately above it.

The interquartile range, therefore, measures only the spread of the middle 50% of values when they are placed in numerical order.

The **standard deviation** is a more sophisticated measure of dispersion since it calculates the average distance of all the scores from the mean. For this reason, it is only used when a precise level of measurement (such as interval level) has been used to gather the data.

Worked Example

Calculate the standard deviation for the following data:

4, 8, 10, 12, 16

First of all, it is necessary to calculate the mean:

The mean = $\frac{4+8+10+12+16}{5}$

Mean = 10

Now the differences of all scores from the mean is calculated by subtracting the mean from each score:

e.g. 4-10 = -6 and so on

giving: -6, -2, 0, 2, 6.

Next, the differences are each squared to get rid of the minus signs

giving: 36, 4, 0, 4, 36.

Now add together and divide by 5 (because there are 5 numbers)

giving: 16.

Because we squared the differences, we now have to square root the answer

giving: 4.

Standard deviation (SD) = 4

Graphs

When you report the results from a piece of research, you will want to present them in a way which shows the overall pattern of your data. These are called **descriptive statistics**. Graphs show the reader any patterns we have found in the data in an easy-to-understand format. We will look at the three most common graphs used in psychological research, namely, the bar chart, histogram and scattergram.

The Bar Chart

Features

- The horizontal axis does not always have a discrete scale but may have nominal labels for each column
- The columns should be separated and of equal width
- The columns can represent single statistics such as the mean or a percentage

Combined Bar Charts

These are used to display two values together. Look at the example below. A student wished to see if the portrayal of gender roles in children's literature had changed over time. She performed a content analysis on children's story books from the 1950s and 1990s. She categorised roles under the following headings:

1. A male performing a traditional male role
2. A female performing a traditional female role
3. A male performing a traditional female role
4. A female performing a traditional male role

The results are represented in a combined bar chart overleaf:

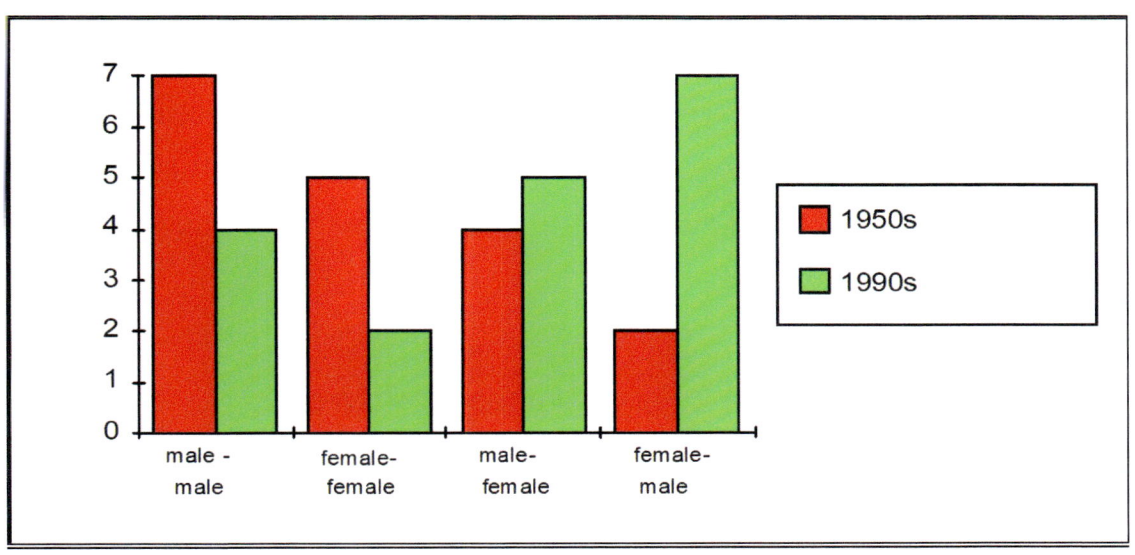

The Histogram

Raw data are difficult to interpret and take up too much space. They can be collated into a table known as a frequency distribution. Below is a frequency distribution showing the ages at which parents report first utterances in their children:

Age (months)	Number of children
13	1
14	0
15	5
16	12
17	37
18	64
19	59
20	83
21	17
22	41
23	12
24	0
25	4
26	5
27	0
Total	340

Suppose we wished to know how many utterances *each child* produced per day; the data set produced would be too large to plot a simple frequency distribution. Such data can therefore be reduced to class intervals, like so:

No. of utterances	No. of children	Cumulative frequency

0-9	3	3
10-19	0	3
20-29	15	18
30-39	43	61
40-49	69	130
50-59	17	147
60-69	24	171
70-79	4	175

The first class interval shows that the number of children speaking 0-9 times a day is 3. As each class interval is scored, the frequency for the class before it is added to give a **cumulative frequency**. This makes sense, since a child who has uttered 39 words also belongs in all the classes before the one in which it appears.

Activity 46

Using graph paper, plot a histogram of the data above.

- Set out the Y axis scale from 0 to 70

- You will need eight columns along the x axis. Each column should use two squares of graph paper. The columns should touch

- Mark the mid-point of each column with the mid-point for the class interval it represents. e.g. the first class is 0-9 and the mid-point is therefore, 4.5. The second class interval is 10-19 and the mid-point is 14.5

- Draw the top of the column level with the frequency (number of children) for each class interval. Note: you do not plot the cumulative frequency. To find it you add the total for all the bars below a particular class interval together

Features

- All categories are represented
- Columns are equal width because they represent equal class intervals
- Empty intervals are plotted

- Columns can be added together to find the total frequency they represent

Scattergrams

A **scattergram** is designed to give a visual impression of the relationship between two variables. Each piece of data is added to the scattergram as a point, usually marked by a cross. The pattern produced indicates the strength and nature of the relationship between the variables.

If the points tend to form a straight line, this indicates a correlation between the variables.

Features

- The more the points cluster around a straight line, the stronger the correlation
- A line running from upper left to lower right shows a negative correlation
- A line running from lower left to upper right shows a positive correlation

Activity 47

Using graph paper, draw scattergrams for the following scores.

1			2			3			4	
A	B		A	B		A	B		A	B
2	2		1	2		1	7		10	1
4	4		2	2		2	5		8	2
5	5		4	3		3	9		6	4
9	9		4	4		5	4		4	5
12	12		5	6		7	8		3	7
13	13		7	7		2	3		0	10

Plot the A column data along the x axis and the B column data along the Y axis. You should find that graph 1 shows a perfect positive correlation; graph 2, a weak positive; graph 3, no correlation; and graph 4, a strong negative correlation.

Primary and secondary data

- Primary data: is collected personally by researchers, for the purposes of their own studies. This can take a wide variety of forms in psychology, and can be either quantitative or qualitative.
- Secondary data: originates from a source other than personal research and can include newspaper articles, books, mass media and the research of other psychologists or social scientists. Psychologists should take caution in the way that they present information gathered from non-academic publications, which could be biased and under-researched.

Meta-analysis

It is common for unaffiliated groups of researchers to be working on the same hypothesis. This means that for many current lines of research, there already exists a large body of data. It is important that this is so, because receiving similar results across different experiments increases the reliability of those results, since it decreases the likelihood that all of the results could have, individually, occurred purely by chance.

However, this means there are also a number of inconsistent studies on a given topic. For example, researchers worldwide are interested in the effect of caffeine on human cognition. The hypothesis of this research is that caffeine does improve cognition in humans. Some of the research generated from this hypothesis shows a smaller effect of improvement on cognition compared to others. And in fact, a small amount of the research shows a very minimal effect, with a few studies even showing no effect or a decreased (rather than increased) effect on cognition. Although we can see that there is a broad consistent trend at work; caffeine does make an improvement to cognition, it is possible to use statistical methods to derive a more precise, numerical estimate of the extent of this effect, and thus to determine causality (e.g., caffeine causes improved cognitive performance in humans). This is known as a **meta-analysis,** and the aim is to establish the extent of either **heterogeneity** (difference) or **homogeneity** (sameness). That is, are there real, underlying differences between the pieces of research in question (in some cases, caffeine does make an improvement to cognition and in others, not), or are the variations in the research in line with what we would expect from chance alone? In the latter case, this would mean that the results are actually the same, with only the natural variability we would expect from chance: caffeine does, in fact, improve cognition in humans. An advantage of a meta-analysis is that by combining studies, small (but nevertheless still clinically significant) results can be detected, which may well be missed in any analysis of a single study.

What are the features of a good meta-analysis?

The quality of the meta-analysis depends on that of the statistical analysis and methodology: the best meta-analysis will include all relevant research through a systematic review of both published and unpublished research, and will also look for the presence of heterogeneity. However, ensuring that the research to be included is relevant can be problematic, since studies can vary greatly in their methodology as well as their outcomes.

This can make it difficult to assess whether a study ought to be included in the meta-analysis, since a significant methodological difference could imply that a different hypothesis is actually being tested. It is also the case that there is a publication bias towards reporting an effect, rather than a lack of effect. This explains why including research in a meta-analysis that has not shown an effect (or a very minimal one) is vital since it will increase the **validity** of the meta-analysis.

This is the extent to which the meta-analysis closely approximates the real world situation, and it is important that this is as high as possible, since the best meta-analysis will be based on research conducted on participant samples which match the true population closely.

Examples of meta-analysis helps to show this in practice: Randall, Oswald and Beier (2014) conducted a meta-analysis on the cognitive phenomenon of 'mind wandering' and to locate relevant research for the meta-analysis, they conducted a keyword search using several databases. They also had an inclusion criteria for the meta-analysis: research had to be on adult participants, though was not restricted by geographical location or cultural context. The research had to include sufficient data needed to calculate the 'correlations between cognitive resources and mind-wandering tor task-related thoughts or between mind-wandering or task related-thoughts and task performance'.

As a result, 'of the 593 studies reviewed, 106 met the initial inclusion criteria.' (p.1417). As can be seen, the inclusion criteria here establish the extent to which the research located by a keyword search on mind wandering is methodologically and statistically similar enough to be suitable to include in the meta-analysis. In a second example, Else-Quest, Hyde and Linn (2010) included cross-national studies on gender variations on mathematical ability on hundreds of thousands of school children, in order to assess both the impact of gender and nationality on both mathematical performance and affect.

Distributions: normal and skewed distributions; characteristics of normal and skewed distribution

Researchers use the frequency data generated from experiments (in quantitative studies) to examine the shape of frequency distributions. For example, researchers may collect data on the height of a class of undergraduate psychologists of the same gender. Variables such as height follow a **normal** distribution. This means that most of the results are concentrated evenly around the mean, with a few people falling at either extreme. This is what the data of class height if plotted as a frequency graph (height on the x axis, frequency on the y axis) would look like:

Normal distribution

Normal distributions can be different shapes, though and still be 'normal'. For example:

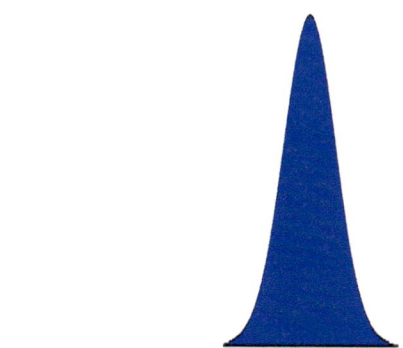

Or

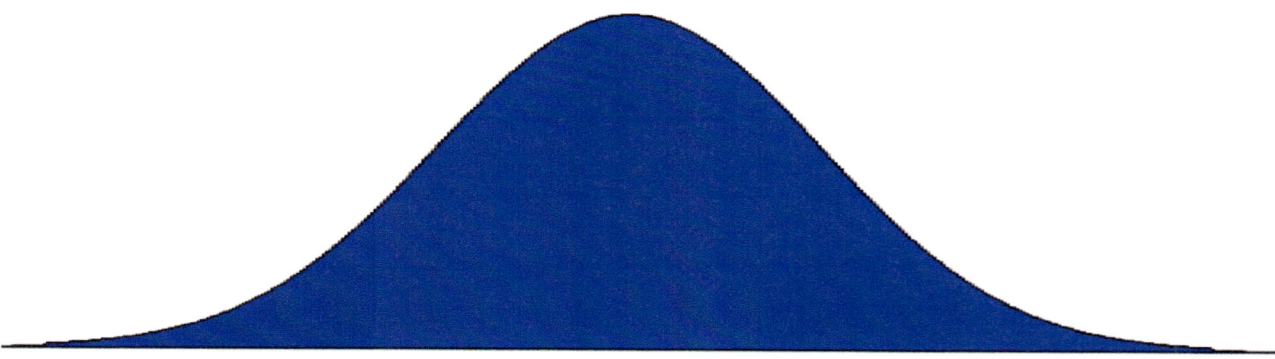

These are the key features of a normal distribution:

- Symmetry around the mean (clearly demonstrated in all three frequency graphs, above) despite the differing shapes.
- Mean, median and mode are all equal
- The area under the normal curve = 1.0
- Both the mean and the standard deviation define the shape of the normal distribution
- Most of the area (95%) under the normal distribution curve is within 2 standard deviations of the mean
- Approximately two thirds of the area (68%) under the normal curve is within 1 standard deviation of the mean

However, not all variables will follow a normal distribution. In statistical analysis, **skewness** is a measure for the skew of a distribution. A **normal** or symmetric distribution will have a **skew** of zero. However, here are two distributions with different directions of skew:

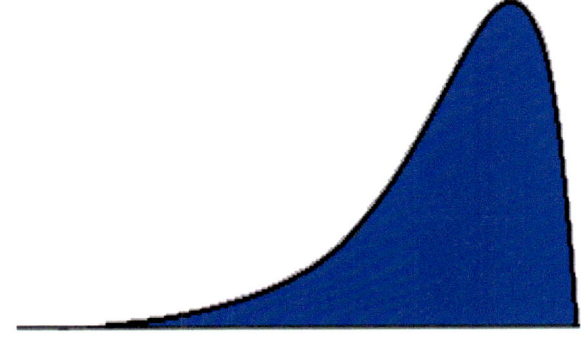

Skewness < 0

This is also known as left-skew (tail to the left) or negative skew.

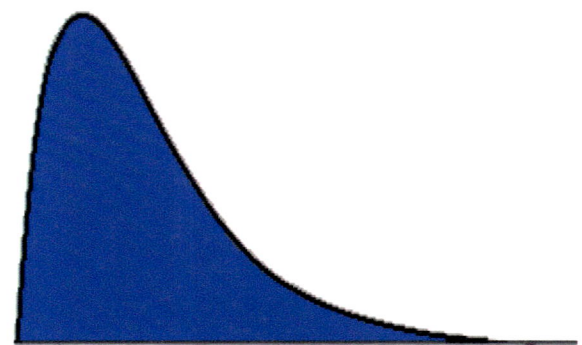

Skewness > 0

This is also known as right-skew (tail to the right) or positive skew.

As you can see, in these distributions the mean and the median will not be equal, due to the long tails (of either direction).

In skewed distributions, data are clustered towards one extreme or the other.

Qualitative Analysis

This involves analysis of non-numerical data generated from observational research and from open questions in interviews and questionnaires. When analysing these types of data, researchers must look for the underlying meaning in what people say or do. They can do this using pure qualitative analysis or by using rating scales or other coding mechanisms to arrange the data into categories and, therefore, make them quantitative.

Pure Qualitative Analysis

This is very time-consuming but does avoid the problem of a particular narrative or behaviour not fitting into a pre-determined category. The process of pure qualitative analysis involves:

- Transcribing the data (in the exact form it was said)
- Reading through repeatedly in order to identify emergent themes

Content Analysis

This technique can be used to analyse transcripts of interviews, TV programmes, newspapers, magazines and websites. The researcher creates a coding system of predetermined categories at the start of the study which is then used to categorise the underlying themes in the material in a consistent manner. The researcher then counts how many times a theme or code word appears. This process translates qualitative data into quantitative (frequency) data which can be analysed in the normal way.

Activity 48

How could a psychologist using content analysis check that allocation of material to coding categories is consistent?

Answer to activity 48

The psychologist could have a second person code the data independently and then check inter-rater reliability.

2.3.3 Inferential Testing

Key Areas:

- **Statistical Testing**
- **Probability and Significance**
- **Factors affecting the choice of statistical tests**

Data Analysis and Reporting on Investigations

Probability

Probability is a measure of how likely something is to occur. Probability (p) is expressed as a number between 0 and 1, where 0 means an event definitely won't happen and 1 means that it definitely will.

It can be calculated as:

$$\text{probability} = \frac{\text{number of particular outcomes}}{\text{number of possible outcomes}}$$

Probability (p) can be expressed as a decimal or a percentage.

Sometimes the probability of an event is conditional on another event occurring. This is called conditional probability.

Significance

Statistical significance is used in hypothesis testing. A **research hypothesis** states that there is a relationship between variables (in a correlation) or a difference between conditions (in an experiment). A **null hypothesis** means that there is no such relationship in the population. If the probability of the events in our sample is greater than chance, then we can reject the null hypothesis.

The probably at which the null hypothesis is rejected (i.e. the probability which is regarded as greater than chance) is called the **level of significance**. This is usually 0.05. The figure of 0.05 has been chosen to minimise the risk of Type 1 and Type 2 errors.

A **Type 1** error occurs when the null hypothesis is rejected, but should have been retained. A **Type 2** error occurs when the null hypothesis is retained, but is false.

Activity 49

1. Calculate the probability of throwing a 6 on a six-sided dice.
2. Why might a level of significance of 0.01 result in a Type 2 error?

1. 0.166 (recurring) or 16.7 %.

2. A 0.01 level of significance might result in a type 2 error because we accept the null at too stringent a level. At a higher level, there may have been a significant result. A 0.01 level of significance would only be used when findings produced might be controversial or may raise ethical issues. In this case, a more stringent level is required.

Dealing with Quantitative Data

Summarising Data

Revise your understanding of range and standard deviation and the use of bar charts, histograms and scattergrams.

Statistical Tests

Psychologists apply various statistical tests when they want to calculate the probability that their results were due to chance. There are many types of statistical tests, and their suitability depends on the type of data.

There are four main types of data:

- Interval data – Interval data is obtained from a measurement scale with equal intervals
- Ratio data – Ratio data is also obtained from a measurement scale with equal intervals, but the scale must also have a true zero point
- Ordinal data – Ordinal data is put in order (1st, 2nd, 3rd, etc.)
- Nominal data – Nominal data is named or put into categories

Summary of Statistical Tests

Chi-square

A chi-square is used to test an association between nominal data which is expressed as frequencies. The data must be independent, and each must only appear once in the sample.

Spearman's Rho

Spearman's rank order correlation coefficient is used to rank pairs of scores. If the ranks are very similar, it shows a positive correlation. If they are opposites, it shows a negative correlation.

Mann-Whitney

The Mann-Whitney test is used for ordinal, interval or ratio data. It can be used when an independent group design has been used.

Wilcoxon

The Wilcoxon matched pairs sign test can be used when the data is ordinal, interval or ratio, and a repeated measure design has been used.

Choosing a Statistical Test

In order to choose a statistical test, a researcher must ask three questions:

- Do I require a test of difference or correlation?
- At what level are my data measured?
- What sort of design did I use?

The flow chart below can help you to decide which test to use:

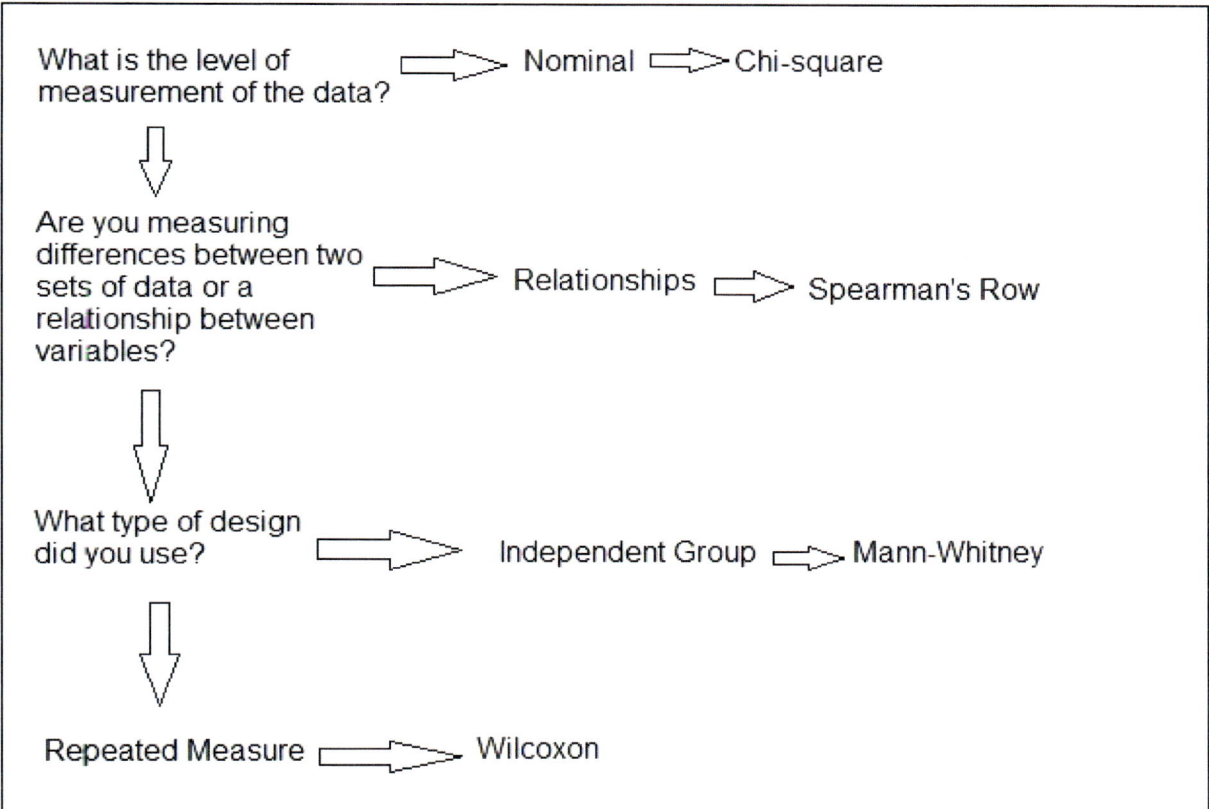

Activity 50

Choose an appropriate test for each of the investigations below:

1. Participants are divided into two groups to determine which therapy is most effective. One group is given Psychoanalysis whilst the other is given Rational Emotive Therapy for a three-month period. After the three months are up, they are given a standardised test to determine their level of psychological functioning.

Level of measurement:

Design:

Type of test needed:

Test chosen:

2.   Participants are asked their preferences for a particular type of teaching method. They are interviewed in college, and the interviewer simply ticks one of the following categories: lecture   notes from board   discussion group   tutorial.

Level of measurement:

Design:

Type of test needed:

Test chosen:

3. A psychologist wishes to determine if aggression is caused by watching violent TV programmes. Children in a residential school are asked to name their five favourite programmes and then have to complete a questionnaire which yie ds an aggression score on a scale of 1-100. The programmes are rated by the researchers on a similar scale where 1 is least violent and 100 is extremely violent.

Level of measurement:

Design:

Type of test needed:

Test chosen:

4. A group of participants are asked to take part in a study which looks at the effects of REM sleep on memory consolidation. The researchers decide to use monozygotic twins in the study since they are likely to have similar sleep patterns. Both groups are given a list of words to learn just before going to sleep. However, one group of participants is woken up each time the EEG shows that they have entered REM. In the morning, the number of words recalled correctly is noted for each of the groups.

Level of measurement:

Design:

Type of test needed:

Test chosen:

5. A psychologist wishes to test people's self-image before and after therapy. He asks them to give a rating of their self-image at the start of the programme and again at the end. Because the rating is subjective, he classes it as ordinal data.

Level of measurement:

Design:

Type of test needed:

Test chosen:

Answer to activity 50

1. Level of measurement - interval

   Design – independent measures

   Type of test needed - difference

   Test chosen – Mann-Whitney

2. Level of measurement - nominal

   Design – independent measures

   Type of test needed - difference

   Test chosen – Chi-square

3. Level of measurement - ordinal

   Design – repeated measures

   Type of test needed - correlation

   Test chosen – Spearman's rho

4. Level of measurement - ordinal

   Design – repeated measures (because it is matched pairs)

   Type of test needed - difference

   Test chosen – Wilcoxon

5. Level of measurement - ordinal

   Design – repeated measures

   Type of test needed - difference

   Test chosen – Wilcoxon

Using Statistical Tests

The value we arrive at when we compute a statistical test is compared to **critical values** in the appropriate table. The tables give different values depending on whether we have used a one tailed (directional) or two-tailed (non-directional hypothesis).

When interpreting the data from tests, it is therefore essential to know whether the hypothesis is one-tailed or two-tailed. A one-tailed hypothesis is a directional hypothesis; it states the direction of the difference or correlation. A two-tailed hypothesis is non-directional. A two-tailed hypothesis therefore specifies a relationship, but not the direction of that relationship.

For example, a hypothesis that states that: "Driving instruction in a simulator will reduce the number of hours of on-road tuition needed before taking a driving test" is one-tailed. It states the direction of the correlation. A hypothesis that: "Driving instruction in a simulator will affect the amount of on-road tuition needed" is two-tailed. It posits a relationship, but not the direction of that relationship.

Using a table of critical values, you will be able to see the level of significance required for a one-tailed and two-tailed hypothesis. At the bottom of the table it will tell you whether the observed value must be **equal to** or **exceed** the critical value given in the table.

Activity 51

Read the material and answer the questions

A preliminary study was carried out to investigate judgements of a female from a photograph. Two separate groups consisting of 1. Older and 2. Younger participants, all working for the same firm, were compared. They were each asked to tick personality characteristics which they had associated with the photograph. The personality characteristics list had 20 items, 10 'feminine' and 10 'androgynous' traits, randomly mixed. Participants were instructed to use as many or as few of the traits as they wished.

A table was compiled of the number of 'feminine' and 'androgynous' traits ticked off by the older and younger participants.

	Feminine	Androgynous
Older	50	49
Younger	48	49

A statistical test showed no significant difference in judgements by the older and younger workers with regard to the selection of feminine traits.

A follow-up experiment was carried out on a mixed age sample randomly selected from the electoral roll. It was an investigation of the primacy effect in judgement of 'femininity' of a female. A video was used of a female giving a self-description. It had two equally timed sections, one using 10 verbally stated 'feminine' traits and the other 10 verbally stated 'androgynous' traits. All the participants saw both sections as a complete sequence. Half the participants (chosen at random) saw the 'feminine' section first, and the other half saw it second. The participants then rated the female on the video for 'femininity' using a ten-point scale, with one as low 'femininity', ten as high 'femininity'. The prediction was that the group who saw the feminine description first would give a higher femininity rating than the group who saw it second. The result was significant at the 0.05 level.

Questions

1. What was the level of measurement of the variables in the preliminary study?

2. What statistical test is appropriate for the preliminary study?

3. What type of sample was used in the preliminary study?

4. What is the independent variable in the follow-up?

5. What is the dependent variable in the follow-up?

6. State an experimental hypothesis for the follow-up experiment.

7. What is the level of measurement of the dependent variable in the follow-up experiment?

8. What statistical test is appropriate for the follow-up experiment?

9. What is an estimate of the type 1 error if we reject the null hypothesis in the fo low-up experiment?

10. Comment on the selection of the follow-up experiment sample.

Answer to activity 51

1. Nominal
2. Chi-square
3. Quota (young and old)
4. Order of presentation of 'feminine' and 'androgynous' traits
5. Ratings of femininity
6. Participants who see the feminine description first will give a higher femininity rating than participants who see the androgynous description first (one-tailed)
7. Ordinal
8. Mann-Whitney
9. 5%
10. Random sampling gives the most representative and valid sample of the target group. However, there are people who are not included in the electoral roll, e.g. homeless people and those in prison or in the armed services. These people are, therefore, underrepresented

Dealing with Qualitative Data

Qualitative data is that which is collected from interviews and surveys, case studies, diaries or notes. This type of data is different to quantitative data and deals with feelings, beliefs and impressions. Qualitative data therefore requires a different, interpretivist approach.

Analysing Data

In order to be able to analyse qualitative data we must be able to code it. The method used and the emphasis on coding will depend on the type of analysis to be carried out. Some of the most common methods of analysis are shown below:

- Interpretive phenomenological analysis – This involves interpreting the meanings different events have for different people

- Grounded theory – Each line of text is coded to find emergent patterns. The way constructs link together can be explored
- Discourse analysis – This method analyses written or verbal discourse. It looks at the social context of discourse and the interaction between speakers

In analysing qualitative data, the researchers recognise the subjectivity of both the participant and the researcher. Often the researcher begins without prior assumptions and looks for patterns that emerge from the data in order to form a theory.

Evaluation

Qualitative data tends to have high external validity but low internal validity and reliability due to the subjective nature of the interpretations made by researchers. Robson (2002) suggests that 'trustworthiness' is a better way to evaluate qualitative data. This involves ensuring that there is an 'audit trail' by which the researchers' decision-making process can be followed (Smith, 2003).

Reporting Psychological Investigations

The report on a psychological investigation must obey certain conventions. It is a formal document with a series of sections. These sections are:
- Title – The title of the report should tell the reader what the report is about
- Abstract – An abstract provides a summary of the report
- Introduction – Explains the background and reason for the research
- Method – An explanation of how the study was conducted
- Results – A summary of the findings
- Discussion – A discussion of the implications of the results
- References – A list of the sources of information used
- Appendices – These are used for further information not included in the body of the report

The published report will become part of the body of scientific knowledge. It is important that the information it contains is detailed enough that other researchers can replicate the study and can fully evaluate the method and findings.

Activity 52

Using a library or online resource, you may like to look for some examples of reports on psychological investigations in order to familiarise yourself with their style and layout.

Tutor Marked Assignment 2

(Mock Exam)

Now go to CloudPort to download your mock exam. Answers should be word processed and uploaded via CloudPort

Please note: If you are pursuing the AS Level qualification only then you will only sit Papers 1 and 2, which correspond to TMAs 1 and 2. If however you are pursuing full A Level qualification you will sit the second set of exam papers which correspond to TMAs 3, 4 and 5. As level no longer counts towards the A level qualification.

3.1 Issues and Debates in Psychology

The topics covered in this section are addressed in various modules throughout the course, so to avoid repetition, what follows is a list of the Key Areas for this unit, after which you will be required to embark upon some research into these various areas of discussion.

- Gender and Culture in Psychology
- Free will and determinism
- The nature-nurture debate
- Holism and reductionism
- Idiographic and nomothetic approaches
- Ethical implications

For this unit complete the following tasks. Using your course file and text book: Research and find examples of studies that illustrate the following debates. Identify the arguments put forward in favour of and against the debates. Include studies to support the points made.

Task 1:

Gender

Universality	Bias

Task 2:

Culture

Universality	Bias

Task 3:

Free Will	Determinism

Task 4:

Nature	Nuture

Task 5:

Holism	Reductionism

Task 6:

Idiographic	Nomothetic

Task 7:

Ethics

3.2 Relationships

If you recall from Unit 3.1.3 on Attachment, we learnt that during the early developmental stages of our lives we can form attachments to primary caregivers and such attachments at an early age can impact significantly upon how we form and develop relationships in later life.

In this unit we will explore how relationships develop and operate by looking at the following areas:

- Evolutionary explanations for partner preferences
- Attraction in romantic relationships
- Theories of romantic relationships
- Virtual relationships in social media
- Parasocial relationships

Partner Preferences

Evolutionary psychology is an area of psychology that is often used to give us a greater understanding of how partner preferences occur and how this relates to sexual selection and human reproduction.

Evolution, put simply, is about change over time. With the innate desire to survive and reproduce, when it comes to partner preferences, from this perspective, people will protect, be possessive and cherish those they consider partners as well as those close to them. This is based on the notion that we intrinsically have a need to pass on our genes.

When it comes to finding a partner or potential mate, psychologists generally accepted that males and females have difference requirements and investments, and these requirements and investments bring with them difference strategies for attracting such a partner.

Parental Investment

When we talk about parental investment, we are referring to the amount of time, energy and involvement parents invest in looking after and caring for their children.

Trivers (1972) defines parental investment as:

"...any investment by a parent in one of his or her offspring that increases the chances that the offspring will survive at the expense of that parent's ability to invest in any other offspring (alive or yet to be born)."

So parents invest in a child in its infancy so as to ensure that parental genes get passed on.

However, the extent of the investment varies according to the sex of the parent. In evolutionary psychology men and women are regarded as having different levels of parental investment.

The extent of the investment can be traced to biological differences in males and females. The gametes produced by females (eggs) are far less numerous than those produced by males (sperm). The difference in terms of the level of production for males and females is referred to as **anisogamy.** On the basis of this it is suggested that male parental investment is lower because of the ease at which males can produce sperm in large quantities. In contrast, because female gametes are harder to produce and less numerous, the parental investment is greater. Anisogamy therefore is seen to be a good indicator of showing the difference between males and females in terms of parental investment.

Females have to be more discriminatory with regard to whom they mate with. If a female mates with the 'wrong' person, in terms of her reproduction this is going to be costly to her (a bit like a waste of eggs!) when compared to a male who has far more gametes at his disposal; as such, if he mates with the 'wrong' person, the cost to him is not so great. It is because of this that Goetz and Shackleford argue that male parental investment is not as great as males can father a high number of offspring with little cost or investment. Also the desire to stay to nurture offspring may also be less when compared to females. Therefore in order to ensure their genes are passed on, males may mate with several females (number is significant in this case). Female investment, being higher, means that she has to choose a quality mate, as opposed to a large number of mates, in order to ensure that the best genes are passed onto her offspring.

Another important factor in terms of parental investment is parental certainty. We've established that male investment tends to be low but we also need to be aware that that makes males fearful of **cuckolding** - investing in children that are not genetically theirs. Daly and Wilson suggest that confidence in a child's paternity by being able to see physical similarities can increase the male investment in the child. This therefore assumes that parental investment in terms of the father is more grounded if the father knows that the child is genetically connected to him. Anderson challenges this view however, by suggesting that men invest equally in biological as well as stepchildren.

Females on the other hand do not have this issue because a female knows that any child she bears is hers, so her parental investment remains high. In humans, fertilization occurs internally, therefore, the female will always know that the child she gives birth to has her genes.

Another factor in terms of parental investment is **cost of investment**. The cost to the male is low as all is required is copulation and a small amount of semen. For females, however, having to carry the embryo inside her means pre-birth investment is higher than that of a male.

Also relevant to this discussion is that of **sexual jealousy**. The issue of sexual infidelity presents significant problems for both males and females in terms of parental investment. Buss (1995) argues that for a man's partner to be unfaithful carries with it the risk of cuckolding, i.e. investing in an offspring that is not genetically his, while a woman whose partner is unfaithful has the concern of resources provided by the male being diverted to other offspring that are not genetically connected to her. Buss goes onto say that sexual jealousy is a technique that is used to prevent infidelity, and men have evolved in a way that the sexual act is the trigger for jealousy, whereas for women it is the shift in the emotional focus of their partner that triggers the jealousy.

Maternal	Paternal
Invests More	Invests less
Choosier	Less choosy
Produces fewer eggs	Fathers unlimited number of children
Parental certainly	Parental uncertainty
Bigger pre/ post birth investment	Minimal biological investment
Indiscriminate mating costly	Indiscriminate mating not costly
Emotional jealousy- loose resources	Sexual jealous- e.g. cuckoldry

Attachment Theory and Relationships

If you recall from our discussion of Attachment theory, early attachment can have a significant impact upon relationships people have and experience later on in life. Therefore as Bowlby (1982) suggests:

- The relationship an infant forms with their primary care giver will form the basis of their future relationships in terms of the internal working model they use as a source of reference
- This will affect their expectations of what relationships are like
- There is a link between early attachment and attitudes toward relationships in later life

Attachment Theory

Childhood Attachment

Secure
- Distress when mother leaves
- Greets mother when she returns

Avoidant
- Does not seek mother when she returns
- Focuses on environment

Ambivalent/Resistant
- Very upset at departure
- Explores very little

Adult Attachment

Secure
- Comfortable in relationships
- Able to seek support from partner

Dismissing
- Greater sense of autonomy
- Tend to cut themselves off emotionally from partner

Preoccupied
- Fears rejection from partner
- Strong desire to maintain closeness

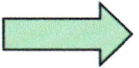

Hazan and Shaver (1987) wanted to look further into the ideas presented by Bowlby in relation to how early attachment could affect future relationships. They did this by devising a 'Love Quiz'.

Aim	Method	Findings	Conclusion
To find out if there was a correlation between infant attachment and future romantic relationships.	'Love Quiz' Self Report Questionnaire with the aim to: 1) Measure the attachment type in childhood 2)Assess the individuals beliefs about romantic love	The responses suggested that there was a high correlation between infant attachment types (refer back to Ainsworth's attachment types) and adult	There was evidence to support the theory that early attachment affected attitudes and approaches to adult romantic relationships. However, they did concede that this

	The questionnaire was printed in a newspaper of which there were 620 replies from people aged between 14 and 82.	romantic love styles.	was not the case in all situations.

Activity 53

Looking at the research carried out by Hazan and Shaver, if we were to evaluate this study under the following headings, what potential criticisms could be made about the research and their findings?

- **Participant memories**

- **Participant perception**

- **Volunteer bias**

- **Reliance on self-reporting**

In 1993 Hazan and Shaver repeated the love quiz and again found a correlation between infant attachment type and adult romantic relationships. However, the correlation was found to be greater in the first study than the later one.

Attraction

Buss *et al* (1990) conducted a cross-cultural study[12] into identifying what characteristics individuals valued when looking for a potential mate. They found

---

[12] 9,474 individuals across 33 countries, 5 islands, 37 cultures with an average age of 23.15 years. The data was collected from two translated questionnaires.

that men prioritised youth and physical attractiveness whereas women prioritised wealth and status.

Attraction and Romantic Relationships

There are many elements that come into play when romantic relationships are being instigated, embarked upon and developed. Humans are said to have a basic need to belong, and as such there is the desire to have regular interaction with others.However, from a psychological perspective, the hearts and flowers associated with romantic relationships is not the starting point of this aspect of the discussion. Rather psychologists suggest that how relationships are formed initially and primarily stems from self interest. According to Bryne and Clore (1970) and their **Reward/Satisfaction Model**, we embark upon relationships because the other person creates positive feelings in us. According to this model, we are drawn toward people who make us feel good about ourselves and fulfil unmet needs, whether this is financially, socially or physically. So, we like people who reward us in some way. The increase and maintenance of this can subsequently lead to relationship formation.

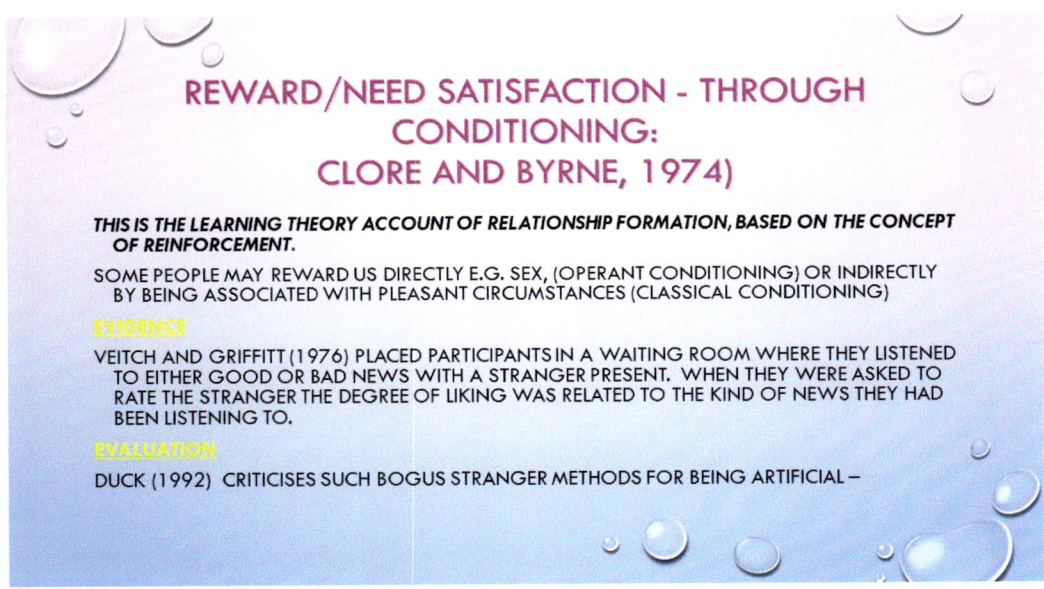

REWARD/NEED SATISFACTION - THROUGH CONDITIONING:
CLORE AND BYRNE, 1974)

THIS IS THE LEARNING THEORY ACCOUNT OF RELATIONSHIP FORMATION, BASED ON THE CONCEPT OF REINFORCEMENT.

SOME PEOPLE MAY REWARD US DIRECTLY E.G. SEX, (OPERANT CONDITIONING) OR INDIRECTLY BY BEING ASSOCIATED WITH PLEASANT CIRCUMSTANCES (CLASSICAL CONDITIONING)

EVIDENCE

VEITCH AND GRIFFITT (1976) PLACED PARTICIPANTS IN A WAITING ROOM WHERE THEY LISTENED TO EITHER GOOD OR BAD NEWS WITH A STRANGER PRESENT. WHEN THEY WERE ASKED TO RATE THE STRANGER THE DEGREE OF LIKING WAS RELATED TO THE KIND OF NEWS THEY HAD BEEN LISTENING TO.

EVALUATION

DUCK (1992) CRITICISES SUCH BOGUS STRANGER METHODS FOR BEING ARTIFICIAL –

Activity 54

Do you think this model applies to all relationships?

What follows are some of the core elements that are addressed within psychology when trying to gain a greater understand of romantic relationships.

Self-Disclosure

In a situation where individuals are interacting in a way that could result in a deeper relationship beyond what could be regarded as superficial, a process of self-disclosure may be evident from their interaction. When it comes to the process of self-disclosure, no one person reveals more about themselves than the other. Ideally, during this interaction one person discloses a bit about themselves, this is then reciprocated, and so on; it is on this basis the relationship can start to build. It also develops trust between the individuals involved.

Physical Attractiveness (including Matching Hypothesis)

Activity 55

Write a list of what you think attracts one person to another.

What is seen to be attractive is generally considered to be very much based on subjective, personal preferences and opinions. Attraction can be influenced by:

- *Proximity* – in that the more people meet and interact with each other, the more likely they are to get close and form relationship bonds

- *Reciprocal Liking* – being aware of the fact that someone likes you can fuel mutual attraction even if there are no real similarities between you and that person

- *Physical Attractiveness* – it is generally agreed that there are some physical traits and characteristics that are considered to be universally attractive[13] and this is referred to as Perceptions of Attractiveness

	Perceptions of Attractiveness
Mealey, Bridgstock, & Townsend (1999); Shackelford and Larsen (1997)	Faces are more appealing if they are symmetrical
Jones (1995) Perrett *et al.* (1998)	Large eyes and a small nose
Cunningham, Roberts, Barbee, Druen, & Wu(1995)	For the more mature - characteristics such as thin cheeks and high cheekbones are considered attractive
Singh (1993) Singh and Luis(1995)	In terms of body shape, a narrow waist-to-hip ratio - an "hourglass" figure, is more attractive in women

However, according to Hatfield, (1966) generally speaking, people are more likely than not to be attracted to individuals who are similar to themselves in terms of physical attractiveness; this is referred to as the **Matching Hypothesis**. Based on this theory, we do not necessarily gravitate toward the person who is considered to be the most attractive: rather, we are drawn to the individual who is most similar to ourselves in terms of physical attractiveness.

---

[13] Sex Differences in Judgments of Physical Attractiveness: A Social Relations, David K. Marcus Rowland S. Miller Sam Houston State University (2010)

When looking at the studies presented above, are there any aspects of the findings that would be open to question?

Filter Model

When deciding whether or not a potential partner is appropriate, people will look at all potential partners i.e. those an individual could possibly have a relationship with. So an individual is looking at what is referred to as the 'Field of Availables'. However, with a 'field' of potentials there has to be a way of eliminating the ineligible and short listing the eligible. According to Kerckhoff and Davis (1962) relationships develop via different filters. This is referred to as the **Filter Model**. According to this model, relationships go through three filters in order to distinguish between candidates that are desirable and potential partners and those that are not. The filters are:

- *Demographic* – here the focus is on the socio-demographic variables such as similar background, location, age, education, religious background and so on. Those who fall outside of these variables are filtered out
- *Attitudes* – this filter enables an individual to establish the extent to which a potential partner has similar beliefs, values, views, and ideas and so on. These are elements that can contribute to positive communication in a relationship. Those who do not share the same or similar attitudes would be filtered out. In fact in a study conducted by Kerckhoff and Davies using self report questionnaires, students who had been in relationships for over 18 months said that attitude similarity was one of the most important factors of a relationship
- *Complimentary Needs* – when a relationship is established, compliments on both sides is an important factor for the maintenance of that relationship. According to Duck (1999) it is through this that individual needs are adhered to

Theories of Romantic Relationships

The maintenance and breakdown of relationships

When looking at the maintenance of relationships, there are three approaches/theories that will be addressed in this section. They are:

- Social Exchange Theory
- Equity Theory
- Rusbult's Investment Model/Theory

Activity 57

Before looking at the three theories referred to previously, what do you think are the features of a successful relationship? In other words what do you think makes a relationship 'work'?

Social Exchange Theory

When people interact, they go through a series of exchanges with others, and according to Thibaut and Kelley (1959) they try to gain the most rewards from the exchange with the minimum cost to themselves. When the interaction results in a reward for the exchange, individuals feel obligated to reciprocate the reward, hence the social exchange. The reward may be in the form of compliments, money, security, sexual interaction and so on. In terms of a positive exchange, the reward could be reciprocated mutually and equally; however, the cost to an individual could be negative and detrimental, and exhibit itself in the form of physical or mental abuse and various forms of loss. In terms of maintaining a relationship, what is considered is whether or not the reward/s outweighs the cost/s and vice versa. If the cost is greater than the reward, this can result in a relationship breakdown.

Whilst this theory does explain some relationship dynamics, later research suggests that being treated fairly in a relationship through a process of negotiation (Equity Theory) is of greater significance than profiting from a relationship.

Activity 58

What criticisms do you think could be made of this theory?

Do relationships operate on the notion of exchange based the idea of reward and loss?

Find some studies or theorists who challenge this theory.

Whilst this theory can be applied to different types of relationships, we have to bear in mind that relationships are complex, and it is difficult to quantify profit/gain and loss/cost. Also, often those in a relationship will put another's needs before their own. As Rubin (1973) said:

"...human beings are sometimes altruistic in the fullest sense of the word. They make sacrifices for the sake of others without any consideration of the rewards they will obtain from them in return."

Equity Theory

As with the Social Exchange Theory, Equity theory (Walster, 1978) agrees that the exchange between individuals in a relationship is about trying to maximise the rewards. Howvere, this is not based on loss and gain but rather to achieve balance and fairness. Therefore, both parties to the interaction benefit mutually. If there is inequity in the relationship and it is not recognised and remedied, this could result in the breakdown of the relationship due to dissatisfaction.

There are three factors that provide the basis for commitment within a relationship. How committed a person is to a relationship is, according to this theory dependent upon:

1. How satisfied they are in the relationship

2. The qualities of alternatives to that relationship

3. How much they have already invested in the relationship

- Satisfaction - How satisfied someone is in a relationship can be as a result of the social exchange or equity. The extent of the level of satisfaction therefore is dependent upon the standards of the individual

- Quality of Alternatives - If there is a more viable and attractive alternative, an individual may feel compelled to opt for the alternative. If there is no eligible alternative, an individual may continue in their existing relationship

- Investment - What a person puts into a relationship, whether this is material, physical, emotionally, is regarded as an investment. Rusbult (1986) suggests that people will continue with a relationship if the rewards of staying in the relationship and the investments made outweighs the cost of being out of it. Also, an individual may still stay in a relationship even if the rewards are not significant, but their investment in the relationship has been so great that they will stick with it

Activity 59

Why do relationships come to an end or go wrong?

Duck's model of relationship breakdown

According to Steve Duck (1982), there are four key phases a relationship goes through prior to a breakdown. They are:

Intra-psychic Phase *'I've had enough of this!'*	An individual begins to think about their relationship and the fact that it is not satisfactory. They may 'vent' their concerns

	to others who do not know the partner personally. The dissatisfaction may be to do with the partner's attitude, behaviour, habits etc., and the aggrieved partner may consider the possibility of not being with the person any longer and think about the benefits of being in another relationship. Whilst an individual may be dissatisfied, they may not go onto the next phase. However, if after this phase the individual continues to be dissatisfied, they will move onto the next phase.
Dyadic Phase *"We need to talk."* *"Who would blame me if I left?"*	This phase is particularly significant in determining how the relationship is to proceed – should they attempt to repair the relationship or should they break up? The dissatisfied party confronts the other party and through this dialogue and negotiation a decision may be made regarding whether or not the relationship should be reconciled and repaired or discontinued. Often this phase challenges the other party's perception of the relationship.
Social Phase *"That's it, I'm done!"*	This is a critical phase. Now everything becomes public and others are 'enlisted' for support. Mutual friends may 'take sides' and comment and give opinions on the relationship by either encouraging the break up or encouraging maintaining the relationship. This therefore has implications for both parties in terms of their social interaction with others, such as mutual friends. At this phase the relationship

	breakdown moves from being a private matter to a social issue. At the point at which the relationship breaks up, the partners (ex) become available to seek other partners.
Grave Dressing Stage *"It was inevitable...I did all I could but I just couldn't make it work."*	Public notification of the end of the relationship with a public post mortem of it that places the individual in a positive light, presenting them as having no choice but to end the relationship. This places the individual in a positive light which has implications for future relationships in terms of how an individual is seen by others. *"Such stories are an integral and important part of the psychology of ending relationships... preparing the person for future relationships as well as helping them out of old ones." (Duck, 1988)*

Note these stages are not exclusive of other elements and discourse that occurs prior to a relationship breakdown. There are various personal reflective and consultative processes that play a part. And whilst presented in a rather clinical manner, one cannot discount the emotional and psychological difficulties that can result from the breakdown of the relationship.

Virtual Relationships in Social Media

Social media have become a significant part of everyday life and social interaction and so it is not surprising that they are seen to have a significant part to play in relationships and relationship development. Social networking sites such as Facebook, Twitter, Instagram and so on have had a marked impact on how we communicate with each other in general, and therefore it is not surprising that such media have had an impact upon romantic relationships. According to research, there are both pros and cons for this increased form of social interaction, particularly when looking at platforms such as Facebook. They are:

Pros	Cons
Because these platforms are easy to access people are able to filter potential mates. Information on an individual is readily available and therefore removes the need to go on several 'dates' in order to establish whether or not there is a real connection. (Warber, and Makstaller, 2013)	There can be a conflict between the partners in terms of publicly displaying the exclusivity of their relationship. For women, declaring their status via a social medium is taken more seriously than for men. It has been suggested that for women a public declaration on mediums such as Facebook portrays exclusivity and seriousness, whereas for men, what is being presented publicly is that his partner is now 'taken' and exclusive to him. However, he may still pursue others because he takes the public declaration of his status less seriously. (Fox and Warber, 2013)
A couples social network can be integrated (Weigel, 2008)	Due to the nature of the information that can be shared (some can over share) this can be a source of jealousy and conflict. Taken out of context, snapshots of interaction, unintentional comments etc. can be misinterpreted causing anxiety and trust issues. (Fox and Warber, 2014; Tokunaga 2015; Muise, , Christofides

	and Desmarais. 2009; Fox, Osborn and Warber,2014)
Often the form of interaction is positive and as such this can enable partners to communicate with each other in a way that cultivates good communication. So not only communicating directly to a partner declarations of love and affection, but also publicly declaring a positive relationship status to others, helps to reinforce the relationship and a commitment to it. (Dainton, 2013).	Over usage of social media can cause relationship conflict. A study by Clayton, Nagurney and Smith (2013) found that high levels of social media (particularly Facebook) usage can cause relationship problems and even lead to break-ups.

Activity 60

Are there any aspects of social networking that these pros and cons have failed to take into account?

Self-disclosure in virtual relationships

As discussed previously self-disclosure is a process of interaction whereby one party discloses information about themselves and the other party reciprocates. The process continues resulting in more personal and in-depth information being disclosed and it is on the basis of this that a deeper relationship can develop. Self-disclosure is often discussed in relation to face-to-face interaction. However, in the light of the increased impact of social media, the issue of self-disclosure has become more complex. As such, research tries to explain how self-disclosure occurs as part of online interaction.

According to Boyd[14] and Ellison (2007) social network sites are:

"... web-based services that allow individuals to (1) construct a public or semi-public profile within a bounded system, (2) articulate a list of other users with whom they share a connection, and (3) view and traverse their list of connections and those made by others within the system."

According to Jai *et al* (2010) part of social networking sites (SNS) success is as a result of self-disclosure:

"With SNS, people's social networks are expanded by connecting to others with shared interests or values based on other users' self-disclosed personal information.... However, the benefits of SNSs cannot be completely achieved if their users do not disclose enough personal information."

When looking at this in terms of relationships, one area that can be used to examine the extent of self-disclosure in terms of social networks is online dating. It has been suggested that individuals who embark upon communicating online tend to have more control over how they present themselves, focussing on the positives and elements that will connect them to someone they are interested in. It enables filtering in a way that does not open them up to awkward face-to-face social interaction. In terms of direct communication using this format, emails and message responses can be constructed in a timescale that enables the respondent to think about their answer or what they want to say. Pictures and images can be edited and retouched. This can be referred to as **impression management**. According to Piwinger and Ebert (2001), impression management occurs when people try to control and present a certain image or idea about themselves in a way that will portray them in a positive light. Social media lends itself quite well to impression management in that what is presented by an individual in terms of 'self-disclosure' is that which the individual wants to present

---

[14] Note this is the correct presentation of this name – no capitals

so as to place them in a positive light. A study of online dating by Gibbs, Ellison and Heino (2006) found that successful online daters used a significant amount of positive self-disclosure coupled with being very open with regard to their intentions.

Activity 61

What evaluations can be offered with regard to the notion of Impression Management?

Do you agree that self-disclosure tends to be 'managed' in this way?

Relationships

These are relationships based on one person spending and investing time and energy on an individual who either does not know them or is completely unaware of their existence, and is often associated with fans and celebrities. The up side of this is that for the individual who is investing their energy in another, there is little chance of rejection (as the celebrity doesn't even know they exist anyway!) and the likes of social media enables an individual to remain 'connected' to the celebrity beyond simply seeing them on television or at a concert, but being able to 'like' a picture they posted or be one of their followers online. Continued access to social networking, with no closing or shut down times, enables an individual 24/7 access to the celebrity. This gives an individual a virtual proximity connection to the celebrity.

Activity 62

Can you think of any potential benefits or problems that can be associated with Parasocial Relationships?

Generally people who embark upon a Parasocial relationship have no psychological issues. However, Keinlen and McCann suggest that people who create such relationships are 'insecurely attached' and as such may be attracted to such relationships because they carry with them less chance of a person being let down or disappointed. Taking this a step further, McCucheon suggests that people who are dissatisfied with their own lives can become somewhat fanatical and try to absorb some of what is lacking in their lives from the lives of the celebrity they have the Parasocial relationship with. This is referred to as Absorption Addiction. Generally, this fanaticism stays at an acceptable level. However, if it develops beyond this, it can manifest itself in the form of an addiction leading to pathology, resulting in activities such as obsession and stalking (Giles and Maltby).

Activity 63

Identify what you think could be considered some positives and negatives associated with Parasocial relationships

3.3 Gender

Paper 3 Option 1

Often the terms sex and gender are used interchangeable, and whilst there are obvious connections, they do have distinctive definitions which invariably determines our understanding of gender from a psychological perspective.

Key Areas:

- Sex and Gender
- The role of chromosomes and hormones
- Cognitive explanations of gender development
- Psychodynamic explanations of gender development
- Social Learning theory as applied to gender development
- Atypical gender development

Sex and Gender

As stated previously the terms sex and gender are often used interchangeable and clearly they are connected. But before we can begin to embark upon a discussion of gender, we need to be clear of the definitions that we will be using here.

Sex	Gender
The biological distinction between males and females e.g. females have *XX* chromosomes and males have *XY* chromosomes; females have ovaries whilst males have testes.	The social and cultural differences, social expectations and norms according to a person's sex.

In psychology the discussion of gender aims to examine the extent to which gender is biologically and socially determined. As a society, our attitudes and our understandings of the social and biological have developed. The once rather straightforward, definitive distinctions of gender in terms of male and females of the past, has become more complex.

Sex Role Stereotypes

People may be biologically born male or female but what constitutes masculine and feminine is learned according to some theories.

The idea of a sex role being masculine or feminine (that which is associated with being male or female) is one that develops and exists as a result of social interaction and social expectations. The shared normative acceptance of what males and females are supposed to be like and supposed to do reinforces our beliefs. Gender associations with certain jobs, for example, females being predominantly associated with being a nursery nurse and males, steel workers, has nothing exclusively to do with biology, but rather social expectations that have been passed on from one generation to the next.

The percentage of workers in each occupation group that are women, April to June 2013, UK

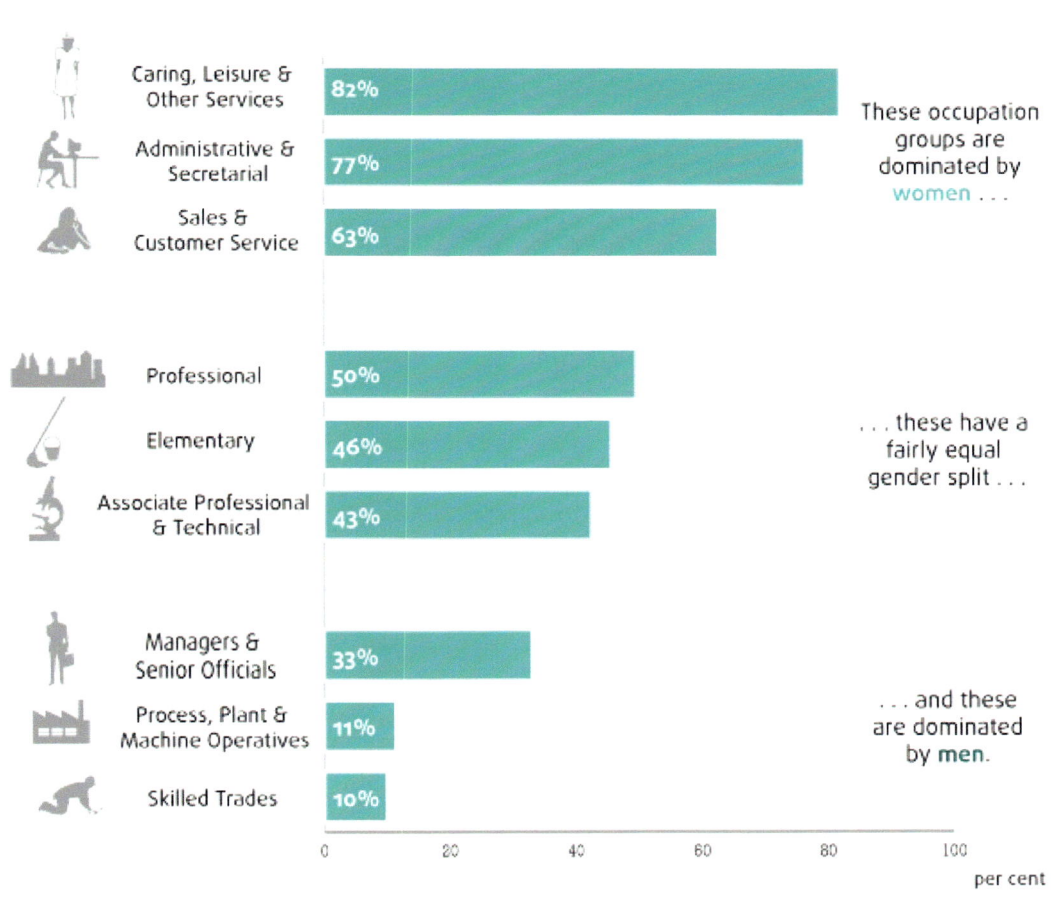

Source: Labour Force Survey - Office for National Statistics

These perceptions of masculine and feminine become sex role stereotypes when people engage in certain beliefs and assumptions about what masculine and feminine is supposed to be. The anthropologist Margaret Mead (1935) studied 3 cultures (Arapesh, Mundugumor, and the Tchambuli tribes of New Guinea (1935)) and found that what is seen to be masculine or feminine was not limited to biology but was culturally determined and defined, and as such this will vary from culture to culture.

Stereotyping

Stereotyping is about categorising and can be regarded as a cognitive process whereby an individual is able to process a lot of experiences and information. The problem arises when stereotyping, and the labelling that goes with it, inhibits what individuals can or cannot do. So a boy saying he wants to be a nursery nurse may be discouraged from doing so because "it's not the masculine thing to do".

The idea of what constitutes masculine and feminine becomes even more complex when we look at **androgyny**.

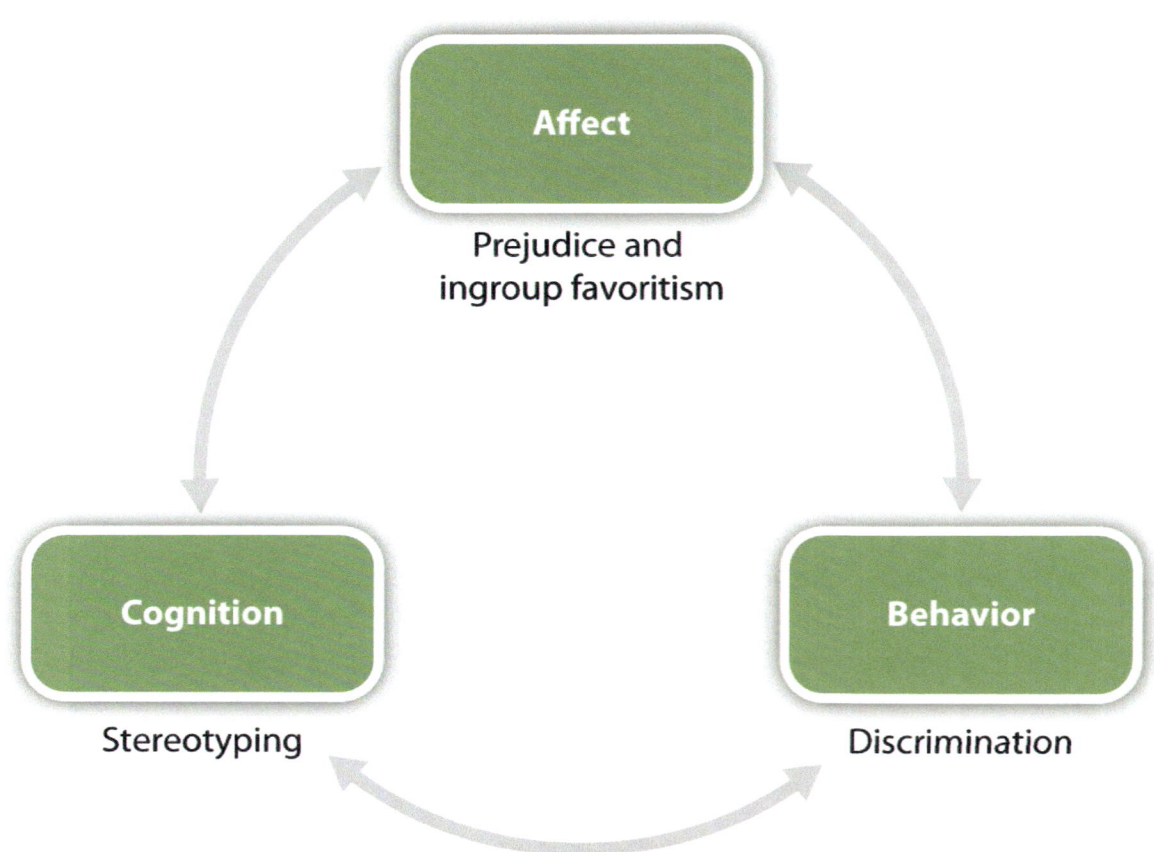

Stereotyping

Consider if being male or female is simply a matter of biology.

Bem (1974) developed the Bem Sex Role Inventory (BSRI), which was a self report questionnaire where participants were asked to rate themselves on a 7 point scale, based on adjectives that were seen as male attributes (strong, aggressive) and female attributes (gentle, warm). 20 of the attributes were male and 20 were female and 20 were indeterminate. The purpose of the questionnaire was to provide empirical research into androgyny. Androgyny is the presence of both masculine and feminine characteristics, and psychological androgyny refers to when a person does not fit into gender stereotype as they have both male and female characteristics. Bem found that individuals who were androgynous scored higher in terms of both masculine and feminine traits, whilst individuals who were sex typed (obviously feminine or obviously masculine) scored higher on either the masculine or the feminine.

From her findings Bem argued that it was better for an individual to be androgynous as they are likely to have better self-esteem and find it easier to adapt to different situations more so than individuals whose sex type was either masculine or feminine. This has been reiterated by Rathus *et al* (2005) who stated: *"People who are psychologically androgynous may be capable of summoning a wider range of masculine and feminine traits to meet the demands of various situations and to express their desires and talents"*.

Note however, psychological androgyny is not to be confused with gender dysphoria, which is when an individual feels as if they are trapped in a body of the wrong sex. Zeldow *et al* (1985) suggested that androgyny, far from making individuals psychologically healthier, was in actual fact masculine traits that were stronger and better adjusted.

Activity 65

Evaluate Bem's theory.

Bem also developed the **gender schema** theory. According to this theory, gender schema is a combination of cognitive development and social learning where an individual is able to make assumptions about what is masculine and feminine. Gender is a way for people (particularly children) to organise the world according to definitions of gender applied to the culture and to assume the identity of the gender appropriate to them.

Evaluation of Bem

Hollway (2002) suggests that it is not individuals who need to change their way of thinking, but rather society as a whole – social change is needed in terms of the amount of unequal power afforded to men and women. It is problematic for Hollway, that masculine traits are seen to be more desirable.

However, on a positive note, what the androgyny approach does offer is a move away from the idea that the only identity available to people in terms of gender is to be either masculine or feminine. Androgyny challenges this by presenting a gender identity that can encompass both the masculine and feminine.

The Role of Chromosomes and Hormones and Atypical Gender Development

From a biological perspective, there is no real distinction to be made between sex and gender as gender is seen to be determined by sex anyway, and there are some schools of thought that suggest that gender is learned, and as such nurture has as much a part to play in gender development. For this part of the discussion we will examine the 'nature' part of gender by looking further at the role played by chromosomes and hormones.

Hormones

The brain produces hormones which are chemicals secreted by glands in the body and carried in the bloodstream. Males and females have the same sex hormones. Androgens are such hormones and are significant in the development of male traits. Therefore the male androgens are Testosterone and Androstenedione.

Often referred to as 'male hormones', they are responsible for the development of testes and penis. Research has shown that androgens cause differences in terms of brain activity e.g. males being more aggressive than female. In the womb during development, when testosterone is released, this brings about the development of male sex organs and the testosterone affects development and behaviour by acting on the hypothalamus, resulting in the masculisation of the brain. As a hormone, testosterone is associated with certain types of behaviour that is regarded as typically male, such as aggression, higher sex drive, competitiveness etc. To demonstrate the distinctive natures of the brain in terms of male and female traits and development, Shaywitz *et al* (1995) used the results of MRI brain scans and found that in terms of the right and left hemispheres of the brain (with the right being associated with non-verbal and spatial skills and the left, language skills), women used both hemispheres whilst men mainly used the right.

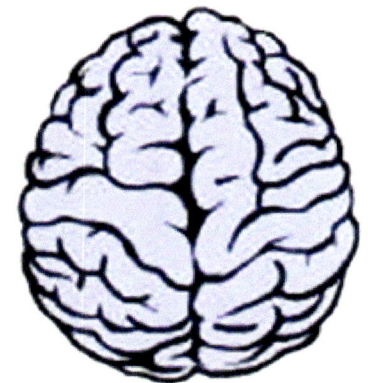

Right Hemisphere		Left Hemisphere
Non-verbal skills		Language skills
Spatial skills		

From brain scans it has been established that each side of the brain has unique and specialised functions and therefore are not identical (laterization).

Another hormone that is significant to this discussion is that of Oxytocin. It is found in both males and females but as with testosterone the amount in which it is found affects behaviour – both physical and psychological. Lower levels of oxytocin are found in males and are associated with ejaculation and sexual behaviour; it also influences social behaviour. Whilst testosterone is associated with strength and aggression, oxytocin can be seen to provide a balance in terms of social behaviour such as connecting with others. In females higher levels of oxytocin are found and it serves two main functions: 1) contraction of the womb during childbirth; 2) lactation. It has also been associated with social behaviour such as sexual arousal, bonding, trust, affection, social recognition, affection etc. Research suggests that this hormone is released during touching and cuddling.

Chromosomes

The sex of a child is determined at the time of conception, and it is chromosomal differences that determine whether or not a child is male or female. Females have XX chromosomes, whilst males have XY chromosomes. In males, it is the Y chromosome that starts the process of the production of testosterone and other male related hormones (androgens). There are 23 pairs of chromosomes (46 in total) and it is the 23rd pair of chromosomes that determines the sex of a child. Therefore, as stated previously if the 23rd pair of chromosomes are XY then the child will be male, if it XX it will be female.

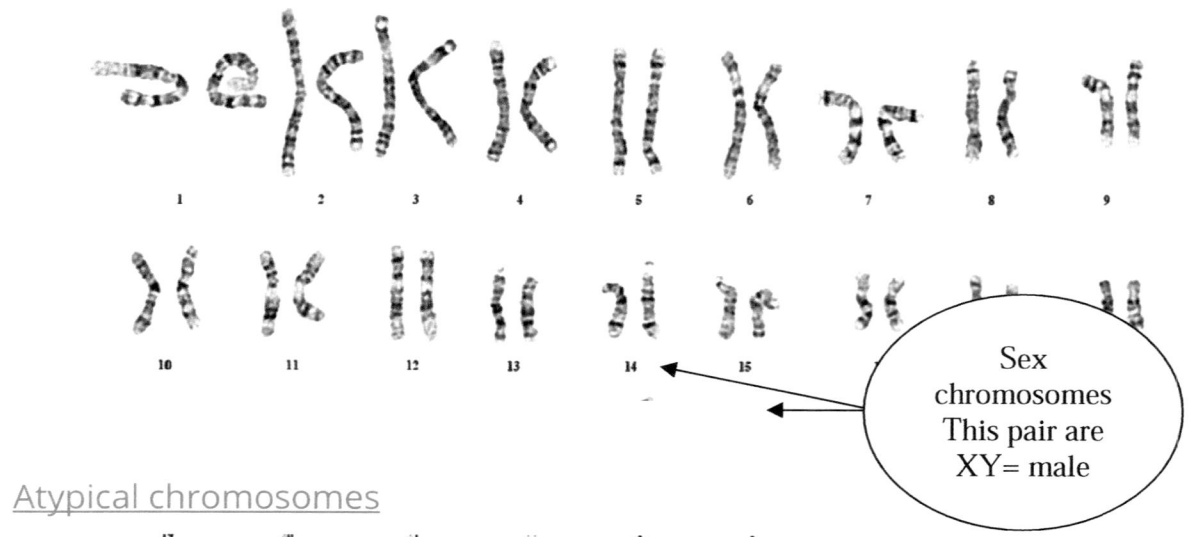

Atypical chromosomes

Atypical chromosomes occur in individuals who are conceived with a chromosomal pattern that is different to those with normal chromosomal development. This has an impact upon these individuals physically, cognitively and socially.

Turner Syndrome is an example of atypical chromosome development. It is a genetic chromosomal disorder that affects only females (1 in 2000) where the second female sex chromosome is either missing or defective. Whilst externally an individual may appear female in appearance, they will be shorter than average, have no or under developed ovaries; a lack of oestrogen, which would result in no menstruation and breast development, is not evident.

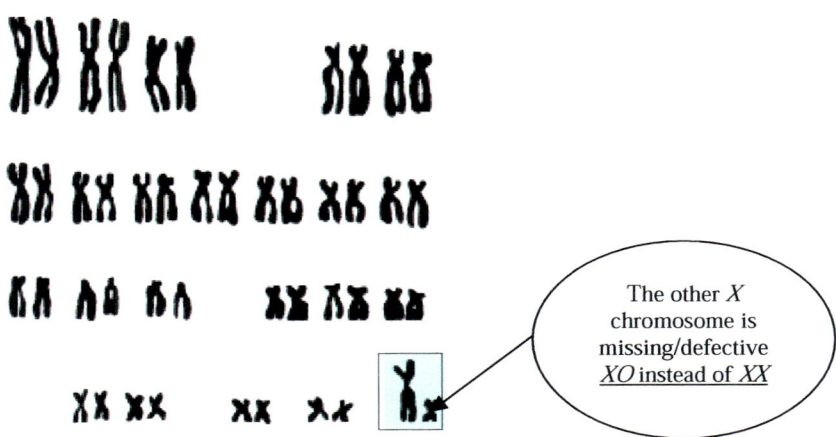

The other X chromosome is missing/defective XO instead of XX

Another example of atypical chromosomal development is Klinefelter's Syndrome. This chromosomal disorder affects males (1 in 600), where they have an excess X chromosomes. So if you recall, the chromosomal pattern should be XX for *female* and XY for *male*. In this case the pattern would look like XXY. Males with this syndrome may externally look male, but they will also be infertile, have enlarged breasts and are usually taller than the average male.

Another atypical chromosome pattern that affects males is the Double Y Chromosome. In this case boys have an extra Y chromosome *(XYY)*. They are characterised as being even taller than males who have Klinefelter's Syndrome. They are also characterised as being very impulsive and have a lower than average IQ.

Gender Identity Disorder

What is clear is that gender development is a complex series of processes - cognitive, biological, physiological, and social. Sometimes, however, an individual may experience somewhat of a disconnection between who they think and feel they are in terms of being male and female, and how they are seen and treated by others. Gender Identity disorder or Gender Dysphoria occurs when an individual experiences distress, discomfort and even confusion due to what they feel is disconnection between their gender identity and their biological sex. This does raise the nature/nurture debate, with no definitive answer as to which is most prevalent when it comes to gender identity. This can occur when, due to the incorrect assignment of a particular gender as in the case of David Reimer.

Case Study

David Reimer (formerly Bruce and Brenda) was a twin who was genetically born a male. However, at six months he suffered a botched circumcision that destroyed his penis. His parents sought the advice of Dr Money, who at the time was a respected psychologist and sexologist, who suggested that his penis and testes should be completely removed and that he should be raised as a girl. This was based on the theory that a boy could be raised as a girl because gender was fundamentally about nurture rather than nature. David received reconstructive surgery, hormone treatment and was renamed Brenda and treated as a girl. Money claimed that the process was a complete success as David was now living as Brenda, unaware of the fact that she had been born a boy. However, the follow up from this, following interviews, suggested the complete contrary to success. Brenda found that she engaged in typically male activity, was very tomboyish in her outlook and activities, dressed in what would be considered typically male clothes, and chose to study mechanics. Bruce, now Brenda was eventually told by his parents what had happened after which he refused to continue with taking female hormones, changed his name to David, had breast reduction surgery and had a penis constructed. David later married and adopted his wife's children (he was unable to have any of his own due to the surgery that was conducted on him as a child).

When interviewed David expressed having felt from an early age that something was not right about his gender.

What this case study seemed to demonstrate is that nurture alone cannot guarantee that a person will see themselves as either male or female. Rather it is a combination of both nature and nurture. If incorrectly assigned, the consequences can be devastating in terms of the trauma caused to the individual.

Activity 66

Evaluate the Reimer Case Study.

Does it provide at least some evidence that nurture is particularly significant?

What issues does it raise as an approach to understanding gender development?

Case Study:

The Batista Family (Imperato-McGinley et al., 1974)

The Batista family had ten children of which four were sons who had changed from being born and growing up as girls into males. When they were born they were born with normal female genitalia and body shape, but by the time they had reached the age of approximately 10, their vaginas had healed over, two testicles descended, and they grew full-size penises. The change had occurred because when they had reached puberty the testosterone levels that had occurred in their bodies gave them the male appearance. Imperato-McGinley et al suggested that their ability to adapt to their now male gender roles was not particularly problematic because the testosterone had masculated their brains. They lived their lives as males, married and did work commonly associated with males. The

Balista boys were genetically male but that did not manifest itself until they reached the age of 10. This study therefore showed that gender identity was programmed naturally from birth.

Cognitive Explanations of Gender Development

In his cognitive development study of gender development, Kohlberg (1966) found that children played an active role in their own gender identity in that at some stage of a child's development they are able to label themselves and categorise others as male or female. According to Kohlberg, a child goes through 3 stages in terms of gender development, and in the final stage a child is able to understand that being male or female is a constant; this is referred to as Kohlberg's Cognitive Development Theory.

By age 2	Stage 1	**Gender Identity**	The child can correctly identify their own sex.
By age 4	Stage 2	**Gender Stability**	The child realises that gender stays the same. The child's understanding of gender is also influenced by external factors e.g. types of dress, hair styles (short for boys, long for girls).
By age 7	Stage 3	**Gender Constancy**	The child understands that gender is independent of external factors and as such is permanent over time and in different situations. So a boy may refuse to wear something that makes him 'look like a girl'.

According to Kohlberg, the stages of gender development is driven by **maturation**, so whatever stage a child is at will determine their understanding of gender. Therefore children will demonstrate sex-type behaviour only when they reach the constancy stage, and once they understand this they then appreciate and understand more attitudes, characteristics and behaviours associated with their gender. Contrary to Kohlberg, Martin and Halverson (1981) suggest that gender typing occurs well before maturation and that gender stereotyping affects behaviour as a child gets older. Slaby and Frey (1975) conducted a study of a sample of 55 two- to five-years olds. The group was divided into high gender constancy and low gender constancy.

They were then presented with a silent film where the screen was split into two. On one side a female model carried out an activity that was gender stereotyped (like baking and being in the kitchen), the other model, a male, also carried out a gender stereotype activity such as changing the tyre on a car. The children were observed and it was found that when watching the eye movements of the children, the researchers found that when compared to children with low level constancy, children with high levels of gender constancy spent more time looking at the model that was of the same sex as themselves.

Activity 67

Write an evaluation of the Slaby and Frey study.

Psychodynamic Explanation of Gender Development

Sigmund Freud (1856-1939) was one of the most influential figures of the early twentieth century. During this time, medicine could offer little explanation for mental disorders and Freud set about looking for underlying unconscious causes. As we have already seen, he believed that we are all born with raw animal instincts (such as the drive for sex, food, and aggression) which have to be tamed to allow us to live in society. During childhood, we go through a series of stages during which we must deal with conflict between our instincts and pressures to conform to the rules of society. Eventually, we learn to subjugate these instincts and become moral citizens.

The Structure of Personality

Note: Much of what follows has already been dealt with but this does provide a good opportunity for revision in another context.

Freud believed that there are three main interacting parts to our basic personality: 'Id', 'Ego', and 'Superego'.

ID	Unconscious	Pleasure principle	Contains raw animal instinct
EGO	Conscious	Reality principle	Delays gratification of instincts until more appropriate time
SUPEREGO	Conscious	Internalises morals and values of society	Makes us feel guilty when we have done wrong and proud when we have upheld our values

Each of the parts can experience conflict, e.g. conflict between innate desires and the need to live in a structured society. If the conflict becomes great enough, it could threaten to overwhelm the ego. Therefore, according to Freud, there are four main ways that the unconscious mind could turn this conflict into an acceptable form.

These are:

- Parapraxes, or slips of the tongue, where some unconscious worry is 'let out' by the person unconsciously substituting a word for the word they meant to say. For example, someone with money problems might say at breakfast 'please pass the money' instead of 'please pass the honey'
- Dreams - The person can dream about the unconscious wish in symbolic form (manifest content) rather than dream about the real worry (latent content) and thereby avoid damaging the sensitive ego. Freud believed

that many dreams were of a sexual nature, e.g. a man worried about being impotent might dream of a broken candlestick or a woman afraid of being raped might dream about her purse being stolen. Here the candlestick and purse represent male and female genitals

- Neurotic symptoms – These arise when too many traumatic memories or wishes have been repressed and threaten to overwhelm the ego. Freud did not make the distinction between neuroses and psychoses, so any abnormal disorder would be classed as a neurotic symptom

- Defence mechanisms - Freud believed that defence mechanisms are used by the ego in the face of conflict. The defences help us to deal with anxiety, prevent us from being overwhelmed by temporary threats or traumas and can provide 'breathing space' in which to come to terms with conflict or find alternative ways of coping. As a short-term measure, they are necessary and normal but, as long-term solutions to life's problems, they are usually regarded as unhealthy and undesirable

Gender Identity

According to Freud our gender identity is the result of strong, unconscious, sexual desires, and we go through what Freud referred to as **Stages of Psychosexual Development.** People go through 5 stages, and at each stage people develop pleasure in one part of the body more than others.

Age	Stage	Description	Fixation
Up to 18mths	Oral	The child's pleasure centre is the mouth, from sucking and biting. Uses mouth to explore the world around them. No gender identity. Indiscriminate sexual drive	Oral adult e.g. a smoker may be over dependent on oral gratification.

1½ - 3 years	Anal	The child's pleasure centre is the anus, which includes the functions associated with it (defecating). Infant gains pleasure and control from retaining or expelling faeces.	A fixation on anal retention may lead to obsession with hygiene and neatness, even perhaps obsessive-compulsive disorder. Alternatively, a fixation on expelling faeces may lead to reckless, careless or disorganised behaviours.
3-6 years	Phallic (discussed in more detail later – Oedipus and Electra Complex)	Interest in own genitalia focusing on the genitals, self-discovery and self-stimulation.	Oedipus complex: intense affection for mother causes rivalry with father and fear of castration. Eventually, boy begins to identify with father. Electra complex: Absence of penis in girls causes penis envy.
6-Puberty	Latency	The child represses interest in sexuality and focuses on social and intellectual development. Psychosexual development enters a latency period and re-emerges at puberty.	Lack of sexual fulfilment in adulthood if become fixated in latency period.
From Puberty onward	Genital	Sexual awareness and focus is reignited.	Sexual desire and pleasure becomes directed toward someone outside of the family.

Case Study

Little Hans

The one and only child studied by Freud was Little Hans (1909) who developed a phobia of horses. Hans was 5 years old and developed his fear after seeing a horse that was pulling a carriage fall over and kick his feet in the air. Little Hans was terrified, and thought that the horse was dead. According to Freud, Little Hans was experiencing unresolved Oedipal conflict (wanting to possess his mother, and seeing his father as a rival) which he had displaced onto horses. The fear of horses, therefore, represented his fear of castration at the hands of his father. The blinkers on the horse reminded Little Hans of his father's glasses, and the black around the horse's mouth reminded him of his father's beard and moustache!

Phallic Stage

This stage is an area of focus as it is at this stage that Freud argues sexual development begins to occur.

Boys	Girls
Oedipus Complex	**Electra Complex**
Sexual desire for the mother	Realisation that they do not have a penis
The father is an obstacle to the fulfilment of the desire, therefore the frustration generated is directed toward the father in the form of aggression and hostility. The boy also experiences **castration anxiety**. Here, the boy is aware that his father is stronger and more powerful than him and as such the boy fears the	The realisation results in the girl believing she has been castrated, and because of this she feels powerless and desires to have a penis (**penis envy**). The girl begins to desire her father because he has a penis and becomes hostile toward the mother because she blames the mother for her not having a penis, but at the

father discovering the desire for the mother as for the boy the consequences will be the father 'castrating' him. This conflict results in the boy rejecting his mother and wanting to be like his father – taking on board the father's identity as part of his own – **internalising** his father and taking on the male **gender identity**. Eventually the desire for the mother is directed toward other women.	same time she is afraid of losing her mother's love and affection if she finds out. After a while she rejects her father and then begins to **identify** with the mother, and the female gender identity is **internalised**. The desire for a penis is repressed and replaced with the desire for a baby.

On the basis of Freud's theory presented above, he also argued that children who are brought up in single parent households are likely to have a weaker gender identity. He went as far as to suggest that a boy brought up by a mother is likely to be homosexual. Rekers and Moray (1990) supported this by suggesting that boys who are brought up without a father figure are more likely to have gender identity issues.

We can link this to gender dysphoria discussed previously, in that this can occur when in infancy as the child is unable to establish a gender identity. If the Oedipus or Electra complex is not resolved appropriately and at the right stage, gender dysphoria may occur because the child is unable to identify with the correct gender role model.

Activity 68

What limitations are there to this psychodynamic approach?

Evaluation

- The theory is based on the unconscious so it is difficult to test

- Freud provides very little evidence to support the theory
- More recent research and statistics would refute that single parent/homosexuality claim. Whilst there has been an increase in single parent families there has not been a significant increase in homosexuality to demonstrate a correlation
- The Little Hans study is very much based on a subjective interpretation
- This approach assumes homosexuality is abnormal and negative – using the notion of 'gender disturbance'
- Does not explain those situations where a child has no connection with either the mother or the father yet is still able to establish a gender identity

Social Learning Theory as applied to Gender Development

Gender differences occur as a result of social interaction and exchanges, therefore psychological differences between men and women are learned. Gender behaviour is learned not just through interaction with family and friends, but through various forms of media and discourse.

Bandura (1977), who we have discussed in previous sections, suggests that observation and imitation is very significant in terms of gender development. Behaviour is learned, and through observations made within the environment around them, people actively process information and are consequently able to understand the correlation between their behaviour and its consequences. In his famous Bobo Doll experiment (1961), Bandura showed that children observe people around them. Those being observed are referred to as 'models', and children's core models are their parents. These models provide the basis for behaviour, which is then imitated by the child e.g. masculine and feminine. Children at the early stages of development are likely to imitate behaviour regardless of the gender associated with it.

As they get older they then model the behaviour of those that they see as similar to themselves (e.g. the same sex). What then happens is that the modelled behaviour is acknowledged externally, positively or negatively, through praise or reprimand. So, if the child models behaviour that is seen to be appropriate for their gender, the child is likely to get praised and this then becomes internally reinforced – the child feels good and desires further approval and as such continues to behave in a way that generates that approval. Note that a child will also be aware of what response others receive if they do or do not behave in a way that is considered acceptable or appropriate. The response of others can influence the extent to which the child will copy the actions of someone else (vicarious reinforcement).

Social Learning theory gender studies

Theorist	Description
McGhee and Frueh (1975)	The more television people engage with, the more likely they are to succumb to gender stereotypes. Therefore heavy viewers of television would have more gender stereotype perception than light or non-viewers.
Gunter (1986)	Children categorised as heavy TV viewers hold stronger stereotyped beliefs than lighter viewers.
Fagot *et al* (1985)	An observational study that found that boys (21-25 months) made fun of boys who played with dolls or with girls. Male and female children were critical of male children who appeared to exhibit 'female' behaviours – more so than female children who exhibited 'male' behaviour.
Martin and Halverson's gender schema theory (GST) (1981)	The theory suggests that children develop gender consistency once they have learnt gender appropriate behaviours, and this is developed through observation. GST has four age related stages.

	- Stage 1 - preschool age – the child develops a gender identity, understanding their own gender. - Stage 2 - age 4-6 – the child views their gender as the in-group and see the opposite sex as the out-group. - Stage 3 - age 8-10 – the child actively presents appropriate behaviours and actions within the in-group. - Stage 4 - adolescence - they use the information observed from the in-group, allowing them to select gender appropriate behaviours for each gender.

The influence of culture

When it comes to culture, what is generally accepted is that there are gender identities and they can be distinctive, usually being either male or female. The differences lie with the extent to which that difference materialises and the nature of gender roles.

Williams and Best (1982) in their study of 30 countries found that there was significant cross cultural agreement in the terms and words used to describe males and females. All 30 countries associated male with strength and activity and female with nurturing and agreeability. So, gender stereotypes were evident in all countries.

Whilst it can be argued that cultural norms determine what is considered to be normal in society in terms of what it means to be male or female, evidence found in studies of Native American cultures have shown that they hold in high regard for those individuals they refer to as "two spirit" people.[15] Two Spirit people were

---

[15] French explorers in North America referred to these individuals as 'berdache", translated as meaning "intimate friend'.

males or females who were androgynous – identifying both with both male and female, they were sometimes referred to as the third gender.

Within Native American cultures, such individuals were highly respected because instead of the emphasis or focus being on whether an individual was male or female, the focus was on the individuals 'spiritual gifts', the spirit world and the gifts that stem from them, this being of paramount importance for this culture. Therefore, if someone was androgynous, far from being stigmatised or vilified, they were revered and respected as they were seen to have been favoured with two spirits and therefore doubly spiritually gifted; they were not just male/masculine or female/feminine: there was also male/feminine and female/masculine. This can be an example of true acceptance of gender diversity, with no one being forced to adhere to a gender identity base on whether or not the individual is biologically male or biologically female.

In terms of partnerships, the Native American cultures studied were very much aware of the practicalities that had to be considered in terms of unions between two people. Two spirited people being doubly gifted could take on work and roles of both the masculine and feminine. A male/feminine would be expected to marry either a female/masculine or a male/masculine in order to ensure balance for the practical provision and division of labour of the household. Likewise a female/masculine would be expected to marry a female/feminine or a male/feminine. No stigma was attached to such unions and, if anything, they were seen as logical and natural.

Figure: A 'male/feminine' from one of the Native American cultures

What the study of the Native American culture demonstrates is that cultural norms dictate what in fact is considered normal within society.

Activity 69

In your own word, write down what the case studies of the Native American cultures discussed previously tell us about gender identity within society.

Hofstede – Cultural Dimensions Theory

In his studies, Hofstede identifies whole societies as either being masculine or feminine, and this is dependent upon the types of values that the society holds. So what he was exmaining here was the degree to which cultures valued certain traits and behaviours. He stated that:

"Masculinity is the opposite of femininity; together, they form one of the dimensions of national cultures. Masculinity stands for a society in which social gender roles are dearly distinct: women are supposed to be more modest, tender, and concerned with the quality of life."

"Femininity stands for a society where gender roles overlap: both men and women are supposed to be modest, tender and concerned with the quality of life." (Hofstede, 2001)

Gender and Media

It has been suggested that there is a correlation between the media and gender stereotypes. Pierce (1993), in content analysis research of magazines between 1987 and 1991 found that in half of the stories, girls have relationship issues and were unable to solve problems with no stories on achievement, whereas boys were portrayed as masculine, sporty, problem solvers. From this it was argued that the media reinforces gender stereotypes.

Activity 70

Try to get hold of some magazines or newspapers (any would do), and as a content analysis exercise, go through each article, advert, anything in the magazines/newspapers, and see if you can identify those that are geared toward males and those toward female. After that go through some of the articles and see if you can identify any words or terminology that are gender specific e.g. 'he looked dashing and smart in his tailored Armani suite, whilst she elegantly glided down the red carpet in a stunning Dolce and Gobbana gown'

Also, note things like articles that are geared toward health and lifestyle or career and money – are they gender biased or quite neutral in the way in which they are presented?

3.4 Cognition and Development

Paper 3: Option1

Introduction

In this section, we will look at the development of thinking skills. We will consider different theories of cognitive development and how they can be applied to education.

Key areas:

- Piaget's theory of cognitive development
- Vygotsky's theory of cognitive development
- Baillargeon's explanation of early infant abilities
- The development of social cognition

Development of Thinking

Cognitive development refers to the development of thinking skills such as reasoning and problem solving.

Jean Piaget (1896-1980)

Piaget originally trained as a zoologist and was able to use his observations of how animals adapt to their environment to describe how children acquire knowledge. He regarded intelligence as a process that developed over time as a result of biological maturation, providing a child with a 'readiness' which allowed him to adapt to his environment.

Piaget believed that children learn about the world through trying different actions and seeing the effects. They store the knowledge in the form of **schemas**, which for very young children may be simple actions such as reaching or grasping. Schemas can be combined into **operations** such as reaching for a toy and grasping it.

Cognitive abilities develop through the processes of assimilation and accommodation. **Assimilation** is the process of fitting new information into an existing schema. **Accommodation** occurs when the new information will not fit into the existing schema. The schema will be altered to fit the new information. Periods when the existing schemas can successfully assimilate most new experiences are called **equilibrium**. Periods where the child encounters many new experiences and constantly needs to adjust their schemas are called **disequilibrium**.

Activity 71

Kitty is in the garden when she points to an aeroplane and says, 'bird'. Her mother explains her error. Describe the process Kitty has gone through to acquire this new knowledge.

When Kitty calls the aeroplane a bird, she is attempting to *assimilate* it into her bird *schema*. Her mother points out her error throwing her into *disequilibrium*. Kitty now makes a new 'aeroplane' schema through the process of *accommodation*; now *equilibrium* is restored.

Piaget found that children do not acquire new schemas in a simple continuous sequence. Children's ways of thinking change as they mature, and since maturation is a biological process; we cannot speed up their learning. For example, a child must babble before it can talk, walk before it can run and pass through puberty before it can become an adult. Piaget identified four broad stages, each with a number of sub-stages. At each stage the child is able to make increasingly complex adaptations. The four stages are: sensorimotor; pre-operational; concrete operational; and formal operational.

Sensorimotor (Birth to 2 years)

During this stage, babies develop their thinking from simple reflex reactions to the use of language at around 2 years. An important part of their development is the recognition of **object permanence** at around 9 months to 1 year. Before this development, when an object is hidden from a child (Piaget covered a toy with a cloth), the child acts as if the object is not there and shows no interest in it. After this development, however, the child will understand that the object is still there, even if it cannot be seen, and will begin to look for the object.

The Pre-Operational Period (2 to 7 Years)

During this stage, children develop language and begin to understand the relationships between objects and words and real and hypothetical situations. They can play games where they imagine and pretend. One of the features of this stage is **animism**, where a child believes that inanimate objects have human feelings. For example, a child might believe that a toy feels sad if left behind at home.

Piaget believed that children at this stage also show **egocentrism** and are unable to understand that others have a different point of view to their own. He also believed that children at this stage were unable to understand the process of **conservation**, meaning that quantities remain the same despite changes in appearance.

For example, if a quantity of water is poured from a short, wide glass into a tall thin glass, Piaget believed that, for a child at the pre-operational stage, it will look like there is more water in the tall, thin glass. Once a child has reached the concrete operational stage they will understand that the quantity remains the same because they know that the increased height of the glass is balanced by its reduced width (**compensation**) and that the water could be poured back into the shorter, wider glass (**reversibility**).

Children at this stage also have difficulty understanding the concept of **seriation**, which means the organisation of objects into a series, e.g. from tallest to shortest. They do not have the logical skills to understand that if object A is bigger than object B, and object B is bigger than object C, that A is also bigger than C, unless they can see the objects all together. They also have difficulty with **class inclusion** tasks and do not understand that, for example, 'pigs' are part of the wider category of 'animals'.

We will look at some of the criticisms of Piaget's research and findings later in this topic.

The Concrete Operational Period (7-11 Years)

Children at this stage are able to carry out the reasoning tasks that pre-operational children have difficulty with. They are able to **decentre**, focussing on the relationship between different factors, such as height and width. The stage is called 'concrete', however, because children can perform these tasks well when they can see the objects involved, but not in abstract terms or for theoretical objects.

The Formal Operational Period (11 Years Onwards)

In this final stage of development, the child develops logical reasoning and abstract thought. Children are able to reason through problems theoretically, without needing to see the objects or to employ trial and error methods.

Piaget's Research

Piaget focused much of his work on the pre-operational stage of development. As we have seen, it was here that he noticed a number of limitations in a child's thinking, including the inability to:

- See things from another's point of view (egocentrism)
- Conserve (understand that quantity remains the same despite changes in appearance)
- Perform Seriation tasks (put objects in order e.g. tallest to shortest)
- Perform class inclusion tasks (the ability to work out how categories of objects relate to one another)

He devised a number of research experiments to test these theories.

Testing Egocentricity

Piaget and Inhelder (1967) constructed the 'three mountains' task to demonstrate egocentricity. They made a 3D model consisting of three mountains, using papier-mâché. Each mountain had a distinctive feature (a cross, a house or snow) to help identify it.

A toy doll was placed at a number of different viewing positions in turn and the child was asked to work out what the doll could see from each position. After each position change, the child was shown a series of photographs (including the correct one) taken from different viewpoints. The child was asked to pick the photograph depicting the doll's view.

Children under the age of seven typically picked the photograph depicting their own view rather than that of the doll, thus demonstrating egocentrism.

Piaget's "3 mountains" egocentrism test:
"Draw how the mountains would look from the doll's point of view."

Testing Conservation

Piaget conducted various tasks to test children's ability to conserve (to know that quantity remains the same despite changes in appearance). One of these was the water experiment that asked children to consider the quantity of water poured from a short, wide glass into a tall, thin glass. Another asked children to estimate quantities using plasticine.

Papalia, Human Development, 7e. Copyright © 1998. McGraw-Hill Companies, Inc. All Rights Reserved.

Piaget's Conservation Task

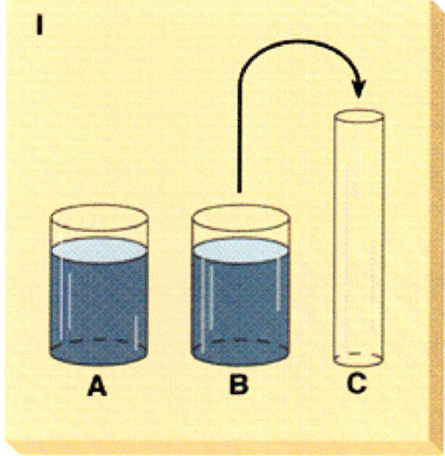
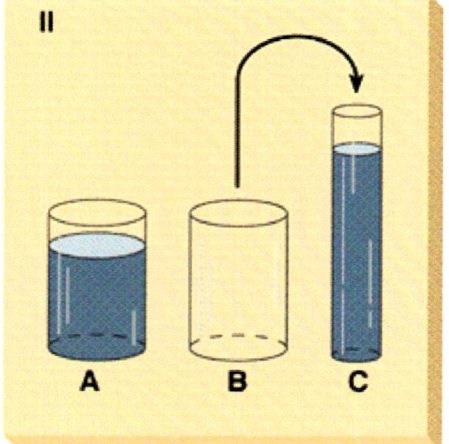

Activity 72

Two 7 year-old boys Jack and Charlie were shown two equal-sized balls of clay. One ball was then rolled into a long sausage shape. The boys were then asked if the two pieces of clay were the same amount. Jack said 'yes', Charlie said 'no'.

i.   Which of Piaget's ideas of cognitive development does this test demonstrate, and on what principle is it based?

ii.   At which of Piaget's stages of development are Jack and Charlie?

Answer to activity 72

i. This test demonstrates conservation. It is based on the ability to decentre (concentrate on more than one aspect.)

ii. Jack is concrete operational and Charlie is pre-operational

Testing Seriation

Piaget showed children stick A which was longer than stick B, then showed them Stick B which was longer than Stick C. Children were then asked about the relationship between Stick A and Stick C (which they had not seen together). Pre-operational children were unable to deduce that Stick A must be longer than Stick C.

Testing Class Inclusion

Piaget used picture cards e.g. five horses and three pigs. Children could count the horses and pigs but experienced difficulty when asked if there were more horses or more animals. This relates to the inability to see 'horses' as a subset of the larger category 'animals'.

Evaluation of Piaget

Piaget has had a wide reaching effect on education theory and practice. In the 1940s and 1950s children sat in rows of single desks and were not allowed to speak. They learned largely by rote e.g. repeating as a class '1x1 is 1, 2x2 is 4' etc. Many subjects involved children copying down large chunks of information which they were expected to learn. Piaget showed that children learn best by having hands-on experience of the world around them. Pre-school children could learn a great deal through play and older children needed to participate in activities which would consolidate the information they had learned. Children were also encouraged to work together as a team. This helped them to learn from each other and to reduce egocentrism.

However, Piaget's methods have been questioned for a number of reasons.

Methodology

1. Clinical Interview - Piaget used a technique he learned when studying Freudian psychoanalysis and applied this when talking to hundreds of children to discover the stages children pass through during their acquisition of cognitive processes. This relies on the children understanding the questions and on the interviewer interpreting what he or she is being told

2. Observation - Piaget observed children playing alone and together in their own natural surroundings to see how they responded to each other and how they played their games. If all six year-old children responded in similar ways to things such as taking turns, obeying rules or changing procedures, they might tell us how six year-olds think. If eight year-olds respond differently, their level of cognitive development must be different. Piaget has been criticised for mainly observing his own children

3. Direct Questioning - Piaget would show a child a 25 cm stick and a piece of string the same length and ask them if the two were the same. Then he would curl up the string and ask if they were the same now. Younger ones said the string was shorter now. Direct questions such as 'What are windows for?' and 'What can we do with a brick?' were used to reveal the way children think and what they know. These may not have been useful in getting the children to understand the task

Tasks Used

Object Permanence Task

Was Piaget's method of hiding a ball under a blanket really showing a lack of object permanence? How do we know? Bower (1977) believes it was demonstrating lack of motor co-ordination rather than object permanence.

Egocentrism: Three Mountains Task

Donaldson believes that the children were unable to complete the three mountains task because they did not understand the situation (it was outside of their schema) rather than because they were limited by egocentrism.

In the 'policeman doll study' carried out by Hughes (1975) children were shown a model of two intersecting walls and asked to position a doll where the policeman could not see it. 90% of children aged between 3 ½ and 5 could complete this task successfully. It may be that this task was more understandable for the children, who understood it in relation to such games as hide and seek.

A conversion task carried out by Paul Light used pasta shells poured between jars. In the standard Piaget test 90% of children could not perform the conversion. However, Light found that when children were given a context for the experiment, their abilities improved. When told that there was a sharp, dangerous edge on the first jar, 70% were able to state that the quantity of pasta had not changed.

However, some have argued that these two experiments do not test the same skills as Piaget's original tasks. For example, the policeman task is a lot easier than the three mountains task.

In addition, a research study by Siegler (1995) found that children can be trained to understand conversion. Their understanding was gradual, rather than a sudden jump in developmental stage.

Some Further Observations

Gelman (1979) has shown that four year-old children often use simpler forms of speech when talking to two year-olds. Would they be able to do this if they were egocentric?

Marvin (1975) found that some four year-olds can choose appropriate presents for their mother's birthday. What would you expect them to choose if they were egocentric?

Bruner (1966) points out that some children use the words 'more' or 'less' when referring to height and length, so in their terms, they are correct when they refer to the taller beaker having 'more' in it. When a child asks for 'more milk' it is used to seeing the level in the glass rise.

Botvin and Murray (1975) have noted that when non-conserving children are placed in a group of conservers, they actually learn the reasoning given and can learn to apply it themselves. This shows that special training techniques may speed children's understanding of conservation but only if they have reached the necessary stage of development.

The Validity of Stages

According to Horn (1976), children can reach later stages without having to go through earlier ones. For example, some children walk without passing through the crawling stage. So the stages are not as rigid as Piaget thought.

In addition, Siegler's study demonstrates the importance of practice and training in speeding up or facilitating cognitive development. Piaget did not take into account the importance of social influences such as language and context on cognitive development, factors emphasised by Vygotsky's theory, discussed later.

Piaget and Education

A Piagetian-inspired curriculum emphasises a learner-centred approach. Piaget advocated active, discovery-based learning environments in our schools. Intelligence grows through the twin processes of assimilation and accommodation; therefore, experiences should be planned to allow opportunities for assimilation and accommodation to occur. Children need to explore, to manipulate, to experiment, to question and to search out answers for themselves. Activity is essential.

However, this does not mean that children should be allowed to do whatever they want. So what is the role of the teacher? Teachers should be able to assess the child's present cognitive level and their strengths and weaknesses. Instruction should be individualised as much as possible and children should have opportunities to communicate with one another, to argue and debate issues. He saw teachers as facilitators of knowledge; they are there to guide and stimulate the students, allow children to make mistakes and learn from them. The teacher should present students with materials and situations according to their stage of development (the concept of readiness) that allows them to discover new learning.

Lev Vygotsky (1896-1934)

There is a growing body of evidence to support the work of Vygotsky. His work centres on the importance of social interaction, language and culture, as well as the role of instruction in development.

The Importance of Social Interaction

- Cognitive skills develop as a child interacts with others (parents, teachers, other adults and peers)
- Interaction enables child to observe others using various problem-solving strategies and cognitive tools
- Notion of child as apprentice
- No specific age-related stages

The Importance of Language

- Transition from simple to complex thinking made possible by language
- Child's use of monologues (talking to themselves) disappears around age 7 when language is internalised
- Two distinct functions:
  - Social speech – used to communicate with others
  - Intellectual speech – used to regulate, plan and think and forms the basis of higher mental functions

Zone of Proximal Development (ZPD)

- Defined as the gap between the tasks that the child can do on their own and those they can do with help
- If tasks are structured within the ZPD and a child is supported to achieve them, they can move forward in terms of their cognitive development

Scaffolding

Vygotsky (perhaps due to his untimely death) did not explain the nature of the support a child should receive in order to progress. Wood, Bruner and Ross (1976) watched mothers and children completing various tasks, and came up with the notion of 'scaffolding' to describe the way in which the mothers supported the child's learning.

In a study by Wood and Middleton (1975) mothers were recorded and observed teaching their children to put together a wooden block puzzle. The study found that the most effective teaching methods were carefully tuned to the child's actions, offering support when needed but allowing them to work on their own when they were able to.

Further Research

Adults as Tutors

In a study by Wertsch (1980), 2, 3 and 4 year-olds were asked to complete a reconstruction task with their mothers. The goal was to build a replica of a truck using a set of pieces of different shapes and colours.

Findings:

1. In about 90% of instances when the mother looked at the model, the child looked too. The children were using social reference to find out what to do

2. The frequency of mother-guided looks declined significantly with age. This supports Vygotsky's idea that the child internalises problem solving skills and shifts from other-regulation to self-regulation

3. Older children appeared to extract the relevant information from maternal looks more efficiently than younger children, which shows that older children have learned how to 'use' an adult for the information they need

Adults as Tutors: Naturalistic Observation

Saxe *et al* (1987)

This study looked at the relationships between mothers' everyday involvements in pre-schoolers' early number activities and the children's number development. They found that the mothers were working at the child's level of ability and then extending it to guide the child towards higher levels of understanding. An example is shown below and consists of counting stairs.

1. Mother counts with child

2. Mother asks "How many have you counted?"

3. Mother asks child to predict how many they will have counted if they go up another step

Importance of Culture

Greenfield and Lave (1982)

Greenfield and Lave studied the learning process of Mexican girls acquiring traditional weaving skills. The girls initially spent over half their time watching the skilled teachers, and they began to weave by co-operating with the teachers. As they became more involved and more competent, co-operative activity increased for a while until the girl was able to take personal responsibility for the work. Adults **scaffolded** the task, providing just the right amount of help to enable the girl to complete it successfully.

Peers as Tutors

Findings from studies of peer tutoring in which children are paired with older children who already have greater skill at a task, show that the tutee's cognitive performance improves after the tutorial session.

Barnier (1989) found improvements in the performance of 6-7 year-olds on spatial and perspective tasks after training by 7-8 year-old tutors.

Cross Cultural Differences in Peer Tutoring

Ellis and Gauvain (1993)

This study compared the performance of Navaho children in northern Arizona with that of Euro-American children from rural Virginia on a peer tutoring task involving a complicated maze game. Nine year-old tutors were taught the task and then had to work in pairs to teach it to seven year-old tutees. The Navaho tutors tended to work co-operatively.

They were more patient and used more non-verbal instruction. Navaho tutors were more content to sit by and observe while their partner taught part of the task, while Euro-American children tended to become bored and disinterested if their partner took over. Overall, the progress the tutees made was similar even though the interaction was considerably different between the two cultures.

Evaluation of Vygotsky's Theory

- Acknowledges individual differences within the same culture and also between people from different cultures
- Emphasises role of social and cultural factors which Piaget overlooked
- Can help explain unusual cases e.g. feral children who have learned to communicate using signs and gestures similar to the animals that raised them
- Lacked empirical support for many years, probably due to the fact that the theory focuses on the *processes* involved in cognitive development and these are more difficult to test. Evidence is now being gathered to support Vygotsky's theory
- Can explain why children can be trained to successfully complete Piagetian tasks at an earlier age
- May have overemphasised the role of social and cultural interaction. Takes no account of biology or the concepts of maturation and 'readiness'. If social interaction were the only influence on cognitive development, we would expect it to occur quicker than it actually does

Vygotsky and Education

Vygotsky's approach to education focuses on instruction and interaction. The teacher's role is to work within the zone of proximal development, scaffolding the child to help them learn new skills. Learning can also be supported by older or more knowledgeable children through the process of peer mentoring. Language and communication are central.

Activity 73

Outline the differences between the theories of Piaget and Vygotsky.

Piaget

- Stresses role of biology, cognitive development depends on maturation and the concept of readiness to progress through a number of developmental stages

- Sees stages as fixed and universal therefore, does not take into account culture

- Sees child as lone scientist

Vygotsky

- Underemphasises biology, social interaction and culture important in helping children to progress within individual ZPD

- Scaffolding and role of parents and peers as teachers important

- Sees child as apprentice

- Communist background influences his ideas on the importance of collective action

Baillargeon (1987)

Piaget argues that object prominence (understanding that an object still exists even if it cannot be seen) develops between 8-12 months. However, Baillargeon's research has shown that this can happen much sooner. Piaget came to his conclusion following observations of 8-12 months old children, where a desirable object was placed before a child for viewing and then the object was covered with a blanket. Piaget found that an infant of between 8-12 months would try to remove the blanket to reveal the object again, and for Piaget this was evidence that the child understood that the object continued to exist even though it was out of sight (object prominence.)[16] Children younger than 8 months rarely tried to remove the blanket. Baillargeon, however, challenges this by pointing out that one of the reasons children under 8 months appear to lack object prominence was

_____

[16] Understanding that the object still existed even if it was no longer visible.

because they may lack the fine motor skills and ability to reach out and remove the blanket. In order to test this Baillargeon devised a test that did not require any motor movement from the child, rather observers looked at the child's response in terms of its increased attention, and the infant would look longer at something.

Violation of Expectation Paradigm

Baillargeon used this approach with the aim to examine a child's ability to understand, predict and interpret the outcomes of the physical world they observe.

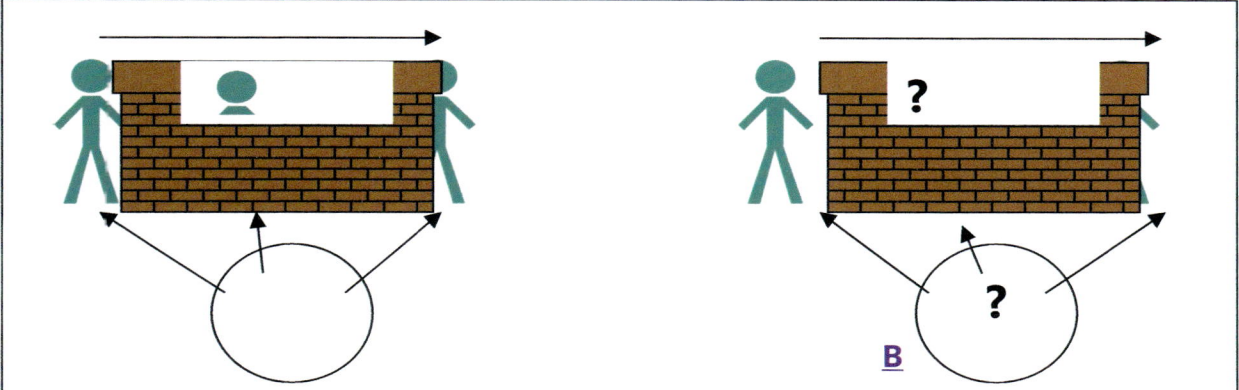

(In the above illustration the circle represents the observing infant)

Baillargeon suggests that children will look longer at something they have not encountered before. In the above illustration an infant is presented with a new situation repeatedly until by looking away the child indicates that the situation is no longer new to them e.g. in **A** the child is presented with a figure moving from one side of the brick wall to the other and as the figure moves from one end to the next the child is still able to see a part of the figure in the gap in the middle of the wall.

Then, an unexpected event is introduced to the situation e.g. **B** as the figure moves from one of the wall to the other; whereas before, part of the figure was visible in the gap, now no part of the figure is visible. The reaction of the child i.e. their staring at the gap, indicating expectation about what should be seen or what should have happened, is evidence of violation of expectation.

Therefore, the child knows that that part of the object (in our illustration this would be the head part of the figure) should have been visible. From her research, Baillargeon found that in contrast to Piaget's theory this level of awareness and understanding could be seen in infants as young as 3 months. Therefore, very young children are able to possess expectations about the physical world and events in systematic and predictable way.

Activity 74

Evaluate the Violation of Expectation Paradigm.

Jerome Bruner (1915 -)

Bruner was influenced by Piaget's work. He agreed that biological organisation underlies cognitive development, and that children actively explore their environment in order to make sense of it. He was also strongly influenced by Vygotsky's ideas and together with David Wood came up with the idea of scaffolding to explain how older children and adults support younger ones when learning a new task.

Bruner's theory is not a stage theory. He believes that adults use three main strategies (modes of representation called enactive, iconic and symbolic) when they solve problems. Although these strategies are acquired in order, we gain the new and more complex strategy *alongside* the old one; it is not replaced as it would be in a stage theory. Adults often use all three modes in order, especially when completing a new task.

Modes of Representation

- Enactive (birth to 18 months) - Representing an object or situation by means of actions e.g. body movements. This mode uses the same actions involved with the object, situation or skill e.g. throwing a frisbee
- Iconic (18months+) - Representing an object or situation by means of mental pictures. Uses sensory images associated with the real situation they represent

- Symbolic (6-7 years old) - Objects or situations are represented by arbitrary symbols e.g. words

Evidence for Transition from the Iconic to the Symbolic Mode of Representation

Bruner and Kenney (1966)

- Aims: To find out at what age children start to use symbolic mode of representation

- Procedure: Children aged 3-7 shown a board divided into 9 squares, on each square was a plastic beaker of different sizes and widths, tallest at back and widest on left. Each child had to look at the beakers and memorise the arrangement. The beakers were then mixed up and children had to:

  ➢ Reproduce the original pattern
  ➢ Transpose the original pattern (arrange them in a mirror image of the original)

- Findings: Most 5-plus year-olds correctly completed the reproduction test. However, few under 7 could complete the transposition task. Most over 7 could complete both tasks

- Conclusion: Supports the view that children on average begin to acquire the symbolic mode at around 7. The task required the ability to mentally transform the visual memory using rules such as 'the thin one goes on the right' etc. In other words, this task required symbolic representation

Evaluation of Bruner

Wood (1988) claims that Bruner's theory stands between those of Piaget and Vygotsky. Bruner's theory places emphasis on language and social experience in cognitive development. He also argues that children learn by actively exploring the world. Unlike Piaget, however, Bruner believes that children of any age can be taught any skill, as long as it is explained to them in a way they can understand. Bruner devised the idea of the **spiral curriculum** as a model for education. In the spiral curriculum, basic skills are taught, repeated and built upon so that the child develops existing knowledge with more complex concepts. **Contingency** is also an important concept, and teaching must be dependent on the ability and behaviour of the child.

Further Evaluation Points

- The flexibility of the different modes of representation is a strength of this theory. It has been confirmed in the classroom that all three modes can be used
- Bruner was responsible for bringing Vygotsky's work to a wider audience and extending some of his thinking (especially through his work on scaffolding).
- The spiral curriculum is widely used and accepted in schools
- Some believed Bruner focused too much on the role of the mother, as many of his early studies involved observing mothers with their pre-school children. His ideas could apply equally to any adult or older child who spends time with a young child

Bruner and Education

- Agrees with Piaget that children learn through enquiry and investigation but rejected the notion of readiness, believing that a child could be taught anything at any time so long as the correct methods were used
- Came up with the 'spiral curriculum', widely used today, in which topics are revisited using different modes of representation until the child has a sophisticated grasp of the subject. For example, a topic on dinosaurs may begin with making a model dinosaur (enactive mode), then watching a film (iconic mode) and finally, reading about dinosaurs from a book (symbolic mode)
- Came up with idea of *contingency* meaning that the method the teacher picks should be contingent on the child's behaviour

- Believed in cognitive acceleration: the idea that children's cognitive development could be speeded up through the teaching of thinking skills. Evidence exists to support this idea (Adey *et al,* 2002)
- States importance of:

  ➤ Structure - Children should be taught underlying principles first

  ➤ Intuitive thought - Children should be taught to think intuitively. Teachers should model intuitive thought and encourage it by using brainstorms or mindshowers at the start of lessons

  ➤ Motivation – Child should be willing to learn and should want to engage with subject materials

Development of Social Cognition

Social cognition focuses on how children think about their social world and their relationships and interactions with others.

To cope with social interactions successfully, we need to be able to understand and predict what other people are thinking or feeling.

Developmental social psychologists are interested in three lines of enquiry:
- What cognitive processes allow us to understand other people?
- How and when do these processes develop?
- What can we learn about these processes by studying individuals with autism and Asperger's syndrome?

Development of the Child's Sense of Self

Most babies love mirrors. If you hold a baby in front of a mirror, she may smile, pat the glass, or even try to kiss her reflection. But young children do not know who the person in the mirror is. She may even think her own reflection is another baby. When are children able to recognise themselves and how do scientists study this?

Lewis and Brooks-Gunn (1979) asked a group of mothers and their babies, aged 9 to 24 months, to play in front of a mirror. First, the researchers watched to see how each baby acted when placed in front of a mirror. Next, each of the mothers pretended to wipe dirt off her baby's face, while they were really putting a small dab of red makeup on the tip of the baby's nose. Then the babies were placed in front of the mirror again, to see what they would do. Would they notice the red spot on their noses? Would they recognize that something was different about their faces and try to wipe off the red spot?

Before 15 months old, babies didn't seem to recognize themselves in the mirror. These babies stared at their reflections and may have found them familiar, but they didn't react any differently when they saw the red spots on their noses. But by 21 months, most infants tried to touch or wipe their nose. These babies knew that they were the baby in the mirror! They had reached a new level of self-awareness and recognised themselves.

The Development of Embarrassment

Tilly is 20 months old, and has just been given a new outfit by her grandmother who helps her put it on, and then stands back to look at her.

"Isn't she cute in that outfit? Everybody look at Tilly in her new outfit!"

Tilly smiles, but she's clearly not comfortable with all the attention. Nervously, she looks down and plays with a button on her dress. She looks around the room, glancing at people, and then looks away again.

Tilly is embarrassed. A few months ago, she might have happily danced in front of a dozen adults, but now her reaction to the attention is different. Embarrassment is a feeling that comes when children are aware that they have become the object of attention (Lewis, 2000). Her father, seeing this embarrassment, takes Tilly out of the spotlight and together they play with a toy.

Tilly's embarrassment shows that she has reached an important new stage in her emotional and cognitive development: she's become more self-aware. Research has found that embarrassment occurs only after self-recognition develops (Lewis, 2000).

Researchers also studied children's self-awareness as a way to learn about emotions, such as embarrassment. First, they used the make-up test to see which of the children tried to touch or wipe the red spots on their noses. Then they over-complimented the children to see if they would get embarrassed. For example, the children were told many times that they were smart, cute, had beautiful hair and lovely clothes. Other children were asked to dance in front of a group of unfamiliar adults. The children who touched their red noses in the mirror were the only ones who showed embarrassment. Those who didn't touch their noses did not show signs of being embarrassed (Lewis, Sullivan, Stranger and Weiss, 1989).

These experiments show that a certain level of self-awareness is needed before children experience emotions like embarrassment. Once children are aware of themselves as individuals, they become more sensitive to the ways people might see them. They also become more aware of how people think differently, and that other people might have feelings that are different from their own. This awareness provides a foundation for emotions like empathy and envy (Lewis, 2000), which are part of a child's social and emotional development.

Striano and Reid (2006) and Berk (2006) show how rapidly social cognition develops from birth:

- 6-10 weeks – Babies are distressed by faces that show no emotion. This shows that they are already accustomed to reading information from faces
- 3 months – Babies make regular eye-contact
- 4-9 months – The parent's gaze is used to switch the baby's attention from one object to another. This is called eye gaze cueing

- 12 -15 months- babies point at objects they want (protoimperative pointing) or that they are interested in (protodeclarative pointing)
- 18 months – Pretend play emerges
- 2 years – A sense of self emerges

Theory of Mind

We constantly rely on our ability to be able to predict other people's thoughts and actions. The ability to do this has been called theory of mind or ToM for short. The term was first coined by Premack and Woodruff (1978) to describe the ability of chimpanzees to deceive their keepers.

ToM allows us to understand the links between beliefs and behaviours and to know that people will often act on beliefs, even if they are false. The development of ToM is seen as crucial to normal social behaviour.

In order to study the development of ToM in children, researchers have used 'false belief' and 'unexpected transfer' tasks. False belief tasks help researchers to assess whether a child can accept that another can hold a false belief. Unexpected transfer tasks help to assess the child's ability to see a situation from another's perspective.

In an unexpected transfer task devised by Wimmer and Perner (1983) children aged 4 and 5 were shown two dolls, Maxi and his mother. Maxi put a bar of chocolate into a blue cupboard and then went out. While he was out, his mother put the chocolate into a green cupboard. The children were asked: 'Where would Maxi look for the chocolate?'

Children aged 4 and under thought that Maxi would look in the green cupboard. Children over 4 would typically say that he would look in the blue cupboard. The children over 4 had developed theory of mind, and understood that Maxi would not know that his mother had moved the chocolate.

Baron-Cohen *et al* **(1985)**

One of the best known false belief studies is that carried out by Baron-Cohen *et al* (1985). This is sometimes called the Sally-Ann task.

Aims	To test the development of theory of mind in normally developing children, children with Down's syndrome and children with autism.
Participants	20 autistic children with an average age of 11 years, 11 months; 14 children with Down's syndrome aged on average 10 years, 11 months; 27 normally developing children, aged on average 4 years, 5 months.
Procedure	The children were told a story involving two dolls called Sally and Ann. Sally put a marble into a basket and, while she was out, Ann moved it into a box. The children were asked: "Where will Sally look for her marble?" (the belief question); "Where is the marble really?" (the reality question); and "Where was the marble at the beginning" (the memory question).
Findings	All the children answered the reality and memory questions correctly. 85% of the normally developing children and 86% of the children with Down's syndrome answered the belief question correctly. However, only 20% of the autistic children were able to answer the belief question correctly.
Conclusions	The autistic children had not developed theory of mind and had difficulties in understanding the perspective of another.
Methodological Issues	This was a well-controlled study where participants were matched for general intelligent and understanding, so that only their social abilities were being tested. However, slight

	differences in how the questions were asked could alter the results.
Ethical Issues	Children cannot give informed consent so parental consent must be obtained. It is important when working with children that they should be treated sensitively, especially if they are atypically developing children who may easily become distressed.

Evaluation of Theory of Mind

- A strength of the Baron-Cohen method is the precise control of variables
- However, the use of dolls with autistic children has been questioned, since it is known that they don't play well. Some children may think that dolls cannot believe things, making the task artificial and lacking in validity
- Baron-Cohen's work has been replicated by other researchers. A meta-analysis of 178 studies by Wellman (2001) has shown that ToM does develop during the pre-school years and is not an artefact of the tasks used
- Bloom and German (2000) state that false belief tasks are too difficult for small children who reason that beliefs should be true. They say that testing of ToM need not require the ability to reason about false beliefs
- Peskin (1992) showed that understanding deception was key to the development of ToM. Children were asked to deceive a nasty puppet who would choose the same sticker as them. The children were then asked to choose the sticker they liked best from a selection of four. Nearly all five year-olds tested had no problem in deceiving the nasty puppet by choosing a sticker other than the one they liked best. Four year-olds quickly learned the deception but three year-olds continued to choose their favourite and were dismayed when the nasty puppet picked it too

Wellman (1990) believes that ToM develops in stages:

Age (years)	Stage
2	Understand others through own desires
3	Perceive beliefs as a representation of the real world
4	Realise that beliefs are not exact copies of the world but can be interpretations which are sometimes incorrect

Charman *et al* (2000) have demonstrated the developmental nature of ToM. They found a correlation between performance on eye-gaze cueing and protodeclarative pointing tasks at 22 months with performance on ToM tasks at 44 months

Perspective Taking

Perspective taking requires an understanding that another person has a different perspective from our own. It is important for the development of moral reasoning. Piaget was one of the first psychologists to investigate perspective taking using the three mountains task. The Sally-Ann task (Baron-Cohen *et al,* 1985) is another example of a perspective taking task.

Flavell *et al* (1990) believe there are two levels of ability in perspective taking:

- Level 1: Children aged between two and three know that another person experiences something differently (perceptual perspective taking)

- Level 2: Children aged between four and five begin to apply complex rules to help them work out what someone else is able to see or experience (cognitive and emotional perspective taking)

Selman investigated perspective taking using short scenarios in which a child must break rules to help another person in need.

Selman used a scenario where Emily is good at skateboarding. However, one day her mother sees her fall from her skateboard and, although Emily is not hurt, her mother bans her from using the skateboard again because it is dangerous. The next day, Emily sees James being pushed to the floor by some other children who have stolen his mobile phone. She can catch up to them and help James, but only if she uses the skateboard. The children are asked whether Emily should use the skateboard and what Emily's mother will say if she does.

The children then had to provide answers and the reasoning behind them. Selman clustered the answers and was able to develop a five-stage model to describe the development of perspective taking.

Stage	Age	Stage Name	Stage Description	Scenario
1	3-6 Years	Undifferentiated Perspective Taking	Child recognises that self and others are different but sometimes confuses the two.	Emily will help James to make him happy. Emily's mum will be happy because Emily has helped James.
2	5-9 Years	Social Informational Perspective Taking	Child understands that a person's reaction to a situation depends on their perspective.	Emily's mum would be angry if she didn't know about the stolen phone. If she explained, Emily's mum might not be angry.
3	7-12 Years	Self-reflective Perspective Taking	Child develops the ability to see things from	Emily's mum will understand why she used the

			another's perspective.	skateboard, so she will not punish Emily.
4	10-15 Years	Third Party Perspective Taking	Child develops the ability to see things from an independent, third party perspective.	Emily shouldn't be punished because she needed to use the skateboard in order to help James.
5	14 Years - Adult	Societal Perspective Taking	The person has developed a broader perspective based on cultural norms, etc.	The theft of the phone was an immoral act, this therefore justifies Emily's use of the skateboard.

Source: This table has been adapted from A2 Psychology (Nelson Thornes, 2009) p. 304

Activity 75

Answer the following questions:

1. **Why do you think there is an age overlap between the stages?**

2. **At what age can a child first 'step into someone else's shoes' and even see themselves through another person's eyes?**

3. **How does this link with Piaget and Kohlberg?**

4. **What happens to the child's ability to see other points of view as they get older?**

1. The overlap between the stages allows for individual differences, i.e. some children develop at a faster rate than others
2. Around the age of seven
3. This coincides with Piaget's ideas of decentration (being able to concentrate on more than one aspect of an object or situation) and Kohlberg's notion of conventional morality - children now begin to internalise the morals of their social group which requires the development of perspective
4. This becomes increasingly broader. Eventually, they understand the idea that the views of a third party can be influenced by a variety of cultural norms and values

Evidence

Longitudinal Study

Keller and Edelstein (1991) conducted a longitudinal study using Selman's original dilemmas. They tested children aged 7, 9, 12, and 15 and found that their responses broadly agreed with Selman's stages. The findings also agreed with Kohlberg's theory of moral development.

Brain Scans

Brain scans show that sensory-motor systems in the brain are involved when taking the perspective of another person. Different areas of the brain are shown to be active when participants are asked to imagine themselves taking the first-person perspective than when taking a bystander perspective.

Evaluation

- Empirical support for the developmental nature of the theory
- Rigorous assessment interviews helps to validate the model
- Application – Pair Therapy helps children and young people with emotional and behavioural difficulties to develop their perspective taking and negotiation skills, which in turn improves their relationships with others

- Kurdek (1977) argues that describing the stages is not enough. More longitudinal research is needed to understand the process of perspective taking
- White, middle-class children used in research. Therefore, ethnocentric and may lack cross-cultural validity

Biological Explanations of Social Cognition

The biological approach to social cognition attempts to find out whether living co-operatively in social groups is hard-wired into our brains. To understand each other, we need to be able to recognise our own and others' emotional states, consider different perspectives and have a ToM, so that we can interpret the actions of others.

So:

- Is there a biological mechanism that ensures we develop the skills we need to live as social animals?

- Have our brains evolved in such a way as to enhance our sociability?

Studies of neurotypicals (those with normal brains), autism, psychopathology (difficulty in empathising with others) and mirror neurones have provided research opportunities.

Area of Research	Biological Evidence
Neurotypicals	Brain scan research by Adolph (2003) has identified several important areas involved in social cognition. Amygdala: Recognises and interprets facial emotions in others. Organises our emotional responses. Parietal cortex: Important in forming self-other distinction. Frontal cortex: Involved in social decision making, planning and reasoning. Motor-related areas: These are involved in control of movement and may be related to social cognition.

	Especially important are areas in the pre-motor cortex in the frontal lobe and the lower part of the parietal cortex.
Autism	The amygdala, frontal cortex and the junction between the temporal and parietal lobes has been found to be abnormal in those with autism (Frith, 2001). Ramachandran and Oberman (2006) found that children who go on to develop autism do not imitate their mothers (e.g. sticking their tongues out) as new-borns.
Psychopathology	Empathy Blair (2003) found a lack of connection between empathising and mentalising in psychopaths. Psychopaths can recognise the emotions of others (mentalising) but they do not empathise with others. Amygdala and orbitofrontal cortex (part of pre-frontal cortex) shown to function abnormally.
Mirror neurons	Mirror neuron research has been conducted on macaque monkeys. It has been observed that, when a monkey observes another monkey reaching for a peanut, the same neurons in the motor cortex fire as if the monkey was reaching for a nut himself. This also occurs if a monkey observes a human reaching for a nut. More surprisingly, it also occurs if the monkey hears a peanut shell being cracked. Researchers believe that this may be the foundation of empathy. Brain scanning studies have shown that observing someone else in pain activates the same brain systems involved in feeling pain (Rizzolatti *et al*, 2006). People who have low scores on empathy scales have a less active mirror neuron system (Gazzola, Aziz-Zadeh and Keysers, 2006) as do people with autism (Oberman *et al*, 2003 and Hadjikhani *et al*, 2006).

Evaluation of the Biological Explanations of Social Cognition

Mirror neuron research suggests that our brains are hard-wired to enable us to live as social animals and that living co-operatively must be an evolutionary adaptation. This idea is further supported by the fact that babies are sociable and seek social interaction soon after birth. As we have seen, new-borns can mimic a parent sticking out their tongue, and those infants who fail to do this often go on to develop autism. However, the research into mirror neurons can only be carried out on monkeys and, therefore, there is no direct evidence of mirror neurones in humans. Indeed, even if there were, the human brain mechanisms underlying social cognition have probably evolved way beyond the mirror neuron system in monkeys. We are far better at deception and perspective taking than monkeys are.

Issues Debates and Approaches

Brain scanning can provide useful information on the brain systems involved in social cognition. However, to rely only on a biological approach is reductionist as it does not take into account the complex emotional and cognitive processes that occur between people.

There is evidence for a significant genetic basis to autism. It could be that autistic children inherit a brain dysfunction that prevents the normal development of social cognition (nature). However, there is also evidence that the correct environmental stimulation can help to overcome some of the problems associated with autism (nurture).

Our understanding of the mirror neuron system is based on studies using non-human animals and, although the science is rigorous, there is still the problem of generalising from animals to humans.

3.5 Schizophrenia

Paper 3: Option 2

Introduction

In this unit, you will learn how schizophrenia is defined and diagnosed and some of the limitations of such classification. We will then study some of the possible causes for schizophrenia, including biological causes, such as genetic and neuroanatomical factors, and some psychological explanations, such a family behaviours. We will then consider some of the possible treatments for schizophrenia.

Key Areas:

- The classification of schizophrenia
- Biological explanations for schizophrenia
- Psychological explanations for schizophrenia
- Therapies
- Approaches, Issues and Debates

What is Schizophrenia?

The word Schizophrenia comes from the Greek *schizen* (split) and *phren* (mind). It is a serious mental disorder affecting about 1% of the population and is characterised by distorted thinking, poor interpersonal skills, impaired emotional responses and a distortion of reality. It is classified as a psychotic disorder, which means that the person's thinking has become 'split' or 'detached' from reality. However, contrary to the way that schizophrenia is usually presented in the media, it not a fragmentation of the person and does not cause a split or multiple personality.

Clinical Characteristics (Symptoms)

There are two main systems used in psychiatry for classifying mental disorders. These are the:

- ICD-10 (International Classification System for Diseases – Tenth Revision) developed by the WHO (used in the UK)
- DSM-5 (Diagnostic and Statistical Manual of Mental Disorders) developed by the American Psychiatric Association (used in the USA)

These two classification systems are broadly similar for schizophrenia.

According to the ICD-10, one symptom from Group 1 or at least two from Group 2 must be present for one month before a diagnosis of schizophrenia is made.

Group 1

(a) Thought withdrawal – Thoughts are being extracted from the person's mind.

Thought insertion – Unwanted thoughts are being inserted into the person's mind

Thought broadcast – Private thoughts are being broadcast to other people.

(b) Delusions of control, influence or passivity – Delusions are distorted beliefs. With delusions of control the person does not believe they are in control of their own thoughts, feelings and will, but that these are being imposed from outside

(c) Hallucinatory voices – These are voices that do not exist but seem very real to the person hearing them. They often take the form of a running commentary on all that the person is doing

(d) Other persistent delusions – These often involve the person believing that they are great religious leaders or other similarly powerful people

Group 2

(a) Persistent hallucinations – Hallucinations are perceptions that occur in the absence of any external stimuli. They often take the form of auditory hallucinations (hearing voices and other sounds that are not there) but they can also involve other senses e.g. touch, sight, taste and smell

(b) Incoherent or irrelevant speech – This happens when the train of thought is disrupted and speech becomes jumbled and meaningless (loose associations). Neologisms (made-up words) may also be inserted

(c) Catatonic behaviour – Unusual body movements including the adoption of odd body postures and sometimes, complete frozen immobility

(d) Negative symptoms – Involve *losses* of emotion, interests, pleasure etc. They are associated with social withdrawal and lack of motivation

Case Studies

Disturbances of Thought and Language

The following illustrates disturbances of thought where the patient may change from one topic to another without any apparent connection between the topics (loose associations).

Psychologist: What have you been thinking about lately?

Patient: I gotta get out of here, the people are talking. They're talking about clocks, maps and triangulating within the neighbourhood. I can understand and see the dangers. I know how people operate, and there isn't any need to be upset.

Psychologist: Why are people talking about maps and clocks?

Patient: It's all part of the family you know, those who are in and the ones who never get to see the words. The deal has to be agreed to by one person, but it doesn't have to last a long time.

Delusions

Delusions may be simple or complex. They can be systematic (tied in with the patient's explanations) or disorganised. Below are examples of delusions from two schizophrenic patients:

Luke

He believed that women could control his erections with their cigarette lighters, which made him angry. He expected to find a better life on another planet and believed that aliens would come and take him there.

Maria

Thought that she was dead. Every day she would dress in black and lie on her bed, motionless, until it was time for dinner.

Disturbances of Perception

This is a patient's account of his own experiences as a student moving into his own flat:

> "I didn't sleep enough; I didn't eat regularly. After four months, I wanted to paint the large white wall in my room. I started to paint a dark forest on the wall, with a reptile on the foreground. I have always been able to hear colours, they transmit vibrations. I can hear black, red and deep brown. During the painting, it was deathly quiet in the room. In this silence, something frightening was slowly growing. Something threatening was coming up. I had the feeling I wasn't alone any more. Then I heard a sound in my ears that didn't come from myself and which I couldn't explain. It was like the squeaking you hear when your ears are closed. It was like an emotion but deeper. I had the feeling something was looking for me."[17]

---

[17] Source: Abnormal Psychology, Kendal *et al*, 1995 Houghton Mifflin

Different Types of Schizophrenia

Some researchers believe that schizophrenia is not a single disorder and have therefore suggested various subtypes. ICD-10 distinguishes between seven different subtypes. The DSM-5, however, has removed all subtypes. The seven subtypes identified in the ICD-10 are:

- Paranoid type – Delusions or auditory hallucinations are present, but thought disorder, disorganised behaviour, or affective (emotional) flattening are not

- Hebephrenic (disorganised type) – Thought disorder and flat affect are both present. Hallucinations and delusions are less structured than in paranoid type. Often begins at a young age

- Catatonic type – A rare type in which the person exhibits unusual movements. They may be almost completely immobile or show marked agitation

- Undifferentiated type – Psychotic symptoms are present but the criteria for paranoid, hebephrenic or catatonic types have not been met

- Residual type – The person has experienced at least one episode of schizophrenia in the past, but is no longer exhibiting significant symptoms.

- Post-schizophrenic depression - A depressive episode arising after a schizophrenic illness. Some low-level schizophrenic symptoms may still be present

- Simple schizophrenia - Insidious and progressive development of prominent negative symptoms with no history of psychotic episodes

Table 1. Types of Schizophrenia

Type	Description
Paranoid	Preoccupation with one or more delusions or frequent auditory hallucinations; cognitive function and affect remain relatively well preserved
Disorganized	Characterized by disorganized behavior and speech
Catatonic	Has at least two of the following features: immobility, excessive or purposeless motor activity, extreme negativism, or peculiarities of voluntary movement
Undifferentiated	Does not have any of the characteristics of paranoid, disorganized, or catatonic schizophrenia
Residual	A continued presence of negative symptoms. More commonly known as *less pronounced symptoms*. DSM-IV-TR criteria are: 1) absence of prominent delusions, hallucinations, or disorganized speech; and 2) presence of negative or positive symptoms

DSM-IV-TR: Diagnostic and Statistical Manual of Mental Disorders, Fourth Edition, Text Revision.
Source: *Reference 1.*

Activity 76

Diagnosing Schizophrenia

Overleaf are some case studies, typical of some of the types of schizophrenia you have met. Read the case studies given below and diagnose the type of schizophrenia the person is suffering from.

1. Todd is only sixteen, but his family have noticed odd behaviours for some time. After starting Tai Chi lessons some months ago, he would assume karate-like positions for long periods of time, seemingly oblivious to what was going on around him. When taken to a hospital, he would assume such postures and the psychiatrist could move his limbs leaving Todd frozen in that posture for minutes at a time. He spoke rarely, and even when he answered questions, little information would be conveyed.

   Diagnosis……………………………………

2. "Suppose for just a minute, that I am right about what is going on," he suggested one day. "You know how the CIA operates. They gather a tiny bit here and a tiny bit there (most of it from available public sources) and they put it together like a giant anagram 'til suddenly, it spells something meaningful." He went on further, stating, "If what I know is going on is true, then it makes sense that everyone denies the truth of what happens. That's the way they would arrange it if they were smart and they are… I'm on to them and they don't know it yet. Everyone looks innocent, sure. But that's the

way they operate. You can't tell me that all the things that have happened are nothing but accidents. I know better."

Diagnosis………………………………………

3. A 24 year-old man was being treated at a hospital for self-inflicted mutilation of his penis, which he explained was the result of trying to get his girlfriend pregnant from a long distance. He spoke about the special symbolism of words and numbers, and stopped to laugh inappropriately at times. He also stated that dwarfs had stuck him with green needles. Once in the hospital, he was loud, threatening and preoccupied with the sexual connotations of objects on the ward. His speech was chatty, spontaneous, loud and laced with delusional material.

Diagnosis………………………………………

Answer to activity 76

1. Todd - Catatonic schizophrenia
2. Paranoid schizophrenia
3. Undifferentiated schizophrenia

Causes of the Disorder

Schizophrenia doesn't usually happen suddenly — rather it is marked by a gradual withdrawal from society and a gradual loss of pleasure in activities and flattening of affect.

Schizophrenia usually develops in early adulthood, although the age of onset is typically five to ten years later in women. It is an episodic illness characterised by periods of illness and periods of relatively normal functioning.

Before an episode of illness, a patient will often enter a prodromal period where they experience anxiety and low mood, and those close to them may notice differences in their behaviour. A period of illness is known as an active phrase, during which the patient will experience symptoms. An episode may last from one to six months and occasionally up to a year.

The outcome for people with schizophrenia is variable, and there is a general lack of consensus amongst clinicians. Recovery depends on a variety of biological, social and psychological factors. One important factor is that schizophrenia is often co-morbid with depression and, tragically, as many as 15% of schizophrenics commit suicide. Generally, those with better inter-episode functioning have a better prognosis.

Issues Surrounding Classification and Diagnosis

A diagnosis of schizophrenia can be very stigmatising. Many individuals face discrimination due to conflation of the illness with the person and inaccurate stereotypes that link the disorder with violence. Szasz (1979) has questioned the concept of mental illness and suggested that diagnosis can be used as a form of social control. There are certainly many controversies associated with the labelling of people as schizophrenics.

Some of the problem involves difficulty in creating a stable diagnostic system. It can be difficult to define the difference between schizophrenia and other disorders and, although some diagnostic tests are effective at distinguishing between different types of psychosis (for example, drug-induced psychosis), it can be particularly difficult to find the boundaries between some mood disorders and schizophrenia. Variations between the symptoms and prognosis of different people diagnosed with schizophrenia have led to the development of the sub-types we have seen above, but these are not used by all clinicians. Boyle (1990) and Bentall (1988) have argued that the concept of schizophrenia is neither reliable nor useful.

Reliability

There have been inconsistencies in how the diagnosis of schizophrenia has been applied over the years. In the 1950s, the term schizophrenia became a catch-all term used to describe any kind of severe mental disorder. The diagnosis was more common in the USA than in Europe due to the use of broader criteria in the early versions of the DSM. Indeed, in America in the 1930s about 20% of patients were diagnosed as schizophrenic, but by the 1950s, this had risen to 80%. During the same period, the rate of schizophrenia diagnoses at the Maudsley Hospital in London remained at a stable 20%.

Classification of illness is only useful if it is based on a reliable system, and the inconsistencies between the early versions of DSM and ICD did much to hamper the development of effective research and treatment into the disorder.

Schneider's First Rank Symptoms

In an attempt to make diagnosis more reliable, Kurt Schneider (1959) came up with what he called first-rank symptoms to help clinicians distinguish schizophrenia from other psychotic disorders. The first-rank symptoms form the basis of the current ICD-10 classification and are as follows:

- Audible thoughts
- Voices heard arguing
- Voices heard commenting on one's actions
- Experience of influences playing on the body
- Thought withdrawal
- Thought insertion
- Thought diffusion (also called thought broadcast)
- Delusional perception

The problem is that although ICD-10 and DSM-5 are very similar, there are still some differences between them. These differences are outlined below:

- DSM requires symptoms to have had a significant impact for six months whilst ICD only requires a period of one month
- ICD emphasises the first-rank symptoms whereas DSM focuses on the course of the disorder and the accompanying functional impairment
- DSM-5 has no subtypes for schizophrenia

There is a fine distinction between some of the types of schizophrenia and some people can begin with symptoms of one type but then begin to show symptoms of another. Also some people will display symptoms which do not readily fit into one of the sub-types. This can weaken the reliability of diagnosis.

For this reason, British psychologists tend to ignore the sub-types and use the overarching diagnosis of schizophrenia although they do make use of the distinction between Type I and Type II syndrome (Crow, 1985):

- Type I syndrome – An acute disorder characterised by mainly positive symptoms (symptoms in addition to a normal individual's behaviour, such as the presence of hallucinations or delusions)

- Type II syndrome – A chronic disorder characterised by negative symptoms (something lacking compared with normal individuals e.g. apathy, flattened mood and poverty of speech)

However, there are problems with this simple distinction since people do not always fit neatly into one or other category. Nevertheless, these two sub-types may have different underlying causes, which may help with research into the disorder.

Type I and Type II

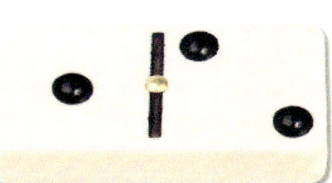

- Another distinction is between Type I and Type II schizophrenia
  - Type I schizophrenia is characterized by positive symptoms
  - Type II schizophrenia is characterized by negative symptoms
- Type I is more acute, as the person functioned normally before the disorder strikes and has a better chance of recovery because Type I can usually be alleviated with drugs, whereas Type II tends to stem from more permanent brain abnormalities

Validity

The large number of categories of schizophrenia raises the issue of validity, i.e. do these subtypes actually exist?

- Dimensional disorder? – Some psychologists argue that schizophrenia should be seen as a dimensional disorder and that classification should reflect the *degree* to which problems are experienced. Some people may experience one of the main symptoms (e.g. hearing voices) but they have strategies to enable them to cope with them and do not feel disabled by them (Romme and Escher, 1989)

- Multiple disorders? – People diagnosed with schizophrenia can present with very different problems. This suggests that there is no single underlying cause for the disorder. In addition, people with schizophrenia respond differently to different types of treatment. For this reason, Bentall (1993) believes the term schizophrenia should be abandoned and each of the symptoms of schizophrenia should be viewed as disorders in their own right

- Differential diagnosis – It can be difficult not only to distinguish between subtypes of schizophrenia but also between schizophrenia and other disorders. For example, drug-induced psychosis is very similar to the symptoms of schizophrenia as are some forms of temporal lobe epilepsy

- Dual diagnosis – It is very common for people diagnosed with one type of disorder to begin to show symptoms of another (called co-morbidity). For example, schizophrenia is often co-morbid with depression. However, this can result in a patient being diagnosed and treated for two disorders when, in fact, they only have one

- Cultural variations – Although schizophrenia is universal (it occurs in all cultures), there are different rates found among different cultures. For example, in the USA and UK, people of African and Caribbean descent are diagnosed more frequently than other groups (Harrison *et al*, 1988)

Issues Debates and Approaches

This could be because classification systems are almost entirely based on white, middle-class social norms, and clinicians misinterpret certain behaviour and expressions as symptoms of schizophrenia. This is an example of ethnocentrism.

Genetic Hypothesis

Schizophrenia has a genetic basis. Controlled genetic studies have shown the risk of developing schizophrenia if a family member already has the disease. The risk is proportional to the amount of genetic material shared, so that the closer the genetic relationship, the higher the risk.

Activity 77

Use the graph below to answer the questions beneath it.

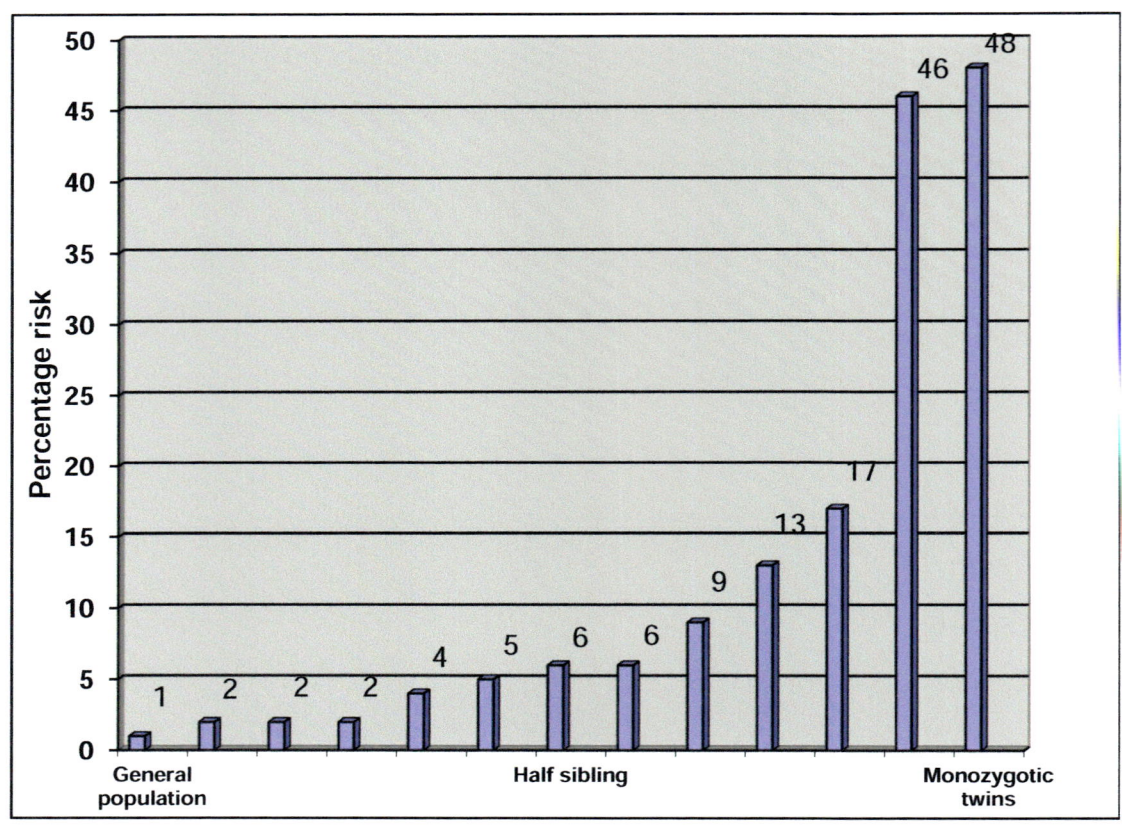

The graph suggests that a closer genetic relationship increases the risk of developing schizophrenia. Using this knowledge, put these family members in the correct place on the graph.

- Grandchild

- Spouse

- Parent

- Offspring of two schizophrenic parents

- Uncle or Aunt

- Offspring of one schizophrenic parent

Answer to activity 77

Genetic risk in order from lowest to highest risk:

- General population
- Spouse
- First cousin
- Uncle / aunt
- Nephew / niece
- Grandchild
- Half sibling
- Parent
- Sibling
- Offspring of one schizophrenic parent
- DZ twin
- Offspring of two schizophrenic parents
- MZ twin

Twin Studies

Shields (1977) reviewed data from twin studies and found an average concordance of 10% for DZ twins (that is a 10% chance of the twin of a schizophrenic going on to develop the disease). The concordance for MZ twins was 50%. He also looked at studies where MZ twins were reared apart or together, and found the concordance rate for both groups was still 50%.

Activity 78

1. What would we expect the concordance between MZ twins to be if genes were wholly responsible for schizophrenia?

2. What does the Shields study tell us about the role of the environment?

3. What conclusions can we draw from this?

4. The Shields study can be criticised on methodological grounds. Using your own knowledge, name four weaknesses of twin studies

Answer to activity 78:

1. 100%

2. The role of the environment is important since the risk even for the spouse of a schizophrenic is slightly higher than that of the general population. This shows the environment has a role in the disorder as we would not expect spouses to share DNA

3. Schizophrenia probably has a genetic basis but requires an environmental trigger (e.g. emotional upheaval or stress of exams) to bring on symptoms. This is the concept of diathesis-stress

4. MZ twin samples often small; different diagnostic criteria often used, making it difficult to compare data from different individuals; zygosity often not reliably established; concordance rates may be calculated differently

Adoption Studies

Heston (1966) looked at a group of 47 adults born to schizophrenic mothers but separated within three days of birth and brought up in an adoptive home. He compared these with normal adoptees brought up in similar socio-economic environments. He found the group from schizophrenic mothers were five times more likely to go on to develop the disease.

Kety *et al* (1975) approached the subject from a different angle. They found 33 adoptees who had schizophrenia and then traced the natural parents to see if they too had the disease. Sure enough, the rate of schizophrenia was higher in the natural parents of the schizophrenic adoptees.

Wender *et al* (1974) found that normal children adopted by families where one of the partners was schizophrenic were no more likely to develop schizophrenia than normal children raised by normal adoptive parents.

Activity 79

1. If a normal child was placed with a family with a long history of schizophrenia, what are their chances of developing the disease in later life? (Give your answer as a percentage.)

2. From the graph, which family relationship would you put most at risk of developing schizophrenia?

3. Placing a child at risk of schizophrenia in a loving, stable home may help to prevent the onset of schizophrenic symptoms. Why do you think this is the case?

Activity 79

1. They have the same risk as a spouse since they share environment but not DNA. The risk is 2%

2. MZ twin of a schizophrenic

3. By removing the 'stress' part of the diathesis-stress model, the child will have less risk of developing the illness. In other words, the child may have a genetic susceptibility but the potential triggers have been minimised

Limitations of Genetic Evidence

- Family studies do not distinguish between environmental (living together) and genetic influence

- Twin studies contain an **equal environment** assumption which is incorrect. MZ twins tend to have environments which are much more similar than same-sex DZ twins, due to their similar appearance, abilities and personalities

- Adoption studies are limited by the problem of **selective placement**. Since many of the countries in which studies have taken place have historically regarded schizophrenia as a genetic defect, it is likely that the most promising adoptive parents would not have been given the children of schizophrenic parents to adopt

- Many of the studies found statistically significant evidence only because they expanded the definition of schizophrenia to include non-psychotic **schizophrenia spectrum disorders**. For example, Kety *et al* (1968) found no cases of chronic schizophrenia among 65 first-degree biological relatives of adopted-away offspring with a schizophrenia-spectrum disorder

- There is a failure to adequately define schizophrenia and schizophrenia-spectrum disorders. Rosenthal *et al* (1971), for example, include manic depression as a schizophrenia-spectrum disorder, though it is categorised in DSM as a completely separate condition

Biochemical Factors

Schizophrenia symptoms are caused by excess of the neurotransmitter dopamine. Evidence for this includes:

- Post-mortems on schizophrenics show unusually high levels of dopamine especially in the limbic system. Seeman (1987) reviewed a number of studies which found between 60 and 110% increase in dopamine receptor density in the brains of schizophrenics

- PET scans of the brains of schizophrenics have revealed a two-fold increase in the density of dopamine receptors compared with the brains of untreated schizophrenics or non-schizophrenic individuals (Wong *et al*, 1986)

- The belief that anti-schizophrenic drugs work by binding to dopamine receptor sites e.g. chlorpromazine which was developed in the 1950s and discovered by chance

- The observation that high doses of amphetamines and L-dopa, both of which enhance the activity of dopamine, can sometimes produce symptoms very similar to the psychomotor disorders seen in certain types of schizophrenia. Dopamine containing neurons are concentrated in the basal ganglia and frontal cortex which are concerned with the initiation and control of movement. Degeneration of the dopamine system produces Parkinson's disease

Issues with the Dopamine Hypothesis

- Phenothiazines (drugs which block dopamine at the synapse) do not work for everyone. They tend to alleviate positive symptoms but not negative symptoms

- L-dopa and amphetamines do not worsen schizophrenic symptoms in every diagnosed individual

- Post-mortems are carried out on people who have been treated for schizophrenia using neuroleptic drugs, often for many years. It is therefore unclear whether an increased dopamine levels are the result of the treatment

- Later PET scans (Farde *et al*) have not replicated Wong's earlier study

- Dopamine may be implicated in causing schizophrenia but it is an insufficient reason on its own

Neuroanatomical Factors

There is growing evidence that schizophrenics may have structural abnormalities in the brain that may cause their symptoms.

Frontal Lobes

Buchsbaum (1990) found that the frontal lobes (important in expressing emotion, planning and initiative) are smaller in schizophrenics compared with normal individuals. PET scans show reduced blood flow in these areas. This agrees with symptoms of altered gait, posture, and abnormal eye movements found in other disorders of frontal lobe dysfunction (Szesko *et al*, 1995).

Ventricles

Ventricles are cavities in the brain which are filled with cerebrospinal fluid. There is evidence to suggest that the ventricles of schizophrenics are considerably larger than in normal individuals, indicating a loss of brain tissue. Andreasen *et al* (1990) made this discovery using CT scans. Interestingly, it was found to be true for men but not women.

Limbic System

The limbic system has a role in emotion. Jernigan *et al* (1991) have found abnormalities in the limbic systems of schizophrenics.

Evaluation of Neuroanatomical Factors

Structural abnormalities have been found more often in those with negative/chronic symptoms (Type II schizophrenia), lending support for the argument that there are two types (Type I: Acute and Type II: Chronic). An argument against this is that people who develop acute symptoms may often go on to develop Type II (Chronic) symptoms. Therefore, rather than there actually being two distinct types, it may be that the types are simply describing the course of the disorder and that brain degeneration is *caused* by schizophrenia rather than brain abnormalities being an underlying factor.

Castner *et al* (1998)

The answer to this argument may lie in a study carried out by Castner *et al* (1998) using monkeys.

Aims: To find out if schizophrenia causes brain changes or if brain changes cause schizophrenia.

Procedure: Monkeys were subjected to blasts of brain-damaging X-rays during foetal development.

Findings: Monkeys showed no ill effects during childhood but developed symptoms of schizophrenia during puberty.

Conclusions: This suggests that brain damage during foetal development caused the schizophrenic symptoms.

Comments: This ties in with the onset of schizophrenic symptoms in humans (i.e. late teens/early adulthood).

Pregnancy and Birth Factors

Winter Births

- An overwhelmingly high proportion of schizophrenics are born in the winter (Procopio and Marriott, 1998)
- Links with viral infections (such as measles, scarlet fever, polio and diphtheria) in the mother, which are more common in the winter months (Jones and Cannon, 1998)

Viral Hypothesis

- Link with mother being infected with influenza A during winter months. 25-30 week foetus most at risk due to accelerated growth of cerebral cortex during this time. Virus may cause gradual degeneration of the brain which becomes apparent at puberty (Mednick *et al,* 1988)

- Support from observation that rises in the rates of schizophrenia tend to coincide with major influenza epidemics (Torrey *et al*, 1988) although other researchers have not been able to corroborate these findings

Birth Complications

- Dalman *et al* (1999) found a positive correlation between birth complications and later development of schizophrenia. Pre-eclampsia was found to be the highest risk factor. Pre-eclampsia is a serious complication in which blood flow to the foetus is restricted causing growth retardation and even death in severe cases. Mother too is at risk, as her blood pressure becomes dangerously high. If left untreated, she can suffer a stroke or kidney and other organ failure

Evaluation of Pregnancy and Birth Factors

- Many studies based on correlational evidence. Therefore it is difficult to establish cause and effect
- If viral hypothesis is true, we would expect MZ twins to have concordance rate of 100% since they share the same genes and the same womb environment and both would be exposed to the virus
- Pre-eclampsia is unlikely to be a cause since it is a common birth complication and most infants from pre-eclamptic pregnancies do not go on to develop schizophrenia

Psychological Explanations for Schizophrenia

Family Models

In the 1950s and 1960s, it was thought that dysfunctional families may play a role in causing schizophrenia. It was proposed that it might be something in the relationships and communication between family members (especially between parents and their children) that could cause withdrawal and emotional instability. If this went unchecked or was severe, then symptoms of schizophrenia could appear.

Fromm-Reichmann (1948) coined the term 'schizophrenogenic' to describe families in which there was high emotional tension, many secrets, close alliances and conspiracies. In addition, Bateson *et al* (1956) describe the double-bind situation in which a parent may give care but in a hostile way. Such contradictory messages can cause the child to develop a false concept of reality. This can cause a child to experience self-doubt, confusion and withdrawal. Such theories began to go into decline in the 1970s as scientists were beginning to find possible genetic causes for the disorder. In addition, psychiatrists were unhappy that the blame that families felt did nothing to improve the family situation. Along with this, came the idea that perhaps the family had become dysfunctional *because* they had to cope with a schizophrenic. So rather than the family causing schizophrenia, perhaps the schizophrenia caused problems within the family.

Therefore, attention turned to the role of the family in the *course* rather than the cause of schizophrenia. Brown (1972) found that patients with schizophrenia were more likely to relapse if the families they returned to had a high level of expressed emotion (EE). EE was assessed by taped interview with relatives and includes high levels of criticism, resentment and over-protectiveness. Research by Tarrier *et al* (1998) supports this finding.

Again, because the research is correlational, it does not establish cause and effect. There have also been criticisms of how EE is measured. However, it seems that negative relationships may make it more likely that children in high-risk groups will go on to develop schizophrenia. Interestingly, high EE has also been found in the families of patients with depression and eating disorders (Kavanagh, 1992).

Comments

The EE model has now become well-accepted in many cultures as a maintenance model for schizophrenia. In fact, treatment programmes for schizophrenia often include training for families in how to control and reduce EE.

Cognitive Explanations

Cognitive psychologists suggest that the profound thought disturbances that characterise schizophrenia may be the *cause* rather than the *consequence* of the disorder. They believe that cognitive impairment in such individuals leads to errors in the processing of information.

More recently, the understanding that such cognitive impairment must have underlying physiological abnormalities has led to two neuropsychological models.

- Faulty cognitive processes (Frith, 1992)
- Failure to activate schemas (Helmsley, 1993)

Frith, 1992

Frith believes that the cause of schizophrenia may lie in a faulty filter between the brain's conscious and pre-conscious processing systems. He postulates that schizophrenics may be aware of pre-conscious thoughts that are not part of the consciousness of normal individuals. For example, in normal individuals, the many sounds around us are analysed and interpreted by pre-conscious mechanisms, and only those which are deemed significant make it into our conscious awareness. For a normal individual, the other sounds are disregarded. Frith believes that it is possible that schizophrenic individuals are partially aware of this process, leading them to hear the erroneous interpretations of sounds that would normally be filtered out by pre-conscious mechanisms.

Frith believes this faulty filter is related to an irregularity of the neural pathways connecting the hippocampus and pre-frontal cortex and is linked to inadequate regulation of dopamine in this part of the brain. Frith has been able to provide some support for this model by demonstrating changes in cerebral blood flow during cognitive tasks in schizophrenic patients. However, the theory is not universally accepted and has been criticised for ignoring environmental factors.

Helmsley (1993)

Helmsley's model for schizophrenia involves difficulties in processing new information into schemas. He believes that schizophrenic patients cannot differentiate between new information and pre-existing schemas and therefore do not know how to categorise stimuli. They may confuse internal events with external stimuli, leading to hallucinations. Helmsley believes this is caused by abnormalities in the hippocampus. As yet, there is no definitive evidence to support this theory.

Therapies for Schizophrenia

Biological Therapies

During the 1950s, a chemical revolution hit the psychiatric profession. Suddenly, patients were taken out of their straitjackets, their behaviour returned to 'normal' and the psychiatric hospital emptied as patients went home to their families. This was all due to the fact that scientists now understood the role of neurotransmitters in both normal and abnormal functioning of the brain.

Neurotransmitters and Synapses

When a nerve impulse gets to the end of an axon, its message must cross the synapse if it is to continue. Messages do not "jump" across synapses. Instead, they are carried across by chemical messengers called **neurotransmitters**. These chemicals are packaged in tiny sacs, or vesicles, at the tip of the axon.

When a nerve impulse arrives at the tip, it causes the sacs to release their contents into the synapse. The neurotransmitters diffuse across the synapse and bind to **receptors** in the membrane of the cell on the other side, passing the signal to that cell by causing special ion channels in the postsynaptic membrane to open.

When it was discovered that too little or too much of these chemicals can give rise to the symptoms of mental disorders, work quickly began to find ways to artificially restore the balance.

Neuroleptics are the most common treatment for schizophrenia. These are also known as anti-psychotic drugs. They work by blocking dopamine receptors, which gradually reduces the levels of dopamine in the brain. This effectively blocks the positive symptoms (hallucinations, delusions, etc.) of the disease. However, the use of neuroleptics has not been without problems, and many people have questioned their appropriateness (is the treatment right for the disorder?) and effectiveness (just how good is it?) for some patients.

Appropriateness and Effectiveness

Appropriateness	Effectiveness
Side-effects of neuroleptics are serious and include drowsiness, visual disturbance, weight changes, dry mouth and depression. Long term use of over seven years produces tardive dyskinesia in 24% of patients. More modern drugs, such as Clozapine, also have fewer side effects but cause damage to the immune system.	Neuroleptics are not effective against negative symptoms (social withdrawal, apathy, etc.)
Adverse effects cause patients to stop taking their medication, leading to a relapse. To avoid this, patients are sometimes injected with the drugs. This takes away their control over their own treatment. There are also wider issues of consent, since people who are very ill may not always be able to understand or consent to treatment.	Neuroleptics reduce symptoms in 6 months. However, symptoms often return if medication is stopped (Rzewuska, 2002).

Monitoring of the effectiveness of drug treatment is very important. Levels of medication may be set at a high level when the patient is in an acute stage of illness but should then be reduced to a maintenance level to minimise the side-effects without suffering relapse. Clinicians need to gauge the dosage carefully.	Not effective in all patients. About 30% do not respond or are intolerant to anti-psychotic drugs. About half of these treatment-resistant patients may respond to Clozapine (Walhbeck *et al*, 1999). However, some patients do not respond to drug treatment at all.

Psychological Therapies

Psychological therapies are useful as a supplement to help patients cope with their everyday lives. Sometimes the situation patients find themselves in (such as the high EE situation discussed earlier) can cause relapse, and it is important to remove or minimise such a situation to give the patient a better chance of recovery. We will now look at some of the psychological therapies.

Psychodynamic Therapy

Psychodynamic therapy involves the patient gaining insight into their past in order to understand their present symptoms. The patient must trust the therapist and must be able to express their thoughts and wishes. The nature of schizophrenic illness, and the difficulties that patients have in expressing themselves, can limit the effectiveness of psychodynamic therapy.

Fromm-Reichman (1948) and Rosen (1947) developed a modified form of psychoanalysis to use with schizophrenic patients, although it is not clear whether this is effective. In fact, psychoanalysis may even be harmful. Tarrier (1990) suggests that the overstimulation caused by psychodynamic techniques can actually cause a relapse in patients. Drake and Sederer (1986) found that patients who had psychodynamic treatment needed longer periods in hospital, developed worse symptoms and were more likely to refuse further treatment.

Social Interventions

There is evidence that social intervention can affect the course of schizophrenia. Wing and Brown (1970) found that female in-patients from wards where they were offered stimulating activities had significant improvements in symptoms over those who were offered no such activities. This finding has been very influential, and hospitals and day-care environments now offer environments that promote self-esteem and personal control.

Milieu Therapy

'Milieu' is a French word which roughly translated means environment. It is a form of social-skills training programme that involves the use of therapeutic communities. Clients join a group of 30 or so people for between 9 and 18 months, and during their stay they are encouraged to take responsibility for themselves and others within the unit. It is thought to be useful in treating personality and behaviour disorders, and is widely used in Scandinavia.

A team of Norwegian researchers looked at how milieu therapy worked in one such unit in Norway. They found that in ways the unit was similar to a traditional nuclear family. The clients were often seen as 'harmed children' and were taught self-management skills.

The staff aimed to provide a caring atmosphere while the clients sometimes seemed to behave in a child-like manner. In a sense, the milieu was 'raising' the clients to transform their 'odd' behaviour and 'nonconforming' lifestyles and produce 'self-governing' individuals. It may involve the use of token economy to reward patients for appropriate behaviour, such as getting up at a reasonable time and refraining from bizarre behaviour.

Social skills training can be used to improve the social behaviour of those with schizophrenia. A training program created by Halford and Hayes (1992) has been used to teach patients conversations skills, conflict management, self-assertion, medication management and employment skills.

Birchwood and Spencer (1999) reviewed research into social skills training and found that it is generally beneficial. However, they also found that some degree of maintenance is necessary, or individuals will often relapse into their former patterns.

Cognitive-behavioural Therapy (CBT)

Tarrier (1987) found that many schizophrenics have developed cognitive strategies to help themselves deal with the distress caused by hallucinations and delusions.

Many use cognitive strategies such as distraction and positive self-talk while behavioural strategies involve shouting or turning up the TV to drown out the voices in their heads.

Therapists have taken some of these ideas and come up with a Coping Strategy Enhancement (CSE) programme to help others with the disorder. It involves two main elements:

- Training
- Symptom targeting

The therapist teaches clients how to improve their own coping strategies and develop new ones. They then get the patient to target a specific symptom and give them homework to focus on developing strategies to deal with it. Eventually, the client should have at least two appropriate strategies for each distressing symptom.

Tarrier *et al* (1993) found a significant improvement in positive symptoms in a group undergoing CSE treatment compared to a group held on a waiting list. CSE may therefore be an effective way to help patients control symptoms.

Beck and Ellis

We met the work of Beck and Ellis in the AS course. Their therapy involves the challenging of irrational beliefs about the self and the situation that are directly responsible for causing distress and negative emotions. Therapy aims to put such beliefs to a reality test by asking the client to provide evidence to support them. When this evidence can't be found, the belief can no longer be supported. The therapist will then encourage the client to replace it with more rational and plausible explanations.

Chadwick *et al* (1996) used this technique of challenging beliefs on an individual who believed he could control events with his mind. He was shown over 50 paused videos and asked what would happen next. When he got every single one wrong, he began to realise that he couldn't make things happen just by thinking them. Kuipers *et al* (1997) have found that this type of therapy can bring about a significant reduction in delusional symptoms.

A form of CBT known as Integrated Psychological Therapy (IPT) has also been used in the treatment of faulty patterns of cognition. In this therapy, patients are taught to evaluate verbal and social cues effectively. This has been shown to result in lower rates of hospitalisation but does not completely eliminate schizophrenic patterns of thinking (Brenner *et al*, 1992).

Family Intervention

Based on the research into high expressed emotion (EE), this therapy is designed to reduce the environmental stresses that make relapse common by helping the whole family to adopt coping skills which help them to live with schizophrenia. The therapy is based on a bond of trust between each family member and the therapist. The family is fully informed about the symptoms, nature and course of the disorder and members are encouraged to share the experiences, frustrations and anger which arise from trying to cope with their loved one. They are also taught to recognise signs of relapse and how to respond.

Pharoah *et al* (2003) conducted a meta-analysis which found that family therapy significantly reduced relapse rates and improves compliance with medication. Obviously it is only appropriate for those patients who are still living with or are in close contact with their families.

Approaches, Issues and Debates

Diathesis-Stress Model: An Interactionist Approach

The interactionist or biopsychosocial approach suggests that the causes of normal as well as abnormal behaviours are a combination of biological, psychological, and sociocultural factors.

The diathesis-stress model is now widely accepted as the most likely cause of schizophrenia. This model sees the cause of schizophrenia as **multifactorial**. In other words, many factors contribute to the disorder, both genetic and environmental. It is thought that an individual inherits a susceptibility to schizophrenia (this may be an imbalance of certain neurochemicals or brain structural abnormalities). This is then triggered by stressful events such as living in a high EE family. This model is helpful in drawing together the different approaches to schizophrenia. It is therefore less reductionist than other approaches since it takes a broad perspective. It is also useful when looking at treatments for schizophrenia since it advocates a multi-dimensional or combined treatment approach e.g. drug treatment supplemented with behavioural and family therapies. Such treatment approaches are often more successful than using drug therapy alone.

Ethical Issues

Some people have criticised the widespread use of drugs to treat schizophrenia and other mental disorders, referring to them as 'chemical straitjackets'. Their argument is that drugs dehumanise people and take away any sense of personal responsibility and control. The ethical issue of informed consent is also relevant here as people in psychiatric hospitals are not always in a position to give fully informed consent about their treatment and for those who are 'sectioned' under the Mental Health Act this right is taken away completely. Sectioning has to balance the needs of the individual with the needs of wider society. For example, some people are considered to be dangerous to others because they may physically attack and must be sectioned to protect the wider community. Such people do not have the right to refuse whatever treatment is deemed appropriate for them. Therapies such as CBT overcome this criticism since, rather than being a passive recipient of treatment, patients on such programmes are actively involved with their treatment.

Tutor Marked Assignment 3

<u>(Mock Exam)</u>

Now go to CloudPort to download your mock exam. Answers should be word processed and uploaded via CloudPort

Please note: If you are pursuing the AS Level qualification only then you will only sit Papers 1 and 2, which correspond to TMAs 1 and 2. If however you are pursuing full A Level qualification you will sit the second set of exam papers which correspond to TMAs 3, 4 and 5. As level no longer counts towards the A level qualification.

4.1 Eating Behaviour

Paper 3 Option 2

In this area of study we will be looking at the various perspectives within psychology that try to explain eating behaviours.

Key Areas:

- Explanations for food preferences
- Neural and hormonal mechanisms involved in the control of eating behaviour
- Biological and Psychological Explanations for anorexia nervosa
- Biological and Psychological Explanations for obesity

Explanations for food preferences

Activity 80

After a long day at work, school, college, etc., and you get home and feel like a snack, what do you reach for?

When you do food shopping (or go with someone who is responsible for food shopping), what do you tend to buy (despite what's on the shopping list)?

There are various explanations as to why we have a preference for certain types of foods over others. The ones we address in this section are:

- Evolutionary explanations
- Biological Explanations
- Social and Cultural Explanations

Evolutionary Explanations

As already discussed in other units, when we talk about evolution we are talking about change and adaptability, all with the goal being to survive. Therefore, in terms of eating behaviour, evolution shows us that those who are able to obtain sufficient food and nutrition have a better survival rate. Humans, it is said, have evolved in a way that their food preferences offer them the best chance of survival.

Activity 81

With the above in mind:

Why do you think some people prefer sweet foods?

Why do you think some people prefer salty foods?

Why do some people prefer food high in fat?

Biologically speaking we can explain the above by looking at **gustation**, the process of tasting food. This can give us some explanation for taste preferences. Through taste we are able to distinguish between tastes such as sweet, salty etc. Biologically the taste receptors on our tongues help us to distinguish one taste from another. Coupled with our sense of smell, the taste buds located on our tongues send information to the brain where the main tastes are identified. They are:

- Sweet

- Salty

- Sour

- Bitter

- Umami (savoury)

When we eat something we may experience a combination of these tastes, and due to the information stored by the brain we can distinguish between the different tastes.

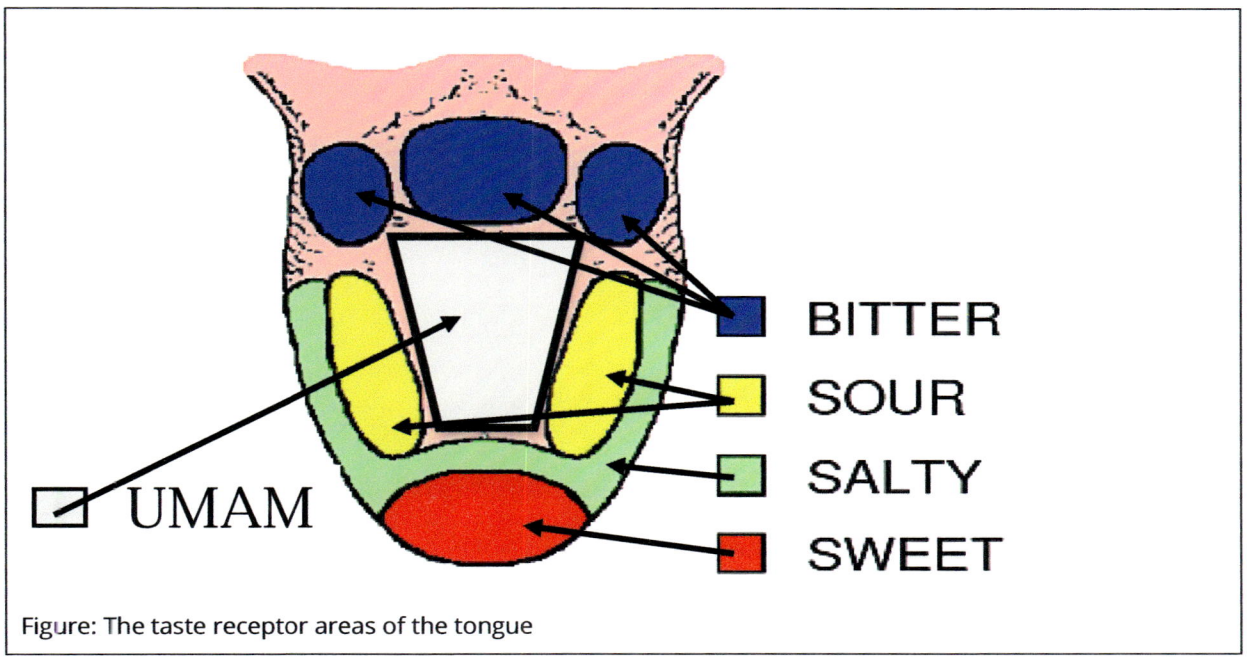

Figure: The taste receptor areas of the tongue

In terms of the evolutionary explanations for these tastes, it has been suggested that they have evolved or developed in the following ways.

Taste	Explanation
Sweet	Sweet foods are associated with food ready for consumption as they are ripe. They also tend to be high in sugars and early humans relied on the consumption of sweet fruits for their survival as they are high in calorific content and as such a good source of energy and fuel. However, today, fruits and berries have been replaced by chocolates, cakes and biscuits. Logue (1991) found that the sweet receptors on the tongue were far more numerous than any other taste receptor, which could explain a preference for sweet foods. Meiselman (1977) found that people of different ages still preferred the taste of sweet foods over other tastes. Desor *et al* (1973) even went as far as to suggest that a 3-day-old baby has a preference for sweet tastes. Studies by Harris (1987) also suggest that babies like sweet tastes.

Salt	Salty foods are an essential part of the diet, and in hot climates our ancestors would need to replace the salts lost during sweating, resulting in a preference for salty foods. Denton (1982) showed that we have innate appetite for sodium, a preference for salty foods, which would be present some evolutionary connection. However, according to Beauchamp (1987) we are not born with an innate preference for salty foods, rather this develops in childhood.
Sour	From a survival perspective, sour foods are an indication that food has gone off and therefore potentially harmful (Steiner).
Bitter	According to Barinaga (2000) bitter foods can be an indication of bacteria formation within the food itself, and like sour foods can be an indication that the food is potentially harmful or poisonous.
Umami	This taste category was introduced by Kikunae Ikeda. Depleting forestation and increased brain development resulted in the consumption of meat and high protein foods. According to Milton (2008) the inclusion of meat has resulted in evolved, active and intelligent brain development. Also some biological evidence suggests that we are in fact designed to eat meat as we have a long duodenum for the absorption of protein (this is the subject of much debate though)

In this part of the discussion it is also appropriate to include preferences (though not directly related to taste specifically) for fatty foods. From an evolutionary perspective according to Burnham and Phelan (2000), fatty foods provided a high level of energy, essential for survival; therefore, the preference for fatty foods stems from times of food scarcity.

Our ancestors did not have the consistent and continuous source of foods we have today, therefore day-to-day survival could go from feast to famine very quickly. Hunting and gathering made our ancestors more active, requiring physical strength for catching food and general survival. As a result it has been suggested that during times of plenty, binge eating would result in the maximum storage of energy for daily needs. So, food high in fats and sugars would be sought out due to the amount of energy they could provide. It has been suggested that this evolutionary left-over is a factor that has resulted in the obesity crisis. Comparatively, our ancestors were active and did not have the readily accessible and quantity of foods we have today, therefore what they consumed would be used as fuel by the body for survival. Our sedentary, convenience, consumer lifestyle does not lend itself to the same levels of energy burning, meaning what we consume in terms of fats and sugars are not expended or burnt of leading to weight gain.

In terms of preferences for spicy foods, this has also been explained from an evolutionary perspective in that spices have antimicrobial properties in that they can kill microorganisms or inhibit their growth. According to Sherman and Hash (2001), in some hot countries spices are used more with meat dishes and less so with vegetable dishes as in hot countries meats can be susceptible to a larger quantity and growth of bacteria, and as such this could explain why spices are used more readily and frequently in meat dishes.

Activity 82

Looking at the evolutionary explanations for food preferences we have just discussed, are there any strengths or weaknesses that you can identify in relation to this perspective?

Evaluation of the Evolutionary Theory

- This approach focuses on nature and therefore does not really address nurture
- It is deterministic in its approach in that it does not explain individual preferences
- As a theory it is hard to test
- Generalisations are problematic, as unlike animals, humans vary significantly in terms of preferences and practices

- It is difficult to apply to modern day eating behaviour as we are no longer in the environment of evolutionary adaptation
- However, this theoretical perspective can explain certain unusual characteristics of our diet

Now we have discussed the evolutionary explanations for certain food preferences, we are going to briefly address **Neophobia** and **Taste Aversion.**

Neophobia

According to Frost (2006), we tend to avoid foods that are unfamiliar to us, but the more we are exposed to them and they become more familiar, the more we are likely to develop a liking for it.

Taste Aversion

Evolutionarily this is said to have developed as part of a survival technique. If we consume something that makes us ill, it stands to reason that we would avoid it or anything like it. Garcia *et al* (1966) conducted an experiment where rats were given saccharine flavoured water, coupled with a bright light and a clicking noise, after which the rats were exposed to radiation which made them ill. They subsequently developed an aversion to the flavoured water. This therefore demonstrated that taste aversion can be learned.

Learning food preferences – Social and Cultural

We've looked at some of the biological (which will be discussed in more detail later) and evolutionary explanations for eating behaviour. Whilst the biological can explain factors such as taste receptors and the evolutionary attempts to provide some explanations (although difficult to prove empirically) for preferences with regard to certain foods, we also need to consider aspects of eating behaviour and food preferences that develop as a result of social conditioning, cultural influences, mood, health concerns and so on.

Elements of tastes can be associated with innate features. As suggested by Birch and Marlin (1999), we have the ability to associate the tastes and smells of food with certain experiences that are either good or bad, and these preferences can be modified. They found that when 2 year olds were exposed to certain foods over a period of six weeks, their preference for that food increased. The greater the exposure to different foods, the more likely a change is to be made from a dislike of these foods to a preference (learned behaviour).

In terms of the social analysis of food behaviour and particularly preferences, not surprisingly, according to Ogden (2007), parents play a key role in a child's attitude toward food. Therefore, the diet of the mother, particularly, provided a role model for food preferences.

In a longitudinal study by Nicklaus *et al* (2004), he studied French children from age 2 to 22, using questionnaires. For approximately 50% of those studied, a correlation was found between childhood to adult food preferences. However, it could be argued that, as a result of later social interaction, peer groups and external influences, some food preferences may change e.g. a preference liking for meat changing to abstinence due to ethical concerns regarding the consumption of meat.

Activity 83

What methodological issues do you think would be associated with this type of longitudinal study that uses questionnaires?

Whilst longitudinal studies can be valuable in providing us with an insight into that which is being studied, one concern that could be raised in relation to a study like the one presented by Nicklaus *et al* is that of **social desirability**. Here the participant, wanting to come across as making healthier or ethically approved of choices, may want to downplay some of their food preferences.

Moving from the social to the cultural preferences when it comes to food, clearly these elements are interlinked, but when looking specifically at culture, we know that different cultures have different views and attitudes toward food. Culture not only determines social interaction associated with eating (who we eat with, when we eat and how we eat) but also determines what we eat and how much. Rozin (1982) said that:

"...there is no doubt that the best predicator of the food preferences, habits and attitudes of any particular human would be information about his ethnic group...rather than any biological measure one might imagine."

Leshem (2009) found that the cultural effects on diets are persistent. Leshem compared Bedouin Arab women, some living in desert encampments and others (at least one generation) living in an urban setting. He also compared both of these groups with a group of urban Jewish women. Despite the easy access to a range of food goods and products, the urban Bedouins still had a diet that was very similar to the desert-living Bedouins. Compared to the urban Jewish women, the Bedouins had a higher intake of proteins, carbohydrates and salt.

Wardle *et al* (1997), found that in European countries basic healthy diets consumption was low (females did better than males). Mediterranean countries ate more fruit and vegetables when compared to England and Scotland. Scandinavian countries ate more fibre when compared to the Portuguese, Spanish and Italians. Wardle said that these differences can be explained by looking at the availability of certain foodstuffs and cultural influences and factors.

Mood

Studies show that a person's mood can influence what they eat and how they eat. Low moods are often associated with comfort eating (note, however, that eating less can also be associated with low moods – 'going off food'). Garg *et al* (2007) conducted an experiment where participants watched a funny film and a 'tear jerker'. Researchers monitored the snack choices people made whilst watching the films.

Afterwards participants were asked to grade their mood on a scale of 1 to 9. The findings suggested that those watching the 'tear jerker' ate more popcorn compared to those who watched the funny film, with more of those participants opting to eat grapes. The findings therefore suggested that the 'low mood' from watching the sad film resulted in comfort eating.

Prior to Garg *et al*, Davis *et al* (1988) said that a low mood in bulimics often preceded binge eating, but unfortunately far from making an individual feel better, they may well experience feelings of guilt following bingeing.

Neural and Hormonal Mechanisms

The body's efficiency is such that it is designed to ensure its own optimal functioning. Therefore, the internal environment of the body is maintained through **homeostasis,** and it utilises mechanisms that <u>detect</u> the internal environment of the body and <u>correct</u> where necessary the internal environment to restore the body's balance.

Therefore, if you are cold, you will shiver; if you are hot you will perspire; if you are dehydrated you will become thirsty; if you need fuel/food you become hungry.

So, when applied to eating, in order for the body function effectively for humans, carbohydrates provide glucose which is the main source of energy.

If we focus on glucose as an example in terms of eating behaviour, when the glucose levels in the body drop the process is as follows:

- The **Lateral Hypothalamus (LH)** is activated, which causes feelings of hunger. An individual will then find a source of food that will result in eating, which will replenish and thus increase the glucose levels
- When the glucose levels in the body increases, this activates the **Vetromedial Hypothalamus (VMH)**. The VMH is located in the hypothalamus and is responsible for feeling full (satiety). When satiety is reached, an individual will no longer feel the need to eat any more
- When the glucose levels drop, the cycle starts again

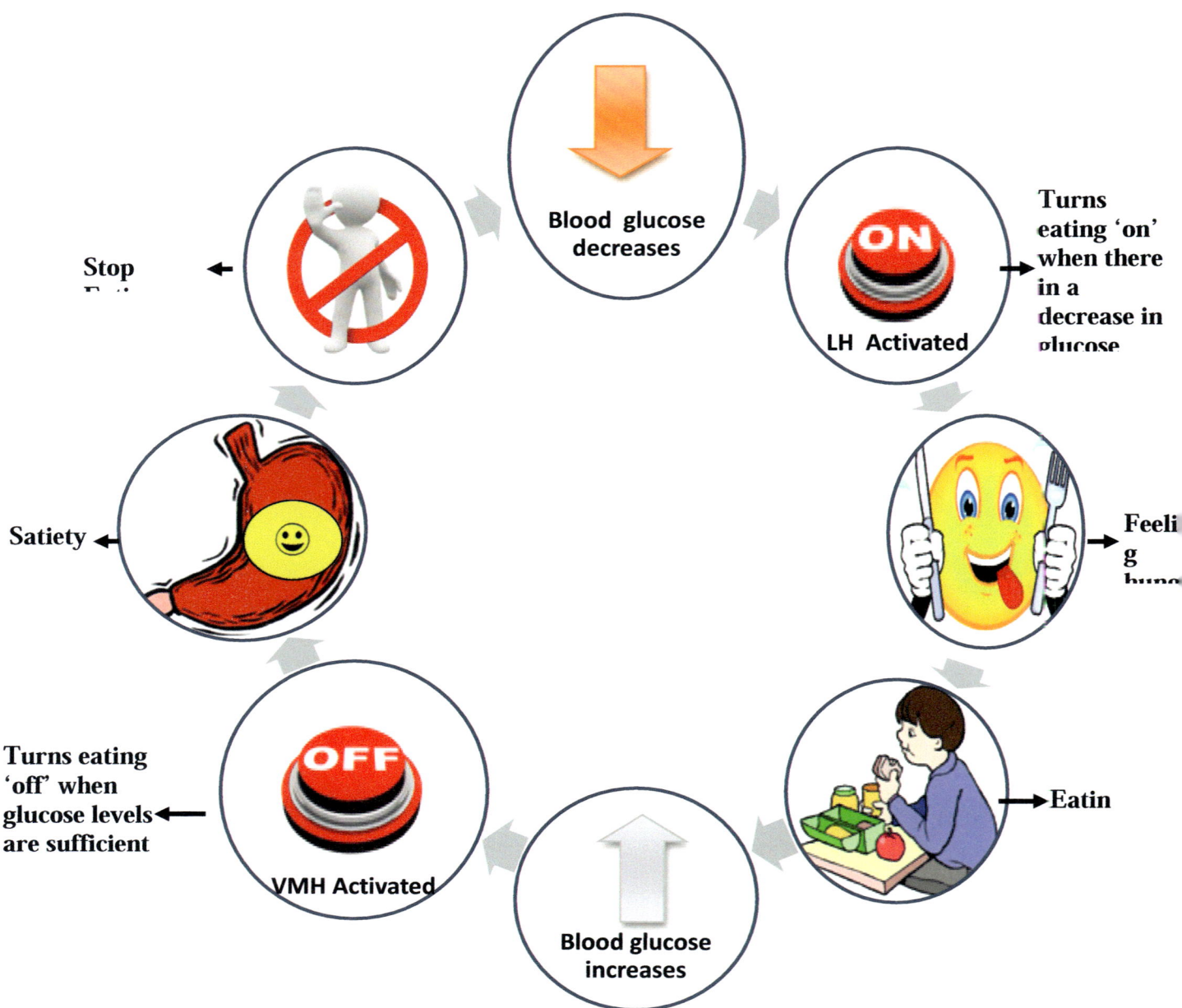

Figure: Eating Cycle

Research shows that the Lateral Hypothalamus (LH) is the activator or 'on switch' for eating behaviour, and as such elicits feeding behaviour. However, if damaged for whatever reason, this causes **aphagia** which is the inability or refusal to swallow or eat food.[18] **Neuropeptide Y** (NPY), which is a neurotransmitter found in the Hypothalamus, was also found to play a very important part in 'turning on' eating. Stanley (1986) and Wickens (2000) found that after injecting the hypothalamus of rats with NPY, this caused them to begin to eat even if they were satiated, resulting in obesity. Research, therefore, of the Ventromedial Hypothalamus (VMH) or 'off switch' in rats, found that, if damaged, this would result in rats over-eating causing **hyperaphagia.** Stimulation of the VMH on the other hand would inhibit eating. But prior to these findings, Gold (1973) found that damage or injury to the VMH on its own did not result in hyperaphagia.

Neural control of cognitive factors

Activity 84

Take a minute or two think about your favourite food/dish. Picture it in your mind. Think about the smell, taste, texture in your mouth. Think about how it makes you feel when you eat it.

After doing the above task, you may have found yourself feeling a little peckish or even outright hungry, or thinking to yourself, 'I fancy a snack'. Reflecting on a time when just thinking about food made you feel hungry is referred to as **cognitive correction**. This cognitive aspect of food includes the mental images we have of food (memories), food related sights, food smells. The neural control of these cognitive factors in hunger are said to have originated from the **Amygdala** and the **Inferior Frontal Cortex**.

Amygdala

It is a set of neurons that is almond shaped and located in the temporal lobe. It is the part of the brain that is involved in emotions such as fear, pleasure, anger and

---

[13] Note: This can occur as a result of a psychological as well as physical issue.

so on. Damage to or an abnormality of the Amygdala can cause imbalance, and this can result in a loss of fear responses, and it can cause anxiety and phobias among other significant responses.

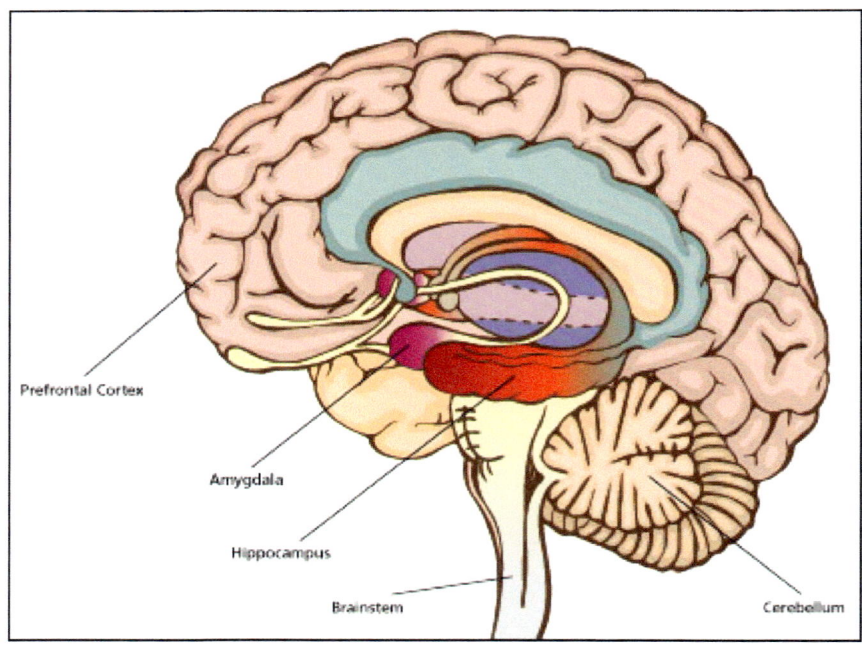

It has been suggested that the Amygdala is responsible for the selection of foods on the basis of previous experience. Rolls and Rolls (1973) found that when they removed the Amygdala in rats, the rats would indiscriminately eat both familiar and unfamiliar foods. This was compared to rats with their Amygdala intact who would initially avoid unfamiliar foods and only consume familiar foods instead.

Inferior Frontal Cortex (IFC)

The IFC receives messages relating to smell, and this is significant as odour has an impact upon the tastes of foods. Therefore, damage to the IFC is said to decrease eating due to the diminished sensory responses.

Leptin

Leptin is a fat hormone that is secreted into the bloodstream to signal to the brain via the hypothalamus that the body has enough fat stored; this in turn decreases appetite after which an individual would stop eating. It is also associated with weight loss. Research with mice found that some mice received two copies of the gene **ob** (obese), known as **ob/ob** mice. These mice had a tendency to over eat, particularly foods high in fats and sugars. Zhang *et al* found that ob/ob mice were either missing or had a defect in the gene that produces leptin. Zhang *et al* found that by injecting the mice with leptin, it caused them to lose weight significantly.

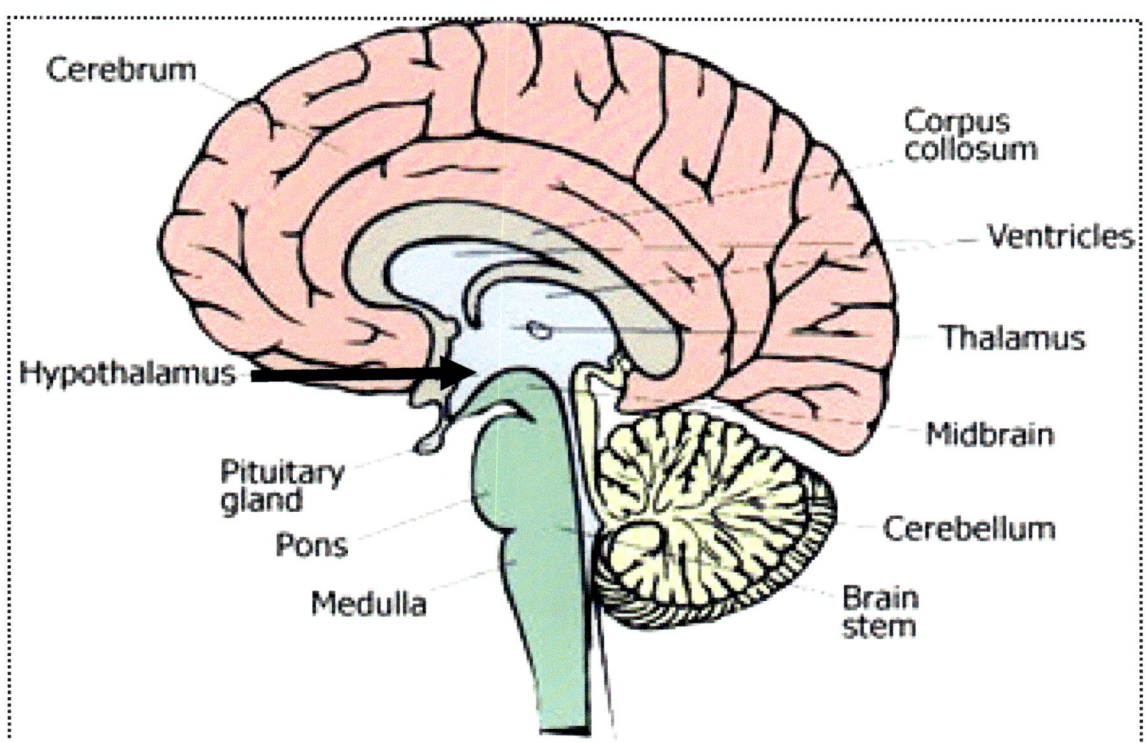

Carlson (2007) also found that mice that did not produce leptin would eat continuously and become obese. Injecting the mice with leptin did reduce how much they ate, and eventually their weight would return to normal. Whilst this can explain to a certain extent eating and weight gain, research also shows that in some cases obese people have normal and in some instances higher than normal levels of leptin, which would suggest that the part of the brain that controls feeding has for some reason become insensitive to the effects of leptin.

Evaluation of a homeostasis explanation

Research shows that damage to the LH causes deficits in other aspects of behaviour, such as thirst and sex and not just hunger. The assumption that the

LH acts as an on switch for eating is reductionist, as it appears there are more complex processes occurring that these explanations do not account for.

Marie *et al* (2005) found that genetically manipulated mice (those injected with NPY) showed signs of hunger. However, manipulating mice so that they did not produce NPY found no subsequent or significant decrease in their feeding behaviour.

As rats and mice were used in the studies, questions can be raised regarding using these findings to generalise about humans. The explanations given are somewhat reductionist with the focus on the biological, with no emotional or evolutionary theories discussed.

It is deterministic in that it does not account for the fact that we do have some control over what we eat: sometimes we choose not eat no matter how tasty the foodstuff smells and likewise we may eat just for the sake of it.

Damage to the Amygdala and the inferior pre frontal cortex could explain the eating abnormalities seen in Kulver-Bucy[19] Syndrome, a rare neural behavioural condition where an individual has an increased appetite and may even attempt to eat things that are not even food e.g. chalk or gravel.

Lotter *et al* suggests that hunger and eating might not be limited to neural control as research shows that the body will produce extra quantities of the hormone Ghrelin in response to stress in order to reduce depressive behaviour, but it does increase the appetite leading to **comfort eating**. This does therefore suggest that blocking the body's response to Ghrelin could assist people in controlling their weight if their consumption is as a result of comfort eating.

Research by Yang *et al* shows that NPY is produced by abdominal fat which suggests that this leads to a cycle where NPY produced in the brain leads to more

_____

[19] (1937)

eating and the production of more fat cells, in turn producing more NPY and more fat cells, and so the cycle continues.

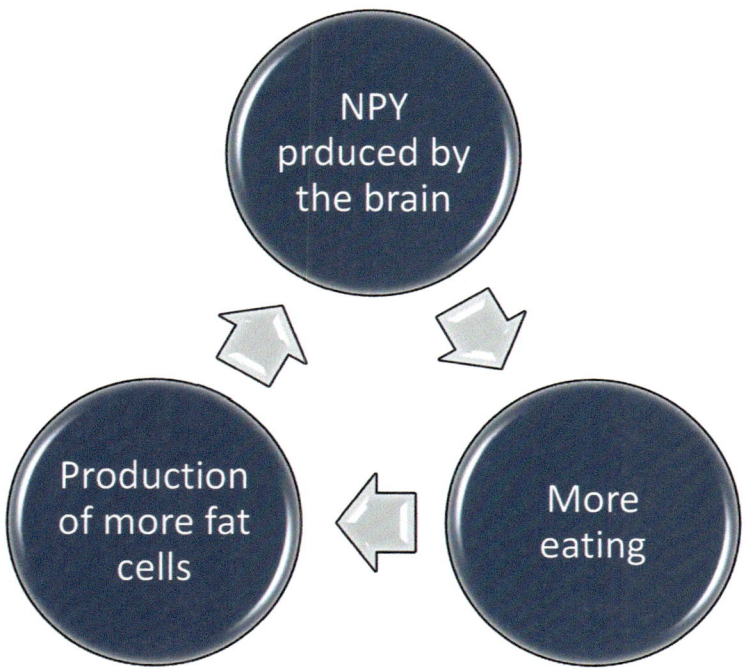

Yang *et al* suggest that it should be possible to treat individuals who produce a lot of NPY with drugs that turn of NPY and therefore prevent obesity.

Activity 85

Can you think of any other limitations to the homeostatic explanation?

Anorexia Nervosa (AN)

Anorexia Nervosa, often referred to as just Anorexia, is an eating disorder characterised by an individual's intense desire to lose weight and an extreme fear of gaining weight. This extreme relationship with food means that sufferers will have a distorted body image and therefore find it difficult to reconcile their perception of their body and what would be regarded as a normal body weight. Sufferers are prone to experience severe health problems, and in some more extreme cases this condition results in death.

Biological Explanations

If you recall, we previously discussed Homeostasis, which is the body's way of maintaining equilibrium in terms of the body's internal environment. Therefore if the body falls below a weight that is 'right' for their body, they will experience feelings of hunger; conversely if an individual goes above a certain weight in order to redress the balance, the individual should feel the need to eat less. Lashley (1938) found that in rats, if there were lesions in certain parts of the hypothalamus that this would affect their appetite – either causing excessive eating or starvation. The findings of this could potentially be used to explain Anorexia Nervosa in humans, in that by implication it is being suggested that there may be a problem with the hypothalamus of those who suffer from this condition.

Neurotransmitters are chemicals in the brain that transmit messages throughout the body, sending different signals and messages throughout the body that enables it to function. So, neurotransmitters will send messages so that the heart knows when to beat, or the lungs to expand and to deflate for breathing, the stomach to digest food and so on. They also affect moods such as those associated with depression or aggression, sleep, levels of concentration and also weight. Problems can occur when the neurotransmitters are not functioning efficiently. Neurotransmitters are either inhibitory (provide balance) or excitatory (to stimulate the brain).

Neurotransmitters			
Inhibitory	OFF	ON	**Excitatory**

Inhibitory is the nervous system's "off switch". But where there is an off switch, there will be an on switch – the excitatory transmitters. There needs be a balance with the messages sent to the brain. If an individual experiences excessive excitation, they can become irritable and restless. Therefore, inhibitory neurotransmitters act like the brakes to the excitatory transmitters, slowing things down. The inhibitory transmitters promote calmness, and decreases aggression. There are different types of inhibitory transmitters, and the one we focus on in this part of the course are GABA, Serotonin and Dopamine.

GABA (Gamma-aminobutyric acid) is a major and most significant inhibitory neurotransmitter in that it prevents the brain from becoming over-stimulated. Research has shown that where GABA is lacking in parts of the brain or the levels are low, individuals may experience anxiety, bipolar disorder and the onset of epilepsy. Conversely, high levels of GABA can cause sedation or such extreme relaxation that this has an impact negatively on a person's ability to function. Overall, research suggests that a dysfunction of the GABA can cause psychological disorders.

If you recall, Serotonin is the neurotransmitter that stabilises mood and helps to regulate cravings, digestion, sleep, concentration and pain. Therefore it has been found that an insufficient amount of serotonin can cause depression and aggression.

Dopamine is a neurotransmitter control found in different parts of the brain and is associated with functions such as voluntary movements, memory, cognitions, mood, sleep among, emotional responses, and focus among other things.

Excitatory transmitters are the 'on switch' regulating the body's functions such movement. It naturally stimulates the body when needed e.g. fight or flight. However, if over-stimulated with no way of switching it off, an individual may spiral out of control.

Dopamine (as discussed earlier) are also excitatory neurotransmitters which among other things are responsible for motivation, and the desire to get things done.

Connection to AN:

Those who restrict their diet have been found to have low levels of dopamine, and with dopamine also being associated with pleasure, it has been suggested that sufferers of AN see weight loss, food deprivation and hunger as desirable.

Research suggests that how neurotransmitters operate can explain how anorexia can occur in some individuals. Neurotransmitters such as serotonin and dopamine are said to contribute to anorexia. Dopamine has been associated with experiences of pleasure, and it has been suggested that in some anorexics, the dopamine levels have been found to be low due to a restricted diet changing the pleasure centre and subsequently causing the individual to see weight loss and the sensation of hunger as a reward. Kaye *et al*, using PET scans of 10 recovering Anorexia suffers and 12 healthy people, found that anorexics had high levels of dopamine and that hunger pains were seen as a pleasurable feeling whereas eating was perceived as negative.

Serotonin is associated with feelings of calm, well-being and satiety. Therefore, increases in this neurotransmitter means that the anorexic can teach themselves not to feel hungry, as the anxiety anorexics experience can be generated by an increase in serotonin and can be abated by associating and justifying reduced food intake and hunger. Reducing the intake of food, therefore, reduces the level of anxiety experienced. Bailer *et al* found that women recovering from AN had significantly higher serotonin activity. They also found that they were more likely to suffer from anxiety.

We do need to note, however, that the numbers of those studied is low, and as such it would be difficult to make a generalisation in terms of anorexic sufferers overall.

Genetic Explanations

According to Strober and Katz (1987), anorexia tends to run in families, and more recent research, such as that conducted by Schork and his team, has also made a genetic connection.

Professor Schork (2013) from the The Sripps Research Institute (TSRI) led a team of 47 scientists in the largest-ever sequencing study of anorexia. The research involved using the genetic information of more than 1,200 anorexia patients and nearly 2,000 non-anorexic control subjects. What was found was the *EPHX2*, which is known to regulate cholesterol metabolism, had a part to play in the condition of anorexia, but it was not clear how *EPHX2*, causing an abnormal metabolism of cholesterol, would trigger or maintain anorexia. Schork did find that people with anorexia often had remarkably high cholesterol levels in their blood, despite being significantly malnourished. Evidence does show that cholesterol, being a basic building block of cells, has an association with mood, therefore it would not be unreasonable to assume that some anorexics may experience positive moods due to high cholesterol because they are not eating. *"The hypothesis would be that in some anorexics the normal metabolism of cholesterol is disrupted, which could influence their mood as well as their ability to survive despite severe caloric restriction."* Schork.[20]

It has been suggested that an anorexic mother-to-be will transmit genetic vulnerability to her unborn child due to a lack of nutrition, impairing the development if the child.

Activity 86

Evaluate the above explanations for anorexia

What are their strengths and what are their weaknesses?

What other variable and factors need to be considered in order to understand the causes of anorexia?

As you can see, there are so many elements and factors that can affect whether or not someone is susceptible to the condition of anorexia, and these are clearly pieces of a rather complex puzzle. Now we are going to look at the psychological explanations given for anorexia.

Psychological Explanations for Anorexia

Overall, whilst it is possible to make biological and genetic connections with anorexia, we do have to consider those aspects of this condition that have occurred as a result of social and psychological factors. For example, how social environments, that family and so on are contributory factors to this condition.

_____

[20] http://www.scripps.edu/news/press/2013/20130911schork.html

Family Systems Theory

According to Bowen, when looking at individuals and individual behaviour, we should not do this without taking into account and examining the family that an individual is a part of; in other words, an individual cannot be fully understood in isolation. With this in mind when looking at eating disorders, we need to also examine the social context in which the affected individual is situated i.e. looking at their family structure and dynamics can offer an insight into why and how they developed an eating disorder.

Family systems theory is one approach that can be applied when trying to understand anorexia. This theory sees individuals as part of a network of relationships and emotional units. So, the aim is to understand the causes of certain behaviour, not just in terms of an individual but also in terms of how that individual interacts with members of a significant group, in this case, the family. All parts of the family are interrelated and as with any unit in order for it to function effectively, there needs to be stability and balance for those who are part of that unit. Therefore, families where the members live together have both implicit and explicit rules and hierarchical structures. The types of rules and the extent to which they are enforced will invariably vary according to the family unit. The best case scenario for a family unit is that the rules and roles are flexible, and this is crucial in terms of resolving issues such as conflicts. Problems can arise in terms of the family dynamics when families are **enmeshed,** and it is this aspect of the family that can be attributed to anorexia. Enmeshment is when an individual or individuals within a family unit is/are allowed very little autonomy or none at all, with obscure and unclear emotional and psychological boundaries. Therefore researchers such as Minuchin *et al* (1978) and Bruch (1991) suggest that eating disorders can occur when a child, usually a teenager, tries to exert their independence but is prevented from doing so because of the perceived threat it would have on the family dynamics – the 'illusion of togetherness'. The adolescent may want to have an identity aside from that of the family and may feel powerless to do so, so they exercise their autonomy and independence in the only way they feel they can – through their own bodies, controlling and monitoring what they eat, how they eat and when they eat – resulting in their developing an eating disorder.

Parental Modelling

Not surprisingly, children will learn certain eating behaviours from their parents through observation and vicarious reinforcement. Brown and Ogden (2004) suggest that there is a link between parents and their children when it comes to consumption of food, eating habits, motivation and body image (i.e. satisfaction/dissatisfaction). The suggestion here is that an attitude to eating is learned (social learning). It is also significant to note that it is the parent/s that has control of the food purchased and given to children.

Activity 87

Do you think that there are any connections that can be made with your eating behaviour and your parents/guardians?
Media reinforcement

Activity 88

It has been suggested by researchers that the media do affect our eating behaviour. With this in mind can you identify 5 positive and 5 negative ways in which the media have an impact on our attitude towards eating?

MacIntryre *et al* (1998) suggest that the media can have a profound effect on what people eat and their attitudes toward food. There is a significant amount of research that shows that the media portray thin as the desired body type that can be equated with beauty, and it is this portrayal of 'beauty' that drives some of the issues associated with adolescence (particularly girls) and how they see their own body image. Jones and Buckingham (2005) found that those with low self-esteem would often compare themselves with the ideal image presented by the media. Goresz *et al* (2001) support the idea that the media present slim as the ideal. In a review of 25 studies, Goresz *et al* found that the ideal portrayed in the media would cause girls 19 years and younger to be dissatisfied with their own bodies, potentially resulting in girls in this age group developing an eating disorder. This factor appears to be a feature of Western adolescence. However, the influence of the media becomes even more apparent when in a study, Fearn (1991) found that when Fijian adolescents had American television introduced to the island, the girls soon became preoccupied with the desire to lose weight and look slim like the image of western women presented on television.

Behavioural explanations

Behavioural explanations for anorexia suggest that it stems from going on a diet, and slimming becomes a habit as a result of stimulus response (classical conditioning). What happens is a cycle where:

- The person goes on a diet to change their eating habits
- They lose weight
- Others notice the difference and compliment and praise the individual
- The individual feels good about themselves and links the controlled eating to weight loss and success
- They continue to control their eating
- They lose more weight
- The cycle continues

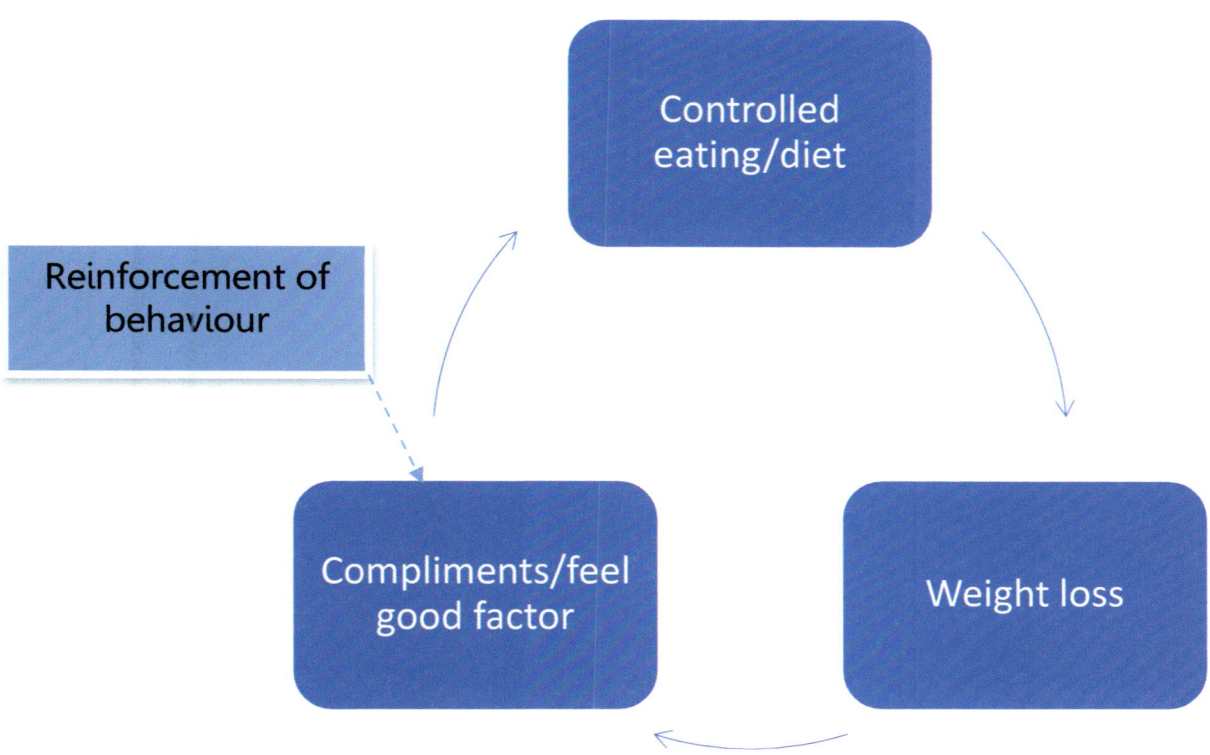

Some researchers, such as Crisp (1967), suggest that anorexia, as a fear of gaining weight, is in fact a **phobia** of weight gain brought about by the impact of social expectations, norms and values.

Cultural influences

Cultural factors also play a significant part in terms of factors such as body dissatisfaction and eating disorders. Powell and Khan (1995) found that black and Asian women had fewer concerns and issues of dissatisfaction in relation to food than white women. But Mumford *et al* (1991) found that Asian girls of school age were more susceptible to eating disorders such as bulimia when compared to white girls. Stiegal-Moore *et al* (1995) found that black women were becoming more concerned with being thin when compared to white women.

Peer influence

Meyer and Gast (2008) conducted a survey of 10 to 12 year olds and found a significant link between eating disorders and peer influence.

Distorted Body Image

We have established from the definition at the beginning of this discussion that anorexia occurs as a result of an individual's low and/or distorted image of their body; even though it is obvious to others that they are underweight, emaciated and fragile, the individual will still consider themselves to be overweight and fat. Garner *et al* (1976) conducted research that found that over half of the anorexics studied would over-estimate their body size when compared to no anorexics who would underestimate their body size.

Biological Explanations for Obesity

Activity 89

Can you think of some of the explanations given for obesity?

Obesity describes when an individual has an excess of body fat. It is estimated that in the UK, approximately 1 in 4 adults and 1 in 5 children (aged 10-11) are obese. Because of this level of obesity, this has been referred to as having reached epidemic proportions. This is a particularly topical area of study due to increasing concern for the rise in obesity.

In our discussion of Anorexia, when looking at neural mechanisms, we established that the hypothalamus is the gland responsible for homeostasis, and it is homeostasis, among other things, that controls eating and eating behaviour.

Neurological Factors

Research has found that stimulating the Lateral Hypothalamus increases eating. When the body needs energy (the blood glucose levels drop), it sends signals to the brain telling it to 'switch on' hunger (the lateral hypothalamus is activated), and the individual will then eat. Glucose levels then go up, the Ventromedial Hypothalamus (VMH) is activated, which turns the hunger impulse off, and satiety is reached and the so the individual stops eating. If there is a fault with this process and the connections, the 'off switch' may not be activated, resulting in the individual not being able to stop the compulsion to eat as they may not be able to tell that they are full.

The hormone Leptin is also a key player in this process. Leptin is secreted by fat cells and regulates appetite by decreasing food intake. Montague *et al* (1997) conducted research looking at two morbidly obsese children (male and female cousins). They were normal weight at birth and did not have any additional health issues. Both children experienced feeling continuously hungry with strong compulsions to eat even if full (hyperaphagia). Montague *et al* found that the leptin levels in the children were extremely low even though the fat levels in their bodies were very high. Therefore a deficiency in the leptin gene was a key factor in the level of obesity in these children. Farooqi *et al* (1999 and 2002) found that notable benefits occurred when the children were given injections of leptin, with reductions in weight and body fat.

Does obesity run in families?

One way in which researchers have attempted to respond to this question is by conducting studies on twins. What follows are some examples of these studies:

Researcher	The study	Findings
Bouchard *et al* (1990)	After establishing what was the normal calorific intake to maintain a healthy weight, 12	All participants gained weight. Weight gain of twins was very similar,

	male MZ twins (identical) were overfed by 1000 calories per day for 84 days.	which suggested that genetics was a key factor in weight gain.
Price and Gottesman (1991)	The level of obesity in 34 separated MZ twins were compared to 38 reared together MZ twins.	MZ Twins reared apart showed a correlation of 0.61 when compared to a 0.75 correlation for MZ twins reared together. The fact that there was very little difference suggested a genetic link.

In terms of family connections in relation to genetics, Stunkard *et al* (1986) conducted an adoption study where 540 adult adoptees in Denmark were compared with both their biological and adoptive parents. They were placed into the categories of Thin, Median, Overweight and Obese. They found that there was a strong correlation in weight between adoptees and their biological parents. There was no correlation between the adoptees' weight and their adoptive parents' in all categories. Therefore, this suggested a strong genetic link between obesity and genetics.

Activity 90

Evaluate the theories above. Identify the strengths as well as the weaknesses that can be associated with the findings presented.

Psychological Explanations for Obesity

In terms of explanations for obesity there are three behavioural factors that can be considered here. They are:

- Disinhibition – over eating as a result of an event trigger, emotional trigger etc.

- Eating as a coping mechanism e.g. comfort eating

- Eating cues – eating is triggered as a result of factors such as time of day ('it's lunch time'), food adverts seen on television, walking or driving past a fast food outlet

According to social learning theory, our attitude toward and behaviour in relation to food is learned from the people we know, particularly those who are significant to us such as parents. Brown and Ogden (2004) found correlations between parents' eating habits and their children's.

Birch and Fisher (2000) suggest a strong connection between the eating habits of a mother and daughter. So, if the mother diets a lot, the daughter is likely to follow the same pattern.

If patterns of dieting are learned and reinforced via various forms of discourse, **restraint theory** suggests that restricting a diet is destined to failure, not only in terms of not being able to continue the diet, but also in terms of gaining more weight.

Activity 91

Think of a time when you were not allowed to have something. Did you not, at some point, want it even more?

Research seems to suggest that restraint has a negative effect. Herman and Mack (1975) found that those who restrained their eating were more likely to consume high calorie meals when compared to those on unrestrained diets. Therefore, trying not to eat or limiting what you can or can't eat increases the chances of over-eating.

This has been explained further by the **boundary model**, developed by Herman and Polivy (1984). According to this model, we not only have biological and physiological boundaries in terms of the amount of food we eat, we also have cognitive boundaries. With the biological and physiological, our bodies will tell us when we need to fuel the body and when we are full, which stem from homeostasis. The **cognitive boundaries** are set by the individual. S/he determines when they eat, how much they eat and the boundaries to restrain eating. Unfortunately, the cognitive boundary in restrained eaters is less than that of the unrestrained eater. The unrestrained eater will eat until they reach satiety, which is biologically and physiologically determined by the body. The retrained eater, however, sets a cognitive boundary, so will eat until they reach that boundary. The problem is, when the individual eats beyond that cognitive boundary, the **disinhibition effect** kicks in. This is the "*What the hell!*" response. The, "*Well, I've already eaten more than I should so I may as well finish the plate!*" This can result in the individual continuing to eat even beyond the biological and physiological boundaries. This also suggests a link between eating restraints and bingeing.

Why do diets fail?

We have previously looked at research and theories that provide explanations for this, but let's delve even further.

Activity 92

List as many well known diets and weight loss programmes that you can. Then list as many reasons as you can to explain why diets fail.

Wegner *et al* (1987) found that when people are asked not to think about a particular thing, they actually did think about it and in some cases more quickly than they would ordinarily. In a study conducted by Wegner *et al*, they asked participants NOT to think of a white bear ringing a bell when they did. Another group were asked to think of a white bear and ring a bell when they did. The findings were that those who were asked not to think of the white bear rang their bell more times than those who were asked to think of the bear.

What does the Wegner study show us in terms of dieting? Well, those on diets will in the main try not to think about the foods they are 'not allowed' to eat, but what tends to happen, as in the white bear experiment, is that they think about what they are not allowed to eat even more. This is what Wegner *et al* calls the **'theory of ironic processes of mental control'** – the irony being, in an attempt to maintain control, an individual can lose control.

Activity 93

Hold this page in front of you. Now, try this:
DO NOT LOOK AT THE PICTURE BELOW FOR 1 MINUTE

This was just a bit of fun. Did you look? If so, how many times? Was it difficult to resist looking? If the theory is correct, being asked not to look at something would have made it more likely that you would, at some point, look.

Whilst the research we have discussed can provide some explanation as to why diets fail, even Wegner accepts that his findings are based on a small scale, experimental study. Also, how would this approach be used to explain those who lose weight and keep it off successfully?

Redden (2008) conducted what became known as the Jelly Bean experiment. 135 participants were put into 2 groups. Each participant was given 22 jelly beans. Group One was given general information on a computer e.g. 'jelly bean 1; jelly bean 7' etc. Group Two were given specific information on a computer e.g. 'jelly bean 8 is cherry flavoured; jelly bean 1 is strawberry flavoured' and so on. He found that participants would get bored with eating jelly beans faster if they only saw general information, but others enjoyed the task more if they saw the details of each jelly bean. This therefore, was used to illustrate the significance of maintaining interest for successful dieting.

So in terms of eating, rather than focusing on just the 'salad', focusing on the specifics on what is in the salad (cherry tomatoes, iceberg lettuce, red onions etc.) would maintain interest, slow down eating and therefore, potentially result in successful dieting.

Ogden and Mills (2008) found that success in weight loss and weight loss maintenance could be attributed to a significant life event such as reaching a milestone age, divorce and so on (provides the motivation needed to maintain).

4.2 Stress

Introduction

In this topic, we will look at stress as a bodily response. We will learn about stress and its effects on the body, including study of the pituitary-adrenal system and the sympathomedullary pathway in outline. We will then look at the effects of stress on the immune system.

Key Areas:

- The Physiology of Stress
- The role of Stress in illness
- Sources of Stress
- Measuring Stress
- Individual differences in stress
- Managing and coping with stress

The Physiology of Stress

Introduction

Stress is a term borrowed from engineering, where it refers to tension placed on a metal by a load. Humans describe stress as both:

- Something in the environment which makes them feel under pressure
- Something they feel as a result of that pressure

The Transactional Model

The most modern psychological view of human stress sees it as a mismatch between the perceived demands of a situation and one's perceived ability to cope. The word 'perceived' is important here, since everyone's idea of what is stressful is different. For example, some people thrive on being busy with many projects on the go at the same time. Others would find this extremely stressful, preferring to finish one project before beginning another. This view of stress is called the Transactional Model. It recognises the role of cognition in the experience of stress and accepts that there are individual differences in how people perceive and react to stressful situations. It also offers cognitive strategies to help people cope.

The General Adaptation Syndrome

Psychologists have not always recognised the role of individual differences in the experience of stress. In the 1930s and 1940s, Hungarian endocrinologist Hans Selye (1956) injected mice with extracts of various organs looking for a new hormone. He soon found that every irritating substance he injected produced the same symptoms (swelling of the adrenal cortex, shrinking of the thymus gland, gastric and duodenal ulcers). He also noted that people with different diseases exhibit similar symptoms. He therefore concluded that it was not the substance that caused the reaction, but the experience of being injected.

He later coined the term 'stress' and came up with a theory called the general adaptation syndrome (GAS) to explain how animals coped with stressors on a physiological level. Selye believed that this response was the same in animals and humans and that it was universal (the response was the same, no matter what the stressor). The GAS has three distinct parts, listed below.

Alarm

When we are surprised or threatened, we have an immediate physical reaction, often called the Fight-or-Flight reaction. This prepares the body for life-threatening situations, channelling away resources from organs such as the digestive system towards more immediate muscular and emotional needs. As levels of stress-related hormones rise, the body is placed on high alert. Heart and breathing rates increase, blood pressure increases and energy reserves are mobilised. This reaction was useful during our evolutionary past when we had to run away from or fight a predator. However, in the modern world, preparation for fight or flight does little to help us cope with a driving test or with the stress of having to meet a deadline. In this respect, the alarm phase is often maladaptive, since the body is prepared but there is no subsequent physical activity to reduce the arousal.

Resistance

As we become used to the stress levels, we initially become more resistant to stress and to illness, which leads us to believe we can easily adapt to these more stressful situations. However, stress hormones and bodily arousal remain high.

Exhaustion

Eventually our bodies literally run out of stress hormones. During this phase, we are no longer able to resist stress. Parts of the body can start to break down and we can suffer from stress-related illness.

HPA and SAM Systems

The GAS is mediated by two different body systems, both involving the adrenal glands and both controlled by a brain structure called the hypothalamus.

The SAM Pathway

The first of these systems is called the sympathetic-adrenomedullary (SAM) pathway:

- Stressor noticed
- Hypothalamus activates sympathetic branch of autonomic nervous system (ANS)
- Sympathetic arousal increases heart rate and blood pressure, slows digestion and mobilises fats and sugars
- Adrenal medulla releases adrenaline and noradrenaline (hormones which maintain sympathetic arousal)

The HPA Response

The second system is a slower (back-up) response known as the hypothalamic-pituitary-adrenal axis (HPA) response:

- Stressor noticed
- Hypothalamus stimulates pituitary gland
- Pituitary gland releases adrenocorticotrophic hormone (ACTH). (The name adrenocorticotrophic comes from *troph* meaning 'to grow' and *adrenocortico* meaning 'cortex or outside of adrenal gland'.)
- Adrenal cortex releases corticosteroids into bloodstream
- Liver releases energy and immune system is suppressed

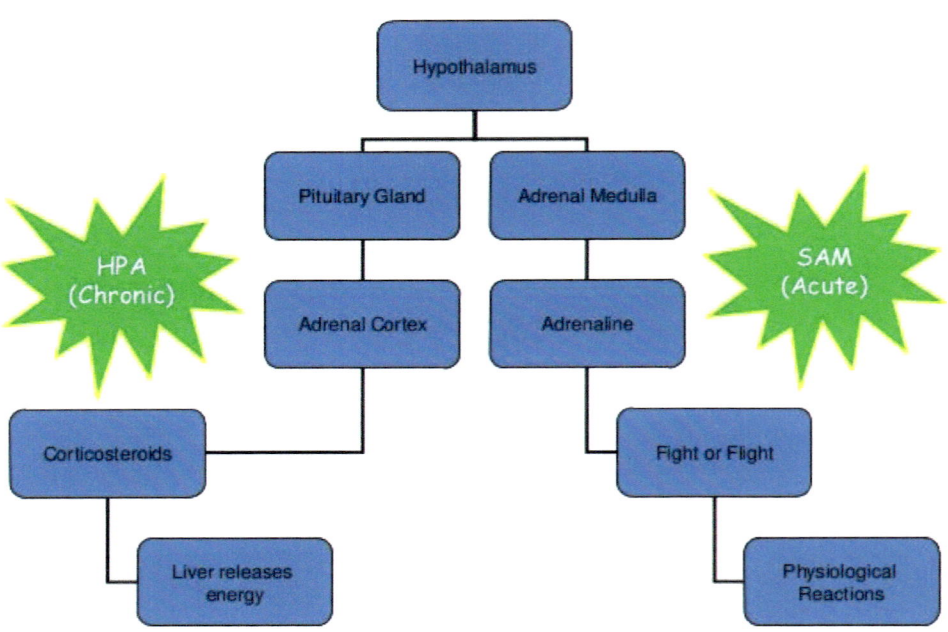

Evaluation

Selye's work has been influential in developing research into stress. He described the SAM pathway and HPA axis and demonstrated the link between chronic stress and illness. However, his work was carried out on animals. Unlike humans, animals lack cognitive awareness of their situation and this makes it very difficult to generalise. He also believed that the GAS was a universal response to all stressors, which is now known to be untrue. Further, stress-related illnesses are now thought to be caused by a long-term increase in stress hormones, rather than a using up of them, such as cortisol, which can damage the body.

Activity 94

1. **Define the following terms:**

    ➢ **Hypothalamus**

    ➢ **Pituitary gland**

    ➢ **Corticosteroids**

2. **The following are features of the pituitary-adrenal system and the sympathomedullary pathway.**

Tick the boxes next to three features of the sympathomedullary pathway.

Noradrenaline	
Pituitary gland	
Adrenal cortex	
Adrenal medulla	
Sympathetic nervous system	

1. Hypothalamus: The hypothalamus is part of the brain that controls the HPA and SAM pathways in response to stress.

Pituitary gland: The pituitary gland is a part of the brain which is controlled by the hypothalamus. It releases hormones and controls glands throughout the body.

Corticosteroids: These are hormones released from the adrenal cortex. They include cortisol, prolonged exposure to which may cause damage to the immune system.

2.

Noradrenaline	√
Pituitary gland	
Adrenal cortex	
Adrenal medulla	√
Sympathetic nervous system	√

The Role of Stress and Illness

Selye believed that in the exhaustion phase of his GAS, the body literally ran out of hormone and could not cope with further stress. We now know that it is not running out of hormone, but prolonged *exposure* to high levels of stress hormones, such as cortisol, which can damage the immune system and lead to illness. Before we study the effects of stress, let's have a closer look at the immune system.

The Immune System

The immune system functions to defend us against viral or bacterial attack. Key players in the immune system are the white blood cells (leukocytes) made in the bone marrow and circulating in the bloodstream. Some of these white blood cells provide non-specific or *natural immunity* by attacking and ingesting any invading bacteria or viruses they happen to come across. Cells which carry out natural immunity include phagocytes, macrophages and natural killer (NK) cells. Other white cells (lymphocytes) are responsible for mounting a specific immune response to a foreign particle (antigen). Lymphocytes can be divided into two classes, T cells and B cells. T cells mature in the thymus gland and are responsible for *cell-based immunity*, while B cells mature in the bone marrow and are responsible for *antibody-based, blood stream (humoral) immunity*. To help them perform their functions, T cells come in different forms:

- *Killer T cells* seek out and destroy cells recognised as foreign (e.g. in transplanted tissues) and cells infected with antigens such as viruses and bacteria
- *Memory T cells* have a system that remembers the chemical characteristics of antigens. If encountered again, the response to that antigen is faster and more effective
- *Helper T cells* respond to infection by stimulating increased production of both T and B lymphocytes

T cells attack antigens which are in the body's cells, but B cells destroy invading agents while they are still in the blood stream and before they enter the body's tissues. They do this by producing large proteins called antibodies which attach themselves to the viruses or bacteria, slow them down and make it easier for them to be destroyed by other immune cells.

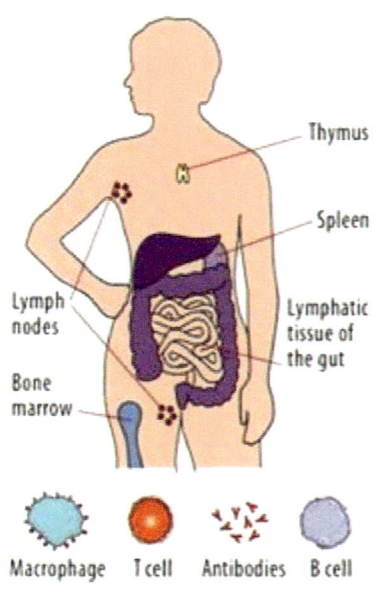

Stress and the Immune System

The immune system is very complicated, and stress-response hormones can affect it directly. For instance, high levels of corticosteroids can shrink the thymus gland, preventing the growth of T cells. The immune system is also more sensitive to stress than was thought. Short-lasting life events, such as brief marital strife, can cause immunosuppression while long-term life stress causes long-term reductions in immune function (Willis *et al*, 1987). On the other hand, exercise, diet and social support can improve immune function. The immune system is self-regulating and will recover once the stressor is removed (Sapolsky, 1994).

The effects of stress on the immune system can be seen in a variety of ways:

- *Infection* - Physiological changes during a stress reaction act to direct resources away from the immune system making it function less effectively. The person is therefore more likely to pick up infection and will take longer to recover from it
- *Indirect effects* – High levels of corticosteroids during periods of chronic stress inhibit immune cell functioning

- *Inflammatory disorders* – Chronic stress affects the immune system's ability to deal with pre-existing inflammatory disorders such as eczema and psoriasis. These conditions get worse

Research Studies

Research studies into stress and the immune system have focused on attempting to measure the effects of stress directly, by measuring levels of immune cells in the blood stream, or indirectly by assessing physical illness or wound healing in stressed individuals.

Laudenslager *et al* (1983) conducted laboratory studies in which rats were given a series of escapable shocks, identical inescapable shocks, or no shock. The rats were re-exposed to a small amount of shock 24 hours later, after which their immune systems were challenged with an antigen and their responses noted. The number of lymphocytes produced in response to the test was reduced in the inescapable shock group but not in the escapable shock group. This suggests that stress does suppress the immune system (in rats at least), especially when it can't be controlled.

Attempting to research the effects of stress on the immune system in humans can be difficult. It is not ethical to deliberately stress humans and measure the effects. Therefore, psychologists have to find situations where stress is occurring naturally and monitor the effects, or rely on people providing an accurate record of all stressful events they have experienced during a given period of time (usually a year).

Measuring immune functioning is also problematic. Researchers can measure physical illness such as cold symptoms or time taken for a wound to heal, but this does not directly relate to the state of a person's immune system. Alternatively, they can measure the number of T cells in a sample of blood, but reduction in T cells does not necessarily mean that the person will be more susceptible to illness. We shall now look at two human studies which examine the effects of stress on the immune system.

Cohen *et al* (1993)

Cohen *et al* designed an experiment to investigate the effect of life stress on susceptibility to the common cold. 394 participants were given a 'stress questionnaire' in which they were asked to rate their levels of stress, the number of stressful life events they had experienced in the previous year and their level of negative emotions, such as depression. They were then exposed to the common cold virus and 82% of the participants became infected. Of those infected, the number who developed full colds was recorded. The people who had been unable to fight off the infection were significantly correlated with the high stress index scores.

The study concluded that stress and negative emotions reduce the effectiveness of the immune system.

Kiecolt-Glaser *et al* (1984)

This study explored the effects of naturalistic stressors (exams) on the function of natural killer (NK) cells. The participants were 75 medical students preparing for their final exams. The level of NK activity in their blood samples was measured one month before the exam (low stress) and during the exam period (high stress). Participants also completed questionnaires on their experience of stressful life events and social isolation.

The study found that the levels of NK cell activity were significantly lower during the period of high stress. It also found that the lowest activity levels were in the students who experienced most social isolation.

The study concluded that naturalistic stressors reduce immune function and that this effect is more pronounced in those who experience higher levels of social isolation.

Evaluation

Although Cohen *et al's* study demonstrated a correlation between stress and ability to resist illness, the researchers did not measure the immune system directly so they cannot say that stress reduces its function. However, Kiecolt-

Glaser *et al* (1984) have shown reduction of natural killer cell activity in medical students experiencing exam stress. These effects were higher in those students who also reported feelings of isolation, or in other words, were already stressed. Another problem with Cohen's study is that it used correlational analysis and, therefore, it is difficult to determine cause and effect. It is also difficult to know whether one part of the stress measure was more important than another in affecting the ability to resist illness.

Other Studies

- Kiecolt-Glaser *et al* (1995): small wounds take longer to heal in carers of Alzheimer's patients
- Cohen *et al* (2005): blister wounds on the arms of married couples heal more slowly after conflictive rather than supportive discussions

Factors Mediating the Effects of Stress

Much research has been carried out to try to understand how stress affects the immune system, and psychologists now realise that the relationship between stress and the immune system is a complex one. For example, some types of short-term stress can *improve* the immune system and different types of stressor can have different effects. In addition, there are age and gender differences in the body's ability to manage stress. An American National Consumer League survey (2003) found that people under the age of 65 were more likely to report being stressed than older people while Segerstrom and Miller (2004) claimed that elderly people may be more vulnerable to stress-related illness because age makes it harder for the immune system to regulate itself.

In terms of gender, the National Consumer League Survey (2003) found that women were more likely to report problems and feelings of stress, and that women show greater immunosuppression following marital conflict - Kiecolt-Glaser *et al* (2001).

Segerstrom and Miller (2004) have carried out a meta-review of over 293 studies into the effects of stress on the immune system. Their findings are summarised in the table below.

Type of Stressor	Effect	Part Involved
Acute (short-lasting)	Upregulation	Natural immunity
Brief naturalistic	No overall ill effects	Shift from cellular to humoral immunity
Chronic (long-lasting)	Downregulation	Natural and Specific immunity
Non-specific life events	Decrease in production	Natural killer cells (over 55s only)

Activity 95

Fill in the blanks using the words below to complete the following conclusion on the effects of stress on the immune system:

Upregulation; specific; infections; GAS; cellular; immunosuppression, immune function; fight; flight; humoral; illnesses.

Acute or short lasting stressors produce an _____ in natural immunity whereas chronic stressors produce a general downregulation in _____.

Natural immunity activation in response to acute stressors fits in with the idea of Selye's ___ and with the idea of _____ or _____. Having a system that can respond rapidly to stressors is adaptive.

Chronic stress activates the immune system beyond what is adaptive. Eventually global _____ occurs, leaving the person vulnerable to stress-related _____ and _____.

Immune changes in response to stress are complex. They can involve shifts from natural towards _____ immunity and, within specific immunity, perhaps shifts between _____ and _____ immunity.

Acute or short lasting stressors produce an _ **upregulation** _ in natural immunity whereas chronic stressors produce a general downregulation in _**immune**_ **function**.

Natural immunity activation in response to acute stressors fits in with the idea of Selye's _ **GAS** __ and with the idea of _ **fight**__ or __ **flight**___. Having a system that can respond rapidly to stressors is adaptive.

Chronic stress activates the immune system beyond what is adaptive. Eventually global _ **immunosuppression**_ occurs, leaving the person vulnerable to stress-related _ **infections** _ and _**illnesses**_.

Immune changes in response to stress are complex. They can involve shifts from natural towards _ **specific** _ immunity and, within specific immunity, perhaps shifts between _ **cellular**_ and _ **humoral**_ immunity.

Stress and the Cardiovascular system

The heart and blood vessels comprise the two elements of the cardiovascular system that work together in providing nourishment and oxygen to the organs of the body. The activity of these two elements is also coordinated in the body's response to stress. Acute stress — stress that is momentary or short-term such as meeting deadlines, being stuck in traffic or suddenly slamming on the brakes to avoid an accident — causes an increase in heart rate and stronger contractions of the heart muscle, with the stress hormones — adrenaline, noradrenaline and cortisol — acting as messengers for these effects. In addition, the blood vessels that direct blood to the large muscles and the heart dilate, thereby increasing the amount of blood pumped to these parts of the body and elevating blood pressure. This is the 'fight or flight response', mentioned previously. Once the acute stress episode has passed, the body returns to its normal state.

Chronic stress, or a constant stress experienced over a prolonged period of time, can contribute to long term problems for the heart and blood vessels. The consistent and ongoing increase in heart rate, and the elevated levels of stress hormones and of blood pressure, can take a toll on the body. This long-term ongoing stress can increase the risk for **hypertension (high blood pressure), heart attack or stroke.**

Repeated acute stress and persistent chronic stress may also contribute to inflammation in the circulatory system, particularly in the coronary arteries, and this is one pathway that is thought to tie stress to heart attack. It also appears that how a person responds to stress can affect **cholesterol** levels.

Other health issues

Stress has also been linked with tension headaches and muscular pains, thought to arise from holding the body in a guarded, 'ready for action' state. Prolonged periods of stress cause strain on the muscles due to a lack of opportunity for proper rest and relaxation.

Depression, weight loss or gain, insomnia and increased use of alcohol/cigarettes/drugs have also been linked to chronic stress and anxiety. These issues carry further risks to general health and wellbeing.

Sources of Stress

There are a number of different sources that can result in different types of stress, such as workplace related stress. The role of personality also factors in our response to stress and ways of managing stress. As we have seen, our experience of everyday stress is firmly rooted in our perception of what is stressful and how able we are to cope. These foundations are laid in childhood and are affected by past experiences as well as individual personality characteristics.

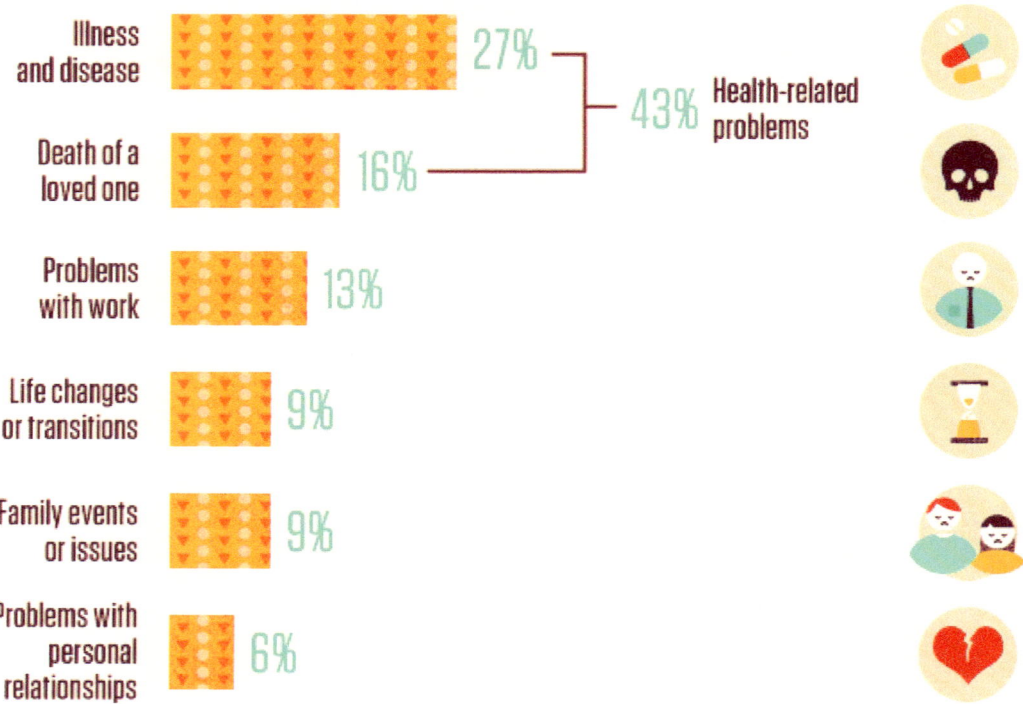

THE MOST COMMON SOURCES OF STRESS

% of people who say they experienced **a major stressful event in the past year** related to...

- Illness and disease — 27%
- Death of a loved one — 16%

43% Health-related problems

- Problems with work — 13%
- Life changes or transitions — 9%
- Family events or issues — 9%
- Problems with personal relationships — 6%

SOURCE: NPR / Robert Wood Johnson Foundation / Harvard School of Public Health: The Burden of Stress in America, March 5-April 8, 2014

Workplace Stress

The relationships between stress, the workplace and physical and mental health were first systematically investigated during the 1970s. In recent years, the workplace has been seen as a major source of stress and consequently stress has overtaken the common cold as the main cause of absence from work (Furedi, 1999). The source of stress experienced in the workplace will depend, for example, on the type of work a person does, how much control they have over their day-to-day activities, how much responsibility they have and the type of work undertaken.

Some common workplace stressors include:

Environment	A work environment that is too noisy or too hot can increase stress. The physical arrangement of the workplace can also affect stress levels. More privacy and personal space decrease stress.
Home-work interface	Balancing the demands of home and work can be very stressful, particularly for parents with small children.
Control	The level of control over workload can affect stress levels. More control leads to lower stress levels.
Workload	Having too much or, interestingly, too little, work to do can cause stress levels to rise.

Now let's look at evidence for each stressor.

Environment

Evans *et al* (2000) found that even low-level noise in open-style offices can result in higher levels of stress, and lower task motivation. Forty experienced female clerical workers were assigned for three hours to either a quiet office or one with low-intensity office noise (including speech). The workers in the noisy office experienced significantly higher levels of stress (as measured by urinary adrenaline), made 40% fewer attempts to solve an unsolvable puzzle, and made only half as many ergonomic adjustments to their workstations, compared to their colleagues in quiet offices. Interestingly, however, the workers themselves did not report higher levels of stress in the noisy office. The findings show open-office noise has modest but adverse effects on physiological stress and motivation and could contribute significantly to health problems such as heart disease (due to elevated levels of adrenaline) and musculoskeletal problems.

Home-Work Interface

Achieving a balance between the demands of the workplace and the demands of home life has become more and more difficult in the last decade, especially since more and more families have both parents working and since technology such as laptop computers and mobile phones have made it easier to stay in contact with work wherever we are. Professor Gary Cooper of UMIST (cited in Stranks, 2005) claims that stress arising from this home-work interface can result in:

- Divided loyalties, where people increasingly have to make decisions in terms of the demands of the family as opposed to the demands of work
- Conflict of work with family demands, especially in the case of overtime work, where people are having to spend more time at work than they do with the family and, consequently, miss out on family activities such as going on trips out and eating together
- Intrusion of problems outside work, where working long hours means that the person is not able to deal with family problems or crisis situations that require his/her attention

Control

Geer and Maisel (1973) showed participants coloured slides depicting victims of violent deaths. One group could stop the slide show by pressing a button whereas the other group had no such control and had to watch the show from start to finish. Stress was measured using the galvanic skin response (GSR) which detects minute changes in electrical conductivity of the skin due to stress. The group who had no control over their viewing had higher GSRs, which suggests they found the viewing more stressful than the other group.

Workload

Steptoe *et al* (2004) found that participants with the highest levels of over-commitment at work had cortisol levels that were an average of 22% higher than those of workers with the lowest levels of over-commitment. In addition, systolic blood pressure was an average of 7 mm Hg higher among over-stressed individuals.

Research Study

Many of these factors interact with each other and with an individual's personality characteristics, as well as their perception of workplace stress. Also, various coping strategies, such as social support and engaging in hobbies, can alleviate some of the negative effects of stress.

The Whitehall Studies

A long-term study of health and workplace stress has been on-going since the 1960s. The Whitehall I study used participants from the London civil service and found that the lower pay grades had twice the rate of illness of the highest pay grade. About a quarter of the difference between these grades could be attributed to risk factors such as smoking and high blood pressure.

In the Whitehall II study, Marmot *et al* (1997) analysed data from over 7000 participants who were followed over five years. They had no heart disease when the study began. The study showed similar results to the Whitehall I study, with the rate of heart disease being 1.5 times greater in the lowest pay grades than the highest pay grades. Although some of the increase could be attributed to risk factors such as smoking, hypertension and obesity, the most significant factor was 'decision latitude' or the sense of control that the participants felt they had over their work.

Conclusions and Evaluation

Marmot *et al*'s study showed that lack of control was related to ill health in their study of male civil servants. But can we generalise their findings to other socioeconomic groups and cultures? Support for Marmot can be found in the following study by Johansson *et al* (1978). They identified a group of high-risk finishers in a Swedish saw mill whose job was to complete the last step in the preparation of timber. Their job was machine-paced, repetitive, highly skilled and isolating. Furthermore, their rate of work determined the wages for the rest of the factory.

When compared to a low-risk group of cleaners, the finishers were found to have more stress-related illnesses such as headaches, and higher levels of absenteeism. They also had higher levels of adrenaline and noradrenaline on work days compared to rest days. This supports Marmot because it shows that the lack of control (machine-paced work) and the high demands placed on them (everyone else's wages depended on their rate of work) led to stress-related health problems in the finishers.

However, in both studies it is not possible to truly understand the part played by life-style factors such as smoking and lack of exercise since these rely on self-report and are therefore often under-reported. In addition, neither of these studies takes individual differences such as personality factors into account. Not all workers who experience low-control and high job demands become ill. We will now turn to research into personality factors and stress.

Measuring Stress

Life Changes and Daily Hassles

In 1967, Thomas Holmes and Richard Rahe developed the Social Readjustment Rating Scale (SRRS) to measure the relationship between life changes and wellbeing.

The SSRS works on the principle that the more we have to adjust to a life event, the more stressful it is. Holmes and Rahe made a list of typical major life events, e.g. death of a spouse, marital separation, gain of new family member, etc. They got hundreds of men and women to rate each item on the list according to how much life adjustment each one would need.

They then ranked the items from those needing most to least adjustment. 'Death of a spouse' came out on top, and this was assigned an arbitrary value (called a life change unit or LCU) of 100. All other items were ranked relative to this life event and given scores according to their rank in the list. Homes and Rahe now had a tool which they could use to investigate the relationship between everyday stress and physical illness. Their study is summarised below.

Rahe *et al* (1970)

Aim

- To find out if the SRRS correlated with onset of illness

Procedure

- 2500 American sailors given the SRRS to complete for previous six months
- Total score recorded for each participant
- Detailed records on health status kept for next six months

Findings

- Positive correlation of 0.118 between life event scores and illness scores

Conclusion

- The greater the number of life events experienced, the greater the likelihood of developing a stress-related illness
- Life events not only factor contributing to illness since correlation very small

Criticisms

- Problem with correlation, cause and effect, perhaps illness (especially mental illness) affects life events and not the other way around
- Limited sample, male US Navy, difficult to generalise to other populations (lacks population validity) and gender biased

Ethics

- Informed consent and full debriefing needed
- Recalling negative life events may *cause* stress to participants

Problems with the SRRS

Other studies using the SRRS have yielded mixed results. Some support Rahe *et al's* findings but others do not. This questions the validity of the scale and asks whether it is a robust tool for measuring everyday stress?

The SRRS failed to take into account individuals' appraisals of particular life events. For example, some people find Christmas very stressful, especially if they are the ones who organise activities and cook for the rest of the family. Others find it the most stress-free time of the year with time to relax and enjoy socialising with family and friends. The SRRS fails to reflect this difference.

Newer life event scales have therefore been devised to take account of individual differences by getting participants to rate life events in terms of whether they see them as positive or negative. Not surprisingly, negative events tend to correlate more with ill health than do positive ones.

Lazarus and colleagues (Kanner *et al* 1981) devised three scales: a 117 item Hassles Scale to give a better measure of the impact of negative events; a 135 item Uplifts Scale (since they realised that positive events can counter the effects of negative ones); and a combined Hassles and Uplifts (HSUPS) Scale containing 53 items worded so that the respondent can indicate whether a given item is a hassle, an uplift, or both.

Examples from the (HSUPS) are given below:

0	1	2	3
None or not applicable	Somewhat	Quite a bit	A great deal

Please circle one number on both sides

How much of a hassle was this for you?

How much of an uplift was this for you?

0 1 2 3		0 1 2 3
0 1 2 3	A. Time spent with family	0 1 2 3
0 1 2 3	B. Enough money for emergencies	0 1 2 3

Research

- Kanner *et al* (1981) found that scores on the Hassles scale correlate with levels of depression
- DeLongis *et al* (1982) found positive correlations with health status for both a life events scale and Hassles scale; although for Hassles, the correlation was greater. Uplifts were unrelated to health outcomes
- Bouteyre *et al* (2007) found a correlation between daily hassles and mental health in a group of first-year university students

Comments

Overall, it would seem that the frequency and type of daily hassles experienced by a person provide a better explanation for physical and psychological health than relatively rare major life events. Daily hassles create persistent irritations, the effects of which can accumulate to give more serious stress reactions such as anxiety and depression (Lazarus, 1999).

Evaluation of Research into Daily Hassles

Most of the data are correlational so it is not possible to draw causal conclusions. However, the research certainly indicates that daily hassles have the potential to adversely affect our health and wellbeing.

Individual Differences in Stress

Personality Factors and Stress

Type A Behaviour

In the early 1960s, a pair of cardiac specialists, Friedman and Rosenman (1976), studied the behaviour of male patients suffering from coronary heart disease (CHD) and found that a personality type (which they called Type A) was consistently linked with an increased risk of developing CHD.

Type A is a form of behaviour exhibited by people who tend to be aggressive, competitive, tense, time-conscious, and generally hostile, whereas Type B is the kind of behaviour exhibited by an easy-going, non-aggressive and non-competitive person. Such people may be less prone to heart disease.

Rosenman *et al* (1976)

Aims

- To investigate the relationship between Type A behaviour and heart disease

Participants

- 3454 middle-aged men on the west coast of America

Procedure

- Participants were characterised as Type A or Type B by structured interview and behavioural signs. Participants were followed up over 8.5 years.

Findings

- During the study there were 257 heart attacks. 69% were in the Type A group.

Conclusions

- Type A individuals were significantly more vulnerable to heart disease, even when high-risk factors such as obesity and smoking were controlled for.

Methodological issues

- The definition of Type A is specific to Western cultures. Gender and cultural factors make the study difficult to generalise. Although some variables that were controlled, it is possible that another significant variable may have been overlooked. This type of real-life study has high ecological validity, but it is not possible to control all variables.

Ethical Issues

- Participants gave informed consent and were fully debriefed. They were not manipulated in any way, so there is little chance of psychological harm.

Comments

Rosenman *et al* demonstrated the first link between personality type and CHD. However, recent research has shown that not all Type A behaviours have an increased risk of heart attack. Dembroski *et al* (1989) Found that only people who exhibit negative behaviours such as chronic hostility are twice as likely to suffer CHD. The reasons for the relationship between hostile behaviour and heart disease are not clear but it has been suggested that the hormones produced during hostility may do some physical damage, or that people who exhibit such negative behaviour do not maintain good health habits, such as exercising and eating a balanced diet.

Hardiness

The research on personality has shown that some aspects of Type A behaviour are correlated with the risk of developing CHD. However, this also means that there are many Type A people who cope very well with their stressful lives and show no ill effects. Kobasa (1979) described the concept of hardiness to explain how such people might cope. She found that people who felt in control, had high commitment and saw problems as challenges rather than stress, and reported fewer stress-related symptoms than those who did not view their lives in this way.

Activity 96

Kobasa used 'the three Cs' of Control, Commitment and Challenge as the basis of a hardiness questionnaire shown below. Have a go at the questionnaire overleaf to test your own hardiness. The higher your score, the hardier you are.

[There is no correct or incorrect answer to this task.]

Based on Kobasa (1979):

Hardiness Questionnaire

0 = strongly disagree

1 = mildly disagree

2 = mildly agree

3 = strongly agree

1. Trying my best at work makes a difference.

0   1   2   3

2. Trusting to fate is sometimes all I can do in a relationship.

0   1   2   3

3. I often wake up eager to start on the day's projects.

0   1   2   3

4. Thinking of myself as a free person leads to great frustration and difficulty.

0   1   2   3

5. I would be willing to sacrifice financial security in my work if something really challenging came along.

0   1   2   3

6. It bothers me when I have to deviate from the routine or schedule I have set for myself.

0   1   2   3

7. The average citizen can have an impact on politics.

0   1   2   3

8. Without the right breaks, it is hard to be successful in my field.

0   1   2   3

9. I know why I am doing what I am doing at work/school/office.

0   1   2   3

10. Getting close to people means I am then obligated to them.

0   1   2   3

11. Encountering new situations is an important priority in my life.

0   1   2   3

12. I really do not mind when I have nothing to do.

0   1   2   3

Scoring:

Numbers in brackets refer to scores for question numbers:

Control =   (1+7) – (2+8)   Max = 6; min = 0

Commitment =   (3+9) – (4+10)   Max = 6; min = 0

Challenge =   (5+11) – (6+12)   Max = 6; min = 0

Hardiness = control score + commitment score + challenge score
The higher your score, the hardier you are.

Kobasa used questionnaires such as the one you have completed to assess the relationship between hardiness and ability to cope with stress. She found that people who have high scores in tests of hardiness are significantly less likely to suffer from stress-related illness than those with low hardiness scores. Her studies of personality and stress have also shown that coping with stress using exercise and social support protected against stress-related illness (Kobasa *et al*, 1985).

Criticisms

Kobassa used mainly Western male white collar workers in her research, so it is difficut to generalise her findings to other cultures and genders. However, it does show that Type A behaviour is not as damaging as first believed and that certain Type A characteristics may actually protect against the effects of stress. This has helped to explain the inconsistent results found in earlier studies of Type A behaviour and heart disease.

The extent to which each of Kobasa's three Cs contributes to the protective effect is unclear. Control, for example, may be an important part of commitment and challenge, rather than being separate from them. Therefore, Kobassa may simply be measuring the role of control in protecting against stress rather than a distinct personality type.

Other Personality Types

Other personality types have been described, each supposedly linking to a different aspect of stress-related illness:

- Eysenck (1988) Type C - Difficulties in expressing emotions and forming social relationships. Linked with cancer
- Denollet (2000) Type D (Distressed) – High levels of negative emotions. Linked with heart disease, especially when combined with social inhibition

Whether these are distinct 'types' remains in question. Nevertheless, research into personality and stress has shown us the kind of behaviour associated with coping with stress and has led to some useful cognitive-behavioural techniques in which people can be taught to engage in less harmful behaviour as a reaction to daily life stress.

Coping with Stress

There are a range of different methods for coping with stress, and the method a person chooses will be related to many different factors such as personality, culture, gender, etc. People are influenced by having observed other family members coping with stress.

The COPE scale (Carver *et al*, 1989) is a research questionnaire which looks at coping styles. Research using coping questionnaires such as this one has shown that people use two main coping strategies to cope with stress. These are:

Problem-focused coping – This tackles the source of the stress using a problem-solving approach, e.g. researching various treatment options for a particular disease (reducing the demands of the stressor), or joining a support group (improving coping resources).

Emotion-focused coping – This Tackles the emotional distress associated with the stress. Typical emotional strategies include denial (a cognitive strategy), venting emotions, smoking, drinking and seeking social support (behavioural strategies).

Activity 97

Read the case study of Janie below:

Janie had been feeling tired and run down for a week. She could not seem to muster enough energy to stay awake past about 9pm and she was falling asleep in class. Since she was sitting her 'A' level exams in two weeks, she thought she had better go the doctor for a check-up and found that she had glandular fever. She would have to have six weeks off college which would mean that she would not be able to sit the exam and would miss all the important revision lessons.

Janie felt upset and disappointed about missing her exams so she telephoned the college to see what they could do. She discovered that work could be sent home for her to complete and that the college would arrange for her to come in for the exams as normal but sit in isolation with her own invigilator. Once she had completed the call, Janie asked her mum to help her make a revision plan. She then went for a nice warm bath. Define the coping strategies used by Janie. Illustrate with examples from the case study.

Managing and Coping with Stress

Type of Stressor

Research has shown that people typically use problem-focused strategies to cope with events over which they have a degree of control, e.g. problems with children, whereas events over which we have no control, e.g. natural disasters, prompt more emotion-focused coping strategies. The consensus amongst researchers is that problem-focused strategies are the most effective, but emotion-focused ones are useful as a short-term measure to deal with the psychological effects of stress. They also help people to deal with situations where problem-focused coping strategies are not an option, e.g. during long-term illness.

Research Studies

Control and Coping

Park *et al* (2004) asked undergraduates to describe their most stressful event, what coping strategies they used and their daily mood. The researchers found that problem-focused coping was most often associated with a positive mood, as long as the stressful event had a high degree of control.

However, it would seem that problem-focused coping does not work for all situations. Fang *et al* (2006) looked at women with a familial risk of developing ovarian cancer. Those women who used problem-focused coping strategies and reported feeling more in control actually suffered more distress over time than those women who used other forms of coping. This would suggest that problem-focused coping only works where there is a high degree of actual rather than perceived control.

Gender

Stone and Neal (1984) reported that women tend to use emotion-focused coping, whereas men tend to use problem-focused coping. Nolen-Hoeksema (1994) found that a ruminative style of coping (thinking and worrying about a problem) was more common in women than in men and more likely to be linked with negative outcomes such as depression.

Do people have a preferred style?

Individual Differences

Tenner *et al* (2000) looked at daily coping styles in patients with chronic pain. They found that patients tended to use emotion-focused strategies in conjunction with problem-focused strategies, suggesting that the styles are not used independently but tend to interact. They also found that the choice of strategy used on a particular day depended on its success in controlling pain the previous day. This means that individuals don't have a characteristic coping style but try out different coping strategies and modify them accordingly.

Psychological Methods of Stress Management

Cognitive-behavioural Therapy

Cognitive-behavioural therapy is based on the understanding that a person's perception of the stressful situation and their ability to cope might be inaccurate. Psychologists have identified certain faulty attributional styles or errors in thinking which make some individuals more susceptible to the effects of stress. For example, a person who thinks: 'I must be perfect in all I do' and 'I have failed one maths test therefore I will never be able to do maths', is exhibiting a demanding cognitive style that they are very unlikely to be able to fulfill. Such negative ways of thinking lead them to overestimate the demands of a situation and underestimate their ability to cope. Cognitive-behavioural therapies are designed to correct these faulty attributional styles and replace them with more rational ones in order to alter a person's ability to cope.

Stress Inoculation Training (Meichenbaum, 1985)

Meichenbaum recognised that clients often have self-defeating attitudes, thoughts and behaviours that make it difficult for them to cope with stressors (see table below). Stress Inoculation Training aims to modify these to make the person better equipped to deal with stressful occurrences.

Thoughts and behaviours that increase or prolong stress (From Meichenbaum, 2007):

A. Self-defeating cognitions	B. Beliefs	C. Blame
1. Seeing oneself as being continually vulnerable 2. Dwelling on negative implications 3. Dwelling on others' views of self	1. Changes are permanent 2. The world is unsafe, unpredictable and untrustworthy 3. The future will be negative	1. Blaming others, with accompanying anger 2. Blaming oneself, with accompanying guilt, shame, and humiliation
D. Comparisons	E. Actions Taken	F. Actions not taken
1. Oneself with others 2. Before with now	1. Being continually hypervigilant 2. Cognitive avoidance (e.g. suppressing unwanted thoughts) 3. Behavioural avoidance (e.g. using substances, withdrawing, avoidant behaviour)	1. Believing that anything positive could come out of situation 2. Retrieving, and accepting data of positive self-identity 3. Seeking social support 4. Protecting oneself from negative, unsupportive stress-engendering environments (e.g. indifference, criticism)

The idea of inoculation comes from vaccination, where a weak dose of a disease provides the body with the ability to fight a future strong dose. Stress Inoculation Training aims to work in a similar way by providing clients with the opportunity to deal with mild forms of a stressor in order to increase their perceived ability to cope with chronic stressors.

There are three stages in Stress Inoculation Training (SIT): conceptualisation; skills training and rehearsal; and application in the real world.

1. **Conceptualisation -** The client works with a therapist to identify sources of stress. This may involve keeping a stress diary

2. **Skills training and rehearsal** - Many forms of stress can be alleviated with appropriate skills training. An example is training in non-verbal communication for people with social anxiety disorder. Relaxation techniques are also used to help clients to reduce bodily responses to stress

3. **Application in the real world -** The client is encouraged to apply the techniques they have learned in real world settings. They are able to evaluate which techniques work best and to learn from experience. There will then be further opportunities for skills training and rehearsal if needed

Evaluation of Stress Inoculation Training

An important strength of Stress Inoculation Training is that it is very flexible. Because it consists of a wide variety of cognitive and behavioural techniques tailored to the individual needs of the client, it can be used to deal with many types of stressor.

It has been found to be successful in helping people deal with the stress of chronic pain, performance anxiety, specific phobias, work related stress (Meichenbaum, 2007), as well as helping athletes deal with the stress of competition (Mace, Eastmen & Carroll, 1986) and helping patients prepare for surgery (Langer, Janis & Wolfer, 1975).

Hardiness Training Kobasa (1982)

As we saw earlier, Kobasa realised that individuals possessing the three Cs (control, commitment, challenge) were better able to cope with stress than those who did not. She therefore used these as the basis for another form of CBT which she called hardiness training. Once again there are three stages.

1. **Focusing** - Clients are trained to spot signs of stress including muscle tension, anxiety and increased heart-rate. This allows them to identify the source of the stress

2. **Reconstruction** - This involves reliving a recent stressful situation, looking at how it was resolved and thinking about the ways in which it went well and how it could have gone better

3. **Self-improvement** - The person is trained to believe they can cope with future stress. Clients are encouraged to take on challenges they can cope with in order that they can succeed. Once they can cope with these challenges, they can take on bigger ones

Activity 98

Explain how you would use hardiness training to help John, below:

John is a personnel manager in a building firm. Recently, due to a downturn in the economy he has had to lay off many employees (a task which he finds really stressful). Recently he had to cope with another round of layoffs during which he reduced the workforce by 1/3. The night before the layoffs, he did not sleep well and at the end of the day he felt so exhausted that he went to bed as soon as he got home. John says the reaction of some of the employees really gets to him as he feels sorry for them but is powerless to help. He has come up with ways to save some of the jobs by job sharing and reducing salaries but, unfortunately, the owner is not interested in his ideas. Remember: You must get John to:

- **Focus**

- **Reconstruct**

- **Self-improve**

As part of the therapy program you design for him.

John's stress may come from the fact that he has little control over the situation and no involvement in the decision making process. However, although John cannot save the jobs, he does control the process of informing the employees that they will be laid-off. He can therefore be encouraged to re-evaluate his role as making the process as painless as possible. This will give him a greater sense of control over the situation.

Focus

At this stage John would learn to become aware of the physical signs of stress, such as increased heart rate. He would begin to notice at which stages of the process he became most tense.

Reconstruct

John would be encouraged to consider what went well and what went less well during the layoffs. For example, are there particular ways of breaking the news that are more successful than others? John would be encouraged to realise that it could have been a lot worse, especially with a less sympathetic manager. By understanding that he handled the situation in best way possible, John will feel more optimistic and positive about handling similar situations in the future.

Self-improve

Although there will always be sources of stress, John will be encouraged to realise that he has dealt with the situation well. This will increase his sense of self-efficacy.

Evaluation of Hardiness Training

Hardiness training has been used successfully to improve health and performance in adult workers and students (Maddi, 1987 and Maddi *et al* 2002). Because it tackles the appraisal of sources of stress, as with other forms of CBT, it reduces the gap between the perceived demands of a situation and a person's perceived ability to cope. However, the concept of hardiness has been criticised since the relative importance of the three factors, control, commitment and challenge, has never been established. The concept of increasing hardiness may simply be the same as increasing personal control. It also involves time, commitment and can be expensive so it is not appropriate for everyone.

Physiological Methods of Stress Management

Drug Treatment

Drugs treat the symptoms of stress and make the person feel better. However, drugs can do nothing to reduce the source of stress or to help the person learn to deal with it. For this reason, drugs are often used as a short-term solution combined with cognitive therapies to help the person better deal with the stress in the future.

The most commonly prescribed drug treatments for stress are:

- Benzodiazepines
- Beta blockers

Each of the drugs targets the symptoms of stress in a different way.

Benzodiazepines, such as Valium and Librium, increase brain levels of an inhibitory neurotransmitter called GABA. As GABA increases, it reduces the output of a range of excitatory neurotransmitters in the brain. This 'quietens' the brain and makes the person feel calmer. Beta blockers work directly on sympathetic nervous system pathways to reduce arousal. During stressful events, adrenaline and noradrenaline bind to beta-adrenergic receptors throughout the body (for example on the surface of the heart) and increase sympathetic arousal. Beta blockers block these receptors and prevent the stress hormones binding. This reduces the physiological reaction to stress.

Strengths

- Drugs treat the symptoms of stress and make it easier to cope

Weaknesses

- However, they do not remove the stressor so physical symptoms will return once treatment stops

- All drugs have side effects and some can create dependency, so they should only be used as a short-term solution

Biofeedback

Biofeedback combines both physical and psychological methods of treating stress by allowing the person to see or hear their physiological response (e.g. heat rate or neck-muscle tension) and use relaxation techniques to reduce it. In a typical biofeedback session, electrodes are attached to the skin. These electrodes then feed information to a small monitoring box that translates the person's responses into a tone that varies in pitch, a visual meter that varies in brightness, or a computer screen that varies the lines moving across a grid. The biofeedback therapist then leads the person in relaxation exercises. Through trial and error, people can soon learn to identify and control the mental activities that will bring about the desired physical changes.

Evaluation

Biofeedback may be highly effective for some individuals, especially children (Attanasio *et al* 1985), in controlling migraine headaches.

However, it is often found to be no more effective than muscle relaxation techniques alone. This suggests that the biofeedback element of the technique is not necessary. Biofeedback is not useful for all stress-related disorders and it can be time consuming and expensive.

Activity 99

Complete the table below:

Stress Management Technique	Advantage	Disadvantage
SIT		
Hardiness Training		
Drug Treatment		
Biofeedback		

Answer to activity 99

Stress Management Technique	Advantage	Disadvantage
SIT	CBT approach that improves both problem-focussed and emotion-focussed coping skills. Effective in many situations, including exam stress and specific phobias.	Requires time and commitment. Expensive and therefore not available to everyone or suitable for everyone.
Hardiness Training	CBT approach that increases sense of personal efficacy. Studies suggest it improves health and performance in adults (Maddi, 1987 and Maddi *et al*, 2002).	Requires time and commitment. Expensive and therefore not available to everyone or suitable for everyone.
Drug Treatment	Effective in short-term.	May lead to dependency. Does not help the client to identify sources of stress or develop coping techniques. Specific side-effects.
Biofeedback	Harmless and no side effects. Shown to be helpful in treatment of tension headaches, especially in children (Attanasio *et al*, 1985).	Requires time and commitment. May be no more effective than relaxation techniques alone.

4.3 Aggression

Introduction

Aggression can be regarded as any type of behaviour with the aim being to cause harm or injury to another. It may not necessarily be accompanied by anger but may have another underlying motive. In this topic, we will begin our study of aggression by looking at some explanations for aggressive behaviour.

Key Areas:

- Neural and hormonal mechanisms in aggression
- Ethological explanations of aggression
- Social psychological explanations of human aggression
- Institutional aggression in the context of prisons
- Media influences on aggression.

Neural and Hormonal Mechanisms in Aggression

Biological Explanations of Aggression

Biological explanations of aggression focus on the idea that some internal, organic factor may make some individuals more naturally predisposed towards aggression than others. The biological approach tends to concentrate on the influence on aggressive behaviour of:

- Genes
- Hormones and neurotransmitters
- Brain structure

Genes

Karyotype

A karyotype is an organized profile of a person's chromosomes. In a karyotype, chromosomes are arranged and numbered by size, from largest to smallest. This arrangement helps scientists quickly identify chromosomal alterations that may result in a genetic disorder. To make a karyotype, scientists take a picture of someone's chromosomes, cut them out and match them up using size, banding pattern and centromere position as guides.

The normal human karyotype has 46 chromosomes:

- 23 derived from each parent
- Sex is determined by X and Y chromosomes
- Males are XY
- Females are XX
- The sex of an offspring is determined by the sex chromosome carried in the sperm

In 1961, Sandberg *et al* identified the 47, XYY karyotype. This karyotype described a male with an extra Y chromosome (the 'super' male). The idea that these individuals were more 'male' than other men led scientists and medical practitioners to believe they would be more aggressive (a trait associated with males).

The reasoning behind this idea included the fact that the Y chromosome is responsible for switching on testosterone production in the male body. Testosterone is responsible for male characteristics (including aggression) and, therefore increased testosterone in the XYY male would lead to such individuals being more aggressive than normal.

Unfortunately, this led to a rather negative stereotype of XYY man. Court-Brown (1965, 1967) even suggested that such individuals should be hospitalised for the safety of themselves and others!

However, Ratcliffe *et al* (1994) have found that testosterone levels are normal in XYY males. Most XYY males have normal sexual development and usually have normal fertility. There are no outward signs of their condition other than that they tend to be taller than normal males and some have learning difficulties, which include delayed language and speech. They are no more aggressive than other males.

The issue has been further examined through animal studies. Nelson (2006) found that selective breeding can cause increased aggression in animals. Earlier research by Cairns (1983) bred highly aggressive mice that would show aggression in middle age (rather than when young or old). These animal studies suggest that aggression can be caused by genetic factors. However, it is difficult to generalise this research to humans. Theilgaard (1984) conducted a study into aggression in XYY men. The study found that there was no consistent link between genotype and aggression. However, the study did find that XYY men were more likely to give aggressive interpretations in thematic apperception tests (similar to ink blot tests). Theilgaard therefore concluded that XYY males might seem more aggressive, but this did not necessarily mean that they were more likely to actually commit violent acts. She emphasised that the situation is complex, with many interrelated factors.

Other Genetic Factors

Monoamine Oxidase A (MAOA) Gene

Sometimes referred to as the 'Warrior Gene', the MAOA gene has been associated with aggressive behaviour. It regulates the metabolism of serotonin in the brain and, if you recall, low levels of serotonin are associated with impulsive and aggressive behaviour.

Brunner *et al* (1993) studied a Dutch family where the males in the family were found to be particularly aggressive, committing acts including rape and arson. It was found that they had abnormally low levels of MAOA. The defective gene was passed on to the male offspring from the X chromosome from their mothers. Therefore, different forms of genes have been identified:

- Low activity – MAOA L = produces less of the enzyme
- High activity – MAOA H = produces more of the enzyme
- Research shows that it is MAOA L that predisposes an individual to aggressive behaviour

Twin and Adoption Studies

Studies in twins provide supporting evidence for this analysis of the MAOA gene.

Twin Studies

That there might be a genetic basis to some aspects of human aggression has been demonstrated in twin studies, which show that aggression is more highly correlated in identical (monozygotic) twins than non-identical (dizygotic) ones.

- McGuffin and Gottesman (1985) – Concordance rate for aggressive and antisocial behaviour of 85% for MZ twins compared with 72% for DZ twins. Therefore, there would seem to be a genetic component

Miles and Carey (1997) findings were:

Type of twin	MZ = Identical	DZ= Non Identical
% of genes shared	Share 100% of their genes	Share only 50% of their genes
Concordance rate for aggressiveness – **living together**		
Concordance rate for aggressiveness – **living apart**		
The higher rate in MZ twins does reinforce the theory of the role of genes		

Note, however, that different studies have been extremely variable in terms of the correlations between twins. Carter (1973) found only a 14% correlation for MZ twins brought reared together. Also:

- Twin studies assume that DZ twins share only 50% of their DNA but if their parents are from similar families living in close proximity, they may share more similar genes than is normally assumed

- MZ twins are likely to be raised in an environment that is more similar than are DZ twins (e.g. being dressed in the same clothes, doing similar activities etc.). Therefore, the environmental influences may be stronger in their case, suggesting that their aggressive behaviour could be the result of nurture rather than nature leading us to consider the importance of environmental as well as genetic factors

What is consistent, however, is that studies show some correlation between aggressiveness of MZ twins when compared to DZ twins, whether or not they are reared together or apart.

Adoption Studies

Another way to tease out the relative roles of genes and environment is to look at children who have been brought up by adoptive parents to see if they are more similar to their natural parents (genes) or their adoptive parents (environment).

- Danish Study – Hutchins and Mednick (1973) reviewed over 14,000 adoptions in Denmark. Found significant positive correlation between the number of violent criminal convictions of biological parents (particularly fathers) and the number of violent criminal convictions in their adopted sons

However:

- Children given up for adoption often display a higher rate of aggressive or antisocial behaviour at the time of their adoption and Tremblay (2003) has found that parents who give up their children for adoption also display higher levels of antisocial behaviour than the general population. Therefore, correlations between biological parents and adoptees could be due to environmental influences *before* the adoption. Also, there may be problems arising from feelings of rejection and abandonment in adopted children

Nevertheless, both the twin and adoption approaches have estimated that about 40% of individual differences in aggression come from genetic factors and that between 50% and 70% come from environmental factors.

Hormones

Testosterone is an androgen (male hormone) produced by the testes. Much scientific and anecdotal evidence has linked this hormone with aggression in males. For example:

- Males have higher levels of testosterone in their bodies than do females (females do have some testosterone) and males are naturally more aggressive.
- Testosterone rises dramatically during puberty, as does aggression
- Male animals of various species show a marked decline in aggression after castration but, if injected with testosterone, show a marked increase (Hutchinson, 1979)
- Animals in the wild are more aggressive during the mating season when testosterone levels are at their highest

The problem is that all of these observations are correlational. Therefore, it would be an equally valid conclusion to say that aggression causes levels of testosterone to rise. To support this idea, Pillay (2006) looked at males and females playing sports and measured their levels of testosterone using saliva samples. He found that both males *and* females playing aggressive sports had high levels of testosterone.

In addition, testosterone is also associated with other more positive traits which don't often get talked about due to its negative stereotype. For example, Kimura (1999) found females with high levels of testosterone had better spatial ability than those with low levels.

Another danger of correlating levels of aggression with levels of testosterone is that is assumes that all individuals will behave in the same way i.e. that increasing testosterone will make all individuals more aggressive. This is a simplistic view which does not allow for individual differences. Harisson *et al* (2000) gave testosterone to men aged 20-50 and then gave them a frustrating computer game to play. Aggressive responses were more frequent in some of the men but not all of them, suggesting that other factors are responsible for the aggressive response.

Models of Testosterone and Aggression

There are two models of testosterone and aggression.

- Basal model – Testosterone causes a person to be more dominant and, therefore, more aggressive
- Reciprocal model – Testosterone varies as a consequence of a person's dominance. As a person gains in dominance, he therefore begins to produce more testosterone

Research carried out by Mazur and Booth (1998) supports both the reciprocal model of testosterone and the basal model.

In a review of a number of studies, they found that men with more testosterone were more likely to be divorced, single, arrested for offences other than driving offences and to use weapons in fights. This could be used to support the basal model of testosterone.

In a study of 2,100 air force veterans over a ten-year period, they found that testosterone levels varied in accordance with life events. The veterans' testosterone levels reduced when they got married and rose when they got divorced. This could be used to support the reciprocal model of testosterone.

Neurotransmitters

Serotonin is a neurotransmitter produced by the pineal gland, deep in the centre of the brain. It plays an important role in the control of appetite, sleep, memory and learning, temperature regulation, mood, behaviour, cardiovascular function, muscle contraction, endocrine regulation and depression. It also influences aggressive and violent behaviour.

Research

- Davidson, Putnam and Larson (2000) – Serotonin serves to inhibit violent behaviour. Observation that violent criminals tend to have lower levels than non-violent ones
- Mice are more aggressive when their serotonin 1B receptors are knocked out.
- Raleigh *et al* (1991) – Decreasing serotonin in vervet monkeys = more aggressive behaviour. Increasing serotonin = less aggressive behaviour and more social behaviour. Also raises monkey's status in the group
- Low serotonin leads to aggression, depression, overeating, alcohol abuse and violent suicide
- Domestic pets selectively bred for low aggression have higher levels of serotonin
- Linnoila and Virkkunen (1992) low levels of serotonin linked to impulsivity and explosive acts of violence

Comments

Once again, the research into serotonin and aggression is correlational, which means it is very difficult to establish cause and effect. Other monkey studies have been conducted in which the effects of increasing serotonin on rank has not been established (Nelson, 2005) and it is well known that SSRIs as a treatment for anxiety disorders and depression (disorders often associated with increased aggression) don't work for everyone and that those suffering from depression don't necessarily become more aggressive. Therefore, serotonin level is just one of a number of complex factors which contribute to aggressive behaviour.

Brain Structure

In humans and animals, three brain structures seem to be important in the initiation and control of aggressive behaviour. These are the amygdala, hypothalamus and frontal cortex.

The amygdala is connected to the hypothalamus and is involved in the fear response. In cats, removal of the amygdala has a taming effect, and you will recall that pre-frontal lobotomy, which cuts the connection between the frontal cortex and amygdala in humans, has a similar effect.

A famous case study was conducted by physician Dr. Harlow on Phineas Gage in 1868. Gage was a railway foreman who suffered a terrible accident when a tamping iron went through the left side of his face and through the top of his head, destroying much of his left frontal lobe. According to Harlow, before the accident Gage was a quiet, hardworking man, but after the accident he became aggressive and impulsive. He was said to have changed so much that his friends described him as 'no longer Gage'.

Gage's example is frequently cited as evidence that the frontal lobe helps to regulate aggression. However, so little is actually known about his personality before or after the accident, or the extent of his injuries, that it is very difficult to form any clear conclusion. It is also impossible to generalise based on the case of only one man.

Further evidence suggests that the amygdala has a role in aggression. Studies of cats (Zagrodska *et al*, 1998) and rats (Potegal, Ferris and Delville, 1994) have found links between the amygdala and aggression.

There are problems in generalising such animal research to humans. However, Potegal *et al* (1994) suggested that the similar brain structures of humans and animals make generalisation viable. Blair *et al* (2001) conducted a study to support the relationship between the amygdala and aggression in humans, where they found a link between psychopathy and damage to the amygdala.

Issues Debates and Approaches

The idea that genes could be responsible for aggressive behaviour is *reductionist* as it does not allow for other influences. It is likely that humans and animals may inherit a tendency to be more aggressive but the environment, e.g. culture, upbringing and experience, will regulate aggressive behaviour. Also the role of hormones, neurochemicals and brain structure will have an influence in the expression of aggressive behaviour.

The idea that increasing certain hormones (e.g. testosterone) and neurotransmitters (e.g. serotonin) can increase aggressive behaviour is **deterministic** since it does not allow for **free will**. Human behaviour is more complicated than simply being a product of levels of hormones and neurotransmitters, since humans experience other influences, such as learning, socialisation and culture. In addition, we have the freedom to make conscious, cognitive decisions about our behaviour.

Much of the work carried out in terms of the biological approach to aggression has been done on animals. The problem with this is that it is often not possible to generalise such findings to humans since we have more complex brains than animals.

Some of the studies, such as cutting out sections of animals' brains to see the effects on aggression, would be considered unethical today and therefore we cannot replicate such work to validate the findings.

Where animal research is carried out, we must question whether the ends (furthering our understanding of human behaviour) justify the means (making animals suffer). Professor Bateson, secretary of the ethical committee of the association for the study of animal behaviour (1986) devised a 'decision cube' considering three elements: the quality of the research, the certainty of benefit and the suffering of the animals involved. Research can proceed where there are no solid blocks, i.e. where the quality of research is high, the certainty of benefit is high (it will alleviate human suffering, for example) and the animal suffering is low.

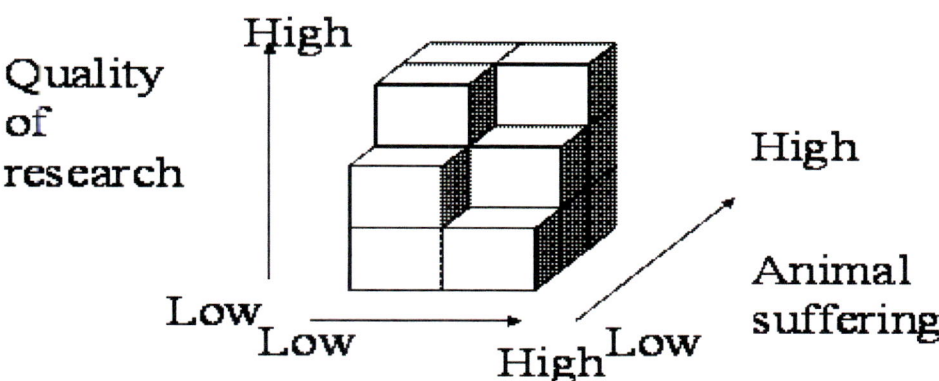

Activity 100

Make a note table to answer the following question:

Compare social and biological approaches to explaining aggression (25 marks).

Remember, you will be assessed on three skill areas:

AO1 = 9 marks for description of the main features of each approach and identifying the differences between them.

AO2/AO3 = 16 marks for discussing the ways in which they are different: such as the amount and robustness of research evidence; similarities and differences relating to assumptions; research methods; and position relative to debates in psychology. To achieve AO2/AO3 marks above basic, you must refer to issues, debates and approaches relevant to this area.

Answer/Example for activity 100

Aggression	Social Approach	Biological Approach
Assumptions	Looks at external causes of aggression such as role of learning, observational learning and modelling, deindividuation and importance of cues.	Looks at internal factors such as genes, hormones, neurotransmitters and brain structure.
Robustness of research	Much research carried out on humans, so can generalise. However, often out of social context in lab: Bandura (social learning theory), Zimbardo (deindividuation) etc. Lab research can lack ecological validity.	Much of the research carried out on animals Raleigh et al (1991) serotonin and Hutchinson (1979) testosterone, plus animal studies on amygdala. Hard to generalise to humans as brains are more complex.
Debates	Reductionist – looks at role of external factors only, although Bandura's cognitive apparatus makes it less so. Deterministic – aggression *caused* by external factors Nature-nurture – suggests nurture most important factor.	Reductionist – looks at role of internal factors. Deterministic – aggression *caused* by genes neurotransmitters etc. Nature-nurture – suggests nature most important factor.
	Although nowadays most psychologists recognise the complex interaction between genes and environment in shaping behaviour e.g. more aggressive children are	

		likely to seek out violent games and aggressive toys than those who are less aggressive (active gene-environment interaction).
Issues	Culturally biased – heavily based on Western society, so tells us little about aggression in other cultures.	Animal studies, animals not as complex as humans. May be other factors. Studies well-controlled and support each other. Problems with ethics of some of the research. Can't replicate today.

Ethological Explanations of Aggression

Ethological explanations see aggression as instinctive, its function is to be adaptive and to ensure survival. The evolutionary approach looks at those behaviours and cognitive processes that we have inherited from our evolutionary past because they enabled our ancestors to survive; in other words, they are adaptive. Evolutionary psychologists support the 'nature' side of the nature-nurture debate.

Aggression as Instinct

Ethologists such as Lorenz believe that aggression is instinctual but see it as a universal, externally-directed drive, possibly connected to a survival instinct, which unites humankind with the animal world. Lorenz (1966) defines aggression as 'the fighting instinct in beast and man which is directed against members of the *same* species'. He relates it to Darwin's notion of the 'struggle for existence'. Lorenz's own study is based largely on his careful research of a variety of animal species, particularly fish and birds and, to a lesser extent, non-primate mammals. In these varied species, he notes a shared instinct to:

- Defend territory from an animal of the same species
- Defeat a competitor for a desired female
- Protect the young and defenceless of the species

Lorenz points out that such aggression serves the animal kingdom well. It:

- Brings about a 'balanced distribution of animals of the same species over the available environment'
- Assures that the gene pool is continually modified toward strength, and enhances the likelihood of the young of a species growing to adulthood
- Preserves the species, regularly improving it to make it more adaptive to the environment

Lorenz also sees a role for aggression in developing the social structure, since it is often used to establish the 'pecking order' or social rank among members of a group. Lorenz sees this as a necessity for developing an advanced social life.

Therefore, aggression has developed in humans as a result of an instinct that has developed evolutionarily. Lorenz defines aggression as:

"...*the fighting instinct in beast and man which is directed against members of the same species.*"[21]

For our ancestors, aggression would occur as a result of two core reasons:

1) With limited food and resources and hostile environment, fighting with conspecifics in order to separate one from another would ensure access to much needed resources –survival of the fittest.

2) The need to procreate - sexual selection created an innate fighting instinct as the strongest aggressor would become the main copulator.

We do need to bear in mind that the theory presented here is based primarily on the study of non-humans (fish and birds), but Lorenz does suggest that whilst aggression is adaptive in most animals (as the need arises and according to the dictates of a given environment),

_____

[21] Lorenz, Konrad. On Aggression. (Marjorie Kerr Wilson, Trans.) New York: Harcourt, Brace & World, Inc., 1966, p. ix.

humans have not developed the instinctive inhibitions that are found in animals. Animals will show signs of submission to a stronger aggressor, and this, according to Lorenz, has evolved meaning that animals will not engage in lethal combat, rather they will fight only until one has submitted to the other or has run away. Humans however are:

"...basically harmless omnivorous creature, lacking in natural weapons with which to kill big prey." (Lorenz)

But in creating weapons for use on others, humans are able to cause harm and death at a distance, resulting in an undeveloped response to submissiveness and the inhibitory instinct of aggression not being developed. Lorenz and others suggest that if aggressive acts were perpetrated using bare hands as opposed to weaponry possibly, the readiness at which aggression can be exhibited in humans would not be so evident. In other words, humans are far *more* aggressive than animals. Cultural and technological advances have outstripped the inhibitory capacities of the human aggressive instinct. Two male mammals fighting over territory or a female do not often fight to the death; the stronger backs off when the weaker acknowledges his loss by exposing a vulnerable body part (an appeasement gesture). Humankind, however, has produced and perfected lethal weapons delivered at a great distance from those being attacked. Sometimes, the attacked do not even know of the attack until the fatal blow has already been struck. Thus they are unable to use such appeasement gestures to avoid destruction.

Evaluation of Lorenz

Some ethologists and psychologists question the idea that there are parallels between animal and human aggression.

For example, Fromm (1973) describes a difference between malign aggression (such as acts of genocide) and benign aggression (a parent defending their young). Furthermore, Nelson (1974) criticises Lorenz for not considering the effects of learning, structural (social) causes and psychological causes on aggression.

Rapoport (1965) also explains how the ability of humans to cease thinking of others as fellow humans makes it easier to attack them. Aggressive acts often therefore stem from the labelling of other people as enemies, rather than from a specific situation. Finally, Tinbergen (1968) thinks it is impossible to generalise explanations of aggression from animals to humans. This is because animal aggression comes from ritualised mating performances, whereas humans exhibit a genuine desire to hurt each other.

Evolutionary Explanations of Human Aggression

The evolutionary approach explains aggression in terms of sexual competition since males have to compete for females so that they can pass on their genes. A major concern of our male ancestors was to find a mate and to hold on to her. Once he had a mate, he would have to make sure that the offspring they raised together were his own (paternity certainty), or any investment he made would be wasted (he would not be passing on his own genes). This would have led to sexual jealousy on the part of the male, designed to protect his genes from female infidelity and cuckoldry (being deceived into bringing up offspring conceived by another man). This inevitably brought males into competition with each other and, according to Carrier (2007), is the root of much male aggression.

Empirical Evidence

Mate Retention and Violence Against Women
Shackelford *et al* (2005)
Aims: To see if mate-retention strategies are correlated with violence.
Procedure: Gave MRI (mate retention inventory) to 461 males and 560 females. The MRI asked about mate-retention strategies and violence commonly used by males against their female partners.
Findings: Two broad types of mate-retention strategy were positively correlated with violence scores.

- *Intersexual negative inducements* - e.g. Shouting at her for looking at another man
- *Direct guarding* - Not allowing her to talk to another man, e.g. at a party

They also found that men who used emotional manipulation were more likely to be violent.

Evaluation: This study supports the idea that there is a correlation between the use of mate-retention strategies and violence and that violence in humans has therefore evolved because it is adaptive in protecting against infidelity and cuckoldry. However, there are limitations associated with correlational research in that they cannot show a causal relationship between the use of mate-retention strategies and violence against women.

The Influence of Jealousy

Further support for this idea comes from the reports of female victims of domestic violence, who often cite extreme sexual jealousy on the part of their male partners as a cause of violence against them (Dobash and Dobash, 1984).

Cascardi and Vivian (1995) conducted research into aggression in relationships, finding that jealousy was the most frequently cited cause. Canary, Spitzberg and Semic (1998) also found that couples reported that jealousy contributed to their anger and aggression.

The situation is complicated by other factors, however. For example, it may be that violent males lack the skills to respond to their feelings of jealousy effectively (Holtzworth, Monroe and Anglin, 1991).

Group Display of Aggression in Humans

Evolutionary Explanations

We are familiar with group display as a strategy used by animals e.g. to ward off a predator. However, in our evolutionary past, group display may well have served an important adaptive function for the individuals making up that group by increasing their chances of survival.

We will look at two different types of group display:

- The behaviour of lynch mobs
- The behaviour of sports crowds

The Behaviour of Lynch Mobs

In the southern states of America, between 1882 and 1930 there were almost 3000 reported lynchings of African-Americans. The scale of this was such that at least one black woman, man or child was murdered almost every week. Two evolutionary explanations given for the behaviour of lynch mobs are:

- The power-threat hypothesis
- Dehumanisation of the victim

The Power-Threat Hypothesis

Blalock (1967) believes that as the minority group membership grows, the majority group will intensify its efforts to maintain dominance. As a consequence, the group's discriminatory behaviour also increases. This fear of 'Negro power' resulted in 'lynch law' as a means of social control. Lynchings intensified after the abolition of slavery, when the ensuing social tension would have left the white population feeling at most risk. Ridley (1997) suggests that group solidarity and discrimination rise dramatically when groups feel at risk.

Evaluation

Clark (2006) studied lynch-mob murders in Sao Paulo, Brazil and found that the victims who were lynched posed no threat either politically or economically to the majority. Therefore, 'fear of the minority' was not a major causal factor.

Dehumanisation

Hyatt (1999) points out that during the lynching and burning of African-Americans, the mob often tried to reduce the victim's body to bits of bone and burned flesh. In other words, the body was reduced to a form barely recognisable as human. In addition, years of racist propaganda had reduced black people to simplistic and animalistic stereotypes. This dehumanisation of the victim fuels the idea that the victim poses a threat and makes violence against them more likely.

Reducing the victim to the status of an animal also makes it easier to kill them, by removing any moral constraints associated with killing other human beings. This tactic was used as part of the propaganda put out by the Nazis during the 1930s and 1940s. This could be an adaptive response which helped our ancestors to protect their territories and families from the threat of neighbouring tribes.

Evaluation

Rothenberg (1998) studied lynch mobs in Guatemala and found evidence consistent with the dehumanisation hypothesis. Enraged crowds often dowsed the bodies of the dead victims with petrol and burned them, dehumanising them even further.

Zimbardo (2007) claims that dehumanisation is crucial to understanding inhuman acts. He also refers to work of Goffman (1959) who stated that a failure to recognise the individuality and humanity of another person facilitates inhumane actions. There are some social psychological alternatives to adaptive theories of human aggression. They focus on the factors existing within a group that might lead to antisocial behaviour.

Influence from the Group

Blumer (1939) saw what he called a **circular reaction** in group behaviour where individuals in the group reproduce the behaviour and emotions of those around them. This intensifies and amplifies the original emotion and behaviour. As we have seen, Le Bon (1896) thought that a contagion occurred within a group, whereby the views of the group become infectious and quickly spread among its members, leading to what he termed a 'collective mind'.

You will recall Le Bon's pathological viewpoint outlined earlier in this section in which he claimed that, once in a crowd, an individual was taken over by the 'collective mind', and the subsequent work on deindividuation which used the effect of reduced inhibitions to explain why a group was more aggressive than an individual.

Activity 101

Summarise the theory of deindividuation using the following key terms to help you:

- **Based on the ideas of**

- **Psychological mechanisms**

- **Loss of self control**

- **Festinger *et al***

- **Loss of individuality leads to**

- **Explains mob violence because**

Activity 101

- Based on the ideas of Gustave Le Bon

- Psychological mechanisms of anonymity, suggestibility and contagion transform an assembly into a 'psychological crowd' in which a 'collective mind' takes possession of the individual

- Loss of self-control causes the individual to become more suggestible to control by the crowd's leader, and capable of performing any act, however atrocious or heroic.

- Festinger *et al* 1952 coin the term 'Deindividuation'

- Loss of individuality leads to loss of self-control which produces emotional, impulsive, irrational, regressive and intense behaviour

- Explains mob violence because, acting as part of a group, individuals will commit the most horrific acts of violence, acts they would never dream of committing alone

Emergent Norm Theory

Developed by Turner and Killian (1957), this theory views crowds as rational and norm-governed.

When a crowd gathers, there is no norm governing the behaviour of the crowd. There is normally no leader or centralised control. The attention of the crowd is drawn towards those that act in a distinctive manner. This distinctive behaviour is taken as the norm, and slowly a norm that governs behaviour emerges. As time passes, the norm becomes entrenched, and there is pressure against non-conformity. Inaction on the part of the crowd is interpreted as being a sign of acceptance of the new norm. Emergent norm theory thus takes into account the fact that crowds communicate and that behaviour in a crowd can be unpredictable.

Support

- Mann *et al* (1982) found that more aggression was shown when people were told the group norm supports it - by the use of loud noise. This supports the emergent norm theory
- Mann *et al* (1982) also found that anonymous participants are more aggressive than identifiable ones, which supports the deindividuation theory

Criticisms of Emergent Norm Theory

- Reicher argues that groups do not coalesce in a normless environment. When groups come together, there is no need for a norm to emerge because they already bring with them a set of norms, e.g. the norm for a group of rock fans coming to watch a Guns and Roses concert would be different from a group of ladies gathering for a WI meeting
- There is limited support for the theory
- It isn't clear how norms emerge

Sports Crowds

A sports crowd is one of the most clearly identifiable groups in society. The members share a common goal and enhance their group identity by wearing their team's colours and learning shared chants and songs to sing on the terraces.

The behaviour of sports crowds can therefore be seen to follow a number of theoretical models. For example, the contagion model might explain booing and cheering by fans, and the dehumanisation of the other team and their fans might lead to acts of violence.

Gutman (1986) notes that no one single theory can explain all aspects of crowd behaviour and that an explanation that incorporates elements of different models seems most logical.

Issues Debates and Approaches

The key tenet of the evolutionary approach is natural selection. Natural selection influences the way species change over time to become better adapted to their environment. It therefore follows that some human behaviours can be explained in terms of the retention of behaviours which have served to increase the 'fitness' of our ancestors. The problem with this approach is that it is reductionist; it sees adaptiveness as the main guiding principle for complex behaviours and fails to take into account social pressures or cognitive processes. It is also **deterministic** as it sees behaviour being genetically determined by past environments, rather than being subject to **free will.** The evolutionary approach is difficult to **falsify** since the concept of adaptiveness is difficult to disprove.

The approach is based heavily on the study of non-human animals, especially those animals which live in some sort of social structure. It is difficult to generalise such examples to humans since, although we too live in complex social structures, our behaviour is also affected by emotion and thought.

Evolutionary explanations therefore suggest that aggression is brought about by an innate desire to reproduce. According to Daly and Wilson (1998), males have evolved in a way that aims to prevent their female partners from procreating with another male, and it is the innate fear of cuckolding or infidelity that can result in jealousy and aggression being exhibited through violence. In research by Dobash and Dobash, they found that in a significant amount of cases involving domestic abuse and violence, the trigger was extreme jealousy on the part of the male partner. In the most extreme cases where the male partner in exercising an evolutionary throwback, that of control over the female partner, sometimes this can go too far resulting in uxoricide (wife killing), the killing being a mistake.

Duntley and Buss (2005) disagreed with Daly and Wilson's explanation that uxoricide is a mistake, arguing that infidelity caused the male partner to feel loss to a competitor, of their partner and also the chance to reproduce, but a competitor gained a partner. So by killing the wife the man may lose a partner, but he has stopped his rival gaining one and exerted his authority.

Social Learning Theory

Social Learning Theory developed from behaviourism. According to the behaviourists, behaviour that is reinforced (rewarded) is likely to be repeated and learned.

Social Learning Theory emphasises that learning occurs in a social environment and that, as well as learning behaviour directly, by being personally rewarded, we can also learn it *indirectly* by observing what happens to other people. Bandura (1977) calls this learning by **vicarious experience** or **observational learning**. For example, a child may see an older brother or sister get what he/she wants from a parent by throwing a temper tantrum. If the child gets what they wanted (i.e. are rewarded for their bad behaviour) the younger child will *imitate* the behaviour in *similar situations*. They are **modelling** the behaviour of the older child. Seeing the tantrum work has acted as a **vicarious reinforcer** for the younger child.

Modelling Behaviour

There are three main stages to the modelling of any behaviour. These are acquisition, instigation and regulation. The stages are summarised as:

- Acquisition – 'See'
- Instigation – 'Try'
- Regulation - 'Internalise'

Activity 102

Here is the scenario with Michael and his brother, which we encountered earlier in the course. Apply the three stages to the scenario:

1. Michael has an older brother whom he admires. Michael's brother is involved with some aggressive boys at school and Michael is worried about how his brother's behaviour is changing. On one occasion, he saw his brother trying to take a younger child's pocket money away from him. His brother and his 'gang' then were able to buy cigarettes with the money. The next day, Michael tried to take money from a smaller child but the child hit him hard on the nose and caused it to bleed. The child's father also came to his house and complained to his parents, causing Michael to be 'grounded' for a week.

Explain Michael's behaviour relating it to the three stages of modelling below:

- **Acquisition**
- **Instigation**
- **Regulation**

Michael sees and mentally represents his brother's behaviour (acquisition). He then tries it out by attempting to steal another child's money (instigation). The fact he was hit by the child and grounded by his parents (punishment) is likely to discourage him from repeating such behaviour in the future (regulation).

Experimental Evidence

Experiment One

Bandura, Ross and Ross (1961) investigated the learning of aggressive behaviour without reinforcement. In a series of experiments, pre-school children observed an adult model interacting either aggressively or non-aggressively with a "Bobo doll" — a weighted, inflatable plastic clown (about the height of the children) that returns to an upright position when hit or pushed over. The study involved observations of the following four groups of children:

Group 1: Watched a *male* acting *aggressively* (6 boys and 6 girls)

Group 2: Watched a *female* acting *aggressively* (6 boys and 6 girls)

Group 3: Watched a *male* acting *non-aggressively* (6 boys and 6 girls)

Group 4: Watched a *female* acting *non-aggressively* (6 boys and 6 girls)

The researchers predicted that children in the first two groups would be more likely to display physical and verbal aggression towards the doll. In addition, they predicted that children would be more likely to imitate the actions of same sex models, so that boys would more readily imitate a male model and girls would imitate a female model. Most of the children already knew how Bobo dolls were supposed to be punched (from television commercials).

From Bandura:

The model exhibited distinctive aggressive acts which were to be scored as imitative responses. The model laid the Bobo doll on its side, sat on it and punched it repeatedly in the nose. The model then raised the Bobo doll, picked up the mallet and struck the doll on the head. Following the mallet aggression, the model tossed the doll up in the air aggressively and kicked it about the room. This sequence of physically aggressive acts was repeated approximately three times, interspersed with verbally aggressive responses such as, "Sock him in the nose...," "Hit him down...," "Throw him in the air...," "Kick him...," "Pow...". (Bandura, Ross, & Ross, 1961, p. 576)

Findings

Overall, boys exhibited more imitative aggression than girls did, which is consistent with gender differences typically found for average levels of physical and verbal aggression. Furthermore, boys were over twice as likely to imitate a male model who had performed physically and verbally aggressive behaviours than a female model who did the same. Girls, on the other hand, were about twice as likely to imitate a female model who had performed physically and verbally aggressive behaviours than a male model who did the same. Lastly, when the models did not perform aggressive behaviours, the children showed few expressions of aggressive behaviours.

Conclusions/Explanations

The type of learning exhibited by these children is called observational learning. This refers to acquired changes in behaviour caused by observing and later imitating the behaviour of another. Bandura and his colleagues concluded that the results of this study showed that learning can take place without reinforcement. Bandura explains that acquisition of the behaviour (remembering what the model did) does not always lead to that behaviour being performed. For the child to later perform the behaviour, he or she must be in a similar situation to that in which the behaviour was observed and be motivated (by reinforcers) to repeat it.

Vicarious Conditioning

Bandura noted that reinforcers need not be direct. Children can learn simply by observing what happens to others. By watching what happens to a model, observers develop an *expectation* about the likely outcome of performing the behaviour themselves. If the models in the study described above had been punished for acting aggressively, the children would have developed an expectation that punishment would follow aggressive behaviour, which would have caused them to be less likely to imitate this behaviour when placed in a room with a Bobo doll.

If, on the other hand, the models had been reinforced for acting aggressively, the children would have developed an expectation that reinforcement would follow aggressive behaviour, which would have caused them to be more likely to imitate this behaviour when placed in a room with a Bobo doll.

Experiment Two

To test this hypothesis, Bandura (1965) filmed adult models acting aggressively towards a Bobo doll. In the film, the model ordered the doll to move, stared at it for a moment in an aggressive manner, and then attacked it:

First, the model laid the Bobo doll on its side, sat on it, and punched it in the nose while remarking, "Pow, right in the nose, boom, boom." The model then raised the doll and pummeled it on the head with a mallet. Each response was accompanied by the verbalization, "Sockeroo stay down." Following the mallet aggression, the model kicked the doll about the room, and these responses were interspersed with the comment, "Fly away." Finally, the model threw rubber balls at the Bobo doll, each stroke punctuated with "Bang." This sequence of physically and verbally aggressive behaviour was repeated twice. (Ibid. pp. 590-591)

Bandura showed these films to pre-school children. He found that, although most of the children had *learned* the aggressive behaviours by watching the models, they did not always perform what they had learned. An important influence on performance of the operant responses was the *consequence* for the model of his aggressive behaviour.

One group of children observed another person reinforcing the model's aggressive behaviour with *praise and treats.* A second group of children observed the other person punishing the model's aggressive behaviour with *scolding and spanking.* Children in the first group were much more likely to imitate the model's aggressive behaviour than children in the second group.

Summary

Children may acquire aggressive behaviour but will not perform it unless they are reinforced or vicariously reinforced for it. Therefore, *the child's social context regulates aggressive behaviour.*

Albert Bandura (1975)

Evaluation of Social Learning Theory

Methodological Issues

- The Bobo doll affords aggression. In other words, its very nature invites you to knock it over and watch it bounce back
- Pre-school children are naturally more aggressive than older children
- Most of the children belonged to colleagues of Bandura – a limited sample
- The children already knew that you were supposed to hit the Bobo doll

Strengths

- Social learning theory can explain inconsistencies in aggressive behaviour, such as how a person may be aggressive in one situation (e.g. at home) but meek and mild in another (e.g. work). This is because they have been rewarded for different types of behaviour in the two different situations
- It also explains how children might be influenced by watching actions on television. (The theory is often used to criticise parents for allowing their children to watch unsuitable programming or the media more generally.)

Weaknesses

- Many of the studies into aggression have been laboratory based and therefore, lack ecological validity
- It ignores the role of biology e.g. effects of testosterone. However, the theory does help to explain why some societies (e.g. the Amish) have little aggression (role of learning over biology)

- It ignores the role of frustration in aggression (Dollard *et al*, 1936) or how the perceived difference between what an individual has and what they think they should have can act as a provocation for aggressive behaviour. (Runciman, 1966)
- Like much of behaviourism, the theory is deterministic. It suggests that the children would repeat the behaviour without thinking about it

Deindividuation

Deindividuation theory is based on the ideas of Gustave Le Bon. In his book "The Crowd" (1895), he proposed that the psychological mechanisms of anonymity, suggestibility and contagion transform an assembly into a 'psychological crowd'. In the crowd the **collective mind** takes possession of the individual. As a consequence, a crowd member is reduced to an inferior form of evolution: irrational, fickle, and suggestible. The individual submerged in the crowd loses self-control and becomes a mindless puppet, possibly controlled by the crowd's leader, and capable of performing any act, however atrocious or heroic. The term 'deindividuation' was coined in the 1950s (Festinger, Pepitone and Newcomb, 1952). Deindividuation theory differs from Le Bon's theory in that, rather than an individual being taken over by a collective mind, it proposes that the loss of individuality leads to a total loss of control, releasing a person from internalised moral restraints to produce emotional, impulsive, irrational, regressive and intense behaviour. Deindividuation theory has been used to explain the collective behaviour of violent crowds, mindless hooligans and lynch mobs in which, acting as part of a group, individuals will commit the most horrific acts of violence, acts they would never dream of committing alone.

Empirical Evidence

Deindividuation and Aggression (Zimbardo, 1969)
- This 1969 study by Zimbardo used female participants

- They were either anonymous and dressed in oversized lab coats and hoods (deindividuated group), or greeted by name and given large name tags (individuated group)
- They were subsequently asked to administer electric shocks to a confederate, with no limits placed on how long they could hold the switch down
- Deindividuated women held the shocks almost twice as long (90 vs. 47 seconds)

Deindividuation and the Internet

Scott (1999)

- This study found that members of internet support groups made more comments overall but fewer group-supportive comments, compared to groups that met physically
- This effect was limited to *anonymous* users

Postmes, Spears and Lea (1998)

- Found that stereotyping, gender typing, and discrimination were higher in anonymous CMC (computer mediated communication) groups than in face-to-face groups

Deindividuation and Cues

Spivey and Prentice-Dunn (1990)

- Found that deindividuation could lead to either pro-social or anti-social behaviour depending on situational factors
- When pro-social environmental cues were present (such as a pro-social model), deindividuated subjects were more likely to behave altruistically
- Deindividuated subjects performed significantly more altruistic acts (gave money) and significantly less antisocial acts (electric shocks) compared to other people when in the presence of a pro-social model

Gergen, Gergen and Barton (1973)

- Found that deindividuation enhanced *affectionate* behaviour. Couples who were deindividuated using a dark chamber displayed significantly more affectionate behaviour such as touching and caressing in comparison to individuated couples in a light chamber. These results imply that deindividuation may be helpful in intimate relationship development

Johnson and Downing (1979)

- Replicated Zimbardo's original deindividuation experiment using females either dressed in bulky lab coats and hood (as in the original) or in nurses' uniform
- Compared with no-disguise controls, the 'nurses' were less aggressive than the anonymous women

Conclusion

Deindividuation cannot always be seen to lead to negative consequences. Indeed, several studies have observed positive results. Bloodstein (2003) observed that stutterers were able to communicate more easily when wearing masks, and Mullen (1986) showed that people were more likely to go to the aid of a victim of violence if they could mask their own identity. As seen above, Gergen *et al* (1973) also found that deindividuation led to an increase in affectionate behaviour. Therefore, deindividuation does not necessarily result in aggression. Postmes and Spears' meta-analysis (1998) suggests that the behaviour of large, anonymous groups is more influenced by 'group norms' than by deindividuation itself.

Explanations of Institutional Aggression

Explanations of institutional aggression look at:

- Situational forces
- Individualistic (dispositional) factors such as personality and upbringing

Situational Forces

In the earlier part of the course, you looked at the situational determinants that could lead to obedience (Milgram) and to the inhumane treatment of 'prisoners' in Zimbardo's prison experiment.

During Zimbardo's experiment, the treatment meted out by one of the 'guards' (Hellmann) was particularly degrading, and yet he came from a middle-class academic family and was described as a 'nice boy' with no history of aggression. He was described as having a friendly disposition which made it easy for him to get along well with others.

Situational factors may have been responsible for Hellman's behaviour. These include:

- Clothing (uniform)
- Anonymity
- Dehumanisation of prisoners
- Lack of instructions to 'guards' on how to manage prisoners
- Cues from media portrayal of prisoner/guard role

Individualistic (Dispositional) Causes

Often, the people in charge of institutions that have been put under the spotlight for having committed inhumane acts will distance themselves from the individuals concerned and point out that it was the work of a few bad police officers or a few bad soldiers. In other words, they blame individual factors, such as the personality or disposition of those few.

This is illustrated nicely by the US television news magazine programme, *60 Minutes II*, broadcast in April 2004. The programme interviewed the then deputy director of Coalition operations in Iraq, Brigadier General Mark Kimmitt, who said:

> "The first thing I'd say is we're appalled as well. These are our fellow soldiers. These are the people we work with every day, and they represent us. They wear the same uniform as us, and they let their fellow soldiers down. Our soldiers could be taken prisoner as well. And we expect our soldiers to be

treated well by the adversary, by the enemy. And if we can't hold ourselves up as an example of how to treat people with dignity and respect, we can't ask that other nations do that to our soldiers as well. So what would I tell the people of Iraq? This is wrong. This is reprehensible. But this is not representative of the 150,000 soldiers that are over here. I'd say the same thing to the American people... Don't judge your army based on the actions of a few."

The situation in Abu Ghraib was very tense; the guards there were military policemen and women (one of the lowest ranking military personnel). They had no mission-specific training and were under the stress of constant bombardment by Iraqi forces. The prison was overcrowded and there were not enough guards to deal with the number of prisoners. This put them under extreme stress which may have led to aggressive and 'out of character' behaviour in some individuals.

However, not everyone at Abu Ghraib responded to the situation in the same way. So what makes one person in a situation commit evil acts while another in the same situation becomes a whistle-blower?

Zimbardo (2008) believes there's no simple answer. He claims it is impossible to predict from individual factors alone whether such an extreme situation as Abu Ghraib will turn someone into a hero whistle-blower or the brutal guard.

He turns again to situational factors similar to those in his Stanford Prison Experiment to explain the atrocities:

- Lack of specific instructions - Guards were told by the military intelligence and CIA to 'soften the prisoners up' and granted permission to 'step over the line' in terms of what is regarded as appropriate behaviour
- Dehumanisation - The prisoners were stripped naked and wore hoods
- Lack of personal accountability – Following higher orders
- Lack of surveillance
- Permission to get away with anti-social actions

- Using army reservists – Low ranking/low esteem makes it easy to seize the opportunity to have power over another individual

Issues Debates and Approaches

The social learning approach to understanding aggression emphasises the role of learning through the observation and imitation of others as well as by direct reinforcement. The strengths of this approach are that it looks at behaviour in its social context rather than in a laboratory, and can, therefore, examine the influence of society and culture in shaping aggressive behaviour. Modern social psychological theories often take into account cognitive factors (e.g. Bandura's mental representation of modeled behaviour) when attempting to explain behaviour. This makes them less **reductionist** than classical behavioural explanations. However, they still don't see a role for biological/genetic factors.

Many social psychological explanations (e.g. Zimbardo's views on institutional aggression) are **deterministic** as they see behaviour being *determined* by the situation. If this is true, we must question whether or not we can hold perpetrators of atrocities, such as those seen as Abu Ghraib, responsible for their actions.

The **nature/nurture** debate is a long-standing debate in psychology. It attempts to determine the extent to which behaviour is governed by our biology (e.g. our genes) and how much is determined by our environment. Nowadays, psychologists accept that genes and environment can interact in complex ways. There is also the idea that we inherit a genetic predisposition to behave in a certain way, but that our experiences can influence this 'blueprint'.

We will now turn to the other side of this debate as we discuss the role of biological factors in aggression.

Media Influences on Social Behaviour

The argument about whether or not being exposed to violence through the media makes children more violent in real-life is one that surfaces from time to time, usually in response to a crime in which the perpetrator copied actions which were from a well-known film or video game.

Essentially, there are two main arguments as to whether or not violence in the media is responsible for such acts.

Argument One

Albert Bandura and Social Learning Theorists

Children imitate some models more than others. Those who appear to be powerful and have higher status are more likely to be imitated. Many television programmes contain acts of violence performed by powerful, attractive models. Therefore, TV can have a very powerful influence on young minds.

Argument Two

Michael Rutter

What children see in their everyday lives is more likely to have an effect than what they see during a few hours of television. In homes where there is parental conflict, the child is more likely to be anxious, and this anxiety may contribute to children's anti-social behaviour.

Influences of TV Violence on Behaviour

Influences on Physiological Responses
- Increased arousal
- Excitation transfer (arousal transferred to real-life situations) (Zillman, 1975)
- Desensitisation (become less and less sensitive to violence) (Huesmann *et al,* 2003)

Influence on Cognitions

- Store scripts (memories) for violent acts
- May 'prime' watchers to behave in a similar way
- Violent acts seen on TV stored as episodic memories in right hemisphere (Murray *et al,* 2007)

Influences on Aggressive Behaviour

- Possible imitation of aggression leading to reproduction of such behaviour in real life

Research Studies

Huesmann *et al* (2003)

Huesmann *et al* (2003) carried out a longitudinal study of 557 boys and girls in Chicago. The study originally asked the children about their favourite television programmes when they were 5-8 years old in 1977, and then asked them similar questions in 1991 when they were in their early twenties. The researchers also used official records to discover whether they had been arrested for any crimes and interviewed a close friend by phone to ask about the participant's levels of aggression.

The study found that there was a significant correlation between watching violent television programmes when young and aggression in both male and female adults. They also found that the more the child identified with same-sex violent models, the more likely they were to exhibit aggressive behaviour in later life. Furthermore, the study found that boys who were classed as high-violence viewers had three times the rate of criminal convictions as the low-violence viewers.

In evaluation, the study's findings are considered robust, as the researchers used a variety of measures to assess aggressive behaviour. It should be remembered, however, that the relationship shown is correlational, not causal.

Gunter *et al* (2002)

Gunter *et al* carried out research into the impact of television on the isolated community of St. Helena. First, the researchers measured the behaviour of the children on the island in 1993, two years before the introduction of television. Using a pre-school behaviour checklist to measure anti-social behaviour, the study found that the children on St. Helena to be 'the best behaved in the world'.

The researchers again returned to the island in 1998 and asked the children to record how much television they watched over a three-day period. They found that the average amount of television watched was 3 hours and 10 minutes a day. On average, this included 95 acts of violence.

The researchers found no overall increase in aggressive behaviour but they did find that specific programme content correlated with increased anti-social behaviour. This was especially true for cartoons. They also found that, on average, boys watched more violent programming and displayed more anti-social behaviour than girls. Interestingly, the children with the highest anti-social behaviour scores before the introduction of television also watched the most cartoons. This suggests that children with a pre-existing interest in violence may select violent programmes to watch.

Comments

These studies do seem to suggest that TV violence does have an effect on children's aggressive behaviour. However, Huesmann *et al*'s study is correlational, and we must be cautious when interpreting the results. The fact that aggressive behaviour correlates with violent TV viewing may simply be showing that naturally aggressive people seek out more violent programmes to watch. It does not mean that watching violence causes aggressive behaviour. This is something that is backed up by Gunter *et al* who found that children with higher antisocial behaviour scores before television was introduced were more likely to watch a large number of cartoons.

However, Anderson and Bushman (2002) have reviewed many different types of study, including lab, field and longitudinal studies, and have found that all these studies suggest that watching violence has a significant effect on later aggressive behaviour. Anderson and Bushman believe that there is a definite relationship, even though not all people who watch violence end up being aggressive themselves. They believe the exact mechanisms have yet to be established.

How Much Violence is on TV?

Obviously, the amount of violence on TV is a concern for parents. Most people believe that there is lot of violence on TV and that the amount shown is steadily increasing. However, Gunter and Harrison (1998) found this not to be the case.

Gunter and Harrison (1998)

Aims: To determine the amount of violence shown on British TV.

Procedure: Monitored 2084 programmes on eight channels over four weeks in October 1994 and January/February 1995

Findings:

- Violence occupied 0.61% of time on terrestrial channels and 1.53% on satellite channels
- 70% of violent acts occurred in drama and films; 19% occurred in children's programmes
- Most violent acts occurred in inner-city locations. The major perpetrators were young, white males
- 1% of programmes contained 19% of all violent acts
- The USA was the most common location for violence (47%), followed by the UK (12%)

Conclusion: Suggests that violence only represents a tiny part of television output, and that it is concentrated in a relatively small number of programmes.

Effects of Watching Pro-social Behaviour

Television has frequently been criticised for showing too much violence and contributing to crime and delinquent behaviour in society. But TV can have many positive effects as a source of information, education and entertainment. Since TV is a very powerful medium, which most children have access to, it makes sense to develop programmes such as *Sesame Street* which aims to increase children's pro-social awareness and skills. A number of studies with children have looked at the effects of pro-social programming:

- Rushton (1975) showed that pro-social attitudes improved after watching pro-social programmes, but the effect only lasted a couple of weeks
- Van Evra (1990) showed a correlation between pro-social programme watching and sharing/co-operative behaviour
- Rosenkoetter (1999) found that young children can grasp a pro-social message so long as they are at the right level of cognitive development. The study also found correlation between the number of sitcoms watched and children's helpfulness

Research Study

Fogel (2007)

Aims: To investigate the effects of watching pro-social behaviour in sitcoms on children aged 8-12.

Procedure: The children were allocated to one of two groups. The first group watched a 30 minute episode of Hang Time and then took part in a 15 minute group discussion with an adult. The second group watched the same episode but didn't discuss it.

Findings: The group who had discussed the episode showed improved scores of pro-social behaviour over the other (control) group.

Conclusion: Watching and discussing TV programmes with adults helps children to gain the maximum pro-social benefit from them.

Evaluation: The study used real programming to give a high level of validity. However, the children knew that they were being observed, possibly leading them to give the desired answers.

Comments

This study appears to show that watching TV with an adult who can explain the content has the greatest benefit for children in terms of developing pro-social attitudes and behaviour.

Influences on Pro-social Behaviour

A meta-analysis conducted by Mares (1996) found four different categories of pro-social behaviour that could be increased by watching pro-social content. The categories included positive interaction, altruism, self-control and anti-stereotyping.

There was a large effect found for altruism and self-control but only when the behaviour was explicitly modelled. The effect for anti-stereotyping was moderate but increased when the programme was followed up by work with counter-stereotypical work in the classroom.

In addition, it was found that pro-social content had more positive effect on girls, and that pro-social messages had more influence on primary age children than on adolescents.

Cole *et al* (2003) looked at the impact of a series of *Sesame Street* programmes designed to teach mutual respect and understanding among Israeli and Palestinian children. 275 four and five year-olds were interviewed before and after the programmes. The 'after' results showed an increase in the use of positive attributes to describe the other group as well as an increase in pro-social justifications to resolve conflicts.

In a more recent study, Mares and Woodard (2005) found that, overall, males and females were equally positively affected by pro-social content and that there were no ethnic or racial differences. They found the effects were stronger among higher socio-economic groups.

Explaining Influences on Behaviour

Theory	Explanation	Research	Works by	Evaluation
Skinner	Direct experience	Operant conditioning	Behaviour that is rewarded is being repeated in the future	Only one of many influences. Social context important too
Social Learning Theory	Vicarious experience	Bussey and Bandura (1984)	Observation and modelling of role models, especially dominant and/or powerful models	Does not take into account cognitive factors
Social Cognitive Observational Learning Theory	Schemas Scripts Normative beliefs	Gerbner *et al* (1994) Guerra *et al* (1995)	Children who watch violent programmes are more likely to view others' behaviour as hostile Children's normative beliefs are related to what they watch on TV	Correlation does not prove causation
Third Variable Theory	Family background	Comstock and Paik (1991)	A 'third' variable may cause both more aggression	

			and more TV watching. Possible variables may include socio-economic status, intelligence and family background	

Summary

Although it is clear that watching anti-social programmes on TV is correlated with future aggressive behaviour, there is little doubt that it is just one of many influences on young children, including family background and socio-economic status. The effects of watching violence on TV have yet to be teased out from these other influences. It would seem that watching pro-social content can be beneficial but undoubtedly the most benefit is derived where there is an adult to explain the content and the behaviour is followed up with real-life activities and discussion.

The Effects of Video Games and Computers on Young People

The impact of violence in computer games differs from that of TV since the player takes an active rather than a passive role. Improved computer graphics mean that the depictions of violence are increasingly realistic.

In June 2007, the game *Manhunt 2* was banned by the British Board of Film Classification. In the game, the player took the role of a mad scientist escaping from an asylum. The game was described by the BBFC as 'brutal, sadistic and bleak'. The game sparked renewed interest in the effects of violence in computer games.

The Effects of Playing Violent Computer Games

The effects of playing violent computer games include:

Effect	Research	Comments
Increased arousal	Tafalla (2007) men and women showed increased Bp/heart rate when the *Doom* game music was playing	Can transfer excitation to outside situations
Reduced helping	Sheese and Graziano (2005) found that players playing a violent version of the game *Doom* chose to exploit rather than help each other in a post-game test	Playing violent games undermines pro-social behaviour
Increased aggressive behaviour, cognitions and feelings	Sherry (2001) found relationship between violent video games and later aggression weaker than that for TV	
	Unsworth *et al* (2007) found no change in feelings of aggression before, during and after playing *Quake II.* Only those already aggressive became more aggressive after playing	Backs up idea that only those with existing aggressive tendencies are affected Positive effects of gaming

	Schie and Wiegman (1997) found no relationship between time spent playing games and level of aggression but positive correlation between time spent playing and child's level of intelligence.	
Desensitisation to Violence	Bartholow (2006) found evidence of reduced brain response (desensitisation) in those used to game violence.	Biological evidence backs up ideas that gaming leads to desensitisation to real-life violence

Research Study

Carnagey, Anderson and Bushman (2007)

Aims: To investigate the effects of playing violent games on later responses to real-life violence.

Procedure: Participants were randomly allocated to one of two groups. The first group played a randomly selected violent game for 20 minutes. The second group played a non-violent game for 20 minutes. All participants then watched a film containing real-life violence, and their physiological responses were measured, including heart rate and galvanic skin response.

Findings: The group who had played the violent game had a reduced physiological response.

Conclusion: Playing violent games desensitises individuals to real-life violence.

Methodological Issues: A well-controlled laboratory study where the measurement of physiological factors over which participants have little control provides a high level of validity. The study used filmed real-life violence and it is likely that there would have been a greater response to immediate rea -life violence.

Explaining the Effects

The General Aggression Model (GAM)

This model was put forward by Anderson *et al* (2000 and 2002) to explain why there are individual differences in vulnerability to playing violent computer games.

Exposure to such games can increase aggression through:

- Arousal – Heightened arousal can lead to aggression
- Cognitions – Violent games may prime aggressive thoughts
- Mood – Playing violent games increases aggressive feelings

These effects depend on multiple input variables, such as:

- Gender
- Personality
- Immediate situation
- Mood
- Aggressive disposition
- Upbringing
- Expectancy bias

Bushman and Anderson (2002) explored the idea that expectancy bias (a belief that others will act in a certain way) could be affected by playing violent games. They gave participants either a non-violent or violent computer game to play and then asked them to complete short stories in which the characters encountered personal problems. Those who had played the violent games tended to complete the stories with more aggressive endings, indicating that they had developed 'hostile expectancy biases'. Of course, it could also mean that the violent games had acted to increase demand characteristics.

Evaluation

The overall pattern in research into the effects of playing violent video games is inconsistent. Some of the research into this area is flawed, and conclusions are not possible on such weak data. There is even evidence that playing violent computer games can be cathartic in that it allows people to discharge feelings of aggression through game playing. This idea has not been adequately tested, and more research needs to be done in this area.

Activity 103

Comment on any issues, debates and approaches that arise from research into the effects of media and computer games on aggressive behaviour.

Answer to activity 103:

Issues:

Ethical considerations have limited the amount of violence to which participants may be exposed, especially if it may have a lasting effect on their behaviour. Researchers can't put people in situations which may increase their level of aggression after the study.

Debates:

Social learning and social cognitive theories suggest that watching violence can influence cognitions. This view is deterministic since it assumes that individuals have no control over their ability to resist media influences.

Social learning approaches can be seen as reductionist since they ignore the role of biology.

Approaches:

The GAM (general aggression model) is a good approach in that it acknowledges the input from individual and situational factors in understanding aggression. This makes it less reductionist than other approaches.

4.4 Forensic Psychology

<u>Paper 3 Option 2</u>

Introduction

Forensic psychology is the interaction between the discipline of psychology and the law. As such the focus is on criminals, their actions and their motives, as well as the legal system, including police work and investigations, legal proceedings e.g. the role of the jury and institutionalisation.

Key Areas:

- Defining Crime
- Offender Profiling
- Biological Explanations
- Psychological Explanations
- Dealing with offending behaviour

Defining Crime

In looking at crime, the consideration here is how criminals become criminals – is it as a result of biological, social or psychological factors? Once an action has been identified as a crime and the person who commits it, as a criminal, forensic psychology examines how the legal system builds a case against an offender, such as eyewitness testimonies (already discussed in the AS), police interviews and interviewing techniques, the courts and how juries reach their verdicts.

Before looking into the above in detail, we need to define 'crime'. According to Blackburn (1993);

"Crimes...are acts attracting legal punishment. [They] are offences against the community."

The English Oxford Dictionary defines crime as:

"...an act punishable by law, as being forbidden by statute or injurious to public welfare...An evil or injurious act; an offence, sin; especially grave of character."

Activity 104

Do these definitions sufficiently explain what crime is?

What would you add, change or take away?

Overall, crime can be regarded as any act that breaches the formal laws of a given society, resulting in formal punishment and/or sanctions being imposed by legal enforcement agencies. Note, what constitutes a crime is dependent upon whether it is judged from a legal or normative perspective, because the definition of crime can be dependent upon various social factors. Therefore the meaning of crime is seen to be a social construct - subject to change and open to interpretation.

Measuring Crime

The British Crime Survey (BCS) and Official Statistics recorded by the police are the primary sources of statistics on crime. Published every year by the Home Office, they provide data on the level of crime and trends in crime. According to the Office for National Statistics (ONS), 2015:[22]

- There were an estimated 6.8 million incidents of crime against households and resident adults (aged 16 and over). This is a 7% decrease compared with the previous year's survey

- There was a 3% increase in police recorded crime compared with the previous year, with 3.8 million offences recorded in the year ending March 2015

- Increase in violence against the person offences were up by 23% compared with the previous year. However, this increase is thought to reflect changes in recording practices rather than a rise in violent crime

- Offences involving knives and sharp instruments increased by 2% in the year ending March 2015

- There has been an increase in assaults (up 13%, from 11,911 to 13,488) and a decrease in robberies (down 14%, from 11,927 to 10,270)

- Weapon possession offences rose by 10% (from 9,050 to 9,951)

- Sexual offences recorded by the police rose by 37% with the numbers of rapes (29,265) and other sexual offences (58,954) being at the highest level since the introduction of

---

[22] http://www.ons.gov.uk/ons/rel/crime-stats/crime-statistics/year-ending-march-2015/index.html

the National Crime Recording Standard in 2002/03. As well as improvements in recording, this is also thought to reflect a greater willingness of victims to come forward to report such crimes

The British Crime Survey (BCS) is a victimisation survey that measures the amount of crime in England and Wales every year, by asking over 51,000 people age 16 and over, about their experiences of crime. This survey is a key source of information as it provides and insight into the levels of crime that are not reported to the police as well as public attitudes to crime. This therefore offers an alternative to official crime statistics. The survey also includes questions about crime related topics such as attitudes toward the police, the criminal justice system and so on.

Because the BCS is based on victim surveys, and therefore includes non-reported crimes, they can provide a more accurate picture of incidences of crime when compared with official statistics. The gap between reported crime and those identified by BCS (unreported and unrecorded crimes) are referred to as The Dark Figure of Crime.

Activity 105

List and explain some of the reasons why people may not report a crime.

Some of the reasons as to why people do not report crime are:

- Some crimes are not regarded as serious enough to report to the police. For example if someone scratches your car with a key, technically that is criminal damage, but would you report it to the police?
- Sometimes people are not even aware that they have been the victim of a crime
- There may be fear of reprisals or revenge if the crime is reported.
- Lack of confidence in the police or the belief that the police will not take it seriously

Some crimes are more likely to be reported:

- Because without a report insurance claims cannot be made or validated
- They are serious crimes and the loss is of a high value
- High profile crimes such as those presented in the media could create a moral panic so the public become more aware of such crimes and reports them more frequently (deviance amplification)

Another way of establishing the extent of crime, apart from the use of official statistics, is Self Report Studies (SRS), also referred to as Offender Surveys. These are questionnaires that ask people to voluntarily record whether or not they have committed any of the offences listed in the questionnaire. The data is then compared to the official statistics on convictions in order to establish the types of crimes people are most likely to be convicted.

Whilst SRS can provide some insight into the extent of criminal activities, one of the problems is that with it being dependent upon an individual admitting to having committed a crime, the respondent may exaggerate (for whatever reason), what they have actually done. Also a respondent may admit to some crimes but not to others – this raises the questions: 'Is the respondent telling the truth'. According to Box (1971), the criticisms of SRS raise concerns about validity, relevance and representativeness.

Activity 106

What other problems could be associated with SRS as an approach to getting statistics on crime?

What are some of the positives associated with using this approach?

Offender Profiling

Offender Profiling can be traced back to the early 1800s when criminal anthropologists attempted to make a connection between physical characteristics and criminal psychology. The Jack the Ripper murders were seen to instigate offender profiling, when Dr Thomas Bond (who performed an autopsy on Jack the Ripper's last victim), in an attempt to identify the killer, embarked on the process of reconstructing the crime, interpreting the behaviour and identify personality characteristics of the perpetrator. All of these elements would provide the basis for police investigation. As such, Bond was regarded as the first ever profiler.

Offender profiling has been defined as:

"... the process of inferring distinctive personality characteristics of individuals responsible for committing criminal acts." Turvey (2002)

"It is an attempt to provide investigators with more information on the offender who is yet to be identified." Egger (1999)

Profiling has developed significantly, and there are two different methods of profiling. They are:

- **The Bottom-up Approach**, also referred to as the **British Method** or Investigative Approach
- **Top-down Approach**, also known as the **FBI** or Organised/Disorganised Crimes

The Bottom-up Approach

The British Approach

This approach is associated with the work of Professor David Canter who devised a way of profiling which is based on putting together a profile from details of the crime scene. It was Canter who prepared the profile that led to the capture of John Duffy, known as 'The Railway Rapist', in 1986.

Between 1982 and 1986, the Metropolitan Police were investigating 24 sexual attacks and three murders that had taken place near railways in North London. The victims' bodies had been burnt, so forensic evidence was difficult to obtain. However, the method of attack seemed to show a link between the rapes and murders. Canter, was invited by the Met to provide a psychological profile of the perpetrator, and he suggested that the perpetrator's profile was as follows:

- Lived in the area
- Lived with a woman
- Aged mid to late 20s
- Right handed
- Semi-skilled or skilled with weekend work; relatively isolated work
- Knowledge of railways

It was Canter's profile that narrowed down the list of suspects leading to the police arresting John Duffy, who was convicted of two murders and five rapes. His characteristics, matched the profile significantly:

- He lived in the area suggested by Canter
- He was recently separated from his wife
- He was in his late 20s
- He was a travelling carpenter
- He worked for British Rail

The investigative approach with its focus on the crime scene aims to identify certain characteristics through the use of statistical techniques, which are then used to identity how likely it is that some of the characteristics co-exist with others at the crime scene – the connection between the characteristics of the offence and the offender. This establishes a baseline from which the investigation can proceed and narrow down the potential list of perpetrators.

Canter (1994), suggests that the main factors of profiling are:

- Interpersonal Coherence – the actions of the offender will be normative or significant to him/her
- Significance of time and place – the offender will choose a particular location and time
- Forensic awareness – if the offender has had previous contact with the police they will try to cover up their tracks in order to mislead investigators. For example, Duffy burnt his victims and it was said that this was something that he had become aware of following a police search of his house after the rape of his wife

Evaluation of the investigative approach

Canter suggests that this approach is more scientific and therefore is potentially more useful for those investigating crimes. However, Copson (1995) argues that the success rate for this approach in catching an offender is minimal, at only 3%.

Alison and Canter (1999) argue that criminal profiling usually takes place after a crime has been committed, which means that as an approach it is reactive. However, it is possible to use profiling proactively, to predict things yet to come.

The Top-down Approach

The FBI Approach

This approach is currently used in the United States, and is based on data to identify key characteristics of serious offenders. FBI research conducted by Douglas, Ressler and Burgess in 1978 aimed to identify significant personality traits of serious offenders and how they differed from non-offenders. In-depth unstructured interviews were conducted with 36 convicted serial killers. Coupled with the interviews, information from the crime scenes also revealed that the crimes committed were either premeditated and planned, or sudden and spontaneous. The conclusion from this research was that crime scene analysis could provide the basis for establishing whether or not the perpetrator was 'organised' or 'disorganised'.

Organised offenders had the following characteristics:

- Above average intelligence
- Socially competent
- Lives with a partner
- Self-controlled
- Angry or depressed at the time of the attack
- Planning is evident from the crime scene

- The victim is a targeted stranger
- Restraints are used on the victim
- Intelligent
- Skilled occupation

<u>Discorganised Offender</u> had the following characteristics:

- Below average intelligence
- Socially incompetent
- Unskilled, unemployed
- First or last born child
- Mental illness
- No signs of planning
- Weapon found at the scene or near the attack
- Victim will be known to the offender
- Quick, brutal attack
- Haphazard, so leaves clues

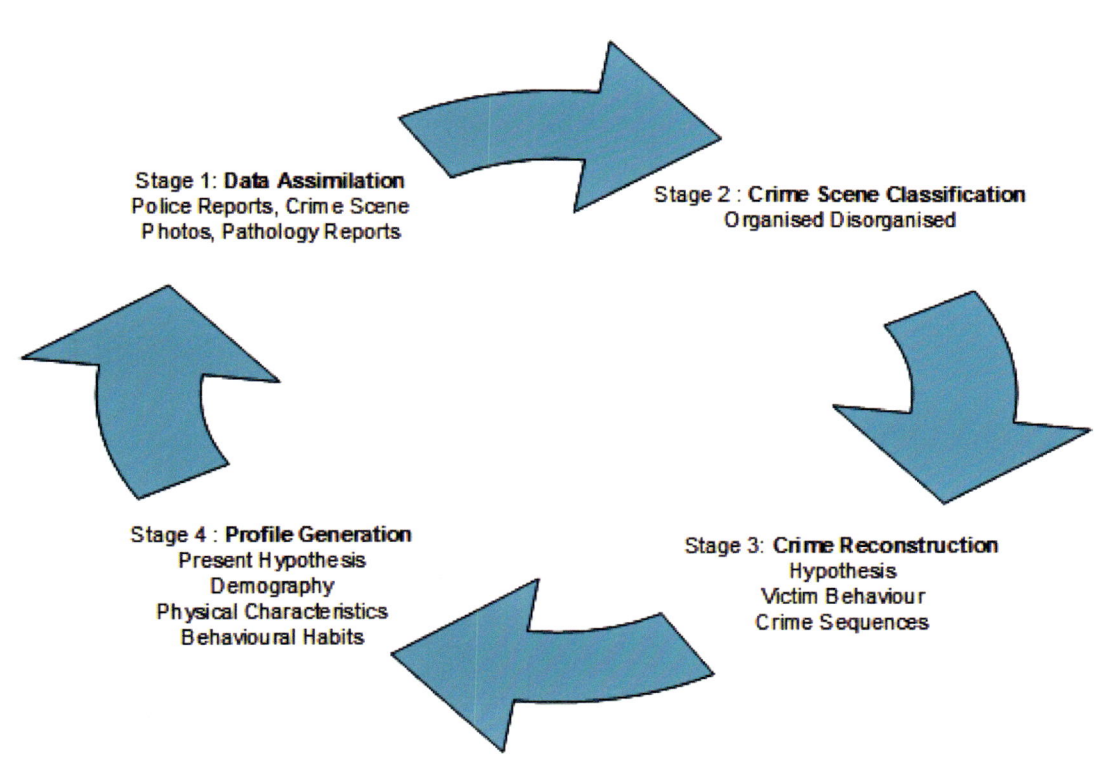

Four main stages in FBI profiling

Overall this approach is based on intuition and as such has been criticised for lacking scientific evaluation; consequently it has been disregarded as a science. Alison and Barrett (2004) argued that this approach relies too much on theories of personality and has

"...many erroneous lay beliefs about consistency of human behaviour and the ability to classify individuals into discrete types."

In terms of the positives of this approach, it can be used to identify common patterns and behaviours and it also tries to understand the motivation behind the crime, which can in turn provide the basis for 'predicting' other crimes.

Geographic Profiling

In addition to offender profiling, there is geographical profiling, which focuses on the location of a crime scene as it can provide the police with essential clues about the offender. Through a process of elimination, this approach assesses and predicts the most likely area that the offender might live, work, socialise, travel and so on. The core concept of geographic profiling is what Zipf (1950) referred to as the principle of least effort. This principle suggests that when a person is considering the possibility of a certain course of action, they will be approach it from the aspect that requires the least amount of effort. Therefore, if distance is an aspect of their activity, subjective and psychological perceptions i.e. familiarity with an area, can be a determining factor in where an individual commits an offence. The Criminal Geographical Technique (CGT) is a computerised system that uses spatial data, which relates to the distance, movement and time to and from the crime scene. It is analysed in order to create a three dimensional model, which can provide some indication of where the offender might live or work. Rossomo devised another form of geographic profiling developed from analysis/profiling software (Rigel), and based on the CGT model. Known as Geographic Information System (GIS), it enables the analysis of the offender's behaviour by incorporating,

"... mathematical models of known offending movement patterns and hunting behaviour, journey to crime distances and includes a method to calculate the relationship between sets of crime locations (e.g. contact, assault, release sites) and offender residence." (Chainey and Ratcliffe, 2005) Canter and Hodge (1997) found that the location of crimes of serial killers in the US and Britain were generally located around their homes. They also found that locations could also be near where they may have been involved in other activities, such as work or leisure. Overall in terms of offender profiling, according to Campbell (1976), there is no concrete evidence that this approach can be used to profile offenders any better than anything else. However, Alison *et al* (2003) argued that the police regard it as invaluable.

Biological Explanations of Offending Behaviour

Are criminals born (nature) or made (nurture)?

Lombroso 1876) stated that criminals had different physical characteristics when compared to non-criminals. He argued that criminals exhibited primitive evolutionary characteristics; this is referred to as the Atavistic Form Theory. Whilst this has been discredited, particularly because there was no evidence to support it, it is still relevant to the discussion in terms of understanding how theories regarding individuals who embark upon criminal activity have developed over time. Lombroso suggested that 40% of criminals were actually 'born criminals', and they could be identified by physical characteristics (skull and facial, body shape). Characteristics included:

- An asymmetrical face
- Large jaw and cheekbones
- Wrinkles
- Cleft palate
- Small ears
- Bloodshot eyes
- Longer than average arms and so on

The picture below is a depiction of what Lombroso considered to be some of the facial features that would identify an individual as a criminal.

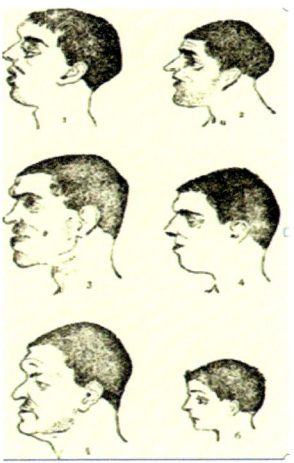

Activity 107

Evaluate Lombroso's 'atavistic form' theory.

A later study by Sheldon (1949) introduced what he considered to be a more scientific approach to explaining aggression and criminal behaviour based on physical appearance. He identified three body types, and these body types could be equated with certain personality types, and therefore make an individual more predisposed to aggression and criminal activity.

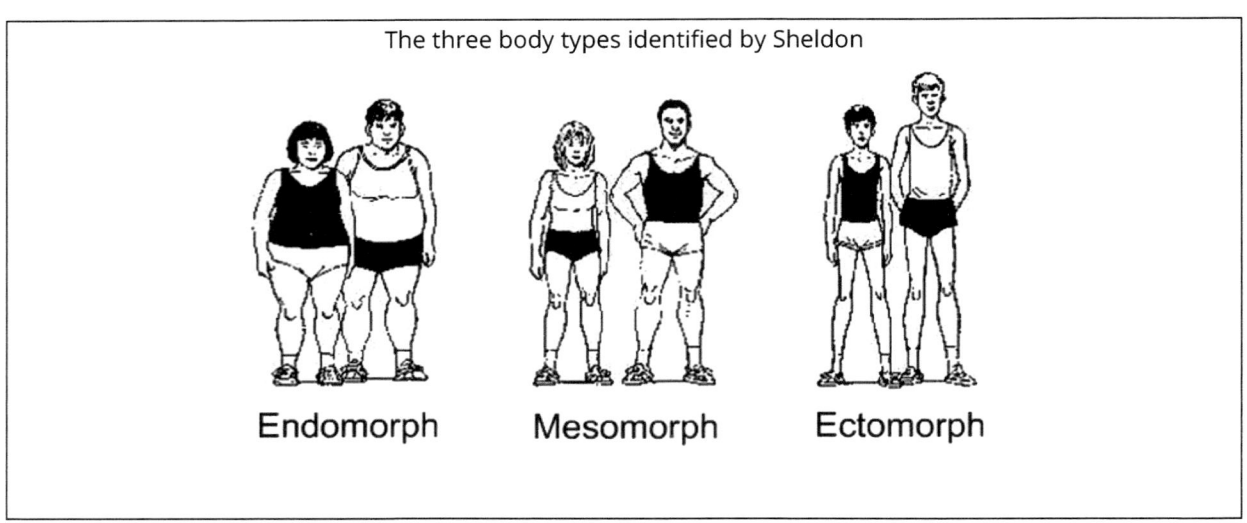

The three body types identified by Sheldon

The three body types identified by Sheldon

Sheldon then studied 200 male college students and 200 male delinquents and rated them according to the body type categories; the results were as presented below:

Body type	Physical characteristics	Temperament	Students	Delinquents
Endomorph	Fat and soft	Relaxed, loving, sociable	3.2	3.4
Ectomorph	Thin and fragile	Solitary, introverted, self conscious	3.4	1.8
Mesomorph	Muscular and hard	Aggressive, selfish, ruthless	3.8	5.4

The results showed that the students generally averaged the same body types; however, this was not the case for the delinquents that showed significantly more Mesomorphs.

Biological explanations

These explanations are based on the theory that genetics can be the basis for criminality. There are a number of ways in which a connection between biology and crime can be made:

- Adoption studies
- Twin Studies
- Chromosomal abnormalities

Adoption Studies

These studies aim to compare criminals with their biological and adoptive parents, to see if a predisposition to criminal activities is as a result of biological factors over environmental ones. Mednick *et al* conducted a study based on adoption records in Denmark from 1924 to 1947, looking at the criminal records of over 4000 males. These records were then compared to the records of the individual's biological and adoptive parents. The findings were, if an individual's biological parents had been convicted of a crime, they were twice as likely to be convicted of a crime themselves when compared to adoptees whose biological parents had not committed a crime.

If unrelated siblings were raised in the same adoptive family 8% of them would both commit crimes. However, if the siblings were related and raised in different adoptive families, 20% would commit a crime/s. If siblings were raised in different adoptive families but had a biological father convicted of a crime, 30% of both of them committed a crime.

Crowe (1972) in a study of 37 American adoptees found that if the biological mother had a criminal record, the child had a 50% chance of getting a record by the age of 18. This was compared to 5%, where the mother did not have a criminal record.

Some studies, however, have demonstrated not only a biological connection but also an environmental one. Bohman (1955), in a study of adoptive and biological parents of children, it was found that 40% of the children who had biological and adoptive parents with criminal records, had convictions when compared to 12% who did if the biological parents had criminal records but not the adoptive parents.

Osborn and West (1979) in their study of the sons of criminals, found that 13% of the sons of non-criminal fathers had committed a criminal offence, and therefore had a conviction when compared to 40% of the sons of the criminals.

Overall, these studies seem to demonstrate a strong link between criminal behaviour and genetics. However, we cannot ignore environmental factors. If only the biological approach is applied, how does this explain individuals who have biological parents who have criminal convictions, yet have not committed crimes themselves? Conversely, there are situations where an individual commits a crime/s but his/her parents do not have criminal convictions. Also figures used for these studies are based on those who have actually been caught and convicted.

According Brennan *et al* (1991):

"In terms of genetics, very little can be learned from . . . family data alone.... The parents have a major influence on the child's environment as well as on his/her genetic makeup; family studies cannot disentangle these hereditary and environmental influences."

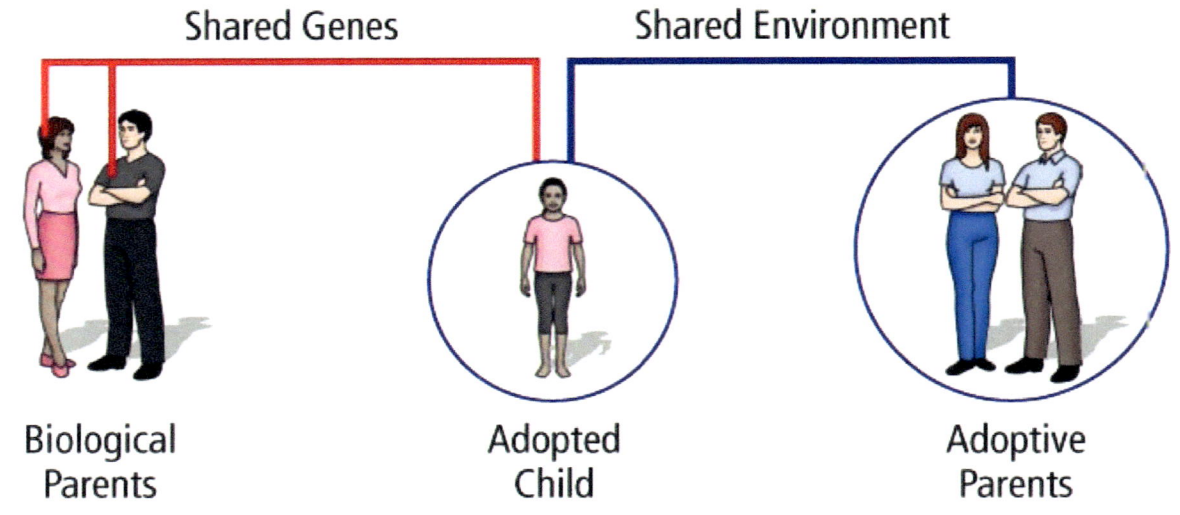

Twin Studies

This starts from the premise that because MZ twins share 100% genetics when compared to DZ twins (50%), these genetic features can be used as a basis upon which to understand the link between genetics and criminal behaviour. Many studies therefore seem to support the claim that an inherited genetic trait can increase the risk of criminal behaviour.

Dalgaard and Kringlen conducted a study on 49 MZ male twins and 89 DZ male twins and found that genetic factors played no part in determining whether or not an individual has a predisposition to crime. They suggested that any similarity between MZ twins was attributable to their shared environment experiences due to their similarity – that of being identical. Carey

(1992), in keeping with this point, suggested that MZ twins may even imitate each other, more so than DZ twins.

Using a sample of 3,586 twin pairs in Denmark, Christiansen(1977) reported 52% of the MZ twins were concordant for criminal behaviour when compared to 22% of the DZ twins. This suggests that the MZ twins inherit some biological characteristic(s) that increases their joint predisposition for criminal involvement.

Activity 108

Consider the following. John has a non-identical twin called Peter. They have been brought up together. Peter is a drug dealer. How likely is it that John will turn to crime?

Chromosomal Abnormalities and Crime

Studies have suggested a connection between XYY abnormality and criminality[23] in that this has been linked to aggression and learning ability. In the 1960s, after blood samples taken from criminals, researchers found that males with the XYY pattern were more likely to be violent and criminal. Whilst providing a genetic explanation for criminality, it was not found to run in families. This chromosomal abnormality and genetic pattern have been found to be linked to violent crime in only a small number of murderers. We do need to bear in mind that as this is such a rare genetic pattern (1 in 1000), it is difficult to have a sufficient enough sample to be able to make a concrete connection to violent crime, criminal behaviour and chromosomal makeup.

Explanations for aggression can also be utilised here in explaining why people commit criminal acts. We will only briefly touch on this here as this was covered in the unit on Aggression. If you recall, the gene MAOA is responsible for regulating serotonin in the brain, and low levels of serotonin has been associated with aggressive behaviour; therefore studies of violent criminals found that some had a defect with MAOA. Brunner (1993) found that in a Dutch family with a history of aggressive criminal behaviour, that the men had extremely low levels of MAOA.

---

[23] This was covered in the Gender unit – please go back and review.

Psychological Explanations

According to Freud, criminal behaviour can be understood by looking at the early childhood experiences of an individual and their unresolved Oedipus and Electra complexes.

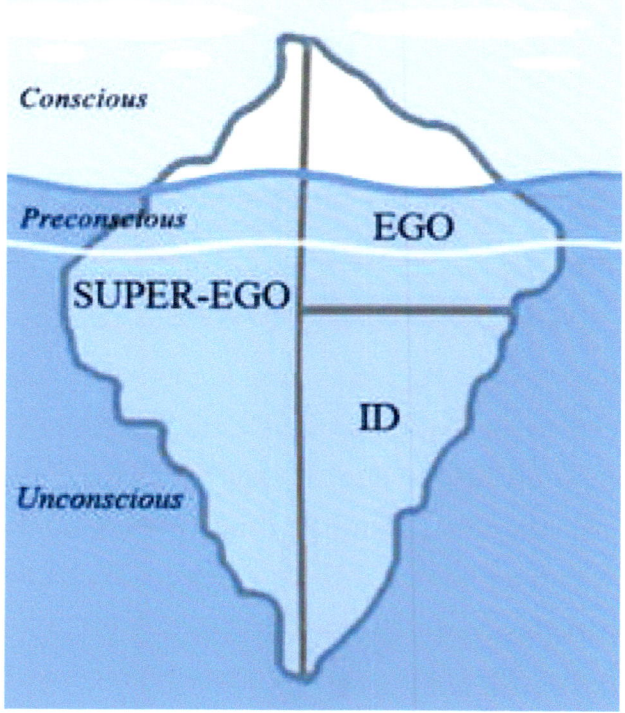

Freud argues that human behaviour is governed by the id, which is the instinctive and primitive part of the personality; as such it needs to be repressed, and this is where the ego and super-ego come into play. According to Freud, by their very nature human beings are intrinsically antisocial. As young children we have anti-social drives, where it is all about us and no one else. As we get older and gain experience of the word the superego forms. This is the part of the personality that is reflective, contemplative, the conscience part of the individual's personality. And the ego is the part that mediates between the id and the superego in reality. It is the part of the individual they call 'self' that seeks to appease the id but in an appropriate way.

The id creates an urge or impulse, but the super ego stops us from acting on that urge/impulse; however, there is still the need for it to be satisfied, so the ego will find legitimate and appropriate ways by which to fulfil the desire, in a way that is not at a cost to others or oneself in a negative way. It is the ego that gives an individual their own sense if identity. How does all of this relate to criminal behaviour?

Well, according to Freud, criminal behaviour can be traced back to faulty parental relations where the ego and superego were not able to develop properly, and because they have not developed properly, this makes it difficult to control the impulses of the id. Bowlby suggested that maternal deprivation at an early age was the cause of delinquent and/or criminal behaviour.

Still on the subject of personality types, according to Eysenck (1977), criminal personality stems from certain personality traits which are biological in origin. He identified four personality traits. They were:

- Extravert – such individuals tended to need excitement
- Introvert – can be withdrawn; no need for excitement
- Emotional stability – as the name suggests this individual would be emotionally stable, calm, emotionally constant
- Neuroticism – unstable, anxious, low self-esteem

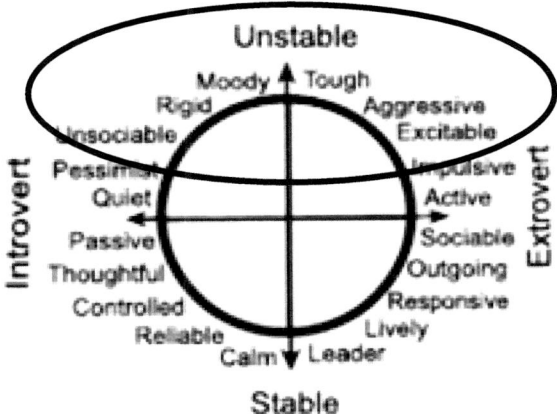

Eysenck argues that those with high levels of introvert/extrovert traits could predispose someone to crime. In fact Eysenck devised the Eysenck Personality Questionnaire to measure these traits, and that those who committed criminal acts scored highly on both the extravert and introvert traits. Eysenck also developed the 'P Scale' (Psychotocism scale). High P scorers would exhibit traits such as aggressive and uncaring behaviour. They would be loners, therefore highly likely to commit criminal acts.

Another element to this discussion that could be used to explain criminal behaviour is the Hostile Attribution Bias. Here an individual will perceive a hostile intent from another even if there is none, or no evidence of it. The individual will assume that others have negative feelings toward them when they do not. In terms of criminal behaviour, this type of personality is reactionary and as such a hostile, physically aggressive reaction to another person can appear to be in response to a provocation when there really wasn't one.

Moral Reasoning

Kohlberg (1981) conducted research into moral development and crime. This was a development upon Freud's theory of development. If you recall, according to Freud, when children are born, they only have the id part of their personality. Therefore for the child everything is about them, they are egocentric. The ego and superego develop later, which are the parts of the personality that is connected to morality and understanding the feelings of others. From this, Kohlberg's theory, the Stages of Moral Development introduced the Heinz Dilemma:

Heinz Dilemma

This was a thought experiment based on the following scenario.

Heinz had a wife who was dying of cancer. A pharmacist had developed a drug that would cure the cancer, and this drug would enable the wife to survive.

The drug cost the pharmacist 1000 (of whatever currency) to make. Heinz approached the pharmacist and asked if he could buy some of the drug, to which the pharmacist responded that Heinz could buy it for 10,000.

Heinz approaches family and friends asking for money to raise the funds needed to buy the drug and manages to get 5000, so he has half the money. Heinz approaches the pharmacist with the 5000 and says that he will pay the remaining 5000 later to which the pharmacist responds by saying that he cannot make any exceptions for Heinz and that he would have to pay the full 10,000 to get the drug.

Activity 109

What should Heinz do?

From this dilemma, Kohlberg was able to work out his theory of moral development. According to the theory there are three levels and six stages to moral development

Level 1	**Pre-Conventional Morality** Stage 1 – <u>Punishment avoidance and obedience</u> – individuals follow rules if it prevents punishment or they can get away with it. Stage 2 – <u>Exchange of favours</u> – individuals begin to understand that they can do things to gain things that they want.
Level 2	**Conventional Morality** Stage 3 – <u>Good boy/girl</u> – individuals make moral decisions on the basis of what actions will please others, particularly authority figures such as parents and teachers. Stage 4 – <u>Law and Order</u> – Individual looks to society for guidelines regarding what is considered to be right and wrong.
Level 3	**Post-Conventional Morality**

	Stage 5 – <u>Social Contract</u> – individual recognises that rules represent agreement among other people about what is appropriate conduct and behaviour - the 'rules' can be transcenced if required. Stage 6 – <u>Universal ethical principle orientation</u> – individual adheres to a small number of abstract universal principles that transcend specific concrete rules; in other words, the individual answers to an inner conscience and may break rules that go against their own ethical principles.

According to Kohlberg very few reach stage 5 and 6.

<u>Kohlberg's study</u>

The aim was to find evidence to support his theory of progression through the Stages of Moral Development. The study was a longitudinal study that started in 1963. Interviews were conducted with 58 middle class and working class boys from Chicago, aged 7, 10, 13 and 16. They were interviewed individually for two hours each, every three years until they were 30 and 36 years old. The youngest boys tended to be in either stage 1 or stage 2 of moral development, whereas older boys were typically in stage 3 and 4. No boys were found to be in stage 6 (Kohlberg later removed stage 6 from his theory). The aim of the study was not really to look at criminal morality, but it did provide the basis of later studies such as those presented by Thornton and Reid (1982). They replicated Kohlberg's study and found that individuals who commit crimes for financial gain had a tendency to display immature levels of morality when compared to those who committed violent crimes.

Differential association theory

This theory was formulated by Sutherland (1995), who argued that criminal behaviour was learnt through interaction with others. That is, individuals learn the norms, attitudes, vales or methods of crime through associating with existing criminals. This theory of deviance is very influential in the social sciences.

Activity 110

Evaluate Kohlberg's Stages of Moral Development

Cognitive Distortion

When looking at cognition in terms of criminal behaviour, the focus is on the thinking patterns of individuals who commit crimes. Yochelson and Samenow (1976) provide a psychodynamic explanation, suggesting that the thinking patterns of criminals are different to non-criminals. Their study consisted of studying 255 criminals, half of whom had pleaded not guilty by reason of insanity. Only 30 completed the interviews of this longitudinal study, over a period of 14 years. The aim was to try to find the root cause of criminal behaviour. Freudian therapy was used to study the changes in cognition over time. 52 different thinking patterns were identified and these were placed into three main categories:

- Crime related thinking errors

- Automatic thinking errors e.g. lack of empathy

- Criminal thinking patterns e.g. power and control

For the most part, criminals are in complete control of their life, therefore criminal behaviour is as a result of choices made by the individual. Often they have a distorted self-image and often take no responsibility for their actions.

Activity 111

Explain further some of the evaluative points made and add a few of your own:

- **High level of subjective attrition – what does this mean?**
- **Sample not cannot be used to make generalisations about the wider criminal population – why?**
- **No control group – why is this an issue?**
- **Focuses only on the psychodynamic perspective – why is this a problem?**
- **Temporal validity is an issue – why?**

Cornish and Clark (1987) argued that criminal behaviour is the result of an individual's rational thought processes, meaning that criminals have thought about their crimes before committing them, applying reason and rational thinking to the process. They will weigh up the pros and cons of committing the crime (a cost/benefit analysis – is the crime worth committing? Does the reward outweigh the risk? However, Hollin (2001) disagrees with Cornish and Clark and suggests that criminal behaviour is mostly opportunistic. Hollin uses the example of the increase in burglaries over the past 20 years. As more people are going out to work, leaving homes empty during the day, criminals are using the opportunity, when it presents itself, to commit burglary.

Dealing with offending behaviour

Once an offender has been convicted, what then has to be addressed is how the criminal justice system will deal with that offender

Custodial sentencing

Sentencing is meant to serve a purpose on terms of responding to the offender's behaviour. There are four aims of sentencing. They are:

Retribution	The punishment fits the crime, so the offender receives a punishment that reflects the seriousness of the offence. Based on the 'eye for an eye' principle.
Deterrence	To deter the offender from committing the offence or one like it again. There are two types of deterrence: General – the sentence given aims to deter others from committing or consider committing an offence. Individual – the aim of the sentence is to deter the individual offender. Home Office figures on recidivism show that 70% of offenders who were given custodial sentences, reoffended within two years of being released.
Rehabilitation	The aim is to 'cure' the offender of their tendency to commit crime. This may present itself in the form of drug treatment, counselling and therapy.
Protection of society	Those who are considered to be serious offenders are taken out of commission by being sent to prison in order to protect society from them.

Whichever approach is applied, they all in some way aim to bring about behaviour modification in an attempt to stop the criminal behaviour from occurring or recurring.

The Psychological effects of custodial sentencing

If you recall, we looked at the Sanford Prison Study conducted Zimbardo (1971). The aim of the study was to investigate how being in prison affected an individual's behaviour. The study took place in a mock prison with 22 male participants who were assigned different roles (either prisoners or prison guards). Prisoners were placed in cells and locked up for 24 hours a day. The experiment was ceased after 6 days, even though it was supposed to have lasted two weeks, due to the extreme psychological distress that was experienced by the 'prisoners' because of the harsh and sometimes brutal treatment they experienced form the 'prison guards'. What could be concluded from this study, even though it did not run for the planned length of time, was that prisons can cause extreme behaviour from both prisoners and prison guards, and as such, prisons can be regarded as institutions that can cause abuse, rebellion, distress and so on. Bartol (1995) found that offenders found prisons to be degrading, demeaning and harsh which invariably has a negative psychological impact on an individual.

In the light of the findings of the above studies, Glaser's (1983) suggestion could be considered to be the more appropriate way forward. Glaser suggests the community type sentences of a more productive and constructive alternative to custodial sentences as prisons can often reinforce certain negative behaviours (hence they sometimes being referred to as the 'Universities of Crime'). As a form of restorative justice, this is seen as a positive alternative to custodial sentences. Sentences such as community service put the offender in a position whereby he/she has to pay back through some form of community programme to society as well as any potential victim.

Restorative justice also enables the victim and offender, with the assistance of a facilitator, to examine what happened, the impact on both sides and what can be done to put things right. The victim is able to say what impact the crime had on them and the harm caused. In this context the offender is required to take responsibility for his/her actions, to apologise and 'put things right' and to be reintegrated back into society.

If an individual is given a custodial sentence, whilst in prison they embark upon a CALM (Controlling Anger and Learning to Manage it) programme. The aim of the programme it to help to reduce the occurrences of anger experienced by the individual (which could have been the root cause of the offence/s they committed). Targeted at male offenders, the individual is required to take part in 24 x two hour sessions which focus on how to solve problems, examining the thought patterns that resulted in the criminal behaviour committed, and how to prevent relapse, among other things. Ireland (2000) studied 50 prisoners who had taken part in the CALM programme. A control group of 37 who had not done the programme was also involved in the study. The aim was to look at the effectiveness of the anger management programme by using cognitive behaviour interviews coupled with questionnaires. The findings were compared, and it was found that those offenders who had taken part in the programme rated themselves as being 'less angry'. This was also supported by the officers who also rated offender as being significantly less angry (92% improvement). The overall conclusion was that in the short term programmes like CALM were effective.

https://www.restorativejustice.org.uk/

4.5 Addiction

Paper 3 Option3

Key Areas:

- Describing addiction
- Risk Factors in the development of addiction
- Nicotine addiction
- Gambling addiction
- Reducing addiction
- Behaviour change

In order to discuss the psychology of addiction, we need a working definition that will provide the basis for our discussion – a starting point. Most definitions refer to the ingestion of a substance or substances (drugs) that becomes habitual and compulsive in the following ways:

'Addiction is the compulsive uncontrolled use of habit-forming drugs.' (Webster's New International Dictionary)

Or

'Addiction is a state of periodic chronic intoxication produced by repeated consumption of a drug, natural or synthetic.' (WHO – World Health Organisation) and in terms of the individual addict:

'An addict is a person addicted to a habit, especially one dependence on a (specified) drug.' (Concise Oxford Dictionary)

Research into addiction has applied broader definitions that go beyond focusing just on substance addictions. Therefore, addiction can be defined as a condition where there is the compulsion to embark upon certain types of behaviour (gambling, shopping, sex - which can be referred to as compulsion addiction), or to take substances (alcohol, nicotine, cocaine - also referred to as substance addiction), persistently, resulting in a level of dependence that can have an impact upon a person's daily activities, functioning and responsibilities. It can also negatively impact upon an individual's physical health and well-being.

There are different usages of the term 'addiction', one of them being **physical addiction** – the person's body adapts to the substance they intake, to the extent that after a while it no longer has the desired effect. The individual therefore develops a tolerance for the substance and eventually, due to the level of tolerance, there is a significant biological reaction if the substance is not used (withdrawal). Also the tolerance could result in more of the substance being used in order to achieve the desire effect. The other usage is **psychological addiction**. Most addictive behaviour can be connected to being emotionally stressed, and therefore treating this type of addiction required an understanding of how it works psychologically.

According to Griffiths (2005), addiction has identifiable components[24] which are:

1. Salience – the addictive behaviour is extremely important to the individual. In fact it can become the most significant thing in their life. They will experience cravings, and even at times when they are not involved in the addictive activity, they are thinking about it

2. Mood modification – has an impact upon the individual's mood in some way e.g. gives them a 'buzz' to face the day or calms them down when they are stressed

3. Withdrawal Symptoms – the individual will experience negative and unpleasant physical and mental side-effects when they stop consuming the substance or embarking upon the addictive activity

4. Tolerance – the individual has to do or consume more in order to have the same effect

5. Conflict – as a result of the addiction the individual may come into conflict with family and friends. Their addictive activity may also come into conflict with other activities such as work

---

[24] Griffiths M. D. (2005). A 'components' model of addiction within a biopsychosocial framework.

6. Relapse – after stopping the individual reverts back to the addiction

Whilst Griffiths suggests that all six components need to be present in order for someone to be regarded as an addict, others have argued that this in fact is not necessarily the case. It is possible for someone to have an addiction and it not necessarily cause a disruption to the individual's life, so there may in fact not actually be any conflict evident. Others suggest that some addicts, depending on the addictions, may not experience any withdrawal symptoms.

Models of addiction, biological, cognitive and social learning or behavioural, attempt to explain addictive behaviour in terms of how it is initiated, how it is maintained and why addicts often experience relapses. So, there are on the basis of this, three stages of addiction development. In summary they are:

- Initiation - the point at which an individual becomes addicted
- Maintenance – even though there are negative consequences, the person continues with the addictive behaviour
- Relapse – the individual may have given up the habit but this is only temporary as they revert back to their addictive behaviour

We will now look at each model in terms of initiation, maintenance and relapse.

Risk Factors

Biological Model of Addiction

According to this model, because each individual has a unique physiological and genetic make-up, some people may have a specific deficiency that predisposes them to addiction; therefore addiction is a specific diagnosis, where an individual is either an addict or they are not – all or nothing! Because it is recognised as a physiological condition there are treatments available to try to combat the addiction, though the predisposition to addiction is irreversible.

Initiation

Initiation is caused by a genetic predisposition or vulnerability, and it is this predisposition that can be triggered by environmental factors such as stress.

Research into twins and families have been conducted in order to try to establish the likelihood of a person developing an addiction based on their genetics – examining the genetic transmission of addictive behaviour.

Agrawal and Lynskey (2008) conducted studies of twins in order to see if there was a genetic connection to addiction. MZ (identical) and DZ (non-identical) twins were studied, and it was found that 30-70% of drug addiction could be genetically explained. They argued that twin studies like this could be a good indicator of a genetic link. As MZ twins, they share the same set of genes. If they are brought up in difference environments (reared apart) for whatever reason, this can provide the basis for looking at the influence of genes over the influence of environment. If, therefore both twins, reared apart, show the same behaviour, the extent to which this can be regarded as genetic (the concordance rate) can be established, with a concordance rate of 100% showing a complete genetic link and 0%, no link at all. So, with a concordance link of 30%-70%, on the basis of this Agrawal and Lynskey could argue a genetic connection was evident.

One of the key benefits of looking at the genetic link in this way is that it enables researchers to, through a process of elimination, identify the specific gene or genes responsible for addiction. Therefore, some may have a genetic predisposition to addiction as a result of deficiencies in the production of the A1 variant, dopamine. If you recall, dopamine is a neurotransmitter linked to pleasure (the pleasure centre of the brain). It becomes activated when some experience unexpected pleasure. As such an individual is likely to become addicted to drugs that give them a 'high' if there is a deficiency in dopamine levels. A significant proportion of drugs stimulate the release of dopamine, thus compensating for any deficiency, increasing dopamine levels artificially. Comings et al (1996) found that nearly 50% of smokers and ex-smokers had a dopamine deficiency when compared to nearly 26% of the general population. We do, however, need to be aware of Comings et al's own conclusion in 1991 that also indicated that individuals who were Autistic or suffered from Tourettes, had the

A1 gene variant. On the basis of this it could not be said categorically that the A1 variant was related to addiction.

Activity 112

Whilst genetic explanations can help us to understand how some addictions can occur, can you identify any aspects of this approach that may be lacking somewhat? In other words, what critiques could be made of this approach?

What this approach does tend to omit, are the environmental factors that can cause addiction. Volkow (2003) argued that just because a person may have a dopamine deficiency, this does not necessarily mean that they would succumb to an addiction. Their surroundings, who they engage with etc., could be such that they are provided with distractions that stimulate them in a way that prevents them from engaging in addictive behaviour e.g. being involved in sporting activities. Therefore social and cultural factors are important elements that need to be taken into account when looking at addiction.

Maintenance

Continued consumption of the drug causes changes in mood, such as experiencing pleasure, calm and so on. When dopamine is the core element here, an individual through the consumption of drugs may feel happier and calmer (a reward by the brain). Therefore continued exposure means that when the activity of taking the drug/s is reduced, so too is the mood change experienced by the individual. The feelings of pleasure derived from taking the drug/s would reinforce the behaviour and result in increasing and continuing it.

However, it has been argued that when exposure is reduced, this causes anxiety and subsequently withdrawal symptoms, and in order to combat this, the individual has to consume more drugs so as to maintain the pleasure they derived from it and to avoid the negative feeling of not taking it. The taking of the drug therefore, becomes more about not having to cope with negative feelings (as the reward circuit of the brain becomes less able to respond to the drug stimulant) if the drug is not taken, and less about the 'enjoyment' of taking it.

Research to support the maintenance theory can be found in studies conducted by Volkow *et al* (2001). They gave adults Ritalin, which is known to raise dopamine levels. Some of those who took it liked it, whilst others found the experience unpleasant. What was found was that those who liked it had fewer dopamine receptors than those who did not. For Volkow *et al* this provided an explanation as to why some individuals who experiment with drugs may succumb to addition. In an experiment with rats, Olds and Milner (1954) had implanted electrodes into the rats' pleasure centre of the brain, and the rats were able to self-administer electrical stimulation via a level in the cage in which they were housed. Olds and Milner found that the rats would use the lever to administer electrical stimulation and would choose the stimulation over other rewards such as food. For Olds and Milner this demonstrated that feelings of pleasure can encourage continued behaviour and thus maintain addiction.

Relapse

Drugs affect the brains ability to function due to permanent changes made as a result of drug use. The prefrontal cortex that is responsible for self-control and may be affected in such a way that the individual is unable to exercise the self-control needed to combat the addiction. Therefore, when they cease taking the drug/s, due to the inability to exercise self-control, they may relapse back into drug taking.

An individual may also return to addictive behaviour in order to prevent or subdue uncomfortable withdrawal symptoms.

Whilst the above can provide some explanation for relapse, they do not fully address the unique individual and social motivations behind an addiction.

Cognitive Model of Addiction

This model focuses on an individual's 'faulty' thinking, which is the judgement, or lack of it, an individual applies when deciding whether or not to embark upon or continue with a certain type of behaviour. For example, with an addiction to gambling, an individual may continue to make a bet despite the likelihood of them winning being remote. They may also apply bad judgement with the view that they are on a 'lucky streak', and therefore continue to gamble, even though the odds are in reality stack against them.

Initiation

The individual may start from the premise that the outcome will be positive. Therefore if we use gambling as an example, the individual may focus on the outcome (large winnings; what could be won) as opposed to the process (placing the bet, sacrificing their own money, 'the house always wins'). Wagenaar (1988) suggested that addicted gambling behaviour often happens because of the individual's overestimation of the level of skill and control they have.

In drug addiction, the individual could lull themselves into a false sense of security that if they only do it once, it will not be harmful or be a problem.

Overall in both scenarios, gambling or drug taking, an individual may overestimate their ability to exercise control and the extent of the outcome e.g. a gambler may underestimate how much they have lost and overestimate how much they have actually won.

Another aspect of the cognitive approach is related to the self-medication model. In terms of drug use, this model is based on the notion that the individual will take drugs in order to treat an adverse psychological symptom. The individual will take the drug under the assumption that it will help alleviate their problem, and whilst the drug may not actually improve the situation e.g. their anxiety, the belief that it will alleviate the symptom is what results in the initiation to the drug.

Southwich *et al* (1981), Brown(1985), Leigh (1987) have all suggested that heavy drinkers had positive expectations about the effects of their alcohol consumption when compared to lighter drinkers, believing that the alcohol will enhance their experience, make them more sociable and less inhibited, resulting in an overall positive view of alcohol consumption.

Maintenance

Addicts often develop a way of thinking (heuristics) that can be used to justify their actions. They can justify their behaviour to themselves by convincing themselves that they are still in control or, for example in terms of losing a bet, that they knew that that was going to be the outcome. They may even say that it wasn't their lucky night because the stars were not in alignment, but '...it'll be better tomorrow.' This passes on the responsibility to external forces beyond their control.

With self-medication, the individual psychological symptom they are trying to combat will become the withdrawal symptom to be avoided should the individual stop their addictive behaviour. Therefore, the individual who takes drugs in order to alleviate anxiety or stress may continue to do so, in order not to experience the anxiety or stress. In the short-term the drug may relieve anxiety and stress but in the long-term it can actually increase anxiety and stress, thereby increasing the need to consume more of the drug (Parrott (1988).

Relapse

Often an individual will relapse because they overestimate their ability to control their behaviour, so the 'one more little flutter' is what will lull them back into addictive behaviour. Or the 'I'll just take this tablet one more time to make me feel better', can soon spiral back into addictive habits and practices. According to Nordgren and Pligt (2009) people believe that they have more control and restraint than they actually have, and addicts with high levels of confidence in their ability to control their addiction often relapse after four months.

Self-efficacy

According to **Bandura (1997),** the extent to which we believe in ourselves (self-efficacy) determines the extent to which we believe in our ability to deal with the effects of a particular type of behaviour – that is a belief,

 "...in one's capabilities to organise and execute the courses of action required to produce given attainments."

Self-efficacy influences the likelihood that specified goals such as trying to give up an addiction, will be achieved (Bandura 1999).

Self-efficacy plays a significant part in determining whether or not an individual engages in addictive behaviours and whether they believe they can do anything about the addiction once it is established. So the belief an individual has in his/her ability to achieve something, or whether or not an individual can give up an addiction, is dependent upon whether or not their self-efficacy is weak (Bandura, 1994).

Activity 113

Identify some of the strengths and weaknesses of the Cognitive Model of Addiction.

Social learning or Behavioural Models

This approach is based on the principle that certain types of behaviour are learned. Social learning is a process whereby behaviour can change and develop according the how they perceive their environment, their interaction and adjusting according to the need of the situation. We therefore learn through our interaction with others and how we engage with the wider society, and this in turns plays a significant role in how we see and think about ourselves and others.

Initiation

If you recall, we looked at classical and operant conditioning, these being ways in which we learn from direct experiences. However, we must also bear in mind that as social beings and through our interaction with others, we often learn a great deal by observing those around us.

Our observations of others exhibiting addictive behaviour can be the initiation part of the process of addiction. Seeing how others respond may result in an individual wanting to replicate in themselves what they have seen in another. For example, you meet up with a friend who you know has been experiencing anxiety, stress and depression and find them to be very 'chilled', calm and even happy. You learn that they have been taking a synthetic drug recommended to them by a friend, and they tell you they only take it when they need it, and they feel great! From you this would have observed what appears to be the positive affect of drugs which, due to your own stress and anxiety levels, may make you inclined to try it yourself.

DiBlasio and Benda (1993) suggested that peers through social learning, have the greatest influence for teenagers who smoke or use drugs.

Maintenance

As discussed previously, this is very much fuelled by the addiction itself. One way maintenance may occur is through the interaction with others, who may also have an addiction. As such there is no motivation to stop, or it may be difficult to stop due to peer pressure.

Relapse

If the addiction takes hold, it may become difficult for an individual to engage with others who are not addicts, such as friend and family; as such, this could be the motivation needed to stop. However, in such instances the addict's social circle may then become other addicts, and this may make the addictive habit too difficult to stop. Peer pressure and feeling compelled to be part of the group may be such that an person who has abstained from the addictive activity may finding themselves relapsing as a result of interacting with those who are still consumers of the addictive activity or substance. It is suggested by researchers that it is almost impossible to be free from addiction without forming new social networks and friendships.

Risk Factors: Stress

The stresses and strains of everyday life can be the trigger for addiction. It can be a way of dealing with and relieving the anxieties generated by problems to do with work, family, relationships, money and so on. Daily stress therefore can act as the initiator for addiction. For example, a glass of wine every evening after work to 'wind down' can then become two glasses, then the bottle, then two bottles and so on, with a developing reliance on alcohol in order to 'unwind'. This can then turn into an active addiction. It starts as something small to relieve stress but over time becomes a problem. These stressors are partially seen to be responsible for initiation, maintenance and relapse of many addictive habits.

If an individual experiences severe stress or trauma, they may be more susceptible to addiction, using the addictive behaviour or substance as a coping mechanism. Driessen *et al* (2008) found that 30% of drug addicts and 15% of alcoholics also suffered from PTSD (Post Traumatic Stress Disorder).

The views presented regarding the stress triggers of addiction do assume that the addiction can alleviate the stress somewhat. However, Hajek *et al* (2010) found that even though smokers said they smoked for stress relief, in fact they found smoking to increase instead of reducing stress. They argued that the stress response could be as a result of the craving for cigarettes and thus made the smoking the problem rather than the solution. So it presented a 'vicious circle': relieving the craving but not the everyday stress it was believed to alleviate.

Cloniger (1987) argues there are different types of alcoholics: those who drink due to stress and tension, who often tend to be females prone to anxiety and depression, and those who drink in order to combat or reduce boredom, more commonly associated with male risk takers. Therefore, Cloniger somewhat challenges the assumption that stress is the only cause of this type of addiction; if it was, there would be no identifiable differences between addicts. He also points out that whilst some may drink following a stressful situation or experience, others may drink in anticipation of a stressful situation or experience (a bit of 'Dutch courage' before the event).

Risk Factors: Peers

Another risk factor for the development of an addiction is that of peers. Social learning theory suggests that individuals learn by watching their peers' behaviours and how they act; this can then lead to an addiction being learned. According to McAlister *et al* (1984) an individual may feel compelled to smoke because of peer pressure. Peers may encourage an individual to 'have a go', so that the individual can gain the approval of their peers as well as believing that to take part would make them accepted, thereby affirming their social identity.

Also, according to Eiser *et al* (1989), teenagers particularly may see the reward for taking up a particular potentially addictive activity, such as smoking, as leading to higher social status and popularity.

In keeping with Bandura's social learning theory, according to Duncan (1995), seeing others who smoke will increase the chances of an individual adopting the same behaviour. Mitchell *et al* (1997) said that teenagers are said to be more likely to begin smoking, stereotypes of smokers are presented in a positive way, and they are likely to be more motivated to imitate what they perceive to be a good thing so as to be part of a their social group.

Risk Factors: Age

We have touched upon adolescents and teens in some of the sections above. In this context, according to Botvin (2000), studies show that teenagers are more vulnerable to develop addictions. Brown *et al* (1997) argues that factors such as peer pressure, romantic connections and so on can be part of the initiation process that causes the addiction to start.

Risk Factors: Family influences

Not surprisingly the influence of family in terms of addiction is very significant, as parents in particular can have a powerful influence on individual actions. Social Learning Theory suggests that children are more likely to become smokers if they have parents that smoke. Ogden (2008) found that children from poor backgrounds were more likely to smoke when compared to children from other social backgrounds.

Activity 114

Why do you think it is the case that children from poor social backgrounds are more likely to smoke than children from other social backgrounds?

Risk Factors: Personality

An individual's personality and the way they behave is another factor that can be associated with addiction. It has been argued that some personality types are more prone to addiction than others. To identify personality types, researchers often use questionnaires to identify them, and then measure the extent to which that personality type will be prone to addiction and addictive behaviour.

Eysenck (1967, 1982) developed what is known as personality dimensions. Based on the responses to questionnaires, he was able to identify the personality type of an individual, and this would provide the basis for making a connection between personal type and addiction. The three personality dimensions were as follows:

Personality Dimension	Link to addiction
Extraversion	**Easily bored and craving excitement. If they are not stimulated enough, they may seek external stimuli in the form of drugs, alcohol, gambling etc. in order to increase the brain's activity.** **Zuckerman (1983) suggests that those addicted to drugs or alcohol are likely to score highly in this personality dimension. Weintraub *et al* (2010), says that people with higher levels of impulsivity have increased levels of dopamine, so they are more likely to become addicts.**
Neuroticism	**They tend to be negative, often experiencing anxiety and depression. They can be moody and reactionary emotionally. In terms of addiction, these individuals may look to**

	taking substances that subdues their levels of anxiety and depression. According to Francis (1996), addicts will score highly in this dimension.
Psychoticism	These individuals can be hostile, lack empathy and even be cruel. They are also reactionary, so will be impulsive and may take risks without due consideration of the consequences of their actions. Such individuals may experiment with substances, not taking into account the potential harm. Or they may do so in order to combat their levels of hostility or negative responses.

Activity 115

Consider whether or not the three personality dimensions presented above provide an adequate explanation as to why some individuals are susceptible to addiction when compared to others.

According to Teeson *et al* (2002), we cannot really be deterministic in our outlook of personality types and addiction and assume that personality type increases the likelihood of addiction. We do need to bear in mind that the addictive behaviour itself can bring about changes in personality.

Overall it can be seen that some correlation between stress and addiction can be made, and can therefore make an individual more vulnerable in terms of developing such an addiction, but a concrete causal connection cannot be fully established. After all, as we have seen above, there are some who would argue that the addiction itself causes stress.

Explanation for Nicotine Addiction

When discussing addictive behaviour, research is often directed to addictions to smoking and nicotine addiction. Statistics shows that a significant number of the population engages in smoking, and of that number, the majority would profess to being addicted. Smoking Statistics:[25]

Adults

- There are about 10 million adults who smoke cigarettes in Great Britain
- This is about a sixth of the total UK population
- In Great Britain, 22% of adult men and 17% of adult women are smokers
- Smoking rates have more than halved since 1974 when 51% of men and 41% of women smoked
- Smoking prevalence is highest in the 25-34 age group (25%) and lowest amongst those aged 60 and over (11%)
- More than half (58%) of all adults report that they have never smoked
- Smoking rates are much higher among poorer people
- In 2013, 14% of adults in managerial and professional occupations smoked compared with 29% in routine and manual occupations

Quitting smoking

- Two-thirds of current smokers would like to stop smoking but only about 30%-40% make an attempt to quit in a given year

Addiction

- 60% of smokers say they would find it hard to last a whole day without smoking
- 69% have their first cigarette of the day within one hour of waking

---

[25] Sourced from ASH (Action on Smoking Health) January 2015; http://www.ash.org.uk/files/documents/ASH_93.pdf

Young people

Two-thirds of smokers start before age 18.

Of those who try smoking, between ⅓ and ½ will become regular smokers.

From the research conducted, it has been established that in order to understand addiction to nicotine we need to look at both the biological model and the learning model.

Biological Model

Initiation

We have seen from previous discussions that dopamine, when released into the brain, triggers signals of reward and pleasure. Nicotine activates receptors which cause the release of dopamine. Therefore, when someone smokes, they experience feelings of pleasure, but the feeling does not last, and after a short period of time there will be a drop in an individual's mood due to the depletion of dopamine. Khaled *et al* (2009) found that smoking long term changes the brain's chemistry, resulting in a smoker experiencing feelings of depression and causing them to want to smoke in order to alleviate the feeling of depression.

Studies show that the nicotine dependence is influenced by genetic factors. Stefansson *et al* (2010) conducted a study of 140,000 participants and found that there was a genetic link to nicotine dependence.

Lerman *et al* (1999) said that those carrying a particular gene (SLC6A3-9) were less likely to take up smoking, and this gene worked in the dopamine system in the brain.

According to **Sabol *et al* (1999),** this gene (SLC6A3-9) was important in enhancing people's ability to stop smoking, and that those not carrying it were more likely to remain as smokers, maintaining their addictive smoking behaviour.

Maintenance and Relapse

In a study of 1214 twin pairs whose aim was to look at environment and genetic contributions to initiation and progression in addiction in adolescence (11 to 19), Fowler *et al* (2007) found that, whilst identifying environmental factors as being an important feature of nicotine addiction at the initiation stage, when it came to heavier use, genetics were found to influence the extent of the addiction.

Tate *et al* (1994) in a sample group of 62 smokers, created 4 sub-groups. By telling some of the groups that they would not experience any adverse effects from not smoking, they found that they reported significantly lower physical and emotional complaints when compared to the other group. Therefore, in terms of maintenance, it was the expectancy of the negative effects of withdrawal (psychological) that would cause a person to continue smoking, even though they had not yet experienced the negative affects anticipated. This negative expectancy was also found to be significant in terms of relapse.

Learning Model

Initiation

Smoking in the past used to be regarded as a 'cool' and sophisticated pastime associated with film stars and celebrities, and it remained a popular activity for some time. Therefore popularity, not just among those in the public eye, but among one's peers, acts as a positive reinforcer. Mayeux *et al* (2008) found that smoking among 16-year-old boys had a positive impact on their popularity some two years later. Smoking may become associated with a desirable experience due to the positive links, such as peer acceptance and an increased social network. Smoking is not only being an individual act but a social experience connecting an individual to others.

Maintenance and Relapse

Repeating the activity of smoking consistently and regularly leads to both social and sensory conditioning; this, coupled with the effects of the nicotine, leads to the continued act of smoking. Giving up smoking can be difficult if an individual's social and peer network consists of other smokers. Smoking can also be ritualistic in that it becomes part of a routine that is compelling and difficult to resist. Cue reactivity is also a significant factor here as this is based on the idea that a craving can be triggered by a cue, such as seeing a packet of cigarette and associating it with the positive effect of the substance that the individual is addicted to. Research shows that when an addict is presented with a variety of cues associated with the addiction, the addict reacts to the thing/s associated with their addiction in a way similar to how they would react to the object of the addictive behaviour. So in smoking, for example, these items might include lighters, cigarettes and ashtrays. In the case of gambling, they might include betting-slips, lottery tickets, betting shops. We have seen in Pavlov's research that a dog can be made to salivate at the sound of a bell; if the bell is associated with food (classical conditioning), so the same principle can be applied to addiction where the craving is generated by the presence of something that is associated with the addictive behaviour. According to Tiffany (1995), addicted related cues are part of the process of maintenance of addiction.

Explanations for Gambling Addiction

Often when people think of gambling they either think of large casinos or more recently online gambling. However, gambling as an activity is far more varied and multi faceted as it involves an individual taking something of value to them (great or small) and risking it on an uncertain event in the hope that they will gain something of greater value. In this section, as with the previous one, we will be examining explanations of gambling addiction, looking at the various models and approaches that attempt to explain how it occurs, why it occurs and what can be done to combat the addiction.

Research commissioned by The Gambling Commission[26] resulted in the British Gambling Prevalence Survey 2010,[27] and they found the following:

- Overall, 73% of the adult population (aged 16 and over) participated in some form of gambling in the past year, which equated to around 35.5 million adults
- There has been a significant increase in participation in gambling activities, e.g. an increase in events other than horse races or dog races with a bookmaker (3% in 1999, 9% in 2010), buying scratch cards (20% in 2007, 24% in 2010), buying other lotteries tickets (8% in 1999, 25% in 2010), gambling online (poker, bingo, casino and slot machine style games) (3% in 2007, 5% in 2010) and gambling on fixed odds betting terminals (3% in 2007, 4% in 2010)
- Men were more likely than women to gamble overall (75% for men and 71% for women)
- Men were more likely than women to take part in most gambling activities. The exceptions were bingo (12% for women and 6% for men) and scratch cards (25% for women and 23% for men)
- Among women, past year gambling increased from 65% in 2007 and 68% in 1999 to 71% in 2010. Among men, past year gambling estimates were higher in 2010 than 2007 (75% and 71% respectively). However, the 2010 prevalence rates were not higher than those observed in 1999 (76%)
- Gambling was associated with age found that gambling participation was highest among those aged 44-64
- Problem gamblers (addicts) were more likely to be male, younger, have parents who gambled regularly and had experienced problems with their gambling behaviour, and be a current cigarette smoker
- The majority of past year gamblers reported that they gambled for the chance of winning big money (83%), '...because it's fun' (78%), to make money (59%) and '...because it's exciting' (51%)

---

[26] Set up under the Gambling Act 2005 to regulate commercial gambling in Great Britain

[27] Sourced from:
http://www.gamblingcommission.gov.uk/pdf/british%20gambling%20prevalence%20survey%202010.pdf

Initiation

When looking at the biological explanation of gambling, it has been suggested that the physical response to gambling stems from how the body responds and prepares itself for an event where there is anticipation and excitement. Physically the heart rate increases, and adrenaline will be realised. In a normal, healthy person, adrenaline is a hormone that is released as a response to an acute stressor. It is part of the natural fight-or-flight response of the body.

There is evidence to show that the burst of energy associated with the release of adrenaline is highly addictive; this where the terms 'adrenaline junkie' stems from. In gambling, the burst of adrenaline comes from the anticipation of the outcome of an event upon which the individual has placed a bet. The bet does not have to be big in order to generate such a physical response. Placing a small amount of money into a slot machine can have the same effect. Therefore, the adrenaline rush is part of the initiation. According to Bergh *et al* (1997), there is a link between addicted gambling, the reward-system, genetics and impulsive behaviour.

Where genetics is concerned, research suggests that addicted gamblers are likely to carry the D2A1 gene, which has been linked to impulsive addictive behaviour. If an individual carries the D2A1 gene, they will have an insufficient amount of dopamine receptors, which means an individual will be deficient in experiencing pleasure and reward from the sort of activities that would give pleasure or reward to others. Comings *et al* (1996) suggests that on this basis, it could well be that some people are born more likely to become problem gamblers than others.

Black *et al* (2006), suggests that addicted gamblers are likely to have an addiction if a first degree relative also has this problem too. This is because the genetic link is closer i.e. they have more genes in common than distant relatives.

In a study of nearly 5000 male and female twins, MZ (identical) twins were twice as likely to both develop a gambling addiction, than DZ (non-identical) twins, thus showing a genetic link.

Maintenance

According to Wray and Dickerson (1981), gamblers who were prevented from gambling often experienced symptoms that resembled withdrawal. The symptoms may not have been as intense as those experienced by individuals addicted to drugs, alcohol or smoking; however, they still experienced symptoms that influenced whether they continued their behaviour.

Examinations of brain activities show that individuals with gambling addictions, when compared to those without, had changes in blood flow in the brain when experiencing different emotions and stimuli.

It seems likely, that the parts of the brain responsible for self-control and decision-making are involved in addictive gambling behaviour.

Relapse

As with other addictive behaviour, to stop carries with it the possibility of withdrawal symptoms, and in terms of gambling this could manifest itself as anxiety, resulting in the reengagement of the activity in order to stave off the anxiety, reverting back to gambling in order to generate and maintain the 'positive' feelings they get from the activity. Also temptation may be difficult to avoid due to reminders of gambling and opportunities to do so, such as advertising.

Cognit ve Model

Gambling can also be explained from a cognitive perspective. It has been argued that gambling addicts often experience deficiencies in their thinking which results in cognitive bias – the belief that due to a positive outcome that happened in the past (the won a bet) they will win again. The tendency is to forget the times they had lost, and focus on the times they won. They have a misguided belief that they control the situation and, as such, can influence the outcome of the gamble. Griffiths (1994) found that gamblers would have irrational thought whilst gambling, such as believing that they had the skills required to win or a 'formula' to control the gambling machines.

Sharpe and Tarrier (1993) state that the physiological effects of gambling, such as excitement (the 'buzz'), occur because of cognitive influences. The excitement generated by gambling with some wins, lead to further gambling, and if gambling continues, cognitive mechanisms become more important in maintaining the behaviour.

Initiation

Gambling can may begin with the positive feelings, generated by a win. This leads to positive thoughts and, once created, these thoughts can be difficult to change. The buzz experienced by gambler enhances positive feelings, reinforcing existing positive cognitions about gambling.

Maintenance

Beck *et al's* 'vicious circle' can be applied here in that gambling may provide the person with a method of improving their mood. With gambling, people tend not to win all the time and in fact most lose money, so they may find themselves experiencing financial difficulties. Not surprisingly this can lead to a downturn in mood, and as a consequence, the gambler embarks upon more gambling to achieve the 'buzz'; they invariably lose money and so the cycle continues – hence the 'vicious circle'.

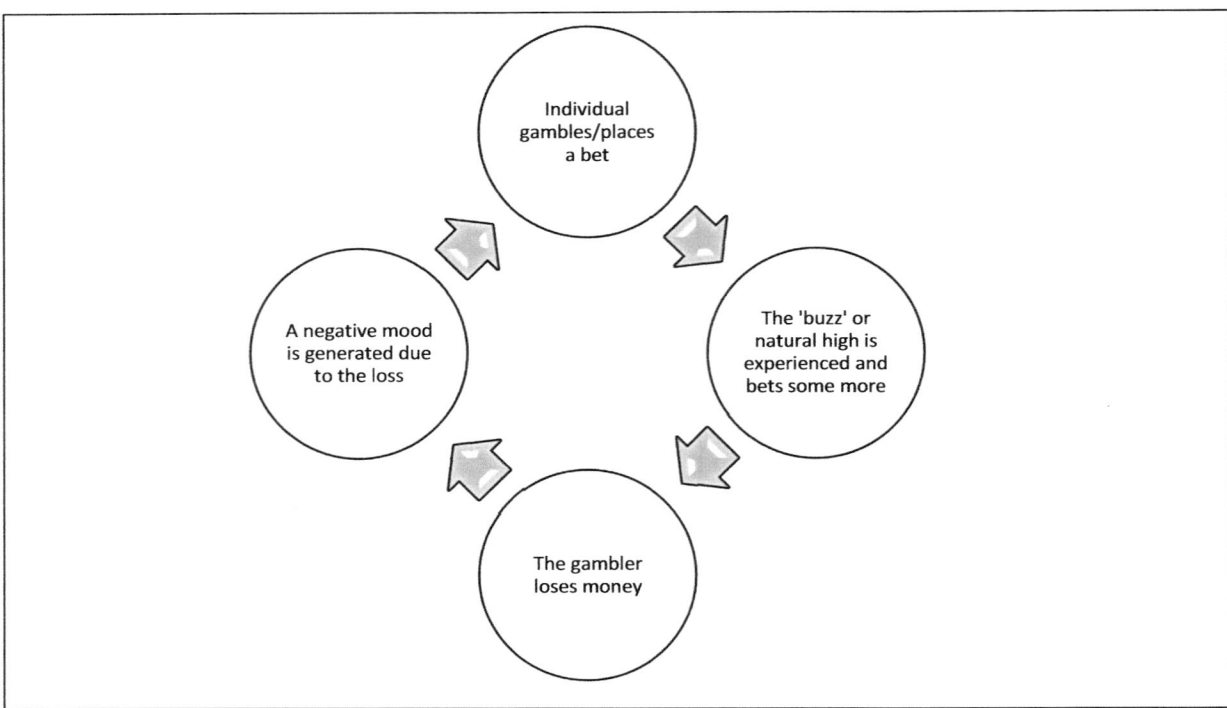

Some do not see gambling as a problem, and therefore do not see why they need to, or should, give it up, in that due to self-efficacy they feel they can stop at any time. There is also the belief that the benefits are such that it can be life changing, and therefore they would not want to miss out on a 'big win' e.g. an addict that plays the lottery and the same numbers every week, may experience some anxiety if they do not get to play their numbers; they could potentially miss out on a big win!

The functions of coping may also explain why people continue to gamble. It may be that they do so because the experience of excitement and the expectancy of the occasional win, hearing stories of 'normal, everyday, people' like themselves winning big, provides the feel good factor – 'it could be you!' These events encourage gamblers to interpret their behaviour positively.

Relapse

The consequences of relapse are seen as the gambler returning to the possibility of winning money. In comparison to other addictions, withdrawal from gambling is seen as relatively painless, and as such the addict may feel that they can stop whenever they want to. But a life without gambling may be considered to be extremely boring, so the motivation to relapse stems from the need to break life's monotony.

Learning Theory

Initiation

This theory or model approaches the issue of gambling from the perspective of operant conditioning, being subject to reinforcement schedules. This is an important element of the learning process in that reinforcement schedules determine how often a behaviour is going to result in a reward. Therefore, in terms of gambling, the addict learns through reward and punishment - the reward being the win, and the punishment being the loss. Reinforcement schedules means that sometimes an instance will be reinforced either every time it happens or in some instances only sporadically. So the person who places coins in a slot machine will not win every time they do so, but rather sporadically. It is this unpredictability as well as the possibility of winning, (having seen it happen to others and maybe having the experience themselves) that overtime develops a strong association. In fact in terms of initiation seeing others win could reinforce the positive feels they associate with gambling and this may be reinforced further by their own occasional win.

Maintenance

The addictive behaviour may continue because of the rewards gained, which could be monetary, or the excitement they may feel from the experience of gambling.

The association of excitement with gambling reinforces the relationship between the two. Whilst winning is infrequent, it is in fact the infrequency that maintains the behaviour. The anticipation can be one of the driving forces behind the gambling behaviour.

Relapse

Not having gambled after a period of time, an individual returning to such activities can be explained in terms of **cue-reactivity paradigm**. References to gambling is very visible and easily accessible e.g. people can now play the National Lottery, but not just by the usual selection of six numbers, but a whole array of other forms of the lottery e.g. Euro millions, scratch cards etc.

Internet gambling is highly publicised, and a person doesn't even have to leave their home to take part e.g. online casinos. Gamblers attempting to give up the habit are bombarded with reminders of their addictive behaviour.

Reducing Addiction

Because of the impact addiction can have on an individual, it is important for there to be ways of dealing with the various forms of addictions discussed previously. Therefore in this section we will be looking at:

- Why it is important to have effective ways of dealing with addictive behaviour
- The methods available for reducing addictive behaviour
- Which methods are considered to be the most effective
- Evaluation of the methods used

Types of Intervention

The types of interventions are:

- Biological
- Psychological
- Public Health

Biological Intervention is associated primarily with drug therapy, and is mostly used with addictions associated with substance abuse.

Agnostic	Antagonistic
The addict is given a milder form of the drug/substance they are addicted to e.g. a heroin addict will be given methadone to treat their addiction; a nicotine addict may be given nicotine replacements such as patches or gum. There are fewer side effects and the withdrawal from the addictive substance is gradual.	Drug therapy that blocks the effects of the substance to which the individual is addicted, resulting in their no longer having the desired effect e.g. naltrexone used as a treatment for opiate and other addictions. Kim and Grant (2001) found that naltrexone could reduce the amount of dopamine in the brain which makes certain addictive behaviour less rewarding.

Both approaches may also use SSRIs (Selective Serotonin Reuptake Inhibitors) which are a form of antidepressants that have fewer side effects when compared to other antidepressants. They work by increasing the serotonin levels in the brain, which, if you recall, tend to be at lower levels in addicts. The outcome is that they have a positive influence on an individual's mood, emotion and sleep.

Activity 116

Evaluate the above forms of drug therapy.

Using your research skills, see if you can find out how effective these approaches are in the treatment of addiction.

Some of the pros and cons of drug therapy:

Pros	Cons
Based on biology	The addict is still reliant on a drug
It is regarded as safer than the opiate or tobacco the individual is addicted to	There can be side effects
It is cheaper than an opiate the individual may be addicted to	The addict can become addicted to the substitute
When alongside behavioural/psychological treatments, this can make process of combating the addiction easier	This form of therapy does not really address the social and psychological issues of the addict
It is deterministic as it removes blame from the addict	Substitutes like methadone can cause death
The process of withdrawal is quicker	There is an illegal market for substitutes such as methadone
	Relapse can occur

Psychological intervention aims to encourage an addict to stop by applying behaviourist and cognitive approaches.

For the behaviourist approach, we will look at the two core elements: Classical Conditioning and Operant Conditioning.

Classical Conditioning	Operant Conditioning
Pavlov: Aversion Therapy Associating the addictive behaviour with something negative. The aim being to create an unpleasant	*Contingency Management* Based on the theory of positive reinforcement. Rewarding positive behaviour.

association between the addict and their addiction.

Owen (2001) – 82 hospitalised alcoholics were given 5 treatments over a period of 10 days. During this time there were given a substance called emetic, which made them feel nauseous and vomit after consuming alcohol they had chosen to consume. They then completed a cognitive and behaviour questionnaire. The participants' responses suggested this approach was effective because their alcohol related behaviour was reduced.

Evaluation:

According to Siegal *et al* (1987), this may work in a supervised and controlled environment, but relapse was very likely once an addict returned to their usual environment. Therefore, it may not have long-term effects.

It also raised issues of ethics in terms of how the participants to this therapy are treated.

Study:

Sindelar *et al* (2007) found that drug addicts who were rewarded with money when testing negative for drugs, reduced the addicts' drug use.

Evaluation:

This approach is not seen to really address how/why the addiction occurred in the first place. It does not therefore address the possibility of an addict replacing one addiction with another.

Overall, this approach directly addresses an individual's behaviour and therefore does have short term positive results; however, in terms of long-term success, it is regarded as lacking. The relapse rate is high and it does not, on its own, really address the underlying causes of, or predispositions to, addiction.

Covert Sensitisation

This was first introduced in the 1960s by Joseph Cautela. It is a form of behav our modification therapy based on the principle that all behaviour is learned. Therefore, in terms of addiction, addictive behaviour can be unlearned.

As with aversion therapy, an aversion stimulus is paired with the addictive behaviour. In terms of convert sensitisation an unpleasant image is coupled with the behaviour in order to prevent the addictive behaviour occurring. During the process of this therapy an addict, with the therapist's guidance, will create a list of aversion images which may include someone vomiting, a diseased lung etc. The image that conjures up the most aversive response is chosen. The addict will then be guided through imagining the process they go through before embarking upon the addictive activity e.g. buying a packet of cigarettes, but just as they are about to enter the shop to by the cigarette, they are asked to imagine an unpleasant consequence (such as seeing a diseased lung inside the packet instead of cigarettes). From this the idea is that the addict learns to associate the addictive behaviour with something unpleasant.

Evaluation:

- Risk free – no adverse physical effects, like actually vomiting
- Relies upon and required the addict to have a vivid imagination

Cognitive Approaches (CBT)

Addiction is a dysfunctional belief. An individual therefore may be unable to control addictive behaviour. For such individuals, what appears to be positive consequences makes them incapable of controlling their addiction. The individual may want to stop the addiction but feel powerless to do so. One reason given for this is that the addict may weigh up the consequences of the act with the act in a way that focuses on the benefits rather than the pitfalls e.g. in drug addiction the benefit focus would be the 'high', in gambling it could be the 'buzz'.

This approach enables an addict to explore and try to understand the feelings and motivations associated with the addictive activity and modify dysfunctional forms of behaviour.

In a 12 week study, comparing CBT (teaching an individual how to avoid risk situations) to drug treatment (anti-depressant) for cocaine addiction, Carroll *et al* (1994) found that whilst both approaches were effective, CBT was more effective in treating individuals with drug addiction (cocaine addiction), and even 12 months later the impact was still notable.

In a study of 290 addicted gamblers who were treated with CBT over a 16 week period, Jiminez-Murcia *et al* (2007) found that after 6 months the success rate was 80%. There were, however, notable drop-out rates and relapses. Ladoucer *et al* (2001) found in a study of gambling addicts that had undergone CBT for the majority of them, they were no longer addicted to gambling. The therapy has improved their belief that they could control their addiction.

Evaluation:

- It is individualised in that it focuses on the need of the individual addict
- It is compatible with other treatments such as drug therapy
- It is a low risk form of therapy with no adverse effects for the addict
- Helps an individual devise skills that can be used in the event of relapse
- Some aspects of a person's thought processes are not just cognitive but can be as a result of a physical issue
- There are no identifiable adverse side effects
- Ladouceur *et al* (2001) found that after gambling addicts received CBT, most no longer had gambling addictions

The Theory of Planned Behaviour (TPB)

Icek Ajzen (1989) introduced the idea of TPB based on the idea that an individual's intention has the most influence on their behaviour. This is another cognitive theory that can be addressed in relation to addiction. According to this approach, beliefs lead to intentions, which then lead to behaviour.

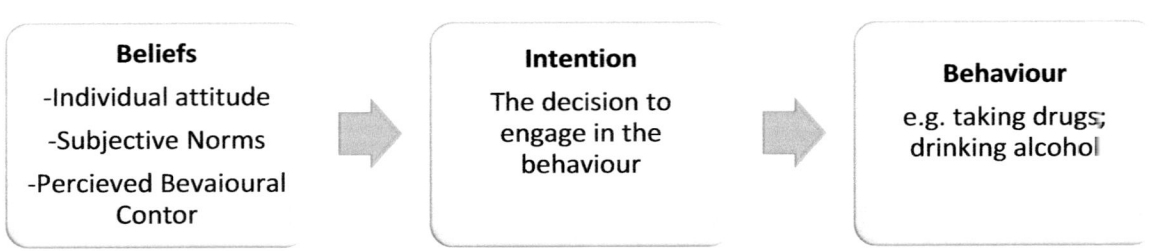

Beliefs
-Individual attitude
-Subjective Norms
-Percieved Bevaioural Contor

Intention
The decision to engage in the behaviour

Behaviour
e.g. taking drugs; drinking alcohol

<u>Intentions</u> **are determined by three variables:**

Individual Attitude	A personal attitude toward something, which will include how desirable a particular type of behaviour is to a person. In terms of addiction, an attitude to alcohol or drugs could be that it will help the individual to relax – a positive consequence – so the positive might outweigh the negative. Slater *et al* (2011): it is possible to change attitudes so as to reduce the use of a drug by stressing that a positive attitude towards it does not correspond with being independent and aspirational – the dependency on it suggests otherwise. However, this approach is all very well and good but only really works if emotions and life situations are not taken into account (Armitage *et al*, 1999)
Subjective Norms	What others may think is significant to the individual. For example, family and friends' attitude to alcohol will impact upon the individual's own attitude to alcohol. If they drink a lot, it may generally be regarded as acceptable.

	Wilson and Kolander (2003): adolescents often have inaccurate subjective norms and believe that more people smoke than is true.
Perceived behaviour control	The extent to which an individual believes they can control their own behaviour. If an individual believes they have a great deal of control the more likely they are to engage in a particular behaviour.
	Godin *et al* (2006): from interviews and surveys of adults it was found that perceived behavioural control was the most important predictor of giving up smoking. That is, that giving up smoking is not easy as it requires a lot of willpower and effort.
	MacDonald *et al* (1996), however, suggested that if we are looking at alcohol addiction, intentions tend to be assessed when the individual is sober, but those intentions can change due to alcohol consumption.

Prochaska's Six-Stage Model of Behaviour Change

Carlo C. DiClemente and J. O. Prochaska introduced a six-stage model of change to help individuals with addictions problems and motivate a change in their behaviour. The six stages of the model are:

- Pre-contemplation
- Contemplation
- Determination
- Action
- Maintenance
- Termination

Pre-contemplation

Individuals in this stage are not even thinking about changing their behaviour, and may not even see it as a problem. They may even think that the opinions of others in terms of their behaviour is exaggerated.

The reasons for this stage are referred to as "the Four Rs":

- Reluctance - individuals do not want to consider change or do not feel the need to change
- Rebellion - these are resistant to being told what to do, particularly as they are invested in continuing with the addictive behaviour
- Resignation - an individual has given up any hope of change and may be overwhelmed by the problem. May even have attempted to stop the addictive behaviour and failed
- Rationalisation - the individual can give plenty of reasons why the addiction is not a problem

Contemplation

Individuals will consider that they have an addiction and that there is a possibility for change, but people who are contemplating change tend not to commit, so they consider it but go no further. They are interested in learning about the addiction and possible treatment. They know that the addiction is causing problems and will be aware of the reasons why the addiction is bad for them. However, even with this awareness, they are still unable to make a decision to change.

Determination: Commitment to Action

Deciding to stop is the key to stage of change. The weighing of up of the 'positives' and negatives of the addiction, finally tips the balance in favour of change. At this stage an individual appears ready to commit and take action.

Preparation

This stage occurs after the commitment to change, where the individual takes appropriate steps, usually with the help of a support plan with appropriate action for change which will include an assessment of the level of difficulty to change. This may also include announcing their intention to others.

Action: Implementing the Plan

The plan is put into action. Usually involves making some form of public commitment by doing things like attending support groups, counselling or treatment. There will also be overt changes in behaviour. Making such public commitments helps the addict get the support they need to deal with and recover from addiction and creates external monitors with family and friends, not only watching the addict but cheering them on.

Maintenance, Relapse and Recycling

In this stage, abstinence is firmly established, and the desire to return to old addictive behaviours becomes less intense and less frequent. The possibility of relapse is always there, and individuals may experience strong urges to revert back to their former behaviour - they may either cope with it or succumb to it.

Termination

This is the goal for an addict: they no longer find the thing they were addicted to a temptation or threat, and they are confident that they can cope without fear of relapse.

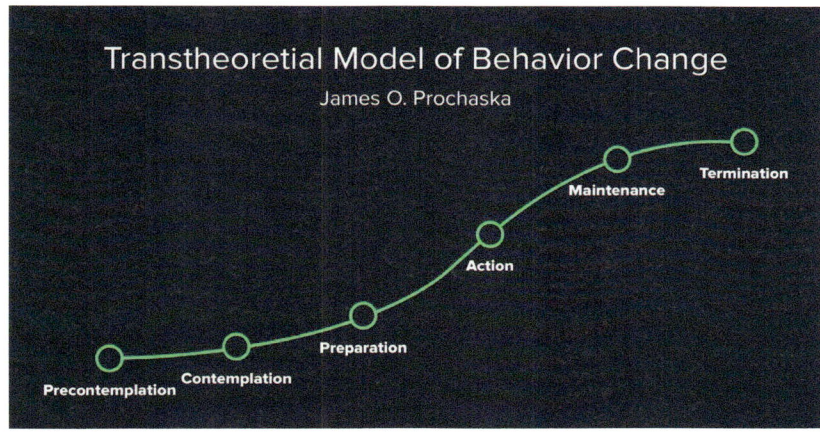

Tutor Marked Assignment 4

(Mock Exam)

Now go to CloudPort to download your mock exam. Answers should be word processed and uploaded via CloudPort

Please note: If you are pursuing the AS Level qualification only then you will only sit Papers 1 and 2, which correspond to TMAs 1 and 2. If however you are pursuing full A Level qualification you will sit the second set of exam papers which correspond to TMAs 3, 4 and 5. As level no longer counts towards the A level qualification.

BV - #0025 - 191219 - C0 - 297/210/45 - PB - 9781326428204